TV Content Analysis

Techniques and Applications

Edited by
Yiannis Kompatsiaris
Bernard Merialdo
Shiguo Lian

CRC Press
Taylor & Francis Group
Boca Raton London New York

CRC Press is an imprint of the
Taylor & Francis Group, an **informa** business
AN AUERBACH BOOK

CRC Press
Taylor & Francis Group
6000 Broken Sound Parkway NW, Suite 300
Boca Raton, FL 33487-2742

© 2012 by Taylor & Francis Group, LLC
CRC Press is an imprint of Taylor & Francis Group, an Informa business

No claim to original U.S. Government works

Printed in the United States of America on acid-free paper
Version Date: 20120202

International Standard Book Number: 978-1-4398-5560-7 (Hardback)

Library of Congress Cataloging-in-Publication Data

TV content analysis : techniques and applications / Yiannis Kompatsiaris, Bernard Merialdo, and Shiguo Lian.
    p. cm. -- (Multimedia computing, communication, and intelligence)
    "A CRC title."
    Includes bibliographical references and index.
    ISBN 978-1-4398-5560-7 (hardback)
    1. Content-based image retrieval. 2. Image analysis. 3. Content analysis (Communication) 4. Video recordings--Abstracting and indexing. 5. Television broadcasting. 6. Internet television. I. Kompatsiaris, Yiannis. II. Merialdo, Bernard. III. Lian, Shiguo.

    ZA4575.T85 2012
    621.388--dc23   2012002067

Visit the Taylor & Francis Web site at
http://www.taylorandfrancis.com

and the CRC Press Web site at
http://www.crcpress.com

Contents

PART III   CONTENT RECOMMENDATION

PART IV   CONTENT QUALITY

PART V   WEB AND SOCIAL TV

PART VI   CONTENT PRODUCTION

Preface

TV content is currently available through various communication channels and devices, for example, digital TV, mobile TV, and Internet TV, and continues to play an important part in our daily life. Social networks also play an important role, providing an additional source of information (user opinions, discussions, user-generated content) relevant to TV content. Both existing applications, such as automatic annotation, classification, and recommendation, and more recent ones, such as TV, web, and Web 2.0 convergence, require the means to efficiently analyze TV programs automatically to enable such applications for content managers and consumers.

This book aims to give a thorough description of TV program analysis techniques, which consist of algorithms, systems, architectures, applications, and overviews, including the latest research results, new emerging approaches, and open issues.

The book is organized in six parts: Part I, Content Extraction, deals with automatic analysis and annotation of TV content, addressing both generic semantics and concepts and TV content–specific ones like commercials. Part II, Content Structuring, includes techniques that are able to identify interesting parts of TV programs and provide direct access to it. Part III, Content Recommendation, discusses the problem of providing users with the most relevant content, solving the problem users face due to the huge amount of TV content available. Part IV, Content Quality, examines visual perception and quality approaches in the multidisplay TV context and in the specific mobile TV scenario. Part V, Web and Social TV, presents approaches and studies for web and TV convergence and on how user-generated content in Web 2.0 applications can be used for enhancing TV services. Finally, Part VI, Content Production, includes chapters on postproduction, visual effects, and presentation standards. Most parts start with a chapter that provides an overview of the area, followed by state-of-the-art approaches focusing on specific issues covered in the part.

Content Extraction

Automatic TV content analysis is very important for the efficient indexing and retrieval of the vast amount of TV content available not only for end users so that they can easily access content of interest, but also for content producers and broadcasters in order to identify copyright violations and to filter or characterize undesirable content. Well-studied techniques such as content-based copy detection (CBCD) and automatic semantic concept detection can be applied in order to solve these problems. However, TV content raises new requirements in both cases. In CBCD, existing global-based descriptors cannot perform well due to transformations in TV content that change the overall appearance such as the addition of logos and banners, picture-in-picture, cropping, etc. Therefore, local-based features are used in order to cope with such variations. Chapter 1 presents a spatiotemporal extension based on local features that takes into account, at the same time, 2D spatial and temporal information. TV content variability is another challenge for machine-learning algorithms used for semantic concept detection. Manual annotation for constructing training sets is time consuming, and classifiers learned on a type or set of TV content are not always efficiently applied to different types of TV programs due to varying distributions. Transfer learning, cross-domain learning, and incrementally updated learning are among the techniques presented in Chapter 2 for addressing these issues. In addition to generic types of annotations, in TV programs specific semantics need to be extracted such as detection and annotation of violent or pornographic scenes in TV movies. With almost everyone having access to TV content nowadays and through a number of end user devices, there is a demand for efficient methods to automatically identify and filter out undesirable content in TV programs. In Chapter 3, low-level single modality (audio, visual, textual) approaches combined with medium-level multimodal fusion approaches and high-level knowledge-based approaches are used not only to reason out the existence of violence (i.e., the binary problem), but also to determine the type of violence (e.g., fight, explosion, murder).

Relevant to extracting useful information from TV content, TV programs contain specific types of information that need to be analyzed. Overlaid graphics, such as text and channel logos and commercials, are among the most typical types of content used extensively in TV. Text and logo detection in Chapter 4 are not applied to the usual indexing and retrieval tasks but to TV-specific applications like visual quality improvement, contrast enhancement during burn-in protection, and customizing text appearance for increased readability. Regarding commercial detection, these include two main categories: explicit advertisements in the form of commercials, that is, short video sequences advertising a product or a service, and indirect advertisements, that is, placement of trademarks and logos that are associated to sponsorships (particularly in sports videos) and product placement. In Chapter 5, near duplicate and CBCD and object recognition techniques are used to detect these two categories. In both cases, computationally efficient techniques are needed to address either the limited processing capabilities when the processing is done in the TV set or the large amount of content when it is done off-line. To address these issues, either hardware-based or appropriately designed algorithms are used.

Content Structuring

While the techniques of Part I emphasize on extracting specific objects, concepts, and semantics from TV programs, there are cases where a user would like to get an overview of the program before watching it. This includes direct access of a specific part of the program, a summary of the program, and, in general, an alternative for the basic fast-forward/backward options. For this purpose, it is useful to have mechanisms that are able to precisely detect the first and the last frames of all the programs as well as the breaks (commercials, trailers, station identification, bumpers) of a given stream, and then annotate all these segments with metadata. To enable these features, each TV program has to be automatically structured, that is, its original structure has to be recovered in order to build the best and most compact overview of the TV program. As described in the overviews of Chapters 6 and 7, there are various categories, as follows: (1) specific methods that make use of prior knowledge of the type of the analyzed TV program and apply this to types of programs like news or sports videos with known and clear structures; (2) generic methods that try to structure a video in an unsupervised way without using any prior knowledge of the video; (3) techniques that analyze the metadata provided with the stream (EPG, EIT); and (4) techniques based solely on analyzing the audiovisual stream. A common step in many approaches is to segment the video document into elementary shots, which are later clustered to longer temporal segments referred to as scenes, story units, video paragraphs, etc. In Chapter 8, a range of techniques is presented together with relevant architectures, metadata representation standards, and applications. Analysis techniques include shot boundary detection, mid-level semantic classifiers of images, speech recognition, speaker segmentation, face detection, near duplicate detection, and clustering methods used, for example, in anchorperson detection and multimodal news story segmentation.

As is described in the overview chapters, there are approaches that target specific types of TV content and exploit prior knowledge about their structure for automatic content structuring. Chapter 9 specifically addresses talk show programs, and while these broadcasts show a wide disparity of aspects, the authors make use of a number of common features: the presence of guests, the polymorphy of the program (a succession of interviews, performances, TV reports, etc.), or the role of the anchorman. A taxonomy of the talk show components is built, including concepts such as the guests, the hosts, the performances, etc., and various automatic or semiautomatic segmentation and detection techniques are applied.

Content Recommendation

Interactive television (iTV) and video-on-demand platforms not only allow access to a large variety of TV programs but also enable users to interact with the TV content and find the program they are interested in. Personalization and recommender systems provide solutions to users' problems, as they are overwhelmed by an abundance of TV channels, programs, and videos. In Chapter 10, an overview of the latest developments in the domain of recommender systems for personalized TV is presented. The categories identified are social-based, collaborative approaches or content-based ones. The chapter also provides a deep understanding of the role played by user-based assessment methods and of the effectiveness of automatic quality metrics (accuracy, errors, coverage, novelty) together with a case study with an IP television provider.

Chapter 11 focuses on the news video domain and how personalization techniques can support users to find the content they are interested in. Users' interactions with such video systems are used to build long-term user profiles that can be used as implicit indicators to identify users' interests. A generic ontology-based representation is used for the creation of structured user profiles. In Chapter 12, the extra dimension, which enables TV content to be available through various devices, is considered. In such cases, the objective is contextualization of the user experience across different devices at different places and time based on the user profile. The chapter considers several devices like iTV, mobile phones, and personal computers (PCs) to access cross-media services.

Content Quality

While there has been significant progress on algorithmic visual quality assessment (QA), in TV content, it is very important to consider the display device being used since there are a number of different displays and formats such as HD TVs, 3D TVs, immersive environments, handheld devices, and so on. Chapter 13 reviews approaches that have been proposed for handheld displays, HD displays, as well as 3D displays and describes how generic objective QA algorithms may be extended to account for the display under consideration. The relationship between content and perceptual quality and the relevance of these findings for algorithm design are also discussed. In Chapter 14, the more specific issue of quality of mobile TV content is presented. Experts from mass media and communication science and from the film academy have cooperated with researchers from computer science to extract critical elements to create a guideline for the production of mobile TV content. Suitability of shot types, camera motions, coding properties, environmental illumination such as night scenes, and several other properties have been estimated by experts.

In both quality-related chapters, it is considered important that display- and mobile-specific QA databases be created for evaluation purposes.

Web and Social TV

Nowadays, there is a strong connection between TV, the web, and Web 2.0. Social TV is concerned with mining information related to TV programs from social media and integrating the results into TV services. In Chapter 15, design, creation, and management of multimedia content from a holistic platform experience are investigated. Understanding what content is accessed where, how, why, and by whom has become essential to create a full TV experience. Chapter 16 analyzes in detail the existing linkage between TV and web content. Focusing on mainstream TV broadcasters in Austria and Finland and choosing 10 Austrian and 10 Finnish TV program formats that feature convergence with the web, the study identifies that there is minimal linkage between TV and web content in both countries and its potential is not well recognized in the marketplace. The reasons are multiple and range from a lack of standards and mechanisms for implementing linkage to inadequate interfaces and input devices. Hence, linear TV content, which limits web content to coexisting web pages, prevails.

Chapter 17 focuses on Social TV and gives an overview of recent social media mining technologies and their applications to TV-related services: efficient techniques for retrieving social media content with relevant discussions on TV shows, sentiment analysis and detection of influential users in social networks related to TV program comments, and integration of the information mined from social media into a Social TV interface.

In all the aforementioned approaches, TV content analysis and data mining, which have been traditionally used for annotation and retrieval, now play an important role in bridging the gap between TV, the web, and Web 2.0.

Content Production

TV production includes important steps such as postproduction, generation of visual effects, and presentation format according to the selected device and channel. Chapter 18 presents a survey of tools and algorithms for interactive video browsing and navigation, with a focus on two important content domains in TV production: news and entertainment content. It is shown that content-based tools can efficiently support specific tasks in the entire chain of manual content management (e.g., content navigation, content selection and filtering, content annotation) and play an important role in facilitating TV postproduction. Among the visual effects used in TV content production, virtual content insertion has been widely used and studied for video enrichment and multimedia advertising. In Chapter 19, an interactive virtual content insertion architecture is presented, which can insert virtual contents into TV programs with evolved animations according to predefined behaviors emulating the characteristics of evolutionary biology. Finally, Chapter 20 addresses the problem of standard and nonstandard presentation formats for TV content. It presents an analysis of the interoperability between interactive content presentation formats for TV, the adaptation issues between these different application formats, and the common scenario for designing iTV contents. The authors suggest the portable content format (PCF), a platform-independent application format for the high-level production of iTV services, which can be easily adapted to any other iTV application format (e.g., HTML and MHP).

Conclusions

It is clear from the chapters presented in this book that TV content analysis and related topics still attract significant attention, and there are a number of requirements and challenges that remain to be addressed. One the one hand is the diversity of TV content; like in many other applications, TV content diversity due to different types of programs, countries, shows, etc., creates limitations to machine-learning approaches based on training examples. On the other hand, many TV programs like news and sports have specific structures and approaches exploiting a priori information about this structure to achieve acceptable performance often without necessarily recurring to sophisticated inference or reasoning techniques once the number of critical parts has been detected with a realistic level of accuracy. In addition, with the wide-scale adoption of new display technologies, devices, and networks, such as HD TVs, 3D TVs, immersive environments, handheld devices, and so on, approaches dealing with QA, user context, and personalization must take into account this multi-environment scenario. Metadata generation still remains an issue since most TV streams have no associated metadata to describe their structure. The associated program guides usually lack precision in time, and details and do not include information about the various parts of the program. Computational efficiency also needs to be addressed due to the huge amount of TV content available or due to the limited capabilities of the TV set when the processing has to be client-based.

In most cases, a common issue is the design and implementation of appropriate evaluation procedures. Large amounts of annotated content are needed, and while TRECVID plays an important role, in many chapters specific TV programs and shows are used. Metrics and test databases are also needed as, for example, in the case of display-specific QA and detailed databases, where databases have been created for this specific purpose. Applications and use cases are also an issue since it is difficult to test research results and approaches with TV providers, although there are projects where this is achieved. Finally, standardization plays an important role. The existence of several standards created problems for application developers, who had to transfer implementations across standards. Standard-independent platforms have now been proposed as a possible solution as lack of standards is hindering development in sectors such as web TV convergence.

The rapid development of digital multimedia technologies is revolutionizing the production and distribution of audiovisual content and expanding the capabilities of TV channels with new types of augmented content, improved presentation, and multiple devices. We hope that this book will serve as a reference for a global view of the current technologies and future trends and will provide a basis to support the continuing development of the domain of digital TV.

Ioannis (Yiannis) Kompatsiaris
Centre for Research and Technology, Hellas
Informatics & Telematics Institute
Thessaloniki, Greece

Bernard Merialdo
EURECOM
Sophia-Antipolis, France

Shiguo Lian
Central Research Institute
Huawei Technologies Co., Ltd.
Shenzhen, China

MATLAB® is a registered trademark of The MathWorks, Inc. For product information, please contact:

The MathWorks, Inc.
3 Apple Hill Drive
Natick, MA 01760-2098 USA
Tel: 508 647 7000
Fax: 508-647-7001
E-mail: info@mathworks.com
Web: www.mathworks.com

Acknowledgments

We would like to acknowledge the help of all those who were involved in the collation process of this book, without whose support the project could not have been satisfactorily completed. Deep appreciation and gratitude is due to the authors of all the chapters for their efforts to achieve a high-quality project.

Special thanks go to the publishing team at Taylor & Francis Group, whose contributions throughout the whole process from inception of the initial idea to final publication have been invaluable. We would like to thank Richard O'Hanley, in particular, for continuously prodding via e-mail to help us keep the project on schedule.

Last but not least, a big and sincere expression of gratitude to our families, for their unfailing support and encouragement during the months it took to give birth to this book.

Editors

Dr. Ioannis (Yiannis) Kompatsiaris is a senior researcher (Researcher B′) with the Informatics and Telematics Institute in Greece. His research interests include semantic multimedia analysis, indexing and retrieval, Web 2.0 content analysis, knowledge structures, reasoning, and personalization for multimedia applications. He received his PhD in 3-D-model-based image sequence coding from the Aristotle University of Thessaloniki in 2001. He is the coauthor of 55 papers in refereed journals, 30 book chapters, 7 patents, and more than 170 papers in international conferences. He is also the coeditor of the book *Semantic Multimedia and Ontologies: Theory and Applications*, the guest editor of six special issues, and has served as a program committee member and regular reviewer for a number of international journals and conferences. Kompatsiaris has been the co-organizer of various conferences and workshops, such as the *ACM International Conference on Image and Video Retrieval* (*CIVR*), *International Workshop on Image Analysis for Multimedia Interactive Services* (*WIAMIS*), and *Summer School on Multimedia Semantics* (*SSMS*). He is also the coordinator of the SocialSensor—Sensing User Generated Input for Improved Media Discovery and Experience, European Integrated Project. He has been appointed as chair of the Technical Committee 14 of the International Association for Pattern Recognition (IAPR-TC14, "Signal Analysis for Machine Intelligence"). Kompatsiaris is a senior member of the IEEE and a member of the ACM.

Bernard Merialdo is a professor in the Multimedia Department of EURECOM, France, and head of the department. A former student of the Ecole Normale Supérieure, Paris, he received his PhD from Paris 6 University and a "Habilitation à Diriger des Recherches" from Paris 7 University. For more than 10 years, he was a research staff, then project manager at the IBM France Scientific Center, working on probabilistic techniques for Large Vocabulary Speech Recognition. He later joined EURECOM to set up the Multimedia Department. His research interests include the analysis, processing, indexing, and filtering of multimedia information to solve user-related tasks. His research covers a whole range of problems, from content extraction based on recognition techniques, content understanding based on parsing, multimedia content description languages (MPEG7), similarity computation for applications such as information retrieval, and user personalization and user interaction for the construction of applications. Merialdo has participated in numerous conference program committees. He is part of the organizing committee for the CBMI workshop. He was editor for the *IEEE Transactions on Multimedia* and chairman of the ACM Multimedia conference in 2002. He often acts as an expert and reviewer for French and European research programs. Merialdo is a senior member of the IEEE and a member of the ACM.

Shiguo Lian received his PhD from Nanjing University of Science and Technology, Nanjing, China. He was a research assistant in City University of Hong Kong in 2004. Since July 2005, he has been a research scientist with France Telecom R&D (Orange Labs), Beijing. He is the author or coauthor of more than 80 refereed international journal and conference papers covering topics such as secure multimedia communication, intelligent multimedia services, and ubiquitous communication. He has contributed 15 book chapters and held 16 filed patents. He has authored the book *Multimedia Content Encryption: Techniques and Applications* (CRC Press, Boca Raton, FL, 2008) and has edited seven books. He was nominated for the prize of "Innovation Prize in France Telecom" and "Top 100 Doctorate Dissertation in Jiangsu Province" in 2006. Lian is a member of the IEEE Communications and Information Security Technical Committee, the IEEE Multimedia Communications Technical Committee, the IEEE SMCS Technical Committee on Soft Computing, and the IEEE Technical Committee on Nonlinear Circuits and Systems. He is on the editorial board of several international journals. He is also the guest editor of more than 10 international journals/magazines. Lian is in the organization committee or the TPC member of refereed conferences, including *IEEE International Conference on Multimedia and Expo* (*ICME*), 2011/2012, *IEEE International Workshop on Multimedia Signal Processing* (*MMSP*), 2011, *IEEE International Conference on Communication* (*ICC*), 2008–2012, *IEEE Global Communications Conference* (*GLOBECOM*), 2008–2012, *IEEE Consumer Communications and Networking Conference* (*CCNC*), 2009, and *IEEE International Conference on Computer Communications and Networks* (*ICCCN*), 2009. He is also a reviewer for refereed international magazines and journals.

Contributors

Alina Elma Abduraman
France Telecom R&D
Orange Labs
Rennes, France

Sabine Bachmayer
Johannes Kepler University Linz
Department of Telecooperation
Linz, Austria

Werner Bailer
JOANNEUM RESEARCH
Institute for Information and
    Communication Technologies
Graz, Austria

Lamberto Ballan
Media Integration and Communication
    Center
University of Florence
Florence, Italy

Riccardo Bambini
Fastweb
Milan, Italy

Andrea Basso
AT&T Labs Research
Middletown, New Jersey

Lee Begeja
AT&T Labs Research
Florham Park, New Jersey

Sid Ahmed Berrani
France Telecom R&D
Orange Labs
Rennes, France

Marco Bertini
Media Integration and Communication
    Center
University of Florence
Florence, Italy

Alan Conrad Bovik
Laboratory for Image and Video
    Engineering
Department of Electrical and
    Computer Engineering
The University of Texas at Austin
Austin, Texas

Shelley Buchinger
Faculty of Computer Science
University of Vienna
Vienna, Austria

Jordi Carrabina
Center for Ambient Intelligence and
    Accessibility of Catalonia
Universitat Autònoma de Barcelona
Bellaterra, Spain

Jean Carrive
National Audiovisual Institute (Ina)
Bry-sur-Marne, France

Teresa Chambel
Faculty of Sciences
Large-Scale Informatic Systems
    Laboratory
University of Lisbon
Lisbon, Portugal

Chia-Hu Chang
Graduate Institute of Networking and
    Multimedia
National Taiwan University
Taipei, Taiwan

Shih-Fu Chang
Electrical Engineering Department
Columbia University
New York, New York

Paolo Cremonesi
Politecnico di Milano, DEI
Milan, Italy

Ovidiu Dan
Lehigh University
Bethlehem, Pennsylvania

Alberto Del Bimbo
Media Integration and Communication
    Center
University of Florence
Florence, Italy

Touradj Ebrahimi
Norwegian University of Science and
    Technology
Trondheim, Norway
and
Ecole Polytechnique Fédérale de
    Lausanne
Lausanne, Switzerland

Ahmet Ekin
Video and Image Processing Group
Philips Research Europe
Eindhoven, the Netherlands

Slim Essid
Télécom ParisTech
Paris, France

Junlan Feng
AT&T Labs Research
Florham Park, New Jersey

Moncef Gabbouj
Tampere University of Technology
Tampere, Finland

David Gibbon
AT&T Labs Research
Middletown, New Jersey

Patrick Gros
Institut National de Recherche en
    Informatique et en Automatique
Centre Rennes-Bretagne Atlantique
Rennes, France

Nuno Guimarães
Faculty of Sciences
Large-Scale Informatic Systems
    Laboratory
University of Lisbon
Lisbon, Portugal

Helmut Hlavacs
Faculty of Computer Science
University of Vienna
Vienna, Austria

Frank Hopfgartner
International Computer Science
   Institute
University of California
Berkeley, California

Patrik Hummelbrunner
Faculty of Computer Science
University of Vienna
Vienna, Austria

Zein Al Abidin Ibrahim
LERIA Laboratory
University of Angers
Angers, France

Wei Jiang
Corporate Research and Engineering
Eastman Kodak Company
Rochester, New York

Ioannis (Yiannis) Kompatsiaris
Centre for Research and Technology,
   Hellas
Informatics & Telematics Institute
Thessaloniki, Greece

Shiguo Lian
Central Research Institute
Huawei Technologies Co., Ltd.
Shenzhen, China

Yu-Tzu Lin
Graduate Institute of Information and
   Computer Education
National Taiwan Normal University
Taipei, Taiwan

Zhu Liu
AT&T Labs Research
Middletown, New Jersey

Klaus Lojka
Mass Media and Communication
   Science
University of Vienna
Vienna, Austria

Alexander Loui
Corporate Research and Engineering
Eastman Kodak Company
Rochester, New York

Karin Macher
Film Academy Vienna
Vienna, Austria

Bernard Merialdo
EURECOM
Sophia-Antipolis, France

Anush Krishna Moorthy
Laboratory for Image and Video
   Engineering
Department of Electrical and
   Computer Engineering
The University of Texas at Austin
Austin, Texas

Matej Nezveda
Faculty of Computer Science
University of Vienna
Vienna, Austria

Walter Nunziati
Media Integration and Communication
   Center
University of Florence
Florence, Italy

Andrew Perkis
Norwegian University of Science and
   Technology
Trondheim, Norway

Thanassis Perperis
Department of Informatics and
    Telecommunications
National and Kapodistrian University
    of Athens
Athens, Greece

Alcina Prata
Faculty of Sciences
Large-Scale Informatic Systems
    Laboratory
University of Lisbon
Lisbon, Portugal

Bernard Renger
AT&T Labs Research
Florham Park, New Jersey

Gaël Richard
Télécom ParisTech
Paris, France

Werner Robitza
Faculty of Computer Science
Entertainment Computing Research
    Group
University of Vienna
Vienna, Austria

Aitor Rodriguez-Alsina
Center for Ambient Intelligence and
    Accessibility of Catalonia
Universitat Autònoma de Barcelona
Bellaterra, Spain

Klaus Schoeffmann
Institute of Information
    Technology
Klagenfurt University
Klagenfurt, Austria

Giuseppe Serra
Media Integration and Communication
    Center
University of Florence
Florence, Italy

Behzad Shahraray
AT&T Labs Research
Middletown, New Jersey

Sofia Tsekeridou
Multimedia, Knowledge and Web
    Technologies
Athens Information Technology
Athens, Greece

Pauliina Tuomi
Tampere University of Technology
Advanced Multimedia Center,
    Pori Unit
Pori, Finland

Roberto Turrin
Moviri, R&D
Milan, Italy

Tinne Tuytelaars
Departement Elektrotechniek
Katholieke Universiteit Leuven
Leuven, Belgium

Félicien Vallet
National Audiovisual Institute (Ina)
Bry-Sur-Marne, France
and
Télécom ParisTech
Paris, France

Luc Van Gool
Departement Elektrotechniek
Katholieke Universiteit Leuven
Leuven, Belgium

Geert Willems
Departement Elektrotechniek
Katholieke Universiteit Leuven
Leuven, Belgium

Julia Wippersberg
Mass Media and Communication
  Science
University of Vienna
Vienna, Austria

Ja-Ling Wu
Graduate Institute of Networking and
  Multimedia
National Taiwan University
Taipei, Taiwan

Junyong You
Norwegian University of Science and
  Technology
Trondheim, Norway

Eric Zavesky
AT&T Labs Research
Middletown, New Jersey

CONTENT EXTRACTION

Chapter 1

Local Spatiotemporal Features for Robust Content-Based Video Copy Detection

Geert Willems
Katholieke Universiteit Leuven

Tinne Tuytelaars
Katholieke Universiteit Leuven

Luc Van Gool
Katholieke Universiteit Leuven

Contents

Detecting (near) copies of video footage in streams or databases has several useful applications. Reuse of video material by different data aggregators can help as a guide to link stories across channels, while finding copies of copyrighted video fragments is of great interest for their rightful owners. Most methods today are based on global descriptors and fingerprinting techniques as they can be computed very efficiently. The downside, however, is that they are inherently not very well suited to detect copies after transformations have been applied that change the overall appearance, such as the addition of logos and banners, picture-in-picture, cropping, etc. To cope with such variations, methods based on local features have been proposed. Most such robust content-based copy detection (CBCD) systems proposed to date have in common that they initially rely on the detection of two-dimensional (2D) interest points on specific or all frames and only use temporal information in a second step (if at all). Here we propose the use of a recently developed spatiotemporal feature detector and descriptor based on the Hessian matrix. We explain the theory behind the features as well as the implementation details that allow for efficient computations. We further present a disk-based pipeline for efficient indexing and retrieval of video content based on two-stable locality sensitive hashing (LSH). Through experiments, we show the increased robustness when using spatiotemporal features as opposed to purely spatial features. Finally, we apply the proposed system to faster than real-time monitoring of 71 commercials in 5 h of TV broadcasting.

1.1 Introduction

Many TV channels around the globe broadcast news, often on a daily basis. For approximately half of their news stories, they all obtain the same video footage from a few big press agencies. Nevertheless, the same material is presented substantially

Figure 1.1 Video footage reuse in broadcasts. All shots were correctly retrieved by our system from a 88+ h database. (Image from Walker, K., *TRECVID 2006*, LDC2006E40, Linguistic Data Consortium, Philadelphia, PA, 2006. With permission.)

different depending on the channel, due to a high level of post-processing: logos and banners are added, items are shown picture-in-picture, gamma-correction, cropping, zoom-in, trans-coding, and other transformations are applied to the raw input data so as to adapt the content to the look and feel of a particular channel, as illustrated in Figure 1.1.

For data aggregators on the Internet, such as news sites collecting information from different channels and presenting it in a unified framework to the user, detecting reuse of the same video footage is a useful tool to link stories across channels, independent of language or political opinion. Likewise, for researchers in broadcasting companies, it may be interesting to retrieve the original video footage based on broadcasted fragments, especially when the metadata are incomplete or missing, which is often the case for older archives.

However, the high level of postprocessing poses specific challenges to the problem of content-based video copy detection. Most of the methods proposed to date are based on global methods and fingerprinting techniques (e.g., [8,15,20]). These work well for exact copies, but have inherently problems with added banners, logos, picture-in-picture, rescaling, cropping, etc. For this reason, specific preprocessing steps are often applied, such as ignoring parts of the video where these additions typically appear, or searching for strong gradients to detect picture-in-picture.

In order to cope with such variations, the use of *local features*, also referred to as interest points, has been proposed in the context of CBCD by [10,11,19,26]. In [10], a detailed comparative study of different video copy detection methods has been performed, including both global and local descriptors. The 2D local features proved indeed more robust than the global features, although they come with a higher computational cost. In the overview, the authors also tested a single local spatiotemporal feature based on the Harris corner detector [17], but the computational cost proved too high to be considered practical.

1.1.1 Local Spatiotemporal Features for Video CBCD

Almost all CBCD systems proposed to date that are based on local features, have in common that they rely on the detection of 2D interest points on specific or all frames of the videos and use the descriptors of the local neighborhood of these points as indices to retrieve the video. Typically, temporal information, if used at all, is added to these features only in a second step. Joly et al. [10] detect local features in key frames only but use information from precedent and following frames as well when computing the descriptor. Law et al. [19] proposed a method for CBCD by means of tracking 2D interest points throughout the video sequence. They use the 2D Harris detector [7] and Kanade–Lucas–Tomasi (KLT) feature tracking software [28]. By using the trajectories, the local descriptor is enhanced with temporal information, while the redundancy of the local descriptors is reduced. The obtained descriptors are invariant to image translation and affine illumination transformations, but are not scale-invariant.

When applying spatial features, the frames that are analyzed are either determined by subsampling (i.e., extracting features from every nth frame), by key-frame selection or a combination of the two. In the case of subsampling, there is no guarantee that the same frames will be selected in both the reference and query videos. Hence, one relies on the assumption that similar features will be found in temporally nearby frames—an assumption which only holds up to some extent and for slowly changing scenes only. For key-frame selection, global methods are typically used (e.g., based on motion intensity) which are often not reliable with respect to specific transformations such as picture-in-picture, the addition of banners, etc. A system that is using key frames is highly dependent on the robustness of the used shot-boundary detection. In this regard, local spatiotemporal features have several advantages:

1. The features are extracted at interesting locations not only spatially but also over time, which makes them more discriminative as well as better localized within the shot.
2. As the spatiotemporal features are detected at *interesting* areas throughout the shot, they allow for an easy and robust alignment between shots by simply finding the corresponding features.
3. The resulting set of descriptors contains information from within the whole shot, rather than focusing on a few selected (key)frames (see also Figure 1.2).
4. By analyzing a spatiotemporal volume instead of spatial planes at certain (key)frames, the performance of the system is no longer dependent on the robustness of the chosen shot-cut detection algorithm.

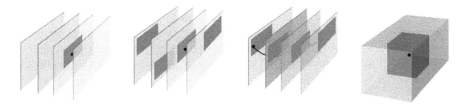

Figure 1.2 **A visual comparison of different local features used in the context of CBCD. In the first three drawings, a 2D feature is detected at a specific (key)frame. The descriptor is computed (from left to right) using solely spatial information; by adding temporal information by including information from neighboring frames; and through tracking. In the right drawing, both the feature's location and scale as well as its descriptor is computed by analyzing the spatiotemporal volume.**

1.1.2 Overview

The remainder of the chapter is organized as follows. We begin with a short overview of previously developed local spatiotemporal features, after which we introduce the proposed Hessian-based spatiotemporal interest point (STIP) detector and discuss the adaptations we have made in the context of video CBCD. Next, in Section 1.3, we describe the proposed disk-based index and query system based on LSH. Section 1.4 contains an experimental evaluation of the system and a comparison of spatial and spatiotemporal features. We test their robustness to artificial transformations and their performance when querying a video stream shot by a handheld camera. We finally apply the system to the task of monitoring commercial airtime (Section 1.5) and conclude in Section 1.6.

1.2 Efficient Local Spatiotemporal Interest Point

Over the recent years, many local viewpoint-invariant features have been extended to the spatiotemporal domain. These take the three-dimensional (3D) nature of video data into account and localize features not only spatially, but also over time.

We start with a short overview of other currently available spatiotemporal detectors and descriptors. Next, we describe in more detail the recently developed spatiotemporal feature detector and descriptor based on the Hessian matrix and discuss the adaptations we made for their use in video CBCD.

1.2.1 Short Overview of Spatiotemporal Interest Points

Laptev and Lindeberg [17] were the first to propose such a spatiotemporal extension, building on the Harris–Laplace detector proposed by Mikolajczyk et al. [22]. This is also the detector that was used in the video copy detection comparison of [10].

However, the extraction of scale-invariant Harris–Laplace features involves a time-consuming iterative procedure that has to be repeated for each feature candidate separately. This is not really suited for video copy detection applications where efficiency is an important aspect. In order to speedup the detection process, these features are typically extracted at a fixed combination of spatial and temporal scales.

Dollár et al. [5], on the other hand, claim that direct 3D counterparts to 2D interest point detectors are inadequate for the detection of spatiotemporal feature points, since true spatiotemporal corners are quite rare. They propose to select local maxima over space and time of a response function based on a spatial Gaussian convolved with a quadrature pair of one-dimensional (1D) Gabor-filters along the time axis. However, their features are not scale-invariant as the size of these *cuboids* needs to be set by the user.

Oikonomopoulos et al. [23] have proposed a spatiotemporal extension of the salient region detector proposed by Kadir and Brady [12]. The features are scale-invariant yet sparse, as was also the case for the original spatial detector.

Also related is the work of Ke et al. [13] on visual event detection. They build on the concept of integral video to achieve real-time processing of video data. However, rather than relying on interest points, they use dense spatiotemporal Haar wavelets computed on the optical flow. Discriminative features are then selected during a training stage. This results in application-dependent features which are, again, not scale-invariant.

Recently, a spatiotemporal extension of the Hessian blob detector [21] has been proposed by Willems et al. [30]. The computed features are scale-invariant in both space and time, as well as invariant to in-plane rotations. Moreover, the coverage of the features can be easily varied from very dense to very sparse, as shown in Figure 1.3b. Most importantly, the features can be extracted and described in an efficient way. These properties make them a good candidate for the task of content-based video copy detection.

Quantitative evaluations of the spatiotemporal Harris–Laplace detector, the Hessian-based detector, and cuboids in [30] and [27] show that the Hessian-based detector outperforms the others for most transformations in terms of repeatability. The latter paper also includes an evaluation of the Hessian-based spatiotemporal descriptor [30], together with the HOG/HOF [18] and HOG3D [16] spatiotemporal descriptors.

1.2.2 Hessian-Based STIP Detector

In [30], Willems et al. propose the use of the Hessian matrix

$$H(\cdot; \sigma^2, \tau^2) = \begin{pmatrix} L_{xx} & L_{xy} & L_{xt} \\ L_{yx} & L_{yy} & L_{yt} \\ L_{tx} & L_{ty} & L_{tt} \end{pmatrix} \tag{1.1}$$

(a)   (b)

Figure 1.3   Hessian-based spatiotemporal features. (a) The two types of box filter approximations for the 2 + 1D Gaussian second order partial derivatives in one direction (left) and in two directions (right). (b) Visualization of the extracted features. The density of features can be varied from very sparse (first and third images) to very dense (second and fourth image), simply by changing the threshold and with minimal effect on the computation time.

for spatiotemporal feature selection, where σ and τ are, respectively, the spatial and temporal scale and L_{ab} denotes a second-order scale-space derivative. The strength of each interest point at a certain scale is then computed by

$$S = |det(H)| \tag{1.2}$$

Part of the efficiency of the detector stems from the fact that the localization and scale selection of the features can be achieved simultaneously with the scale-normalized determinant of the Hessian. It is further shown in [30] that, in D dimensions, the determinant of the scale-normalized Hessian, with $\gamma = 1$, reaches an extremum at the center of a Gaussian blob $g(\mathbf{x}; \boldsymbol{\sigma}_0)$ with $\boldsymbol{\sigma}_0 = [\sigma_{0,1}, \ldots, \sigma_{0,D}]$, for scales

$$\tilde{\sigma} = \sqrt{\frac{2}{D}} \sigma_0 \tag{1.3}$$

Since computing the determinant of the Hessian at many positions and scales can become computationally prohibitive, all Gaussian second-order derivatives are approximated with box filters, as shown in Figure 1.3a. In this regard, the implementation can be seen as a spatiotemporal extension of the 2D SURF [1] features. Box filters can be computed very efficiently in constant time using an integral video structure [13], the spatiotemporal extension of integral images.

Finding interest points boils down to detecting local extrema in the 5D space defined by the position (x, y, t), spatial scale σ, and temporal scale τ.

1.2.3 Hessian-Based STIP Descriptor

The descriptors are again an extended version of the SURF descriptor [1]. Around each interest point with spatial scale σ and temporal scale τ, a rectangular volume is defined with dimensions $s\sigma \times s\sigma \times s\tau$ with s a user-defined magnification factor. The volume is subsequently divided into $M \times M \times N$ bins, where M and N are the number of bins in the spatial and temporal direction, respectively. These bins are filled by a weighted sum of uniformly sampled responses of the three axis-aligned Haar wavelets d_x, d_y, d_t. Each bin stores the 3D vector $v = \left(\sum d_x, \sum d_y, \sum d_t \right)$. The descriptor can be made in-plane rotation-invariant if needed.

For more in-depth information on the detector and descriptor, we refer the reader to [30].

1.2.4 Adaptations for Video CBCD

Robust video CBCD poses many challenges as a myriad of post-processing transformations can be applied to the original video material before it is broadcasted. The editing of rushes, rescaling, color correction, a superposition of a lower third or logo, compression, picture-in-picture are just some of the possible changes that can occur. However, rotating a video clip is rarely, if ever, an applied transformation. Secondly, we assume that clips are shown at their original speed, which is not always true, as e.g., televised sporting events often show replays in slow motion. As a result, invariance to in-plane rotation and changes in the temporal scale are as such not required. For this reason, we choose to use a rotation-variant descriptor and fix the temporal scale of the detector to the smallest possible kernel width of nine frames. By fixing the temporal scale, we reduce the search space from five to four dimensions, which speeds up the detection significantly. The acquired features are still robust to a certain degree of time dilation, however, as shown in Section 1.4.4. We choose for magnification factor $s = 3$, which means that each descriptor is computed over 27 frames. This allows us to detect and match features in shots with a minimum length of about 1 s. We search over three octaves in the spatial domain, with five scales per octave, and divide the region around the interest point in $4 \times 4 \times 3$ bins, creating a 144-dimensional* descriptor. The proposed detector can extract features from videos in NTSC resolution at about 45 fps.

1.3 Disk-Based Pipeline for Efficient Indexing and Retrieval

1.3.1 Pipeline Overview

Figure 1.4 gives an overview of our processing pipeline. Long videos to be stored in the database are first cut into smaller segments. We use the term *segment*, and not *shot*, as we do not require the video to be split along shot boundaries. For each segment, we then extract local spatiotemporal features and store these in our database, based on an index that is a combination of a segment index and a feature

---

* $4 \times 4 \times 3$ bins $\times 3$ dimensions per vector $= 144$.

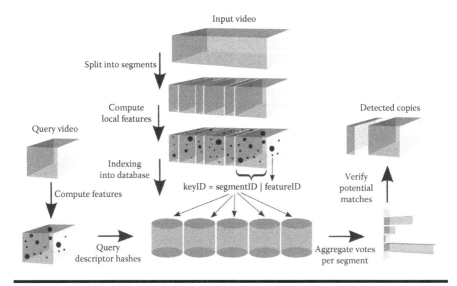

Figure 1.4   An overview of the pipeline used in this chapter. We refer the reader to the text for more details.

index. When a query video is presented to the system, the same process is repeated. The database retrieves all possible matches for each of the extracted spatiotemporal features of the query video, and returns a ranked list of relevant reference segments based on the amount of aggregated votes. At this point, a RANSAC-based scheme can be used to further verify the spatiotemporal consistency between the query segment and the returned reference segments.

1.3.2 Indexing and Retrieving High-Dimensional Data

Indexing and retrieving high-dimensional data on a large scale is far from trivial as exact nearest-neighbor searches suffer from the *curse of dimensionality*. Over the years, several schemes have been introduced which perform approximate searches to overcome this hurdle.

LSH [9] is such an approximate high-dimensional similarity search scheme. It is able to avoid the curse of dimensionality by hashing the descriptors through a series of projections onto random lines and concatenating the results into a single hash. The probability of collision between such hashes is much higher for descriptors that are near to each other in the high-dimensional space. Typically, several hash databases are combined to improve the probability of finding correct matches.

Ke et al. [14] were the first to implement an on-disk version of LSH in the context of near-duplicate image retrieval. In order to minimize disk access, they combine queries in batches. By sorting both the batches and the on-disk database, only one sequential scan through the database is needed per batch as first the smallest hash value will be encountered (if it exists in the database), and so on. In a second step, the matched descriptors need to be checked for outliers as LSH matches with respect to L1.

More recently, Joly et al. [10] proposed a distortion-based probabilistic similarity search where they partition the space of the relatively small descriptors using a Hilbert space filling curve. While the proposed scheme could handle over 40.000 h of video, a recent adaptation using a Z-Grid [25] allows for the evaluation of 120.000 h of video.

The NV-tree, proposed by Jonsson et al. [11], is another disk-based approach for efficient approximate nearest neighbor search. The scheme combines partitioning the descriptors into small segments by projecting them on random lines, similar to LSH, with B^+-tree structures that allow for efficient aggregation of ranking. NV-trees are able to perform approximate nearest neighbor search in constant time and can be used in a distributed setup [3].

1.3.3 Disk-Based p-Stable LSH

We use an on-disk LSH indexing scheme, as proposed by Ke et al. [14], yet with some notable changes that speed up the process and allow for more accurate matches.

First, we implemented a variant of the original LSH scheme based on p-stable distributions [4]. Since this variant works directly with the L2 norm, it removes the need to access the descriptors in order to check for outliers. Secondly, as our descriptors lie on a unit hypersphere, we divide the randomly selected projection lines by the square root of the dimension, roughly normalizing each line. Due to this small change, we can swap the parameter W with the parameter N, the number of subdivisions of the radius of the hypersphere.

Next, we construct the key identifier in such a way that both the video segment identifier as well as the features identifier within that segment can be extracted from this one key. This enables votes to be cast per video segment without the need to read auxiliary data. Only in the case when the transformation between two segments is required, need the features be loaded into memory. In the following experiments, we show that a RANSAC procedure is not really necessary to correctly detect the copies in the TRECVID2006 dataset [29] with a high degree of certainty. Each key identifier is stored inside the corresponding hash bucket together with an additional check-sum hash to discriminate between different features within the same bucket (see [14]).

Finally, when the database has been created, we further divide the list of ordered buckets into fixed-size blocks and record the offsets to each block, together with the bucket index at the start of that block. Instead of linearly reading all buckets that make up the database in order to find the matches to each query feature hash in the batch, the offsets are used to compute the next possible block that could contain a matching hash value. As the bucket indices in the database are ordered, the next block is invariably positioned in the part of the database we have not yet scanned. By using these offsets, most parts of the database are never read, reducing the search time tremendously since at most one small block per feature has to be loaded from disk into memory. The list of offset and start indices is kept in memory at all time.

1.4 Experimental Evaluation

1.4.1 Setting Up the Experiment

In order to test the performance of our proposed spatiotemporal features, we used over 88 h of video from the TRECVID2006 dataset containing news broadcasts* by American channels. All experiments and timings in this paper are done on a Intel 2.4 GHz Core2 Quad processor with 4 GB of memory running Linux with a 1 TB 7200 rpm hard disk.

The same pipeline, depicted in Figure 1.4, is used to include reference videos into the database and to process video clips for querying. In a first step, shot-cut detection [24] is applied, resulting in approximately 41,400 segments. This algorithm has linear complexity and uses both global motion compensation and adaptive thresholding for detecting shot cuts. While it exhibits a high detection rate for abrupt cuts, it has problems detecting smooth cuts leading to under-segmentation. From each segment features are computed. We extract on average 180 features per second, which is similar to the amount of features used by [3]. In the case of reference videos, these features are stored in the LSH database together with a key identifier. From this identifier, both the segment as well as the feature within that clip can easily be obtained. In all our experiments, we use 20 (L) randomly chosen hash databases where each hash is computed from 16 (K) random projections. Each projection is then divided into roughly 200 bins within the unit hypersphere.

The resulting database holds about 53 million features. The disk access time (seeking and reading) and the overall query time is shown in Figure 1.6a. The figure also includes the timings of a second database containing over 105 million features, almost double in size. As can be seen, the query times are no longer linear dependent on the size of the database. Furthermore, using a larger batch of query features reduces the seek time per feature.

Upon querying a video segment, we extract the interest points and create a batch of hashes for each of the 20 databases. Whenever a match is detected in a database, a vote is cast for the corresponding reference segment. After all votes have been aggregated, we end up with a list of possible copies of the query clip together with a ranking, the number of votes each clip received. It should be noted that, unlike with NV-trees [11], LSH is not rank-based and as such we cannot use rank aggregation. However, if a query feature is matched to a same reference feature in

---

* In NTSC resolution. The length of the segments ranges between 1 and 48 s.

several databases, these concurring votes give a higher probability that both features are nearest neighbors. In a final step, false errors can be pruned by applying a RANSAC scheme to find the translation and spatial scale between the query clip and a potential copy. However, this step should be avoided if possible since it can be a slow process and requires both reference and query features to be loaded into memory.

1.4.2 Comparison between Spatial and Spatiotemporal Features

For 2D features, we use upright, 64-dimensional SURF [1] features. We search for interest points over three octaves, as we do for the spatiotemporal features. Similar to [3], we detect the 2D features at every 12th frame of a clip and compute a 4×4 bins 2D descriptor.

We created a full database of the 88+ h of video for both feature types, while making sure that both databases have a comparable size. More information on the databases can be seen in Figure 1.5.

To evaluate the features, we randomly selected 13 video clips from the full database and manually obtained the ground-truth—all (partial) copies of these clips within the database. Besides itself, each query clip has between 2 and 30 copies inside the database. We would like to note here that the shot-cut detection, discussed earlier, is solely applied to split the original 30 min to 1 h news broadcasts into manageable segments. Using the spatiotemporal features, the pipeline is not dependent on the quality of shot cuts. Indeed, many cuts are erroneous or missed and many segments contain different scenes. This is no problem, however, as even small 1 s segments can be detected successfully by the spatiotemporal features.

In Figure 1.6B, we show several precision-recall curves for the 2D SURF features (a) and the spatiotemporal features (b). The black curve is obtained by simply using the total amount of votes for each clip as a threshold. Next, we only look at votes that have support from two or more databases. By counting only concurring votes, the probability is higher that the matched features are indeed nearest neighbors. We can clearly see that this improves the performance for both feature types. However, if this threshold is set too high many matches are being discarded, again deteriorating the performance.

Feature type	#Hours	Avg #Entries	Total disk space
SURF	88+	44M	11.5 GB
Spatiotemporal	88+	53M	14.9 GB

Figure 1.5 **Information on the databases used in the experiments.**

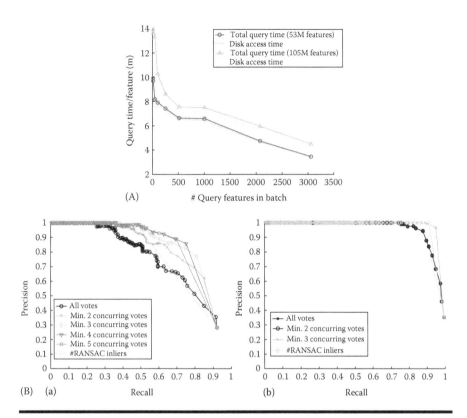

Figure 1.6 **(A) On average disk access and query time per feature (in ms) for a single hash database in function of the query batch size. The queries are performed on a database containing 105M (⬆) and 53M (⊖) features. While the query time increases slightly for larger databases due to longer seek times, the query time per feature can be reduced drastically by increasing the batch size. (B) Precision-recall curves for spatial (a) and spatiotemporal (b) features.**

As the detector and descriptor of each SURF feature is solely dependent on the data inside one frame, their discriminative power is lower than that of the spatiotemporal features. This causes the features to trigger on frames that contain similar content, but depict a different scene. Indeed, many segments that are shot from the same event, yet on different instances or from different views, are often matched using SURF features. While this can be a valuable property, it is clearly not desirable in the context of strict CBCD. Furthermore, the dataset itself is challenging. Almost all news channels display a lower third, or chyron, which is superimposed onto the lower portion of the frame. These graphics trigger the detection of many features and often will result in a possible match between clips solely due to the lower third. While in some scenarios, this could be solved by cropping all videos before indexing and querying, it still is an important part of the footage.

Relying on the inliers after RANSAC does not impact the performance for the spatiotemporal features, but deteriorates the score for the spatial features. The reason is that the amount of wrong matches can be quite high. While there are enough correct matches to consistently vote for the correct copy, RANSAC breaks down when the percentage of wrong matches become too high. Furthermore, sometimes a very small overlap between videos is correctly detected, yet the matches give not enough info to find the corresponding transformation.

1.4.3 Robustness to Transformations

Next, we test the robustness of the feature types by applying several transformations to randomly selected video segments, which are subsequently used as query. Figure 1.7 (top row) shows an example of the applied transformations. As before, the ranking is based on the votes that appear at least twice within the hash databases. The obtained precision–recall curves are presented in Figure 1.7 (bottom row).

As both features types are scale-invariant (in the spatial dimensions), it is not surprising they are very robust against subsampling the video resolution. Gaussian noise and gamma correction also have little impact on the performance. However, the spatial features behave poorly against the addition of salt and pepper noise, although precision seems to have increased for low recall values. Without noise, some reference videos are incorrectly identified as copies because they share the same lower third with the query video. After applying the noise, these reference videos no longer match, resulting in the improved precision at low recall.

The spatiotemporal features, however, are fairly resilient against this attack. Since the detector works over nine frames, the random noise applied to each separate frame is largely canceled out. This robustness that is obtained by working in the

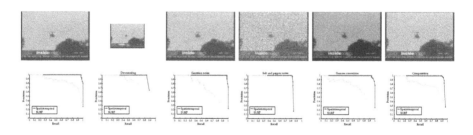

Figure 1.7 Applied transformations. From left to right: an original frame, sub-sampled to half the resolution, Gaussian noise (std. var. 20), salt and pepper noise (20% filled), gamma correction of 1.6, video compression to 5 kbit/s. On the bottom row, the PR curves of both feature types are shown for each transformation. (Image from Walker, K., *TRECVID 2006*, LDC2006E40, Linguistic Data Consortium, Philadelphia, PA, 2006. With permission.)

spatiotemporal domain can also be seen, although in a lesser way, when compression is applied.

1.4.4 Video Copy Detection from Handheld Shooting

We now apply video copy detection to a more challenging real-life transformation. For this, we use a handheld webcam* to record 15 s of one of the reference video while it is being displayed on a monitor. The webcam has a resolution of 320×240 and records at 12 fps. Since we assume, as discussed before, that there is no time dilation, we generate the query video by simply duplicating each frame, giving us a near 25 fps frame rate. Furthermore, the webcam records the video at an oblique angle distorting the frames. Finally, additional jitter is added by holding the camera in hand.

The recorded movie contains four reference shots. From each shot a frame is shown in Figure 1.8a. In Figure 1.8b, two frames are shown with the detected spatiotemporal and spatial features. The spatial features are detected every 12th frame.

Checking the database reveals that, from the four reference shots, seven copies exist in total. The seven highest ranked retrieved reference segments obtained via

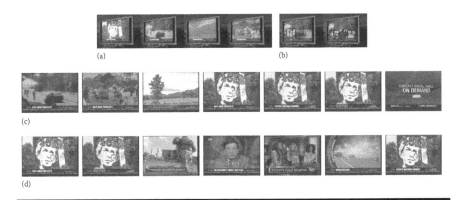

Figure 1.8 Detected videos from a recording using a handheld webcam. (a) Four frames from the recorded video. The video covers several topics. (b) Detected spatiotemporal (left) and spatial (right) features. (c) The seven highest ranked retrieved video clips using spatiotemporal features. (Image from Walker, K., *TRECVID 2006*, LDC2006E40, Linguistic Data Consortium, Philadelphia, PA, 2006. With permission.) (d) The seven highest ranked retrieved video clips using spatial features. (Image from Walker, K., *TRECVID 2006*, LDC2006E40, Linguistic Data Consortium, Philadelphia, PA, 2006. With permission.)

---

* Logitech QuickCam.

the spatiotemporal and spatial features are displayed in Figure 1.8c and d. The ranking was based on those votes which appear at least twice within the 20 hash databases.

The amount of votes retrieved by both feature types was very low. This is the result of the color changes and affine transformation that heavily distort the surrounding of each interest point. However, as can be seen in Figure 1.8, the spatiotemporal features still detect five of the seven available copies in the top 6, while the spatial features were only able to detect three. Both feature types fail to detect the third reference clip shown in Figure 1.8a. This segment is rather short and blurry and proved difficult to describe by either feature types. Besides transformations, the actual content of a clip has a very large influence on the performance. The robustness and descriptiveness of the spatiotemporal features clearly have a positive influence on the result.

1.5 Application: Monitoring Commercial Airtime

We finally apply the pipeline in the context of commercial airtime monitoring. In this setting, one or more broadcast streams are being continuously scanned for the occurrence of any commercial that resides in a reference database. As it is equally important to know the exact broadcast time for each commercial, a good (temporal) alignment with the input video is required.

The commercial reference database contains 71 ads that were recorded from five different Greek TV channels. The commercials all have a length between 7 and 46 s, except for one that lasts 113 s. The query set consists of five 1 h video streams from two Greek channels that were recorded on a different day than the ads. Both ads and query videos have an image resolution of 360 × 288 (half PAL) and are encoded in MPEG-2 at 1.5 Mbit/s and 25 fps.

As the ads are all relatively short, we do not split each of them up into shots but extract the features from one spatiotemporal volume. We again limit the features to a fixed temporal scale in order to speed up the computations. Generating 20 independent hashes per feature and 16 projections per hash results in a reference database of 548 MB.

The 1 h video streams, on the other hand, are split up into segments. In order to show that the system is independent of good and consistent detection of shotboundaries, we perform two experiments. For the first experiment, we use shot-boundary detection [24], while for the second, we simply split each video into segments of 250 frames. Next, we use each segment as the query video to our system. After all votes are aggregated, a geometrical check between the features of the query video and the corresponding features of each matched commercial is performed by estimating the transformation between the two segments using RANSAC. As commercials are always shown at their original frame rate, a simple model with four parameters (spatial and temporal offsets and a spatial scale factor) suffices.

When enough inliers are found, the query segment is labeled as containing at least a partial copy of the commercial. The exact position and length of the copied part is easily obtained by computing the bounding box of the inlier features. We ignore matches where the area of the spatial bounding box is less than 1% of the dimension of the query video.* Thanks to the use of local spatiotemporal features, we can thus directly obtain the alignment between segments (if it exists), even if they are not cut along the same shot boundaries. This is an important advantage with respect to systems that find matches between (key)frames, where further steps are needed to detect groups of frames that constitute a copy (e.g., the creation of 2D Hough histograms [6], dynamic programming [2] or even highly specialized algorithms depending on the length and content of the query and reference videos [32]).

In our first experiment, the 5 h of query video were split into 3166 segments. As can be seen in Figure 1.9a, the overall computation time for both feature extraction and copy detection is faster than real-time. The system found 273 segments that contained part of a commercial. No false positives were detected, resulting in a precision of 100%. The obtained recall was 76%, as 86 segments containing part of an ad were missed. Two reasons can explain the bulk of the missed segments: the occurrence of very short shots (less than a second) and shots that contain an almost static scene. In both cases, few or none spatiotemporal features are detected and RANSAC will mostly fail.

A commercial in a video stream is typically split into multiple segments. As we already have located those segments (and the parts within each segment) that constitute a copy, we simply group segments that are matched to the same commercial

#Frames	#Features	Feature Extraction + Copy Detection (s)	Total (fps)	Speedup w.r.t. real-time
89,831	896,113	1458 + 342 = 1800	49.9	2.0
74,856	1,410,568	1614 + 372 = 1986	37.7	1.5
89,819	1,047,924	1384 + 268 = 1652	54.4	2.1
89,874	1,192,072	1837 + 345 = 2182	41.2	1.6
89,900	1,026,331	1722 + 271 = 1993	45.1	1.8

(a)

Detected	Ground truth	Full	Reedited	Partial	Branding
Full	35 / 32	– / 1	3 / 2	– / –	
Reedited	– / 2	4 / 3	– / –	– / –	
Partial	1 / 2	– / –	4 / 4	8 / 3	
Missed	– / –	– / –	– / 1	– / 5	

(b)

Figure 1.9 Monitoring commercial airtime. (a) Some statistics for each of the 5 h of query video. The copy-detection process is faster than real-time. (b) The confusion matrix which summarizes the results of the commercial detection using shot-boundary detection (left) and segments of uniform length (right).

---

* As the ads inside the database are also recorded broadcasts, they contain a channel logo. In some cases, the same logo is matched between two otherwise unrelated segments. These occurrences are easily identified, however, as the area containing the matched features is very small.

and have the same temporal offset. Although most segments are aligned with an accuracy below one frame, we allow for a temporal offset of maximally five frames. For every group, we compute the overlap percentage (OP) as the ratio of the sum of the frames of the matched segments to the number of frames of the reference ad. We distinguish between three types of detected copies:

1. *Full copies*: The commercial has been broadcasted in its entirety. Since some relevant segments are sometimes missed, we assign this type when we have found copies for at least 85% of the commercial (OP ≥ 0.85).
2. *Partial copies*: Commercials from the same company often share some shots containing e.g., the company's logo. Some examples of these shared shots can be seen in Figure 1.10. We assign this type when OP < 0.85. In most cases, however, the overlap ratio lies around 0.10.
3. *Reedited commercial*: Sometimes several versions of the same commercial are made, e.g., an alternative version with different content to keep the audience interested, or a shortened version. While those types of copies are hardly ever mentioned in the literature on video CBCD, they can be easily detected in our system. This type is chosen when two or more groups, that match to the same commercial, are temporally close together (less than a minute). An example of a detection of a reedited version of a commercial in the database is shown in Figure 1.11, which shows the query segments at the top and the relevant commercial at the bottom. We refer to the figure for more information.

The overall performance of the commercial monitoring is shown in Figure 1.9b. Of the 36 commercials that were broadcasted in full, 35 were found. A single commercial was classified as partial as it ended with two highly static shots that account for 18% of the length of the commercial. The three types of copies were detected with an accuracy of 92.7%, with no false or missed detections. All reedited and partial occurrences were correctly detected. Finally, one commercial, which was broadcasted three times and is shown in Figure 1.12, was incorrectly classified as a

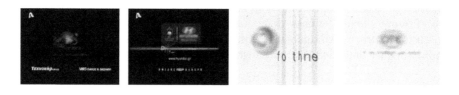

Figure 1.10 Four examples of short *branding* shots which are shared between different commercials and result in the detection of partial copies.

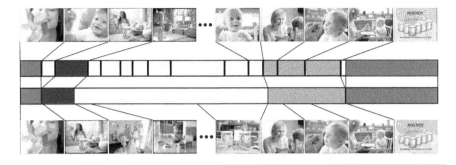

Figure 1.11 An example of a correctly detected reedited copy of a reference commercial. The top and bottom row show frames from the query video and reference commercial respectively. The second and third row respectively depict the segmented query video and the relevant commercial along the time dimension. Six segments contain copies of the reference commercial. We are dealing with a reedited commercial as the alignment of the segments with the reference ad falls apart into three groups (the first and last segment belong to the same group), shown in different shades of gray. Note that for the six segments that match, we show the first frame that contains inlier features, and not the first frame of the segment (the detected boundary) which might not be the same.

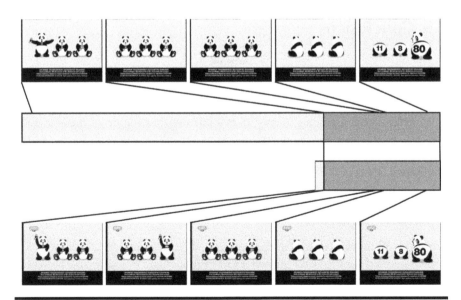

Figure 1.12 An incorrect detection. A part of the query video (top two rows) is incorrectly matched to the reference ad (bottom two rows). It can be clearly seen that the matched frames from the second and third segments are actually not copies. See the text for more information.

full copy. The broadcasted version is almost three times as long as the commercial in the database and shares the last two shots. However, due to the simplistic cartoon drawings together with the sparse motion, many of the spatiotemporal features in the second and third segment have been incorrectly detected as inliers by the RANSAC algorithm. This results erroneously in an overlap of more than 85%.

The second experiment splits the query videos into 1740 segments of equal length. Since the segments are relatively long (10 s) with respect to the average shot cut in a commercial, we apply the RANSAC procedure in a slightly different way. After each successful RANSAC, all features inside the matched bounding volume are removed from the list of matched features and the RANSAC procedure is repeated. This allows us to find multiple copies of the same commercial inside one segment, which can occur for reedited videos. However, adding this flexibility can also lead to erroneous classification of full copies as reedited versions, since some ads contain two or more (almost) duplicate shots. Another consequence of using long query segments is that very short copies are not detected since the percentage of votes for these copies no longer exceeds the threshold.* This mostly occurs for branding shots since they are not only short but also often contain sequences of static frames, which do not contain spatiotemporal features. Most of the mentioned issues could be avoided by choosing a shorter uniform length. As in the previous experiment, no full or reedited ads were missed and only one partial copy could not be found.†

1.6 Conclusions

In this chapter, we have presented a new method for content-based video copy detection based on local spatiotemporal features. By fully exploiting the video's spatiotemporal information, we have a robust system that utilizes highly discriminative local features and that is not dependent on accurate shot-boundary detection or complex frame grouping. A new disk-based implementation of p-stable LSH has been proposed where the query time increases sublinearly with the size of the database. The system has been successfully applied to the task of commercial airtime monitoring. Parts of this work were previously published in [30,31].

Acknowledgments

We thank Wim Moreau for the manual ground-truth annotation. This work has been supported by the IBBT project PISA (Production, Indexing and Search of Audio-visual material) and the IWT-SBO project AMASS++.

---

* The threshold is set for all experiments to 10%.
† The missed partial copy consisted of the last 3 s of the ad shown in Figure 1.12 which does not contain much spatiotemporal information.

References

1. H. Bay, T. Tuytelaars, and L. Van Gool. Surf: Speeded-up robust features. In *Proceedings of the 9th European Conference on Computer Vision*, Graz, Austria, 2006.
2. D. Borth, A. Ulges, C. Schulze, and T. M. Breuel. Video copy detection providing localized matches. In *GI-Informatiktage 2009*, Bonn, Germany, pp. 19–22. Gesellschaft für Informatik e.V., 2009.
3. K. Dadason, H. Lejsek, F. Ásmundsson, B. Jónsson, and L. Amsaleg. Videntifier: Identifying pirated videos in real-time. In *Proceedings of the 15th International Conference on Multimedia*, Augsburg, Germany, pp. 471–472. ACM, 2007.
4. M. Datar, N. Immorlica, P. Indyk, and V. S. Mirrokni. Locality-sensitive hashing scheme based on p-stable distributions. In *Symposium on Computational Geometry (SOCG)*, June 9–11, 2004, New York, pp. 253–262. ACM Press, 2004.
5. P. Dollár, V. Rabaud, G. Cottrell, and S. Belongie. Behavior recognition via sparse spatio-temporal features. In *VSPETS'05*, Beijing, China, pp. 65–72, 2005.
6. M. Douze, A. Gaidon, H. Jégou, M. Marszałek, and C. Schmid. Inria-lears video copy detection system. In *TRECVID Workshop*, November 17–18, 2008, Gaithersburg, MD.
7. C. Harris and M. Stephens. A combined corner and edge detector. In *4th ALVEY Vision Conference*, Manchester, U.K., pp. 147–151, 1988.
8. X.-S. Hua, X. Chen, and H.-J. Zhang. Robust video signature based on ordinal measure. In *Proceedings of the International Conference on Image Processing (ICIP'04)*, Singapore, Vol. 1, pp. 685–688, October 2004.
9. P. Indyk and R. Motwani. Approximate nearest neighbors: Towards removing the curse of dimensionality. In *ACM Symposium on Theory of Computing*, Dallas, TX, pp. 604–613. ACM Press, 1998.
10. A. Joly, O. Buisson, and C. Frelicot. Content-based copy retrieval using distortion-based probabilistic similarity search. *IEEE Transactions on Multimedia*, 9(2):293–306, 2007.
11. B. Jonsson, H. Lejsek, and L. Amsaleg. The eff2 project: Towards efficient and effective support for large-scale high-dimensional indexing. In *International Workshop on Content-Based Multimedia Indexing, 2007 (CBMI '07)*, Lisboa, Portugal, pp. 1–10, June 2007.
12. T. Kadir and M. Brady. Scale, saliency and image description. *International Journal of Computer Vision*, 45(2):83–105, 2001.
13. Y. Ke, R. Sukthankar, and M. Hebert. Efficient visual event detection using volumetric features. In *Proceedings of the International Conference on Computer Vision (ICCV '05)*, Beijing, China, Vol. I, pp. 166–173, 2005.
14. Y. Ke, R. Sukthankar, and L. Huston. An efficient parts-based near-duplicate and sub-image retrieval system. In *ACM International Conference on Multimedia*, New York, pp. 869–876. ACM Press, 2004.
15. C. Kim and B. Vasudev. Spatiotemporal sequence matching for efficient video copy detection. *IEEE Transactions on Circuits and Systems for Video Technology*, 15(1):127–132, January 2005.

16. A. Kläser, M. Marszałek, and C. Schmid. A spatio-temporal descriptor based on 3d-gradients. In *British Machine Vision Conference*, Leeds, U.K., pp. 995–1004, September 2008.

17. I. Laptev. On space-time interest points. *International Journal of Computer Vision*, 64(2):107–123, 2005.

18. I. Laptev, M. Marszalek, C. Schmid, and B. Rozenfeld. Learning realistic human actions from movies. In *IEEE Conference on Computer Vision and Pattern Recognition (CVPR '08)*, Ancharage, U.K., pp. 1–8. IEEE, June 2008.

19. J. Law-To, O. Buisson, V. Gouet-Brunet, and N. Boujemaa. Robust voting algorithm based on labels of behavior for video copy detection. In *Proceedings of the 14th Annual ACM International Conference on Multimedia*, October 23–27, 2006, Santa Barbara, CA. ACM, 2006.

20. Y. Li, J. Jin, and X. Zhou. Video matching using binary signature. In *Proceedings of the International Symposium on Intelligent Signal Processing and Communication Systems (ISPACS '05)*, Hong Kong, pp. 317–320, December 2005.

21. T. Lindeberg. Feature detection with automatic scale selection. *International Journal of Computer Vision*, 30:79–116, 1998.

22. K. Mikolajczyk, T. Tuytelaars, C. Schmid, A. Zisserman, J. Matas, F. Schaffalitzky, T. Kadir, and L. V. Gool. A comparison of affine region detectors. *International Journal of Computer Vision*, 65(1–2):43–72, 2005.

23. A. Oikonomopoulos, I. Patras, and M. Pantic. Spatiotemporal salient points for visual recognition of human actions. *IEEE Transactions on Systems, Man, and Cybernetics — Part B: Cybernetics*, 36(3):710–719, 2006.

24. M. Osian and L. Van Gool. Video shot characterization. *Machine Vision and Applications*, 15(3):172–177, 2004.

25. S. Poullot, O. Buisson, and M. Crucianu. Z-grid-based probabilistic retrieval for scaling up content-based copy detection. In *Proceedings of the ACM International Conference on Image and Video Retrieval (CIVR '07)*, July 09–11, 2007, Amsterdam, the Netherlands, pp. 348–355. ACM, 2007.

26. J. Sivic and A. Zisserman. Video Google: A text retrieval approach to object matching in videos. In *Proceedings of the International Conference on Computer Vision*, Nice, France, Vol. 2, pp. 1470–1477, October 2003.

27. J. Stöttinger, B. T. Goras, T. Pönitz, N. Sebe, A. Hanbury, and T. Gevers. Systematic evaluation of spatio-temporal features on comparative video challenges. In *Workshop on Video Event Categorization, Tagging and Retrieval, in Conjunction with ACCV*, Queenstown, New Zealand, 2010.

28. C. Tomasi and T. Kanade. Detection and tracking of point features. Technical Report CMU-CS-91-132, Carnegie Mellon University, Pittsburgh, PA, April 1991.

29. K. Walker. *TRECVID 2006*. LDC2006E40. Linguistic Data Consortium, Philadelphia, PA, 2006.

30. G. Willems, T. Tuytelaars, and L. Van Gool. An efficient dense and scale-invariant spatio-temporal interest point detector. In *Proceedings of the 10th European Conference on Computer Vision*, Marseille, France, 2008.

31. G. Willems, T. Tuytelaars, and L. Van Gool. Spatio-temporal features for robust content-based video copy detection. In *Proceeding of the 1st ACM International Conference on Multimedia Information Retrieval (MIR'08)*, British Columbia, Canada, pp. 283–290. ACM, 2008.
32. Z. Zhao and X. Liu. A segment-based advertisement search method from TV stream. In *2nd International Conference on Future Computer and Communication, (ICFCC'10)*, Wuhan, China, Vol. 2, May 2010.

Chapter 2

Cross-Domain Learning for Semantic Concept Detection

Wei Jiang
Eastman Kodak Company

Alexander Loui
Eastman Kodak Company

Shih-Fu Chang
Columbia University

Contents

Automatic semantic concept detection has become increasingly important to effectively index and search the exploding amount of multimedia content, such as those from the web and TV broadcasts. The large and growing amount of unlabeled data in comparison with the small amount of labeled training data limits the applicability of classifiers based upon supervised learning. In addition, newly acquired data often have different distribution from the previous labeled data due to the changing characteristics of real-world events and user behaviors. For example, in concept detection tasks such as TRECVID [19], new collections may be added annually from unseen sources such as foreign news channels or audiovisual archives. There exists a non-negligible domain difference. To improve the semantic concept detection performance, these issues need to be addressed.

In this chapter, we investigate cross-domain learning methods that effectively incorporate information from available training resources in other domains to enhance concept detection in a target domain by considering the domain difference.* Our contribution lies in twofolds. First, we develop three approaches to incorporate three types of information to assist the target domain: the *cross-domain support vector machine* (*CDSVM*) algorithm that uses previously learned support vectors; the *prediction-based method* that uses concept scores of the new data predicted by previously trained concept detectors; and the *adaptive semi-supervised SVM* (AS^{3}VM) algorithm that incrementally updates previously learned SVM concept detectors to classify new target data. Second, we provide a comprehensive summary

---

* Data sets from different domains generally have different data distributions. It may be more appropriate to use the term "data distribution." We use "domain" to follow the notation in previous work.

and comparative study of the state-of-the-art SVM-based cross-domain learning methods.

Cross-domain learning methods can be applied to classify semantic concepts in various types of data. For instance, we can assign semantic labels to images, videos, or *events* that are defined as groups of images and videos in this chapter. With regard to the three approaches we propose here, the CDSVM and AS^3VM algorithms are irrelevant to the specific data type. In other words, they directly work with feature vectors that are extracted to represent the underlying data. The prediction-based method, on the other hand, is developed for classifying event data, where the prediction hypotheses generated by previously trained concept detectors are used as features.

We extensively evaluate the proposed approaches over two scenarios by using four large-scale data sets: the TRECVID 2005 development data set containing 108 h of videos in different languages from international broadcast news programs; the TRECVID 2007 data set containing 60 h of videos from news magazines, science news, documentaries, and educational programming videos; Kodak's consumer benchmark set containing 1358 videos from actual users representing different consumer groups; and Kodak's consumer event data set containing 1972 events from actual users. In the first scenario, we use information from the TRECVID 2005 development data to enhance concept detection over the TRECVID 2007 data. Both data sets contain TV program videos, and we evaluate the cross-domain learning performance of using TV news videos to help classify TV documentary videos. In the second scenario, we use the TRECVID 2007 set to enhance concept detection over Kodak's consumer video and event data. We evaluate the prediction-based method and the AS^3VM algorithm, respectively. We aim to test the cross-domain learning performance when there is significant domain difference, i.e., using TV programs to help classify consumer data. Experimental results show that compared with several state-of-the-art alternatives, the proposed approaches can significantly improve semantic classification in both scenarios.

2.1 Survey of Cross-Domain Learning for Concept Detection

We first define our learning problem. The goal is to classify a set of K concepts $C_1, \ldots, C_K$ in a data set $\mathcal{X}$ that is partitioned into a labeled subset $\mathcal{X}_L$ (with size $n_L \geq 0$) and an unlabeled subset $\mathcal{X}_U$ (with size $n_U > 0$), i.e., $\mathcal{X} = \mathcal{X}_L \cup \mathcal{X}_U$. Each data point $\mathbf{x}_i \in \mathcal{X}_L$ is associated with a set of class labels y_{ik}, $k = 1, \ldots, K$, where $y_{ik} = 1$ or -1 indicates the presence or absence of concept C_k in $\mathbf{x}_i$. A data point $\mathbf{x}_i$ can be an image, a video, or an event (a set of images and videos grouped together). In addition to $\mathcal{X}$, we have a previous data set $\mathcal{X}^{old}$ (with size $n^{old} > 0$), whose data characteristics or distribution is different from but related to that of $\mathcal{X}$, i.e., $\mathcal{X}$ and $\mathcal{X}^{old}$ are from different domains. A data point $\mathbf{x}_j \in \mathcal{X}^{old}$ can also be an image, a video, or an event. A set of classifiers (represented by a set of parameters Θ^{old}) have been learned using the old domain data $\mathcal{X}^{old}$ to detect another set of K^{old} concepts $C_1^{old}, \ldots, C_{K^{old}}^{old}$. Intuitively, there are several different scenarios to study. From the data type point of view, the target data $\mathcal{X}$ and the old-domain data $\mathcal{X}^{old}$ can have the same data type, or $\mathcal{X}$ and $\mathcal{X}^{old}$ can have different types of data. From the concept point of view, the target concepts $C_1, \ldots, C_K$ can be the same as the old-domain concepts $C_1^{old}, \ldots, C_{K^{old}}^{old}$, or $C_1, \ldots, C_K$ can be different from $C_1^{old}, \ldots, C_{K^{old}}^{old}$.

Cross-domain learning has been proposed recently as a technique to leverage information from the previous domain to enhance classification in the target domain. Such information can be selected data points or learned models from the previous domain. Several cross-domain learning methods have been developed for concept detection [5,6,10,21], and they all deal with the scenario where $\mathcal{X}$ and $\mathcal{X}^{old}$ have the same type of data, and the target concepts $C_1, \ldots, C_K$ are the same as old-domain concepts $C_1^{old}, \ldots, C_{K^{old}}^{old}$ (i.e., C_k is the same as C_k^{old}, and $K = K^{old}$). The CDSVM [11] and AS³VM algorithms we develop in Sections 2.2 and 2.3, respectively, deal with this scenario too. In Section 2.4, we describe our prediction-based method [9] that studies the scenario where data in $\mathcal{X}$ are events while data in $\mathcal{X}^{old}$ are images or videos, and $C_1, \ldots, C_K$ can be different from $C_1^{old}, \ldots, C_{K^{old}}^{old}$. In the following, we first briefly summarize the previous work, followed by some discussions of our approaches.

2.1.1 Standard SVM

Without cross-domain learning, the standard SVM classifier [20] can be learned based upon the labeled subset $\mathcal{X}_L$ to classify unlabeled data $\mathcal{X}_U$ and future unseen test samples. For each concept C_k, given a datum $\mathbf{x}$ the SVM determines its corresponding label by the sign of a decision function $f(\mathbf{x})$. The optimal hyperplane gives the largest margin of separation between different classes and is obtained by solving the following problem:

$$\min_{\mathbf{f} \in \mathcal{H}} Q^{svm} = \min_{\mathbf{f} \in \mathcal{H}} \left\{ \gamma ||\mathbf{f}||_2^2 + \frac{1}{n_L} \sum_{i=1}^{n_L} (1 - y_{ik} f(\mathbf{x}_i))_+ \right\}, \qquad (2.1)$$

where

$(1 - y_{ik} f(\mathbf{x}_i))_+ = \max(0, 1 - y_{ik} f(\mathbf{x}_i))$ is the hinge loss

$\mathbf{f} = [f(\mathbf{x}_1), \ldots, f(\mathbf{x}_{n_L})]^T$

$\mathbf{x}_i \in \mathcal{X}_L$

γ controls the scale of the empirical error loss that the classifier can tolerate

The simplest way to perform cross-domain learning is to learn new models over all possible training samples $\tilde{\mathcal{X}} = \mathcal{X}^{old} \cup \mathcal{X}_L$, i.e., the *combined SVM*. The primary motivation is that when the size of $\mathcal{X}_L$ is small, the target model will benefit from a high count of training samples present in $\mathcal{X}^{old}$ and, therefore, hopefully be more stable than a model trained on $\mathcal{X}_L$ alone. However, this method is computationally expensive if $\mathcal{X}^{old}$ is large. Also, the influence of new data in $\mathcal{X}_L$ may be overshadowed by the large amount of data in $\mathcal{X}^{old}$.

2.1.2 Semi-Supervised Approaches

One intuitive way to improve the combined SVM is to use semi-supervised learning. By incorporating knowledge about the unlabeled data $\mathcal{X}_U$ into the training process, semi-supervised learning methods [1,4,20,23] can obtain better classifiers to classify test data. One most popular branch of semi-supervised learning is to use graph regularization [4,23]. A weighted undirected graph $\mathcal{G}^d = (\mathcal{V}^d, E^d, \mathbf{W}^d)$ can be generated for the data set $\mathcal{X}$, where $\mathcal{V}^d$ is the vertices set and each node corresponds to a data point, E^d is the edges set, and $\mathbf{W}^d$ is weights set measuring the pairwise similarities among data points. To detect a concept C_k, a binary classifier is trained as follows. Under the assumption of label smoothness over $\mathcal{G}^d$, a discriminant function f is estimated to satisfy two conditions: the loss condition—it should be close to given labels y_{ik} for labeled nodes $\mathbf{x}_i \in \mathcal{X}_L$; and the regularization condition—it should be smooth on graph $\mathcal{G}^d$. Among graph-based methods, the *Laplacian SVM (LapSVM)* algorithm [1] is considered one of the state-of-the-art approaches in terms of both classification accuracy and the out-of-sample extension ability. Let $\mathbf{f} = [f(\mathbf{x}_1), \ldots, f(\mathbf{x}_{n_U+n_L})]^T$ be the vector of discriminant functions over $\mathcal{X}$. LapSVM solves the following problem:

$$\min_{\mathbf{f} \in \mathcal{H}} \left\{ \gamma_A \|\mathbf{f}\|_2^2 + \gamma_I \mathrm{tr}\left(\mathbf{f}^T \mathbf{L}^d \mathbf{f}\right) + \frac{1}{n_L} \sum_{\mathbf{x}_i \in \mathcal{X}_L} (1 - y_{ik} f(\mathbf{x}_i))_+ \right\}, \tag{2.2}$$

where $\mathbf{L}^d$ is the Laplacian matrix computed from $\mathbf{W}^d$.

Semi-supervised learning methods such as LapSVM can be applied directly to cross-domain learning problems by using $\tilde{\mathcal{X}} = \mathcal{X}^{old} \cup \mathcal{X}_L$ as the combined training data. However, due to the non-negligible domain difference, the classifier may still be biased by $\mathcal{X}^{old}$. Also, such methods usually have high computation cost, especially for large-scale problems.

2.1.3 Feature Replication

The feature replication approach [5] uses all training samples from both $\mathcal{X}^{old}$ and $\mathcal{X}$, and tries to learn generalities between the two data sets by replicating parts of the original feature vector, $\mathbf{x}_i$, for different domains. Specifically, we first zero-pad the dimensionality of $\mathbf{x}_i$ from d to $d(N + 1)$ where N is the total number of adaptation domains (in our experiments $N = 2$). Next we transform all samples from all domains as:

$$\hat{\mathbf{x}}_i^{old} = \begin{bmatrix} \mathbf{x}_i^T & \mathbf{0} & \mathbf{x}_i^T \end{bmatrix}^T, \quad \mathbf{x}_i \in \mathcal{X}^{old}; \quad \hat{\mathbf{x}}_i^{new} = \begin{bmatrix} \mathbf{x}_i^T & \mathbf{x}_i^T & \mathbf{0} \end{bmatrix}^T, \quad \mathbf{x}_i \in \mathcal{X}.$$

During learning, for each concept C_k a model is constructed by using the transformed training data from both $\mathcal{X}^{old}$ and $\mathcal{X}$. However, due to the increase in feature dimensionality, there is a large increase in model complexity and computation time for both training and evaluation.

2.1.4 Domain Adaptive Semantic Diffusion

The domain adaptive semantic diffusion (DASD) algorithm [10] aims to improve classification of $\mathcal{X}_U$ by using affinity relationships among the K semantic concepts while considering the domain-shift problem. An undirected graph $\mathcal{G}^c = (\mathcal{V}^c, E^c, \mathbf{W}^{c,old})$ is defined to capture semantic concept affinity relations over the old domain. $\mathcal{V}^c$ is the vertices set, each node corresponding to a concept, E^c is the edges set, and $\mathbf{W}^{c,old}$ is the concept affinity matrix. Each entry W_{kl}^c gives the edge weight (representing the affinity relation) between C_k and C_l. Define the normalized graph Laplacian matrix $\mathbf{L}^{c,old}$:

$$\mathbf{L}^{c,old} = \mathbf{I} - \mathbf{D}^{c,old\,-1/2} \mathbf{W}^{c,old} \mathbf{D}^{c,old\,-1/2}, \tag{2.3}$$

where $\mathbf{D}^{c,old}$ is a diagonal matrix whose entries are row sums of $\mathbf{W}^{c,old}$. DASD makes an assumption of local smoothness over $\mathcal{G}^c$, i.e., if two concepts have high similarity defined in $\mathcal{G}^c$, they frequently co-occur (or have similar discriminant functions) in data samples. Let $\mathbf{F} = \begin{bmatrix} \mathbf{f}_1^c, \ldots, \mathbf{f}_K^c \end{bmatrix}$ be the discriminant functions over $\mathcal{X}$ for all concepts, $\mathbf{f}_k^c = [f_k(\mathbf{x}_1), \ldots, f_k(\mathbf{x}_{n_L+n_U})]^T$. The initial $\mathbf{F}$ is usually composed by discriminant functions generated by concept detectors that are trained from the old data $\mathcal{X}^{old}$. DASD solves the following problem to get refined $\tilde{\mathbf{F}}$ and $\mathbf{W}^{c,new}$ by iteratively updating the initial $\mathbf{F}$ and $\mathbf{W}^{c,old}$:

$$\min_{\tilde{\mathbf{F}}, \mathbf{W}^{c,new}} \frac{\mathrm{tr}(\tilde{\mathbf{F}}^T \mathbf{L}^{c,new} \tilde{\mathbf{F}})}{2}. \tag{2.4}$$

The major issue of DASD is the lack of the out-of-sample extension ability, i.e., $\tilde{\mathbf{F}}$ is optimized over the available unlabeled data $\mathcal{X}_U$, and the learned results cannot be easily applied to new unseen test data. Therefore, DASD does not have the incremental learning ability. This largely limits the applicability of DASD in many real problems.

2.1.5 Adaptive SVM (A-SVM)

The A-SVM algorithm [21] adapts classifiers Θ^{old} learned from the previous domain to classify $\mathcal{X}$ with the out-of-sample extension ability and incremental learning ability, without the requirement of retraining the entire model using data $\mathcal{X}^{old}$ from the previous domain. For a concept C_k, A-SVM adapts the old discriminant function f^{old} learned from $\mathcal{X}^{old}$ to classify the current data $\mathcal{X}$. The basic idea is to learn a new decision boundary that is close to the original decision boundary and can separate new labeled data. This is achieved by introducing a "delta function" $\Delta f(\mathbf{x}) = \mathbf{w}^T \mathbf{x} + b$ to complement $f^{old}(\mathbf{x})$. The final discriminant function over a datum $\mathbf{x}$ is the average of $f^{old}(\mathbf{x})$ and $\Delta f(\mathbf{x})$. $\Delta f(\mathbf{x})$ can be obtained by minimizing the deviation between the new decision boundary and the old one, as well as minimizing the classification error over new labeled data.

One potential problem with this approach is the regularization constraint that the new decision boundary should not be deviated far from the old-domain classifier. It is a reasonable assumption when $\mathcal{X}$ only moderately deviates from $\mathcal{X}^{old}$, i.e., $\mathcal{X}$ has similar distribution with $\mathcal{X}^{old}$. When $\mathcal{X}$ has a different distribution but comparable size than $\mathcal{X}^{old}$, such regularization can be problematic and can limit classification performance.

2.1.6 Overview of Our Methods

In this chapter, we develop three different cross-domain methods to use three different types of information from the old domain to help classification in the new target domain. For data incorporation, instead of using all training data from $\mathcal{X}^{old}$ like combined SVM, we selectively use a fewer number of important data from the old domain to help classify new data. For classifier adaptation, instead of relying upon target labeled data $\mathcal{X}_L$ alone such as A-SVM, we incrementally update Θ^{old} by considering unlabeled data $\mathcal{X}_U$. For the prediction-based method, we incorporate prediction hypotheses generated by previously trained models from the old domain to enhance classification in the new domain.

2.2 CDSVM for Data Incorporation

In this section, we describe our CDSVM algorithm that learns a new decision boundary based upon the target labeled data $\mathcal{X}_L$ to separate the unlabeled data $\mathcal{X}_U$ and future unseen test data, with the help of $\mathcal{X}^{old}$. For a concept C_k, let $\mathcal{U}^{old} = \left\{ \left(u_1^{old}, y_{1k}^{old} \right), \ldots, \left(u_{n^{s,old}}^{old}, y_{n^{s,old}\, k}^{old} \right) \right\}$ denote the set of $n^{s,old}$ support vectors that determine the decision boundary and $f^{old}(\mathbf{x})$ be the discriminant function already learned from the old domain. The learned support vectors carry all of the information about $f^{old}(\mathbf{x})$; if we can correctly classify these support vectors, we can correctly classify the remaining samples from $\mathcal{X}^{old}$ except for some misclassified training samples. Therefore, instead of using all data from $\mathcal{X}^{old}$ directly, we only incorporate these support vectors $\mathcal{U}^{old}$ from the old domain. In addition, we make the assumption that the impact of each data in $\mathcal{U}^{old}$ can be constrained by neighborhoods. The rationale behind this constraint is that if a support vector u_j^{old} falls in the neighborhood of the target data $\mathcal{X}$, it tends to have a distribution similar to $\mathcal{X}$ and can be used to help classify $\mathcal{X}$. Thus the new learned decision boundary needs to take into consideration the classification of this support vector. Let $\sigma\left(u_j^{old}, \mathcal{X}_L\right)$ denote the similarity measurement between the old support vector u_j^{old} and the labeled target data set $\mathcal{X}_L$, our optimal decision boundary can be obtained by solving the following optimization problem:

$$\min_{\mathbf{w}} \frac{1}{2}||\mathbf{w}||_2^2 + C\sum_{i=1}^{n_L}\epsilon_i + C\sum_{j=1}^{n^{s,old}} \sigma\left(u_j^{old}, \mathcal{X}_L\right)\bar{\epsilon}_j$$

$$s.t.\ y_{ik}(\mathbf{w}^T\phi(\mathbf{x}_i) + b) \geq 1 - \epsilon_i, \epsilon_i \geq 0, \forall\ \mathbf{x}_i \in \mathcal{X}_L,\ y_{jk}^{old}\left(\mathbf{w}^T\phi\left(u_j^{old}\right) + b\right)$$

$$\geq 1 - \bar{\epsilon}_j, \bar{\epsilon}_j \geq 0, \forall\ u_j^{old} \in \mathcal{X}^{old}, \tag{2.5}$$

where $\phi(\cdot)$ is a mapping function to map the original data into a high-dimension space.

In CDSVM optimization, the old support vectors learned from $\mathcal{X}^{old}$ are adapted based upon the new training data $\mathcal{X}_L$. The adapted support vectors are combined with the new training data to learn a new classifier. Let $\tilde{\mathcal{X}} = \mathcal{U}^{old} \cup \mathcal{X}_L$, Equation 2.5 can be rewritten as:

$$\min_{\mathbf{w}} \frac{1}{2}||\mathbf{w}||_2^2 + C\sum_{i=1}^{n_L + n^{s,old}} \tilde{\sigma}(\mathbf{x}_i, \mathcal{X}_L)\epsilon_i$$

$$s.t.\ y_{ik}(\mathbf{w}^T\phi(\mathbf{x}_i) + b) \geq 1 - \epsilon_i, \epsilon_i \geq 0, \forall\ \mathbf{x}_i \in \tilde{\mathcal{X}}$$

$$\tilde{\sigma}(\mathbf{x}_I, \mathcal{X}_L) = 1, \forall\ \mathbf{x}_i \in \mathcal{X}_L, \tilde{\sigma}(\mathbf{x}_i, \mathcal{X}_L) = \sigma(\mathbf{x}_i, \mathcal{X}_L), \forall\ \mathbf{x}_i \in \mathcal{U}^{old}. \tag{2.6}$$

The dual problem of Equation 2.6 is as follows:

$$\max_{\alpha_i} L_D = \sum_{i=1}^{n_L + n^{s,old}} \alpha_i - \frac{1}{2}\sum_{i=1}^{n_L + n^{s,old}}\sum_{j=1}^{n_L + n^{s,old}} \alpha_i\alpha_j y_{ik}y_{jk}K(\mathbf{x}_i, \mathbf{x}_j)$$

$$s.t.\ \epsilon_i \geq 0, \mu_i \geq 0, 0 \leq \alpha_i \leq C\tilde{\sigma}(\mathbf{x}_i, \mathcal{X}_L), \alpha_i\left[y_{ik}(\mathbf{w}^T\phi(\mathbf{x}_i) + b) - 1 + \epsilon_i\right]$$

$$= 0, \mu_i\epsilon_i = 0, \forall\ \mathbf{x}_i \in \tilde{\mathcal{X}} \tag{2.7}$$

where

$K(\cdot)$ is the kernel function

$K(\mathbf{x}_i, \mathbf{x}_j) = \phi^T(\mathbf{x}_i)\phi(\mathbf{x}_j)$

Equation 2.7 is the same as the standard SVM optimization, with the only difference that:

$$0 \le \alpha_i \le C, \forall\, \mathbf{x}_i \in \mathcal{X}_L, \quad 0 \le \alpha_i \le C\sigma(\mathbf{x}_i, \mathcal{X}_L), \forall\, \mathbf{x}_i \in \mathcal{U}^{old}.$$

For support vectors from the old data set $\mathcal{X}^{old}$, weight σ penalizes those support vectors that are located far away from the new training samples in the target data set $\mathcal{X}_L$.

Similar to A-SVM [21], in CDSVM we also want to preserve the discriminant property of the new decision boundary over the old data $\mathcal{X}^{old}$, but our technique has a distinctive advantage: We do not enforce the regularization constraint that the new decision boundary is similar to the old one. Instead, based upon the idea of localization, the discriminant property is addressed only over important old data samples that have similar distributions to the target data. Specifically, σ takes the form of a Gaussian function:

$$\sigma\left(u_j^{old}, \mathcal{X}_L\right) = \frac{1}{n_L} \sum_{\mathbf{x}_i \in \mathcal{X}_L} \exp\left\{-\beta \left\| u_j^{old} - \mathbf{x}_i \right\|_2^2\right\}. \tag{2.8}$$

Parameter β controls the degrading speed of the importance of support vectors from $\mathcal{U}^{old}$. The larger the β, the less influence of support vectors in $\mathcal{U}^{old}$ that are far away from $\mathcal{X}_L$. When β is very large, a new decision boundary will be learned solely based upon new training data from $\mathcal{X}_L$. When β is very small, the support vectors from $\mathcal{U}^{old}$ and the target data $\mathcal{X}_L$ are treated equally and the algorithm is equivalent to training an SVM over $\mathcal{U}^{old} \cup \mathcal{X}_L$ together. With such control, the proposed method is general and flexible. The control parameter, β, can be optimized in practice via systematic validation experiments. CDSVM has small time complexity. Let O_L denote the time complexity of training a new SVM based upon labeled target set $\mathcal{X}_L$. Because the number of support vectors from the old domain, $\mathcal{U}^{old}$, is generally much smaller than the number of training samples in target domain or the entire old data set, i.e., $n^{s,old} \ll n_L$ and $n^{s,old} \ll n^{old}$, CDSVM trains an SVM classifier with $n^{s,old} + n_L \approx n_L$ training samples, and this computational complexity is very close to O_L. Therefore CDSVM is in general faster than combined SVM or semi-supervised approaches.

2.3 AS³VM for Incremental Classifier Adaptation

In this section, we study the scenario where there are only a few (or even none) training samples available in the new domain, i.e., $\mathcal{X}_L$ is a small (or empty) set. In such a case, it is difficult to obtain a satisfactory classifier by using previous cross-domain learning methods. For example, both CDSVM and A-SVM rely mainly on $\mathcal{X}_L$ and will suffer from small sample learning. Combined SVM or semi-supervised learning will be biased by $\mathcal{X}^{old}$ since the old training data dominate the entire training set. We develop an AS³VM algorithm to accommodate this scenario. The main idea is to directly adapt the old classifiers Θ^{old} by using both $\mathcal{X}_L$ and $\mathcal{X}_U$, without retraining classifiers over all of the data. It is also desirable that such adaptation has the out-of-sample extension ability and can be conducted incrementally.

Before introducing the detailed AS³VM algorithm, we first make our cross-domain learning problem more general. For each labeled data $\mathbf{x}_i^{new} \in \mathcal{X}_L$, we have a set of labels y_{ik}^{new}, $k = 1, \ldots, K$. Instead of requiring $y_{ik}^{new} = 1$ or -1, here y_{ik}^{new} can take three values, 1, 0, or -1, where $y_{ik}^{new} = 1 (-1)$ indicates that $\mathbf{x}_i^{new}$ is labeled as positive (negative) to the concept C_k, and $y_{ik}^{new} = 0$ indicates that $\mathbf{x}_i^{new}$ is not labeled for C_k. That is, it is not necessary that each $\mathbf{x}_i^{new}$ is fully labeled to all K concepts. This is a frequent situation in reality because users commonly only annotate a few important concepts to a datum. Unless they are required to do so, users are reluctant to provide full annotation due to the burden of manual labeling.

2.3.1 Discriminative Cost Function

The previous concept detectors Θ^{old} are trained to separate data $\mathcal{X}^{old}$ in the old domain. To maintain this discriminative ability, we want the learned new models Θ^{new} to be similar to Θ^{old}. This is the same assumption used in some previous cross-domain methods such as A-SVM [21] described in Section 2.1.5. Therefore, the first part of the joint cost function that our AS³VM minimizes is the following:

$$\min_{\Theta^{new}} ||\Theta^{new} - \Theta^{old}||_2^2. \qquad (2.9)$$

Specifically, SVMs are used as concept detectors from the old domain. According to the Representer Theorem [20], the discriminant function $f_k(\mathbf{x})$, which is learned from the old domain of a datum $\mathbf{x}$ for a concept C_k, is given as:

$$f_k(\mathbf{x}) = \sum_{\mathbf{x}_i \in \mathcal{X}^{old}} \mu_{ik} K(\mathbf{x}_i, \mathbf{x}) = \mathbf{K}(\mathbf{x}; \mathcal{X}^{old})^T \mathbf{u}_k, \qquad (2.10)$$

where
  $K(\cdot)$ is the kernel function
  $\mathbf{K}(\mathbf{x}; \mathcal{X}^{old})$ is a vector composed by kernel functions of $\mathbf{x}$ against all data in $\mathcal{X}^{old}$
  $\mathbf{u}_k = [\mu_{1k}, \ldots, \mu_{n^{old}k}]^T$ (n^{old} is the size of $\mathcal{X}^{old}$)

Define $\mathbf{U}^{old} = [\mathbf{u}_1, \ldots, \mathbf{u}_K]$. The $n^{old} \times K$ matrix $\mathbf{U}^{old}$ contains all parameters learned from the old domain to generate discriminant functions for classifying K concepts.

Our goal is to learn a new matrix $\mathbf{U}^{new} = \left[\tilde{\mathbf{u}}_1, \ldots, \tilde{\mathbf{u}}_K \right]$ that is similar to $\mathbf{U}^{old}$. Thus Equation 2.9 can take the form:

$$\min_{\mathbf{U}^{new}} ||\mathbf{U}^{new} - \mathbf{U}^{old}||_2^2, \tag{2.11}$$

where $|| \cdot ||_2$ is the Hilbert–Schmidt norm. The new discriminant function of classifying $\mathbf{x}$ for a concept C_k is given by:

$$\tilde{f}_k(\mathbf{x}) = K(\mathbf{x}; \mathcal{X}^{old})^T \tilde{\mathbf{u}}_k. \tag{2.12}$$

Now let us incorporate the new labeled data $\mathcal{X}_L$ into the aforementioned process. $\mathcal{X}_L$ can be added directly into the set of support vectors by assigning a set of parameters $\mathbf{u}_i^{new} = \left[\mu_{i1}^{new}, \ldots, \mu_{iK}^{new} \right]^T$ to each data sample $\mathbf{x}_i^{new} \in \mathcal{X}_L$, where:

$$\mu_{ik}^{new} = \begin{cases} \eta \cdot \min_i(\mu_{ik}), & y_{ik}^{new} = -1 \\ y_{ik}^{new} \cdot \max_i(\mu_{ik}), & \text{others} \end{cases}. \tag{2.13}$$

Parameter μ_{ik} is the parameter in original $\mathbf{U}^{old}$, and $0 \leq \eta \leq 1$ is a weight added to the negative new labeled samples. Due to the unbalancing between positive and negative samples in some real applications, i.e., negative samples significantly outnumber positive ones for some concepts, we may need to treat positive and negative samples unequally. The weight μ_{ik}^{new} assigns more importance to the newly annotated data in $\mathcal{X}_L$ compared with old support vectors in $\mathbf{U}^{old}$. This is especially useful for small-size $\mathcal{X}_L$ since we need to emphasize the few newly labeled target data to obtain a good target classifier.

Let $\mathbf{U}^L = \left[\mathbf{u}_1^{new}, \ldots, \mathbf{u}_{n_L}^{new} \right]$. We can obtain the new amended parameter matrix $\hat{\mathbf{U}}^{old} = [\mathbf{U}^{old}{}^T, \mathbf{U}^L{}^T]^T$. Equation 2.11 can be directly rewritten to the following:

$$\min_{\mathbf{U}^{new}} ||\mathbf{U}^{new} - \hat{\mathbf{U}}^{old}||_2^2, \tag{2.14}$$

which is the first part of the cost function AS^{3}VM optimizes.

2.3.2 Graph Regularization on Data Points

In order to use the large amount of unlabeled data in the new domain to assist classification, we incorporate the assumption of graph smoothness over data points from the semi-supervised learning, i.e., close-by points in the feature space should have similar discriminant functions. Let undirected graph $\mathcal{G}^d = (\mathcal{V}^d, E^d, \mathbf{W}^d)$ denote the graph over $\mathcal{X}$ in the new domain, where $\mathcal{V}^d$ is the vertices set and each node corresponds to a data sample, E^d is the edges set, and $\mathbf{W}^d$ is the data affinity matrix.

Each entry W_{ij}^d measures the similarity of $\mathbf{x}_i$ and $\mathbf{x}_j$. Then we have the following cost function:

$$\min_{\tilde{\mathbf{F}}} \frac{1}{2} \sum_{\mathbf{x}_i, \mathbf{x}_j \in \mathcal{X}} W_{ij}^d \left\| \left(\frac{\tilde{\mathbf{f}}_i^d}{\sqrt{d_i^d}} \right) - \left(\frac{\tilde{\mathbf{f}}_j^d}{\sqrt{d_j^d}} \right) \right\|_2^2. \tag{2.15}$$

$\tilde{\mathbf{F}} = \left[\tilde{\mathbf{f}}_1^d, \dots, \tilde{\mathbf{f}}_{n_U+n_L}^d \right]^T$ contains the discriminant functions of $\mathcal{X}$ over all K concepts. $\tilde{\mathbf{f}}_i^d = [\tilde{f}_1(\mathbf{x}_i), \dots, \tilde{f}_K(\mathbf{x}_i)]^T$ comprises discriminant functions over $\mathbf{x}_i$. d_i^d is the degree of graph $\mathcal{G}^d$ over node $\mathbf{x}_i$. By substituting Equation 2.12 into Equation 2.15, we obtain:

$$\min_{\mathbf{U}^{new}} \frac{1}{2} \mathrm{tr} \{ \mathbf{U}^{new\,T} \mathbf{K}(\mathcal{X}^{old}; \mathcal{X}) \mathbf{L}^d \mathbf{K}(\mathcal{X}; \mathcal{X}^{old}) \mathbf{U}^{new} \}, \tag{2.16}$$

where $\mathbf{L}^d$ is the normalized graph Laplacian matrix:

$$\mathbf{L}^d = \mathbf{I} - \mathbf{D}^{d-1/2} \mathbf{W}^d \mathbf{D}^{d-1/2}. \tag{2.17}$$

$\mathbf{D}^d$ is a diagonal matrix whose entries are row sums of $\mathbf{W}^d$. $\mathbf{K}(\mathcal{X}; \mathcal{X}^{old})$ is the kernel matrix of data set $\mathcal{X}$ against data set $\mathcal{X}^{old}$, and $\mathbf{K}(\mathcal{X}; \mathcal{X}^{old}) = \mathbf{K}(\mathcal{X}^{old}; \mathcal{X})^T$.

2.3.3 Solution

We can combine the cost functions Equations 2.14 and 2.16 into a joint cost function to minimize by our AS³VM algorithm:

$$\min_{\mathbf{U}^{new}} Q^{AS^3\,VM}$$

$$= \min_{\mathbf{U}^{new}} \left[\|\mathbf{U}^{new} - \hat{\mathbf{U}}^{old}\|_2^2 + \left(\frac{\lambda^d}{2} \right) \cdot \mathrm{tr} \{ \mathbf{U}^{new\,T} \mathbf{K}(\mathcal{X}^{old}; \mathcal{X}) \mathbf{L}^d \mathbf{K}(\mathcal{X}; \mathcal{X}^{old}) \mathbf{U}^{new} \} \right]. \tag{2.18}$$

By optimizing $Q^{AS^3\,VM}$ we can obtain a new parameter matrix $\mathbf{U}^{new}$ that constructs classifiers to classify all K concepts. By taking the derivative of the cost $Q^{AS^3\,VM}$ with respect to $\mathbf{U}^{new}$ we can obtain:

$$\frac{\partial Q^{AS^3\,VM}}{\partial \mathbf{U}^{new}} = 0 \Rightarrow 2\mathbf{U}^{new} - 2\hat{\mathbf{U}}^{old} + \lambda^d \mathbf{K}(\mathcal{X}^{old}; \mathcal{X}) \mathbf{L}^d \mathbf{K}(\mathcal{X}; \mathcal{X}^{old}) \mathbf{U}^{new} = 0$$

$$\Rightarrow \mathbf{U}^{new} = \left[I + \frac{\lambda^d}{2} \mathbf{K}(\mathcal{X}^{old}; \mathcal{X}) \mathbf{L}^d \mathbf{K}(\mathcal{X}; \mathcal{X}^{old}) \right]^{-1} \hat{\mathbf{U}}^{old}. \tag{2.19}$$

The AS^{3}VM algorithm has several advantages. First, AS^{3}VM can be conducted with or without the presence of new annotated data from the new domain. That is, when $n_L = 0$, $\hat{\mathbf{U}}^{old} = \mathbf{U}^{old}$, AS^{3}VM is still able to adapt old classifiers to the new domain by using Equation 2.19. This is in comparison to most previous domain-adaptive methods that rely upon new annotated data. Second, AS^{3}VM allows incremental adaptation. This extends the algorithm's flexibility in real applications because multimedia data sets (and their annotations) are usually accumulated incrementally. The major computation cost is from the matrix inversion, which is about $O((n^{old})^3)$.

2.4 Prediction-Based Concept Score Incorporation

In this section, we develop a cross-domain learning system to adapt concept scores predicted by previously trained concept detectors from the old domain to the new domain. In the preceding two sections, the CDSVM and AS^{3}VM algorithms apply to the situation where both the target data $\mathcal{X}$ and the old data $\mathcal{X}^{old}$ have the same data type, and the target concepts are the same as the old-domain concepts, i.e., they work with feature vectors extracted from underlying data points, and such data points can be images, videos, or events. Different from these two methods, here we study the scenario where the target data $\mathcal{X}$ are events while the old data $\mathcal{X}^{old}$ are images or videos. An event is defined as a set of photos and/or videos that are taken within a common period of time, and have similar visual appearance. For example, an event can be composed by photos and videos taken by any user at the 2009 commencement of a university. Events are generated from unconstrained photo and video collections, by an automatic content management system, e.g., an automatic albuming system. We want to assign one or multiple semantic labels to each event to describe its content, such as "wedding" and "graduation." In other words, the old domain data type is a building element of the target domain data type, i.e., images and/or videos are building elements of events. Therefore, semantic concept detectors previously trained based on the old domain data can generate prediction hypotheses over the target data, and such hypotheses can be used as features to represent the target data. As a result, the target concepts $C_1, \ldots, C_K$ that we want to label to the event data can be different from the old-domain concepts $C_1^{old}, \ldots, C_{K^{old}}^{old}$ for which previous detectors are trained to generate prediction hypotheses.

Semantic classification of events has several characteristics. First, an event can contain both photos and videos, and we need to process photos and videos simultaneously. Second, the algorithm needs to accommodate errors resulting from automatic albuming systems. For example, in Figure 2.1, a photo irrelevant to "parade" is mistakenly organized into a "parade" event. Third, events taken by different users, although from the same semantic category, can have quite diverse visual appearances, e.g., as shown in Figure 2.1, data from two "parade" events can look very different. In comparison, occasionally we do not have enough event data for robust

Figure 2.1   Two event data taken for different "parade" events, which have quite different visual appearances. These events are generated by an automatic albuming system, and in the event on the right a photo irrelevant to "parade" is mistakenly organized into this event. (From Jiang, W. and Loui, A., Effective semantic classification of consumer events for automatic content management, in: *SIGMM Workshop on Social Media***, Beijing, China, pp. 35–42, 2009.)**

learning, e.g., in Kodak's consumer event collection we use in our experiment, there are only 11 "parade" events for training. The small sample learning difficulty may be encountered. This drives us to solicit help from cross-domain learning where we can borrow information from outside data sources to enhance classification.

2.4.1 Overview of Our System

Addressing the aforementioned characteristics, we develop a general two-step *event-level feature* (ELF) learning framework, as described in Figure 2.2. In the first step each image (a photo or a video keyframe) is treated as a set of data points in an elementary-level feature space (e.g., a concept score space at the image level or a low-level visual space at the region level). In the second step a unified ELF learning procedure is used to construct various ELFs based upon different elementary features. The ELF representation models each event as a feature vector, based upon which classifiers are directly built for semantic concept classification. The ELF representation is flexible to accommodate both photos and videos simultaneously, and is more robust to difficult or erroneous images from automatic albuming systems compared to the naive approach that uses image-level features to obtain classifiers straightforwardly.

Using the general ELF learning framework, we conduct cross-domain and within-domain learning for semantic indexing in event data, as described in Figure 2.3.

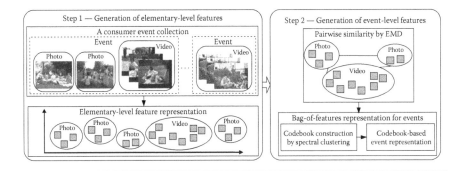

Figure 2.2 The general ELF learning framework. In the first step, each image (a photo or a video keyframe) is treated as a set of feature points in an elementary-level feature space, and then in the second step, an ELF representation can be constructed. (From Jiang, W. and Loui, A., Effective semantic classification of consumer events for automatic content management, in: *SIGMM Workshop on Social Media*, Beijing, China, pp. 35–42, 2009.)

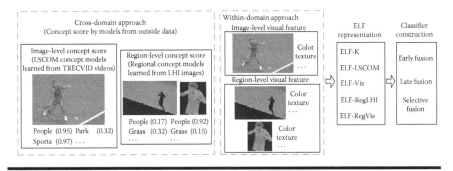

Figure 2.3 The overall framework of our concept detection approach over event data. (From Jiang, W. and Loui, A., Effective semantic classification of consumer events for automatic content management, in: *SIGMM Workshop on Social Media*, Beijing, China, pp. 35–42, 2009.)

Complex target semantic concepts are usually generated by the concurrence of elementary constructive concepts. For example, "wedding" is a complex concept associated with people, park, etc., evolving with a certain pattern. Based upon this idea, we adopt the PRED framework [5] for cross-domain learning. That is, a set of models detecting a set of elementary concepts $C_1^{old}, \ldots, C_{K^{old}}^{old}$ are built based upon the old data source, and are applied to the current data to generate concept occurrence predictions. Such predictions are then used as features to represent the current data and to learn semantic concept detection models in the current domain. In practice, we incorporate two sets of concept detection scores from pretrained models over two different old data sources, at both image and region level. They are the TRECVID 2005 news video set [19] with a 374-concept LSCOM ontology [14], and the LHI image-parsing ground-truth set with a 247-concept regional ontology [22]. Within-domain approaches use low-level visual features over entire images or image region segments as elementary-level features. The cross-domain and within-domain ELFs complement and cooperate with each other to improve classification.

2.4.2 ELF Learning Process

Assume that we have a collection of photos and videos from consumers, which is partitioned into a set of events. The partition is based upon the capture time of each photo/video and the color similarity between photos/videos, by using previously developed automatic albuming systems such as [13]. Let E^t be the tth event, which contains m_p^t photos and m_v^t videos, and I_i^t and V_j^t be the ith photo and jth video in E^t, respectively. We define that both photos and videos are *data units*, represented by **x**. For example, event E_t contains $m^t = m_p^t + \tilde{m}_v^t$ data units. Our goal is to assign E^t with semantic categories $C_1, \ldots, C_K$.

We first develop a *bag-of-features* (BoF) representation at the event level to describe each event as a feature vector, based upon which semantic concept detectors can be directly built. The BoF representation has been proven effective to detect generic concepts for images [18], where images are first represented by an orderless set of local descriptors (e.g., SIFT features), and then through clustering a middle-level vocabulary is constructed. Visual words in the vocabulary are treated as robust and denoised terms to describe images.

In our event classification problem, for each semantic concept C_k, e.g., "wedding," we have M events $E^1, \ldots, E^M$ that contain this concept. A vocabulary can be constructed by clustering all data units from these M events into N words. Each word can be treated as a pattern that is a common characteristic for describing all events that contain C_k. To accommodate both photo and video data units, the similarity-based spectral clustering algorithm [16] is adopted to construct the vocabulary.

Specifically, the consumer video generally contains only one shot, and keyframes can be uniformly sampled from the videos. Let $I_{j,l}^t$ be the lth keyframe in video V_j^t. Each photo I_i^t or keyframe $I_{j,l}^t$ can be represented as a set of feature points in the elementary-level feature space. For example, I_i^t is a single-point set with an image-level low-level visual feature $\mathbf{f}\left(I_i^t\right)$, or a multipoint set with region-level low-level visual features $\left\{ \mathbf{f}\left(r_{i1}^t\right), \ldots, \mathbf{f}\left(r_{iG}^t\right) \right\}$ where each r_{ig}^t is a region from image I_i^t described by a feature vector $\mathbf{f}\left(r_{ig}^t\right)$.

By treating each data unit as a set of feature points in the elementary feature space, the *earth mover's distance* (EMD) [17] can be adopted to measure the similarity between two data units (feature point sets). Note that there are many ways to compute the distance between two sets of feature points, e.g., the maximum/minimum distance. These methods are easily influenced by noisy outliers, while EMD provides a more robust distance metric. EMD finds a minimum weighted distance among all pairwise distances between the two sets of feature points subject to weight-normalization constraints, and EMD allows partial matching between data units, which can alleviate the influence of noisy outliers. The pairwise EMD distance $D(\mathbf{x}_i, \mathbf{x}_j)$ between two data units $\mathbf{x}_i$, $\mathbf{x}_j$ can be converted to pairwise similarity based upon the Gaussian function: $S(\mathbf{x}_i, \mathbf{x}_j) = \exp\left(-D(\mathbf{x}_i, \mathbf{x}_j)/\beta\right)$, where β is the mean of all pairwise distances among training data units.

Given the pairwise similarity matrix over data units from the M events that contain semantic concept C_k, spectral clustering can be applied to find clusters of these data units. We adopt the algorithm developed in [16] where the number of clusters N can be determined automatically by analyzing eigenvalues of the similarity matrix. Each obtained data cluster is called a word, and all the clusters form a vocabulary. Let W_j be the jth word, and let $S(\mathbf{x}, W_j)$ be the similarity of a datum $\mathbf{x}$ to word W_j calculated as the maximum similarity between $\mathbf{x}$ and the member data units in W_j. Assume that event E^t contains m^t data units in total, the entire event E^t can be represented by a BoF feature vector $\mathbf{f}_{bof}(E^t)$ as: $\mathbf{f}_{bof}(E^t) = [\max_{\mathbf{x} \in E^t} S(\mathbf{x}, W_1), \ldots, \max_{\mathbf{x} \in E^t} S(\mathbf{x}, W_N)]^T$.

2.4.3 Semantic Concept Classification with Multitype ELFs

The aforementioned ELF learning framework is very flexible. Different types of elementary-level features can be used to generate ELFs.

2.4.3.1 Cross-Domain ELFs

We further categorize the cross-domain ELFs as image-level or region-level, i.e., concept detectors from external data sets are learned at the image or region level to generate the image-level or region-level elementary concept spaces.

2.4.3.1.1 Image-Level Concept Space

We use the TRECVID 2005 development set [19] with a 374-concept LSCOM ontology [14] to generate a concept-score-based ELF at the image level. The LSCOM ontology contains 449 multimedia concepts related to objects, locations, people, and programs. The entire TRECVID 2005 development set is labeled to this ontology. By using visual features [3] over the entire image, i.e., 5×5 grid-based color moments, Gabor texture, and edge direction histogram, 374 SVM concept detectors are learned based upon the TRECVID data, detecting 374 concepts with high-occurrence frequencies in LSCOM. These 374 concepts are the old-domain concepts $C_1^{old,trec}, \ldots, C_{374}^{old,trec}$, and we apply the 374 concept detectors to obtain the concept detection probabilities for each image I (a photo or a video keyframe) in the current event data set. These probabilities represent I in a concept space with a feature

vector formed by concept scores $\mathbf{f}_\iota(I) = \left[p\left(C_1^{old,trec}|I\right), \ldots, p\left(C_{374}^{old,trec}|I\right) \right]^T$.
Each photo is a single-point set and each video is a multipoint set in the concept space. Then the ELF learning process described in the second step of Figure 2.2 can be used to generate the ELF over the LSCOM ontology, which is called *ELF-LSCOM*.

2.4.3.1.2 Region-Level Concept Space

Region-level features provide detailed object information to describe the image content, which is complementary to global image-level features. In the regional approach, each image I is segmented into a set of regions $r_1, \ldots, r_G$, and each region can be represented by a feature vector in the elementary region-level feature space. Thus, both photos and videos are treated as multipoint sets, and the ELF learning procedure from the second step of Figure 2.2 can be conducted to obtain ELF representations.

To generate region-level concept scores, we need external region-level concept detectors. In this work, the LHI image-parsing ground-truth data set (the free version) [22] is used to build region-level concept detectors. The data set contains images from six categories: manmade object, natural object, object in scene, transportation, aerial image, and sport activity. These images are manually segmented and the regions are labeled to 247 concepts. Low-level visual features, i.e., color moments, Gabor texture, and edge direction histogram, are extracted from each region. By using each region as one sample, SVM classifiers are trained to detect the 247 region-level concepts corresponding to the old-domain concepts $C_1^{old,LHI}, \ldots, C_{247}^{old,LHI}$. These detectors generate concept detection scores for each automatically segmented region in our event data. Then an ELF representation (*ELF-RegLHI*) can be learned based upon the region-level concept scores.

2.4.3.2 Within-Domain ELFs

The use of concept score space has been proven effective for semantic annotation by several previous works [7,8]. However, low-level visual features are still indispensable, especially when we only have a limited concept ontology. Because in practice we cannot train a concept detector for every possible concept, low-level visual features can capture useful information not covered by the available concept detectors.

Within-domain visual-feature-based approaches can also be categorized as using image-level or region-level visual features. With image-level visual features, each image I is represented as a low-level visual feature vector. Then each photo is a single-point set and each video is a multipoint set, based upon which an ELF (*ELF-Vis*) can be generated. Specifically, we use the same low-level visual features as the ones to obtain image-level concept detection scores. Using region-level visual features, each region is represented as a low-level visual feature, and the entire image is a multipoint set in the regional feature space (as is a video), based upon which we generate an ELF (*ELF-RegVis*). In practice, we also use the same low-level visual features as the ones to obtain region-level concept detection scores. In addition, we use the concept detectors trained from Kodak's consumer benchmark video set with a 21-concept consumer ontology [12] to generate concept detection scores as elementary-level features to construct the ELF. We call this ELF representation *ELF-K*. This is treated as a within-domain learning approach, since both Kodak's benchmark videos and Kodak's event data are from the same consumer domain.

2.4.3.3 Classification with ELFs

By now we have five ELFs: ELF-K, ELF-LSCOM, ELF-RegLHI, ELF-Vis, and ELF-RegVis. Individual classifiers can be built over each ELF, and improved performance can be expected if we appropriately fuse these ELFs. In early fusion, we concatenate these ELFs into a feature vector to train classifiers. In late fusion, we combine classifiers individually trained over ELFs. We can also use selective fusion, i.e., forward feature selection. In selective early fusion, we gradually concatenate one more ELF at one time based upon the cross-validation error to choose the optimal combination of features. Similarly, in selective late fusion we gradually combine one more classifier trained over individual ELFs.

In Section 2.6.2, we will evaluate the concept detection performances of the prediction-based method over real event data from consumers, where both individual ELFs and their combinations are tested. From the result, the selective fusion can obtain more than 70% performance gain compared with individual ELFs.

2.5 Experiments: Cross-Domain Learning in TV Programs

We evaluate the CDSVM algorithm over two different TV program data sets. The first data set, $\mathcal{X}^{old}$, is a 41,847-keyframe set derived from the development set of TRECVID 2005, containing 61,901 keyframes extracted from 108 h of international broadcast news videos. The target data set, $\mathcal{X}$, is the TRECVID 2007 data set containing 21,532 keyframes extracted from 60 h of news magazine, science news, documentaries, and educational programming videos. We further partition the target set into training and test partitions with 17,520 and 4,012 keyframes, respectively. The partition is at the video level, i.e., keyframes from the same video will be in the same set. The TRECVID 2007 data set is quite different from the TRECVID 2005 data set in program structure and production value, but they have similar semantic concepts of interests. All keyframes are manually labeled for 36 semantic concepts, originally defined by LSCOM-lite [15]. Both data sets are multi-label sets, i.e., each keyframe may be labeled to multiple semantic concepts. One-vs.-all classifiers are trained to classify each concept. For each keyframe, three types of low-level visual features are extracted: grid color moments over 5×5 image grids, Gabor texture, and edge direction histogram. These features are concatenated to form a 346-dim feature vector to represent each keyframe. Such features, although relatively simple, have been shown effective in detecting generic concepts, and considered as part of standard features in semantic concept detection [3].

We compare CDSVM with several different alternatives in this section: the SVM trained using TRECVID 2005 data alone (SVM 05), the SVM trained using TRECVID 2007 data alone (SVM 07), the combined SVM trained using the merged TRECVID 2005 and 2007 data, the feature replication method [5], and the A-SVM method [21]. To guarantee model uniformity, all SVM classifiers use the RBF kernel $K(\mathbf{x}_i, \mathbf{x}_j) = \exp\left\{-\gamma||\mathbf{x}_i - \mathbf{x}_j||_2^2\right\}$ with $C = 1$ and $\gamma = 1/d$, where d is the feature dimension of $\mathbf{x}$. The LibSVM source code [2] is used and is modified to include sample independent weights, described in Equation 2.7.

Figure 2.4 shows the comparison of detection performances over 36 concepts by using different algorithms. The performance measurements are *average precision* (*AP*) and *mean average precision* (MAP). AP is the precision evaluated at every relevant point in a ranked list averaged over all points; it is used here as a standard way of comparison for the TRECVID data set. MAP is the averaged AP across all concepts. From the figure, we can see that comparing MAP alone, the proposed CDSVM outperforms all other methods. This is significant not only because of the higher performance, but also because of the lower computation complexity. In addition, out of the three evaluated cross-domain learning methods, CDSVM is the only

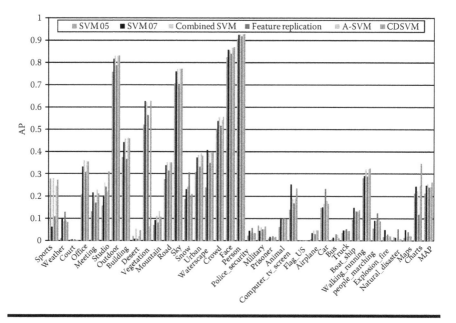

Figure 2.4   Result comparison: from TRECVID 2005 set to TRECVID 2007 set.

one that improves over the target model and the combined SVM, while the other two, both feature replication and A-SVM, cannot. This phenomenon confirms our assumption that a judicious usage of data from the old domain is critical for learning robust target models. Because A-SVM pursues moderate modification of the old model instead of pursuing large-margin classification over the target domain, when the number of target training data is large to train a relatively good classifier, such moderate modification may be not as effective as retraining a target model directly. Feature replication, on the other hand, uses all of the old data without selection, may be biased by the old data, and suffer from the high dimensionality of the replicated feature.

2.6 Experiments: From TV Programs to Consumer Videos

We conduct two sets of experiments to evaluate the AS^3VM algorithm and the prediction-based method over three data sets: the TRECVID 2007 data set, Kodak's consumer benchmark video set [12], and Kodak's consumer event data set [9]. Kodak's consumer benchmark set contains 1358 videos from about 100 actual users representing different consumer groups. A total of 5166 keyframes are sampled from these videos and are labeled to 21 consumer concepts. Kodak's event set contains 1972 consumer events, which are generated from the automatic albuming system described in [13], and are labeled to 10 semantic categories. The details, such as definitions of these semantic categories and descriptions of the event data, can be found in [8].

2.6.1 AS^3VM for Semantic Concept Detection

Kodak's set and the TRECVID 2007 set are from different domains. Among the 36 concepts annotated over the TRECVID data, 5 concepts are similar to the consumer concepts annotated over Kodak's benchmark data. They are animal (animal), boat-ship (boat), crowd (crowd), people-marching (parade), and sports (sports), where concepts in parentheses are defined for Kodak's set. We adaptively apply the 5 SVM concept detectors trained over TRECVID 2007 data to Kodak's benchmark data by using the AS^3VM algorithm. The performance measures are AP and MAP. We evaluate two scenarios where we do not have new labeled data or have some labeled data, from Kodak's consumer set. Algorithms in these scenarios are marked by "(n)," and "(l)," respectively, e.g., "(n) AS^3VM" and "(l) AS^3VM." Figure 2.5 shows the performance comparison in the first scenario where we compare AS^3VM with semi-supervised LapSVM [1] and original SVM (directly applying TRECVID-based SVMs). For LapSVM, we treat the TRECVID 2007 data as training data and Kodak's consumer data as unlabeled data. This is one intuitive alternative of learning classifiers that use information from both data sets without new annotations. The

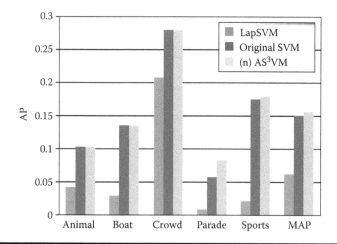

Figure 2.5 From TRECVID 2007 set to Kodak's benchmark set: without new annotation.

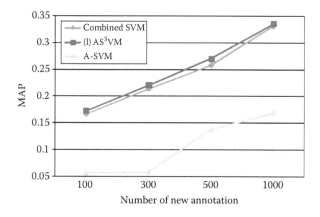

Figure 2.6 From TRECVID 2007 set to Kodak's benchmark set: with new annotations.

results show that A^3SVM can improve the performance of original TRECVID-based SVMs by about 4% in terms of MAP on a relative basis. LapSVM, which treats both data sets as from the same distribution, does not perform well due to the non-negligible domain difference.

Figure 2.6 shows the performance comparison in the second scenario with different numbers of annotated data from the new domain. A set of randomly selected data in Kodak's benchmark set are provided to users, and for each data one concept is randomly chosen for users to annotate. The annotation rate is pretty low, i.e., from 0.4% to 4% when we have 100–1000 annotations compared with 5166×5 annotations to fully annotate the entire target set. Results in Figure 2.6 are the averaged results over 10 random runs. Here we compare AS^{3}VM with two other alternatives: the combined SVM using all labeled data from both the TRECVID 2007 set and Kodak's benchmark set, and the cross-domain A-SVM [21] of adapting TRECVID-based SVMs to Kodak's data using new labeled data. The figure shows that AS^{3}VM can effectively improve the classification performance by outperforming the combined SVM. In comparison, A-SVM cannot improve detection because it updates classifiers only based upon the few labeled samples that are often biased. The results indicate the superiority of our method by both using information from unlabeled data and adapting classifiers to accommodate the domain change.

2.6.2 Prediction-Based Method for Concept Detection in Events

From Kodak's consumer event set, a total of 1261 events are randomly selected for training, the rest for testing. AP and MAP are still used as performance measures.

Figure 2.7 gives the individual AP and the overall MAP using different individual ELFs. From the result, different types of ELFs have different advantages in classifying

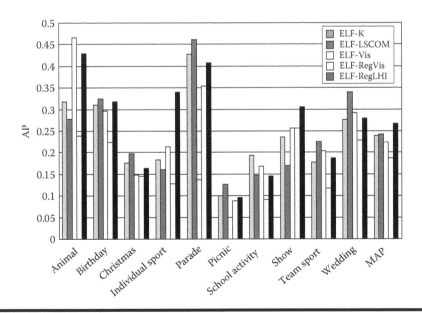

Figure 2.7 Performances of individual ELFs. (From Jiang, W. and Loui, A., Effective semantic classification of consumer events for automatic content management, in: *SIGMM Workshop on Social Media*, Beijing, China, pp. 35–42, 2009.)

different semantic categories. In general, image-level concept scores (ELF-K and ELF-LSCOM) perform well over complex semantic concepts such as "birthday," "parade," "picnic," "school activity," and "wedding," which are composed of many constructive concepts, e.g., wedding consists of wedding gowns, suits, park, flowers, etc. The concept scores capture the semantic information about occurrences of these constructive concepts. On the other hand, ELF-Vis performs extremely well over semantic categories that are determined by only one or a few concepts, such as "animal," where the detection scores for other constructive concepts are not so helpful. Similarly, ELF-RegLHI performs well over complex semantic categories in general, and it works very well over those semantic categories having strong regional cues, e.g., "individual sport" or "show," where detection of sport fields or stages helps greatly.

In terms of image-level concept scores, the large ontology (ELF-LSCOM) outperforms the small one (ELF-K), although concept detectors for the latter are trained with consumer videos that are more similar to our consumer event data than the TRECVID data. This confirms that a large ontology can provide rich descriptors to represent the media content and a large external data source can be quite helpful. Specifically, ELF-LSCOM gets very good results over "parade," "team sport," and "wedding." This is because the TRECVID news videos and the LSCOM ontology provide good detectors for many constructive concepts related to parade (e.g., protest, demonstration, etc.), sports (e.g., basketball, football, etc.), and well-suited people (e.g., corporate leader, government leader, and so on).

Figure 2.8 shows performances of different fusion methods, and the best individual ELF is also given for comparison. From the result, consistent performance improvements can be achieved over every semantic concept when we combine different ELFs by either early or late fusion, i.e., about 35% gain in MAP compared to the best individual ELF. In addition, by selectively combining different ELFs, further performance gain can be obtained. Compared to the best individual ELF, the selective fusion can attain more than 70% MAP improvement.

2.7 Conclusion

We study the cross-domain learning issue of incorporating information from available training resources in other domains to enhance concept detection in a target domain. We develop three approaches: the CDSVM algorithm that uses previously learned support vectors; the AS^3VM algorithm that incrementally updates previously learned concept detectors; and the prediction-based method that uses concept scores predicted by previously trained concept detectors. Experiments over both TRECVID data from TV programs and Kodak's consumer videos demonstrate the effectiveness of our approaches.

In general, all three methods are developed to deal with relatively large domain differences. However, if the domain difference is very large, the prediction-based

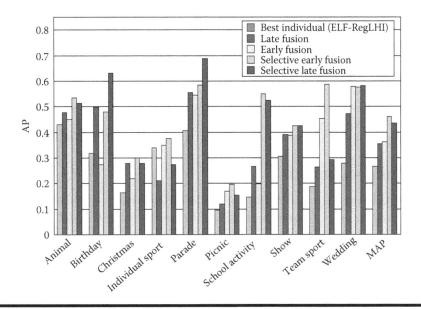

Figure 2.8 Performances of different fusion methods. Significant improvements can be achieved by selectively combining different ELFs. (From Jiang, W. and Loui, A., Effective semantic classification of consumer events for automatic content management, in: *SIGMM Workshop on Social Media***, Beijing, China, pp. 35–42, 2009.)**

method is more robust than the other two. The reason is that compared to incorporating old data or updating old models, using concept scores of new data as features to train new classifiers is less sensitive to the distribution change between old and new domains. On the other hand, if there are very few training data available in the new domain, and the domain difference is not very dramatic, the AS^{3}VM algorithm tends to work better than the other two. This is because AS^{3}VM relies on both the old models and the new data structure to obtain updated classifiers while the other two mainly rely upon the insufficient new training data.

In addition, both CDSVM and AS^{3}VM deal with the scenario where we have the same type of data in both the target and the old domains. Also, the set of concepts that we want to detect in the target domain and the old domain are the same. These two methods work with the abstract feature vectors generated from the underlying data points. The prediction-based method, on the other hand, deals with the scenario where we have different types of data in the target and the old domains. Since the concept prediction scores generated from the old-domain models are used as features, the target concepts can be different from the old-domain concepts.

In terms of computation complexity, both CDSVM and AS^{3}VM are faster than the combined SVM in general, especially with large-scale old domain data $\mathcal{X}^{old}$. This is because CDSVM only incorporates a part of the old data (previously learned support vectors), and AS^{3}VM relies on a matrix inversion instead of solving the QP problem. As for the prediction-based method, the major time complexity lies in the computation of the ELFs, including extraction of elementary-level features and construction of vocabularies. For example, to compute the region-level concept scores, we need to segment images and apply previous region-based concept detectors to the segmented regions. Luckily, a lot of computation can be conducted off-line during the training process, and the evaluation is still reasonably fast.

Acknowledgments

This work was supported in part by a Kodak fellowship from Eastman Kodak Company (to the first author) and NSF CRI Award No CNS-07-51078.

References

1. M. Belkin, P. Niyogi, and V. Sindhwani. Manifold regularization: A geometric framework for learning from labeled and unlabeled examples. *Journal of Machine Learning Research*, 7(11):2399–2434, 2006.
2. C.C. Chang and C.J. Lin. LIBSVM: A library for support vector machines. *ACM Transactions on Intelligent Systems and Technology*, 2(3), Article 27, 2011. Software available at: http://www.csie.ntu.edu.tw/~cjlin/libsvm
3. S.F. Chang, W. Jiang, W. Hsu, L. Kennedy, D. Xu, A. Yanagawa, and E. Zavesky. Columbia University TRECVID-2006 video search and high-level feature extraction. *NIST TRECVID Workshop*, Gaithersburg, MD, 2006.
4. O. Chapelle, B. Scholkopf, and A. Ziene. *Semi-supervised Learning*. MIT Press, Cambridge, MA, 2006.
5. H. Daumé. Frustratingly easy domain adaptation. In: *Proceedings of the 45th Annual Meeting of the Association of Computational Linguistics*, Prague, Czech Republic, pp. 256–263, 2007.
6. L. Duan, I.W. Tsang, and D. Xu. Domain transfer SVM for video concept detection. In: *Proceedings of the IEEE Computer Society Conference on Computer Vision and Pattern Recognition*, Miami, FL, pp. 1375–1381, 2009.
7. S. Ebadollahi, L. Xie, S.F. Chang, and J. Smith. Visual event detection using multi-dimensional concept dynamics. In: *Proceedings of the 2006 IEEE International Conference on Multimedia and Expo*, Toronto, Ontario, Canada, pp. 881–884, 2006.
8. W. Jiang and A.C. Loui. Semantic event detection for consumer photo and video collections. In: *Proceedings of the 2008 IEEE International Conference on Multimedia and Expo*, Hannover, Germany, pp. 313–316, 2008.
9. W. Jiang and A.C. Loui. Effective semantic classification of consumer events for automatic content management. In: *SIGMM Workshop on Social Media*, Beijing, China, pp. 35–42, 2009.
10. Y.G. Jiang, C. Ngo, and S.F. Chang. Semantic context transfer across heterogeneous sources for domain adaptive video search. In: *ACM Multimedia*, Beijing, China, 2009.

11. W. Jiang, E. Zavesky, S.F. Chang, and A.C. Loui. Cross-domain learning methods for high-level visual concept classification. In: *Proceedings of the IEEE International Conference on Image Processing*, San Diego, CA, pp. 161–164, 2008.
12. A. Loui, J. Luo, S.F. Chang, D. Ellis, W. Jiang, L. Kennedy, K. Lee, and A. Yanagawa. Kodak's consumer video benchmark data set: Concept definition and annotation. *ACM SIGMM International Workshop on MIR*, Augsburg, Germany, pp. 245–254, 2007.
13. A. Loui and A. Savakis. Automated event clustering and quality screening of consumer pictures for digital albuming. *IEEE Transactions on Multimedia*, 5(3):390–402, 2003.
14. LSCOM lexicon definitions and annotations version 1.0. DTO challenge workshop on large scale concept ontology for multimedia, Technical Report 221-2006-7, Columbia University ADVENT, March 2006.
15. M. Naphade, L. Kennedy, J. Kender, S.F. Chang, J. Smith, P. Over, and A. Hauptmann. A light scale concept ontology for multimedia understanding for TRECVID 2005, IBM Research Technical Report, 2005.
16. A. Ng, M. Jordan, and Y. Weiss. On spectral clustering: Analysis and an algorithm. In: *Proceedings of the NIPS*, Vancouver, BC, Canada, 2001.
17. Y. Rubner, C. Tomasi, and L.J. Guibas. The earth mover's distance as a metric for image retrieval. *International Journal of Computer Vision*, 40(2):99–121, 2000.
18. J. Sivic and A. Zisserman. Video google: A text retrieval approach to object matching in videos. *Proceedings of the IEEE International Conference on Computer Vision*, Nice, France, pp. 1470–1477, 2003.
19. A.F. Smeaton, P. Over, and W. Kraaij. Evaluation campaigns and TRECVid. In: *Proceedings of the Eighth ACM International Workshop on Multimedia Information Retrieval, MIR'06*, October 26–27, 2006, Santa Barbara, CA, pp. 321–330, 2006.
20. V. Vapnik. *Statistical Learning Theory*. Wiley-Interscience, New York, 1998.
21. J. Yang, R. Yan, and A. Hauptmann. Cross-domain video concept detection using adaptive SVMs. In: *Proceedings of the ACM Multimedia*, Augsburg, Germany, pp. 188–197, 2007.
22. B. Yao, X. Yang, and S.C. Zhu. Introduction to a large scale general purpose ground truth data set: Methodology, annotation tool and benchmarks. In: *Proceedings of the IEEE International Conference on Energy Minimization Methods in Computer Vision and Pattern Recognition*, Ezhow, China, 2007.
23. X. Zhu. Semi-supervised learning literature survey. Computer Sciences Technique Report 1530, University of Wisconsin-Madison, Madison, WI, 2005.

Chapter 3

TV Content Analysis and Annotation for Parental Control

Thanassis Perperis
National and Kapodistrian University of Athens

Sofia Tsekeridou
Athens Information Technology

Contents

3.1 Introduction

Although controversial, television is probably the most common medium of information and entertainment. Everyone has access to TV content through a number of end user devices (TV sets, mobile phones, PCs) and over a number of different communication channels, but still limited control over the received content. Personalization services enhancing the overall viewers experience are nowadays made possible and offered by a number of media service providers. However little progress has been noted on the development of intelligent, efficient, human-like technological solutions for automatic identification and filtering of undesirable broadcasted TV content, which could further facilitate the protection of sensitive user groups (e.g., children). To better understand the underlying processes and provide a more intuitive description of the benefits and functionalities arising from such technologies, an example use case is presented involving Bob and Mary's family—themselves and their two children, a daughter, Pat, who is still a kid, and a son, Tom, who is a teenager. This use case further illustrates how advanced TV content filtering services will operate. In this use case, Bob has just bought a brand new TV set with content filtering capabilities. He plugs it to the power source and turns it on. The *profile settings* screen appears. Bob creates four distinct user profiles for each one of his family members and browses through a *harmful content* hierarchy to select the corresponding content that should be filtered out for each one of them, including himself. As Pat is still a kid, all content classified as harmful should be filtered out; thus the top class of the hierarchy is selected. As Tom is a teenager, who likes action movies with *fights* and *explosions* and is old enough to watch *partial nudity*, the corresponding harmful content subclasses are deselected for him. However *sexual actions*, *total nudity*, and *murders* are disallowed. Mary does not like *murders*, *blood splatter*, and *boxing*; therefore, the corresponding classes are selected for her to be filtered out. Finally, Bob creates an empty profile for himself, as he wishes to view any type of received content. The next step is to filter out (i.e., skip or blur) the selected categories of received content for the corresponding user profile. For this purpose, the TV set (or set-top box) is accompanied by dedicated filtering software, that further allows for user profile storage and harmful TV content filtering on mobile phones and PCs, providing thus the desired protection from objectionable content for Bob and Mary's family.

Enabling such content filtering on the fly is not a trivial task. Before proceeding to the technical difficulties, an elementary question has to be first effectively addressed:

What kind of content is considered harmful? The answer seems straightforward: *violence and pornography*, but the diversity of violent and pornographic actions is enormous and their characterization is quite subjective, creating difficulties in the definition and identification of such content unambiguously. For example, we may define as violence any action or situation, that may cause pain, suffering, physical or mental harm to one or more persons, injury to animals, fire, explosion or destruction of nonliving objects and as pornography any situation containing molestation, nudity, or sexual actions. Having concluded to an adequate definition of harmful TV content, one has to deal with the technical difficulties of the identification problem, involving audiovisual analysis, content annotation, content and metadata delivery, and finally content filtering at the user side. Unlike content annotation standards (TV-Anytime, MPEG-7, POWDER), content delivery and consumption standards (MPEG-21, TV-Anytime) and standards enabling content filtering (XML, MPEG-7, OWL) being currently mature enough, the main obstacle to enable effective TV content filtering is the lack in most cases or the limited extent of prior TV programs annotations to facilitate such process. Ideally those are created during the content production life cycle, but this is not always applicable. Production metadata are either missing, mostly because their manual creation is a heavy time-consuming task, or are insufficient for higher level content filtering, since they are usually targeted in genre characterization or viewer's age indication rather than in more detailed content, at shot or scene level, description. Consequently, the need is identified at the content provider's side for an automated offline content analysis and annotation process.

In the sequel, we initially elaborate on a number of existing TV and video analysis techniques for harmful content (e.g., violence and pornography) detection and annotation (Section 3.2). Each method is reviewed as to its positive and negative features, its estimated performance and the level of extracted semantics. In more detail, we initiate our investigation from low-level single modality (Section 3.2.1) (audio, visual, textual) approaches, proceed with medium-level multimodal fusion approaches (Section 3.2.2), and conclude with high-level knowledge-based approaches (Section 3.2.3). As the latter presents a promising case for which limited published work exists, the implementation of a complete semantic-based harmful content detection framework (Section 3.3), combining audiovisual processing (Sections 3.3.1 and 3.3.2) with OWL ontologies and SWRL rules (Sections 3.3.3 and 3.3.4), is presented in more detail. The framework is experimentally evaluated (Section 3.3.5) for the problems of binary and multiclass violence detection at the minimum defined temporal segment level (i.e., 1 s duration) and at the shot level. The aim is to automatically determine the type of depicted violence (e.g., fight, explosion, murder), at the corresponding temporal granularity level, by logically combining violent clues extracted from audio and visual modalities, thus supplying content providers with automated movie violence annotators and end users with high-level parental control through personalized filters.

3.2 TV Content Analysis for Harmful Content Detection

Detecting harmful content in TV/video data, which are complex in nature, multi-modal, and of significant size is not an easy task and requires extensive and efficient analysis. Although quite different, in terms of the exploited modalities and methodology specific details, most of the proposed approaches in the literature fall in the *pattern recognition* discipline [1]. Generally pattern recognition algorithms such as classification algorithms classify a set of objects into a number of predefined categories. Thus one has to answer the following questions:

Which categories to classify to? The set of predefined categories depends on the problem at hand and the desired level of the extracted semantics. In the case of harmful content detection one has to deal either with the binary (i.e., violence vs. nonviolence) or with the multiclass (i.e., gunshots, explosions, fights, screams, etc.) version of the problem.

What to classify? The answer in this question varies depending on the perspective someone views it. Hence from the segmentation perspective we classify *objects* and from the analysis perspective we classify vectors of *features* (i.e., numerical values, statistics) extracted from *objects*. In terms of video analysis, an object is defined as either a structural or a logical temporal segment. Specifically objects of the first category are frames, frame areas, or shots (i.e., a set of consecutive frames taken with a single camera) whereas objects of the second one are scenes (i.e., a set of consecutive shots displaying the same event), or audio frames (usually fixed duration segments of the auditory modality conveying the same audio event). Extracting the aforementioned types of objects are hard-to-solve subproblems of the overall process. Since image, video, and audio segmentation methodologies are out of the scope of this chapter and the interested reader is referred to [2–4] and the PASCAL visual object classes (VOC) challenge [5] for image segmentation [6,7], and TRECVid's corresponding task [8] for shot boundary detection, [9] for scene detection, and [10] for audio segmentation. From the analysis perspective aforementioned *objects* are characterized and classified by a set of measurable quantities (e.g., mean value, median, etc.), extracted from their low-level physical properties (e.g., pitch, luminance), which are defined as *features* in the literature. Feature generation and selection are also very important subproblems of the overall classification process. In short, one has to generate and select a set of feature values that optimally represent each one of the predefined classes and facilitate good discrimination among them. The reader is referred to [1] for further details.

How to classify? Video object classification raises the following issues: (a) Is a single- or a multimodal approach adopted? In the first case feature extraction is performed on a single modality (audio or visual), whereas in the second one on both of them. (b) In the multimodal approach, how is fusion performed from both modalities? At the feature level (i.e., early fusion) or at the decision level (i.e., late fusion)? (c) Is a supervised or an unsupervised classification algorithm employed? In the first case a large pre-annotated dataset is used for classifier training and classes are predefined, whereas in the second one similar object clusters are automatically created without training or classes predefinition. (d) Which specific classification algorithm/methodology is the optimal one for the problem in question? Many alternatives exist like Bayesian networks, k-nearest neighbor (kNN) classifiers, Gaussian mixture models (GMM), Markov models, support vector machines (SVM), neural networks (NN), decision graphs, automata, and a variety of others. According to data characteristics or the actual classification problem or performance trade-offs of the final application, the appropriate algorithm is selected.

In this section we provide a concise review of TV content (video) analysis techniques for harmful content detection, elaborating further on the aforementioned issues. Our aim is not to give extensive methodological details but to briefly sketch the studied approaches, comment on the achieved semantics level and familiarize the readers with fundamental concepts and performance conclusions. Although significant progress in the domain is achieved through the benchmarking activities of TRECVid [11], that evaluate the accuracy of several concept detectors on the identification of some violence-related concepts like riots, gunshots, explosions, fire, physical violence, the description of the corresponding methodologies is omitted because they do not directly aim toward harmful content identification for filtering applications, but examine the problem from a more generic point of view. Taking under consideration that most of the examined approaches use a distinct TV series and movies dataset, an objective performance comparison and evaluation is rather difficult to be achieved. Thus performance results are roughly discussed, in terms of precision and recall measures (whenever they are available), and mainly compared on the level of extracted semantics.

3.2.1 Extracting Harmful Clues from a Single Modality

In TV (video) content, violent and pornographic actions usually appear as a combination of simultaneous or consecutive events in auditory and visual modalities whereas accompanying textual data (e.g., subtitles, metadata, overlaid text) can provide valuable hints on the perceived content. The idea of dividing the main problem into smaller ones to optimally detect the desired semantics from the corresponding data stream is adopted in single modality approaches. Before proceeding with the review part of this chapter, in Table 3.1 we summarize related literature based on the achieved level of extracted semantics. It is observed that the set of detected harmful events/concepts is rather limited mostly due to limitations of low-level analysis algorithms. Further, approaches to tackle the detection of psychological/mental violence, which may be extremely harmful for sensitive user groups, are missing. Such content is difficult to automatically identify because of the inability to extract the actors emotional state or characterize it as sets and sequences of specific audio and visual clues.

Table 3.1 Overview of Achieved Semantics per Adopted Methodology

	Audio	*Visual*	*Multimodal*	*Ontological*
Violence	[12,15]	[24–26,31]	[55,57,58]	[70,71], [Section 3.3]
Fights/punches/ kicks	[16]	[30]	—	[70,71], [Section 3.3]
Screams/cries/ shout	[12,16,22,23]	—	—	[70,71], [Section 3.3]
Gunshots/ explosions	[12,16,17,20,23]	—	—	[70,71], [Section 3.3]
Pornography	—	[39,40,44,46]	[54]	—

3.2.1.1 Audio Analysis Approaches

Analyzing audio is significantly easier than visual analysis and provides valuable hints on the identification of gunshots, explosions, screams, music, speech, etc.; however related literature for pornography detection is missing, while it is fairly limited for violence detection. One of the first audio-based approaches appears as part of the MoCA* (movie content analysis) project in [12]. In this work, gunshots, explosions, and cries detection is examined from the implementation perspective. In particular, the development of an *audio content processing toolbox*, composed of biological and physical properties analysis algorithms, in the context of a movie analysis framework, is presented. Biological algorithms simulate the human process of sound perception, by computing the frequency dependent response of a specific nerve cell. This is achieved using a fourth-order *gammatone* filter [13] on the frequency domain of the audio signal. Exploiting the cell model of [14], the filtered signal is transformed into response probabilities and the *onset, offset*, and *frequency transitions* measures are computed. The former ones indicate how fast the nerve cell reacts to the signal and the latter ones localize glides in frequency. Physical properties analysis algorithms perform volume, frequency, pitch, and beat analysis to exploit the corresponding audio signal's physical properties. Namely statistics of *amplitude, frequency, pitch, onset, offset*, and *frequency transition* are computed to construct a 30D feature vector for each 30 ms window of the examined audio stream. Biological and physical properties measures, in combination, define a unique signature for each 30 ms audio segment. This signature is compared by means of Euclidean distance thresholding, against a ground truth database containing pre-calculated signatures of gunshots, explosions and cries, to identify the segment's nearest class. In terms of precision

---

* http://pi4.informatik.uni-mannheim.de/pi4.data/content/projects/moca/

(the recall measure is not provided) this method achieves 81% for gunshot, 51% for cry, and 93% for explosion detection leading to an overall of 75% for the binary problem.

Giannakopoulos et al. extensively studied both the binary and the multiclass version of audio-based violence detection in [15–17] and seem to have defined the state of the art in the domain. In [15], a detailed examination of *energy entropy*, *short time energy*, *zero crossing rate* (ZCR), *spectral flux*, and *spectral rolloff* features and their ability to discriminate violent from nonviolent audio segments is presented. The selected feature set, using support vector machines [18,19] for the classification process, proved satisfactory, achieving a total of 85.5% and 90.5% for precision and recall, respectively. An extended 12D feature set additionally employing *MFCCs* (Mel-frequency cepstral coefficients), *spectrogram features*, *chroma coefficients* and *pitch*, aiming at constructing discriminative feature spaces for three nonviolent (music, speech, others) and three violent classes (gunshots, fights, screams), was adopted in [16]. The devised multiclass approach follows the one versus all paradigm, that essentially divides the main problem in K ($K = 6$) binary subproblems (e.g., gunshot vs. no gunshot, speech vs. no speech). Each binary classifier is constructed as a Bayesian network fusing the mid-level decisions of three k-nearest neighbors (k-NN) classifiers, trained to distinguish between a class and its complement, with respect to a randomly selected 4D feature subvector. Thus six class probability estimations are drawn for every audio segment under investigation and the winner is the class with the highest probability. The achieved recall and precision values are 78.7% and 70.6% for gunshots, 69.1% and 65.6% for fights, 74.1% and 75.9% for screams, producing an increased overall performance of 90.8% and 86.6% for binary violence detection. In [17] the efficiency of dynamic programming in increasing gunshots detection accuracy through boundary correction is explored. The idea, initially presented in the context of speech/music discrimination of radio recordings, is to maximize a function defined to return a score given a sequence of segments and the respective class labels. The initial segmentation of the audio stream is performed by means of the multiclass approach [16]. Gunshot event detection results are significantly improved achieving 78.8% precision and 90.6% recall.

Although surveillance applications seem irrelevant with the problem at hand, we argue that they can be employed, with slight modifications, for harmful TV content detection, especially for surveillance videos shown during news, in live coverage of riots or war scenes (the Gulf War was broadcasted on TV), in reality shows (Big Brother, etc.), using fixed cameras and sensors. In contrast to preproduced TV programs, audio-based surveillance approaches have further to deal with the additional environmental noise included in the audio signal. The Gaussian mixture model approach for *gunshot* detection, in surveillance or homeland security applications, of [20] examines the negative effects of noise to the detection accuracy. Principal component analysis [21] tackles the selection of 13 uncorrelated features from *short time energy*, *spectral centroid*, *spectral spread*, the first eight *MFCCs* and their first and second derivatives. Finally two distinct Gaussian mixture models (GMMs) are trained (one for each class, e.g., gunshots, normal) using the expectation maximization algorithm. A comparative study of GMMs and SVMs, in the context of *shout* detection, using a common set of *MFCC, linear prediction coefficients* (LPC) and *perceptual linear prediction coefficients* (PLP) features is presented in [22]. The authors conclude that in terms of identification performance the GMM approach outperforms the SVM one. GMMs are also employed in [23] devising a *scream* and *gunshot* detection system in noisy environments. Two GMM classifiers, each tackling a binary subproblem (i.e., screams vs. noise and gunshots vs. noise), are trained and run in parallel. A logical OR function provides the identified event. Special attention was given on optimally discriminating the classes under investigation, by means of a two-step procedure combining *scalar* and *vectorial* feature selection. This system achieves 90% precision and 92% recall in a dataset of noisy and clear sounds.

3.2.1.2 Visual Analysis Approaches

The visual modality conveys a much richer set of semantics; however, their identification is a much more challenging and difficult task. First of all, one has to deal with the intrinsic spatiotemporal nature. Displayed events are constantly evolving and physical or artificial objects are randomly moving during TV program broadcasting. Their *localization, recognition,* and *tracking* are core, hard-to-tackle subproblems of visual analysis. Secondly, *editorial effects* (gradual or abrupt shot cuts), *camera movements* (pan, tilt, zoom), *overlaid artificial objects* (textual or not), and *visual effects* (explosions, complex actor movements) further increase the semantics extraction difficulty. Finally the employed *compression* standard (MPEG, H.264, raw) greatly affects the design and in some cases the performance of the detection algorithms.

One of the first approaches attempting visual-based violence detection appears in [24]. The authors bring forward a simple yet efficient idea: *Action movies have a strong component of short shots with significant inter frame variations* (i.e., high activity in short shots). Furthermore, they argue on the superiority of higher level semantics, compared to binary ones (i.e., violence vs. nonviolence) for retrieval and filtering applications. Thus they devise a feature set, providing a continuous video content rating scale, which is composed of (a) the *average shot activity,* measuring interframe differences resulting from camera motions and lighting variations by means of *tangent distance* and (b) the *shot length,* measuring the shot duration. Experimentation with a movie trailers dataset, which results in plotting the extracted feature values, shows that the selected features lead to good discrimination between violent and nonviolent trailers and further classify the latter based on the inherent degree of action. However, no results are presented in terms of recall and precision and no attempt to further characterize movie violence at shot level. The notion of high motion activity in short shots is also employed in the *state machine*–based approach for action sequence detection presented in [25]. Namely, motion vectors extracted from P-frames of MPEG-1 video sequences along with visually similar and temporally related shot clusters feed the state machine to track action sequences. The interpretation of the term *action* in terms of fights, gunshots, chases, robbery, crashes, along with the examined dataset (only 8 out of 57 sequences were not depicting violent content), pose a strong correlation with violence detection. In terms of recall and precision, the action detection system achieves a total of 95% and 62%, respectively; however, identification of the specific violent event (i.e., fight, gunshot, etc.) is not explored.

Intense motion in connected skin or blood pixel areas might be indicative of fighting or punching or stabbing scenes. In [26] the authors exploit this idea to devise an automated modular system that tackles the binary violence detection problem in MPEG encoded streams. The first module detects shot boundaries. The second one employs *self-organizing maps* [27,28] to classify pixels as skin or blood. The third isolates blood and skin pixel connected areas and maintains only those of significant size. Finally, the fourth module employs the *pixel change ratio map* (PCRM) [29], essentially computing *pixel motion intensity* per shot. Namely, the algorithm computes the amount of movement for every pixel during the shot under investigation. Shots with highest motion intensity are kept for further PCRM computation on the contained skin and blood components, to localize intense movement and provide valuable hints for violent acts detection. Experimentation on three violent movies provided rather conflicting results. Namely, 100% for recall and precision is achieved for the *Gladiator* movie, 58.33% and 46.67%, respectively for *Kill Bill*, and 100% and 50% for a segment of *Passion of Christ*. Taking under consideration the diversity of examined movies in terms of action and editorial effects, we argue that this method is not adequate for fast paced movies with a lot of blood (i.e., *Kill Bill*), for which it needs further refinement.

In [30], the authors attempt to exploit limps orientation and abrupt head speed changes to identify person on person violent actions (i.e., kicks, punches, etc.). Initially, *Gaussian background subtraction* detects moving object silhouettes and extracts their bounding boxes. Then, a set of measures, like *mean* number of pixels and *standard deviation* of black pixels, are computed from projection histograms of bounding boxes' parts and compared against a pretrained lookup table of 20 human models to identify person silhouettes. Simple geometrical rules applied, on the detected silhouettes, are used to localize upper human body parts (head, neck) and limps orientation, for tracker initialization and kicks/punches detection, respectively. Head movements tracking is performed by means of *color sums of squared differences* while motion abrupt changes in magnitude and direction are detected using *acceleration measure vector* and *jerk* (third derivative of head speed). Although the authors aim for movie violence detection, the undertaken experimentation assumes a simplified version of the problem using static camera, background settings, and predetermined view of the two actors, causing thus system failure when at least one of the actors falls or when multiple actors appear in the scene.

The newest approach on binary violence detection, further concentrating on fights detection, appears in [31]. The authors inspired from textual information extraction employ the *bag of visual words* [32] model for features representation and support vector machines for segments classification. Each visual word represents, in the form of a feature vector, a pattern appearing in the training dataset. To define the bag of visual words, a K-means clustering algorithm is adopted to organize spatiotemporal feature vectors into similarity groups by computing Euclidean distances. Two distinct feature sets are used in this work for comparison reasons: (a) *scale invariant features* (SIFT) [33] and (b) *spatiotemporal interest points* (STIP) [34]. The SIFT feature set results in 80.9% and 94.74% for recall and precision, respectively, while the STIP feature set achieves an increased total of 99.54% for both measures.

Although significant progress appears in violence, major intrinsic difficulties on the one hand and questionable opinions that it is a taboo or a solvable, simply through skin detection, problem, on the other hand, prevented equivalent advances on the pornography detection domain. Current approaches mostly exploit *skin* and *motion patterns* extraction toward identifying nudity and sexual acts, respectively. With respect to skin detection, a good starting point are the works presented in [35,36] the first one surveying existing such methodologies and the second one evaluating 21 color spaces and their performance on nudity detection. Skin color statistics along with self-organizing maps (SOM) in the first and Adaboost algorithm in the second case are further exploited in the nipple detection systems presented in [37,38], respectively. A comparative study of motion pattern extraction, image classification, and a combined approach for pornography detection is presented in [39], while skin detection alone is used in the automatic pornography filtering system of [40]. In the first case, five different methods, each one returning a pornography existence likelihood score for the movie under question, are benchmarked and compared against a large video database. Image (i.e., keyframe) classification employs SVMs with two distinct feature sets—one related with a histogram-based skin detection process (average skin probability, skin pixel ratio, size of skin blobs) and another related with a patch-based bag of visual words extraction process [41]. The motion patterns extraction process employs decision tree classification with *periodicity*-related features and SVM classification with *motion histogram* features [42]. The fusion step computes the *weighted sum* of the single methods classification scores. Experimental results (in terms of error rate) prove the motion analysis superiority against image classification and reveal significant performance increase for the fusion approach. In the second case, an empirical rule initially excludes frames near the shot boundary or frames with global motion as non-pornographic ones. The remaining frames are first segmented into homogeneous color regions and the weighted skin amount, by means of color histograms, is computed for each area. Then a size filter maintains, for further processing, only frames displaying large skin regions. Finally, seven *invariant moments* [43] are computed for them and compared against a predefined obscene and benign image database, using *weighted Euclidean* distances. This system achieved a total of 96.5% and 64% for recall and precision, respectively, in a large video dataset composed of a mixture of pornographic scenes.

The idea to combine unsupervised clustering with supervised learning mimicking the human ability to easily perform an accurate coarse categorization of random objects with little observation, and proceed to finer discrimination after further examination of results, is demonstrated in the pornography detection system of [44]. During the unsupervised clustering step *latent Dirichlet allocation* (LDA) [45] extracts the hidden relationship of training frames inferring thus an LDA model, roughly categorizing the training dataset into small topic clusters, by means of maximum membership probability. Finer discrimination is achieved during the supervised learning phase, where each clustered set is trained to generate multiple smaller SVM models. Finally, an adaptive Bayesian approach fuses inferred LDA membership probability with the SVM predicted one, deriving thus the final pornography score. The employed features in this hierarchical LDA-SVM system are *global color histogram* for the top layer coarse categorization clustering and *color moments* along with *edge histograms* for the finer discrimination process. The system achieved a recall rate of $\approx 93\%$ and a precision rate of $\approx 90\%$. A totally different and unique approach on pornography detection, involving users in the process, is presented in [46]. In this work, the aim is not to automatically detect pornography but to integrate a set of visual analysis tools in a software application, in order to assist police investigators to identify child pornography in large image and video databases. The implemented tools on the one hand tackle face, nudity, and salient patches detection adopting a histogram-based Naïve Bayesian classifier and a generic object detection framework, based on the work of [47], respectively. On the other hand, they enhance searching and browsing, exploiting a 101 concepts lexicon to add shot-based video semantic indexing and an intelligent thread-based video browsing and playback technique to assist and speed up the video/image viewing process.

3.2.1.3 Textual Approaches

Textual information accompanies TV programs either directly in the form of subtitles, closed caption, overlaid text, textual signs in the recorded scene or indirectly in the form of teletext, metadata, and transcripts. Although textual modality analysis, detecting inappropriate words or phrases, measuring their appearance, analyzing their syntax, semantics or even emotion, could provide significant clues for violent (physical and psychological) or pornographic content identification, both in single- and multimodal approaches, related literature is totally missing. However for the interested reader significant progress appears in more constrained domains. A review of several text retrieval approaches and their employed components (e.g., retrieval models, text sources, similarity measures), in the domain of broadcasted news, is presented in [48]. Bag of words representing closed captions extracted also from news broadcasts were used in [49]. In [50,51] closed caption stream and superimposed texts were exploited for sports semantic description and interesting events detection in Formula-1 races, respectively. A weakly supervised algorithm exploiting screenplay and closed captions to parse a movie into a hierarchy of shots and scenes, aiming further for object tracking and action retrieval, is presented in [52]. Finally continuous streams of timed words transcribed from audios recordings, as an additional clue for video event detection, were used in [53].

3.2.2 Combining Low- to Medium-Level Extracted Clues in Multimodal Approaches

Single modality harmful content detection approaches produce satisfactory results. However, taking into consideration that violent or pornographic actions rarely appear in isolation (i.e., only in one of the modalities), the potential of *multimodal* approaches toward increasing the detection accuracy or the level of extracted semantics has to be explored. *Multimodal* approaches tackle the problem at hand by means of single modality analysis *fusion*, that either combines single modality features in a unique multimodal representation, feeding machine learning algorithms to extract combined semantics (*early fusion*) or couples extracted audio, visual, and textual mid-level semantics to achieve higher level of abstraction and improve semantics extraction accuracy (*late fusion*). Despite the apparent advantages of multimodal approaches the reported literature is fairly limited, especially for the pornography case. The only approach employing multimodality in the pornography detection problem is presented in [54]. The added value of this work is not to devise a complete solution and present experimental results (a real-time filtering approach is left for future development), but to propose a set of specific (some of them novel) audio and visual features optimally discriminating pornographic content. In particular, the authors prove that in addition to *skin* detection, *homogeneous motion* and *sound periodicity* features, extracted in real time, provide significant pornographic clues.

One of the first binary violence detection approaches, combining audio and visual clues in a rather perceptual than systematic way appears in [55]. Namely, *Gaussian modeling* is employed for soundtrack classification into violent and nonviolent segments and the *energy entropy* criterion for gunshots or explosions identification. *Spatiotemporal dynamic activity* measure (initially presented in [24]), abrupt luminance changes, and predefined color tables extract visual clues like activity, gunshots/explosions, and blood, respectively. The designated audiovisual signatures are perceptually fused for violent shots detection.

The idea of *co-training* [56] is employed in [57,58] for binary movie violence detection. The co-training algorithm is a weakly supervised approach, generating reliable classifiers when a limited training dataset is available and applied when extraction of conditionally independent and sufficient feature sets (views) from the data under investigation is possible. In TV content analysis, audio and visual information comprise the two different data views. In the first case, a *linear weighted model* combining visual measures (motion intensity, flame explosion and blood in terms of yellow and red tone areas, respectively) and a pLSA (probabilistic latent semantic analysis)-based classifier, employing common audio features (e.g., ZCR, MFCC, pitch, spectrum flux, etc.) with a per-shot threshold are trained. These two independent classifiers along with the training and the testing samples feed the co-training algorithm. During the experimental evaluation on a five movie dataset, this approach achieved a mean of 83% and 92% for precision and recall, respectively. In the second case the co-training is used to determine the set of violence candidate shots, extracted at the first stage of the method. A set of motion activity features based on tensor histograms [59] form the visual view, while spectrum features (denoting high power/energy) along with SVM-based speech classification results (a negative feature on violence detection) from the audio one. The candidate shots are further processed by a group of SVM classifiers, each one trained to identify gunshots, explosions, car racing, screams, crashes, swords, and fights from the audio modality. Although the devised SVM concept detectors enable higher level of semantics extraction, the evaluation step addresses only the binary version of the problem, achieving a total of 80% precision and 91% recall.

3.2.3 Higher Level Semantics Extraction: The Role of Ontologies

Examining the reported research on harmful content detection, we conclude that the extracted semantics are not at the desired level for higher level harmful TV content filtering applications. Most approaches tackle either the binary or constrained instances of the multiclass problem and are rather tailor-made. In addition, there is a lack of interest on incorporating automatic annotation processes in terms either of MPEG-7* or of ontological representations. Years of research on various domains (e.g., sports, news, medical) of video analysis has acknowledged the demand for a complete and unified approach detecting and representing displayed events, actions, and objects. Narrowing down this conclusion for the problem of harmful content detection, violence and pornography should be detected by means of a unified approach exporting various levels of semantic abstractions, employing state-of-the-art audio, visual, and textual mid-level concept detectors, using domain knowledge, ontologies, and reasoning for higher level semantics inferencing, annotation, and filtering. Ontologies [60,61] as a real-world concepts representation formalism, in the form of hierarchies, logical relations and rules, play a crucial role on communicating higher level semantics among machines and human beings. Current semantic web research trends (e.g., POWDER†) attempt to exploit ontologies, binded with documents (i.e., images, texts, videos, music, or combinations), to provide an intelligent and human-oriented data manipulation. Deploying semantic web trends in the context of TV content analysis for annotation and filtering is a

---

* http://mpeg.chiariglione.org/standards/mpeg-7/mpeg-7.htm
† http://www.w3.org/TR/powder-dr/

very challenging task. Significant progress in the domain is achieved through the BBC Program ontology,* developed to publish BBC programs information in the semantic web. Further the NoTube project[†] focuses on employing web standards and semantics, to enhance TV content distribution and consumption through high-level personalization services creation. However these approaches employ ontologies at program's overall description level and are not sufficient for detailed content description at the shot or the scene level, enabling advanced filtering capabilities. Such approaches appear mostly to enhance semantic searching applications in simplified and constrained domains like medical [62,63], sports [64,65], and surveillance [66] videos whereas limited work appears in the domain of movies and TV series for harmful content detection. An ad hoc ontological approach, exploiting video event representation language (VERL) [67] along with video event markup language (VEML), for surveillance, physical security, and meeting video event detection applications, emerged as a result of the ARDA event taxonomy challenge project [68]. In addition, an interesting approach aiming toward extracting and capturing the hierarchical nature of actions and interactions, in terms of *context free grammars* (CFG) rather than ontologies, from raw image sequences appears in [69]. To the best of our knowledge, the only approaches, directly employing multimedia and domain ontologies for multimodal video analysis, in the context of harmful content identification, was our preliminary works for violence detection presented in [70,71]. In the following section, we present an extended and complete version of [70] and extend the experimental results of [71], both for binary and multiclass violence detection, at the minimum defined temporal segment level (i.e., 1 s duration) and at the shot level.

3.3 Knowledge-Based Framework for Violence Identification in Movies

The presented ontological (Figure 3.1) approach[‡] is a direct application of the proposed framework in [70], further elaborating, extending, and implementing each of the involved modules. Our aim is not to devise high-quality, low-level analysis processes, but to propose an open and extendable framework, combining existing single modality low- to mid-level concept detectors with ontologies and SWRL[§] rules, to identify and formally annotate an *extensive range of complex violent actions* in video data. We identify as major processes of the system, a preprocessing/segmentation step, a visual analysis step, an audio analysis step, each one interconnected with

---

* http://www.bbc.co.uk/ontologies/

† http://notube.tv/

‡ This work has been supported by the Greek Secretariat for Research and Technology, in the framework of the PENED program, grant number TP698.

§ Employed ontologies and SWRL rules are available through http://hermes.ait.gr/PenedHCD/

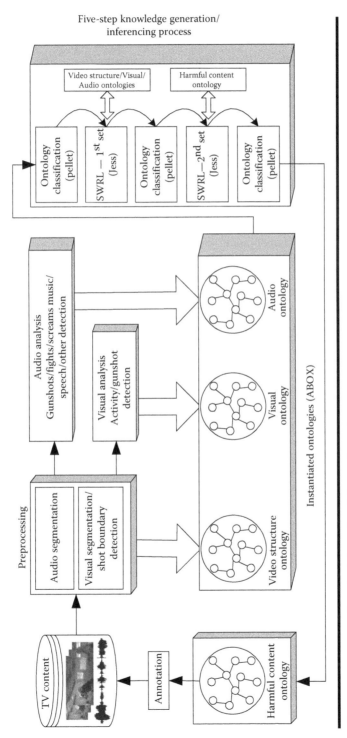

Figure 3.1 Proposed methodology for violence detection.

the corresponding data ontology, an Inferencing procedure and a harmful content domain ontology. Speaking in terms of knowledge engineering, low-level analysis extracts *basic facts* — *basic truth* that holds for the corresponding TV/video content data, while ontologies define *complex* and *terminological* facts that hold for the examined domain in general. Thus an explicit knowledge base is formed and the scope of the five-step inferencing procedure is to draw new implicit conclusions/knowledge during each step. In the following, we further elaborate on the implementation decisions adopted for each of the aforementioned processes.

3.3.1 Preprocessing — Segmentation Semantics

Preprocessing tackles the task of temporal audiovisual segmentation and feeds the corresponding low-level analysis algorithms. The role of segmentation is threefold: (1) Define the temporal annotation units, (2) feed low-level analysis with temporal segments of predefined duration, (3) preserve a common time reference and extract sequence and overlapping relations, among visual and audio segments, for the temporal reasoning procedures. Thus, both modalities are initially segmented into fixed duration segments (1 s as the minimum event duration), as defined from the low-level, modality-specific algorithms, and then grouped into the corresponding shots to preserve the synchronicity and time reference, further forming the annotation units. The task of shot boundary detection is performed by means of a local content adaptive thresholding approach, as the one employed in [72]. In short, local color histogram-based interframe differences and their mean values are computed on a 5D (i.e., five consecutive frames) temporal window. If the current difference is maximum in the examined window and is greater than twice the mean window value, a shot cut is detected. Although such an approach seems outdated (see [6,8] for more recent approaches), it produces accurate and satisfactory results on action and violent content that, based on common filmmaking techniques, employ short shots with hard cuts. Further the devised window-based adaptive threshold avoids over-segmentation that usually arise on slow gradual camera movements and simple edit effects, as zoom-ins and zoom-outs.

For interoperability reasons of the segmentation process with modality-specific and domain ontologies, the overall methodology demands for a video structure ontology (Figure 3.2), capturing temporal and structural semantics along with authoring information. In short, an example of the core classes is *VSO:MultimediaDocument** that defines the class of documents containing combinations of audio, visual, and textual information. Although our final target is to provide complete ontological representation for a multitude of multimedia document (e.g., streaming videos, web pages, images, audio recordings) currently, the only implemented subclass is the one representing movie/TV series content, defined

---

* VSO stands for *video structure ontology* and is used as prefix for every element of the structure ontology.

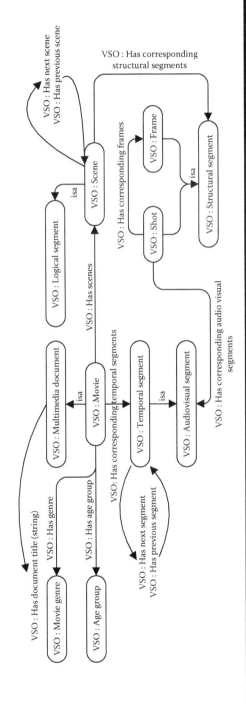

Figure 3.2 Video structure ontology.

to include individuals instantiating the corresponding property axioms with at least one temporal and at least one structural segment. In addition, datatype properties (i.e., VSO:hasDocumentTitle, VSO:hasTotalFrameNumber, VSO:hasFrameRate) capture authoring information. For further interoperation with existing metadata annotations (e.g. TV-anytime) providing overall content description, in terms of intended age groups or genre classification, corresponding axioms *VSO:hasAgeGroup*, *VSO:hasGenre* were included in the ontological definition. *VSO:TemporalSegment* categorizes segments (in our case of 1 s duration) exploiting either the auditory or visual modality or both to convey meaning associated with a temporal duration. Structurally every video is a sequence of shots (i.e., single camera capturing) and every shot is a sequence of frames. Logically, every video is a sequence of semantically meaningful scenes, each one composed of consecutive shots. Thus *VSO:StructuralSegment* defines content's elementary structural and *VSO:LogicalSegment* subsumed logical segments. The last two classes and their property axioms serve as the main interconnection point with the low-level analysis algorithms and are the first to be instantiated, initiating thus the inferencing procedure. Obviously there is a strong interconnection of the video structure ontology with an MPEG-7 one. Thus we have incorporated, with property axioms, an extended version with the MPEG-7 audio part version of Jane Hunter's ontology [73], aiming further for automated MPEG-7-based annotation.

3.3.2 Audiovisual Semantics

To optimally combine multimedia descriptions with the violence domain ontology, the knowledge representation process has further defined modality violence ontologies (audio, visual) that essentially map low-level analysis results to simple violent events and objects (medium-level semantics). Adopting a top-down approach, the modality-specific ontologies comprise an important "guide" for low-level analysis algorithms. Namely, they define what to search or try to extract from raw data. Although concept detectors using statistical, probabilistic, and machine learning approaches are extensively studied in the literature, it is not yet possible to extract whatever a knowledge engineering expert prescribes. Consequently, the corresponding ontologies contain a broader set of potential for extraction concepts, further prioritizing low-level analysis research toward developing novel concept detectors. Taking under consideration the intrinsic difficulties of low-level analysis, providing erroneous results in some cases, the long-term target is to connect a broad set of concepts/events/object detectors with the modality-specific ontologies, providing thus a cooperative mechanism toward increasing the detection accuracy.

3.3.2.1 Visual Semantics

The visual ontology (Figure 3.3) defines, in a hierarchical way, the set of objects/events—possibly related with harmful content—identified during visual

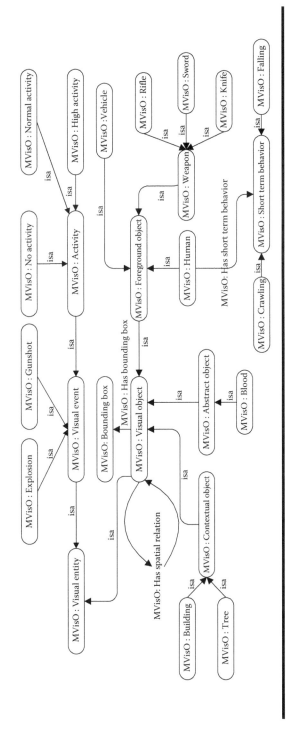

Figure 3.3   Visual ontology: objects and events.

analysis Although a much broader set of low- to mid level semantics is already defined, for interoperability with the employed visual analysis algorithms reasons, we focus our attention on the actually extracted visual clues. In particular, each fixed duration segment is classified in one of three activity (low, normal, high) and two gunshot (gunshot, no-gunshot) classes. Thus, the simple human events and visual objects ontological classes of interest are *MVisO:HighActivity,** *MVisO:NormalActivity*, *MVisO:NoActivity*, *MVisO:Gunshot*, *MVisO:noGunshot*, and *MVisO:Face*.

The activity detection process initially computes, in a per segment basis, the *average overall motion*, *variance of motion*, and *average degree of overlap of the detected people* (i.e., faces) features. The former ones are computed by the corresponding *motion vectors* while the latter by the face detection and tracking component. The face detection component employs a set of Haar-like features and a boosted classifier to detect people in the scene [74] while the tracking component employs the hierarchical fusion algorithm devised in [75]. To increase face detection robustness, the histogram-based skin detection algorithm of [76] filters out objects with minimum skin content. Finally, the classification process is performed by means of a weighted kNN (k-nearest neighbor) classifier that computes the segment likelihood to attain high, normal, or no activity content. Measuring abrupt changes in the illumination intensity can provide valuable hints on the existence of fire, explosions, or gunshots. Thus, the *maximum luminance difference* and *maximum luminance interval* features are used to train a distinct weighted kNN classifier discriminating between gunshot and no-gunshot segments. For further details on the visual analysis components the reader is referred to [71].

3.3.2.2 Audio Semantics

Additional clues increasing the harmful content detection accuracy exist in the auditory modality. Contrary to visual, in audio semantics the ontological definition covers the full set of extracted mid-level semantics. Thus the audio classes (Figure 3.4) of interest are *MSO:Screams,†* *MSO:Speech*, *MSO:Gunshot*, *MSO:Fights*, *MSO:SharpEnviromentalSound*, and *MSO:SmoothEnviromentalSound*. The audio analysis process involves a variant of the "one-vs-all" (OVA) classification scheme presented in [16] (see brief description in Section 3.2.1.1), on a segment basis, in order to generate a sequence of three violent (*gunshots*, *fights*, and *screams*) and four non-violent (*music*, *speech*, *others1*: environmental sounds of low energy and almost

---

* MVisO stands for *movie visual ontology* and is used as prefix for every element of the visual ontology.

† MSO stands for *movie sound ontology* and is used as prefix for every element of the sound ontology.

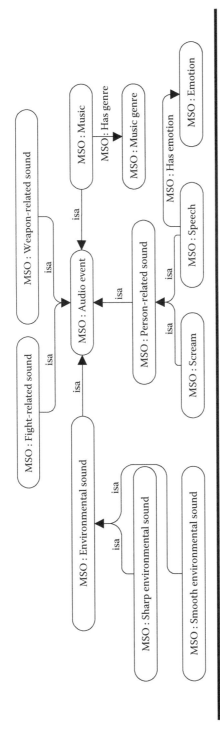

Figure 3.4   Audio ontology.

stable signal level like silence, background noise, etc., and *others?*· environmental sounds with abrupt signal changes like thunders or closing doors) audio class probabilities for each segment.

3.3.3 Domain Ontology Definition

An effective formal representation of the harmful content domain knowledge in all its complexity, abstractness, and hierarchy depth, to drive corresponding acts detection, has never been attempted before. We have made a step forward toward this direction. The ontology definition has resulted from an extended investigation through close observation of mostly violent* acts in video data collected from TV programs, movies, streaming videos, news, and security camera captures. The harmful content domain ontology† (Figure 3.5) includes the definition of numerous high-level concepts as a set of related spatiotemporal entities (i.e., actions, events, objects) irrespective of low-level analysis algorithms. Taking under consideration the inability of employed audio and visual analysis algorithms to extract the broad set of violence-related modality-specific semantics (i.e., guns, swords, vehicles, contextual objects, body parts, emotional state, simple actions, events, etc.), we are forced to limit our description and experimentation on the set of attained mid-level semantics. In addition due to *open world reasoning* in OWL,‡ we cannot identify nonviolence directly using simple *negation as failure* reasoning. Therefore the domain ontology further aims on the identification of a number of non-harmful classes like dialogue, actions/activity, and scenery.

3.3.4 Inferencing Procedure

Having the extracted low- to mid-level semantics, and the corresponding loosely coupled, using common terms, equivalent classes and object property axioms, ontological descriptions, we have to tackle with the issue of *fusing and interchanging semantics from different modalities*, toward inferring more complex, abstract, and extensive violent cases represented in the domain ontology. Thus there is a need for a cross-modality ontological association mechanism between modality-specific and domain ontologies, further increasing the semantic extraction capabilities of low-level analysis. Toward this direction we investigate the usage of SWRL rules§ combined in a five-step inferencing procedure with ontological reasoning. SWRL

---

* The ontology definition covers both violence and pornography; however, the implementation of low-level analysis algorithms for pornography clues detection is not yet completed and in this chapter we focus our attention on the violence subclass.
† HCO stands for *harmful content ontology* and used as prefix for every element of the domain ontology.
‡ Every logical statement might be true unless there is a definition that proves it is false.
§ http://www.w3.org/Submission/SWRL

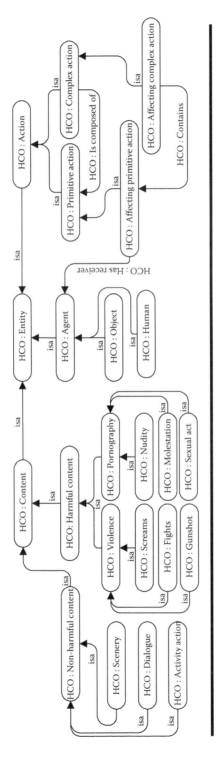

Figure 3.5   Harmful content ontology.

(a Horn-like rule language combining OWL with RuleML), on the one hand, can reason about OWL instances (individuals) in terms of OWL classes and properties and is mostly used to increase the OWL expressivity. Ontological reasoning, on the other hand, implements consistency checking, classification, and instance checking services, which is usually achieved using one of the existing reasoners (in our case Pellet [77]). Although manual SWRL rule construction is a tough procedure, especially for such a complicated domain like harmful content detection, we explore the potential for cross-modality representation of violent spatiotemporal relations and behavioral patterns. Since SWRL and OWL do not yet formally support reasoning under uncertainty, we attempt to capture such semantics by simply thresholding the corresponding datatype relations with SWRL built-in axioms.

Speaking in terms of description logic (DL) [78], the involved ontologies define the conceptual representation of the domain in question, forming thus the *terminological box* (TBox) of our knowledge base. Taking into consideration that the inferencing procedure attempts to reclassify modality individuals to the violence domain ontology, the definition of the *assertional box* (ABox)—the set of individual definitions in terms of TBox's concepts, roles and axioms—is mandatory. In the examined field of application, the ABox derives directly from the segmentation and audio/visual analysis algorithms, forming the basic facts in terms of individuals representing segments, frames, events, and objects along with the corresponding low-level numerical values and occurrence/accuracy probability results. Essentially, the instantiated model captures existing and extracted knowledge for the TV content in question. Based on this explicit knowledge, the five-step inferencing procedure is applied. Each ontological reasoning step draws implications that could possibly trigger the execution of a new rule set. Similarly, each rule execution implies fresh knowledge exploited by subsequent ontological reasoning steps. Namely, the process is as follows:

Step-1: During ontology instantiation, individuals are subclassed under *owl:Thing*; thus, the main purpose of this step is to check the consistency of the instantiated VSO model and assert each individual's initial class, according to TBox's necessary and sufficient conditions.

Step-2: The first SWRL rule set, composed of 35 rules, is applied. Datatype property axioms expressing arithmetic probabilities and numerical values are translated to object property axioms, instantiated with classes and instances from the modality-specific ontologies (e.g., assign the winner class). In addition, instantiation of the extracted video structure is performed (i.e., shots are related with the corresponding segments and segments with the corresponding frames). In Table 3.2 an example rule of this category is provided.

Step-3: Consistency checking and classification services on the implied modality-specific models are applied.

Step-4: The second SWRL rule set (see Table 3.3 for an example) composed of 39 rules is applied. Implied audio and visual mid-level semantics are combined using commonsenselogic, spatiotemporal relations and simplified conclusions drawn from

Table 3.2 Inferring *MSO:Fight* Using SWRL

Description	SWRL Rule
If	
?as is an Audio Segment	VSO:AudioSegment(?as) ∧
?gsp is the probability of gun-shot existence	VSO:hasAudioGunshotProbability(?as, ?gsp) ∧
?fp is the probability of fight existence	VSO:hasFightProbability(?as, ?fp) ∧
?shsp is the probability of Sharp Sound existence	VSO:hasSharpSoundProbability(?as, ?shsp) ∧
?smsp is the probability of Smooth Sound existence	VSO:hasSmoothSoundProbability(?as, ?smsp) ∧
?sp is the probability of Speech existence	VSO:hasSpeechProbability(?as, ?sp) ∧
?m is the probability of Music existence	VSO:hasMusicProbability(?as, ?m) ∧
Fight probability is greater than Gunshot probability	swrlb:greaterThan(?fp, ?gsp) ∧
Fight probability is greater than Music probability	swrlb:greaterThan(?fp, ?m) ∧
Fight probability is greater than Speech probability	swrlb:greaterThan(?fp, ?sp) ∧
Fight probability is greater than Sharp Sound probability	swrlb:greaterThan(?fp, ?shsp) ∧
Fight probability is greater than Smooth Sound probability	swrlb:greaterThan(?fp, ?smsp)
Then	
Fights are detected in ?as	→ VSO:hasAudioEvent(?as, MSO:fight)

low-level analysis modules (i.e., confusion matrices) for cross-modality reasoning, further mapping video segments in one of the domain ontology classes.

Step-5: In this final step, consistency checking and classification services on HCO are applied to infer violent and nonviolent segments (instances reclassify from children to parents) on the one hand and extended semantics (instances reclassify from

Table 3.3 Identifying a Nonviolent (Activity/Action) and a Violent (Fighting) Segment

Description	SWRL Rule
If	
?avs is an Audio Visual Segment	VSO:AudioVisualSegment(?avs) ∧
?ms is an individual of audio class Music	MSO:Music(?ms) ∧
?ha is an individual of visual class High-Activity	MVisO:HighActivity(?ha) ∧
In ?avs music is detected	VSO:hasAudioEvent(?avs,?ms) ∧
In ?avs high activity is detected	VSO:hasVisualEvent(?avs,?ha)
Then	
?avs is an action segment	→ HCO:ActivityAction(?avs)
Description	SWRL Rule
If	
?avs is an Audio Visual Segment	VSO:AudioVisualSegment(?avs) ∧
?f is an individual of audio class Fights	MSO:Fights(?g) ∧
?f is an individual of visual class High-Activity	MVisO:HighActivity(?ha) ∧
In ?avs fights are detected	VSO:hasAudioEvent(?avs,?f) ∧
In ?avs high activity is detected	VSO:hasVisualEvent(?avs,?ha)
Then	
?avs is a fights segment	→ HCO:Fighting(?avs)

parents to children) on the other hand. Since the first classification case is straightforward (e.g., every fight segment is also a violent one) we will further describe the second case using a simple example. In Table 3.4 we demonstrate the definition of *MVO:PersonOnPersonFighting* and *MVO:MultiplePersonFighting* using necessary and sufficient conditions. During classification every fighting segment displaying exactly two persons (identified by their faces) is finally classified as instance of *MVO:PersonOnPersonFighting* and every fighting segment displaying more than three persons is finally classified as instance of *MVO:MultiplePersonFighting* producing thus higher level of semantics. In addition following the path from an instance to the root of HCO a complete description of the corresponding segment is produced.

Table 3.4 Identifying Person-on-Person-Fighting and Multiple-Person-Fighting

HCO:Fighting Subclasses Definition	Necessary and Sufficient Conditions
HCO:PersonOnPersonFighting	HCO:Fights ∧ HCO:displaysObjects some MVisO:Face ∧ HCO:displaysObjects exactly 2
HCO:MultiplePersonFighting	HCO:Fights ∧ HCO:displaysObjects some MVisO:Face ∧ HCO:displaysObjects min 3

3.3.5 Implementation and Experimentation

The presented ontological approach was developed using MATLAB® and the OpenCV library* for audio/visual feature extraction and classification, Protégé† for the definition of ontologies and SWRL rules, Pellet [77] and Jess‡ for ontology reasoning services and rules execution, and finally Jena semantic web framework§ for ontologies instantiation and synchronization of the knowledge generation life cycle. For evaluation purposes, 50 videos¶ have been extracted from 10 different movies (see Table 3.5). The aim during the dataset creation was to cover the set of violent and nonviolent semantics/concepts to be extracted (i.e., gunshots/explosions, fights, screams, scenery, action/activity, dialogue), emphasizing on the non-violent ones to make the evaluation process more accurate. The corresponding training phases of audio and visual modules used a different video dataset of the same movies whether

Table 3.5 Movie Dataset

Movie	Duration	Movie	Duration
American Ninja	8.9 min	Usual Suspects	55.12 s
Friday the 13th	28.5 min	Matrix Reloaded	22.25 min
Heroes (TV series)	19.7 min	Terminator I	21.9 min
Kill Bill I	13.9 min	Pulp Fiction	4.1 min
Nochnoy Dozor	22.1 min	Mississippi Burning	2.4 min

---

* http://sourceforge.net/projects/opencvlibrary/
† http://protege.stanford.edu
‡ http://www.jessrules.com/
§ http://jena.sourceforge.net/
¶ Videos and annotations are available upon request. For more information visit http://hermes. ait.gr/PenedHCD/

the ontology and rules development performed irrespective of data. The total duration of the test data is 2.5 h. The video streams have been manually annotated by three persons, using the Anvil* video annotation research tool to generate ground truth data for performance evaluation. In more detail, these persons annotated, in a per event basis, those parts of the videos that contained violent content. According to manual annotations, 19.4% of the data was of violent content. The mean execution time for fully running the aforementioned process[†] is approximately 75 min for every 10 min of video. However, the execution time strongly varies depending on the movie structure. For example, the knowledge generation life cycle in 1 min of *Kill Bill* having constantly interchanging shots of very short duration (i.e., a large number of VSO instances) is more time consuming than the same process in 10 min of *Friday the 13*[th] having a small number of long shots. We estimate that it is possible to highly reduce running time by optimizing the ontology instantiation and query processes and by parallelizing audio and visual analysis algorithms, and the corresponding modality-specific ontology classification processes.

Tables 3.6 and 3.7 demonstrate the achieved experimental results for the binary and multiclass violence detection problem in a per segment (1 s duration) and in a per shot basis. The multiclass results are drawn only from the correctly classified as violent segments. For comparison with the single modality approaches purposes in Table 3.6, we further demonstrate the achieved performance of low-level audio and visual analysis algorithms for the binary problem. The performance measures are computed by means of **Precision** (i.e., the number of correctly detected violence segments, divided by the total number of detected violence segments), **Recall** (i.e., the number of correctly detected violence segments divided by the total number of **true** violence segments), *mean accuracy*, and F_1 *measure* $(F_1 = (2 \cdot P \cdot R)/(P + R))$. To investigate the potentials of the approach in the case of ideal low-level analysis algorithms, producing 100% accurate results, and detect possible drawbacks for further enhancements, we have conducted a series of experiments artificially altering the low-level analysis results based on the manual annotations. In the first case only the audio modality extractions were artificially varied (ArtA) (e.g., extracted probability values of 1 s segments annotated as screams varied as 1.0 for screams and 0 for fights, speech, etc.), in the second case only the visual one (ArtV) (e.g., extracted probability values of 1 s segments annotated as fights varied as 1.0 for high activity and 0 for gunshots, normal activity, etc.) and in the third case both (ArtAV) of them. Taking under consideration that experimentation with artificial varied input data, conducted only on the manually annotated as harmful content, the precision metric is omitted in this case.

The observation of segment-based results leads to the conclusion that the ontology-based approach results in enhanced performance, with respect to the

---

* http://www.anvil-software.de/
[†] Experimental evaluation performed on an Intel(R) Core(TM)2 Duo CPU T9400 At 2.53 GHz with 3.00 GB of RAM.

Table 3.6 Segment-Based Binary and Multiclass Detection Performance Measures

	Recall	Precision	F_1	Mean Accuracy	ArtA(**R**)	ArtV(**R**)	ArtAV(**R**)
Audio-binary	82.9%	38.9%	53%	61%	—	—	—
Visual-binary	75.6%	34%	46.9%	54.8%	—	—	—
Violence inference	91.2%	34.2%	50%	62.7%	98.7%	79.4%	98.2%
Fights inference	61.6%	68.2%	64.8%	64.9%	79.8%	41.0%	98.1%
Screams inference	41.4%	33.5%	37.1%	37.4%	100%	37.5%	100%
Shots-explosions inference	63.3%	38.2%	47.6 %	50.7%	99.8%	100%	100%

Table 3.7 Shot-Based Binary and Multiclass Detection Performance Measures

	Recall	Precision	F_1	Mean Accuracy	ArtA(**R**)	ArtV(**R**)	ArtAV(**R**)
Violence inference	61.07%	68.80%	64.7%	64.93%	66.8%	55.1%	81.8%
Fights inference	68.72%	89.9%	77.89%	79.31%	95.7%	57%	96.3%
Screams inference	25.0%	41.17%	31.10%	33.08%	54.5%	41.0%	82.41%
Shots-explosions inference	89.39%	40.68%	55.91%	65.03%	90.1%	97.3%	97.5%

binary detection problem, compared to the audio-based and visual-based ones. With respect to the multiclass problem (high-level semantics), the performance (Table 3.6) is satisfactory considering the unconstrained nature of the video data in the test set. The shot-based approach (Table 3.7) further increases the detection accuracy both for the binary and the multiclass problem, except for the case of screams. Screams are usually localized in short video segments and their detection is not actually aided from visual modality or neighboring segments. Thus the shot based approach, classifying longer video segments, using temporal relations among corresponding 1 s segments, tend to overlook scream detection triggering rules as a trade-off for increasing shot-based fights and gunshots detection accuracy. The overall recall rate in the artificially altered input case is highly increased, except in cases of screams and fights identification when varying visual modality's extraction results, because of the uncertainty in audio analysis actual results. In the case of screams, employed visual analysis algorithms assist the identification process only by means of face detection, thus the mapping of modality-specific concepts through SWRL to the domain ontology strongly depends on the achieved audio semantics. In the case of fights identification SWRL rules demand for visual high activity detection and audio fights detection. However, high activity detection is strongly related with action/activity shots inferencing; thus, the audio analysis results play significant role in triggering the correct rule set. Further the quality of shot-based results seem worse than the segment-based ones, because in order to reproduce the actual identification process, the artificial variation performed at the 1 s segment basis. Thus artificial are combined with extracted data affecting the set of applied SWRL rules and consequently the overall identification process. Since a direct comparison of our approach with the reported literature is not feasible, due to experimental evaluation in different datasets, we comment only on the level of achieved semantics. Single- and multi-modal approaches are unable to extract higher level of semantics with respect to harmful content annotations. The ontological approach attempts to fill in this gap by tackling an extensive range of such semantics. The achieved performance is greatly affected, on the one hand, by the low contribution of the visual-based analysis and, on the other hand, by the inability to handle and take advantage of mid-level probabilistic detection results (accuracy of detection, or probability of occurrence in a segment or shot). Further improvements on these directions are under investigation.

3.3.6 Extensions—Future Work

Intrinsically the proposed approach is an offline process perfectly adapted to the TV environment. Specifically the low-level analysis modules at first, and the inferencing procedures secondly run at content provider servers, producing the corresponding ontological annotations that will be transmitted along with the TV signal. However, in the age of social networks (e.g., Facebook), streaming video services (e.g., YouTube), and peer-to-peer services (e.g., torrents), all types of videos are uncontrollably available to sensitive user groups. Thus one has to explore the poten tials of applying this approach in such environments. In the case of streaming videos the use case scenario is fairly similar. Namely, when a video is uploaded it is automatically annotated on the server side and the produced ontological annotations are further published on the web, in machine readable format (i.e., POWDER), following the linked data principles, for future use. Further the inferencing procedure exploits user intervention either by exploiting their comments and tags, that form the textual modality, to increase the detection accuracy or by devising an interactive process to determine misclassifications, retrain the low-level classifiers, learn new ontology concepts and cross-modality mapping rules. In the case of downloadable videos, the corresponding software executes at the home gateway during "sleep" time, to annotate downloaded videos for later viewing. Taking under consideration that video annotation is a one-time process, assistive communities and user groups over the web provide the produced annotations in machine-readable format for others to easily find and use. Of course, in the case of homemade videos using cell phones, video cameras etc., there is a need for much finer low-level analysis processes.

As already mentioned in the introduction of Section 3.3, the devised framework follows an open and extensible design pattern. The modality-specific ontologies serve as interconnection points with an extended set of low- to mid-level concept/objects/events detectors, a limited set of whom is currently developed. Thus to further extend the accuracy and semantics extraction ability of the framework, either in the harmful content or in other domains (i.e., sports, news), all one has to do is to extend the set of concept detectors and increase the SWRL rule set to map modality-specific individuals in the corresponding domain ontology. We are currently developing such detectors to increase visual analysis accuracy in fights and gunshots detection, to detect sexual actions/nudity and to identify dialogues, scenery, and action/activity scenes. Although the video structure ontology (VSO) offers interconnection with TV programs description metadata (e.g., genre, intended age group), either in the form of TV-anytime or other metadata, that could assist the overall identification process by biasing a set of rules (i.e., movies of wars can bias SWRL rules toward gunshot/explosion detection against fights detection), our experiments currently do not formally exploit such information. Design of corresponding experiments is in progress along with formal exploitation of low-level probabilistic results in terms of fuzzy reasoning. Finally investigation of clustering techniques is performed to increase detection granularity (i.e., enable scene detection from shots) on the one hand and to examine automatic SWRL generation potentials on the other hand.

3.4 Conclusions

In this chapter, we have reviewed existing research on harmful TV content identification, exploiting either a single- or a multimodal approach. Although most of them produce interesting results, we argue that the single modality approaches fail to identify complex multimodal semantics while the multimodal ones require extensive training procedures. In addition none of the examined approaches encapsulate annotation processes for semantic-based filtering applications. We have proposed a complete ontological framework for harmful content identification and experimentally evaluated the violence detection case. The presented approach performs better than the employed audio and visual ones, for the 1 s segment-based binary violence detection problem, by means of recall rate, and achieves a small boosting in terms of mean accuracy. The performance is significantly increased both for the binary and the multiclass problems in the shot-based approach. We notice that for the *fight* class we achieve the best results whereas for the *screams* class the worst. This happens on the one hand because audio analysis algorithms produce the most accurate hints for fights identification and on the other hand because visual analysis does not actually aid screams identification. Summarizing the low value of attained results is greatly affected by the following facts: (a) Extracted visual analysis clues are not at the desired level, since activity classification is rather generic for specific concepts identification and detection of violence-related objects (i.e., guns, swords, knifes) and human actions (i.e., punch, kick) remains unfeasible. (b) Extracted audio and visual mid-level clues are biased toward nonviolence (i.e., five violent classes: audio-gunshot, screams, fights, high activity, visual-gunshot and seven non-violent: music, speech, smooth environmental sound, sharp environmental sound, no activity, normal activity, no gunshot). (c) Uncertain single modality results are treated as certain. Apparently the devised approach does not yet produce results at the desired accuracy for real parental control applications. However, taking into consideration the results of artificially varied experiments, demonstrating the potentials of such an approach, in combination with the aforementioned negative facts, we conclude that the attained results are really promising both for the binary and multiclass violence detection problems and that the main advantage of using such an ontological approach still remains the higher level semantics extraction ability, using an unsupervised procedure and commonsense reasoning.

References

1. S. Theodoridis and K. Koutroumbas, *Pattern Recognition*, 4th edn., Academic Press, Boston, MA, 2008.
2. K. McGuinness and N. E. O'Connor, A comparative evaluation of interactive segmentation algorithms, *Pattern Recognition*, 43, 434–444, Feb. 2010.
3. M. P. Kumar, P. H. S. Torr, and A. Zisserman, OBJCUT: Efficient segmentation using top-down and bottom-up cues, *IEEE Transactions on Pattern Analysis and Machine Intelligence*, 32, 530–545, 2010.
4. R. Timofte and L. J. V. Gool, Four color theorem for fast early vision, in *Proceedings of the 10th Asian Conference on Computer Vision*, Queenstown, New Zealand, vol. 6492 of *Lecture Notes in Computer Science*, pp. 411–424, Springer, 2010.

5. M. Everingham, L. J. V. Gool, C. K. I. Williams, J. M. Winn, and A. Zisserman, The PASCAL visual object classes (VOC) challenge, *International Journal of Computer Vision*, 88(2), 303–338, 2010.

6. J. Yuan, H. Wang, L. Xiao, W. Zheng, J. Li, F. Lin, and B. Zhang, A formal study of shot boundary detection, *IEEE Transactions on Circuits and Systems for Video Technology*, 17, 168–186, Feb. 2007.

7. K. Choroś and M. Gonet, Effectiveness of video segmentation techniques for different categories of videos, in *Proceedings of the 2008 Conference on New Trends in Multimedia and Network Information Systems*, Amsterdam, The Netherlands, pp. 34–45, IOS Press, 2008.

8. A. F. Smeaton, P. Over, and A. R. Doherty, Video shot boundary detection: Seven years of TRECVid activity, *Computer Vision and Image Understanding*, 114, 411–418, Apr. 26, 2010.

9. C. Petersohn, Logical unit and scene detection: A comparative survey, *Multimedia Content Access: Algorithms and Systems II*, 6820(1), 682002, 2008.

10. E. Peiszer, T. Lidy, and A. Rauber, Automatic audio segmentation: Segment boundary and structure detection in popular music, in *Proceedings of the 2nd International Workshop on Learning the Semantics of Audio Signals*, Paris, France, 21 June 2008.

11. A. F. Smeaton, P. Over, and W. Kraaij, High-level feature detection from video in TRECVid: A 5-year retrospective of achievements, in *Multimedia Content Analysis, Theory and Applications*, Springer Verlag, pp. 151–174, New York, 2009.

12. S. Pfeiffer, S. Fischer, and W. Effelsberg, Automatic audio content analysis, in *Proceedings of the Fourth ACM Multimedia Conference*, Boston, MA, pp. 21–30, ACM Press, Nov. 1996.

13. M. Cooke, *Modelling Auditory Processing and Organisation (Distinguished Dissertations in Computer Science)*, Cambridge University Press, Cambridge, U.K., 2004.

14. R. Meddis, Simulation of mechanical to neural transduction in the auditory receptor, *Journal of the Acoustical Society of America*, 79, 702–711, Mar. 1986.

15. T. Giannakopoulos, D. I. Kosmopoulos, A. Aristidou, and S. Theodoridis, Violence content classification using audio features, in *Advances in Artificial Intelligence, 4th Helenic Conference on AI, SETN 2006*, Crete, Greece, vol. 3955 of *Lecture Notes in Computer Science*, pp. 502–507, Springer, 18–20 May 2006.

16. T. Giannakopoulos, A. Pikrakis, and S. Theodoridis, A multi-class audio classification method with respect to violent content in movies, using Bayesian networks, in *IEEE International Workshop on Multimedia Signal Processing*, Crete, Greece, 2007.

17. A. Pikrakis, T. Giannakopoulos, and S. Theodoridis, Gunshot detection in audio streams from movies by means of dynamic programming and Bayesian networks, in *Proceedings of the 33rd International Conference on Acoustics, Speech, and Signal Processing*, Las Vegas, NV, pp. 21–24, IEEE, 2008.

18. I. Steinwart and A. Christmann, *Support Vector Machines*, 1st edn., Springer Publishing Company, Incorporated, New York, 2008.

19. S. Abe, *Support Vector Machines for Pattern Classification*, 2nd edn., Springer Publishing Company, Incorporated, London, U.K., 2010.

20. C. Clavel, T. Ehrette, and G. Richard, Events detection for an audio-based surveillance system, in *International Conference on Multimedia and Expo*, Amsterdam, The Netherlands, pp. 1306–1309, IEEE, 6–8 July 2005.

21. S. Wold, Principal component analysis, *Chemometrics and Intelligent Laboratory Systems*, 2(1), 37–52, 1987.

22. J.-L. Rouas, J. Louradour, and S. Ambellouis, Audio events detection in public transport vehicle, in *Proceedings of the 9th International IEEE Conference on Intelligent Transportation Systems*, Toronto, Ontario, pp. 733–738, IEEE, 17–20 Sept. 2006.

23. G. Valenzise, L. Gerosa, M. Tagliasacchi, F. Antonacci, and A. Sarti, Scream and gunshot detection in noisy environments, in *Proceedings of the 15th European Signal Processing Conference*, Poznan, Poland, pp. 1216–1220, 3–7 Sept. 2007.

24. N. Vasconcelos and A. Lippman, Towards semantically meaningful feature spaces for the characterization of video content, in *International Conference on Image Processing*, Washington, DC, vol. 1, pp. 25–28, 1997.

25. B. Lehane, N. E. O'Connor, and N. Murphy, Action sequence detection in motion pictures, in *Knowledge-Based Media Analysis for Self-Adaptive and Agile Multi-Media, Proceedings of the European Workshop for the Integration of Knowledge, Semantics and Digital Media Technology*, London, U.K., QMUL, 25–26 Nov. 2004.

26. C. T. Clarin, J. A. M. Dionisio, M. T. Echavez, and P. C. Naval, DOVE: Detection of movie violence using motion intensity analysis on skin and blood, in *Proceedings of the 6th Philippine Computing Science Congress*, Quezon City, Philippines, pp. 150–156, Computing Society of the Philippines, 2006.

27. T. Kohonen, The self-organizing map, *Proceedings of the IEEE*, 78, 1464–1480, 1990.

28. T. Kohonen, J. Hynninen, J. Kangas, and J. Laaksonen, SOM_PAK: The self-organizing map program package, Tech. Rep., Helsinki University of Technology, Laboratory of Computer and Information Science, FIN-02150 Espoo, Finland, 1996.

29. H. Yi, D. Rajan, and L.-T. Chia, A new motion histogram to index motion content in video segments, *Pattern Recognition Letters*, 26(9), 1221–1231, 2005.

30. A. Datta, M. Shah, and N. D. V. Lobo, Person-on-person violence detection in video data, in *Proceedings of the 16th International Conference on Pattern Recognition*, Quebec City, QC, Canada, IEEE Computer Society, 2002.

31. F. D. M. de Souza, G. C. Chávez, E. A. do Valle Jr., and A. de A. Araújo, Violence detection in video using spatio-temporal features, in *Proceedings of the 23rd SIBGRAPI Conference on Graphics, Patterns and Images*, Gramado, Brazil, pp. 224–130, IEEE Computer Society, 30 Aug.–03 Sept. 2010.

32. J. Yang, Y.-G. Jiang, A. G. Hauptmann, and C.-W. Ngo, Evaluating bag-of-visual-words representations in scene classification, in *Proceedings of the 9th ACM SIGMM International Workshop on Multimedia Information Retrieval*, Augsburg, Germany, pp. 197–206, ACM, 24–29 Sept. 2007.

33. D. G. Lowe, Distinctive image features from scale-invariant keypoints, *International Journal of Computer Vision*, 60, 91–110, Nov. 2004.

34. I. Laptev, On space-time interest points, *International Journal of Computer Vision*, 64(2–3), 107–123, 2005.

35. V. Vezhnevets, V. Sazonov, and A. Andreeva, A survey on pixel-based skin color detection techniques, in *Proceedings of the 13th International Conference on Computer Graphics and Vision*, Moscow, Russia, pp. 85–92, 5–10 Sept. 2003.

36. A. Abadpour and S. Kasaei, Pixel-based skin detection for pornography filtering, *Iranian Journal of Electrical and Electronic Engineers*, 21–41, Jul. 2005.

37. P. Fuangkhon, Neural network-based nipple detection for obscene pictures, *WSEAS Transactions on Computers*, 4, 1138–1145, Apr. 2005.

38. Y. Wang, J. Li, H. Wang, and Z. Hou, Automatic nipple detection using shape and statistical skin color information, in *Advances in Multimedia Modeling*, vol. 5916 of *Lecture Notes in Computer Science*, pp. 644–649, Springer, 2010.

39. C. Jansohn, A. Ulges, and T. M. Breuel, Detecting pornographic video content by combining image features with motion information, in *Proceedings of the 17th International Conference on Multimedia*, ACM Multimedia, Vancouver, BC, Canada, pp. 601–604, ACM, 19–24 Oct. 2009.

40. C.-Y. Kim, O.-J. Kwon, W.-G. Kim, and S.-R. Choi, Automatic system for filtering obscene video, in *Proceedings of the 10th IEEE International Conference on Advanced Communication Technology*, vol. 2, Phoenix Park, Korea, pp. 1435–1438, Feb. 2008.

41. J. Sivic and A. Zisserman, Video Google: A text retrieval approach to object matching in videos, in *Proceedings of the 9th IEEE International Conference on Computer Vision*, vol. 2, Nice, France, pp. 1470–1477, IEEE Computer Society. 13–16 Oct. 2003.

42. A. Ulges, C. Schulze, D. Keysers, and T. M. Breuel, A system that learns to tag videos by watching YouTube, in *Proceedings of the 6th International Conference on Computer Vision Systems*, Santorini, Greece, vol. 5008 of *Lecture Notes in Computer Science*, pp. 415–424, Springer, 12–15 May 2008.

43. J. Flusser and T. Suk, Pattern recognition by affine moment invariants, *Pattern Recognition*, 26(1), 167–174, 1993.

44. S. Tang, J. Li, Y. Zhang, C. Xie, M. Li, Y. Liu, X. Hua, Y. Zheng, J. Tang, and T.-S. Chua, Pornprobe: An LDA-SVM based pornography detection system, in *Proceedings of the 17th International Conference on Multimedia*, Vancouver, BC, Canada, pp. 1003–1004, ACM, 19–24 Oct. 2009.

45. D. M. Blei, A. Y. Ng, and M. I. Jordan, Latent Dirichlet allocation, *Journal of Machine Learning Research*, 3, 993–1022, 1993.

46. P. T. Eendebak, W. Kraaij, S. Raaijmakers, E. Ranguelova, O. de Rooij, A. Thean, and M. Worring, Visual tools for assisting child pornography investigators, in *Proceedings of NEM Summit*, St. Malo, France, Oct. 2008.

47. C. Schmid and R. Mohr, Local grayvalue invariants for image retrieval, *IEEE Transactions on Pattern Analysis and Machine Intelligence*, 19, 530–535, May 1997.

48. R. Yan and A. G. Hauptmann, A review of text and image retrieval approaches for broadcast news video, *Information Retrieval*, 10(4–5), 445–484, 2007.

49. W.-H. Lin and A. Hauptmann, News video classification using SVM-based multimodal classifiers and combination strategies, in *Proceedings of the Tenth ACM International Conference on Multimedia*, Juan les Pins, France, pp. 323–326, ACM Press, 2002.

50. N. Nitta, N. Babaguchi, and T. Kitahashi, Generating semantic descriptions of broadcasted sports videos based on structures of sports games and TV programs, *Multimedia Tools Applications*, 25(1), 59–83, 2005.

51. V. Mihajlović, M. Petković, W. Jonker, and H. Blanken, Multimodal content-based video retrieval, in *Multimedia Retrieval (Data-Centric Systems and Applications)*, Springer, pp. 271–294, Berlin, Germany, 2007.

52. T. Cour, C. Jordan, E. Miltsakaki, and B. Taskar, Movie/script: Alignment and parsing of video and text transcription, in *Proceedings of the 10th European Conference on Computer Vision*, Marseille, France, Lecture Notes in Computer Science, Springer, 12–18 Oct. 2008.

53. A. Amir, S. Basu, G. Iyengar, C.-Y. Lin, M. R. Naphade, J. R. Smith, S. Srinivasan, and B. L. Tseng, A multi-modal system for the retrieval of semantic video events, *Computer Vision and Image Understanding*, 96(2), 216–236, 2004.

54. N. Rea, C. Lambe, G. Lacey, and R. Dahyot, Multimodal periodicity analysis for illicit content detection in videos, in *IET 3rd European Conference on Visual Media Production*, London, U.K., pp. 106–114, Nov. 2006.

55. J. Nam, M. Alghoniemy, and A. H. Tewfik, Audio-visual content-based violent scene characterization, in *International Conference on Image Processing*, Chicago, IL, vol. 1, pp. 353–357, IEEE, 4–7 Oct. 1998.

56. A. Blum and T. Mitchell, Combining labeled and unlabeled data with co-training, in *Proceedings of the 11th Annual Conference on Computational Learning Theory*, Madison, WIsconsin, pp. 92–100, ACM, 1998.

57. J. Lin and W. Wang, Weakly-supervised violence detection in movies with audio and video based co-training, in *Advances in Multimedia Information Processing—PCM 2009, 10th Pacific Rim Conference on Multimedia Proceedings*, Bangkok, Thailand, vol. 5879 of *Lecture Notes in Computer Science*, pp. 930–935, Springer, 15–18 Dec. 2009.

58. Y. Gong, W. Wang, S. Jiang, Q. Huang, and W. Gao, Detecting violent scenes in movies by auditory and visual cues, in *Advances in Multimedia Information Processing—PCM 2008, 9th Pacific Rim Conference on Multimedia Proceedings*, Tainan, Taiwan, vol. 5353 of *Lecture Notes in Computer Science*, pp. 317–326, Springer, 9–13 Dec. 2008.

59. C.-W. Ngo, T.-C. Pong, and H. Zhang, Motion analysis and segmentation through spatio-temporal slices processing, *IEEE Transactions on Image Processing*, 12(3), 341–355, 2003.

60. T. R. Gruber, A translation approach to portable ontology specifications, *Knowledge Acquisition—Special Issue: Current Issues in Knowledge Modeling*, 5, 199–220, Jun. 1993.

61. N. Guarino, Formal ontology, conceptual analysis and knowledge representation, *International Journal of Human-Computer Studies*, 43(5/6), 625–640, 1995.

62. J. Bao, Y. Cao, W. Tavanapong, and V. Honavar, Integration of domain-specific and domain-independent ontologies for colonoscopy video database annotation, in *Proceedings of the International Conference on Information and Knowledge Engineering*, Las Vegas, NV, pp. 82–90, CSREA Press, 21–24 Jun. 2004.

63. J. Fan, H. Luo, Y. Gao, and R. Jain, Incorporating concept ontology for hierarchical video classification, annotation, and visualization, *IEEE Transactions on Multimedia*, 9(5), 939–957, 2007.

64. M. Bertini, A. D. Bimbo, and C. Torniai, Automatic video annotation using ontologies extended with visual information, in *Proceedings of the 13th ACM International Conference on Multimedia*, ACM Multimedia, Singapore, ACM, 6–11 Nov. 2005.

65. L. Bai, S. Lao, G. J. F. Jones, and A. F. Smeaton, Video semantic content analysis based on ontology, in *Proceedings of the 11th International Machine Vision and Image Processing Conference*, Maynooth, Ireland, pp. 117–124, IEEE Computer Society, 5–7 Sept. 2007.

66. L. Snidaro, M. Belluz, and G. L. Foresti, Domain knowledge for surveillance applications, in *Proceedings of the 10th International Conference on Information Fusion*, Quebec, Canada, pp. 1–6, 2007.

67. A. R. J. Francois, R. Nevatia, J. Hobbs, and R. C. Bolles, VERL: An ontology framework for representing and annotating video events, *IEEE MultiMedia*, 12(4), 76–86, 2005.

68. B. Bolles and R. Nevatia, A hierarchical video event ontology in OWL, ARDA Challenge Workshop Report, 2004.

69. M. S. Ryoo and J. K. Aggarwal, Semantic understanding of continued and recursive human activities, in *Proceedings of the 18th International Conference on Pattern Recognition*, Hong Kong, pp. 379–382, IEEE Computer Society, 20–24 Aug. 2006.

70. T. Perperis, S. Tsekeridou, and S. Theodoridis, An ontological approach to semantic video analysis for violence identification, in *Proceedings of I-Media'07 and I-Semantics'07. International Conferences on New Media Technologies and Semantic Technologies (Triple-i: i-Know, i-Semantics, i-Media)*, Graz, Austria, pp. 139–146, 5–7 Sept. 2007.

71. T. Perperis, T. Giannakopoulos, A. Makris, D. I. Kosmopoulos, S. Tsekeridou, S. J. Perantonis, and S. Theodoridis, Multimodal and ontology-based fusion approaches of audio and visual processing for violence detection in movies, *Expert Systems with Applications*, 38, 14102–14116, Oct. 2011.

72. S. Tsekeridou and I. Pitas, Content-based video parsing and indexing based on audio-visual interaction, *IEEE Transactions on Circuits and Systems for Video Technology*, 11, 522–535, Apr. 2001.

73. J. Hunter, Adding multimedia to the semantic web-building an MPEG-7 ontology, in *Proceedings of the First Semantic Web Working Symposium*, Stanford University, Pala Alto, CA, pp. 261–281, 2001.

74. R. Lienhart and J. Maydt, An extended set of Haar-like features for rapid object detection, in *Proceedings of International Conference on Image Processing*, Rochester, NY, pp. 900–903, 22–25 Sept. 2002.

75. A. Makris, D. Kosmopoulos, S. S. Perantonis, and S. Theodoridis, Hierarchical feature fusion for visual tracking, in *IEEE International Conference on Image Processing*, vol. 6, San Antonio, TX, pp. 289–292, 16 Sept. – 19 Oct. 2007.

76. M. J. Jones and J. M. Rehg, Statistical color models with application to skin detection, *International Journal of Computer Vision*, 46(1), 81–96, 2002.

77. E. Sirin, B. Parsia, B. Cuenca Grau, A. Kalyanpur, and Y. Katz, Pellet: A practical OWL-DL reasoner, *Web Semantics: Science, Services and Agents on the World Wide Web*, 5(2), 51–53, 2007.
78. F. Baader, D. Calvanese, D. L. McGuinness, D. Nardi, and P. F. Patel-Schneider, eds., *The Description Logic Handbook: Theory, Implementation, and Applications*, Cambridge University Press, Cambridge, U.K., 2003.

Chapter 4

Robust, Hardware-Oriented Overlaid Graphics Detection for TV Applications

Ahmet Ekin

Philips Research Europe

Contents

Overlaid graphics, such as text and channel logos, are extensively used in television (TV) programs to provide additional information to the audiovisual content. In the literature, their automatic extraction has mainly been considered in non-TV applications, such as for automatic video indexing and retrieval. In this chapter, we propose algorithms for automated detection of overlaid graphics with limited computational and memory resources of a TV set. Specifically, we deal with text and logo detection, and introduce novel applications that use their results for visual quality improvement, contrast enhancement during burn-in protection, and customizing text appearance for increased readability.

4.1 Introduction

Graphics are overlaid onto TV content to provide supportive information and to further attract audiences' interests. Since the overlaid content differs from the natural content both in their low-level visual properties and high-level information, the accurate segmentation of visual TV content into natural and overlaid graphics assists in applications for high-level content analysis as well as for low-level processing. For example, video indexing and retrieval applications have been using text information for understanding the content [1,2], whereas, although less known, the same segmentation information can be used to adapt the enhancement parameters for improving the visual quality of the TV content. The latter type of applications requires methods that can be implemented on TV architecture with given memory and processing constraints, such as with only limited lines of memory and no support for temporal data, which result from the desire to minimize the manufacturing cost of TV sets. In this chapter, we will propose methods for fast and efficient detection of overlaid text and channel logos and present applications that make use of them.

We first briefly present the TV content properties and hardware constraints that are relevant to the algorithmic choices we have made. After that, we describe a hardware-oriented, overlaid text detection algorithm that differs from the existing approaches in its assumption of available computational and memory resources. The proposed algorithm takes advantage of text properties along a horizontal line with a fast-computable maximum gradient feature and models the texture properties of overlaid text in a block with SVM. The two approaches and other cues are combined in a decision tree to provide a final decision. A fully integer-based processing and shortcuts like bit shifting have been adopted for memory conservation and for the reduction of costly division operations, respectively.

In Section 4.4, we introduce a generic TV channel logo detection algorithm. It is generic in the sense that it is able to detect various types of logos, such as static, moving, transparent, and opaque. The algorithm uses a cinematic rule that is often practiced by the professionals in the positioning of the camera and the placement of the main actors in the scene. The logos are modeled as outliers from the scene model represented as color histograms. The detected logos can be used for content segmentation, such as identification of commercial segments, but also for display protection that aims at protecting displays (particularly plasma displays) from burning-in. The burn-in problem refers to the ghostly appearance of long-time static scenes on the display even after the display is turned off. It is caused by permanent deformations in the chemical properties of some display types and requires their renewal. Since some or all pixels of a channel logo stay in the same location, logo detection can help localize the operating region of burn-in protection algorithms.

In Section 4.5, we present applications that use the outputs of text and logo detection algorithms. The first application concerns the enhancement of perceived image quality where the detected text regions undergo a different type of enhancement compared with the natural content. In the second application, we use text and logo detection results to preserve the contrast during display burn-in protection. Finally, we use the detection results to modify the text properties to improve readability, which is especially useful for people with visual impairment. In Section 4.6, we conclude the chapter by summarizing the presented work and explaining possible future work.

4.2 Properties of Content and the TV Architecture

The content properties, the quality of the data, and the given computational and memory constraints are three important variables that affect the methodologies employed in the image analysis part. The TV content is often produced by professionals; hence, many of the accepted production rules, such as positioning of the actors in the scene, apply to the TV content. Furthermore, the natural content is typically the preferred content; hence, text and logos are often overlaid onto the natural content in a structured manner, such as aligned text lines and captions at the bottom or on the side of the screen, to minimize the chance of covering the important content. This attribute differs from the more unstructured nature of text in web images and is considered in our text detection algorithm. Furthermore, the content is of high quality without excessive compression artifacts. It is commonly accessible in a decoded format directly in the YUV color space; hence, we do not use any compressed domain features that have been used for text detection in earlier works [1–4].

Figure 4.1 The local area for the line in white is highlighted (a total of 11 lines); we use only the information from the local region for text detection and verification. (From Ekin, A., Local information based overlaid text detection by classifier fusion, in *Proceedings of the IEEE ICASSP*, Toulouse, France, 2006. With permission. Copyright 2006 IEEE.)

In this context, memory refers to the size of the image buffer as the number of image lines available for processing at a single instant. A typical TV chip often only supports sequential data access for some part of the frame at a given instant. For example, to process a pixel at frame position (x, y), one has access only to a limited number of pixels above and below the pixel position. In Figure 4.1, we highlight the available data to process the pixels on the white line.

In this work, we mainly refer to the buffer size of 11 lines, five lines above and below the current line, although the presented algorithms are generic in the sense that the methodology is not fixed to a specific value of this parameter. In general, the implication of having access to only the limited part of the content is that text larger than the given number of lines will not be wholly accessible during text detection; hence, the detection of text with large font size becomes problematic. We will propose solutions to detect larger font sizes than the available memory in the next section. Furthermore, for cost-effective implementation, we have implemented fully integer processing with as few divisions as possible by replacing the divisions with bit shifts.

4.3 Detection of Overlaid Text by Classifier Fusion

In this section, we propose a hardware-oriented overlaid text detection algorithm (slightly modified version of the algorithm in [5]). In general, overlaid text detection involves two steps: (1) text candidate extraction and (2) text verification. In the first stage, the smallest spatial processing units, such as pixels and blocks, are processed independently from each other to compute their text likelihood values. In the second stage, spatially connected detections are merged for region-level morphological analysis, for example, by using region bounding box information. In one or both of these steps, the state-of-the-art text detection algorithms rely on nonlocal information, which, in some cases, can be the whole image/video frame information. In this work, we define the locality as the number of image lines that is equal to the hardware memory size. For example, Figure 4.1 highlights the local region for the white line. This value is 11 lines in our case. The memory size could be much less than the height of the text, but the width equals the image width.

Earlier text detection algorithms exploit color connectedness (connected component [CC]–based approaches) and/or textural features of text [6–8]. Machine-learning tools, such as neural nets [9], or support vector machines (SVM) [10–12], have also been applied to determine the text and non-text boundaries. These algorithms automatically learn text characteristics in a selected feature space from labeled text and non-text training data. In general, the existing algorithms utilize nonlocal information mainly during multiresolution image analysis (for large-sized text detection), in text segmentation (for extraction of word and text line boundaries), and postprocessing (for suppression of false alarms) steps. Having constraints not applicable to the existing approaches, we propose an integrated framework that employs a CC-based and a texture-based algorithm. The CC-based algorithm utilizes character-based features in the horizontal direction; hence, it processes each image line independently from the others. In contrast, texture-based algorithm uses block-based features; hence, it makes use of both horizontal and vertical neighbor information. In order to take advantage of machine-learning tools, an SVM with a linear kernel has been trained to make the text and non-text decisions for the texture-based algorithm. We also propose a height-independent horizontal scaling for size-independent text detection. In the verification stage, we use a novel decision tree approach to integrate detection results with color and edge features for the detection of bounding boxes. As a result, the proposed algorithm is able to robustly detect text whose height can be five times bigger than the vertical extension of the memory content.

4.3.1 Edge-Based Preprocessing

The insertion of text onto video should result in large changes in the intensity and color, so that the viewers can read the overlaid text regardless of the natural content. We use this feature to eliminate non-text regions to speed up the processing. We first detect horizontal, $G_h(x, y)$, and vertical, $G_v(x, y)$, derivatives at each image location (x, y) by applying a 2×2 mask. After that, the edge strength, $ES(x, y)$, is computed for the pixel (x, y) as in Equation 4.1, where we use fast-computable L1 norm. The pixels having edge strength greater than the adaptively computed threshold value, $GThr_{High}$, are assumed to include text regions if there are any in an image. The value of $GThr_{High}$ is determined as a function of the average edge strength as shown in Equation 4.2, where the value k is a constant coefficient ($k = 5$ often suffices not to lose any pixels at the text boundaries). Figure 4.2 demonstrates the output of this stage proving that strong edges should exist at the transitions between text and natural video content transitions:

$$ES\left(x, y\right) = \left|G_h\left(x, y\right)\right| + \left|G_v\left(x, y\right)\right| \tag{4.1}$$

$$GThr_{High} = \frac{k}{M \times N} \sum_{x=1}^{M} \sum_{y=1}^{N} ES\left(x, y\right) \tag{4.2}$$

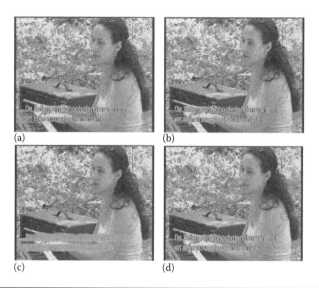

Figure 4.2   The results of different stages of text detection pipeline (top left to bottom right): (a) strong edge detection, (b) CC-based analysis, (c) SVM-based detection, and (d) combined final result. (From Ekin, A., Local information based overlaid text detection by classifier fusion, in *Proceedings of the IEEE ICASSP*, Toulouse, France, 2006. With permission. Copyright 2006 IEEE.)

4.3.2 CC-Based Character-Level Analysis

When analyzed at a character level, text regions show (1) large gradients that have opposite signs at character-to-background and background-to-character transitions and (2) a horizontally smooth single colored region within a character stroke (this allows for variations of text color change from character to character but not within a character). In this section, we present a method that exploits these observations to detect text regions by processing image intensity in lines with at least one strong edge identified along the line.

The maximum gradient difference (MGD) feature proposed in [13] can boost the first characteristics of the overlaid text. This feature computes the difference between the maximum and the minimum horizontal gradient values in a window. The key idea behind the feature is that if a window is large enough to include background-to-character and character-to-background transitions, there will be a large positive and a large negative gradient, respectively, if the character is brighter than the background. Otherwise, two large gradients will still occur, but the positive gradient will refer to character (darker)-to-background transition. The window length should be large enough to accommodate the smallest detectable font size. In [13], text regions are identified as those having large MGD by comparing the MGD value with a predefined threshold value. However, this tends to merge the text regions with the line structures in the background. Furthermore, the maximum and the minimum are sensitive to noise.

To remedy the earlier problems, we modify the MGD by integrating the color smoothness constraint (the second observation) and verifying the relative location and magnitude of the positive and negative gradients. For the color smoothness within the character, we require low gradient values at the locations between the large gradients, which should ideally be at the character-to-background borders. This will reduce the false alarms; but, to prevent the merging problem between the end of the text and the possible line structures in the background, we also add the location and magnitude constraints to the MGD. The location constraint makes sure that the large positive and negative gradients occur at the opposite sides of the window center. The magnitude constraint verifies that there is not a big discrepancy between the magnitudes of the largest positive and the negative gradients by checking that the smaller one, in the absolute sense, is bigger than the half of the larger one. Figure 4.2b shows a sample result of this step where the pixels having high text likelihood are highlighted.

4.3.3 Texture-Based Text Detection by SVM

In the previous section, we processed each line independently from their vertical neighbors. As a result, some false alarms may occur at locations that do not have horizontal textures but have only strong vertical edges. To incorporate local texture information, we introduce a block-based texture analysis. The text likelihood of the processed block is computed by a pretrained SVM [14]. This type of analysis adds the power of machine learning to the algorithm.

For texture-based analysis, a set of features in a window of fixed size, 11×11 in our case, are extracted. We compute two features per pixel: magnitudes of the horizontal and vertical gradients. When a machine-learning tool, such as an SVM, is used, a supervised training stage is needed to train the classifier with the selected features. This is done offline and only once. After the training of the classifier, when a new image is presented, the same set of derivative features are extracted and fed into the classifier that determines the text likelihood of the input feature vector. In order to detect text of varying size, multiresolution analysis of the image, as shown in Figure 4.3, is needed. The results across multiple scales are integrated to decide whether a site can be text or not. In our case, the multiresolution analysis is impossible because the limitation of the number of available image lines does not allow scaling in the vertical direction. This presents a unique challenge for the detection of text independently from size. To this effect, we propose to scale the group of lines only in the horizontal direction. This makes scaling independent of the number of available lines. Figure 4.4 shows the proof of the height invariance of the proposed scaling method. In contrast to the usual multiresolution as shown in Figure 4.3, this is a suboptimal solution. However, our thorough analysis has shown that proposed scaling method robustly detects text when the length of a word is

Figure 4.3 The traditional multiresolution scheme requires larger number of lines in lower resolution for the same window size (shown in white in the pictures; window is enlarged for better visualization). (From Ekin, A., Local information based overlaid text detection by classifier fusion, in *Proceedings of the IEEE ICASSP*, Toulouse, France, 2006. With permission. Copyright 2006 IEEE.)

Figure 4.4 The proposed height-preserving multiresolution approach uses the same number of lines for the same window size (shown in white; window is larger than 11 × 11 for better visualization of the concept). (From Ekin, A., Local information based overlaid text detection by classifier fusion, in *Proceedings of the IEEE ICASSP*, Toulouse, France, 2006. With permission. Copyright 2006 IEEE.)

large enough (3–4 letters). The reason for such robustness stems from the fact that the classifier identifies large variations in texture (measured by the derivatives) as text. When the text is large, the window in the original image is not big enough to capture those variations; hence, scaling is necessary. The proposed horizontal scaling fits close characters into the window so that they can be identified as text.

For the detection, we use three scales as shown in Figure 4.4. The detection result from the first scale is accepted as text when the SVM result is greater than zero. The second and third scales are only accepted if the SVM detection result is greater than

0.5. In this way, we can detect text whose height is as large as five times the processed image lines. Figure 4.2 shows the result of texture-based detection with SVM. In order to speed up processing, we use a linear kernel for the SVM. This makes it possible to define the classification with a cross-correlation operation. Furthermore, we apply the SVM only to the strong edges that are detected.

4.3.4 Text Verification by a Decision Tree

In the text verification stage, we aim to decide whether individual detections from character and texture analysis can be accepted as text and, at the same time, we attempt to determine the most accurate boundary of the text region. In addition to the detection results, we also use color cues and strong edge count for the final decision. Since we have to decide locally, the steps below are executed for each group of lines (a group of lines is shown in Figure 4.1). If there is any detection from both stages, we apply the following steps to extract text regions where we extract features to make the final text and non-text decisions with a decision tree:

1. Find the regions both texture-based and CC-based algorithms have classified as text.
2. Compute the start and the end points of each text region determined in the texture-based analysis. Before this, a dilation operation is applied to merge close disconnected regions.
3. Determine the dominant text color from the results of character-based detection.
4. Starting from the center of each region found in step 2, use CC-based algorithm to refine the start and the end of the selected region, and compute the length of the region.
5. Find the regions that are identified as text by the CC-based algorithm, but not supported by the SVM result. Rerun SVM over the scaled version of each such region with a lower threshold.
6. Use the length of the region bounding box, the position of the box in the frame, the number of separate regions in a line, the results of SVM, the mean and standard deviation of strength of the edges in the region, the mean and standard deviation of MGD as features in a decision tree to accept the block as text or not.

4.3.5 Text Detection Performance

In order to evaluate the proposed algorithm, we have used video clips downloaded from the publicly available Open Video Project site [15] and video data captured in Philips from various TV channels. In Table 4.1, the details of the dataset are given. The total length of the video content in the dataset is close to 10 h. More importantly, especially in the Philips dataset, we have a large amount of variation

Table 4.1   The Properties of Text Detection Evaluation Dataset

Dataset	Number of Video Clips	Total Length (min)
Open Video Project	29	81.3
Philips set	252	518.2

(genre, TV channel, time of data collection) that provides sufficient representation of the TV content. In each video clip, we made sure that there is at least one frame with text so that we could test the detection accuracy over different content types. Different from the Philips dataset, the clips from the Open Video Project set have compression artifacts that are not typically observed in the high-end TV content and they are mostly of size 352×240 whereas the clips in the Philips set are of size 720×576. For each video clip in the two datasets, we determined two frames with text and two frames without text where the selected frames preferably belonged to different scenes or at least had the largest frame-to-frame intensity difference among the candidate pairs. In the frames with text (58 frames from Open Video Project and 504 frames from the Philips set), we manually identified 3242 text bounding boxes.

To determine the SVM parameters, we prepared a training dataset of text and non-text images. In a separate dataset of 124 images, some of which are shown in Figure 4.5, we manually identified the bounding boxes of text blocks. For the non-text samples, we used non-text parts of the 124 images and additional 262 images that do not contain any text region. We initially trained the SVM with the text and non-text samples from the 124 images. In this case, we selected the non-text samples from the regions with high edge strength. Afterward, we tested the classifier in the additional 262 images without any text. Any misclassified regions as text were included into our training set before another round of training. This training, classification, and extension of training dataset steps were repeated until the classifier performance did not change significantly.

The proposed text detection algorithm was tested on the dataset explained in Table 4.1. The ground truth text bounding boxes were considered correctly detected if more than 85% of the box was classified as text by the algorithm. In other cases, we labeled them missed. Text regions detected by the algorithm were considered as false detections if at least 70% of the region was not considered as text in the ground truth. The other cases were regarded as localization inaccuracy and not included in the statistics.

In Table 4.2, the performance of the algorithm has been reported in precision, defined in Equation 4.3, and recall, defined in Equation 4.4, rates as a function of text height (in pixels). On the overall dataset, the algorithm achieves a precision rate of 88.2% and a recall rate of 92.1%. Some results from the algorithm, shown in Figure 4.6, where the detected text regions are highlighted, show the robustness

Figure 4.5 Some of the training images used in the training of SVM, and in the optimization of some of the thresholds, such as edge strength, and MGD value.

Table 4.2 The Precision and Recall Rates of the Proposed Text Detection Algorithm

Text Size [min, max]	Precision Rate (%)	Recall Rate (%)
[8, 70]	88.2	92.1
[8, 12]	86.8	93.2
[12, 25]	90.2	91.4
[26, 35]	91.1	88.2
[36, 50]	93.1	81.4
[51, 70]	95.1	75.3

of the proposed algorithm to such artifacts as well as variations in background. We observe that the precision rate increases with the increased font size meaning that the likelihood of false detections is lower for large font sizes. Figure 4.7 is an example for the detection of large-sized text. The text "Markte Morgen" is more than five times larger than the number of image lines available for processing. However, as expected,

Figure 4.6 The sample results from the text detection algorithm on moving text. (From Ekin, A., Local information based overlaid text detection by classifier fusion, in *Proceedings of the IEEE ICASSP*, Toulouse, France, 2006. With permission. Copyright 2006 IEEE.)

Figure 4.7 The sample results from the content in the Philips set. (From Ekin, A., Local information based overlaid text detection by classifier fusion, in *Proceedings of the IEEE ICASSP*, Toulouse, France, 2006. With permission. Copyright 2006 IEEE.)

the opposite effect was observed in the recall rate. The proposed algorithm could detect less of the large font sizes than the small font sizes. This is generally not a major problem for the text enhancement application because the visual quality of large text regions is often at more acceptable levels compared with that of smaller text regions that need to be enhanced. The other reasons for the missed text are small width of the text block, such as single digits, and low contrast between the background and the text. Since the proposed text detection algorithm mainly operates in the luminance channel, text that has very small contrast in the luminance channel may not be detectable. In Figure 4.8, an example to a text that our algorithm missed is shown:

$$\text{Precision} = \frac{\text{Number of correctly detected text boxes}}{\text{Total number of detected text boxes}} \qquad (4.3)$$

$$\text{Recall} = \frac{\text{Number of correctly detected text boxes}}{\text{Total number of ground truth text boxes}} \qquad (4.4)$$

(a)   (b)   (c)

Figure 4.8 An image where text is most distinguishable in the color channel (original—(a), histogram equalized for display—(b)), but it has very low contrast in the luminance channel (c).

4.4 Detection of TV Channel Logos by Using Cinematic Cues

In this section, we present a TV channel logo detection algorithm that is robust to motion and transparency characteristics of channel logos that can be static opaque, animated opaque, static transparent, and animated transparent. The majority of the existing logo detectors assume logos as static and opaque, or at most mildly transparent, and they aim to detect most consistently appearing region in time by using temporal intensity differences. When the assumed model and the content characteristics are similar, logos can be detected; however, the following cases may limit the detection accuracy: (1) If the scene is stationary, the algorithm has to wait for a long time until there is significant motion in the scene to separate logo from the content. (2) The logo may be inserted over a completely stationary segment, such as vertical/horizontal black bars. (3) The logo may be animated, hence, moving. (4) The logo intensity/color characteristics may periodically change (e.g., brightness change in the CNN logo). (5) Temporal information may not be supported in the hardware.

The earlier logo detection algorithms typically handled one type of logos or proposed different algorithms for each case. In [16–19], change detection algorithms were used for extracting logo regions. In [16], the average pixel gradient is computed from multiple key frames, and then high gradient regions are extracted to detect logos. In addition to static logos, background is assumed to be non-textured. In [17], 30–60 s of waiting time was necessary to uniquely identify stationary logos in sports video. In [18], when four frame corners contain large number of pixels with no-change (measured as having a difference value of zero), it is assumed that those segments correspond to logos. In [20], the min–max difference was proposed to detect static-opaque logos. Only the min value is used for static-transparent logos that have to be brighter than the background to be detected. Transparent logos were also handled in [21] by a neural scheme. The type of logos and the removal of them from the content also received interest [22–24]. In [25], logo templates are first computed by other cues, such as slow-motion segments in sports video, and then templates are matched to detect the logo in the other segments.

In contrast to these approaches, we do not make any assumptions about the motion and transparency characteristics of the logos. We observe that since logos are graphical objects that are artificially inserted over the video content, they should deviate from it. To this effect, we model logos as outliers from the scene. The proposed algorithm uses purely spatial information; hence, it can detect logos independently of their motion characteristics (the presented approach improves over the algorithm presented in [26] and has been tested on a larger set of data).

4.4.1 Computation of the Scene Model by Color

Since logos are artificial additions to the video content, their characteristics should deviate from the natural content. We first estimate the local video scene model by multiple color histograms. We use local models because frame-level representation of video content is generally too coarse to be a reliable model in logo detection.

We assume that one or more channel logos are positioned in one or more corners of the frame. We have not seen any violation of this assumption in TV content. For each of the corners, we estimate a scene model by using the neighboring pixels to the respective corners. We use the Golden Section Rule (GSR) [27] to define the corners and their neighbors because GSR is a cinematic technique commonly utilized by professionals. GSR recommends horizontal and vertical division of the frame in 3:5:3 proportions and positioning of the main objects at the intersections of the GSR lines (or in the center area for a single object in the scene) [27]. The content captured from CNN in Figure 4.9 is perfect according to GSR because the heads of the two reporters are at the intersections.

Following the numbering notation in Figure 4.9, logos occur only in regions 1, 3, 7, and 9. We compute the scene models of each region from the pixels in the closest region; for example, the model of region 1 is computed from the pixels in regions 2, 4, and 5. We define one color histogram in the readily available YUV space for each of the four corners (total of four histograms, H_1, H_3, H_7, and H_9 for regions 1, 3, 7, and 9, respectively). We apply a quantized Gaussian kernel in 2D to

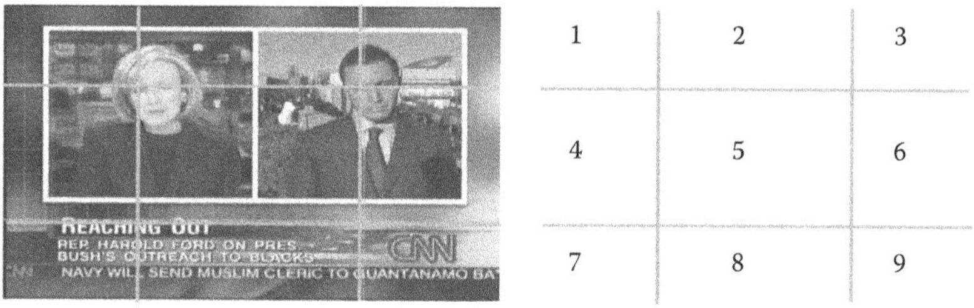

Figure 4.9 3:5:3 spatial division of the frame by GSR and the numbering scheme we use to refer to the regions.

weigh the pixels based on their L1 distance from the logo regions. As a result, each histogram gets a decreasing contribution by increasing distance from the respective corners. Finally, we normalize the histograms.

4.4.2 Identification of the Outliers

In order to identify individual logo pixels, we compute the deviation value from the scene model. One of the methods to identify outliers in a sample is to define the values above the Nth percentile as outliers [28]. We compute the distance of each pixel in the candidate logo areas to the corresponding color scene model by Equation 4.5, where $d_i(x, y)$ is the color distance of the pixel (x, y) with luminance Y_{xy}, and chrominance U_{xy} and V_{xy} to the ith scene model H_i. The function $Q_i()$ computes the ith histogram index of the input luminance–chrominance values, and $H_i(k)$ is the histogram entry of the ith histogram (scene model). In Figure 4.10, the result of this stage is shown for typical TV content:

$$d_i(x, y) = 1 - H_i \left(Q_i \left(Y_{xy}, U_{xy}, V_{xy} \right) \right) \tag{4.5}$$

4.4.3 Extraction and Verification of Logos

The final stage of the proposed logo detection algorithm is the analysis of the spatial distribution of outliers and comparison of this distribution with the models of logo pixels spatial distribution. Logos that consist of characters, such as the CNN logo in Figure 4.9, result in separate, disconnected outlier pixels whereas a pictorial logo usually results in a single blob that is significantly larger than the other outlier blobs. We detect the former type of logos by using two-stage vertical/horizontal projections and the latter type of logos by identifying blobs that have significantly larger size than the other blobs. In both cases, we make sure that the candidate region conforms to certain morphological constraints.

In order to detect a logo by using vertical/horizontal projections, we first identify the start and the end segments of pixel clusters in the vertical direction. This

Figure 4.10   Logo detection algorithm uses Golden Section Rule to compute a scene model.

stage involves iteratively finding the peak of the histogram, and then computing the vertical start and the end coordinates of the cluster that contains the peak value. After a vertical cluster is identified, the peak of the unassigned vertical projection pixels is found and the process repeats until all vertical clusters are identified. After this first step, the horizontal projection of each segment is computed and the horizontal start and end points of the clusters are found. In the final stage, aspect ratio, filling ratio, height, and width of the bounding box about the cluster are verified to detect a logo. We also compute the cleanliness of the region around the bounding box, B_i, by counting the number of outliers in the area between B_i and the enlarged box whose center is the same as B_i and width and height is 1.25 times the width and height of B_i. The decision rules are set as follows: bounding boxes whose aspect ratio is greater than 1.1, with a cleanliness score less than 0.05, height greater than 1.8% of the video height (excluding black bars), and filling ratio greater than 0.5, are labeled as logo boxes. A decision tree could also be formed by training.

For the pictorial logo score, we search for a blob with size significantly larger than all the others. For that purpose, we first find connected regions and then merge close, vertically or horizontally similar blobs. We found the proposed object-based dilation by bounding box features rather than pixel-based dilation to be more noise-robust because the latter may merge blobs from different objects. Finally, we compute the peak saliency ratio by dividing the size of the largest blob to the average size of all the other blobs, and compare it with a certain threshold (we set this to 7 in our experiments) to find the logo-candidate blob.

4.4.4 Logo Detection Performance

We measured the performance of the proposed logo detection algorithm over 562 frames that belong to 63 different channels. Among these 63 logos, 40 are static opaque (342 frames), 16 are static transparent (188 frames), and 7 are animated opaque (32 frames). We could not find any animated-transparent logos to include to our database.

For the algorithm, we had to set several parameters: (1) the histogram bin size for the model, (2) the histogram bin size for the color distances of the pixels to the models in the outlier detection step, and (3) the threshold percentile value for the outlier detection. For the first threshold, we determined that $8 \times 8 \times 8$ YUV results in robust performance whereas larger quantization values are very coarse and not discriminative enough. We quantized the distance values to scene models to 1000 intervals and defined N to be 90th percentile, and accepted it only if it is greater than 0.9.

In Table 4.3, the precision and recall rates achieved by the proposed algorithm were shown. The precision rate (also related to false positives) does not vary with the logo type and is above 90% in all cases. The recall rate, however, is dependent on the logo type. With static-opaque logos, we could achieve a recall rate higher than 90%. This rate reduces to 85.6% for the animated logos. This is because animation

Table 4.3   The Precision and Recall Rates of the Logo Detection Algorithm

Logo Type	Precision Rate (%)	Recall Rate (%)
Static opaque	92.5	91.2
Animated opaque	92.3	85.6
Static transparent	91.7	75.1

Figure 4.11   Sample logo detection results for pictorial and text logos, and the corresponding outlier maps.

may result in small-sized logos in different viewpoints that cannot be detected by our binary logo model approach. The static-transparent logos are detected with a recall rate of 75.1%. In this part, since a transparent logo also includes part of the background, its distance to the background model is smaller. This is the main reason for the lower detection performance.

In Figures 4.11 and 4.12, we show some frames with correctly detected logos, and also the detected outlier pixels in Figure 4.11. From the logos in Figure 4.11, the RTL logo can be problematic for the existing algorithms because background has little or no motion during the entire sequence. The transparent ZDF logo was also detected because its color properties deviate from the scene. The National Geographic logo is a textual logo and was detected by our model-based approach. In Figure 4.13, we show detection results for the video frames that are several frames apart from each other. In the first frame, the algorithm could detect logo, but also player in the lower left corner was detected. In the second frame, the logo is still detected but the player was out of view; hence, false detections can be removed when the temporal detections are integrated. As long as the scene is dynamic, false alarms can be removed quickly by using temporal consistency of detections within a given video shot; if the false alarm is caused by a static object, it can be removed after a shot transition.

Figure 4.12 **Further logo detection results independently of logo location, motion content, and logo opacity.**

Figure 4.13 **A misclassified foreground region in the lower-right corner can be corrected when the detections from other frames are considered. In the scene, only the actual logo region is consistently detected.**

4.5 Applications for TV

In this section, we propose three applications that use the results of the text and logo detection algorithms.

4.5.1 Enhancement of TV Graphics for Improved Visual Quality

Traditional pixel-based image/video enhancement methodologies adapt their parameters to the image data at the low-level content without being concerned about the medium- or high-level content. For example, a commonly used nonlinear sharpening technique is luminance transient improvement (LTI) [29], and it makes edges steeper and creates sharp transitions at the beginning and end of each edge. As a result, the perceived sharpness is increased. The LTI algorithm steepens the edge. In the process, it modifies picture values on both sides of the edge center, that is, dark samples are getting darker and bright samples brighter. The downside of this effect is that it increases the width of lines due to gamma correction, which can become annoying for very thin lines. To prevent this, a simple but effective solution is used; the original signal is offset and the second-order derivative is added [29]. In case of a black line, a positive offset is added, and in case of white line, a negative offset is added.

In general, the peaking and LTI settings provide good quality images in many cases. But, for text, default LTI and thinning settings may degrade the text quality and produce very thin, difficult-to-read characters, a much thicker black background that may even dominate the normal text, and ghost effects for some characters as shown in Figure 4.14. With the use of object-based optimized settings, these unwanted effects are eliminated and other desired effects can be achieved (Figures 4.15 and 4.16).

Figure 4.14 The artifacts caused by high peaking and LTI settings include thicker dark background and ghost effect in text regions.

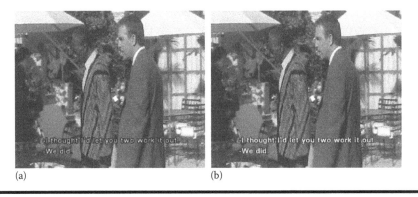

(a)   (b)

Figure 4.15 The result of traditional enhancement approach (a) and text-adaptive enhancement (b).

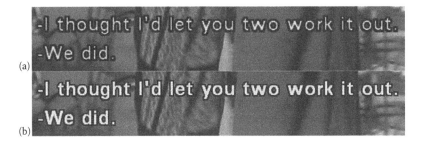

Figure 4.16 The zoomed view of Figure 4.15. The text-adaptive enhancement approach (b) results in better signal quality in both text and non-text regions.

4.5.2 Simultaneous TV Burn-In Protection and Text Contrast Enhancement

The burn-in effect is a well-known problem for display devices and results from the appearance of static scenes on a display for long times. To mitigate the burn-in effect, some solutions, such as moving the static scene within a predefined spatial window, for example, "Pixel Orbiting" of Sony [30], and reducing the contrast of the static scene, have been proposed. These methods reduce the overall quality of images and make the content more difficult to understand. More adverse affects are observed in static text regions because reduction in the quality and contrast of text can be easily noticed and may even prevent the intelligibility of text. In this section, we propose a partitioning-based contrast reduction algorithm to preserve the quality and relative contrast of text during display burn-in protection.

Contrast-changing algorithms for burn-in protection map the pixels from their original range $\left[I_{\min}^{\text{org}}\ I_{\max}^{\text{org}}\right]$ to the new range $\left[I_{\min}^{\text{new}}\ I_{\max}^{\text{new}}\right]$. The difference between the highest and lowest pixel luminance or color values $\left(\Delta_{\text{org}} = I_{\max}^{\text{org}} - I_{\min}^{\text{org}},\right.$ $\left.\Delta_{\text{new}} = I_{\max}^{\text{new}} - I_{\min}^{\text{new}}\right)$ is the measure of contrast. If $\Delta_{\text{org}} < \Delta_{\text{new}}$, then the transformation increases the contrast; otherwise, assuming Δ_{org} is not equal to Δ_{new}, it decreases the contrast. Most burn-in protection algorithms employ some variation of contrast reduction methodology. The problem, however, is that content characteristics and quality are not preserved during this process. One such popular content is text and logos as explained in the earlier sections and to preserve the text quality and readability, we propose a partitioning-based contrast reduction algorithm. In the following, we describe the algorithm for a single-channel (intensity) image. Although the extension to multichannel (color) images is straightforward, some precautions have to be taken during that transformation.

The pixel intensity in an 8-bit channel can assume values in the range [0, 255]. In a window that corresponds to the static region, we first compute the range of the pixel values by finding the minimum and the maximum intensity values $\left[I_{\min}^{\text{org}}\ I_{\max}^{\text{org}}\right]$. As explained earlier, a typical burn-in protection algorithm reduces the contrast by mapping the original pixel value range to a new range $\left[I_{\min}^{\text{new}}\ I_{\max}^{\text{new}}\right]$ such that the new contrast is significantly less than the original contrast. For burn-in protection application, one approach is to set $I_{\min}^{\text{new}}$ to zero to guarantee the lowest possible pixel value; hence, the problem we would like to solve is to optimize the text quality when mapping the pixel value range from $\left[I_{\min}^{\text{org}}\ I_{\max}^{\text{org}}\right]$ to $\left[0\ I_{\max}^{\text{new}}\right]$.

We propose to transform the intensity values of the text and non-text pixels differently. In this process, the range $\left[0\ I_{\max}^{\text{new}}\right]$ is partitioned to $\left\lfloor 0\ I_{\max}^{R1}\right\rfloor$ and $\left\lfloor I_{\min}^{R2}\ I_{\max}^{R2}\right\rfloor$ referring to two regions where one interval is background region and the other is the text region. If the text is brighter than the background, the lower interval, $\left\lfloor 0\ I_{\max}^{R1}\right\rfloor$, corresponds to background (non-text) in the static scene. If text is darker than background (inverse text), then the same interval is composed of text pixels. The boundaries of the intervals are defined by parameters C_1, C_2, and C_3, as in

Equation 4.6, where $0 \leq C_1 \leq 1.0$ and $0 \leq C_2 \leq C_3 \leq C_1$:

$$I_{max}^{R2} = C_1 \times I_{max}^{new}$$
$$I_{max}^{R1} = C_2 \times I_{max}^{R2} \qquad (4.6)$$
$$I_{min}^{R2} = C_3 \times I_{max}^{R2}$$

Some of the values of the three parameters (C_1, C_2, and C_3) have interesting outcomes:

- $C_2 = C_3$: The outcome is the same as the traditional contrast reduction approach.
- $C_2 = 0$ and $C_3 = C_1$: Maximum attainable contrast because all background pixels assume the lowest pixel value while all the text pixels assume the value of maximum allowable intensity value, which is still very much less than 255.
- $C_1 < 1$: The user further turns down the pixel value. This may be useful for aggressive protection of the screen as well as to black out or aggressively shade some static segments, such as logos.

For content with color, we could extend the previous approach by processing each color channel independently. The disadvantage of such a procedure is that the color content may be degraded considerably. As a better solution, the dynamic ranges of background and text are computed for each color channel. Then, separate pixel value ranges are defined for each color channel so as to keep the relative values among them intact. As described earlier, the user also has the flexibility to adjust the parameters C_1, C_2, and C_3.

Here, we show the results for inverse text on a gray image (Figure 4.17), normal text on an intensity image (Figure 4.18), and normal text in a color image (Figure 4.19) with also some variations of the parameters. These results have been obtained by mapping the original content in the static segment to the range where

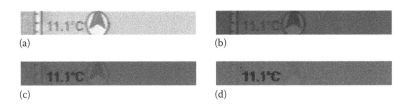

(a)

(b)

(c)

(d)

Figure 4.17 (a) Original image, (b) direct contrast reduction resulting in low contrast, (c) ($C_1 = 1$, $C_2 = 0.25$, and $C_3 = 0.5$), and (d) the result of higher contrast settings ($C_1 = 1$, $C_2 = 0$, and $C_3 = 0.75$) and $I_{max}^{new} = 50$.

(a) (b) (c)

Figure 4.18 Original image (a), the result of general contrast reduction method (b), and the result of the proposed method (c) with $C_1 = 1$, $C_2 = 0$, and $C_3 = 1$ and $I_{max}^{new} = 50$.

(a) (b) (c)

Figure 4.19 Original image (a), the result of general contrast reduction method (b), and the result of the proposed method (c) with $C_1 = 1$, $C_2 = 0$, and $C_3 = 1$ and $I_{max}^{new} = 50$.

the highest pixel value is 50 (approximately 5–1 (255–50) reduction in intensity to protect the display from burn-in effect). The proposed method enhances the contrast between the background and the text during burn-in protection compared with the traditional contrast reduction. The results also show that the optimal parameters may be content-dependent. For example, the use of aggressive contrast separation is visually more pleasing when the text is brighter than the background as in Figure 4.18 than the inverse text case in Figure 4.17.

4.5.3 Modification of Text for Improved Readability

Overlaid text provides interesting information for the users; hence, text characters must be easily readable independently from the source of the content. However, the state of the art does not treat displaying text in video in a special manner; hence, the readability of text in video relies heavily on the assumption that the preferences of the content owners, such as the size of the text and the velocity of the scrolling text, are favorable for the display and the visual ability of the viewers. The large variations in the visual abilities of the users require personalized approaches. To this effect, we propose a method that makes it possible for the viewers to customize the appearance of overlay video text on the display medium being used by adjusting the properties of text, such as its size and color, which appear in a user-defined location, able to make the same text appear in another location for a certain amount of time, and able to apply the *customized settings* independent of broadcaster. Furthermore, the viewers may adjust the speed of the moving (scrolling) text, may freeze it for a certain amount of time, and even completely remove it.

We use the results of the text detection algorithm in Section 4.3. For a pixel-accurate map, we first binarize the text region into text and non-text. Afterward, a morphological closing operation, whose result is shown in Figure 4.20, and a connected-component labeling algorithm are applied to the resulting text mask to

Figure 4.20 Processing the text region for word and character region segmentation.

Figure 4.21 Coloring of the video text, and coloring, enlarging the font size, and adding motion to the text.

segment individual words. The closing operation joins separate characters in words while connected-component labeling algorithm extracts connected regions, that is, words in this case.

At this stage, we can change the color of the text as in Figure 4.21. For other operations, we need to remove the original text and we do not aim implementation on a TV architecture in this part and use a suboptimal text removal algorithm in the sense that, in some cases, the removal of text may result in visible artifacts. We use an enlarged text mask shown in Figure 4.20 that is obtained after the application of a morphological closing operation to the original text mask. The primary reason to use an enlarged mask is that the original mask may be thinner than the actual text line and, hence, may result in visible visually unpleasant text pieces in the text-removed image. Our approach to fill text regions is to use an iterative scheme where the median color of the non-text pixels in a large enough neighborhood of each pixel is used to fill the text regions (window size is 23×23 for a 720×576 image).

Figure 4.22   A side-by-side visual comparison of the improvement as a result of the proposed approach.

After the binarization and the removal of the text, the binarized map can be modified and inserted onto the image. There are many possibilities to change the appearance of the text, including changing the color, font size, location, and so on. The size of the text in the subsampled image is made even larger than the subtitle text size in the original image by converting the static text to moving text. As demonstrated in Figure 4.21, originally static subtitle text is transformed to a larger moving text with a different color. In Figure 4.22, we juxtaposed the original resized image where the readability of the text is poor and the resized image with large-sized scrolling subtitle text.

4.6 Conclusions

In this chapter, we presented novel algorithms for detection of overlaid text and channel logos by considering the properties of the TV architecture, production rules, and content properties. We showed that text as large as five times the vertical extension of memory content can be detected. Since the visual quality of the text with larger size is not degraded by the image enhancement algorithms, this upper limit for text size is not critical for text enhancement application. In the text detection, we also mainly used only luminance information (because of the initial specifications). Text with only distinguishable properties in chrominance may occur. In these cases, the proposed algorithm may miss the text; hence, color information can be considered as a future work. With the logo detection algorithm, we could detect logos of different types, such as transparent, animated, or static, as long as logo has different color properties from the natural content. After that, we demonstrated applications that use the outputs of these algorithms for enhancing visual quality, providing better contrast during burn-in protection, and improving the readability of text. All these applications provide means to treat overlaid graphics and natural contents differently, which are essentially formed in separate steps of video production.

References

1. K. Jung, K.I. Kim, A.K. Jain, Text information extraction in images and video: A survey, *Pattern Recognition*, 37:977–997, 2004.
2. R. Lienhart, Video OCR: A survey and practitioner's guide, in *Video Mining*, Kluwer Academic Publisher, Alphen aan den Rijn, the Netherlands, pp. 155–184, 2003.
3. Y. Zhong, H.-J. Zhang, A.K. Jain, Automatic caption localization in compressed video, *IEEE Transactions on Pattern Analysis and Machine Intelligence*, 22(4):385–392, 2000.
4. X. Qian, G. Liu, H. Wang, R. Su, Text detection, localization, and tracking in compressed video, *Signal Processing: Image Communication*, 22:752–768, 2007.
5. A. Ekin, Local information based overlaid text detection by classifier fusion, in *Proceedings of the IEEE ICASSP*, Toulouse, France, 2006.
6. N. Dimitrova, L. Agnihotri, C. Dorai, R. Bolle, MPEG-7 Videotext description scheme for superimposed text in images and video, *Signal Processing: Image Communication*, 16:137–155, 2000.
7. J.-C. Shim, C. Dorai, R. Bolle, Automatic text extraction from video for content-based annotation and retrieval, in *Proceedings of the IEEE International Conference on Pattern Recognition*, Brisbane, Queensland, Australia, Vol. 1, pp. 618–620, 1998.
8. C.W. Lee, K. Jung, H.J. Kim, Automatic text detection and removal in video sequences, *Pattern Recognition Letters*, 24:2607–2623, 2003.
9. R. Lienhart, A. Wernick, Localizing and segmenting text in images, videos and web pages, *IEEE Transactions on CSVT*, 12(4):256–268, 2002.
10. K.C. Kim, H.R. Byun, Y.J. Song, Y.W. Choi, S.Y. Chi, K.K. Kim, Y.K. Chung, Scene text extraction in natural scene images using hierarchical feature, in *Proceedings of IEEE ICPR*, Cambridge, U.K., 2004.
11. D. Chen, J. Odobez, J.-P. Thiran, A localization/verification scheme for finding text in images and video frames based on contrast independent features and machine learning methods, *Signal Processing: Image Communication*, 19:2005–2017, 2004.
12. K.I. Kim, K. Jung, J.H. Kim, Texture-based approach for text detection in images using support vector machines and continuously adaptive mean shift algorithm, *IEEE Transactions on Pattern Analysis and Machine Intelligence*, 21(12):1631–1639, 2003.
13. E.K. Wong, M. Chen, A new robust algorithm for video text extraction, *Pattern Recognition*, 36:1397–1406, 2003.
14. C. Cortes, V. Vapnik, Support vector machines, *Machine Learning*, 10(3):273–297, April 1995.
15. The Open Video Project, http://www.open-video.org/ (accessed on September 2004).
16. A. Albiol, M.J.C. Fulla, A. Albiol, L. Torres, Detection of TV commercials, in *Proceedings on IEEE ICASSP*, Montreal, Quebec, Canada, May 2004.
17. D. Zhang, R.K. Rajendran, S.-F. Chang, General and domain-specific techniques for detecting and recognized superimposed text in video, in *Proceedings of IEEE ICIP*, Rochester, NY, September 2002.
18. N. Dimitrova, T. McGee, J.H. Elenbaas, E. Leyvi, C. Ramsey, D. Berkowitz, Apparatus and method for locating a commercial disposed within a video stream, U.S. Patent 6,100,941, July 1998.

19. N. Ozay, B. Sankur, Automatic TV logo detection and classification in broadcast videos, in *Proceedings of the European Signal Processing Conference*, Glasgow, U.K., 2009.

20. T. Hargrove, Logo detection in digital video, http://toonarchive.com/logo-detection/ (accessed on March 4, 2005).

21. S. Duffner, C. Garca, A neural scheme for robust detection of transparent logos in TV programs, *Lecture Notes in Computer Science—II*, 4132:14–23, 2006.

22. J.R. Cozar, N. Guil, J.M. Gonzales-Linares, E.L. Zapata, E. Izquierdo, Logo-type detection to support semantic-based video annotation, *Signal Processing: Image Communication*, 22(7–8):669–679, August–September 2007.

23. K. Meisinger, T. Troeger, M. Zeller, A. Kaup, Automatic TV logo removal using statistical based detection and frequency selective inpainting, in *Proceedings of the European Signal Processing Conference*, Antalya, Turkey, 2005.

24. W.-Q. Yan, J. Wang, M.S. Kankanhalli, Automatic video logo detection and removal, *Multimedia Systems*, 10(5):379–391, 2005.

25. H. Pan, B. Li, M.I. Sezan, Automatic detection of replay segments in broadcast sports programs by detection of logos in scene transitions, in *Proceedings of IEEE ICASSP*, Orlando, FL, May 2002.

26. A. Ekin, R. Braspenning, Spatial detection of TV channel logos as outliers from the content, in *Proceedings of Visual Communications and Image Processing*, San Jose, CA, Vol. 6077, 2006.

27. G. Millerson, *The Technique of Television Production*, 12th edn., Focal, New York, 1990.

28. V. Barnett, T. Lewis, *Outliers in Statistical Data*, 2nd edn., John Wiley & Sons, Great Britain, U.K., 1990.

29. G. de Haan, *Video Processing*, University Press, Eindhoven, the Netherlands, pp. 186–187, 2004.

30. Y. Ono, Image display control apparatus and image display control method, US Patent 7,719,530, May 2010.

Chapter 5

Commercial and Trademark Recognition

Lamberto Ballan
University of Florence

Marco Bertini
University of Florence

Alberto Del Bimbo
University of Florence

Walter Nunziati
University of Florence

Giuseppe Serra
University of Florence

Contents

5.1 Introduction

In this chapter we discuss the problem of detecting and recognizing the two main categories of advertisement present in television videos: explicit advertisement in the form of commercials, that is, short video sequences advertising a product or a service, and indirect advertisement, that is, placement of trademarks and logos, that is associated with sponsorships (particularly in sports videos) and product placement.

The first type of advertisement is still the most common one, but the latter type is now evolving in a form that is being shown more and more, mostly for advertising TV shows on the same channel, as an ad overlay at the bottom of the TV screen. In this new form the trademark is transformed in a "banner," or "logo bug," as they are called by media companies. Figure 5.1 shows three frames: one taken from a commercial, one from a sport video showing placed trademarks, and one grabbed from a news program showing a logo bug in the lower right corner of the image.

There are several motivations for the development of methods for the recognition of commercials and trademarks in TV videos, mostly related to economical reasons. In fact, given the high costs for commercial broadcasts and trademark placement, media agencies and sponsors are extremely keen to verify that their brand has the level of visibility they expect for such an expenditure, and want to be sure that if they paid to have a commercial aired at a certain time it was effectively done so [1]. Other motivations may include marketing analysis, for example, to evaluate the impact of a campaign measuring sales [2] or other behaviors like website access after the airing of a commercial, or for business intelligence, for example, to estimate

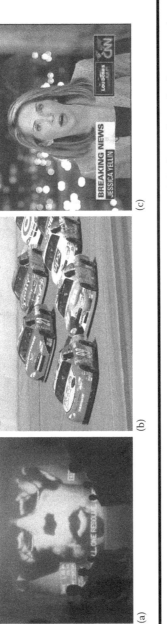

Figure 5.1 Examples of TV advertisement: (a) still image of the Apple "1984" commercial; (b) trademark placement in a sport event; (c) logo bug in a news program.

the expenditures in the advertisement of a competitor (also called "competitive advertising"). Motivations may also be related to sociological studies analyzing, for example, the impact of certain commercials on people's behavior [3]. The techniques that will be described in the following sections are intended to be used in application scenarios where the only available media are the (somehow digitized) audio/video stream as received by set-top boxes and TV, without relying, for instance, on cues or metadata that could be purposely embedded in the digital media used for transmission.

The two types of advertisement introduced above require different and specialized techniques, in order to be recognized: In the first case we have to deal with a short span of television programming (called "commercial," "TV ad," or "spot"), whose length may vary from a few seconds to a few minutes, and our goal is to identify its appearance in a video stream. The problem of recognizing the presence of a commercial segment in a video stream can be assimilated to that of dealing with near-duplicate and content-based copy detection: the commercial to be detected is the "original" video, while the broadcasted version may differ due to some editing or transmission artifacts. In the second type of advertisement we have to deal with a small portion of a video frame, and the problem is to match some views of the trademark or logo bug with parts of the frame, identifying its appearance both in space and time. Detecting the presence of a specific logo is highly correlated with the problem of (specific) object recognition: issues related to occlusion, to scale, pose, and lighting variations, fully apply to our case.

Furthermore, several other practical problems have to be dealt with: the video quality is generally low, especially when considering interlaced video, and the number of high-definition television (HDTV) channels is still relatively small; these facts lead directly to the need of developing techniques that are invariant to the largest possible set of photometric and geometric disturbances. On the other hand, due to the large number of broadcast material to be analyzed in commercial/trademark automatic analysis applications, it is required to have computationally efficient methods and compact representations of the models to be retrieved.

The chapter is structured as follows: the problem of commercial recognition is addressed in Section 5.2, with a discussion of state-of-the-art approaches on detection (Section 5.2.1), recognition and modeling (Section 5.2.2), semantic analysis (Section 5.2.2.4); then a system for fast commercial detection based on a combination of compact descriptors based on the MPEG-7 standard is thoroughly discussed in Section 5.2.3. Trademark detection is analyzed in Section 5.3. Early works on the problem are presented in Section 5.3.1, while state-of-the-art approaches that can be applied in real-world images and videos are presented in Section 5.3.2. A thorough presentation of a complete system that can be executed in quasi-real time is given in Section 5.3.3. Conclusions for the whole chapter are drawn in Section 5.4.

5.2 Commercial Recognition

The problem of recognizing commercials is related to many general video processing and analysis tasks, like scene detection, video segmentation, feature extraction, and indexing [4,5]. Scene segmentation and shot detection are required to identify the segments of the video stream that are candidates to contain a spot [6,7]. Typically spots are grouped together in commercial segments; each commercial is often separated from the others and from the normal TV program by a number of black frames [8,9]. In other cases broadcasters hide their superimposed logo during the commercials [10,11]. Also audio features can be used to detect the presence of a commercials segment: the black frames that separate them have no audio [12] while during the commercials the audio level is typically higher than during the normal TV program [1]. Audio and visual features can be fused together to improve commercials segmentation and identification [13].

Once a commercial segment candidate has been selected, it is required to compute a similarity measure with the video segments taken from (usually large) database, and the system must return relevant matches. For instance, a company may need to search for its video commercials (or for other companies' commercials) within an entire day of broadcast transmission, from several TV channels, and without browsing the entire recorded video material. As such, a *video signature* (also called *fingerprint*) is typically extracted from each segment, and is stored into the database. At run time, a query video signature is compared with all the signatures stored in the database, and most similar results are returned. The problems that have to be solved are thus that of extracting a suitable signature from a video clip, and how to use it to perform matching [14].

There are some general requirements that the signature should meet. First, the signature must be representative of the clip it refers, while being at the same time as compact as possible [15,16]. Second, the signature must be robust to a wide range of disturb, generated from different encoding schemes, different image and video formats, etc. Finally, it would be desirable to take advantages of well-established, standard image and video descriptors, in order to easily compare videos coming from heterogeneous sources.

Other important considerations are related to the metric used to compare signatures extracted from two different video sequences [17–19]. As for all modern multimedia retrieval systems, the metric must be flexible enough to enable similarity matching. Another desirable property would be to allow the user to query the system with a short, "summarized" version of the video clip of interest (e.g., the trailer of a movie, or a short version of a commercial), and let the system retrieve the video the clip belongs to. Considering "spots" it is quite common that for a spot there exist several versions with different durations, for example, a 30 s spot has reduced versions of 20 or 15 s, created by further editing of the original video.

Commercials/trademark applications need also to face scalability-related issues, that is, how to deal with very large (end ever growing) video archives; this problem is more relevant when addressing near duplicate and copy video detection [20–23] in web-scale archives like YouTube, but it must be considered (e.g., to reach real-time performance) in the case of commercial detection [24,25].

5.2.1 Commercial Detection

The first problem to address in commercial recognition is the identification of the candidate sequences that may contain spots in the broadcast video stream; this problem is akin to scene recognition, although it can be eased by the presence of certain characteristics that favor the identification, either imposed by local regulation that, for example, require the presence of a commercial block introduction sequence as in Germany [8], or by common practices of broadcasters, that add visual cues to distinguish the normal programs from the commercials.

The most common practices are the introduction of a certain number of black frames (typically between 5 and 12) between TV programs and commercials blocks, and within the blocks themselves; another common practice is the disappearance of the broadcaster's logo during the commercials. These characteristics have been exploited by several authors, either alone or combined, and have been observed in TV streams of Germany, Italy, Spain, USA, China, Japan, and Australia, among the others. References [4,8,26–28] used the detection of monochrome black frames. The detection of presence and disappearance of TV logos has been used in [5,10,13].

Another common practice, perhaps the most irritating for viewers, is the increase of the audio volume during commercials, combined with silence during the sequences of black frames between the spots. This characteristic has been recently used in [29,30], where audio energy windows are used for advertisement boundary detection. A combination of visual and audio characteristics for commercials segmentation has been used in [9,31].

Some approaches skip the problem of commercials detection and rely solely on shot segmentation, either checking each sequence of the video stream [7,24,28,32,33] or by learning, using a fusion of audiovisual cues, which shots are more likely to contain commercials, as in [12].

5.2.2 Commercial Representation and Modeling

5.2.2.1 Descriptors

The problem of defining a video clip's signature has been widely investigated, and is still currently researched because of its applicability to content-based copy and near-duplicate detection, which have recently become urgent problems since the inception of systems that allow web-based video distribution and collection, as YouTube.

In early approaches, several researchers have proposed various kinds of simple global keyframe descriptors, based usually on color and edge cues. In [8], the color coherence vector was used to characterize keyframes of commercials clip. A similar approach was followed in [34], with the addition of the use of the principal components of the color histograms of keyframes for commercial recognition. Color histograms, compressed with PCA, have been used in [6]. More recent works along these lines introduced more sophisticated descriptors, or combinations of descriptors. In [35], the combination of color and edge-based features was considered. This work also proposed the use of inverted indices to detect copies of a video clip. A hashing mechanism based on color moment vectors to efficiently retrieve repeated video clips was proposed in [36] and also in [24]. In [37], a lookup table was used to store fingerprints based on mean luminance of image blocks. In [38] and [28] color was proposed in combination with the *ordinal measure* (originally proposed for the problem of stereo matching), to define a binary-valued signature of the video. Dominant color, Gabor filters, and edge densities have been used in [5]. HSV color and edge histograms have been recently used in [33]. A combination of global visual features, like MPEG-7 CLD, EHD, and others, has been recently proposed for duplicate video detection in large databases in [39]. Typical limitations of approaches based on global image descriptors are related to the difficulties of dealing with image distortions occurring either at global or local level. In addition, the discriminacy of some of these techniques rapidly decreases with the growing of the collection to be searched.

To overcome limitations of image descriptors, people have proposed to include motion-based feature in the repertoire of descriptors, either at frame level, or at local, object-like level. For instance, in [40], the concept of *video strands* was used to create spatiotemporal descriptions of video data. These video strands encapsulate the movement of objects within half-second segments of a video sequence. In [4], has been proposed the use of video editing features like cuts, considering the fact that, at least when compared to news videos, commercials have a faster paced editing and a larger number of cuts. A drawback is related to the fact that not every video segment might be suitable for this type of techniques.

Some approaches rely on audio only. In particular, [32] uses 64 dimensions zero-crossing rate features; [29] uses units of energy envelope, to cope with the fact that energy is less robust to noise than frequency domain features; Fourier coefficients have been used in [30] because of their direct applicability to raw signal and low computational cost. Audio-based approaches obviously fail when it is required to search a video collection which includes contents that have been dubbed in different languages.

Audio and visual features have also been combined to increase the robustness of the system. In [12], global visual features like edge change ratio and frame differences are combined with audio features like MFCCs and short-time energy.

In [31], audio features were also used as part of the signature. The authors also performed a comprehensive experimental validation on the TRECVID dataset.

The use of local features, like interest points, is more common in the approaches for near-duplicate sequences detection, like in [41,42], where trajectories of interest points are used as features to create the video fingerprint or like in [43] where interest points selected using Hessian-Affine detector and represented with PCA-SIFT descriptor have been used.

5.2.2.2 Modeling and Matching

In [38], commercials are compared only to sequences that have the same length, using a specific metric to handle the compact ordinal descriptor of each frame. The same approach, which does not consider possible errors in video segmentation or the fact that commercials may be edited, has been followed in [29]. Comparison of sequences of keyframes has been used in [7]; this approach allows to cope only with the shortening of the shots of the commercial.

A way to handle videos that may differ for some subsequences, for example, like those due to reediting of the original video stored in the database, is to use a metric belonging to the class of the edit distances. The use of the edit distance in the context of video matching was proposed in [17] and, specifically for commercial recognition, in [8]. Since then, variations have been proposed over the basic formulation [19]. Typically features' descriptors are quantized to obtain a sequence of discrete symbols (sometime referred as *visual words*), prior to perform matching. Approximate string matching has been used also in [16,27], and has been adapted to video copy detection in [21]. Dynamic time warping has been used to find the optimal alignment of audio signatures of commercials in [30].

Hashing has been used in [24] because of its constant computational complexity, and the authors experimented with different hashing functions. Locality-sensitive hashing (LSH) has been used in [32,33]. More recently [44,45], similarity measures for near-duplicate detection have been derived from metrics used in information retrieval, such as *tf/idf* weighting: in text mining application, this weight is a statistical measure used to evaluate how important a word is to a document in a collection or corpus. This definition has been translated in the image context using the concept of visual words introduced above.

SVM classifiers have been proposed in [12] to classify shots containing commercials and those containing normal programs.

5.2.2.3 Scalability

A critical problem of near-duplicate and content-based copy detection is how to deal with web-scale databases. This problem is less important when dealing with commercial recognition since a real-time system just needs to check the presence of a relatively limited number of commercials in a video stream. To speed the similarity evaluation, based on edit distance, in [21] has been introduced a pruning mechanism inspired by the FASTA algorithm employed in bioinformatics to find similar DNA sequences. In [28], differences of sequence durations are used to reduce comparisons, although this risks to miss the detection of edited spots. A dual-stage temporal recurrence hashing algorithm for commercial recognition in very large databases has been recently proposed in [25]. The issue of descriptor size has been addressed in [23], where compact frame descriptors are created through aggregation of local descriptors. With the growing interest of major search engines in duplicate or near-duplicate image and video detection, parallel algorithms have been introduced to perform analysis of massive quantities of data *in the cloud*, in particular by adapting *map/reduce* strategies to decompose the problem [46]: In this framework, the problem is initially chopped into a number of smaller subproblems (*map* step), which are distributed to *worker* computational nodes. The output of these nodes is then fed back to the master node, which combines the results in a way to get the output of the original problem (*reduce* step).

5.2.2.4 Semantic Analysis

Some authors have tried to directly encode semantic aspects in the retrieval process [13,47–49]: In these approaches, the visual content of the image or video is mapped to semantic concepts that are derived by various sources of information. In [47], the principles of *semiotics* are used to characterize the video at semantic level, by means of a weighted average of individual semiotic categories. In [48], categorization is obtained by querying public textual search engines using keyword automatically extracted from transcripts or audio features. A similar type of multi-modal approach has been proposed in [13], where a set of mid-level features are used to categorize the commercial in one of five predefined classes, following a supervised-learning strategy. More recently [49], semantics have been modeled as a latent random variable using the *probabilistic latent semantic analysis* framework, or PLSA [50]. PLSA was originally proposed as a generative model to discover topics from document corpus. As a statistical model, a PLSA model attempts to associate a latent variable (or aspect) with each observation (occurrence of a word in a document). Again, in the image context words are substituted by the occurrences of visual symbol derived from quantization of local features.

5.2.3 Sample Approach

As case study let us review thoroughly a real-time approach for commercials recognition [27]. One of the main issues that has to be solved is the decision on the type of features to be used: They need to have a low computational cost to achieve real-time performance and do not have to be ad hoc to be usable in a domain that sports a large variability like commercials. To this end we have selected an effective and efficient combination of features and features' descriptors, taken from the well-established MPEG-7 standard. Using these descriptors allows video content provider to easily index their content with freely available tools, without ambiguity; moreover it also enable to match clips taken from various sources and from different organizations, provided that a suitable general purpose metric is employed, using a common representation based on a ISO standard.

The proposed method is based on the combination of three MPEG-7 descriptors, namely, the *scalable color descriptor* and the *color layout descriptor* for global color and color layout, and by the *edge histogram descriptor* for textures. These descriptors are collected for each frame, and their sequences constitute the clip signature. To match two signatures, a variation of the edit distance [51] is employed, in order to cope with clips that may differ for small subsequences. The edit distance, or Levenshtein distance, is a metric widely used in information theory to compute the distance between two strings. It is given by the minimum number of operations needed to transform one string into the other, where an operation is an insertion, deletion, or substitution of a single character; these operations have a counterpart in video editing techniques and thus edit distance is very well suited to cope with them, more than other techniques that are more suitable to handle time or speed variations like dynamic time warping. However, the use of edit distance has some potential drawbacks, since it is not completely clear how one should choose the number of symbols for videos of generic type. In contrast to the existing works based on edit distance, and as a second contribution of the proposed approach, we avoid this discretization step, relying directly on the distance used to compare two "symbols" (in our case, two frame descriptors, which are compared using an appropriate metric) for deciding on the cost of transforming one string into another.

The video clip matching system is performed in two phases. In the first one an indexing process generates the signatures, composed by MPEG-7 descriptors, for the clips that are to be retrieved. In the second phase the target video that has to be analyzed is processed to extract the same features, and these are used to measure similarity with the signatures. There are no special requirements on the video format used to create the index or the target video, since the descriptors are extracted from decompressed frames. Moreover, experiments showed that even frame sizes as low as PAL QCIF (192×144) can be used in both phases, thus easing the achievability of real-time performance. The descriptors used capture different aspects of the video content [52], namely, global color, color layout, and texture and are computationally inexpensive. Motion descriptors have not been used in order to be able to perform recognition in real time. However, the temporal aspects of video are implicitly considered using the edit distance to match the video sequences.

The MPEG-7 features that have been selected are suitable for the creation of fingerprint since they meet the important requirements of fast calculation, compact representation, good discriminative power, and tolerance to small differences due to signal degradation. To reduce the space occupation of the stored MPEG-7 descriptors, due to the verbosity of the XML format, it is possible to use the BiM (Binary Format for MPEG-7) framework; in fact BiM enables compression of any generic XML document, reaching an average 85% compression ratio of MPEG-7 data, and allows the parsing of BiM encoded files, without requiring their decompression. In the following we provide a short discussion on these descriptors and the metrics used to match them.

5.2.3.1 Scalable Color Descriptor (SCD)

The SCD is a color histogram in the HSV color space, uniformly quantized into bins according to tables provided in the MPEG-7 standard normative part, encoded using the Haar transform. Its binary representation is scalable since it can be represented with different bits/bins, thus reducing the complexity for feature extraction and matching operations. Increasing the number of bits used improves retrieval accuracy. This descriptor can be extended into the GoF/GoP (group of frames/group of pictures) color descriptor, thus allowing it to be applied to a video segment. In this case two additional bits allow to define how the histogram is calculated before applying the Haar transform. The standard allows to use average, median, or intersection. In the first case, adopted in this work, averaging of the counters of each bin is performed; the result is equivalent to computing the aggregate histogram of the group of pictures and performing normalization. The median histogram is equivalent to compute the median of each counter value of the bins, and may be used to achieve more robustness with respect to outliers in intensity values. The intersection histogram requires the calculation of the minimum counter value of each bin, and thus the result is representative of the "least common" color traits of the group of pictures.

SCD descriptors can be matched both in the histogram domain and in the Haar domain using the L1 norm, although it has to be noted that results of the L1 norm-based matching in the Haar domain are not the same of the histogram. Generation of the Haar coefficients is computationally marginal with respect to histogram creation, and their matching is equal in complexity to histogram matching; thus, to avoid the reconstruction of the histogram from the descriptor we have used matching in the Haar domain, using 128 bits/histogram.

5.2.3.2 Color Layout Descriptor (CLD)

This descriptor represents the spatial distribution of color in an extremely compact form (as low as 8 bytes per image can be used), and thus is particularly interesting for our scope, because of computational cost of matching and space occupation. The input picture is divided in an 8×8 grid and a representative color in the YCrCb color space for each block is determined, using a simple color averaging. The derived colors are then transformed into a series of coefficients using a 8 × 8 DCT. A few low-frequency coefficients are selected using zigzag scanning and then quantized. Since the calculation of the descriptor is based on a grid it is independent from the frame size.

To match two CLDs ({DY, DCr, DCb} and {DY', DCr', DCb'}), the following distance measure is used [53]:

$$D = \sqrt{\sum_i w_{yi} \left(DY_i - DY_i'\right)^2} + \sqrt{\sum_i w_{bi} \left(DCb_i - DCb_i'\right)^2}$$

$$+ \sqrt{\sum_i w_{ri} \left(DCr_i - DCr_i'\right)^2}$$

where

DY_i, DCb_i, and DCr_i are the ith coefficients of the *Y, Cr,* and *Cb* color components

w_{yi}, w_{bi}, and w_{ri} are the weighting values, that decrease according to the zigzag scan order

5.2.3.3 Edge Histogram Descriptor (EHD)

This descriptor represents the spatial distribution of five types of edges (four directional and one nondirectional). This distribution of edges is a good texture signature even in the case of not homogeneous texture, and its computation is straightforward. Experiments conducted within the MPEG-7 committee have shown that this descriptor is quite effective for representing natural images. To extract it, the video frame is divided into 4 × 4 blocks, and for each block an edge histogram is computed, evaluating the strength of the five types of edges and considering those that exceed a certain preset threshold. Values of the bins are normalized to [0, 1], and a nonlinear quantization of the bin values results in a 3 bits/bin representation. Overall the descriptor consists of 80 bins (16 blocks and 5 bins per block), and is thus quite compact.

The simplest method to assess similarity between two EHDs is to consider the 3-bit numbers as integer values and compute the L1 distance between the EHDs.

The combination of the three descriptors discussed above creates a robust signature, which comprises global and local features that describe syntactic aspects of video content, and yet is still compact and computationally inexpensive. Moreover, it is standard and can be easily reproduced using the MPEG-7 XM Experimentation Model software, freely available.

5.2.3.3.1 Video Clip Matching

Our goal is to be able to perform approximate clip matching, evaluating similarity of video sequences even in case that the original video has been reedited. This case may occur since often several variations of the same commercial are produced, usually creating shorter versions from a longer one. This may happen also with *video rushes* (the first unedited sequence that is filmed), from which a smaller section is usually selected to be used. Another case may be that of identifying sequences that have a variable length such as those containing anchormen in a news video, those that compose a dialog scene in a movie, or slow motion versions of a sequence like the replay of a sport highlight.

In our approach we extract the features used to create the commercial's fingerprint from the clip A that has to be analyzed, and consider both its feature vector and the fingerprint of the commercial B to be recognized as vectors composed by three strings, one for each feature. All the strings of A will have length m and those of B will have length n.

To evaluate the similarity of the video clips we consider each corresponding couple of corresponding strings and calculate an approximate distance. The three distances are used to calculate the Manhattan distance between the clips, and if the distance is bigger than a minimum percentage of the length of the clips then they are matched.

The approximate distance between the strings is evaluated using the Sellers algorithm [54]. This distance is similar to the Levenshtein edit distance, and adds a variable cost adjustment to the cost of gaps, that is, to insertions and deletions. Using this distance, and tailoring the costs of the edit operation appropriately, it is possible to adjust the system to the specific clip matching task. For example, if there is need to detect appearances of a long rush sequence, that is likely to be shortened in the video editing process, deletions could be considered less expensive than insertions. A simple dynamic programming implementation of the algorithm, as that shown in [51], is $O(mn)$ in time and $O(min(m, n))$ in space, but other algorithms can reduce time and space complexity. Given the short length of commercials, the complexity of the algorithm does not pose any problem. From the edit operations cost formula of [51], and considering the cost matrix C that tracks the costs of the edit operations needed to match two strings, we can then write the cost formula for the alignment of the a_i and b_j characters of two strings as:

$$C_{i,j} = min(C_{i-1,j-1} + \delta(a_i, b_j), C_{i-1,j} + \delta_I, C_{i,j-1} + \delta_D)$$

where

$\delta(a_i, b_j)$ is 0 if the distance between a_i and b_j is close enough to evaluate $a_i \approx b_j$
    or the cost of substitution otherwise

δ_I and δ_D are the costs of insertion and deletion, respectively

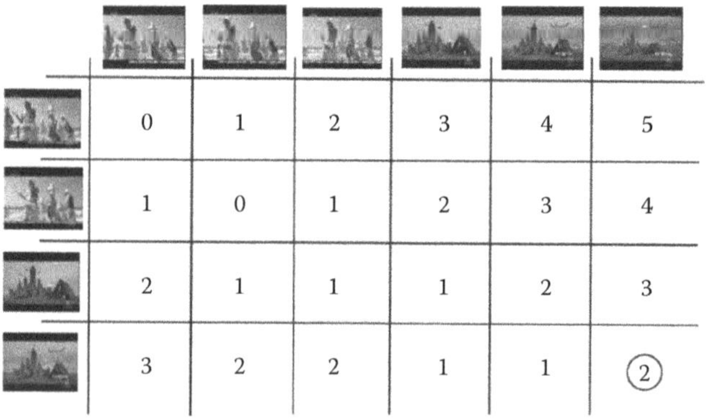

	0	1	2	3	4	5
	1	0	1	2	3	4
	2	1	1	1	2	3
	3	2	2	1	1	(2)

Figure 5.2 **Simplified example of edit distance calculation performed using CLDs between two edited versions of the same commercial. The top row shows part of a commercial, the left column shows a reduced version. The table contains the $C_{i,j}$ costs, where $\delta(a_i, b_i)$, δ_I, and δ_D have value 1. The circled number is the distance between the two sequences. (From Bertini, M. et al., Video clip matching using MPEG-7 descriptors and edit distance, in *Proceedings of ACM International Conference on Image and Video Retrieval (CIVR)*, Tempe, AZ, 2006. ACM 139-2006, http://www.acm.org/publications/policies/copyright_policy#Retained)**

Figure 5.2 shows a simplified example of edit distance calculation between a part of a commercial and a shortened version of the same commercial, using the CLDs.

The alphabet of the strings has size equal to the dimensionality of features, but it has to be noted that it has no effect in terms of computational time or size on the string similarity algorithm, since only the cost of the edit operations are kept in memory, and the only operation performed on the alphabet characters is the check of their equality, using the appropriate distance described for each feature in the above paragraphs. This approach allows us to overcome a limitation of string matching; in fact usually a difference between symbols is evaluated using the same score, that is the distance between symbol 1 and 2 is the same between symbol 1 and 10. In our case instead, when comparing two CLDs, for example, a close match could be evaluated as an equality, without penalizing the distance.

The calculation of similarity can be stopped earlier, when the required similarity threshold has been reached, to speed up processing.

5.2.3.3.2 Experimental Results

The clip matching approach described in the previous section is independent with respect to the domain of the videos. According to each domain the most appropriate clip selection algorithm should be used, ranging from simple shot detection to other methods that may select sequences composed by more shots. The clip selection algorithm used to extract the commercials to be matched is based on detection of black frames that appear before each commercial, as noted in [8].

About 10 h of videos was acquired from digital TV signal and from different European and international broadcasters, at PAL frame rate and size, and frame resolution was scaled down to PAL QCIF (192 × 144 pixels). Forty different commercials were selected and added to the test database. Videos were converted to MPEG-1 and 2 format using FFMpeg and Mainconcept MPEG Pro encoders, at different quality, to test the robustness with respect to compression artifacts and noise. In our prototype application (implemented in C++ under Linux, without any use of multithreading that would greatly improve speed through parallel computation of features), the system took about 3 s (on average) to extract the signature of a PAL QCIF clip of length 30 s. At query time, the system took less than half second to perform a single comparison between two of such signatures.

Figure 5.3 shows the average similarity between pairs of corresponding commercials, where one of the spots was corrupted by a range of photometric or geometric disturbance: high video compression, contrast, crop, and blur. These corruptions

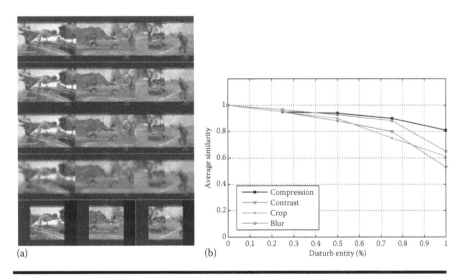

(a)   (b)

Figure 5.3 (a) Keyframes from a sample sequence. The top row shows the reference commercial. Subsequent rows show keyframes taken from the commercial with the maximum level of disturb applied. From top to bottom: original, contrasted, compressed, blurred, and cropped versions. (b) Average similarity between 100 corresponding clips versus the entity of various disturbs on the original signal. (From Bertini, M. et al., Video clip matching using MPEG-7 descriptors and edit distance, in *Proceedings of ACM International Conference on Image and Video Retrieval (CIVR)*, Tempe, AZ, 2006. ACM 140-2006, http://www.acm.org/publications/policies/copyright_policy#Retained)

affect differently the descriptors used in the system: (1) blur affects mainly EHD; (2) contrast affects both SCD and CLD, but at a certain level starts to affect also EHD; (3) compression affects more EHD, due to the typical blocking effect of MPEG video; (4) crop affects more EHD and CLD, since they are based on local representations while SCD is less affected since it is a global feature. Since we do not have a natural way to express the entity of all the types of disturbance, the *x*-axis represents this measure relatively to the maximum level of the disturb that was applied. Such maximum level is shown in the right column for some sample keyframes of a test sequence. All of the corrupted versions of the commercials were obtained using the program Avidemux, on a dataset of about 100 video clips taken from various sources. Clips were originally encoded at a frame rate of 1000 kbps, and the maximum compression was obtained setting a fixed bitrate of 50 kbps. The graph shows how similarity gracefully degrades for all kinds of disturb, thanks to the fact that descriptors are typically not affected all together by these disturbs. As can be expected, most critical disturbs are those that heavily influence the photometric properties, such as large changes in contrast.

5.2.3.3.3 Discussion

In this section we have presented a TV commercial recognition algorithm that uses a robust video fingerprint based on standard MPEG-7 descriptors. Apart from detection of commercials in TV broadcasts the proposed approach can be used also to solve the generic problem of near-duplicate clip matching, such as identification of structural elements like dialogs in movies or appearance of anchorman or interviews in news videos. The descriptors that compose the fingerprint capture several syntactic aspects of videos are easily computed and compact enough to be used in large databases. Experiments have shown that the approach is suitable for real-time recognition.

Use of edit distance as a base for the approximate match allows to cope with reedited clips (e.g., the common shorter versions of commercials), or clips that have different frame rates. While the proposed method can be directly adopted to solve the matching problem efficiently in small databases, additional effort must be made to complete the representation with a suitable indexing scheme, which would make possible matching clips in very large video databases, like online video sharing services, without performing exhaustive search.

5.3 Trademark Detection

Currently, verification of brand visibility in a video is done manually by human annotators that view a broadcast event and annotate every appearance of a sponsor's trademark. The annotation performed on these videos is extremely labor-intensive, usually requiring the video to be viewed in its entirety several times, and subjective. Moreover, manual annotations of this type are usually limited to the annotation of the *appearances* of a given trademark (i.e., a particular trademark *appears* at a particular timecode). Because of their popularity and the amount of related sponsorships investments, sports videos are for sure the ones that are more investigated for this kind of analysis [55–59]. Just as an example, the television coverage of the 2006 FIFA World Cup was aired in a total of 43,600 broadcasts across 214 countries and territories, generating a total coverage of 73,072 h; this is an increase of 76% on the 2002 event and a 148% increase on 1998. The analysis of a similar huge amount of material is nowadays unfeasible for a manual procedure. This fact becomes evident as we observe that the best human annotators can annotate approximately a sports video by considering only four different trademarks in real time (i.e., 1 h of video requires 1 h of annotation for four trademarks). But annotations are typically required for between 20 and 30 trademarks for each sport video, requiring the annotator to view it multiple times or requires that multiple human annotators check the same video in parallel. In any case, a 1 h video typically requires around six man-hours to be fully annotate.

Automatic annotation of trademark promises to significantly reduce the human labor involved in annotating. Furthermore, automatic annotation can provide a richer information than those currently performed by humans. Some methods are able, for example, to compute metrics on the duration of each trademark appearance as well as an estimation of the size it occupies in the image or frame.

5.3.1 Early Approaches

The early work on automatic trademark detection and recognition addressed the problem of assisting the registration process. Since a trademark has to be formally registered, the idea of these approaches is to compare a newly designed trademark with archives of already registered ones, in order to ensure that it is sufficiently distinctive and avoid confusion [60]. Historically, the earliest approach was Kato's Trademark system [61]. Its idea is to map normalized trademark images to an 8×8 pixel grid, and calculate a histogram (called *GF-vector*) for each image from frequency distributions of black and edge pixels appearing in each cell of the grid. Matching between logos was performed by comparing the respective GF-vectors. An other notable system was Artisan [62] that achieves trademark retrieval using shape similarity. In this approach Gestalt principles were used in order to derive rules allowing individual image components to be grouped into perceptually significant parts. In [63], the authors proposed a method to retrieve trademarks using query by rough sketches. They characterize regions as either solid or line-like, extracting boundary contours for the former and skeletons for the latter. These descriptions are used to compare the overall image similarity between the query and stored images. More recently, in [64] the authors proposed a system that combines global Zernike moments, local curvatures and distance to centroid features in order to describe logos. In [65], a query-by-example retrieval system was proposed; logos are described by a variant of the shape context descriptor [66] and are then organized by a LSH indexing structure, aiming to perform approximate k-NN search in high dimensional spaces in sub-linear time.

In this scenario it is usually assumed that the image acquisition and processing chain is controlled so that the images are of acceptable quality and are not distorted. For this reason, all these methods use synthetic images and rely on global logo descriptions, usually related to their contours or to particular shape descriptors.

5.3.2 Trademark Detection and Recognition in Real-World Images/Videos

In the last years novel works on logo detection and recognition in real-world images/videos have emerged; they are mainly targeted to automatically identify products (such as groceries in stores for assisting the blind or product on the web) [67,68] or, as previously introduced, to verify the visibility of advertising trademarks (e.g., billboards or banners) in sports events [55–58]. Nevertheless, there are few publicly available datasets to evaluate and compare the most recent retrieval approaches, except the recent *BelgaLogos* dataset [59].

However, the trademark detection and recognition problem in natural image collections is extremely hard, due to the relatively low resolution and quality of images (e.g., due to compression artifacts, color subsampling, motion blur, etc.) and also to the fact that trademarks are often small and may contain very few information. Moreover, their appearance is often characterized by occlusions, perspective transformations, and deformations (see the examples in Figure 5.4). The problem of detecting and tracking billboards in soccer videos has been initially studied in [55], with the goal of superimposing different advertisements according to the different audiences. Billboards are detected using color histogram back-projection and represented using a probability density function in an invariant color space estimated from manually annotated video frames. The focus of this work is on detection and tracking rather than recognition. In [69], logo appearance is detected by analyzing sets of significant edges and applying heuristic techniques to discard small or sparsely

Figure 5.4   Realistic examples of trademark images characterized respectively by a bad light condition (Coca-Cola), a deformation (Starbucks), and an occlusion (Pepsi).

populated edge regions of the image. Subsequently, the same authors extended this work [70] by dealing with logos appearing on rigid planar surfaces with an homogeneously colored background. Video frames are binarized and logo regions are combined using some heuristics. The Hough transform space of the segmented logo is then searched for large values, in order to find the image intensity profiles along lines, and logo recognition is performed by matching these lines with the line profiles of the models. In [71], candidate logo regions are detected using color histogram back-projection and then are tracked. Multidimensional receptive field histograms are finally used to perform logo recognition; for every candidate region the most likely logo is computed and thus, if a region does not contain a logo, the precision of identification is reduced. In [72,73], logos are represented defining an extension of the color-edge co-occurrence histogram (CECH) [74], which captures both the color and spatial relations between color pixels, by introducing a color quantization method based on the HSV color space.

Recently, interest points and local descriptors have been successfully used in order to describe logos and obtain flexible matching techniques that are robust to partial occlusions as well as linear and nonlinear transformations. The first approach of this type, proposed in [57], achieves trademark detection and localization in sports videos; each trademark is described as a bag of local features (SIFT points [75]) which are classified and matched with the bags of SIFT features in video frames. Localization is performed through robust clustering of matched features. Following a similar approach, a SIFT point representation is exploited in [59] for detecting logos in natural images. In order to refine their detection results, authors also included geometric consistency constraints by estimating affine transformations between queries and retrieved images. Furthermore, they use a contrario adaptive thresholding in order to improve the accuracy of visual query expansion. This method puts a model assumption about the possible transformation (i.e., homography) between reference logos and test images. Though it might not capture the actual inter-logo transformation, for example when logos are deformed (e.g., a logo on a T-shirt), perspective deformations are captured by a homography model. This is an important point, since in practice logos are usually affected by this kind of transformations. In [76], the authors proposed a logo detection method, following the idea previously introduced by [77] for object categorization and retrieval, by data mining association rules that capture frequent spatial configuration of quantized SIFT features at multiple resolutions. These collections of rules are indexed in order to retrieve representative training templates for matching, nevertheless image resolution is a major limitation. In [78], is presented a two-stage logo detection algorithm which also achieves localization by adapting a spatial-spectral saliency to improve the matching precision. A spatial context descriptor is introduced in order to estimate the spatial distribution of the set of matching points. The system is able to find the minimum boundary round of matched points and to partition it into nine areas. This information is used to describe the distribution of these feature points using a simple nine-dimensional histogram.

5.3.3 Sample Approach

As case study we review in detail an automatic system for detecting and retrieving trademark appearances in sports videos [57]. This system has been designed to attain a quasi-real-time processing of videos. Broadcast sports video is recorded directly to DVD. This video and a collection of static trademark images are then processed to extract a compact representation based on SIFT feature points. The results of this processing are stored in a database for later retrieval. All of the trademarks are then matched against the content extracted from every frame of the video to compute a "match score" indicating the likelihood that the trademark occurs at any given point in the video. Localization is performed through robust clustering of matched feature points in the video frames. These time series are used to retrieve intervals of the video likely to contain the trademark image. Retrieved segments are shown in a user interface used by a human annotator who can then validate this automatic annotation (see Figure 5.5 for a screenshot of the application).

5.3.3.1 Trademark Appearances

One of the distinctive aspects of trademarks is that they are usually planar objects and contain both text and other high-contrast features such as graphic logos. In sports videos they are often occluded by players or other obstacles between the camera and the trademark. Often the appearance of trademarks is also characterized by

Figure 5.5 A screenshot of the visualization application. The user can configure how detected trademarks are visualized on the video frame. The rows at the bottom indicate, in different colors, the timeline of detected trademarks in the video.

(1) *perspective deformation* due to placement of the camera and the vantage from which it images advertisements in the field; (2) *motion blur* due to camera motion, or motion of the trademark in the case of trademarks placed, for example, on Formula One cars or jerseys of soccer players. Since blur is indistinguishable from a change in scale, a scale-invariant representation is essential.

To obtain a matching technique that is robust to partial occlusions, we use local neighborhood descriptors of salient points. By combining the results of local, point-based matching we are able to match entire trademarks. Local texture and important aspects in trademarks are compactly represented using SIFT features [75], because they are robust to changes in scale, rotation, and (partially) affine distortion. Trademarks are so represented as a bag of SIFT feature points. Each trademark is represented by one or more image instances. More formally, trademark T_i is represented by the N_i SIFT feature points detected in the image:

$$T_i = \left\{ \left(x_k^t, y_k^t, s_k^t, d_k^t, \mathbf{O}_k^t \right) \right\}, \quad \text{for } k \in \{1, \ldots, N_i\},$$

where x_k^t, y_k^t, s_k^t, and d_k^t are, respectively, the x- and y-position, the scale, and the dominant direction of the kth detected feature point. The element $\mathbf{O}_k^t$ is a 128-dimensional local edge orientation histogram of the SIFT point. The superscript t is used only to distinguish points from trademarks and video frames. An individual point k from trademark i is denoted by T_i^k.

Each frame, V_i, of a video is represented similarly as a bag of M_i SIFT-feature points detected in frame i:

$$T_i = \left\{ \left(x_k^v, y_k^v, s_k^v, d_k^v, \mathbf{O}_k^v \right) \right\}, \quad \text{for } k \in \{1, \ldots, M_i\},$$

and where each element is defined as above for trademarks. Again, the super-script is used to distinguish video frame points from points detected in trademark images.

The local orientation histogram portions ($\mathbf{O}_k^v$ and $\mathbf{O}_k^t$) of the feature points are then used for the matching procedure, as described in the next section. This allows to define a feature descriptor that may result in robust to geometric distortions and scale changes. Note also that the coordinates x and y of the feature points are not used during the matching phase, while they are then utilized only for trademark localization.

5.3.3.2 Detection and Localization of Trademarks

Trademark detection is performed by matching the bag of local features representing the trademark with the local features detected in the video frames. In order to minimize false positive detections we use a very conservative threshold. In particular, for every point detected in trademark T^j, we compute its two nearest neighbors in the points detected in video frame V_i:

$$N_1\left(T_j^k, V_i\right) = \min_q \left\|\mathbf{O}_q^v - \mathbf{O}_k^t\right\|$$

$$N_2\left(T_j^k, V_i\right) = \min_{q \neq N_1\left(T_j^k, V_i\right)} \left\|\mathbf{O}_q^v - \mathbf{O}_k^t\right\|. \tag{5.1}$$

Next, for every point in the video frame we compute its *match score*:

$$M\left(T_j^k, V_i\right) = \frac{N_1\left(T_j^k, V_i\right)}{N_2\left(T_j^k, V_i\right)}, \tag{5.2}$$

that is the ratio of the distances to the first and second nearest neighbors.

SIFT points are selected as being good candidate matches on the basis of their match scores. The *match set* for trademark T_j in frame V_i is defined as:

$$M_i^j = \left\{k \mid M\left(T_j^k, V_i\right) < \tau_1\right\}, \tag{5.3}$$

where τ_1 is a suitable chosen threshold (we empirically fix it to 0.8 in all of our experiments).

This methodology gives very good results in terms of robustness. In fact, a correct match needs to have the closest matching descriptor significantly closer than the closest incorrect match, while false matches, due to the high dimensionality of the feature space, have a certain number of other close false matches. Figure 5.6 shows two matching examples in different sport domains.

In order to make the final decision that the trademark T_j is present in the frame V_i, a certain percentage of the feature points detected in the trademark has to be matched according to Equation 5.3. This task is done by thresholding the *normalized match score*:

$$\frac{\left|M_i^j\right|}{\left|T_j\right|} > \tau_2 \iff \text{trademark } T_j \text{ present in frame } V_i.$$

Analysis of the precision–recall curves obtained using different values of τ_2, and different trademarks, allows to determine the best choice for this threshold (see Section 5.3.3). Experiments on several different trademarks and sports have shown that a value of 0.2–0.25 is a reasonable choice.

Trademark localization is performed by a robust estimate of the features point cloud. Let $F = \{(x_1, y_1), (x_2, y_2), \ldots, (x_n, y_n)\}$ be the matched point locations in

Figure 5.6 Two examples of the "traditional" SIFT matching technique. (From Bagdanov, A.D. et al., Trademark matching and retrieval in sports video databases, in *Proceedings of ACM International Workshop on Multimedia Information Retrieval (MIR)*, Augsburg, Bavaria, Germany, 2007. ACM 3/2007, http://www.acm.org/publications/policies/copyright_policy#Retained)

the frame. The robust centroid estimate is computed by iteratively solving for (μ_x, μ_y) in

$$\sum_{i=1}^{n} \psi(x_i; \mu_x) = 0, \quad \sum_{i=1}^{n} \psi(y_i; \mu_y) = 0$$

where the influence function ψ used is the Tukey biweight:

$$\psi(x; m) = \begin{cases} (x - m)\left(1 - \frac{(x-m)^2}{c^2}\right)^2 & \text{if } |(x - m)| < c \\ 0 & \text{otherwise} \end{cases} \quad (5.4)$$

The scale parameter c is estimated using the *median absolute deviation from the median*:

$$\text{MAD}_x = \text{median}_i(|x_i - \text{median}_j(x_j)|).$$

Once the estimation of the robust centroid is done, the distance of each matched point to the robust centroid is computed according to the influence function (Equation 5.4). Points with a low influence are excluded from the final match set. Figure 5.7 reports a schematization of the robust trademark localization procedure.

Some example matches found in different sports videos using this technique are shown in Figure 5.8. Notice that the technique is quite robust to occlusions, scale variation, and perspective distortion. Note also that the model trademark used in the second row is a synthetic trademark image. The distinctive structure in the text of the trademark is enough to discriminate it from other trademarks and background noise.

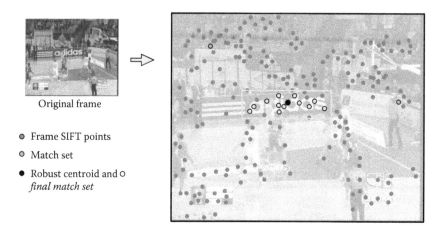

Original frame

⊕ Frame SIFT points

◎ Match set

● Robust centroid and ○
final match set

Figure 5.7   An example of robust trademark localization. Points in cyan are those selected as finale trademark points set; points in green are SIFT matched points with a low influence and so excluded from the final match set.

5.3.3.3 Experimental Results

To calibrate and evaluate our proposed technique we perform several experiments. Three full videos of three different sports (each one is approximately 90 min long) were used for an evaluation of the performance of the approach. The first video is related to a MotoGP motorcycle race. The second one is related to a volleyball match and contains significantly different trademarks and characteristics than the MotoGP video. In fact, sports like volleyball and basketball presents a lot of situations with occlusions or partial appearance of the trademarks. The last one is of a soccer match (taken from italian *Serie A*); in this case there are often trademarks at low resolution with few SIFT feature points. We refer to this collection of videos as SPORTS-VIDEOS dataset. The examples in the top row of Figure 5.8 are from the MotoGP video, those in the middle row are from the volleyball, and those in the bottom row from the soccer video.

The MotoGP video was manually annotated for the presence of a number of trademarks, to analyze the effects of all the parameters of the proposed algorithms. These annotations were performed at the frame level, and each trademark appearance is associated with an interval in the ground truth. The performance of the approach is evaluated in terms of two standard metrics that is, *precision* and *recall*, defined as:

$$\text{precision} = \frac{\text{\# correct trademark detections}}{\text{\# trademark detections}},$$

$$\text{recall} = \frac{\text{\# correct trademark detections}}{\text{\# trademark appearances}}.$$

Figure 5.8 **Some example matches. The leftmost column contains the trademark model annotated with its detected SIFT feature points. The other three columns contain a portion of a video frame where a match was found. Points indicated in cyan are those selected as "good" matches according to Equations 5.3 and 5.4. (From Bagdanov, A.D. et al., Trademark matching and retrieval in sports video databases, in *Proceedings of ACM International Workshop on Multimedia Information Retrieval (MIR)*, Augsburg, Bavaria, Germany, 2007. ACM 5/2007, http://www.acm.org/publications/policies/copyright_policy#Retained)**

Figure 5.9 gives an overview of the performance of the algorithm on the MotoGP video for six trademarks over a range of normalized match score thresholds. Also shown in the plots of Figure 5.9 are the precision and recall performances as a function of the frame sampling rates. Results are shown for 2.5, 5, and 10 fps. Note that in these plots, the recall plots are the ones that start at or around 1.0 and *decrease* as the normalized match threshold is increased. In most cases, a recall of about 85% can be obtained at a precision of around 80% with values of τ_2 varying between 0.2 and 0.25. The experiments performed on soccer and volleyball videos have shown that this value of the threshold can be used also for these other sports. Increasing the frame sampling rate predictably impacts the recall of the results. It is interesting, however, that the precision of the retrieved results is not adversely affected. This indicates that the matching technique has a very low false-positive rate. In cases such as Tissot and Kerakoll, the poor performance is related to the fact that the model trademarks have relatively few feature points detected in them, causing the normalized match score to become unreliable.

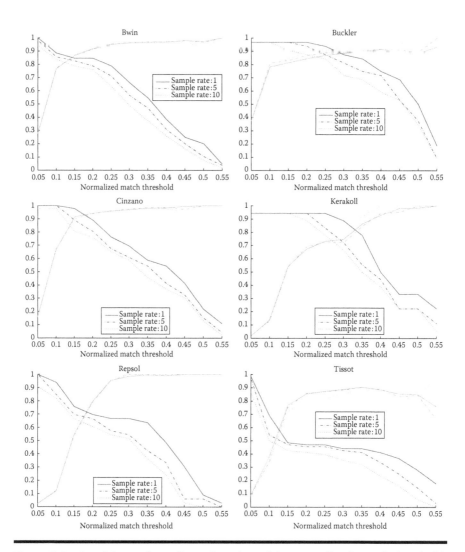

Figure 5.9 Precision and recall as a function of the normalized match threshold. Note that as the threshold increases, more matches are *excluded*. Because of this, recall usually begins at or around 1.0 and is inversely proportional to the normalized match threshold.

We have also experimented with different types of trademark prototypes used for matching. In some cases, the textual and graphical structure of a trademark is enough to distinguish it. In Figure 5.10 are shown results comparing matching performance on synthetic trademarks and on trademark instances cropped directly from the video. In these plots, "bwin1" and "cinzano1" refer to the synthetic images (shown to the right of Figure 5.10). In the case of precision, we can see that, for

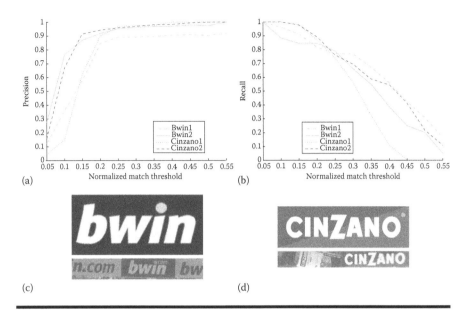

Figure 5.10 Comparison of precision between synthetic trademarks and trademarks cropped from actual video frames. (a) Precision. (b) Recall. (c) Bwin trademarks. (d) Cinzano trademarks. (From Bagdanov, A.D. et al., Trademark matching and retrieval in sports video databases, in *Proceedings of ACM International Workshop on Multimedia Information Retrieval (MIR)*, Augsburg, Bavaria, Germany, 2007. ACM 7/2007, http://www.acm.org/ publications/policies/copyright_policy#Retained)

low values of the normalized match threshold, the synthetic images perform worse than those selected from the video itself. This is due to the fact that many other trademarks consisting of mostly text and graphics are confused for the synthetic trademark models. Recall is affected as well, though not as significantly as precision.

Finally, we have conducted some preliminary experiments using SURF features instead of SIFT since they can speedup our method. To this end, we have replicated the same experimental setup on the SPORTS-VIDEOS dataset. Our results shows that at the same recall values there is a breakdown in precision performance of around 11%.

5.3.3.4 Discussion

In this study case, we analyzed an approach to automatically detect and retrieve trademark occurrences in sports videos. A compact representation of video and trademark content, based on SIFT features, ensures that the technique is robust to occlusions, scale, and perspective variations. In our SPORTS-VIDEOS dataset, on average, a recall rate of better than 85% can be achieved with a precision of approximately 60%. Our robust clustering procedure enables accurate localization of trademark instances and makes the technique robust to spuriously matched points in the video frame, by requiring spatial coherence in the cluster of matched points. Preliminary experiments on sports videos in different domains confirm that the technique can effectively retrieve trademarks in a variety of situations. Results on Formula One races, for example, are comparable to the results presented here for MotoGP. For sports such as soccer and volleyball, however, the approach suffers from the fact that trademarks are usually viewed from a wide-angle vantage and appear at a much lower resolution than in MotoGP and Formula One. This fundamentally limits the ability to detect enough feature points on the trademarks in the video. A possible solution to this problem is to double the resolution of each video frame before processing. However, this has the adverse effect of greatly increasing the amount of time required to detect feature points and perform matching on the (greatly inflated) sets of features.

5.4 Conclusions

In this chapter, we have reviewed the state of the art in commercial and trademark recognition in videos, providing an in-depth analysis of two real-time and quasi-real-time systems. The main issues that have to be solved for commercials recognition regard the problem of scalability, that is, how to recognize the presence of a commercial in a web-scale archive; this problem will become more and more important as video is going to be distributed also through Internet channels and not only using TV channels. Regarding trademark recognition, the main issues are the improvement of recall and scalability. In this case, the problem of scalability is related not only with the number of videos but also with the high number of variations of the same trademark, and with the limits of the robustness of local descriptors to the strong scene variations that occur in sports videos.

References

1. B. Satterwhite and O. Marques. Automatic detection of TV commercials. *IEEE Potentials*, 23(2):9–12, April–May 2004.
2. J.Y. Ho, T. Dhar, and C.B. Weinberg. Playoff payoff: Super bowl advertising for movies. *International Journal of Research in Marketing*, 26(3):168–179, 2009.
3. H.G. Dixon, M.L. Scully, M.A. Wakeeld, V.M. White, and D.A. Crawford. The effects of television advertisements for junk food versus nutritious food on children's food attitudes and preferences. *Social Science & Medicine*, 65(7):1311–1323, 2007.
4. J.-H. Yeh, J.-C. Chen, J.-H. Kuo, and J.-L. Wu. TV commercial detection in news program videos. In *Proceedings of IEEE International Symposium on Circuits and Systems (ISCAS)*, Kobe, Japan, May 2005.

5. L.-Y. Duan, Y.-T. Zheng, J. Wang, H. Lu, and J. Jin. Digesting commercial clips from TV streams. *IEEE MultiMedia*, 15(1):28–41, January–March 2008.

6. J. Sánchez, X. Binefa, J. Vitrià, and P. Radeva. Local color analysis for scene break detection applied to TV commercials recognition. In *Proceedings of International Conference on Visual Information Systems (VISUAL)*, Amsterdam, the Netherlands, 1999.

7. J.M. Sánchez, X. Binefa, and J. Vitrià. Shot partitioning based recognition of TV commercials. *Multimedia Tools and Applications*, 18:233–247, 2002.

8. R. Lienhart, C. Kuhmunch, and W. Eelsberg. On the detection and recognition of television commercials. In *Proceedings of IEEE International Conference on Multimedia Computing and Systems (ICMCS)*, Ottawa, Ontario, Canada, 1997.

9. D.A. Sadlier, S. Marlow, N. O'Connor, and N. Murphy. Automatic TV advertisement detection from MPEG bitstream. *Pattern Recognition*, 35(12):2719–2726, 2002.

10. A. Albiol, M.J. Ch, F.A. Albiol, and L. Torres. Detection of TV commercials. In *Proceedings of IEEE International Conference on Acoustics, Speech, and Signal Processing (ICASSP)*, Montreal, Quebec, Canada, 2004.

11. J. Wang, L. Duan, Z. Li, J. Liu, H. Lu, and J. Jin. A robust method for TV logo tracking in video streams. In *Proceedings of IEEE International Conference on Multimedia & Expo (ICME)*, Toronto, Ontario, Canada, 2006.

12. X.-S. Hua, L. Lu, and H.-J. Zhang. Robust learning-based TV commercial detection. In *Proceedings of IEEE International Conference on Multimedia & Expo (ICME)*, Amsterdam, the Netherlands, 2005.

13. L.-Y. Duan, J. Wang, Y. Zheng, J.S. Jin, H. Lu, and C. Xu. Segmentation, categorization, and identification of commercial clips from TV streams using multimodal analysis. In *Proceedings of ACM International Conference on Multimedia (ACM MM)*, Santa Barbara, CA, 2006.

14. A. Hampapur and R. Bolle. Comparison of distance measures for video copy detection. In *Proceedings of IEEE International Conference on Multimedia & Expo (ICME)*, Tokyo, Japan, 2001.

15. T.C. Hoad and J. Zobel. Fast video matching with signature alignment. In *Proceedings of ACM International Workshop on Multimedia Information Retrieval (MIR)*, Berkeley, CA, 2003.

16. J. Zobel and T.C. Hoad. Detection of video sequences using compact signatures. *ACM Transactions on Information Systems*, 24:1–50, January 2006.

17. D.A. Adjeroh, I. King, and M.C. Lee. A distance measure for video sequences. *Computer Vision and Image Understanding (CVIU)*, 75(1):25–45, 1999.

18. S.H. Kim and R.-H. Park. Ancient algorithm for video sequence matching using the modified Hausdorff distance and the directed divergence. *IEEE Transactions on Circuits and Systems for Video Technology (TCSVT)*, 12(7):592–596, 2002.

19. Y.-T. Kim and T.-S. Chua. Retrieval of news video using video sequence matching. In *Proceedings of Multimedia Modelling Conference*, Melbourne, Victoria, Australia, 2005.

20. J. Law-To, A. Joly, and N. Boujemaa. INRIA-IMEDIA TRECVID 2008: Video copy detection. In *TREC Video Retrieval Evaluation Notebook*, Gaithersburg, MD, 2008.

21. M.-C. Yeh and K.-T. Cheng. Video copy detection by fast sequence matching. In *Proceedings of ACM International Conference on Image and Video Retrieval (CIVR)*, Santorini Island, Greece, 2009.

22. H.-K. Tan, C.-W. Ngo, R. Hong, and T.-S. Chua. Scalable detection of partial near-duplicate videos by visual-temporal consistency. In *Proceedings of ACM International Conference on Multimedia (ACM MM)*, Beijing, China, 2009.

23. M. Douze, H. Jégou, C. Schmid, and P. Pérez. Compact video description for copy detection with precise temporal alignment. In *Proceedings of the 11th European conference on Computer Vision: Part I, ser. ECCV'10*. Springer-Verlag, Berlin/Heidelberg, Germany, 2010, pp. 522–535. [Online]. Available: http://portal.acm.org/citation.cfm?id=1886063.1886103

24. A. Shivadas and J. Gauch. Real-time commercial recognition using color moments and hashing. In *Proceedings of Canadian Conference on Computer and Robot Vision (CRV)*, Montreal, Quebec, Canada, 2007.

25. X. Wu, N. Putpuek, and S. Satoh. Commercial film detection and identification based on a dual-stage temporal recurrence hashing algorithm. In *Proceedings of International Workshop on Very-Large-Scale Multimedia Corpus, Mining and Retrieval (VLS-MCMR'10)*, Firenze, Italy, 2010.

26. A.G. Hauptmann and M.J. Witbrock. Story segmentation and detection of commercials in broadcast news video. In *Proceedings of Advances in Digital Libraries Conference*, Santa Barbara, CA, 1998.

27. M. Bertini, A. Del Bimbo, and W. Nunziati. Video clip matching using MPEG-7 descriptors and edit distance. In *Proceedings of ACM International Conference on Image and Video Retrieval (CIVR)*, Tempe, AZ, 2006.

28. Y. Li, D. Zhang, X. Zhou, and J.S. Jin. A confidence based recognition system for TV commercial extraction. In *Proceedings of ADC*, Ballarat, Victoria, Australia, 2007.

29. D. Zhao, X. Wang, Y. Qian, Q. Liu, and S. Lin. Fast commercial detection based on audio retrieval. In *Proceedings of IEEE International Conference on Multimedia & Expo (ICME)*, Hannover, Germany, 2008.

30. H. Duxans, D. Conejero, and X. Anguera. Audio-based automatic management of TV commercials. In *Proceedings of IEEE International Conference on Acoustics, Speech, and Signal Processing (ICASSP)*, Taipei, Taiwan, 2009.

31. P. Duygulu, M.-Y. Chen, and A.G. Hauptmann. Comparison and combination of two novel commercial detection methods. In *Proceedings of IEEE International Conference on Multimedia & Expo (ICME)*, Taipei, Taiwan, 2004.

32. N. Liu, Y. Zhao, and Z. Zhu. Coarse-to-ne based matching for audio commercial recognition. In *Proceedings of International Conference on Neural Networks and Signal Processing (ICNNSP)*, Zhenjiang, China, 2008.

33. N. Liu, Y. Zhao, and Z. Zhu. Commercial recognition in TV streams using coarse-to-ne matching strategy. In *Proceedings of Advances in Multimedia Information Processing (PCM)*, Shanghai, China, 2010.

34. R. Mohan. Video sequence matching. In *Proceedings of IEEE International Conference on Acoustics, Speech, and Signal Processing (ICASSP)*, Seattle, WA, 1998.

35. A. Hampapur and R. Bolle. Feature based indexing for media tracking. In *Proceedings of IEEE International Conference on Multimedia & Expo (ICME)*, New York City, NY, 2000.

36. K.M. Pua, J.M. Gauch, S.E. Gauch, and J.Z. Miadowicz. Real time repeated video sequence identification. *Computer Vision and Image Understanding (CVIU)*, 93(3): 310–327, 2004.

37. J. Oostveen, T. Kalker, and J. Haitsma. Feature extraction and a database strategy for video fingerprinting. In *Proceedings of International Conference on Visual Information Systems (VISUAL)*, Hsinchu, Taiwan, 2002.

38. Y. Li, J. Jin, and X. Zhou. Matching commercial clips from TV streams using a unique, robust and compact signature. In *Proceedings of Digital Image Computing: Techniques and Applications (DICTA)*, Cairns, Australia, 2005.

39. A. Sarkar, V. Singh, P. Ghosh, B. Manjunath, and A. Singh. Efficient and robust detection of duplicate videos in a large database. In *IEEE Transactions on Circuits and Systems for Video Technology (TCSVT)*, 20(6):870–885, June 2010.

40. D. DeMenthon and D. Doermann. Video retrieval using spatio-temporal descriptors. In *Proceedings of ACM International Conference on Multimedia (ACM MM)*, Berkeley, CA, 2003.

41. S. Satoh, M. Takimoto, and J. Adachi. Scene duplicate detection from videos based on trajectories of feature points. In *Proceedings of ACM International Workshop on Multimedia Information Retrieval (MIR)*, Augsburg, Bavaria, Germany, 2007.

42. X. Wu, M. Takimoto, S. Satoh, and J. Adachi. Scene duplicate detection based on the pattern of discontinuities in feature point trajectories. In *Proceedings of ACM International Conference on Multimedia (ACM MM)*, Vancouver, British Columbia, Canada, 2008.

43. X. Wu, A.G. Hauptmann, and C.-W. Ngo. Practical elimination of near-duplicates from web video search. In *Proceedings of ACM International Conference on Multimedia (ACM MM)*, Augsburg, Germany, 2007.

44. O. Chum, J. Philbin, M. Isard, and A. Zisserman. Scalable near identical image and shot detection. In *Proceedings of ACM International Conference on Image and Video Retrieval (CIVR)*, Amsterdam, the Netherlands, 2007.

45. O. Chum, J. Philbin, and A. Zisserman. Near duplicate image detection: min-hash and tf-idf weighting. In *Proceedings of British Machine Vision Conference (BMVC)*, London, U.K., 2008.

46. E.Y. Chang, H. Bai, and K. Zhu. Parallel algorithms for mining large-scale rich-media data. In *Proceedings of ACM International Conference on Multimedia (ACM MM)*, Vancouver, British Columbia, Canada, 2009.

47. C. Colombo, A. Del Bimbo, and P. Pala. Retrieval of commercials by semantic content: The semiotics perspective. *Multimedia Tools and Applications*, 13(1):93–118, 2001.

48. Y. Zheng, L. Duan, Q. Tian, and J. Jin. TV commercial classification by using multi-modal textual information. In *Proceedings of IEEE International Conference on Multimedia & Expo (ICME)*, Toronto, Ontario, Canada, 2006.

49. J. Wang, L. Duan, L. Xu, H. Lu, and J.S. Jin. TV ad video categorization with probabilistic latent concept learning. In *Proceedings of ACM International Workshop on Multimedia Information Retrieval (MIR)*, Augsburg, Bavaria, Germany, 2007.

50. T. Hofmann. Probabilistic latent semantic indexing. In *Proceedings of ACM International Conference on Research and Development in Information Retrieval (SIGIR)*, Berkeley, CA, 1999.

51. G. Navarro. A guided tour to approximate string matching. *ACM Computing Surveys*, 33(1):31–88, 2001.

52. B. Manjunath, J.-R. Ohm, and V. Vasudevan. Color and texture descriptors. *IEEE Transactions on Circuits and Systems for Video Technology (TCSVT)*, 11(6):703–715, June 2001.

53. E. Kasutani and A. Yamada. The MPEG-7 color layout descriptor: A compact image feature description for high-speed image/video segment retrieval. In *Proceedings of IEEE International Conference on Image Processing (ICIP)*, Thessaloniki, Greece, 2001.

54. P.H. Sellers. The theory and computation of evolutionary distances: Pattern recognition. *Journal of Algorithms*, 1(4):359–373, 1980. [Online]. Available: http://www.sciencedirect.com/science/article/B6WH3-4D7JN56-4T/2/2b859d72a68774d0a51959fda148c6b3

55. F. Aldershoff and T. Gevers. Visual tracking and localisation of billboards in streamed soccer matches. In *Proceedings of SPIE*, San Jose, CA, 2004.

56. N. Ichimura. Recognizing multiple billboard advertisements in videos. In *Proceedings of IEEE Pacific-Rim Symposium on Image and Video Technology*, Hsinchu, Taiwan, December 2006.

57. A.D. Bagdanov, L. Ballan, M. Bertini, and A. Del Bimbo. Trademark matching and retrieval in sports video databases. In *Proceedings of ACM International Workshop on Multimedia Information Retrieval (MIR)*, Augsburg, Bavaria, Germany, 2007.

58. A. Watve and S. Sural. Soccer video processing for the detection of advertisement billboards. *Pattern Recognition Letters*, 29(7):994–1006, 2008.

59. A. Joly and O. Buisson. Logo retrieval with a contrario visual query expansion. In *Proceedings of ACM Multimedia (ACM MM)*, Beijing, China, 2009.

60. J. Schietse, J.P. Eakins, and R.C. Veltkamp. Practice and challenges in trademark image retrieval. In *Proceedings of ACM International Conference on Image and Video Retrieval (CIVR)*, Amsterdam, the Netherlands, 2007.

61. T. Kato. Database architecture for content-based image retrieval. *Proceedings of SPIE Image Storage and Retrieval Systems*, 1662:112–123, 1992.

62. J.P. Eakins, J.M. Boardman, and M.E. Graham. Similarity retrieval of trademark images. *IEEE Multimedia*, 5(2):53–63, 1998.

63. W.H. Leung and T. Chen. Trademark retrieval using contour-skeleton stroke classification. In *Proceedings of IEEE International Conference on Multimedia & Expo (ICME)*, Lausanne, Switzerland, 2002.

64. C.-H. Wei, Y. Li, W.-Y. Chau, and C.-T. Li. Trademark image retrieval using synthetic features for describing global shape and interior structure. *Pattern Recognition*, 42(3):386–394, 2009.

65. M. Rusiñol and J. Lladós. Efficient logo retrieval through hashing shape context descriptors. In *Proceedings of International Workshop on Document Analysis Systems*, Boston, MA, 2010.

66. S. Belongie, J. Malik, and J. Puzicha. Shape matching and object recognition using shape contexts. *IEEE Transactions on Pattern Analysis and Machine Intelligence (TPAMI)*, 24(4):509–522, 2002.

67. M. Merler, C. Galleguillos, and S. Belongie. Recognizing groceries in situ using in vitro training data. In *Proceedings of IEEE CVPR SLAM-Workshop*, Minneapolis, MN, June 2007.

68. Y. Jing and S. Baluja. Pagerank for product image search. In *Proceedings of WWW*, Beijing, China, 2008.

69. B. Kovar and A. Hanjalic. Logo appearance statistics in a sport video: Video indexing for sponsorship revenue control. In *Proceedings of SPIE*, San Diego, CA, 2002.

70. R.J.M. Den Hollander and A. Hanjalic. Logo recognition in video by line profile classification. In *Proceedings of SPIE*, pp. 300–306, 2004.

71. F. Pelisson, D. Hall, O. Ri, and J.L. Crowley. Brand identification using Gaussian derivative histograms. *Machine Vision and Applications*, 16:41–46, 2003.

72. R. Phan, J. Chia, and D. Androutsos. Unconstrained logo and trademark retrieval in general color image database using color edge gradient co-occurrence histograms. In *Proceedings of IEEE International Conference on Acoustics, Speech, and Signal Processing (ICASSP)*, Las Vegas, NV, 2008.

73. R. Phan and D. Androutsos. Content-based retrieval of logo and trademarks in unconstrained color image databases using color edge gradient co-occurrence histograms. *Computer Vision and Image Understanding (CVIU)*, 114(1):66–84, 2010.

74. J. Luo and D. Crandall. Color object detection using spatial-color joint probability functions. *IEEE Transactions on Image Processing (TIP)*, 15(6):1443–1453, 2006.

75. D.G. Lowe. Distinctive image features from scale-invariant keypoints. *International Journal of Computer Vision*, 60(2):91–110, 2004.

76. J. Kleban, X. Xie, and W.-Y. Ma. Spatial pyramid mining for logo detection in natural scenes. In *Proceedings of IEEE International Conference on Multimedia & Expo (ICME)*, Hannover, Germany, 2008.

77. T. Quack, V. Ferrari, B. Leibe, and L. Van Gool. Efficient mining of frequent and distinctive feature configurations. In *Proceedings of International Conference on Computer Vision*, Rio de Janeiro, Brazil, 2007.

78. K. Gao, S. Lin, Y. Zhang, S. Tang, and D. Zhang, Logo detection based on spatial-spectral saliency and partial spatial context. In *Proceedings of IEEE International Conference on Multimedia & Expo (ICME)*, New York City, NY, 2009.

CONTENT STRUCTURING

Chapter 6

TV Program Structuring Techniques

A Review

Alina Elma Abduraman
Orange Labs

Sid Ahmed Berrani
Orange Labs

Bernard Merialdo
EURECOM

Contents

6.1 Introduction

The objective of this chapter is to present the problem of TV program structuring and its applications in real-world services and to provide a panorama of existing techniques.

Due to the high number of television channels and their various audiovisual content, the amount of broadcasted TV programs has grown significantly. Consequently, data organization and tools to efficiently manipulate and manage TV programs are needed. TV channels broadcast audiovisual streams, in a linear way, 24/7. This makes the content available only at the broadcast time. Services like Catch-up TV and PVRs remove this constraint and allow users to watch previously broadcasted TV programs. To enable these services, TV programs have to be extracted, stored, indexed, and prepared for a later usage. Additional indexing steps are also required. After choosing a program, the user might want to get an overview of the program before watching it. He or she might also want to directly access a specific part of the program, to find a certain moment of interest or to skip a part of the program, and go to the following one or even to the final one. These features represent an alternative for the basic fast forward/backward options. The value of these features was explored by Li et al. [25], where users were provided with such capabilities for a wide variety of video content. The results showed that the users found the ability to browse video content very useful for the reasons of time saving and the feeling of control over what they watched.

Program extraction requires a macro-segmentation of the TV stream. Macro-segmentation algorithms generally rely on detecting "inter-programs," which include commercials, trailers, jingles, and credits. These are easier to detect as they have a set of common properties related to their duration and visual and audio content. The idea is to detect these inter-programs and to deduce the long programs as the rest of the stream. Metadata (like EIT or EPG) can be used afterward to annotate the programs.

As for nonlinear TV program browsing and summary generation, the original structure of TV programs has to be recovered and all possible moments of interest have to be precisely tagged. A similar option exists on DVDs, where an anchor-point indicates the different chapters of the video. But in order to obtain such a representation, a human observer is required to watch the entire video and locate the important boundaries. Obviously this could be done in the case of TV programs also, but these preprocessing steps are costly and highly time consuming, especially when dealing with large amount of TV programs, as is the case in real-world services. One challenge is hence to develop content-based automatic tools for TV program structuring. These tools will allow the easy production of information that will give to the users the capability to watch programs on demand or to watch just the parts of the programs they are interested in. As mentioned earlier, another important field where TV program structuring is extremely useful is video summarization [31,32,42]. Video summarization techniques can use the structure of the program and its moments of interest in order to build the best compact overview of the TV program.

A video can be analyzed at different granularity levels. The elementary level is the image/frame, generally used to extract features like color, texture, and shape. The next level is represented by shots, basic video units showing a continuous action in both time and space. Shots are separated by editing effects called transitions. A transition can be abrupt, namely, *cut*, and groups directly successive shots, or *gradual*, and groups together successive shots by different editing effects like dissolve, wipe, fade, etc. Shot boundary detection is the process of identifying the transitions, abrupt (cut) or gradual, between the adjacent shots. Shot boundary detection techniques were intensively studied and a lot of methods have been proposed [53]. The shot, however, is not a relevant level to represent pertinent parts of a program as it usually lasts few seconds and has low semantic content. A video may have hundreds or thousands of shots, which is not practical for human navigation. Therefore, high-level techniques are required to group video shots into a more descriptive segment of the video sequence. These techniques are classified into two wide categories: *specific methods* and *generic methods*.

Specific methods exploit the prior knowledge of the domain in order to construct a structured model of the analyzed video. They can be applied only to very specific types of programs like news, sports programs, series, advertisements, etc. On the other hand, generic methods try to find a universal approach for the structuring of videos independent of their type and based only on their content features.

The rest of the chapter is composed of two main parts presented in the next two sections. They discuss in more detail each of the two types of approaches, the different techniques that were proposed in the literature for their implementation, and their strengths and weaknesses.

6.2 Specific Approaches

Authors who propose specific methods consider that a universal solution for high-level video analysis is very difficult, if not impossible, to achieve [13]. Low-level features generally used for indexing video content are not sufficient to provide a semantically meaningful information. In order to achieve sufficient performance, the approaches have to be specifically adapted to the application. Bertini et al. [3] consider that in order to ease the automatic extraction of high-level features, the specific knowledge of the different types of programs must be considered. Thus, many researches have focused on very specific types of programs like sports programs, movies, advertisements and news broadcasts. The methods they propose are specific methods. Specific methods make use of prior knowledge of the type of the analyzed TV program in order to extract relevant data and construct its structure model. They are supervised as they generally require the prior creation and manual annotation of a training set used to learn the structure. A class of TV programs that are often analyzed by specific methods are sports programs. These have a very well-defined structure. The rules of the game provide prior knowledge that can be used to provide constraints on the appearance of events or the succession of those events. These constraints are very helpful to improve the accuracy of the event detection and categorization. Another class of programs that are most appropriate for this kind of systems are news programs, as they also have a very clear structure. They are produced using almost the same production rules: they consist generally in a succession of reports and anchorperson shots. Specific methods analyze the temporal (the set, reports, advertising, forecast, etc.) and spatial (images with the anchorperson, logos, etc.) structures. Most of the work relies on finding the anchorperson shots and then deducing the sequences of shots representing the reports.

We focus on these two categories of TV programs (sport and news) for the specific approaches as they are the most representative for their class and discuss them in more detail in the next sections.

6.2.1 Approaches for Sports Program Structuring

Sports videos have been actively studied since the 1980s. Due to the fact that sports events attract a large audience and have important commercial applications, they represent an important domain of semantics acquisition. Sports videos are generally broadcasted for several hours. People who miss the live broadcast are often interested in the strongest moments only. Motivated by this need of the users, broadcasters should automatically select and annotate the relevant parts of the video in order to recover the structure and create a table of content that would allow a direct access to the desired parts. Sports videos are characterized by a defined structure, specific domain rules, and knowledge of the visual environment. All these make possible the extraction of the video structure, allowing nonlinear browsing. We distinguish two levels in the sports video analysis: segment and event. In the first case, the objective is to split the video into narrative segments like *play* and *break* through a low-level analysis of the video. The second one assumes a higher-level analysis of the video and its objective is to identify the interesting moments (highlight events) of the sports video. Both of them are predetermined by the type of sport. For example, an event in the case of soccer might be the detection of the goal while for tennis this will be the match points. Therefore, in order to accomplish these objectives the use of prior knowledge is needed. This prior knowledge may be related to the type of the analyzed sport (i.e., game surface, number of players, game rules) but also to the production rules for the video program (i.e., slow-motion replay, camera location and coverage, camera motion, superimposed text [45]).

6.2.1.1 Low Level Analysis of Sports Videos

As mentioned earlier, the first level of semantic segmentation in sports videos is to identify the *play* and *break* segments. For the class of field ball games, a game is in play when the ball is in the field and the game is going on. Out of play is the complement set, when the action has been stopped: ball outside the field, score, audience, coach, play stopped by the referee, etc. Generally any sports game can be segmented into these two mutually exclusive states of the game. The interest in obtaining such a segmentation is that it allows play-by-play browsing and editing. It also facilitates further high-level analysis and detection of more semantically meaningful units as events or highlights. It is claimed that highlights are mainly contained in a play segment [41]. The occurrence of audiovisual features in play/break (P/B) segments show remarkable pattern for different events. For example, a goal event usually happens during a play segment and it is immediately followed by a break. This break is used by the producers to emphasize the event and to show one or more replays for a better visual experience. As a result, the goal event can be described by a pattern that can be defined using the play and break structure. Another benefit of using P/B segmentation is that it reduces significantly the video data (no more than 60% of the video corresponds to a play), as stated in [46]. A sports video is actually composed of continuous successions of play and break sequences. Two major factors influence the sports video syntax: the producer and the game itself. A sports video benefits of typical production rules. Most of the broadcasted sports videos use a variety of camera view shots and additional editing effects such as replay and on-screen captions to describe the sports video content. The different outputs of camera views have successfully been used for P/B segmentation. An example is in [11] where shots are classified in to three classes: long shot, in-field shot, and close-up or out-of-field shot (see Figure 6.1). A long shot displays the global view of the field hence it serves for localization of the events in the field. An in-field medium

(a)   (b)   (c)   (d)

(e)   (f)   (g)   (h)

Figure 6.1   View types in soccer: (a,b) Long view, (c,d) in-field medium view, (e,f) close-up view, and (g,h) out-of-field view.

shot is a zoomed-in view of a specific part of the field and it contains usually a whole human body. A single isolated medium-length shot between two long shots corresponds to a play while a group of nearby medium shots correspond to a break in the game. The replays are also considered medium shots. A close-up shot shows the view of a person and in general indicates a break in the game. Also, out-of-field shots that show the audience, the coach, etc., indicate a break in the game. The classification is made automatically, based on the ratio of grass color pixels (G) for the close-up and out-of-field shots, which have a small value of G. Because the limit between medium or long shots is questionable for the frames with a high value of G, a cinematographic algorithm (golden section composition) is used in order to classify them as long view or in-field medium shots. An analysis of frame to frame change dynamics is performed in order to detect the replays. The same approach is used in [41] where P/B sequences are segmented using the output from camera view classification and replay detection. The camera view classification is performed on each frame using the playing field (or dominant) color ratio, which measures the amount of grass pixels in the frame. As replays are often recognized as play shots because of the global view, even though they should be included as breaks (as they are played during breaks), replay detection is applied to locate additional breaks and to obtain more accurate results. The algorithm is tested on soccer, basketball, and Australian football videos.

In [9], Duan et al., use a mid-level representation, between low-level audiovisual processing and high-level semantic analysis. First, low-level visual and audio features are extracted and a motion vector model, a color tracking model, and a shot pace model (that describes the production rules, effect on the shot length) are developed. These models are then used in a supervised learning algorithm in order to classify shots into predefined classes, e.g., Player Close-up, Field View, Audience. SVM is also used to classify game-specific sounds, e.g., applause, whistling. The semantic classes are specific to the nature of the analyzed sport and are further used to construct a temporal model for representing the production rules of the sport. The sports video shot sequences are partitioned into two logical segments, namely, *in-play segments* (IPS) and *out-of-play segments* (OPS), that occur in successive turns. Based on the temporal model and the semantic shot classes, the in-play and out-of-play segments are determined by checking the shot transition pattern. The approach has been tested on five field ball–type sports. In Xie et al. [46], a stochastic method based on HMMs is proposed for P/B sequence detection. As in previous approaches, dominant color ratio is used, this time along with motion intensity in order to identify the view type of each frame of a soccer video. Motion intensity gives an estimate of the gross motion in the whole frame including object and camera motion. A wide shot with high motion intensity often results from a play, while static wide shot usually occurs during the break in a game. Six HMM models are created for the respective game sequences. Using a sliding window, the likelihood for each of the pretrained (play and break) models is retained. A dynamic programming algorithm is used for the temporal segmentation depending on the transition probabilities between the P/B and the likelihood of each segment to belong to one of the two classes (play or break). The experimental evaluations showed improvement of the performance of the HMM-based algorithm compared to the discrete, rule-based one studied in a previous work of the author [49]. In the last cited one, heuristic rules were used in detecting the view type of the sequences in order to obtain P/B segmentation. The rules took in to consideration the time duration of each view and its relative position in time.

HMMs can also be modeled in a multistream approach [48] to classify shots of soccer or volleyball videos. A multistream is obtained by combining multiple single-stream HMMs and introducing the weight for each stream. For soccer videos, the first stream is the motion feature vector and the second is the color feature vector of each frame. For volleyball videos the processing is similar excepting the features used.

6.2.1.2 High-Level Analysis of Sports Videos

Highlight events in sports videos are composed of the most interesting moments in the video that usually capture the users attention. They represent the exciting scenes in a game, i.e., the goal in a soccer match, the tennis match points, or the pitches in baseball. A lot of research has focused on the detection of interesting events in sports videos, most of it employing rule-based annotation and machine learning or statistics-based annotation. The modalities used to acquire the semantics are either individual or multiple modalities. The main sources of information used for the analysis are the video and audio tracks (because crowd cheers, announcer's excited speech, and ball hits are highly correlated with the exciting segments). Also, editing effects such as slow-motion replay, or close caption information that accompanies the sports program and that provides information of the game status, are used for detecting important events. Within each of these, the features used for the program segmentation may be general (i.e., shot boundary detection) or domain specific (i.e., the center line on a soccer field is vertical or almost vertical in frame [52]). As the highlights are specific to each type of sport, most of the approaches make use of sport-specific features. The features used for semantic analysis of sports videos can also be considered as cinematic or object-based features. The cinematic ones are those that result from the production rules, such as camera views and replays. Sport video production is characterized by the use of a limited number of cameras on fixed positions. The different type of views are very closely related to the events in the video and for each type of sport a pattern can be identified. As an example, during a rally in a tennis video, a global view of the camera, filming the entire court is selected. Right after the rally, a close-up of the player that just scored a point is captured [20]. In the soccer videos a goal is indicated by a close-up on the player who just carried out the important scene, followed by a view of the audience and a slow-motion replay. Moreover, starting from close-up shots, the player's identity can be automatically annotated using face recognition techniques and based on textual cues automatically read from the player's jersey or from text caption [4].

For the case of object-based features, they are used for high-level analysis of sports videos. Objects are described by their color, texture, shape, and motion information. Using even more extensive prior knowledge, they are localized in different frames and their motion trajectories are identified and used for the detection of important events. As example in diving videos, player body shape segmentation and transition is used to represent the action [26].

As a result, high-level analysis in sports videos can be done based on the occurrences of specific audio and visual information that can be automatically extracted from the sports video.

6.2.1.2.1 Rule-Based Approaches

Many of the existing works on event detection use rule-based approaches to extract a predictable pattern and construct, manually or automatically, a set of rules by analyzing the combination of specific features. In order to analyze different sports, Duan et al. [9] used a mid-level representation, between low-level audio-visual processing and high-level semantic analysis. As described in the previous section, predefined semantic shot classes are used to facilitate high-level analysis. Based on production rules, a general temporal model is developed and coarse event (in-play)/nonevent (out-of-play) segments are identified. Richer events are classified in a hierarchy of *regular events*, which can be found in the transitions between in-play and out-of-play segments, and *tactic events* that usually occur inside the in-play segments. To identify the regular events, the semantic shot classes and audio keywords are exploited in order to derive heuristic rules according to game-specific rules. For example, a soccer goal occurs if there are many *close-up* shots, *persistent excited commentator speech* and *excited audience*, and long duration within the OPS segment. For tennis, events like serve, return, score, etc., are detected by analyzing audio keywords like *hitting ball* and *applause* to compute the ball hitting times and the intervals between two ball hits and the applause sound at the end of court view shots. Because of the use of audio keywords, the precision in detecting some events (i.e., goal for soccer) can be low due to the confusion from the loud environmental audience sound. Tactic events are strongly dependent on the game-specific knowledge and are detected using object features. To identify *take the net* and *rally* in tennis games, player tracking is employed. Player tracking and its movement over time also used by Kim et al. [23] to detect the locations where the play evolution in soccer games will proceed, e.g., where interesting events will occur. A ground-level motion of players at each step is extracted from individual players movement using multiple views and a dense motion field is generated. Using this field the locations where the motion converges are detected. This could represent an important application for automated live broadcasting. Player localization is viewed as a K partite graph problem by Hamid et al. [18]. Nodes in each partite of the graph are blobs of the detected players in different cameras. The edges of the graph are a function of pair-wise similarity between blobs observed in camera pairs and their corresponding ground plane distances. The correspondence between a player's blob observed in different cameras is treated as a K-length cycle in the graph. Yu et al. [52] use players motion intensity, along with other object features and low-level features, to rapidly detect the boundary of interesting events indicated by the gamelog. The instant semantics acquisition and fast detection of event boundaries are important for the two interactive broadcast services for the live soccer video they propose. The first one is a *live event alert* service that informs mobile viewers of important events of a live soccer game, by providing a video clip of the event with a time lag between 30 s and 1.5 min. The second one is *the on-the-fly language selection* and allows users to choose their preferred contents and preferred language. To improve the accuracy of event boundaries detection, object features are used. The center line of a soccer field is detected based on the knowledge that this line is vertical or almost vertical in every frame. The goal mouth is also detected based on prior knowledge: the two posts are almost vertical, the goal posts and goal bar are bold line segments and compared with the center line and side lines and the goal posts are shorter line segments. Guziec [17] tracks also specific objects, as the ball during pitches in baseball games, to show as replays if the strike and ball decisions were correct. The implemented system was launched in 2001 during *ESPN's Sunday Night Baseball* and it tracked pitches with an extremely low failure rate. The real-time tracking involves the use of extensive prior knowledge about the game and system setup (i.e., camera locations and coverage). Considering that object-based features are computationally costly, Ekin et al. [11] try to use more cinematic features to detect certain events in soccer videos and employ the object-based ones only when needed, to increase the accuracy. Therefore, after classifying shots and segmenting the video into P/B segments (see previous section), events like goal, red-yellow cards, and penalties are detected. For goal detection, a pattern is computed using only cinematic features, resulted from common rules used by producers after goal events. The red-yellow cards are indirectly identified by locating the referee by their distinguishable colored uniform. The penalty box is detected based on the *three-parallel-line rule* that defines the penalty box area in the soccer field. All these approaches use an extensive prior knowledge of the game and production rules. Most of them are based on manual observation and heuristic knowledge. In order to reduce the amount of knowledge used for sports video analysis and make the framework more flexible for different sports, Tjondronegoro et al. proposed in [41] a knowledge-discounted event detection approach in sports videos. The highlights contained in each P/B sequence are classified using a set of statistical features (e.g., sequence duration, break ratio, play ratio, replay duration, near goal ratio, excitement ratio, and close-up view ratio) calculated from the P/B sequence. During a training phase, each of the predefined events were characterized using the set of statistics and the heuristic rules were constructed. To classify which highlight is contained in a P/B segment, a score is used for each statistical feature. The value of each calculated feature is compared to the trained one, and if the value falls within the trained statistics of the highlight, the corresponding score is incremented. The highest score will indicate the most likely highlight contained in the P/B segment.

6.2.1.2.2 Machine Learning–Based Approaches

Other approaches that try to use a modest quantity of prior knowledge, only needed for selecting the features that match the most with the event, are approaches based on machine learning. For example, hidden Markov models, which have been proven to be effective for sequential pattern analysis, can be used to model tennis units like *missed first serve, rally, break*, and *replay* based on the temporal relationship between shots and with respect to editing and game rules [21]. Visual features are used to characterize the type of view of each shot. HMMs are also utilized to recognize the action and index highlights in diving and jump game videos [26]. The highlight in diving videos is described by the entire diving action. As the action occurs many times in the video and the distance between two action clips is regular, these are detected by motion segmentation and a hierarchical agglomerative clustering. Then the action is recognized based on body shape segmentation and shape transitions modeled by continuous HMMs. The Baum-Welch algorithm is used to train the HMMs and the Viterbi algorithm is used to calculate each model's output probability. The model with the maximum probability is the recognition result. The HMMs can also be modeled in a multilayered approach to detect events like *offence at left/right court, fast break at left/right court*, etc., in basketball videos [48]. Instead of detecting and tracking objects, the statistical learning approach is used to build semantic models based on a set of motion features. HMMs are also used to model audio sequences. In [45], the plopping sound is modeled with HMMs in order to identify the highlights in diving sports videos. As it has been proven that browsing highlight with contextual cues together is preferred, slow-motion replay and game statistics information in superimposed captions are extracted. It might happen that announcer's exciting speech and audience applause exceed the plopping sound, making it hard to take a correct decision. Special sound effects like announcer's excited speech (detected using learning machines) and ballhits (detected using directional templates) have also been employed to detect highlights in baseball programs [37]. A probabilistic framework is used to combine the two sources of information. If an audio segment has a high probability to be an excited speech segment and occurs right after a frame that has a high probability to contain a baseball hit, then it is very likely for the segment to be an exciting (highlight) segment. Audio and video markers together are used in [47] to detect highlights in sports videos like soccer, baseball, and golf. A Gaussian mixture model has been generated for each predefined audio class (applause, cheering, commentator's excited speech, music) and used to identify the audio markers. For the visual ones, an object detection algorithm such as Viola and

Jones has been used to detect the pattern in which the catcher squats waiting for the pitcher to pitch the ball in baseball games, the players bending to hit the golf ball in golf sports and appearance of the goal post in soccer games. Other approaches for event/highlight detection in sports videos propose the use of neural networks to classify shots into predefined classes and utilize them for further processing [1], or AND-OR graphs to learn a storyline model from weakly labeled data using linguistic cues annotations and visual data [16].

6.2.2 *Approaches for News Program Structuring*

A second class of programs very appropriate for the specific systems are the news programs. Compared to the sports programs, the work related to news programs is much more extensive and dates for a long time. This might be partially due to their regular structure that makes the analysis much easier. Indeed, most news videos exhibit a similar and well-defined structure (Figure 6.2).

They usually start with a general view of the set during which the anchorperson announces the main titles that will be developed later (the highlights). The rest of the program is organized as a succession of TV reports (stories) and segments where the anchorperson announces the next topic. Each story generally begins with an anchorperson segment that provides the general description of the event and continues with a more detailed report and sometimes interview segments. At the end of a story an anchor segment may reappear to give a summary or conclusion. Most news broadcasts end with reports on sport, weather, and finance. Commercials may also appear during the broadcast.

6.2.2.1 *Shots Classification*

The fundamental step in recovering the structure of a news program is to classify the shots into different classes (anchorperson, report, weather forecast, interview, etc.).

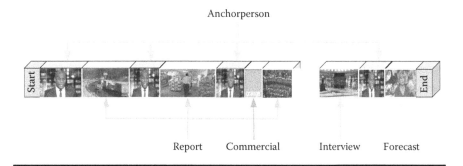

Figure 6.2   The structure of a TV news program.

Then, based on this classes video segmentation into story units can be performed. Detecting anchorperson shots plays an important role in most of the news video segmentation approaches. The anchorperson shots exhibit a lot of characteristics that make their detection easier. Early approaches used properties like the fact that the same anchorperson appears during the same news program and the background remains unchanged during the entire shot. They also considered that anchorperson shots are usually filmed with a static camera so the anchorperson will always be situated in the same place of the image. Furthermore, each TV channel has representative semantic objects, like logos or captions with the anchorperson's name, which are displayed only during news program. All of these made possible the detection of anchorperson shots by **template matching techniques** based on weighted similarity measures and model images. Zhang et al. [56] proposed a spatial structure model for the anchorperson frame based on a composition of distinctive regions: the shape of the anchorperson, the caption of reporters names, and the logo of the broadcast channel that appears in the top right part of the image. Recognizing an anchorperson shot involves testing every frame over a frame model, which in turn means testing each frame against the set of region models. However, constructing a set of model images is difficult due to variations from one TV station to another and the matching algorithm is time consuming. Gunsel et al. [15] proposed also semantic object detection and tracking (i.e., faces and logo) using a region matching scheme, where the region of interest is defined by the boundary of the object. The detection of anchorperson shots lies here on a face detection technique, highly used in this purpose. The possible regions where anchorpersons might be situated are extracted using skin detection (color classification) and histograms intersection. These regions are then compared to templates stored in the application database. The prior knowledge of the spatial configuration of the objects included in these shots is used to limit the region of interest during skin detection. The system has some limitations, as it is difficult to track occluded or transparent semantic objects. Also, the interview shots can be confused with anchor shots if the interviewed person has the same spatial position as an anchorperson. In [24], once faces have been detected, procedures including face position analysis, size filter, and dress comparison are used to reduce the possibilities of erroneous identification. In [2], a robust face detector approach is implemented by means of color segmentation, skin color matching, and shape processing. Heuristic rules are then used to detect anchorperson, report/interview and outdoor shots (e.g., one or two face close-ups with a static background are classified as single or double anchor). Uncontrolled illumination conditions can interfere with skin-color model, making the classification rates smaller for report/interview shots. In order to avoid using a model for the anchorperson shot recognition, another property of the anchorperson shots is exploited by researchers for detecting these shots: their recurrent appearance during an entire news broadcast. Based on the fact that shots of the anchorperson are repeated at intervals of variable length and that their content is very similar, Bertini et al. [3] propose a **statistical approach**. They compute for each shot the *shot lifetime*, as "the shortest temporal interval that includes all the occurrences of a shot with similar visual content, within a video." The shots that have the lifetime greater than a threshold are classified as anchorperson shots. Based on the assumption that both the camera and anchorperson are almost motionless in anchor shots, the statistical approach is refined by the use of motion quantity in each shot. A subclassification of anchorperson shots (like *weather forecast*) is obtained considering the speech content of anchorperson shots. High-level information about the shots being broadcasted is also extracted from close captions text. The frequency of occurrence of anchorperson shots and their similarity are also used in [35] where a clustering method is used to group similar key frames into two groups. The smallest group will represent the anchorperson group. The neighboring shots that have key frames with the same label are merged together. A different approach based on frame statistics models frames with HMMs [10]. Feature vectors deriving from color histogram and motion variations across the frames are computed and used to train the HMMs. An HMM is built for each of the predefined six content classes (i.e., newscaster, begin, end, interview, weather forecast, report) and four editing effect classes. Frames are then classified by evaluating the optimal path resulted from the Viterbi algorithm. The system has real-time capabilities as it works three times faster than real time. Other approaches use SVM to identify anchorperson shots. In [28], the first anchorperson shot in the video is detected using key frames frequency and similarity. For each shot, a region of three other neighboring shots on both sides is taken into account for features computation. An SVM is then trained to identify other anchor shots, using features like distance from anchorperson template, semantic text similarity, shot length distance, average visual dissimilarity, and minimum visual dissimilarity between the shots of left and right region. Chaisorn et al. [5–7] define 13 categories (e.g., anchor, 2anchor, interview, sport, finance, weather, commercial) to cover all essential types of shots in typical news videos. First, commercials are eliminated using a heuristic approach based on black frames, still frames, cut rate, and/or audio silence. Weather and finance are then identified using a histogram matching algorithm. Finally, a decision tree is employed to perform the classification of the rest of the shots using a learning-based approach and temporal (audio type, motion activity, shot duration) and high-level features (human faces and video text) extracted from video, audio, and text. The same principle is used in [12]. As anchorperson is one of the most important shot categories, they add a similarity measurement module that uses the background similarity detection to reduce the errors that might appear when identifying the anchorperson shots (anchor shots can easily be confused with speech/interview as they all have similar face features). Thresholds need to be defined for each tested broadcast channel. Gao and Tang [13] classify video shots into anchorperson shots and news footage shots by a graph-theoretical cluster (GTC) analysis. Since anchorperson key frames with identical models have the same background and anchorperson, they thus have similar color histogram and spatial content. Based on this similarity the anchorperson key frames of each model will be grouped together into subtrees of the graph and distinguished from the individually distributed news footage shots.

6.2.2.2 TV News Story Segmentation

Once the shots are classified, a more challenging task is to segment the broadcast into coherent news stories. This means finding the boundaries of every story that succeeds in the video stream. Using the prior knowledge on the structure of a news broadcast and the classified shots, Zhang et al. [55] and Gao and Tang [13] use a temporal structure model to identify the different stories in the broadcast. Ko and Xie [24] extracts boundaries of anchorperson and non-anchorperson shots and use them next to metadata from the video structure to classify the news segments into six predefined categories (e.g., opening animation, headlines, preview, anchorperson greeting, news stories, weather forecast, and closing scene). As TV channels have different programming and scheduling formats for the news videos, before performing the categorization, metadata from every channel need to be determined by separately analyzing each structure. In [15], consecutive anchorperson-news footage shots are combined into *news units* according to a set of predefined rules. For example, *the anchorperson shot(s) followed by a commercial are combined with the last news unit, the news footage shot(s) following a commercial are considered a part of the next news unit*, etc. In [30], dynamic programming is used to detect *relevant video segments* (important situations) by associating image data and language data. For each of the two clues, several categories are introduced. Intermodal coincidence between the two clues indicates important situations. A considerable number of association failures are due to detection errors and time lag between close caption and actual speech. Other approaches use finite state automatons [22,27] or HMMs to model shot sequences and identify story boundaries. Chaisorn et al. [6,7] represent each shot by a feature vector based on the shot category, scene/location change, and speaker change and model it with ergodic HMMs. A similar approach is used in [12]. In addition, a pre-segmentation module based on heuristic rules is added to join together intro/highlights shots or weather shots that can be seen as a single story logical unit. Because in the output of the analysis using HMMs in [6,7] there were embedded pattern rules, in [5] a global rule induction technique is used instead of HMMs. Pattern rules are learned in a form similar to the if-then-else syntax, from training data. The results are slightly lower compared to the use of HMMs but this method has reduced computational cost and complexity. Text is also highly used for story boundaries detection in news videos. An example is in [34] where a fully automatic television news summarization and extraction system (ANSES) is built. Shots are merged into story units based on the similarity between text keywords, extracted from the teletext subtitles that come along with the broadcast. The assumption made is that story boundaries always coincide with shot boundaries. Keywords are extracted from the subtitles and tagged with their part of speech (noun, verb, etc.). Each type of word has a score. A similarity measure is computed and each text segment is compared to each of its five neighbors on either side. When the similarity exceeds a certain threshold, the segments and their corresponding video shots are merged. In [28], closed captions text along with video stream is used to segment TV news into stories. For text, the latent Dirichlet allocation (LDA) model is used to estimate the coherence of a segment and thus provide its boundaries. The assumption made is that *each document is represented by a specific topic distribution and each topic has an underlying word distribution.* In this manner, a coherent segment (containing only one story) will have only a few active topics, while a noncoherent segment (that contains more than one story) will have a comparatively higher number of active topics. Using the same vocabulary as for the training corpus and a fixed number of topics, the likelihood of a segment is computed and used as a score for performing the text segmentation task. For the video-based segmentation, anchorperson shots are identified (as described in the previous section) and story boundaries are identified based on the assumption that a story always begins with an anchorperson shot. The two detected boundaries from both approaches are fused using the "or" operator in order to improve the accuracy of story segmentation. The main drawback of the approach is that words that did not appear during training are dropped and whenever an anchorperson shot has been missed, the story boundary will also be missed.

6.3 Generic Approaches

Generic methods are independent of the type of the video and try to structure it in an unsupervised way, without using any prior knowledge. Due to the fact that they do not rely on a specific model, they are applicable to a large category of videos. The restraints of a certain domain are no longer available. As already mentioned in the introduction, the first step into building a structured description of a video is to segment it into elementary shots. A shot is the smallest continuous unit of a video document. But shots are too small and too numerous to assure an efficient and relevant structure of a video. Therefore, in order to segment the video into semantically richer entities, shots need to be grouped into higher-level segments, namely, *scenes*. A scene is generally composed of a small number of shots all related to the same subject, ongoing event, or theme [45,54]. However, the definition of a scene is very ambiguous and depends on the subjective human understanding of its meaning. In the literature they are also named "video paragraphs" [19], "video segments" [43,54], "story units" [38,50,51], or "chapters" [39]. Existing scene segmentation techniques can be classified in two categories: the ones using only visual features and others using multimodal features. Both of them compute the scene segmentation either by clustering the shots into scenes based on their similarities (using the similarities inside a scene), or by emphasizing the differences between the scenes. Even though the goal is the same, the differences appear in the choice of the parameters and their thresholds. The challenge lies thus in finding the appropriate set of features that would lead to a correct identification of the scenes in a video. An objective evaluation of these methods assumes the existence of a ground truth (GT) at the scene level. But this GT is human generated so it is hard to make a reliable comparison of the performance of different approaches based on subjective judgments.

6.3.1 Visual Similarity–Based Scene Segmentation

A first group of scene segmentation approaches is based on the visual similarity between the shots of the video document. In this manner, Yeung and Liw [50] use two metrics of similarity based on color and luminance information to match video shots and cluster them into scenes. From these metrics, a dissimilarity index is derived and based on it a proximity matrix for the video shots is built. The algorithm first groups the pairs of shots that are the most similar and then proceeds to group the other shots by their proximity values (dissimilarity indices). The main drawback of this approach is that it may happen that two shots belonging to different scenes are found visually similar and thus grouped into the same cluster (e.g., several scenes can take place in the same room, or several shots show the same person but were taken far apart in time). Therefore, the visual similarity of shots alone is not sufficient to differentiate the context of a shot and to produce a good structure of the video. In order to overcome this difficulty, time-constrained clustering was proposed. The general idea is to group successive shots into meaningful clusters along the temporal dimension so that all the shots in a scene are relevant to a common event [45]. Different approaches have been proposed in the literature, most of them are based on the principle of scene transition graph (STG). Yeung and Yeo [51] use an STG in order to segment videos into story units. The nodes are clusters of visually similar shots and the edges indicate the temporal flow of the story. A fixed temporal threshold is used to delimitate distant shots. In this way only shots that fall within the time window can be clustered together. An edge exists between two nodes only if there is a shot represented by the first node that immediately precedes a shot represented by the second node. The *cut edges* are used in order to partition the graph into disjoint subgraphs. Each subgraph represents a story unit. The variation of clustering parameters (e.g., time window parameter) is also discussed. Rasheed and Shah [36] exploits the same idea of an STG. They construct a weighted undirected graph called shot similarity graph (SSG). Each node represents a shot. Edges between the shots are weighted by their color and motion similarity and also with the temporal distance. Scene boundaries are detected by splitting this graph into subgraphs, so as to maximize the intra-subgraph similarities and minimize the inter-subgraph similarities. The choice of the values for the visual dissimilarity threshold and temporal parameter can generate over/under-segmentation depending on the length and type of video. This problem is discussed in [57] where a similar approach is implemented, but, moreover, the temporal parameter is estimated as depending on the number of shots in the video. When the shot number is large, the temporal parameter should increase so as to avoid the over-segmentation and vice versa.

In [54], another approach for scene segmentation is proposed, based on the Markov chain Monte Carlo (MCMC) algorithm. Based on the visual similarity between all pairs of shots in the video, each shot is assumed to have a likelihood of being declared a scene boundary. The scene boundaries are first initialized randomly and then automatically updated based on two types of updates: diffusion (shifting of boundaries) and jumps (merging or splitting two adjacent shots). Finally, the shots with the highest likelihood in their neighborhoods are declared as scene boundary locations. The method does not require the use of any fixed threshold (resolving the problem of over/under-segmentation).

As montage and cinematic rules are widely used by producers to put shots together into coherent stories, Tavanapong and Zhow [40] introduce a more strict definition of the scene based on continuity editing techniques in film literature. First, visual features are extracted from two predetermined regions of the key frames. These regions were carefully chosen to capture the essential area of frames according to the scene definition. A "background" region will be used to identify shots in the same setting and a "two corners" region to detect events like the traveling event. For each key frame a feature vector is computed. Guided by the strict definition and predefined editing rules (background criterion, upper corner criterion, lower corner criterion), the extracted features are compared in order to cluster together shots of the same scene.

6.3.2 Multimodal Similarity–Based Scene Segmentation

A second category of methods use the combination of features extracted from video, audio, and/or text in order to segment videos into scenes. Therefore, in [33] a scheme for identifying scenes by clustering shots according to detected dialogs and similar settings and audio was developed. Shots are recovered from the video and values for each semantic feature are calculated: background and cuts are identified for audio, frontal face detection is used for recovering the shot/reverse shot pattern for dialog determination, and color and orientation for settings determination. Shots are merged into scenes based on computed distances with respect to each feature. This results in different types of scenes depending on the underlying feature. The scenes of different types are also combined to construct better setting scenes, by merging the clusters that overlap into clusters of maximum size. Difficulties were encountered in audio sequence detection based on speech. The experiments showed also that the merging of all the features does not significantly improve the performance.

In [8], a different approach based on video and audio attention is proposed to automatically detect scenes in videos. Attentive video features are extracted and used to segment the video into shots. Scene changes are detected based on the Euclidean distance among attentive audio features of two neighboring shots. The shots whose audio distance is lower than a threshold are merged into a scene.

In [38], two multi-modal automatic scene segmentation techniques are proposed (audio and video), both building upon the STG. First, a visual STG is created as in [51] and the cut edges are identified as the set of scene boundaries. Second, audio analysis is employed and a similar audio-based STG is constructed, in parallel to the video STG. The technique proposed for combining the results of the two graphs involves the creation of multiple video and audio graphs using different construction parameters each time. A measure of confidence is computed for each boundary between shots, which was identified as scene boundary over the total number of generated video STGs and separately on the total number of audio STGs. These confidence values are linearly combined and all shot boundaries for which the resulted confidence value exceeds a threshold will form the set of scene boundaries. The approach was tested over only three documentary films and research still needs to be done for the optimization of the weights controlling the combination of the audio and visual graphs. In [14], audio and visual features are extracted for every visual shot. Using these features and a support vector machine (SVM) each shot boundary is classified as scene change/non-scene change. The drawback of this method is that it requires the availability of sufficient training data.

Based on the fact that scenes in videos are constructed by producers based on some cinematic rules, Wang and Chua [44] use the concept of continuity to model these rules and extract the scene boundaries. After segmenting the video into shots, the framework successively (from lower level to higher level features) applies the concept of visual, position, camera focal distance, motion, audio, and semantic continuity to group into scenes the shots that exhibit some form of continuity. An example of relation between cinematic rules and continuity might be that "visual continuity exists between shots with similar background" but "similar background models the scenes that happen at the same time and in the same location." For the case of audio continuity, "the same scene should possess the similar environment sound and dialog by the same speakers, especially for dialog scenes." The framework is tested using the first three levels of continuity to extract the scenes defined using most common cinematic rules.

Yamamoto et al. [39] propose another approach for semantic segmentation of TV programs based on the detection and classification of corner subtitles. These are considered as indicating the structure of a program based on the fact that they stay on the screen and switch at semantic scene changes. Corner subtitle with similar features are grouped as relative subtitles based on their color, location on the screen, and segment location on the time axis. Chapter points are then detected according to the distribution of the relative subtitles. Three patterns of the program are manually defined according to broadcasted TV programs.

6.4 Conclusion

As stated in the introduction, TV program structuring is very important for a better understanding and an efficient organization of the video content. It facilitates tasks like video indexing, video classification, and summarization and provides fast and nonlinear access to relevant parts of the programs (nonlinear video browsing). Its domain of applicability is very vast: in sports videos for the detection of moments of interest (e.g., goal in a soccer match, pitches in baseball) and also for kinematic analysis for sports professionals training purposes [26], in news broadcast programs to identify the different stories and/or build personalized TV news programs [29], in entertainment TV shows to recover their structure and identify the main parts allowing the browsing inside such programs, in films to provide the chapters of the film, and in home videos to permit the organization of the videos related to certain events. All the methods presented in the previous sections try to solve one or more of these requirements. Both specific and generic approaches have strengths and weaknesses. In the case of specific methods, although they give promising results, they can be applied to only very specific types of programs. They are characterized by a lack of generality due to the use of rules, templates, or learning algorithms based on a previous analysis of the specific videos. Also, when dealing with videos more complex than news or sports videos, the computation cost could increase and an important knowledge in the domain will be needed.

On the other hand, generic methods try to structure a video without using any prior knowledge in the domain. But because the definition of a scene is very ambiguous and depends on the human understanding of its meaning, it is difficult to find an objective one, that would cover all users interests. This is why it is hard to compare the performance of the existing approaches and develop a better one. An objective evaluation would assume the existence of a ground truth (GT), whereas this GT is human generated and so depends on human judgment.

Even so, the advances in the field offer, as best as possible, solutions to the problems in the video content domain. A great amount of work continues to be done, with the goal to propose methods that are completely unsupervised and require as minimum human intervention as possible. Services like Catch-up TV, which make use of these approaches, become more and more interesting for the TV providers and their clients, so their practical applicability is very important for the close future.

References

1. J. Assfalg, M. Bertini, C. Colombo, and A.D. Bimbo. Semantic annotation of sports videos. *IEEE MultiMedia*, 9(2):52–60, April 2002.
2. Y.S. Avrithis, N. Tsapatsoulis, and S.D. Kollias. Broadcast news parsing using visual cues: A robust face detection approach. In *IEEE International Conference on Multimedia and Expo*, Singapore, Vol. 3, pp. 1469–1472, August 2000. IEEE, New York.
3. M. Bertini, A. Del Bimbo, and P. Pala. Content-based indexing and retrieval of TV news. *Pattern Recognition Letters*, 22(5):503–516, April 2001.
4. M. Bertini, A. Del Bimbo, and W. Nunziati. Automatic detection of player's identity in soccer videos using faces and text cues. In *14th Annual ACM International Conference on Multimedia*, Santa Barbara, CA, pp. 663–666, October 2006.

5. L. Chaisorn and T.-S. Chua. Story boundary detection in news video using global rule induction technique. In *IEEE International Conference on Multimedia and Expo*, Toronto, Ontario, Canada, pp. 2101–2104, July 2006.

6. L. Chaisorn, T.-S. Chua, and C.-H. Lee. The segmentation of news video into story units. In *IEEE International Conference on Multimedia and Expo*, Vol. 1, Lausanne, Switzerland, pp. 73–76, August 2002.

7. L. Chaisorn, T.-S. Chua, and C.-H. Lee. A multi-modal approach to story segmentation for news video. *World Wide Web*, 6(2):187–208, 2003.

8. A. Chianese, V. Moscato, A. Penta, and A. Picariello. Scene detection using visual and audio attention. In *ACM International Conference on Ambi-Sys Workshop on Ambient Media Delivery and Interactive Television*, Quebec, Canada, February 2008.

9. L.-Y. Duan, M. Xu, T.-S. Chua, Q. Tian, and C.-S. Xu. A mid-level representation framework for semantic sports video analysis. In *ACM International Conference on Multimedia*, Berkeley, CA, pp. 33–44, November 2003.

10. S. Eickeler, F. Wallhoff, U. Iurgel, and G. Rigoll. Content based indexing of images and video using face detection and recognition methods. In *IEEE International Conference on Acoustics, Speech and Signal Processing*, Vol. 3, Salt Lake City, UT, pp. 1505–1508, May 2001.

11. A. Ekin, A.M. Tekalp, and R. Mehrotra. Automatic soccer video analysis and summarization. *IEEE Transactions on Image Processing*, 12(7):796–807, July 2003.

12. Y. Fang, X. Zhai, and J. Fan. News video story segmentation. In *12th International Multi-Media Modelling Conference*, Beijing, China, pp. 397–400, January 2006.

13. X. Gao and X. Tang. Unsupervised video-shot segmentation and model-free anchor-person detection for news video story parsing. *IEEE Transactions on Circuits and Systems for Video Technology*, 12(9):765–776, September 2002.

14. N. Goela, K. Wilson, F. Niu, and A. Divakaran. An SVM framework for genre-independent scene change detection. In *IEEE International Conference on Multimedia and Expo*, Beijing, China, pp. 532–535, July 2007.

15. B. Gunsel, A. Ferman, and A. Tekalp. Temporal video segmentation using unsupervised clustering and semantic object tracking. *Journal of Electronic Imaging*, 7(3):592–604, 1998.

16. A. Gupta, P. Srinivasan, J. Shi, and L.S. Davis. Understanding videos constructing plots learning a visually grounded storyline model from annotated. In *IEEE Conference on Computer Vision and Pattern Recognition*, Miami, FL, June 2009.

17. A. Guziec. Tracking pitches for broadcast television. *Computer*, 35(3):38–43, March 2002.

18. R. Hamid, R. Kumar, M. Grundmann, K. Kim, I. Essaz, and J. Hodgins. Player localization using multiple static cameras for sports visualization. In *IEEE Conference on Computer Vision and Pattern Recognition*, San Francisco, CA, pp. 731–738, June 2010.

19. A.G. Hauptmann and M.A. Smith. Text, speech and vision for video segmentation: The infomedia project. In *AAAI Fall Symposium, Computational Models for Integrating Language and Vision*, Cambridge, MA, November 1995.

20. E. Kijak. *Structuration multimodale des vidos de sports par modles stochastiques.* PhD thesis, Universit de Rennes 1, Rennes, France, 2003.
21. E. Kijak, L. Oisel, and P. Gros. Hierarchical structure analysis of sport videos using HMMS. In *International Conference on Image Processing*, Vol. 3, Barcelona, Spain, pp. 1025–1028, September 2003.
22. J.-G. Kim, H.S. Chang, Y.T. Kim, K. Kang, M. Kim, J. Kim, and H.-M. Kim. Multimodal approach for summarizing and indexing news video. *ETRI Journal*, 24(1):1–11, 2002.
23. K. Kim, M. Grundmann, A. Shamir, I. Matthews, J. Hodgins, and I. Essa. Motion fields to predict play evolution in dynamic sport scenes. In *IEEE Conference on Computer Vision and Pattern Recognition*, San Francisco, CA, pp. 840–847, June 2010.
24. C.-C. Ko and W.-M. Xie. News video segmentation and categorization techniques for content-demand browsing. In *Congress on Image and Signal Processing*, Hainan, China, pp. 530–534, May 2008.
25. F.C. Li, A. Gupta, E. Sanocki, L.W. He, and Y. Rui. Browsing digital video. In *ACM Computer-Human Interaction*, Hague, the Netherlands, pp. 169–176, 2000.
26. H. Li, J. Tang, S. Wu, Y. Zhang, and S. Lin. Automatic detection and analysis of player action in moving background sports video sequences. *IEEE Transactions on Circuits and Systems for Video Technology*, 20(3):351–364, March 2010.
27. A. Merlino, D. Morey, and M. Maybury. Broadcast news navigation using story segmentation. In *ACM International Conference on Multimedia*, Seattle, WA, pp. 381–391, November 1997.
28. H. Misra, F. Hopfgartner, A. Goyal, P. Punitha, and J.M. Jose. TV news story segmentation based on semantic coherence and content similarity. In *16th International Multimedia Modeling Conference*, Chongqing, China, pp. 347–357, January 2010.
29. B. Mrialdo, K.-T. Lee, D. Luparello, and J. Roudaire. Automatic construction of personalized TV news programs. In *Seventh ACM International Multimedia Conference*, Orlando, FL, pp. 323–331, October 30–November 5, 1999.
30. Y. Nakamura and T. Kanade. Semantic analysis for video contents extraction—Spotting by association in news video. In *ACM International Conference on Multimedia*, Seattle, WA, pp. 393–401, November 1997.
31. P. Over, A.F. Smeaton, and G. Awad. The TRECVID 2007 BBC rushes summarization evaluation pilot. In *International Workshop on TRECVID Video Summarization*, Augsburg, Germany, September 2007.
32. P. Over, A.F. Smeaton, and G. Awad. The TRECVID 2008 BBC rushes summarization evaluation. In *Second ACM TRECVid Video Summarization Workshop*, Vancouver, BC, Canada, pp. 1–20, October 2008.
33. S. Pfeiffer, R. Lienhart, and W. Efflsberg. Scene determination based on video and audio features. *Multimedia Tools and Applications*, 15(1):59–81, September 2001.
34. M.J. Pickering, L. Wong, and S.M. Rger. ANSES: Summarisation of news video. In *Proceedings of the Second International Conference on Image and Video Retrieval*, Urbana, IL, pp. 425–434, July 2003.

35. J-P. Poli. *Structuration automatique de flux televisuels.* PhD thesis, Universite Paul-Cezanne Aix-Marseille III, France, 2007.

36. Z. Rasheed and M. Shah. Detection and representation of scenes in videos. *IEEE Transactions on Multimedia*, 7(6):1097–1105, December 2005. ISSN 1520-9210.

37. Y. Rui, A. Gupta, and A. Acero. Automatically extracting highlights for TV baseball programs. In *ACM International Conference on Multimedia*, New York, pp. 105–115, October 2000.

38. P. Sidiropoulos, V. Mezaris, I. Kompatsiaris, H. Meinedo, and I. Trancoso. Multi-modal scene segmentation using scene transition graphs. In *17th ACM International Conference on Multimedia*, Beijing, China, pp. 665–668, October 2009.

39. K. Yamamoto, S. Takayama, and H. Aoki. Semantic segmentation of TV programs using corner-subtitles. In *IEEE 13th International Symposium on Consumer Electronics*, Kyoto, Japan, pp. 205–208, May 2009.

40. W. Tavanapong and J. Zhou. Shot clustering techniques for story browsing. *IEEE Transactions on Multimedia*, 6(4):517–527, August 2004.

41. D.W. Tjondronegoro and Y.-P.P. Chen. Knowledge-discounted event detection in sports video. *IEEE Transactions on Systems, Man, and Cybernetics, Part A: Systems and Humans*, 40(5):1009–1024, September 2010.

42. B.T. Truong and S. Venkatesh. Video abstraction: A systematic review and classification. *ACM Transactions on Multimedia Computing, Communications, and Applications*, 3(1):1–37, February 2006.

43. E. Veneau, R. Ronfard, and P. Bouthemy. From video shot clustering to sequence segmentation. In *15th International Conference on Pattern Recognition*, Vol. 4, Barcelona, Spain, pp. 254–257, September 2000.

44. J. Wang and T.-S. Chua. A cinematic-based framework for scene boundary detection in video. *The Visual Computer*, 19(5):329–341, 2003.

45. J. Wang, L. Duan, Q. Liu, H. Lu, and J.S. Jin. A multimodal scheme for program segmentation and representation in broadcast video streams. *IEEE Transactions on Multimedia*, 10(3):393–408, April 2008.

46. L. Xie, P. Xu, S.-F. Chang, A. Divakaran, and H. Sun. Structure analysis of soccer video with domain knowledge and hidden Markov models. *Pattern Recognition Letters*, 25(7):767–775, May 2004.

47. Z. Xiong, X.S. Zhou, Q. Tian, Y. Rui, and T.S. Huangm. Semantic retrieval of video—Review of research on video retrieval in meetings, movies and broadcast news, and sports. *IEEE Signal Processing Magazine*, 23(2):18–27, March 2006.

48. G. Xu, Y.-F. Ma, H.-J. Zhang, and S.-Q. Yang. An HMM-based framework for video semantic analysis. *IEEE Transactions on Circuits and Systems for Video Technology*, 15(11):1422–1433, November 2005.

49. P. Xu, L. Xie, S.-F. Chang, A. Divakaran, A. Vetro, and H. Sun. Algorithms and system for segmentation and structure analysis in soccer video. In *IEEE International Conference on Multimedia and Expo*, Tokyo, Japan, pp. 721–724, August 2001.

50. M.M. Yeung and B. Liu. Efficient matching and clustering of video shots. In *International Conference on Image Processing*, Vol. 1, Washington, DC, pp. 338–341, October 1995.

51. M.M. Yeung and B.-L. Yeo. Time-constrained clustering for segmentation of video into story units. In *13th International Conference on Pattern Recognition*, Vol. 3, Vienna, Austria, pp. 375–380, August 1996.

52. X. Yu, L. Li, and H.W. Leong. Interactive broadcast services for live soccer video based on instant semantics acquisition. *Visual Communication and Image Representation*, 20(2):117–130, February 2009.

53. J. Yuan, H. Wang, L. Xiao, W. Zheng, J. Li, F. Lin, and B. Zhang. A formal study of shot boundary detection. *IEEE Transactions on Circuits and Systems for Video Technology*, 17(2):168–186, February 2007.

54. Y. Zhai and M. Shah. Video scene segmentation using Markov chain Monte Carlo. *IEEE Transactions on Multimedia*, 8(4):686–697, August 2006.

55. D.-Q. Zhang, C.-Y. Lin, S.-F. Chang, and J.R. Smith. Semantic video clustering across sources using bipartite spectral clustering. In *IEEE International Conference on multimedia and expo (ICME)*, Taipei, Taiwan, pp. 117–120, June 2004.

56. H.J. Zhang, Y.H. Gong, S.W. Smoliar, and S.Y. Tan. Automatic parsing of news video. In *International Conference on Multimedia Computing and Systems*, Boston, MA, pp. 45–54, May 1994.

57. Y. Zhao, T. Wang, P. Wang, W. Hu, Y. Du, Y. Zhang, and G. Xu. Scene segmentation and categorization using n-cuts. In *IEEE Conference on Computer Vision and Pattern Recognition*, Minneapolis, MN, pp. 343–348, June 2007.

Chapter 7

About TV Stream Macro-Segmentation

Approaches and Results

Zein Al Abidin Ibrahim
University of Angers

Patrick Gros
Institut National de Recherche en Informatique et en Automatique

Contents

In the last few decades, digital TV broadcasting has witnessed a huge interest from users against the traditional analog transmission. Many facilities have been already provided for capturing, storing, and sharing digital video content. However, navigating within TV streams is still considered as an important challenge to be faced. From a user point of view, a TV stream is represented as a sequence of programs (P) and breaks (B). From a signal point of view, this stream is seen as a continuous flow of video and audio frames, with no external markers of the start and the end points of the included programs and no apparent structure. Most TV streams have no associated metadata to describe their structure, except the program guides produced by TV channels. These program guides lack precision, since TV channels cannot predict the exact duration of live programs, for example. In addition, they do not provide any information about breaks like commercials or trailers. To cope with this problem, TV stream macro-segmentation or structuring has been proposed as a promising solution in the domain of video indexing. TV stream macro-segmentation consists in precisely detecting the first and the last frames of all programs and breaks (commercials, trailers, station identification, bumpers) of a given stream, and then in annotating all these segments with some metadata. This can be performed by (1) analyzing the metadata provided with the stream (EPG, EIT), or (2) analyzing the audiovisual stream to detect the precise start and end of programs and breaks. In this chapter, we aim at providing a survey of the existing approaches in this field. Then, we discuss and compare the results of the different approaches to see how to benefit from the advantages and to overcome the limitations of each of them.

7.1 Introduction

With the recent exponential growth of digital technologies and today's Internet, multimedia content (text, still images, animation, audio, video, rich-media) has become of common use. Video can be considered as the most challenging content, as it combines the main modalities (image, sound, text) in an integrate stream. Many techniques have already been proposed in order to capture, store, and share such content. This allowed the development of storage systems able to archive very large amount of video. However, accessing, retrieving, and browsing video information from such archives is still problematic and remains an active subject of research.

Usually, to retrieve or access a video content, users are reduced to use the "rewind" and "forward" operations to search the part of interest or to find a particular object in the video. This is an inefficient, time-consuming, and a very complicated process as soon as the video is long. To remedy this situation, a lot of work has already been done in this domain. One relevant proposition in order to access a video content is to imitate the textual-book access methods [1]. In a book, the reader can efficiently access the content using the *table of content* (ToC) without reading the whole document. The ToC captures the semantic structure of the book, while the entries of this table serve as cues for the reader to find the chapters or sections of interest and to go directly to their right locations in the document. On the other hand, if a reader has a specific question (query), he can consult the *index* of the book and directly access the sections addressing that question. So, the ToC helps the reader to browse the book, while the *index* helps him to retrieve the information from the book. We can map this idea to video content: With a ToC, browsing a video or retrieving information from it should become much easier. Constructing tables of video content thus appears as a simple way to facilitate the user's access to a specific content in a video stream. Several propositions to create such a video ToC have been already proposed in the literature, in which this process is named *video content segmentation*, video content structuring, or video structure analysis. Many of these techniques share a common limitation. They are restricted to a single genre of videos, while users' needs exist for a very wide range of video genres. As an example, TV is one of the main sources of video. A TV stream is a succession of various kinds of video segments (movies, news, TV games, different sports, commercials, weather forecasts, etc.). Consequently, besides accessing and retrieving data in a specific segment, the goal of a ToC is also to detect the boundaries of these segments in the continuous stream. This process is called TV stream macro-segmentation.

Normally, TV channels produce a stream before broadcasting it. They should thus be able to provide precise metadata about what is broadcasted (start, end, name, description of each program) without any difficulties. This would solve the TV stream macro-segmentation problem. However, in practice, most TV streams have no associated metadata to describe their structure, except the electronic program guide (EPG) or the event information table (EIT), which lack precision and cannot be used directly without additional processing. Besides, different reasons prevent TV channels from associating precise metadata with the broadcasted streams. First, TV stream production is a very complex process supported by many persons and many systems. Furthermore, some changes may occur at any minute. Saving and forwarding the metadata associated with the stream production is a very hard and costly task. On the other hand, even if such metadata were available, TV channels would not provide them to users, because it could allow third parties to archive and build novel TV services (TVoD, catch-up TV) in the absence of any agreement with the TV channel. Moreover, delivering precise metadata to viewers would open them the possibility to skip commercials that are the first financial source of TV channels (in recorded streams or catch-up TV service) [2].

The objective of this chapter is to provide a clear presentation of the TV stream macro-segmentation domain, to justify its importance, and to present the recent works that have been already proposed in the literature. To this aim, we organize the rest of this chapter as follows. In Section 7.2, we explain the difference between video content segmentation and TV stream macro-segmentation. The possible applications of the latter are presented in Section 7.3. While Section 7.4 justifies the need of automating the macro-segmentation process and provides an overview of the different types of metadata and their reliability, Section 7.5 is dedicated to review the methods proposed in the literature and ends by discussing their performance. Finally, Section 7.6 concludes the chapter.

7.2 From Video Content Segmentation toward TV Stream Macro-Segmentation

7.2.1 Video Content Segmentation

Video content segmentation or structuring has been defined as the hierarchical decomposition of videos into units and the construction of their interrelationships [3]. In other words, similarly to text documents that can be decomposed into chapters, paragraphs, sentences, and words, videos can be segmented into units like scenes, shots, sub-shots, and key-frames. In an analogous way, the video content segmentation problem can be considered as a classification one. For example, shots can be classified in several classes in order to obtain the video scenes that can be, in their turn, classified to obtain the video stories and so on.

In order to apply the hierarchical decomposition of video, the latter should have structured content. Rui et al. define in [4] a structured content as being a video that can be produced according to a script or to a plan and can be edited later. Unfortunately, some video content is not structured or exhibits a poor structure such as some sports (e.g., soccer) or such as surveillance videos. A proposition to cope with this issue was to structure the nonstructured (or semi-structured) videos into logical units as play/break sequences instead of the six-level hierarchy. In sports video (soccer), a game is in play if the ball is inside the field and the game is going on. Break represents the case when the ball is outside the field (read [5–7] for more information). In surveillance video, a play is the period in which some activity is detected (read [8] for more information about video surveillance).

In the structured content, the six-level video units are defined as follows:

1. *Video*: Flow of video and audio frames presented at a fixed rate.
2. *Story or group of scenes*: Several scenes that capture continuous action or series of events. This element is relevant for some video genres such as news reports and movies.
3. *Scene*: A series of shots that is semantically related and temporally adjacent. It is usually composed of a series of shots recorded in the same location.

4. *Shot*: A sequence of frames that are recorded continuously with the same camera.
5. *Sub-shot or micro-shot*: A segment in a shot that corresponds to the same camera motion. Each shot may be composed of one or more consecutive sub-shots depending on the camera motion.
6. *Key-frame*: The frame that represents a shot or a sub-shot. Each shot and sub-shot may be represented by one or more key-frames.

Figure 7.1 shows how video content can be represented using the six-level hierarchy (video, story, scene, shot, sub-shot, key-frame). Each unit of a level in the hierarchy is the result of the decomposition (segmentation) of a unit in the upper level (segmentation-based) and the composition of several units in the lower level (classification-based). The only exceptions are key-frames, which are a sparse component of sub-shots.

The literature is very rich in techniques that address one or several levels of this hierarchy (segmentation-based or classification-based approaches). The reader can refer to [3,4,9–13] for more information about the segmentation techniques and to [14,15] for reviews of video classifications.

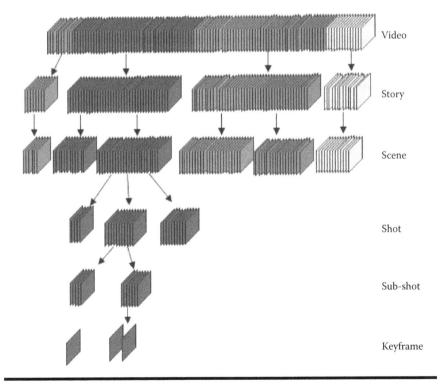

Figure 7.1   ToC: the six-level video content hierarchy.

7.2.2 TV Stream Macro-Segmentation

Nowadays and with the appearance of TV streams that contain several heterogeneous programs, this hierarchy faces several challenges. First, we agree with [16] that a stream contains a large number of scenes (or even stories) that makes the tasks of browsing and retrieval time-consuming. Moreover, hierarchical video content decomposition has been designed for a video from the same genre. Unfortunately, TV streams contain various types of programs that are successively achieved in a single continuous video stream. Programs may be separated and interrupted with breaks. Moreover, a program may be related to other programs having the same type (i.e., same TV series). In addition, a program may be composed of several other programs.

For such cases, the six-level hierarchical structure should be updated in order to take into account TV streams. In a first step, a simple solution that copes with this problem is to consider the TV stream as a sequence of programs (P) and breaks (B). Thus, the table of content for TV streams should be specialized to take these items (P and B) into consideration. In other words, the traditional ToC is specialized into TvToC which contains an additional level representing programs and breaks. Using this level, the viewer can skip programs that do not interest him or navigate deeply in others. This TvToC may be completed by another level that represents program collections. This level may be done by categorizing the macro-segmented programs of the TV streams (i.e., [14,17]). Figure 7.2 shows the possible extension of the traditional ToC. The six-level hierarchy may be applied on each program of the Program/Break sequence (first extended level) or on any video of the various collections (second extended level). The TvToC idea opens the door on new definitions of TV streams, programs, breaks, and the domain of TV stream macro-segmentation:

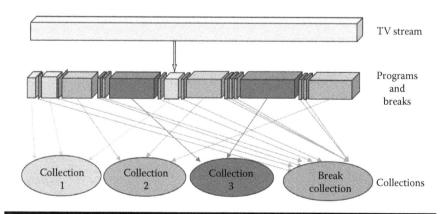

Figure 7.2   TvToC: the possible extension of traditional ToC.

TV stream: Defined as contiguous sequence of video and audio frames produced by TV channels. It is composed of a series of heterogeneous programs (P) and breaks (B) without markers at the signal level of the boundaries of the programs and the breaks. Two consecutive programs are usually, but not always, separated by breaks. Each program may be also interrupted by breaks.

Break (B): Every sequence with commercial aim such as commercials, interludes, trailers, jingles, bumpers and self-promotions. In some references [2,18] breaks are also called inter-programs or non-programs.

Program (P): Every sequence that is not of break type (movies, TV games, weather forecasts, news). Programs have culture, informative or entertainment aim. Sometimes, a program may be composed of several parts separated by break sequences.

TV stream macro-segmentation: Known also as TV stream structuring is the process of precisely detecting the first and the last frames of all the programs and breaks of the stream and in annotating all these segments with some metadata. As a consequence, TV stream macro-segmentation allows user to recover the original macro-segments that construct the continuous stream.

7.3 Applications

Motivated by the huge video content of TV stream broadcasting channels, TV stream macro-segmentation has become a very important domain in the recent years. In this section, we highlight some interesting applications in which macro-segmentation can interfere to facilitate their tasks and provide better performance:

1. *Archiving*: The first application that takes benefit from TV stream macro-segmentation is the archive management for the TV broadcasting. This operation is done in several countries in the world including the French National Audiovisual Institute (INA), Beeld en Geluid in Netherlands, NAA in Finland, BBC in the UK, RAI in Italy, and many other organizations. For example, the INA institute is responsible for archiving all programs broadcasted on all French TV channels and radios. By 2010, INA records the streams of 100 French TV channels 24/7 [19]. Since September 2006, INA has archived 540.000 h of TV per year [20]. Unfortunately, the recorded streams should be indexed for further retrieval, which is done manually by the INA institute. Each program in each stream is annotated with its start time, end time, summary, and other information. This process can be automated (or at least semiautomated) using TV stream macro-segmentation.

2. *Legal regulation*: In France, the Conseil Superieur de l'Audiovisuel (CSA) monitors the number and duration of commercial breaks. Other examples are the European Platform of Regulatory Authorities (EPRA) in Europe and the Federal Communications commission (FCC) in the United States. To

avoid doing this task manually, TV stream macro-segmentation can provide the boundaries of breaks and thus get the total number and duration of commercials broadcasted on a TV channel each day for further monitoring.

3. *Statistics/analytics*: The audience measurement (i.e., Mdiametrie in France or Nielsen Media Research in the United States) is one of the possible applications that may take advantage of the TV stream macro-segmentation. In France, Mdiametrie measures the TV audiences by equipping the television of some audiences (some samples) with a box. This box registers information about the watched programs each day. The registered information is uploaded each night to the Mdiametrie server. To get accurate statistics, Mdiametrie should have the precise start and end of each program in each watched stream in order to provide accurate statistics.

4. *IPTV services*: The Internet protocol television (IPTV) services may be classified in three categories:

   (a) The time-shifted programming: catch-up TV (replays a TV show that was broadcasted hours or days ago) or start-over TV (replays the current TV program from its beginning). If the precise boundaries of programs are not available, the service (catch-up and start-over) will provide to users the imprecise boundaries of the requested TV program. The viewer will be obliged to do the fast-forward or the back-forward operation in order to reach the precise start of the desired program. This problem can be avoided using a macro-segmentation solution.

   (b) TV on demand (TVoD): a system that allows users to select and watch/listen TV content on demand. IPTV technology is often used to bring video on demand to televisions and personal computers. The TV programs in the TVoD are broadcasted as TV streams before putting them on disposal. The non-presence of tools that can conserve the accurate information about the broadcasted programs when composing streams obliges TV channels to macro-segment TV streams after broadcasting it in order to get the recover its initial structure for further retrieval using the TVoD service.

   (c) The network personal video records (nPVR): a network-based digital video recorder stored at the provider's central office rather than at the consumer's private home. It is similar to a digital video recorder except it stores its content on a network instead of a local hard disk. In this service, the nPVR should have the precise boundaries of the program to be recorded. The availability of TV stream macro-segmentation solution that can perform a live detection of the start and end of programs permits the nPVR to shift the recording to the precise boundaries of the requested program.

5. *Video analysis*: Most of the video analysis methods proposed in the literature are highly dedicated and depend on the type of the video analyzed, for example, a method that detects highlights in a soccer game or structures a news video in Newscaster/Report sequences. To do so, the content should be homogeneous.

Heterogeneous programs in a TV stream should be separated (manually or automatically using TV stream macro-segmentation) and then appropriate analysis methods can be applied on each program according to its type.

6. *Skipping commercials in the recorded streams*: The availability of the precise start and end of commercials provided by the macro-segmentation gives viewers the possibility to skip them while watching the recorded streams.

7.4 Toward Automatic TV Stream Macro-Segmentation

Generally, most of the video content analysis tasks that can be achieved by automatic tools are done manually by humans before. For example, TV stream macro-segmentation can be done by human annotators who search the boundaries manually and then tag them. This can be done online or off-line as mentioned in [2]. In the online mode, annotators should watch the stream 24/7 and each time the program or the break ends, they tag the start and the end of it, and then they put a description of the broadcasted program, or break segments. In the off-line mode, streams will be saved first and then annotators watch them, tag the start and the end of programs and breaks, and then label them. In both cases, annotators use adequate software to facilitate the tasks. The off-line mode is widely used, especially in the case of TV stream annotation such as in the INA archive institute.

As we can notice, manual annotation is very expensive and it can be hardly handled by human annotators due to the large amount of video content. In addition, the automatic approaches may be, for some problems, more precise than the manual ones. For example, Manson and Berrani present in [2] their experience of manual annotation. They have taken more than one working day to annotate one day of TV stream and the results present some imprecision and contain errors. To cope with the problems of manual annotation, it was indispensable to start stepping into the development of some new methods to handle the TV stream macro-segmentation automatically or at least to facilitate the task of manual annotation.

The first proposition in this domain was derived from the fact that TV channels provide metadata about the structure of the TV stream. Although these metadata can be considered as a semiautomatic solution for TV stream macro-segmentation, they cannot replace the automatic tools. To understand the reason, we present the different available types of metadata. In addition, we discuss the limitations that prevent them from being (alone) sufficient for the macro-segmentation process.

7.4.1 Metadata

TV streams metadata is a label that describes the "storytelling" of the broadcasted stream. It is provided by TV channels for informing audiences about the current or forthcoming broadcasted programs. The metadata is an important source of information that deserves to be included in any automatic TV stream macro-segmentation system. It contains valuable, but not reliable, information that may help to structure the stream. Before presenting studies about the reliability of such metadata, the reader should take an idea about the types of metadata that may be broadcasted with TV streams.

7.4.1.1 Types of Metadata

Usually, TV channels provide two types of metadata with their broadcasted streams:

- Metadata associated and broadcasted with the stream
- Metadata available on websites or in markets

These two types are dedicated to give information about the broadcasted programs but not about the breaks.

7.4.1.1.1 Associated Stream Metadata

This type of metadata depends on the standards and the broadcasting modes (analog or digital).

In analog TV, teletext [21] (or what is called the closed caption in the United States) provides additional or interpretive information to viewers who want to access it. For example, teletext in Europe contains information such as transcription of the audio of a program, news, weather forecasts, program guides for 1 week or more. A system that could signal the precise start and end time of a program was developed for analog TV in Europe. This system is the program delivery control (PDC) that properly controls video recorders using hidden codes in the teletext service [22]. With PDC, if we want to record a TV program that has been delayed or rescheduled, the video recording will automatically be rescheduled too. However, in some European countries other programs have been used to the same purpose, such as VPS (video programming system) in Germany.

In digital TV, the metadata are called event information tables (EITs). An EIT is a group of data elements that is transmitted with the stream and contains the details of specific TV programs, including the program name, start time, duration, genre, summary, and possibly other information. The EITs are used by the middleware of the set-top box to create an on-screen EPG. EIT has two types:

1. The EIT schedule that stores the TV program for many days, and that allows the creation of an EPG. These tables are rarely provided.
2. The EIT present/following that is the most common type. This EIT provides details about the current program and also about the following one.

Except the PDC system, broadcasted metadata are static and are not updated or modified if changes occur in the schedule. Consequently, these metadata cannot be used alone for stream macro-segmentation. Likewise, PDC cannot be used for TV macro-segmentation because it is rarely available. This is because it allows users to skip commercials that represent the first financial source for TV channels as we have already mentioned. In addition, PDC is standardized for analog TV while it is not the case for digital TV. The digital TV has its own system for program tagging, in which the metadata are provided via the running status table (RST), which is, unfortunately, rarely implemented.

7.4.1.1.2 Metadata Available on the Web or in Markets

The EPGs are available on the Internet or in markets. Generally, they provide the TV stream schedule for the coming week. Tvtv, emapmedia, and plurimedia are examples of Internet sites selling EPGs. Meanwhile, ZguideTV is a software that gathers the EPGs from several magazine sites in France. Whatever is the technology that provides the EPGs (Internet sites or software), these EPGs can be queried through web services and are always available.

7.4.1.2 Reliability of Metadata

The first question a reader may ask is why these metadata are not sufficient to macro-segment TV streams. The answer is that they are incomplete and also they lack precision. Several studies have been made on TV metadata to discover their reliability and bring to light their insufficiency to replace the automatic TV stream analysis without any preprocessing step. An example is the correction process that had been made in [23] over the metadata, before being able to use it for TV stream macro-segmentation. However, many approaches in the literature have proven that such metadata can be used as complementary information in the TV stream macro-segmentation process in order to annotate program segments [2,18,25]. Next, we explain the incompleteness and the imprecision limitations of the metadata that prevent them from being sufficient for automatic TV stream macro-segmentation.

7.4.1.2.1 Incompleteness of Metadata

The first study of the incompleteness of metadata is the one presented by Berrani et al. in [26]. The idea is to count the number of programs that have been broadcasted and those announced in the metadata. A 24 h of France2 TV stream has been stored, segmented, and labeled manually. They identified 49 programs and they distinguished between short programs (less than 10 min) and long programs (longer than 10 min). The distinction permits authors to measure if the incompleteness affects short programs or may cover also long ones. Figure 7.3 shows the obtained results. As we can notice in the figure, the EPG does not mention most of the short

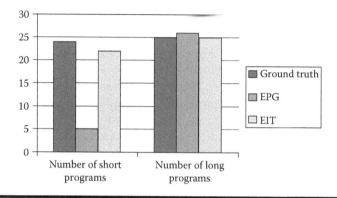

Figure 7.3   Incompleteness of metadata.

programs and EIT is more complete than the EPG. The authors have also discovered that three programs announced in the EPG (four in EIT, respectively) have not been broadcasted.

The second study of the incompleteness of metadata is presented by Poli in [19]. It concerns the EPG metadata provided by four TV channels over 4 years of broadcasting. In this study, the author depends on modeled EPG instead of the ground truth (GT) one, due to the large amount of metadata involved in the study. In consequence, the results approximate the incompleteness to 65%. In addition, this study shows that the EPGs stay stable over a long period of time.

7.4.1.2.2 Imprecision of Metadata

Like the incompleteness study of metadata, Berrani et al. present in [26] a complementary study measuring the imprecision of metadata and using the same 24 h TV stream. The aim is to estimate the mean of the temporal shift between broadcasted programs and announced ones. The authors compute the program time-shift between EPG, EIT, and GT (EPG with GT, EIT with GT, and EPG with EIT). The results show that 40% of the programs start more than 5 min earlier or later than announced in the EIT.

Contrarily to the first study applied on 1 day of TV stream, Berrani et al. present a second study done on 5 months of France2 metadata. The study concerns only programs having stable opening credits that have been detected automatically. News, magazines, TV games, and TV series are examples of such programs. Figure 7.4 resumes the obtained results. The obtained results prove the imprecision of the metadata even for news programs that attract the most number of audiences. Results have been illustrated clearly in Figure 7.5 using a histogram to show the distribution of temporal imprecision and the number of related time-shifted programs.

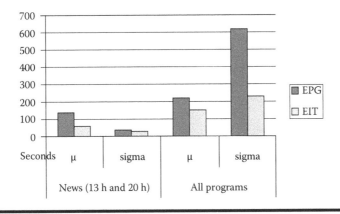

Figure 7.4   Imprecision of metadata.

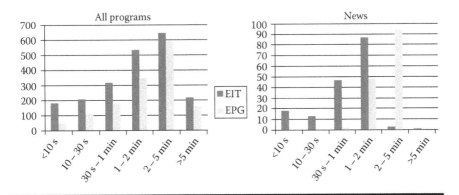

Figure 7.5   Histogram of the temporal time-shift.

The histogram shows that only 10% of the announced programs in the EIT and EPG have about 10 s of time-shift. On the contrary, 40% of the EIT and EPG programs have more than 2 min of time-shift. As a conclusion, we can notice that TV channels do not provide reliable metadata with their daily streams. These metadata may be incomplete and temporally imprecise. In addition, they may contain errors and sometimes are not available. Consequently, metadata are insufficient and cannot replace the automatic or even the manual TV stream macro-segmentation process. Moreover, in some cases, these metadata need to be corrected before integration in any video content analysis process. However, they are still considered very valuable for automatic TV program annotations. This is because of their ease of use, especially for long programs that are usually presented in the metadata. Although metadata suffer from less of reliability, to our knowledge, all the existing TV stream macro-segmentation methods that annotate programs are based on them [2,18,25]. One proposition that may cope with this limitation of metadata is to use the speech transcription [27,28]. However, besides its complexity, this method may also not be very advantageous in terms of reliability.

In this section, we could realize the necessity of implementing new automatic methods for TV streams macro-segmentation. Thus, in the next section we aim at detailing the different methods that have been already proposed to handle this issue.

7.5 State of the Art

The TV stream macro-segmentation problem has not been extensively addressed in the literature. Most of the methods focus on structuring a single program or a collection of programs without dealing with a stream containing several heterogeneous programs.

The macro-segmentation process is usually divided into two complementary tasks:

- The stream is segmented in program/break sequences, where the precise start and end of programs and breaks are provided.
- Each segmented program is labeled with metadata in order to identify it and to facilitate the retrieval of information from the stream.

The first task can be done using different approaches:

1. Segmenting the stream into logical units and then classifying each segment as a program or a break segment [2,25]. These segments may be of different granularities (key-frame, shot, scene). Then, consecutive segments of the same type are fused.
2. Searching the start and the end of program segments basing on the detection of discontinuities in the homogeneities of some features [29], modeling the boundary between programs and breaks [30], or detecting the repetition of opening and closing credits [16].
3. Searching the start and the end of break segments by recognizing them in a reference database [18] or based on their repeated behavior [2,25,31]. The latter should be followed by a classification step in order to separate repeated program segments from break ones.

The second task of the TV stream macro-segmentation is to annotate each program with metadata. This metadata can be derived from the following:

1. The metadata provided by TV channels with the stream such as the EPG or the EIT (e.g., [2,18,25])
2. The metadata extracted from the signal such as the use of audio transcription (e.g., [32]), the analysis of the teletext, or the recognition of pre-annotated programs or opening/closing credits

The TV stream macro-segmentation methods of the literature are classified into two main categories:

1. Methods that are based on the almost exclusive use of the metadata available with the stream [19]. In this category, the audiovisual stream is partially processed in order to refine the prediction of the boundaries. This prediction is generally computed from the metadata. Such methods are top-down approaches because they start the analysis from high-level information (EPGs). In the rest of the chapter, these methods are noted as metadata-based methods.
2. Methods that use the audiovisual content to macro-segment TV streams. Such methods are noted as content-based, and they can be considered as bottom-up approaches. In their turn, these methods can be categorized into two subclasses:
   (a) Methods that search the boundaries of the programs themselves. This type of methods is noted as program-based methods [16,29,30,33].
   (b) Methods that detect breaks, which may separate consecutive programs. These methods are called break-based methods [2,18,25].

In the rest of this section, we present the different methods of the literature and provide their advantages and disadvantages. Then, we conclude the section by presenting the results obtained by each method and by discussing its efficiency.

7.5.1 Metadata-Based Methods

As we have already mentioned, the methods in this category mainly use metadata to macro-segment TV streams. The signal is marginally used at the end of the method for refinement purposes only. A prototype of this category is the method developed by Poli in [19].

Poli proposes a statistical approach for predicting the structure of the stream. His aim is to use a large set of already annotated data to learn a model of the program guide, and thus of the stream structure. His idea relies on the assumption that TV channels respect some regularity in their program plans in order to preserve and increase their audience.

In this approach, a contextual hidden Markov model (CHMM) and a regression tree are used to learn the model that predicts the start time, the duration, and the genre of all programs and breaks appearing during a week. Poli uses the HMM to model the transition between programs, where each program is represented by its genre. Obviously, the genre of a program does not depend only on the genre of the precedent one, but on the broadcast context. This context may be reduced to the time of the day and the day of the week. Classical HMMs cannot represent such a broadcast context and consequently provide poor results in terms of program genre and duration predictions [19]. To overcome this problem, Poli proposes an extension of the HMM called contextual HMM (CHMM). In this extension, the transition between states takes into account the genre, the time of the day, and the day of the week of a given instant of the broadcast. Depending on the genre and the contextual information of a broadcast, a regression tree is used to predict the minimum, the maximum, and the average duration of this broadcast. The models are built on 1 year of corrected EPGs and tested on 1 week (1 year in Poli's thesis).

The originality of Poli's approach comes from the idea that stream structure can be predicted from previous broadcasts. Moreover, the results prove the efficiency of the proposal. In contrast, the first and main drawback is that it requires a huge amount of annotated data for the learning stage (up to 1 year for each channel). Secondly, the method extensively depends on the fact that TV channels have a stable stream structure over years, which makes the approach unable to structure correctly the days containing special events or not following the standard structure: The structure learned on 2004 proved to be relevant to predict the structure of the stream of 95% of the days of 2005. An additional step may be required afterward to analyze the stream since the prediction may not be perfect. However, this work proves that, on the channels used, the stream structure is stable over years.

To our knowledge, this is the only approach that structures TV streams basing mainly on the metadata. Literature contains some other methods that also use the metadata not for macro-segmentation aims, but for other purpose such as personalizing and recommending program to viewers [34–37], creating stream program summaries [38], or indexing TV programs [39].

7.5.2 Content-Based Methods

This category contains the methods that depend on the audiovisual content for applying macro-segmentation. We classify those methods into two subclasses: a class that focuses on the detection of program boundaries (program-based), and a class that extracts break segments (break-based).

7.5.2.1 Program-Based Methods

An example about the program-based methods is the one proposed by Liang et al. [16]. The authors start from the assumption that, when considering two consecutive days, a given program starts and ends approximately at the same time with the same opening and closing credits. As a consequence, their method relies on the repetitive behavior of the opening and closing credits of programs in order to detect their start and end time. They construct program boundary models by detecting the repeated shots in different days. Then, they use the constructed models to segment a TV stream recorded from the same TV channel into programs. In order to test the system, 10 TV streams recorded from CCTV-4 from 17h00 to 21h00 were used (four TV streams for training and six for testing). This system gives excellent results in terms of precision and recall near 100%. On the opposite side, this method was accompanied with several drawbacks:

- The method assumes that all programs have an opening and a closing credit, which is unfortunately not verified by many programs. For example, on French television, constructing a macro-segmentation method that is based on this assumption would not be a good idea.
- Basing on the opening and closing credits of programs (if present) does not permit the detection of commercials that may interrupt programs. Thus, the solution proposed is not a complete TV stream macro-segmentation one. This approach may not be preferment when applying on more complex streams and cannot take into account any possible change of TV schedule that may occur because the models are already constructed.
- Although authors have used a 6-day CCTV-4 Chinese TV stream, we would have been more interested by tests that are not restricted only on the period from 17h00 to 21h00 because the remaining parts of the day, to our knowledge, are less structured.

Like Liang et al., Wang et al. propose in [30] a method basing on the opening and closing credits of programs. They propose a method that detects special images called *program oriented informative images* (POIM). These POIM are frames containing logos with monochrome backgrounds and big text characters. From the authors' point of view, these POIM appear in opening and closing credits and at the end of commercial segments. The authors combine these POIM with auditory and textual information to reject false alarms and retain the most pertinent POIM. The used features feed an SVM classifier in order to find the transitions between programs and reject all the other transitions in the stream. Experiments are made on the TRECVID 2005 corpus and the method seems to be able to detect the boundaries of the programs and the breaks. Even then, we can notice several drawbacks:

- The POIM can be used to detect the boundaries of programs with opening and closing credits and breaks that end with logos. The method would be unable to detect boundaries that do not contain these special features.
- The method does not address the problem of programs that are segmented in several parts. It does not combine the parts of the same program that would be over-segmented due to the presence of commercials inside it.
- The stream that is used to validate the approach is made by concatenating several videos that are taken from the TRECVID 2005. In other words, authors have not used a real TV stream recorded from a TV channel.

Contrarily to the methods proposed in [16,30], El-Khoury et al. propose an unsupervised method based on the fact that each program has homogeneous properties [29]. Consequently, the programs are extracted by detecting the discontinuities of some audiovisual features. The authors start from the idea that during a program, a selected set of features behaves in a homogeneous manner, so that their value distributions can be modeled by a Gaussian law. Moreover, the features of two consecutive programs follow two different Gaussian laws [29]. The authors use a GLR-BIC (*generalized likelihood ratio - Bayesian information criterion*) audio segmentation method that was designed for speaker diarization [40]. The proposed method detects the most probable changes between two homogeneous zones. It provides a segmentation using visual features, then audio features, and afterward the two segmentations are merged. The break segments cannot be detected because of their short duration. The method was tested on 120 h of French TV stream recorded continuously during 5 days and promising results have been obtained. The importance of this method led out from the fact that it is unsupervised and can be applied for several video-processing tasks like speaker diarization, shot detection, program segmentation, etc. Moreover, the homogeneity feature is a stable one that is not affected by any changes in TV broadcasts. However, this method was also accompanied with several limitations:

- Short programs may not be detected and bias the results.
- Merging consecutive extracts of a program that has been over-segmented is not addressed.

Continuing with the homogeneity properties, Haidar proposes a method that uses similarity matrices [33]. The author's aim in this work was to define a similarity measure (SM) of two audiovisual documents that could be of long duration (a day long stream, e.g.). The idea is to measure the similarity between document styles [41]. It can be applied to detect total similarity (near duplicate detection), or partial similarity (quantitative, qualitative, temporal). To compare two documents, a set of audiovisual features is used for constructing a set of similarity matrices, one for each feature. In a second step, the set of SM are merged to obtain one SM that represents the distance between these two documents. As application, the author provides the SM coming from the comparison of a long day stream with itself in order to structure it. The image of the SM shows effectively the structure of the stream. The assets of the method are as follows:

- The method is independent from the video type, the used features, and the duration of the documents.
- It can be applied for various applications such as stream macro-segmentation, video copy detection, and other applications.
- It is an unsupervised approach that does not need any training step.

Even though the author shows visually the structure of the stream, by printing the similarity matrix, the main limitation of this method is that the structure is never extracted and represented explicitly. The extraction of this structure from the SM is certainly not so trivial, and the method, even if promising, is not complete.

7.5.2.2 Break-Based Methods

Contrary to the program-based methods, break-based ones handle the problem in an opposite way. Instead of extracting or searching the boundaries of the programs, they try to extract or detect the boundaries of breaks, a task that may be easier than the former one. They use the fact that TV channels separate consecutive programs by breaks or even by some specific audiovisual frames (monochromatic frames or others). Finding the break boundaries allows the inference of the start and end of programs. Using this assumption, methods should handle the problem that the same program may be interrupted by breaks, and, thus, may be over-segmented into several parts. In this case, the parts of the same program should be merged in order to retrieve the whole program.

As presented before, TV channels present several types of breaks: commercials, trailers, station identification, bumpers. The literature is very rich with methods that are dedicated for commercial detection. These methods do not address the problem of TV stream macro-segmentation itself, but they are always in the kernel of any break-based method. Commercial detection approaches are simply extended in order to detect all types of breaks. Commercial detection approaches can be categorized into three clusters:

1. Detecting commercials using multimodal features [42–48]
2. Detecting commercials present in a collection of preregistered commercials [46,49]
3. Detecting commercials based on their repetitive behaviors [50–52]

The last two categories have been already used in the literature to extract breaks for TV stream macro-segmentation, where they have been called recognition-based and repetition-based approaches. In all the methods of these two types, the macro-segmentation process is composed of four steps:

Step1: Detection of repeated audiovisual sequences in the TV stream. The underlying idea is that breaks and especially commercials have repetitive behaviors.

Step2: Classification of the detected repetitions to differentiate P (program) segments from B (break) ones. As a matter of fact, the detected repetitions may be of diverse natures: breaks, program segments like opening and closing credits, programs broadcasted twice, small programs like weather forecast, etc. As a consequence, the repetitions do not provide enough information to get a clear structure of the stream and a classification step is required.

Step3: Segmentation of the whole stream in P/B sequences based on the classified repetitions.

Step4: Annotation or labeling the so-far-extracted segments.

7.5.2.2.1 Recognition-Based Extraction of Breaks

To our knowledge, [18] is the first complete (and pioneer) recognition-based solution for the TV stream macro-segmentation problem. Step1 (detect repetitions) and Step2 (classification) are performed using a recognition-based method. The author uses a reference video dataset (RVD) that contains shots that are manually annotated and classified as P or B. He uses a perceptual hashing technique in order to recognize the shots of the TV stream that exist in the RVD (rebroadcasted or repeated shots) in real time. The hashing function is built upon a visual signature derived from the DCT coefficients [53].

After the recognition step, the set of recognized shots are used in a second step to macro-segment the stream in P/B sequences (Step3). The author adds to the recognized shots, the segments that contain simultaneous silence and monochromatic frames (noted as separations) and that may be present at the beginning and the end of the commercials.

The segmentation step (Step3) is composed of three stages: pre-segmentation, classification, and merging:

1. *Pre-segmentation*: All the segments that are recognized as breaks are retrieved from the stream.
2. *Classification*: The remaining segments of the stream are classified as P segments or B ones based on their duration (B=segments less than 1 min, P=segments greater than 1 min).
3. *Merging*: The consecutive B segments are merged into one segment.

Finally, the obtained macro-segmentation of the stream is aligned with the EPG that is provided with the stream, by using a dynamic time-wrapping (DTW) algorithm in order to annotate the programs (Step 4).

The proposed method is applied on a 22-day long TV stream recorded from the France2 TV channel from May 9 to May 30, 2005. The first day is used as the RVD and the remaining days to test the system.

The proposed method offers several advantages:

■ It is a rare example of a complete method for TV stream macro-segmentation.
■ The method is validated on a real and long continuous TV stream and the results are categorized among the most interesting ones in the domain.
■ The provided programs are annotated automatically.

Even then, the method has three important drawbacks:

■ The RVD has to be created and annotated manually for each TV channel. It should contain sufficient number of breaks in order to achieve a precise TV stream macro-segmentation.

■ The performance of the method is related to the used RVD. The number of recognized breaks decreases with time. In other words, the efficiency of the method requires updating the RVD regularly. Even then, an automatic technique has been proposed by the author to update the database periodically, and thus to face the continuous change of breaks over time. The experimental data set that is used to this aim is not long enough to validate the updating approach.

■ The macro-segmentation step is based not only on the recognized shots, but also on a set of separation segments (simultaneous presence of silence and monochromatic frames). However, the experimentations that have been done by Ibrahim and Gros in [25] show that the separation segments have a big effect on the efficiency of the results. Additionally, the results do not decrease immediately and maintain some stability even if the number of recognized shots decreases. Moreover, the separations may not be present in all TV streams and may not be present in future TV streams.

7.5.2.2.2 Repetition-Based Extraction of Breaks

Based on the fact that breaks have repetitive behaviors, several repetition-based TV stream macro-segmentation approaches have been proposed [2,25,31]. The approaches of [25,31] have used hashing tables with audio or video signatures in order to detect repeated segments while [2] has implemented a cluster-based approach.

In [31], authors use silence detection and robust audio hashing in order to detect repetitions in the audio track (Step 1). These repetitions are classified as advertisements if their length is between 5 s and 2 min while the others are discarded. The remaining segments of the stream are classified as program segments if their length is more than a fixed threshold (Step 2). The classified segments are then used to provide the whole segmentation of the stream. The authors consider that a program is interrupted by breaks of short duration. Meanwhile, these breaks will be of a long duration when they are broadcasted between two different programs. This simple rule is used to merge two consecutive segments that belong to the same program (Step 3). The proposed method is applied on three TV streams of 12, 9, and 11 h.

This study gave good results, but even then it still suffers from several limitations:

■ Authors justify the use of the audio track by the fact that audio can overcome the limitation of the time-consuming video decoding. Using audio is a good idea, but it should be noticed that video decoding is not so time-consuming nowadays. Moreover, detecting audio segment boundaries is not quite easy. To this reason, many recent researches have been already done to use video signatures instead. In addition, video signatures may be more robust than audio ones since the audio signal is very sensitive to noise and this may affect the repetition detection.

■ Authors assume that repetitions of length between 5 s and 2 min are advertisements, but this is not always the case (e.g., opening and closing credits of news programs in France). To circumvent such strict assumptions about the type of repetitions, which may not be always verified, novel approaches have been proposed in [2,25]. These approaches have added a new step into their macro-segmentation solutions only to handle the problem of repetitions, classification. This step is consecrated to separate the program repetitions from the break ones.

■ The rules used in the segmentation step (Step 3) are very specific and their effectiveness is not clearly evaluated, for example, by a comparison with the ground truth. Authors do not give any information about the measures that have been used to evaluate the approach. In addition, the system was validated using three different streams, where only a part of the day is selected. Such validation may bias the results especially that TV streams may be more structured in some parts of the day than others.

■ Finally, the programs that have been segmented by this method have to be annotated manually. Moreover, the metadata provided with the stream (e.g., EPG) which are an interesting source of information, are not used.

Other novel complete solutions for macro-segment TV streams are proposed by Ibrahim et al. in [24,25] and Manson et al. in [2]. These methods show that it is possible to learn the structure of the stream from the raw data. Somehow, they make a link between Naturel's technique [18] and Poli's [19].

Ibrahim and Gros in [25] propose an extension of Naturel's approach [18] that overcomes its main limitation (the use of the RVD). The same video signature is used in a hashtable in order to retrieve the shots that are repeated more than once in the stream, in real time. These shots are then processed in order to merge consecutive repeated shots that belong to the same content (e.g., same commercial). The repeated sequences are then classified in order to separate program repetitions from break ones using several well-known classifiers and sampling methods. The authors propose two types of segment descriptions: segment-based and repetition-based. On the other hand, to macro-segment and annotate the programs, authors use the algorithm that has been proposed in [18]. The method is applied on a 3-week TV stream, and the results that have been obtained were very close to the results of [18], even though they showed more stability over time. The main drawback of this method is the need of some annotated sequences to train the classifiers. Furthermore, the approach of [25] does not handle the problem of live TV broadcast macro-segmentation, as [2] does. The reader may refer to [25] for a complete description of Ibrahim et al.'s method and a complete comparison with Naturel et al.'s one [18].

In [2], a micro-clustering technique is used to detect the repeated sequences of the stream (refer to [54] for details). The idea is to gather similar key-frames basing on visual features in the same clusters. Each segment of the stream (repeated and non-repeated) is characterized by a set of local, contextual, and relational features. Then, all the segments of the stream are classified in Step 2 using inductive logic programming (ILP) to separate P segments from B ones. The results issued from Step 2 provide the whole segmentation of the stream in P/B sequences [55]. Finally, the DTW is used in Step 4 to align the segmentation with the EPG in order to annotate the program segments. This method was applied on a 2-week corpus of French TV channel.

Here, we list the advantages of this method:

- It is fully automatic and can perform a live TV stream macro-segmentation.
- It is applied on a TV stream of significant duration and the authors obtain good results.

In addition to the previous advantages, we should mention several drawbacks:

- The method needs 7 days of manually annotated data to train the ILP system in order to extract the ILP rules.
- The ILP that is used to classify segments restricts the usable information to the local context of each segment. Taking into account the contextual information of all occurrences of each repeated segment in the stream adds a considerable improvement to the results as presented by [25]. But this may also forbid the use of the live TV stream macro-segmentation solution.

7.5.3 Comparison of Approaches: Results and Discussion

Ideally, in order to compare the different TV stream macro-segmentation approaches of the literature, each one should be tested on the same data sets and use the same metrics of evaluation. The state of the art presented earlier shows that different approaches have used different data sets in their experimentations (except [18,25]). For example, TV streams used to test the methods are of different durations. They vary from 1 day [16] to several weeks [25]. In addition, these approaches did not measure their results using the same methods. Some have used the precision and recall (or *F*-measure), while others have provided the mean of temporal shifts between extracted programs and the real broadcasted ones. This makes the comparison between the reviewed approaches more difficult. Thus, it is not easy to tell which one provides the best overall results. However, some features still can help the reader to determine the best approach (or approaches) from his point of view, for example, the type of method (metadata-based, program-based, or break-based), the amount of data used for the training phase, the length of the tested TV stream, or the solution provided to annotate the programs (if any).

Among the characteristics presented earlier and based on our experiences in the domain, the tested-stream length and continuity can be considered as a very important feature for the evaluation step. This is because some parts of the day are more structured than others. For example, the period of [18h00-22h00] is more structured than [12h00-16h00] as the former corresponds to a larger number of audience than the latter. Thus, TV channels tend to respect the announced schedules for this very competitive time slice. An example about a long continuous TV stream is a 6-h one that is recorded in the period of [12h00-18h00]. In contrast, the stream recorded in the periods of [12h00-15h00] and [18h00-21h00] is not a continuous one because the period [15h00-18h00] is missing.

The features used by each method could be added in the comparison table, in addition to the advantages, disadvantages, and results obtained.

Before launching the discussion, we present a summary of the experimentations done by each approach and the results obtained. Then, we discuss the efficiency of the methods.

7.5.3.1 Results

The aim of this section is to summarize the experimentations done by the approaches to validate their systems. Specifically, we focus on three main points: (1) corpus, (2) measures, and (3) results.

Different measures have been used to evaluate the systems:

1. Program-based precision (P_p^p simplification for program-based evaluation of programs), recall $\left(R_p^p \right)$, and F-measure $\left(F_p^p \right)$: These measures are made at the program level:

$$P_p^p = \frac{Number\_of\_correctly\_found\_programs}{Total\_number\_of\_found\_programs}$$

$$R_p^p = \frac{Number\_of\_correctly\_found\_programs}{Total\_number\_of\_programs\_to\_be\_found}$$

$$F_p^p = \frac{2 * P_p^p * R_p^p}{P_p^p + R_p^p}$$

2. Frame-based precision, recall, and F-measure: Contrary to the previous item, these measures are made at the frame level. They are used to evaluate the P/B segmentation and programs annotation. There is a measure per class (P_p^f for frame-based program precision and P_b^f for frame-based break precision), which are computed using the same method. The program (break,

respectively) segmentation precision, recall, and F-measure are noted as P_p^f, R_p^f, F_p^f (P_b^f, R_b^f, F_b^f, respectively) and are defined as follows:

$$P_p^f = \frac{Number\_of\_frames\_correctly\_classified\_as\_program\_frames}{Total\_number\_of\_frames\_classified\_as\_program\_frames}$$

$$R_p^f = \frac{Number\_of\_frames\_correctly\_classified\_as\_program\_frames}{Total\_number\_of\_frames\_to\_be\_classified\_as\_program\_frames}$$

$$F_p^f = \frac{2 * P_p^f * R_p^f}{P_p^f + R_p^f}$$

3. Temporal accuracy (TA): The average of temporal shifts, between extracted programs from one side and the real broadcasted ones from the other side. This measure concerns the extracted programs only, and gives an idea about the imprecision of the provided segmentation.
4. Boundary-based precision (P^{bd}), recall (R^{bd}), and F-measure (F^{bd}): These measures are made at the boundary level:

$$P^{bd} = \frac{Number\_of\_correctly\_detected\_boundaries}{Total\_number\_of\_detected\_boundaries}$$

$$R^{bd} = \frac{Number\_of\_correctly\_detected\_boundaries}{Total\_number\_of\_boundaries\_to\_be\_detected}$$

$$F^{bd} = \frac{2 * P^{bd} * R^{bd}}{P^{bd} + R^{bd}}$$

5. The F-measure defined in the evaluation campaign ARGOS [56]: The idea is to match each segment of the ground truth with the longest overlapping segment obtained as a result. The latter is matched only once and the temporal intersection between matched segments is identified:

$$F^{arg} = \frac{2 * |matched\_intersection|}{|Ground\_truth| + |Results|}$$

Table 7.1 gives a summary of the corpus, measures, and results of each approach. In order to present an implicit and comprehensible summary that helps the reader to compare approaches, we were obliged, for some approaches, to present an approximation of the efficiency of each approach due to the absence of a global value of the efficiency. For example, [18,25], authors provide a curve of the precision and recall for each day. Similar to that, Manson et al. [2] decompose the day into six intervals. They provide the TA of the beginning (end, respectively) of extracted programs. To

Table 7.1 Summary of the Papers Experimentations

Papers	Corpus	
	Training	*Test*
[19]	One year	One week
[16]	4 TV streams (17h00 to 21h00)	6 TV streams (17h00 to 21h00)
[30]	3000 POIM images to train the classifier	5 TV streams from TRECVID 2005 (15 h each)
[29]	One hour to tune GLR-BIC parameters	5 days
[18]	One day as RVD	20 days
[2]	One week to train the ILP rules	7 days
[25]	30% of annotated repeated sequences in a 3-week stream to train the classifiers	21 days

Papers	Measures	Results	
		P/B segmentation	*Labeling*
[19]	(1), (3)	P_p^p=97%, TA=17 s	P_p^p=97%
[16]	(1), (3)	P_p^p=95.8%, R_p^p=100%, TA=28 s	None
[30]	(4)	P^{bd}=88%, R^{bd}=91.5%, F^{bd}=89.2%	None
[29]	(5)	F^{arg}=90.5%	None
[18]	(2)	F_p^f≈99%, F_b^f≈90%	F_p^f≻88%, F_p^f≺96%
[2]	(3)	Not available	TA≈3 m 35 s
[25]	(2)	F_p^f≈98%, F_b^f≈90%	F_p^f≻90%, F_p^f≺96%

compute one value that measures the efficiency over the whole test stream, we were obliged to compute the average of the provided values.

As we can see in Table 7.1, comparing the approaches is one of the hardest tasks, especially if they have not validated their systems using the same corpus and the same measures. However, we can still highlight the advantages and disadvantages of each approach that may facilitate the comparison task. From our point of view, the approaches presented in the state of the art may be classified in to four clusters:

1. The first cluster gathers approaches that do not provide a clear and complete TV stream macro-segmentation solution or that are based on some nonevident assumptions [16,30,33].
2. The second cluster contains methods that are based on a reference video database [18] or need a lot of data to train the structure model [19].
3. The third cluster is composed of the unsupervised methods [29,31].
4. The fourth cluster gathers methods that replace the RVD by a stage where the structure is learned from raw data [2,25].

The major drawback of the approaches in the first cluster is that they base on assumptions that are not always true. In addition, the solution proposed is not a complete one, because they may not provide the boundaries of all the programs and do not detect the boundaries of all breaks. The approaches of the second cluster are very efficient regarding the results they obtain. Even then, their efficiency is constrained by the amount of annotated data they use. In addition, these systems should be updated with time.

7.5.3.2 Discussion

From our point of view, the approaches of the third and fourth clusters are the most efficient for several reasons:

- They provide a complete TV stream macro-segmentation solution and are less constrained by a priori information (assumptions) contrarily to the methods of the first cluster.
- El-Khoury et al. and Zeng et al. [29,31] provide unsupervised solutions while Manson and Berrani and Ibrahim and Gros [2,25] replace the RVD by a stage where the structure of the stream is learned from raw data. Even if the training step requires the manual annotation of a longer stream extract, up to several days, the extracted information from this ground truth is structural and has a much longer validity (at least several months) than in Naturel's work [18].
- Their systems are validated on a real continuous TV stream (except [31]) and they provide good results.

Comparing the approaches of the third and fourth clusters, the authors of [29] and [31] propose an unsupervised approach that may favor them over [2,25]. However, the approach in [29] cannot extract programs of short durations, the provided programs are not annotated, and the results of [2,25] are better than its results. In contrast, the results obtained by Zheng et al. in [31] are competitive to [2,25]. Additionally, the repetitive behavior of breaks, used by Zheng et al., makes the extraction of breaks easier and more efficient than the extraction of programs. The main problem of the method proposed in [31] is that they consider the repeated sequences with durations between 5 s and 2 min as advertisements. This assumption is not always correct during the day and for all the TV streams. The experiments done in [2,25] contradict completely this assumption. They present the classification problem as the most important step in the macro-segmentation chain. Moreover, the programs provided are not labeled.

Although [2,25] are more preferment than [29,31], they need a supervised learning stage. This point has been addressed in some recent researches, but up to now, these complete unsupervised techniques have been unsuccessful for stream segmentation basing on break-based techniques.

7.6 Conclusion

Our objective in this chapter was to provide the reader with a clear definition about the TV stream macro-segmentation domain, and to present the most important recent works that have been already proposed in the literature. To this aim, we first presented how traditional video content segmentation methods were insufficient for the long-period and heterogeneous-content TV streams, which leads to implement the novel technology of TV stream macro-segmentation. This technology allows users to recover the original macros that construct any heterogonous continuous TV stream. We saw in this chapter how the manual macro-segmentation process is very time-consuming and laborious. We highlighted also the incompleteness and the imprecision of the metadata that prevent them from being sufficient for automatic TV stream macro-segmentation. This was the main motivation that opened the door on a rich state of the art in the domain of automatic TV stream macro-segmentation.

In this state of the art, we presented the different methods that have been grouped into two categories: metadata-based methods and content-based ones. In this latter, the classification is refined into two subclasses. The first one contains methods that extract programs, while the second gathers methods that are based on breaks detection.

In order to compare the proposed approaches, at the end of our chapter, we provided a summary of the experimentations that has been done in the different research papers. In addition to these experiments, we also used the advantages and drawbacks of each method to give a more reliable classification of the different approaches. We categorized these approaches in four clusters, where one of the four seems to contain, from our point of view, the most generic, novel, and promising methods.

References

1. Y. Rui, T.S. Huang, and S. Mehrotra. Constructing table of content for videos. *Constructing Table of Content for Videos*, 7(5):359–368, September 1999.
2. G. Manson and S.A. Berrani. Automatic TV broadcast structuring. *International Journal of Digital Multimedia Broadcasting*, 2010:16, January 2010.

3. M. Wang and H. Zhang. Video content structuring. *Scholarpedia Journal*, 4(8): 9431, 2009.

4. Y. Rui, Z. Xiong, R. Radhakrishnan, A. Divakaran, and T.S. Huang. A unified framework for video summarization, browsing and retrieval. Technical report, MERL Technical Report, September 2004.

5. T. D'Orazio and M. Leo. A review of vision-based systems for soccer video analysis. *Pattern Recognition*, 48(8):2911–2926, August 2010.

6. D. Tjondronegoro, Y.-P.P. Chen, and B. Pham. The power of play-break for automatic detection and browsing of self-consumable sport video highlights. In *Proceedings of the sixth International ACM Multimedia Information Retrieval Workshop (MIR'04)*, New York, October 2004.

7. L. Xie, P. Xu, S.-F. Chang, A. Divakaran, and H. Sun. Structure analysis of soccer video with domain knowledge and hidden Markov models. *Pattern Recognition Letters*, 25(7):767–775, May 2004.

8. M. H. Ali, A.A. Shafie, H. Fadhlan, and M.A. Roslizar. Advance video analysis system and its applications. *European Journal of Scientific Research*, 41(1):72–83, 2010.

9. A. Hanjalic. Shot-boundary detection: Unraveled and resolved? *IEEE Transactions on Circuits and Systems for Video Technology*, 12(2):90–105, February 2002.

10. R. Lienhart. Reliable transition detection in videos: A survey and practitioner's guide. *International Journal on Image Graphics*, 1(3):469–486, 2001.

11. I. Koprinska and S. Carrato. Temporal video segmentation: A survey. *Signal Processing: Image Communication Journal*, 16(5):477–500, January 2001.

12. C.G.M. Snoek and M. Worring. Multimodal video indexing: A review of the state-of-the-art. *Multimedia Tools and Applications*, 25(1):5–35, January 2005.

13. K.W. Wilson and A. Divakaran. Broadcast video content segmentation by supervised learning. *Multimedia Content Analysis*, Springer, Heidelberg, pp. 1–17, 2009, ISBN: 978-0-387-76569-3.

14. D. Brezeale and D.G. Cook. Automatic video classification: A survey of the literature. *IEEE Transactions on Systems, Man and Cybernetics*, 38(3):416–430, May 2008.

15. M. Roach, J. Mason, L. Xu, and F. Stentiford. Recent trends in video analysis: A taxonomy of video classification problems. In *Proceedings of the International Conference on Internet and Multimedia Systems and Applications, IASTED*, Honolulu, HI, August 2002.

16. L. Liang, H. Lu, X. Xue, and Y.P. Tan. Program segmentation for TV videos. *Proceedings of the IEEE International Symposium on Circuits and Systems*, Kobe, Japan, pp. 1549–1552, May 2005.

17. Z.-A.-A. Ibrahim, I. Ferrane, and P. Joly. A similarity-based approach for audiovisual document classification using temporal relation analysis. *EURASIP Journal on Image and Video Processing*, 2011:Article ID 537372, March 2011.

18. X. Naturel, G. Gravier, and P. Gros. Fast structuring of large television streams using program guides. *Proceedings of the Fourth International Workshop on Adaptive Multimedia Retrieval*, Geneva, Switzerland, pp. 223–232, March 2006.

19. J.P. Poli. An automatic television stream structuring system for television archives holders. *Journal of Multimedia Systems*, 14(5):255–275, September 2008.

20. X. Naturel and P. Gros. Dealing with television archives: Television structuring. INRIA Research Report, No. 7301, Mai 2010.

21. European Telecommunication Standard Institute. Enhanced Teletext Specification. Standard 300 706 Edition 1, May 1997.

22. European Telecommunication Standard Institute. Television systems; Specification of the domestic video Program Delivery Control system (PDC). Standard 300 231 Edition 2, April 1998.

23. J.P. Poli and J. Carrive. Television stream structuring with program guides. In *Proceedings of the IEEE International Symposium on Multimedia*, San Jose, CA, pp. 329–334, December 2006.

24. Z.-A.-A. Ibrahim, P. Gros, and S. Campion. AVSST: An automatic video stream structuring tool. In *Third Networked and Electronic Media Summit Conference*, Barcelona, Spain, October 2010.

25. Z.-A.-A. Ibrahim and P. Gros. TV stream structuring. *ISRN Signal Processing Journal*, 2011(Article Id 975145):17, April 2011.

26. S.A. Berrani, P. Lechat, and G. Manson. TV broadcast macro-segmentation: Metadata-based vs. content-based approaches. In *Proceedings of the ACM International Conference on Image and Video Retrieval*, Amsterdam, the Netherlands, pp. 325–332, July 2007.

27. R. Jin and A.G. Hauptmann. Automatic title generation for spoken broadcast news. In *Proceedings of the IEEE International Conference on Multimedia*, San Diego, CA, pp. 1–3, March 2001.

28. A. Messina, L. Boch, G. Dimino, W. Bailer, P. Schallauer, W. Allasia, M. Groppo, M. Vigilante, and R. Basili. Creating rich metadata in the TV broadcast archives environment: The Prestospace Project. In *Proceedings of the International Conference on Automated Production of Cross-Media Content for Multi-Channel Distribution*, Leeds, U.K., pp. 193–200, December 2006.

29. E. El-Khoury, C. Senac, and P. Joly. Unsupervised segmentation methods of TV contents. *International Journal of Digital Multimedia Broadcasting*, Hindawi Publishing Corporation, March 2010.

30. J. Wang, L. Duan, Q. Liu, H. Lu, and J. S. Jin. A multimodal scheme for program segmentation and representation in broadcast video streams. *IEEE Transactions on Multimedia*, 10(3):223–232, Geneva, Switzerland, March 2006.

31. Z. Zeng, S. Zhang, H. Zheng, and W. Yang. Program segmentation in a television stream using acoustic cues. In *Proceedings of the International Conference on Audio, Language and Image Processing*, Shangai, China, pp. 748–752, July 2008.

32. C. Guinaudeau, G. Gravier, and P. Sbillot. Improving ASR-based topic segmentation of TV programs with confidence measures and semantic relations. In *Proceedings of the 11th Annual Conference of the International Speech Communication Association, Interspeech' 10*, Makuhari, Japan, pp. 1365–1368, September 2010.

33. S. Haidar. Comparaison des Document Audiovisuels par Matrice de Similarit. PhD thesis, University of Toulouse 3-Paul Sabatier, September 2005.

34. L. Ardissono, C. Gena, P. Torasso, F. Bellifemine, A. Chiarotto, A. Difino, and B. Negro. Personalized recommendation of TV programs. In *The Advances in Artificial*

Intelligence, Pisa, Italy, Volume 2829 of *Lecture Notes in Computer Science*, pp. 474–486, 2003.

35. H. Lee, J.G. Kim, S.J. Yang, and J. Hong. Personalized TV services based on TV-anytime for personal digital recorder. *IEEE Transactions on Consumer Electronics*, 51(3):885–892, August 2005.

36. L.A. Nickum. Personal preferred viewing using electronic program guide. US Patent, No. 7617512, url: http:www.freepatentonline.com/7617512.html, November 2009.

37. M. Rovira, J. Gonzalez, A. Lopez, J. Mas, A. Puig, J. Fabregat, and G. Fernandez. Indextv: A MPEG7 based personalized recommendation system for digital TV. In *IEEE International Conference on Multimedia and Expo*, Taipei, Taiwan, pp. 823–826, June 2004.

38. Y. Kawai, H. Sumiyoshi, and N. Yagi. Automated production of TV program trailer using electronic program guide. In *Proceedings of the ACM International Conference on Image and Video Retrieval*, Amsterdam, the Netherland, pp. 49–56, July 2007.

39. Z. Liu, D.C. Gibbon, and B. Shahraray. Multimedia content acquisition and processing in the miracle system. In *IEEE Consumer Communications and Networking Conference*, Las Vegas, NV, pp. 272–276, January 2006.

40. E. El-Khoury, C. Senac, and P. Joly. Speaker diarization: Towards a more robust and portable system. In *IEEE International Conference on Acoustics, Speech and Signal Processing (ICASSP)*, Honolulu, HI, pp. 489–492, June 2007.

41. S. Haidar, P. Joly, and B. Chebaro. Mining for video production invariants to measure style similarity. *International Journal of Intelligent Systems*, John Wiley & Sons, Inc, 21(7):747–763, July 2006.

42. A. Albiol, M. J. Fulla, A. Albiol, and L. Torres. Detection of TV commercials. In *Proceedings of the IEEE International Conference on Acoustics, Speech, and Signal Processing*, Montreal, Quebec, Canada, pp. 541–544, May 2004.

43. N. Dimitrova, S. Jeannin, J. Nesvadba, T. McGee, L. Agnihotri, and G. Mekenkamp. Real time commercial detection using MPEG features. In *Proceedings of the International Conference on Information Processing and Management of Uncertainty in Knowledge-Based Systems*, Annecy, France, pp. 1–6, July, 2002.

44. L.Y. Duan, J. Wang, Y. Zheng, J.S. Jin, H. Lu, and C. Xu. Segmentation, categorization, and identification of commercial clips from TV streams using multimodal analysis. In *Proceedings of the 14th Annual ACM International Conference on Multimedia*, Santa Barbara, CA, October, 2006.

45. X.S. Hua, L. Lu, and H.J. Zhang. Robust learning-based TV commercial detection. In *Proceedings of the IEEE International Conference on Multimedia and Expo*, Amsterdam, the Netherlands, pp. 149–152, July 2005.

46. R. Lienhart, C. Kuhmunch, and W. Effelsberg. On the detection and recognition of television commercials. In *Proceedings of the IEEE international Conference on Multimedia Computing and Systems*, Toronto, Ontario, Canada, pp. 509–516, June 1997.

47. T. McGee and N. Dimitrova. Parsing TV program structures for identification and removal of non-story segments. In *Proceedings of the SPIE Conference on Storage and Retrieval for Image and Video Databases*, San Jose, CA, pp. 243–251, January 1999.

48. S.A. Sadlier, S. Marlow, N. O'Connor, and N. Murphy. Automatic TV advertisement detection from MPEG bitstream. *Journal of Pattern Recognition Society*, 35(12):2719–2726, January 2002.

49. J.M. Sanchez, X. Binefa, and J. Vitria. Shot partitioning based recognition of TV commercials. *Journal of Multimedia Tools and Applications*, 8(3):233–247, December 2002.

50. P. Duygulu, M.Y. Chen, and A. Hauptmann. Comparison and combination of two novel commercial detection methods. In *Proceedings of the IEEE International Conference on Multimedia and Expo*, Taipei, Taiwan, pp. 1267–1270, June 2004.

51. G.M. Gauch and A. Shivadas. Finding and identifying unknown commercials using repeated video sequence detection. *Journal of Computer Vision and Image Understanding*, 103(1):80–88, July 2006.

52. M. Covell, S. Baluja, and M. Fink. Advertisement detection and replacement using acoustic and visual repetition. In *Proceedings of the IEEE International Workshop on Multimedia Signal Processing*, Victoria, British Columbia, Canada, pp. 461–466, October 2006.

53. X. Naturel and P. Gros. Detecting repeats for video structuring. *Multimedia Tools and Application*, 38(2):233–252, May 2008.

54. S.A. Berrani, G. Manson, and P. Lechat. A non-supervised approach for repeated sequence detection in TV broadcast streams. *Signal Processing: Image Communication*, special issue on *Semantic Analysis for Interactive Multimedia Services*, 23(7):525–537, 2008.

55. G. Manson and S.A. Berrani. An inductive logic programming-based approach for TV stream segment classification. In *Proceedings of the IEEE International Symposium on Multimedia*, Berkely, CA, pp. 130–135, December 2008.

56. P. Joly, J. Benois-Pineau, E. Kijak, and G. Quenot. The ARGOS campaign: Evaluation of video analysis and indexing tools. *Signal Processing: Image Communication*, Special Issue on *Content-Based Multimedia Indexing and Retrieval*, 22(7–8):705–717, 2007.

Chapter 8

Large-Scale Analysis for Interactive Media Consumption

David Gibbon
AT&T Labs Research

Andrea Basso
AT&T Labs Research

Lee Begeja
AT&T Labs Research

Zhu Liu
AT&T Labs Research

Bernard Renger
AT&T Labs Research

Behzad Shahraray
AT&T Labs Research

Eric Zavesky
AT&T Labs Research

Contents

8.1 Introduction

Over the years the fidelity and quantity of TV content has steadily increased, but consumers are still experiencing considerable difficulties in finding the content matching their personal interests. New mobile and IP consumption environments have emerged with the promise of ubiquitous delivery of desired content, but in many cases, available content descriptions in the form of electronic program guides (EPGs) lack sufficient detail and cumbersome human interfaces yield a less-than-positive user experience. Creating metadata through a detailed manual annotation of TV content is costly and, in many cases, this metadata may be lost in the content life cycle as assets are repurposed for multiple distribution channels. Content organization can be daunting when considering domains from breaking news contributions, local or government channels, live sports, music videos, documentaries up through dramatic series and feature films. As the line between TV content and Internet content continues to blur, more and more long tail content will appear on TV and the ability to automatically generate metadata for it becomes paramount. Research results from several disciplines must be brought together to address the complex challenge of cost effectively augmenting existing content descriptions to facilitate content personalization and adaptation for users given today's range of content consumption contexts.

This chapter presents systems architectures for processing large volumes of video efficiently, practical, state-of-the-art solutions for TV content analysis and metadata generation, and potential applications that utilize this metadata in effective and enabling ways. A brief synopsis of chapter highlights is included in the following to serve as guidance for the reader as several topics are given a deeper discussion.

- *System Architecture:* A flexible system architecture supports a range of applications including both on-demand retrieval of assets ingested as files as well as real-time processing of IP multicast MPEG-2 transport streams. Transcoding and segmentation is performed at both ingest and delivery phases to meet the system design parameters of optimizing storage and supporting content repurposing for a range of user devices including desktop browsers, mobile phones, tablets, and STBs.
- *Media Analysis:* Starting from a high-level program structure discovery, programs are segmented at several scales using the detection of similar segments with SBD, mid-level semantic classifiers of images, speech recognition, speaker segmentation, face detection, near-duplicate detection, and clustering methods. These elementary segmentations are then combined to perform anchorperson detection and multimodal news story segmentation for easier program navigation and indexing.
- *Clients and Applications:* Standards compliant metadata (e.g., EPG, PSIP, MediaRSS, MPEG-7) is ingested, augmented, and made available to client applications. Over 200,000 TV programs have been indexed by the proposed system and media processing results are available in XML form for each asset. Indexing systems with web service interfaces provide rapid access to this detailed metadata for content collections to facilitate the creation of highly dynamic applications from complex analytical scenarios to mobile retrieval environments.

The remainder of this chapter is organized into three main sections as follows: Section 8.2 describes systems and architectures to support content processing at scale, Section 8.3 discusses techniques for processing TV content, and Section 8.4 outlines a few applications that are enabled by TV content processing, ranging from those targeted to expert users for detailed content analysis to those intended for novice users for entertainment applications utilizing multiple device environments.

8.2 System Architectures for Content Processing

The increasing relevance of automatic content processing methods as a key component for multimedia services requires the development of sophisticated, large-scale
content processing system architectures. Such architectures rely on well-known
service-oriented architecture (SoA) concepts with the needed extension specific to
content processing, and are necessary to process large amounts of content from
real-time feeds or existing archives and to analyze and publish content rapidly for
immediate search. While the transactional nature of SoA is very effective for some
of the tasks in a content processing architecture, other media-intensive workflows
are characterized by a series of specific requirements. For example, the individual
content processing modules can range between computationally very light and of a
stateless transactional nature (i.e., converting a metadata format) to extremely computationally intensive (i.e., asset transcoding) and may take a considerable amount
of time. In addition, asset management, large data transfer, and large data storage
are generally involved, requiring the separation of the metadata and the media processing paths for efficiency. Furthermore, specific consideration needs to be given to
maintain coherence of media formats and profiles. Finally, content security including content watermarking and DRM must be taken into account for every step of
the media workflow. In the discussed architectures, the workflows are media-aware
to address these issues.

A high-level system architecture is presented in Figure 8.1. The architecture
separates the media-specific path (indicated by solid arrows in Figure 8.1) from the

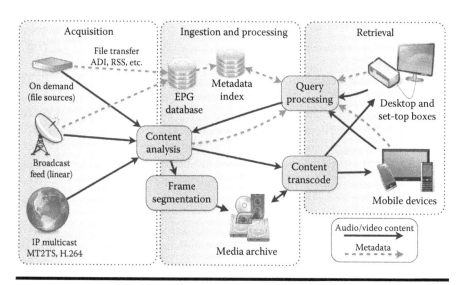

**Figure 8.1 High-level system architecture briefly describing all stages of content
analysis.**

metadata path (dashed arrows in Figure 8.1). Metadata that is still embedded in the media is separated at the ingestion phase. Two separate communication buses, one for media and one for metadata, allow for the proper process pipelining in order to maximize efficiency and meet requirements for a variety of applications. The system architecture in Figure 8.1 is distributed and reconfigurable and can process live ingested media streams and static media collections. This architecture handles media acquisition, content processing, indexing, and publishing for a variety of heterogeneous devices. The ensemble of the modules is orchestrated by a task flow management component that exploits parallelism whenever possible. A central scheduler manages load balancing among the servers and has the capability of task prioritization. Each module is exposed as a web service, implemented with industry-standard interoperable middleware components. For more information, readers can consult a detailed description of the architecture in [16].

8.2.1 Web Services Model

With the increasing availability of high-bandwidth connectivity, the opportunities for content analysis, services have surfaced in desktop, mobile, and set-top environments alike. This is a formidable challenge because each environment may have unique demands for content acquisition, representation, retrieval, and delivery. An increasingly popular way to bridge these environments is using web-based services following either a SOAP-based or REST-based design models that leverages lightweight data formats like MediaRSS (XML) or JSON. Web services allow generic access to both acquisition (the Internet, a camera, DTV feed, desktop computer, etc.) and consumption (a mobile phone, a television, etc.) devices to offload heavy resource and complex computational requirements onto a remote location, as illustrated in Figure 8.2. Web services naturally fit into "cloud" computing or storage architectures, where network connectivity, throughput, and some security demands are assumed to be satisfied by service providers as a prerequisite of their offering.

As illustrated earlier, there are a few core components for content analysis systems exposed via web services. First, the most critical (and only visible) component is a services controller that acts as a middle layer, mapping requests from different clients into functionality requests for underlying systems. This middle layer exposes a simple yet intuitive API that adds additional security provisioning to internal system functions and is capable of routing a request to any number of distributed resources that are hidden within the web service. These capabilities correctly vet access to internal resources and allow a single web service to efficiently distribute requests according to system load. Second, a set of computers (either physical or virtual), referred to as nodes, capable of executing analysis functions on a piece of content are located within the web service. Nodes can be added in an ad hoc fashion to execute one or many of the processing functions required. For example, some nodes with a large local storage capacity and a fast processor

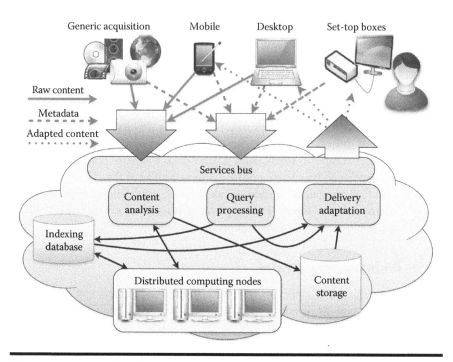

Figure 8.2 Typical web-service configuration, offering a generic interface to many platforms and offloading indexing, analysis, and storage requirements to a decentralized location.

may be ideal for video analysis whereas other nodes with a large memory capacity may be better suited for complex numerical analysis. Next, an indexing database that stores metadata and low-level features for a set of content is stored within the web service and is accessible only to other internal systems. Similar to the internal computation nodes, this indexing database also can be distributed to better accommodate different request loads if needed. Finally, to complete a media web service, a reliable content storage and delivery system is needed. The only responsibilities of this system are to store incoming content and queries and to deliver that content in a format that the requesting client can interpret. As the number of devices, operating systems, and content codecs fluctuate across clients, it is critical to have a content delivery system capable of satisfying all playback requests. These systems can transcode content to all possible formats required (i.e., decode to a raw format and re-encode to a target format) either preemptively off-line or online in a live, adaptive streaming fashion. Although, online transcoding no longer requires elaborate systems with costly dedicated hardware, the cost of digital storage is also continually declining. Thus, a system designer must be cognizant of the expected number of users and requests for his or her application before choosing one configuration.

8.2.2 VoD Ingest Model

In more traditional architectures such VoD content is analyzed in a distributed manner from static repositories. In these architectures, content ingestion and processing are two separate phases that include a large amount of intermediate storage and potentially involve content transcoding. Such architectures do not suffer from high latency and in general do not have streaming and real-time requirements. However, with the increased need for content analysis, and in particular the volume of content derived from broadcast or multicast sources that needs to be processed, real-time and streaming requirements need to be factored in, leading to more complex system architectures.

8.2.3 Linear and Continuous Ingest Model

We define linear and continuous ingestion models framework where metadata and content is ingested continuously in time in a linear fashion and where the result of the content processing is readily available for consumption. Every element of a linear and continuous ingestion architecture must be designed to minimize end-to-end latency. Relevant content analysis results corresponding to a point in the ingested media stream need to be available for consumption in a bounded time interval for applications such as content-based search, advanced content-based services, content monitoring, etc. Media processing profiles are defined to match content analysis loads with available processing resources. The architecture dynamically adapts from one profile to another in a graceful manner. As an example, transcoding parameters can be changed dynamically or accuracy of speech to text indexing can be traded off versus execution time. For real-time processing, content storage is minimized if not eliminated completely and content must be processed in a real-time manner with minimal buffering and state. Unlike the VoD ingest case, the continuous ingest model precludes any media processing that uses multiple passes with large windows. In order to meet some of these requirements, the usage of specialized processing software and hardware nodes may be required. Such nodes may require demultiplexed elementary streams from the original content or encapsulation format conversion may be required in some cases. This may be implemented by a preprocessing service that prepares the media prior to invoking the main processing services.

8.2.4 Role of Standards

Taking a modular approach to media processing architecture design allows individual components to be optimized more easily and simplifies reconfigurability to support a wide range of applications. Well-defined standards for data representation are critical for successful system operation, and open standards enable interoperability among research groups and industry vendors. This applies not only at the transport and basic data marshaling level through the use of such standards as TCP/IP, HTTP, XML, and REST, but also up through the application layers as well. Of course supporting a range of media encoding specifications and media container formats is a requirement for any media processing system. Beyond this, standardizing the representation of the results of media analysis in addition to basic content descriptions enables content creators and media consumption applications to interoperate harmoniously.

8.2.4.1 Electronic Program Guide Metadata

The role of TV content analysis may be viewed as that of extracting enhanced content descriptions that augment available high-level descriptions. Although other external sources may be available such as less dynamic Internet knowledge repositories, generally the most reliable descriptions are provided by EPGs that accompany TV programming offered over the air, cable, or IP networks. These enhanced descriptions increase the quality of experience for users, for example, by improving content discovery by providing more data to search and personalization systems. Standards are critical for the exchange of content descriptions among the content analysis subsystem and other service components as well as the interoperability between different systems. EPG data is typically managed in relational databases but exchanged in XML format. Various methods have been devised to efficiently deliver EPG metadata via multicast communications [6]. Program descriptions and scheduled broadcast event information can also be delivered in an encapsulated form with the content. For example, terrestrial broadcasts in the United States use the ATSC Program and System Information Protocol to deliver program guide information to receivers [13]. The data model is most easily represented in an XML schema which facilitates reuse of data types and extension to support representation of detailed content analysis results harmoniously. For instance, the Alliance of Telecommunications Industry Solutions/IPTV Interoperability Forum (ATIS IIF) EPG specification [30] incorporates schemas from TV-Anytime [2] as well as MPEG-7 [20] and includes, for example, classification schemes for role codes defined by the European Broadcast Union (EBU) [3]. In addition to the global program descriptions, TV-Anytime allows for specification of metadata describing segments of a program which, for example, could be used for subtopics in a documentary. Going further, a recent effort in MPEG-7 [30] defines a profile for representation of automated content processing results. This will be a natural extension to the existing EPG standards which already use MPEG-7 data types.

8.2.4.2 Representation of Automatically Extracted Metadata

The current evolution and performance of content analysis tools and its imminent mass-scale market adoption stresses the importance of a standardized representation of automatically extracted metadata. In this context, the EBU P/SCAIE [1,29] metadata group has designed a new MPEG-7 audiovisual profile for the description of complex multimedia content entities. This profile accommodates a comprehensive structural description of the content, including also audio and visual feature descriptions obtained via automatic metadata extraction. The profile also defines a set of semantic constraints on the selected tools, which resolve ambiguities in modeling the description and support system interoperability. The description tools in this profile can be used to describe the results of various kinds of media analyses with visual and audio low-level features. Consequently, the information resulting from the media analyses, such as shot/scene detection, face recognition/tracking, speech recognition, copy detection and summarization, can be used in a wide range of applications such as archive management, news, new services for new media, and many academic projects handling a large scale of video content. Citing a practical use case discussed earlier in this chapter, copy repetition detection is implemented through AudioVisual Segments cross-reference (through the Relation element of AudioVisual Segment), and by the use of the appropriate term chosen from Segment Relation Classification Scheme to specify the kind of copy/transformation. For more detail, the reader can refer to the examples reported in [1].

8.2.4.3 Media Encoding and Delivery

While several media-encoding formats may be used for content archival, and new formats are constantly being developed, there has been some convergence toward H.264 for a wide range of video encoding applications. H.264 is often used in conjunction with an MPEG-2 transport stream for delivery on IPTV networks, or is encapsulated in an MPEG-4 file format for web applications. Individual implementations must balance design trade-offs when selecting particular encoding parameters; for example, HTTP adaptive streaming and precise random access may suggest considerable use of reference frame structure with frequent intra-coded frames, but at the cost of increased storage and bandwidth requirements.

8.2.4.4 On-Demand Metadata

Global metadata in the form of an EPG is used to describe scheduled broadcast time and program-level information about programs. The on-demand consumption paradigm is gaining popularity in the TV realm and web media has been predominantly on demand for many years. While some of the same program description data types may be used for both EPG and VoD (or CoD for content on demand) applications, in practice other standards for CoD have emerged, such as the Cable Labs VoD metadata specifications [5] in the broadcast space or MediaRSS [4] and its variants in the web space. These data models not only include program descriptions, but also support publishing functions such as specifying content purchase options and periods of availability.

8.3 Media Analysis

At the core of every content processing system is a battery of techniques for media analysis. To address the many different forms of media like still images, audio podcasts, live or broadcast video, and highly edited content, media analysis is broken down into different stages that all produce bits of information, called *metadata*, that can be easily transmitted and stored within a processing architecture. Automated media analysis methods can generate detailed metadata that augments existing manually created content descriptions to enable a range of video services. Algorithms may operate on individual media streams, including audio, video, or text streams from subtitles or closed captions. Multimodal processing techniques process media streams collectively to improve accuracy. This section presents several methods that have applicability to a broad range of TV content genres. Most of the media processing functions discussed here have been the subject of research study for a number of years and interested readers are encouraged to consult the references for a more in-depth treatment. However, to convey solutions to a few issues encountered in media processing algorithms in this domain, some sections are explored with more detail.

8.3.1 Media Segmentation

Dividing media streams and programs into smaller segments facilitates media retrieval, browsing, and content adaption for mobile device applications. For some content sources such as TV news programs, a hierarchical program structure can be extracted [19], as shown in Figure 8.3. This program structure, whether determined automatically by content analysis or manually by user annotation, enables other content analysis routines to more precisely understand and process the different syntactic structure of a TV program. For example, non-news programs (i.e., soap operas and sitcoms) may have story segments like an introduction, action, and conclusion instead of topic segments, but both of these segmentations provide strong cues for the underlying syntax of a program. While some program analysis systems may require a detailed syntactical understanding of a programs structure, the methods described here focus on high-performance detection of elementary syntax analysis, such as shots and commercial breaks.

8.3.1.1 Shot Boundary Detection

In a video sequence, a visual shot corresponds to the act of turning a camera on and off of a scene, person, or object and results in a group of adjacent frames whose content is homogeneous. SBD facilitates further video content analysis and it is an important component in video indexing, query, and browsing systems. Due to fast global or local motion, camera operations, complex lighting schemes, camera instability, and combinations of a variety of video editing effects, shot boundary detection (SBD) is

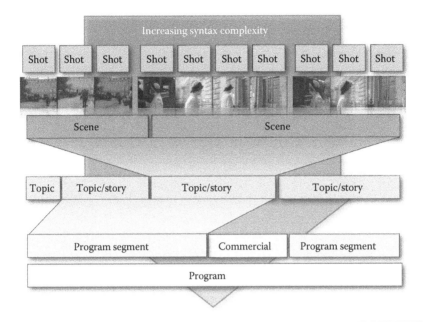

Figure 8.3   Typical TV program structure.

still a challenging task. One of the most established platforms for SBD was the SBD task evaluated yearly in TRECVID from 2001 to 2007. TRECVID is a workshop hosted by the National Institute for Standards and Technology (NIST) organized to objectively evaluate international academic and industrial research labs in numerous video analysis tasks [35]. Interested readers can find the state-of-the-art approaches reported in these workshops.

One approach for SBD and classification [25] is illustrated in Figure 8.4. A set of independent detectors, targeting the most common types of shot boundaries, are designed. This figure shows the detectors for cut, fade in, fade out, fast dissolve (less than 5 frames), dissolve, and subshot introduced by global motion. Subshot detection is valuable for providing accurate representations of video in cases such as with long camera pans where the visual contents have changed significantly within a single shot. Essentially, each detector is a finite state machine (FSM), which may have different numbers of states to detect the target transition pattern and locate the transition boundaries. The modular design of the system allows for easy addition of additional detectors to tackle other types of transitions that may be introduced during the production process. A support vector machine (SVM) based transition verification method is employed in several detectors, including cut, fast dissolve, and dissolve detectors. Finally, the results of all detectors are fused together based on the priorities of these detectors. The detectors utilize two types of visual features: intra-frame and inter-frame features. The intra-frame features are extracted within a

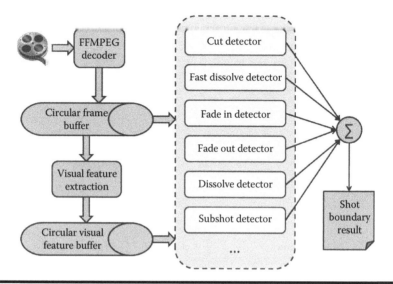

Figure 8.4   Overview of the shot boundary detection system.

single frame, and they include color histogram, edge, and related statistical features. The inter-frame features rely on the current frame and one previous frame, and capture the motion-compensated intensity matching errors and histogram changes. For more detailed information about the implementation of these detectors, please refer to [25].

8.3.2 Audio Processing

Most systems utilizing audio processing for TV content indexing focus on the speech within a program. While this narrow scope may unusual, it is unusual for musical scores, specific sounds (i.e., sound effects like laugh tracks), and environmental audio to significantly contribute to the indexing of TV content because of their brief and heterogenous nature. However, some visual techniques, discussed later in Section 8.3.4, like semantic concepts and duplicate detection can be aided by the addition of generic audio detection methods.

8.3.2.1 Speaker Segmentation and Clustering

Speaker segmentation is important for ASR and audio content analysis. For example, with information about different speaker segments, ASR systems can dynamically adapt utilized models and parameters for different speakers to improve overall recognition accuracy. Additionally, information about different speaker segments provides useful cues for indexing and browsing audio content. These cues can be taken

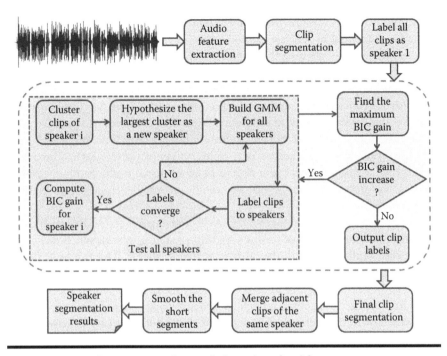

Figure 8.5   Speaker segmentation and clustering algorithm.

advantage of to organize and index TV content. The overall system for speaker segmentation and clustering is depicted in Figure 8.5. The algorithm uses mel-frequency cepstral coefficients (MFCC) and Gaussian mixture model (GMM) to model the acoustic characteristics of speakers. The Bayesian information criterion (BIC) is adopted to locate the speaker boundaries and determine the number of speakers [11]. The kernel, indicated by the round cornered rectangle in the middle of the figure, proceeds iteratively. At each iteration, BIC gain induced by splitting segments of one speaker into two speakers is computed and the speaker whose split produces the maximum BIC gain is found. If that gain is positive, then the number of speakers is increased for the next iteration. If not, the iteration terminates and the process is complete. The speaker boundaries and speaker models are refined iteratively while speaker segments are split (see the embedded dashed line rectangle), until the speaker labels converge.

8.3.3 Closed Caption Processing

While not all content descriptors that are supplied with or extracted from content are in textual form, linguistic information plays a major role in indexing, retrieval, and adaptation of content. Closed captioning that is provided with most TV programs is a major source of this information. Because of some issues related to proper timing and formatting of closed captions, effective content searching and adaptation requires additional processing of the raw captioning information. These requirements are addressed by properly aligning the captions with audio information by employing speech recognition, and restoring the proper case through linguistic processing.

A significant portion of TV content is closed captioned in real time, as it is being broadcast. This is, of course, necessary for live events such as sports or breaking news programs, but since this mode of captioning is less time consuming to produce than off-line captioning, it is used for content from other genres as well. While real-time captioning provides an invaluable service to hearing impaired viewers and broadens the audience to include non-fluent listeners and to public multi-monitor viewing contexts, the process inherently includes significant variable latency (e.g., 3–10 s) and paraphrasing.

Optimizing the user experience for content-based retrieval of TV content and the performance of multimedia processing algorithms requires accurate synchronization of the closed caption text with the other media components. This can be achieved using speech processing either using edit-distance minimization on the one-best word hypothesis from large vocabulary ASR or by using forced alignment methods similar to those used in acoustic modeling. Systems using either of these approaches must be robust to the presence of background music and mismatches between the closed caption text arising from paraphrasing and must deal with program segments for which no captioning is available.

8.3.3.1 Web Mining for Language Modeling

When adapting content for viewing on a range of display devices, correct text capitalization is an important factor in determining the quality of the transcripts obtained from closed captioned text [6,10]. An N-gram language model generated using a large corpus of AP newswire data provides a baseline model for case restoration. Keeping this data up to date requires timely discovery and mining of recently published documents to learn new information and incorporate it into the models and web resources described by RSS are a good source of such documents. However, as the sources vary widely in terms of content formatting, processing is required to extract the relevant textual components and detect breaks at sentence boundaries. The result of the processing (Figure 8.6) shows that readability is greatly improved.

8.3.4 Image Processing

While audio processing largely helps to index content with speech, multimedia content from TV news programs, documentaries, or home videos often lacks rich descriptions of the actual scenes and subjects within an image. Fortunately, a number of techniques have matured to generate a mid-level representation of content,

Original CC text	HUNDREDS OF FAMILIES HAVE FOUND THEM-SELVES IN NEW YORK CITY WHERE THEY'RE GETTING A HEARTFELT BIG APPLE WELCOME.
Case restored CC	Hundreds of families have found themselves in New York City where they're getting a heartfelt Big Apple welcome.

Figure 8.6   Closed caption case restoration.

including general scene information, detect the presence of people or repeating characters, and even locate similar frames and video segments within a single program that can help to identify repeated thematic information.

8.3.4.1 Semantic Concepts

One problem encountered when indexing video content is the inability for existing metadata to adequately describe that content. Often, the way a computer indexes content (i.e., using low-level features) and the way a human would describe it (i.e., using high-level textual keywords) are quite different. This problem is referred to as a semantic gap, and is due to computational limitations in content representation [36]. Mid-level semantic concepts, often realized as machine-learned visual classifiers, are one increasingly popular way to resolve this disparity because they combine knowledge from a set of machine features and human labels over a common dataset. Additionally, mid-level semantic concepts can aid in indexing of content if it does not include title and description information or an audio track, which respectively provide textual keywords and transcripts from speech recognition.

The core stages traditionally employed when using semantic classifiers are as follows:

1. Define the lexicon or names of concepts: As research in the area of formally defined concept classifications has progressed, an increasing number of ontologies have been developed that define concepts and categories based on language [12], popular concepts for consumer media [27], and generic concepts common in broadcast news [23]. In the presented work, the latter option was chosen and the Large Scale Concept Ontology for Media (LSCOM) definitions are used to describe a library of concepts because each offers an additional piece of mid-level information that can be used to index the target content. However, it should be noted that the detection performance for some of these concepts was poor, which was most commonly attributable to infrequency of training data, or greatly varying appearance of the subjects.
2. Obtain human labels and machine features: After defining a set of concepts, both human-provided labels and machine features are required. Although

other techniques have sought to leverage social tags from popular photo sharing sites [12], the presented system utilized the relevant and nonrelevant labels from 374 LSCOM [23] and 100 MediaMill [37] concept definitions that were provided for 160 h of multilingual broadcast news from the TRECVID2005 development set [35]. To reduce the annotation required to achieve a given level of accuracy, active learning may be employed in an interactive and iterative manor. Alternatively, other sources of labeling such as social tagging may be leveraged, but here methods such as consensus labeling are required to reduce labeling error.

3. Train machine models for classification: The final step is to train a set of classifiers, and in this system one SVM was trained for each feature and concept pair. Optimal low-level image features can also vary dramatically, features were derived from prior work: three global features (grid color moments, Gabor texture, and edge direction histogram [7]) and one local feature (keypoints soft-quantized into a bag-of-words representation [41]). To produce a single concept score, each SVM is evaluated, normalized with a sigmoid, and then averaged across features.

One example usage of semantic classifiers is to aide in interactive search in a filtering fashion [41]. In this use case, the user starts with a single textual or concept-based query and then refines the query by expanding it to include another concept (a logical OR operation) or exclude a concept (a logical NOT operation). This system was evaluated over 314 h of TV content and demonstrated a gradual increase in precision up to a point, as illustrated in Figure 8.7. After this critical point (which varies per query), the noisy nature of the semantic classifiers begins to degrade performance.

8.3.4.2 Face Detection

Detecting the presence of people in video can provide valuable information for determining the structure of the content and is useful in creating visual summaries. For example, in news programs, detecting the presence of the anchorperson and reporters can be used as a part of the process of segmenting the content into individual news stories. This facilitates retrieval or repurposing of content by converting long-form content into shorter units for consumption on mobile devices. Applications may discard repeated images of the anchorperson in order to provide more informative visual summaries containing images representing news events filmed on location. Face detection is the task of detecting human faces in arbitrary images or videos. In the simplest case, face detection in video can be performed by treating the video as a sequence of still images (frames) from which it is composed and by performing face detection on each frame. Such an approach may be suitable for

Concept filter	Precision @ 40	Precision @ 100
Baseball only	0.050	0.020
Or athlete	0.175	0.250
Or sports	0.375	0.340
Not soccer	0.525	0.440
Or running	0.600	0.540
Or grandstand	0.600	0.420

(a)   (b)   (c)

Figure 8.7 **For a system utilizing semantic concepts as filters in an interactive search process, precision scores for different results set sizes and visual illustrations of results at each stage with relevant images marked with a white square in the lower right corner. Performance continues to improve until a point (here, the addition of *grandstand*) where the noisy nature of the concept classifiers begins to overpower useful relevance scores. (a) *Baseball* only, (b) or *athlete* or *sports*, and (c) not *soccer* or *running*.**

applications that not only require faces to be detected, but also need to track the motion of the individual faces between consecutive frames.

While the Viola–Jones algorithm [39] has been widely used for detecting faces in an image, more recent work involves online learning of faces and their identification in real-time [33]. Earlier methods include fast template matching using iterative dynamic programming combined with tracking [26], neural network-based techniques [32], and sparse network of linear functions technique of Roth et al. [31].

8.3.4.3 Face Clustering

The state of the art in face detection and identification is now mature enough to act as a complementary piece of semantic information extracted during the analysis process. Face identification can provide valuable nonlinguistic information that can be used to retrieve video segments in which a particular person appears like finding popular characters, locating the principal cast of a video, finding multiple characters appearing together, and even finding characters in particular outfits. When highly accurate identification is not possible, or no prior information is available about the faces that are present in a video program, information related to the appearance of the same faces in different segments has proven highly effective in deriving higher level semantic information. In user-generated videos, one can search for specific points in videos where certain family members appear or search for segments of videos that contain certain combinations of family members.

Several face clustering algorithms have been proposed in the literature. Antonopoulos et al. [8] propose using a dissimilarity matrix from preexisting face clusters; Fitzsgibbon and Zisserman [14] use joint manifold distance; Tao and Tan [38] propose dividing face sequences by pose and then applying additional constraints obtained from domain knowledge. There are other methods that have been proposed in [18,24,31,40].

The approach discussed in the following uses hierarchical agglomerative clustering (HAC) to generate clusters of faces from a video or multimedia presentation. It employs a hybrid technique that uses Eigenfaces, face, and torso information during the clustering process. This provides richer and more stable results than any of the single methods alone [9]. To cluster the detected faces, the face and torso region below the face are used. Patterns of clothing in the torso regions are trivially detected (an offset from the face) and they are more differentiable among different persons. A weighting is applied to the torso with the assumption that same person within one video (e.g., TV news program) wears the same clothes. In total, features are weighted from two regions: an icon region and torso region, as shown in Figure 8.8.

Features from these three regions are extracted to measure the dissimilarity among faces. For the icon and torso regions, several features are computed: color moments in *Luv* color space (9 features), the Gabor texture features (mean and standard deviation) in a combination of three scales and four directions (24 features), and the edge direction histogram in 16 bins (17 features, including one bin for nonedge pixels). These 50-dimensional low-level features can effectively represent the color and texture patterns in these regions. For face region i, its icon and torso features are denoted by I_i and T_i, respectively. In this approach, the distance between any

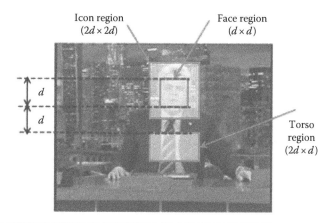

Figure 8.8 Icon and torso regions are defined in terms of the face location and size.

two face, icon, or torso pairs is simply the Euclidean distance $FD(i,j)$, $ID(i,j)$, or $TD(i,j)$. However, to emphasize the uniqueness of each person's face region, face features are first mapped into a basis derived from an Eigen analysis of faces inspired by the Eigenface concept [14]. An average face and M Eigenfaces are denoted by Ψ and u_n, where $n = 1, \ldots M$, respectively. For face F_i, its Eigenface components $\omega_i = (\omega_n^i, n = 1, \ldots M)$ are computed by $\omega_n^i = u_n^T(F_i - \Psi)$. All faces from one video are analyzed as a set to compute Ψ and u_n (where M is preset to 16) after resizing face regions to 50×50. Finally, the Euclidean distance for a face is computed using a vector of the ω components that correspond to that face. Although not analyzed here, for more generic (but possibly less discriminable features), Eigenface models can also be learned from a larger corpus.

8.3.4.4 Duplicate Detection

Duplicate detection is the process of detecting images or segments from specific content that may be included in other content. Duplicate image and video detection is essential for copyright monitoring, business intelligence, and advertisement monitoring. However, in addition to these applications, duplicate detection can serve as a powerful mechanism that enables the discovery of content of interest from large content repositories bases on a short sample. At a high level, there are two distinct approaches to duplicate detection. The first approach is watermarking, which embeds some kind of watermark in the original image. For this method to be effective, the embedded watermark needs to be robust to a number of transformations that are applied during processing to survive such transformations. Examples of such transformations include re-encoding, scaling, and changes in intensity or color. The watermark also needs to be imperceptive such that it does not hurt the visual quality of the original image or video. The second approach involves detecting the duplicated image or video purely based on the content itself. This approach is applicable in a wider range of applications since it does not require the initial step of embedding a watermark in the content. Due to this distinct advantage, this chapter focuses on the latter approach.

Many methods have been proposed for near-duplicate detection, and they can be generally grouped into two categories: global visual feature based and local visual feature based. The first category relies on visual features that are extracted from the entire image, including color, texture, edge, etc. [28]. These features usually reflect the global characteristics of the image, and the feature dimension is low. The advantage of this category is the high efficiency, yet the disadvantage is the low robustness. Simple image transformations, for example, Gamma correction and insertion of big patterns, can easily devastate the performance. The second category relies on salient local feature points that can be repeatedly detected after severe image transformations, for example, heavy re-encoding and rotation. The commonly adopted visual features include Scale-invariant feature transform (SIFT), Speeded Up Robust Features (SURF), and Maximally Stable Extremal Regions

(MSER) [22]. Usually thousands of such features are detected in an image, and the overall feature dimension is high. Methods in this category usually deliver high detection performance, and they can also find sub-image duplicates. The obvious disadvantage is that they are hard to scale. One remedy for the scalability issue is to adopt the bag of visual words approach [34], which converts the high dimension visual features into quantized labels, and treats them as words in a document. Traditional information retrieval techniques can be straightforwardly applied. Such methods usually provide satisfactory performance with much less computational complexity. While the near-duplicate detection method presented here is in the first category, it has been augmented by a grid mechanism that improves the reliability of the general global visual feature based approaches.

Figure 8.9 is a high-level representation of a one possible duplicate image detection algorithm implementation. Each image is partitioned into 4 × 4 pixel grid, and within each grid a set of global features is computed [16], including the color moments in *Luv* color space [10], the Gabor texture features (mean and standard deviation) in a combination of three scales and four directions, and the edge direction histogram in 16 bins. For efficient image comparison in the entire video collection, the Locality-Sensitive Hashing (LSH) approach was employed [7]. For each image, 64 hashing values are computed based on global image features. The LSH values

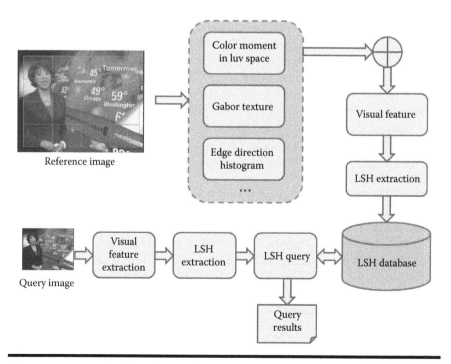

Figure 8.9   Near-duplicate image detection algorithm.

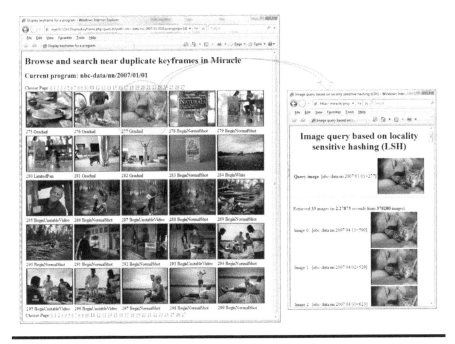

Figure 8.10   **Near-duplicate keyframe detection system.**

of all reference images are saved in a database. The LSH values of each test image are used to query the database. Figure 8.10 presents a prototype system for finding near-duplicate images. All keyframes extracted from the "NBC Nightly News" and the "ABC World News Tonight" programs in 2007 have been indexed. In total, there are about 400,000 keyframes. The panel on the left-hand side shows the user interface for browsing all keyframes in a certain TV program. The user can select any of them and search near duplicates in the database. In this example, the third keyframe in the first row is chosen as the query keyframe, and the duplicate detection results are listed in the panel on the right hand side. The query time is about 2 s, which is indicative of this approach's efficiency.

8.4 Clients and Applications

Previous sections in this chapter focused on the discussion of core content analysis methods and system architectures to support (i.e., store and index) the information from those methods. With the discussed tools and system architecture as a foundation, content in various formats can be analyzed in either an asynchronous or live fashion and delivered to an application over a standards-compliant web services interface. This section provides a brief look at a few example applications and their implementations, which use different quantities of the produced metadata for a range of tasks from generic mash-up applications to user-centric mobile retrieval.

8.4.1 Retrieval Services

Following the design shown in Figure 8.2 as a template, web services interface to the query, analysis, and delivery systems were created using the Python language and the CherryPy software library.* These services permit the viewing of content captured from broadcast television and analyzed by a set of distributed nodes in a real-time fashion. Services executing analysis routines for shot segmentation, speech recognition, semantic concept classification, duplicate image detection, and face recognition are performed in parallel by a set of nodes that can independently be enabled or disabled to provide a richer user experience that can be replayed in mobile, desktop, and set-top environments. This client personalization is possible because each of the underlying analysis routines are exposed with a generic web services interface that is client agnostic. This system was also deployed to simultaneously record, analyze, and index metadata (using the SOLR Lucene environment†) for four broadcast television channels and generic user-generated content (i.e., personal images, home videos, generic Internet content) on one high-performance computer, respectively. Verifying the design aforementioned guidelines, multiple content analysis tasks are consolidated into a single physical resource because the web service is capable of distributing each analysis task of any form to a number of ad hoc processing nodes. Finally, subsequent web service requests for semantic classification were made asynchronously to process a decade of content that was captured before this analysis technique was even available. This capability is possible because each analysis request is atomic, mimicking web-based REST requests that allow stateless operations to occur non-deterministically.

8.4.2 Content Analytics

The media archive and associated extracted metadata can serve a wide range of applications including entertainment, broadcast monitoring, and complex analytics. Two analytical interfaces are discussed in the following demonstrating a comprehensive playback view and a program aggregated view for spotting content anomalies.

Figure 8.11 depicts a user interface for presenting and interacting with the metadata that has been extracted from a TV program. A search component facilitates content selection and once a particular asset is selected, the metadata that is extracted is displayed on an interactive timeline. Other visualizations such as the results of face detection and clustering are made available by utilizing a tabbed

---

* CherryPy - http://www.cherrypy.org/
† SOLR - http://lucene.apache.org/solr/

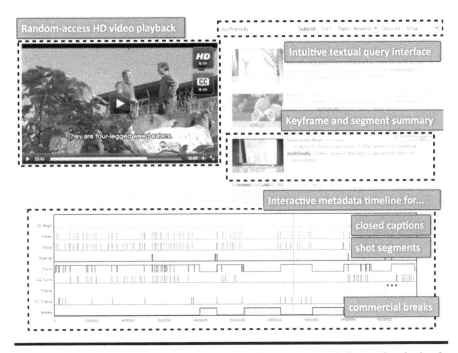

Figure 8.11 Comprehensive analytics view demonstrating full search, playback, and inspection capabilities.

structure on the web page. An "analytics" tab shows summary statistics derived from the media processing so that the selected asset can be compared with other assets along a number of dimensions (e.g., shots per minute, percentage of shots with people, words spoken per minute, etc.). The video window allows the replay of H.264 encoded video at HD and SD resolutions that are streamed using RTMP and can be rendered using Adobe Flash. The same streams may also be rendered in HTML 5 browsers that support this video format. Closed captions are encoded in the W3C Timed Text Markup Language (TTML) [15]. The extracted metadata is available for export to various standard formats, including MediaRSS and MPEG-7.

In a second illustration in Figure 8.12, the automatically detected commercial segments from two popular evening talk shows are visualized. The top and bottom bar charts depict the location and duration of commercial segments in the program "Late Night with Jimmy Fallon" and the program "The Tonight Show With Jay Leno," respectively. This simple metadata visualization demonstrates that there is high amount of variance in the start and duration of commercial segments during the "Jimmy Fallon" show compared to the relatively stable commercial segment position and duration during "Jay Leno." Although some plot locations may be attributed to detector errors, the likely explanation for these differences is the requirement for the

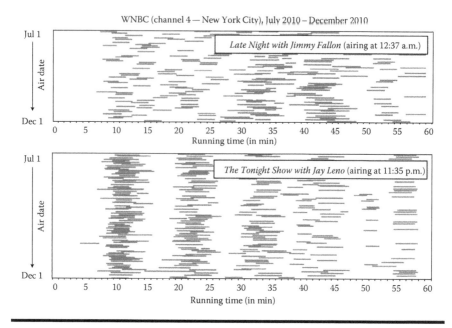

Figure 8.12 Visualization of detected commercial segments aligned to program running time, from air dates spanning 6 months in 2010, and used to detect content anomalies.

content provider to provide relatively specific time slots for both local and nationwide advertising campaigns. While this example focuses on commercial data, almost any other metadata field can be quickly visualized to facilitate the easy discovery of content anomalies and patterns over varying timescales.

8.4.3 Mobile and Multiscreen Video Retrieval

In the previous section, interfaces intended for professional analysis for actionable information from either a single asset or a collection of assets was described. Now a system for TV content analysis can be used to create compelling user experiences for content discovery and consumption for novice users on mobile devices. In a mobile scenario, the primary challenges arise from the limited user interface capabilities of the mobile device. Similarly, in a TV viewing usage context for entertainment purposes, a keyboard and mouse-based interface is not appropriate. Here, the assumption is made that the systems engineering challenges of securely delivering appropriately transcoded media streams to a range of devices have been addressed. For the applications that are envisioned, video delivery subsystem support random access and stream handoff are required, but these capabilities are emerging in the marketplace via IPTV services or for on-demand content at

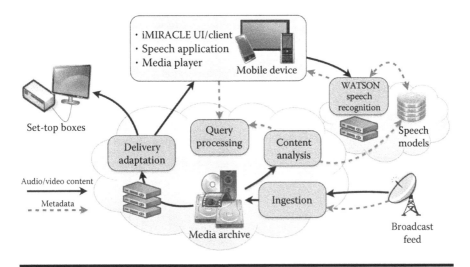

Figure 8.13   iMIRACLE Architecture supports mobile and IPTV clients.

least, with best effort IP systems (over the top). With these capabilities, mobile users can preview or watch video on a mobile device (mobile phone or tablet) and then send the video to the big screen in the living room for shared viewing. To address the aforementioned challenges, the use of spoken natural language queries as part of a multimodal interface to allow users to search for previously recorded TV content on mobile devices is proposed. The architecture detected in Figures 8.13 and 8.14 is utilized and extended with additional capabilities to handle spoken queries with interactive response requirements. Turning to research in multiscreen video retrieval and consumption, a prototype system (called iMIRACLE) was designed and implemented that allows the users to search for previously recorded video. Once the desired video has been retrieved, it can be played on the mobile device, or sent to another display screen such as a set-top box (STB) connected to a TV monitor.

The iMIRACLE architecture is shown in Figure 8.13. Broadcast feeds (ATSC/ MPEG-2) are ingested and processed by the content/media analysis components described in Section 8.3. During processing, closed caption extraction and alignment, metadata (title, station, genre, airdate, etc.) extraction, indexing, scene change detection, and content-based sampling techniques are executed. The extracted metadata and closed caption data are used to build new speech models daily for cloud-based automatic speech recognition (ASR) engine (here, AT&T WATSON [17]) and natural language understanding (NLU) [21]. The speech models are hierarchical language models (HLM) that parse components of a multi-constraint speech query. A top-level speech grammar is used in conjunction with five sub-models where each sub-model handles a different constraint (title, station, genre,

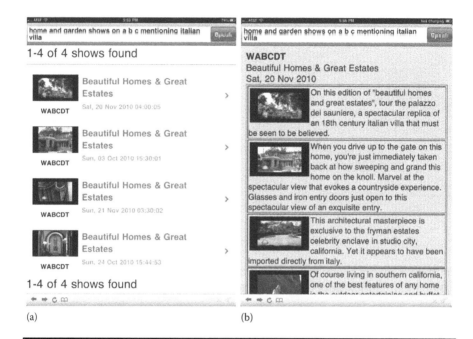

(a)   (b)

Figure 8.14 **Interfaces demonstrating programs matching a speech query (a) and the ability to randomly access automatically detected topic segments of any program (b).**

time, and content). Metadata is used to create sub-models and the closed captioning is used to create content sub-models.

A prototype system was constructed and evaluated on an Apple iPad as the mobile device. Using a mobile device, the mobile user might speak "home and garden shows on ABC mentioning Italian villa." First, the audio is streamed to the cloud, and the WATSON engine performs the ASR and NLU functions. The speech recognition output is "home and garden shows on a b c mentioning Italian villa" and the NLU teases apart the different constraints of the query. In this case, the genre is "home and garden," the station is "ABC," and the content search term is "Italian villa." The system then uses this information to form a search query (one parameter for each constraint). The mobile device will then receive a list of TV programs from the query processing component that match the search criteria, as shown in Figure 8.14a. This example demonstrates the benefits of using speech to create search queries with multiple constraints. Empirically, users have noted that speaking queries is faster than typing them and the use of natural language during query formulation facilitates the combination of multiple constraints with little effort. Figure 8.14a depicts the results of this query, consisting of four programs that meet the user's search criteria, where the user can select a program to view more details about the selected program. At this point, the user can browse the content thumbnails and associated text and initiate the replay of the video with a single touch on one of the thumbnails, as shown in Figure 8.14b. The delivery adaptation module in Figure 8.13 streams the H.264 encoded video (HTTP live streaming) to the mobile device. Alternatively, the user can choose to view the content on the TV, where the delivery adaptation module will stream a higher quality H.264 encoded version of the video (using RTSP streaming) to the STB. Thus, the mobile user can preview the video on the mobile device or can throw the video to the TV STB.

As a final example of how TV content analysis can create personalized interfaces that facilitate content consumption, an application intended for tablet devices is demonstrated. Today's mobile devices support touch screen interfaces and include highly capable graphics that when combined with high-speed data networking, can render compelling rich media interfaces for content exploration and selection. Figure 8.15 shows a screen capture from a mobile device rendering results in response to a user-specified topic of interest (in this case, the topic was Yankees). Rather than developing a customized user interface, a standards compliant image browser* is used to provide rapid perspective transformations with simulated momentum to

Figure 8.15   Graphical, highly interactive browsing of TV content on a mobile device.

---

* Cooliris - http://www.cooliris.com

render an intuitive user interface. The application seamlessly submits queries to the media retrieval services which deliver personalized thumbnail sets and video metadata represented in MediaRSS format. The video content can be selected and previewed and consumed on the mobile device or displayed at high resolution on a connected TV. This example demonstrates the value of processing TV content to create enhanced video service capabilities that allow viewers to quickly navigate to content of interest.

8.5 Conclusions

In this chapter, some of the state-of-the-art methods for TV content analysis were presented. Starting from a holistic analysis of incoming program data, this chapter iterates over the key components of a content analysis engine: automatic shot segmentation, audio analysis for speech, alignment of caption data, semantic classification of scenes, and near-duplicate detection in a large-scale database. Although the purpose of each discussed method may be different, the underlying goal of producing useful, distinctive metadata for describing content is common throughout all components. Additionally, with fully implemented and deployed algorithms in continuously running systems, one can assert that these methods have been optimized for scalability and easy integration in existing IPTV services. The system architecture proposed in this chapter not only embodies these existing services, but has been created such that it easily accommodates unforeseen future approaches in an intuitive modular fashion. Wherever possible, all methods have also been organized and orchestrated in a scalable and efficient Service oriented Architecture (SoA) that is media-aware. This important distinction has allowed the proposed architectures to both preserve and leverage existing metadata capabilities (i.e., closed caption extraction from analog or digital signals) while simultaneously adapting ingestion routines to accommodate new codecs and media formats. Finally, as a real-world evaluation of the architecture and underlying metadata, several service concepts as well as heterogeneous clients have been described supporting multiscreen content consumption scenarios and services.

References

1. ISO/IEC JTC/SC/WG 15938-9:2005/PDAM 1 information technology multimedia content description interface part 9: Profiles and levels, amendment 1: Extensions to profiles and levels. 2005.
2. ETSI TS 102 822-3-1 V1.4.1 (2007–11), Broadcast and On-line Services: Search, select and rightful use of content on personal storage systems (TV-Anytime); Part 3: Metadata; Sub-part 1: Phase 1 Metadata schemas. 2007.
3. EBU study of content analysis-based automatic information extraction in production, first call for technologies. June 2009.

4. Yahoo! Media RSS Specification 1.5.0, September 2009.

5. Cablelabs content 3.0 specification version 1.1, md-sp-contentv3.0-i01-100812. August 2010.

6. O.M. Alliance. Service guide for mobile broadcast services. *Candidate Version*, 1, 2008.

7. A. Andoni and P. Indyk. Near-optimal hashing algorithms for approximate nearest neighbor in high dimensions. 2006.

8. P. Antonopoulos, N. Nikolaidis, and I. Pitas. Hierarchical face clustering using SIFT image features. In *IEEE Symposium on Computational Intelligence in Image and Signal Processing, 2007 (CIISP 2007)*, Honolulu, HI, pp. 325–329, 2007. IEEE, New York.

9. L. Begeja and Z. Liu. Searching and browsing video in face space. In *11th IEEE International Symposium on Multimedia, 2009 (ISM'09)*, San Diego, CA, pp. 336–341, 2009. IEEE, Washington, DC.

10. C. Chelba and A. Acero. Adaptation of maximum entropy capitalizer: Little data can help a lot. *Computer Speech & Language*, 20(4):382–399, 2006.

11. S.S. Chen and P.S. Gopalakrishnan. Speaker, environment and channel change detection and clustering via the Bayesian information criterion. In *Proceedings DARPA Broadcast News Transcription and Understanding Workshop*, Lansdowne, VA, 1998.

12. J. Deng, W. Dong, R. Socher, L.J. Li, K. Li, and L. Fei-Fei. Imagenet: A large-scale hierarchical image database. In *IEEE Computer Vision and Pattern Recognition (CVPR)*, Miami, FL, 2009.

13. M. Eyer. PSIP: Program & System Information Protocol. 2002.

14. A.W. Fitzgibbon and A. Zisserman. Joint manifold distance: A new approach to appearance based clustering. In *Proceedings of IEEE Computer Society Conference on Computer Vision and Pattern Recognition*, Madison, WI, 2003.

15. G. Adams (ed.). Timed text markup language (ttml) 1.0. November 2010.

16. D. Gibbon and Z. Liu. Large scale content analysis engine. In *Proceedings of the First ACM Workshop on Large-Scale Multimedia Retrieval and Mining*, Beijing, China, pp. 97–104, 2009. ACM, New York.

17. V. Goffin, C. Allauzen, E. Bocchieri, D. Hakkani-Tur, A. Ljolje, S. Parthasarathy, M. Rahim, G. Riccardi, and M. Saraclar. The AT&T Watson speech recognizer. In *Proceedings of ICASSP*, Philadelphia, PA, 2005, pp. 1033–1036. Citeseer, 2005.

18. P. Huang, Y. Wang, and M. Shao. A new method for multi-view face clustering in video sequence. In *IEEE International Conference on Data Mining Workshops, 2008 (ICDMW'08)*, Pisa, Italy, 2008, pp. 869–873. IEEE, New York.

19. Q. Huang, Z. Liu, A. Rosenberg, D. Gibbon, and B. Shahraray. Automated generation of news content hierarchy by integrating audio, video, and text information. In *Proceedings of Acoustics, Speech and Signal Processing*, Phoenix, AZ, Vol. 6, pp. 3025–3028, 1999.

20. International Standards Organization (ISO). Information technology – multimedia content description interface—part 5: Multimedia description schemes, ISO/IEC 15938-5:2003 (MPEG-7). 2003.

21. M. Johnston and S. Bangalore. Finite-state multimodal integration and understanding. *Natural Language Engineering*, 11(2):159–187, 2005.

22. Y. Ke, R. Sukthankar, and L. Huston. Efficient Near-duplicate detection and sub-image retrieval. In *ACM Multimedia*, New York, October 2004. ACM, New York.

23. L. Kennedy, A. Hauptmann, M. Naphade, A.H.J.R. Smith, and S.F. Chang. Lscom 1.5. lexicon definitions and annotations version 1.0. In *DTO Challenge Workshop on Large Scale Concept Ontology for Multimedia*, Columbia University, New York, NY, pp. 217–2006, 2006.

24. Z. Li and X. Tang. Bayesian face recognition using support vector machine and face clustering. In *CVPR'04 Proceedings of the 2004 IEEE Computer Society Conference on Computer Vision and Pattern Recognition*, Washington, DC, 2004.

25. Z. Liu, D. Gibbon, E. Zavesky, B. Shahraray, and P. Haffner. AT&T research at trecvid 2006. In *Notebook Paper. NIST TRECVID Workshop*, Gaithersburg, MD, 2006.

26. Z. Liu and Y. Wang. Face detection and tracking in video using dynamic programming. In *Proceedings of the 2000 International Conference on Image Processing, 2000*, Vancouver, BC, Canada, Vol. 1, pp. 53–56, 2000. IEEE, New York.

27. A. Loui, J. Luo, S.F. Chang, D. Ellis, W. Jiang, L. Kennedy, K. Lee, and A. Yanagawa. Kodak's consumer video benchmark data set: Concept definition and annotation. In *Proceedings of the International Workshop on Multimedia Information Retrieval*, pp. 245–254, 2007. ACM, New York.

28. Y. Maret, F. Dufaux, and T. Ebrahimi. Image replica detection based on support vector classifier. In *Optical Information System III, SPIE*, Vol. 5909, pp. 173–181. SPIE, 2005.

29. A. Messina, R. De Sutter, W. Bailer, M. Sano, J.-P. Evain, P. Ndjiki-Nya, A. Linnemann, B. Schrter, and A. Basso. Some changes to wd on mpeg-7 audiovisual description profile (AVDP). ISO/IEC JTC1/SC29/WG11 MPEG2010/M18150, October 2010.

30. E. Mikoczy, D. Sivchenko, B. Xu, and J.I. Moreno. IPTV systems, standards and architectures: Part II-IPTV services over IMS: Architecture and standardization. *Communications Magazine, IEEE*, 46(5):128–135, 2008.

31. D. Roth, M. Yang, and N. Ahuja. A SNoW-based face detector. In *the Conference on Advances in Neural Information Processing Systems (NIPS)*, Denver, CO, 2000.

32. H.A. Rowley, S. Baluja, and T. Kanade. Neural network-based face detection. *IEEE Transactions on Pattern Analysis and Machine Intelligence*, 20(1):23–38, 1998.

33. J. Sivic, M. Everingham, and A. Zisserman. Who are you?-Learning person specific classifiers from video. In *IEEE Conference on Computer Vision and Pattern Recognition, 2009 (CVPR 2009)*, Miami, FL, pp. 1145–1152, 2009. IEEE, New York.

34. J. Sivic and A. Zisserman. Video Google: A text retrieval approach to object matching in videos. In *International Conference on Computer Vision*, Beijing, China, pp. 1470–1477, January 2003.

35. A.F. Smeaton, P. Over, and W. Kraaij. Evaluation campaigns and TRECVid. In *Proceedings of the 8th ACM International Workshop on Multimedia Information Retrieval*, Santa Barbara, CA, pp. 321–330, 2006. ACM, New York.

36. A.W.M. Smeulders, M. Worring, S. Santini, A. Gupta, and R. Jain. Content-based image retrieval at the end of the early years. *IEEE Transactions on Pattern Analysis and Machine Intelligence*, 22(12):1349–1380, 2000.

37. C. Snoek, M. Worring, D. Koelma, and A. Smeulders. Learned lexicon-driven interactive video retrieval. *Image and Video Retrieval*, 4071:11–20, 2006.

38. J. Tao and Y.P. Tan. Face clustering in videos using constraint propagation. In *IEEE International Symposium on Circuits and Systems, 2008 (ISCAS 2008)*, Seattle, WA, pp. 3246–3249, 2008. IEEE, New York.
39. P. Viola and M. Jones. Robust real-time object detection. *International Journal of Computer Vision*, 57(2):137–154, 2002.
40. N. Vretos, V. Solachidis, and I. Pitas. A mutual information based face clustering algorithm for movies. In *2006 IEEE International Conference on Multimedia and Expo*, Toronto, Ontario, Canada, pp. 1013–1016, 2006. IEEE, New York.
41. E. Zavesky, Z. Liu, D. Gibbon, and B. Shahraray, Searching videos in visual semantic spaces, in *Semantic Computing*, (eds. P.C.-Y. Sheu, H. Yu, C.V. Ramamoorthy, A.K. Joshi, and L.A. Zadeh), John Wiley & Sons, Inc., Hoboken, NJ. doi: 10.1002/9780470588222.ch16, May 3, 2010.

Chapter 9

High-Level TV Talk Show Structuring Centered on Speakers' Interventions

Félicien Vallet
National Audiovisual Institute (Ina)
Télécom ParisTech

Slim Essid
Télécom ParisTech

Jean Carrive
National Audiovisual Institute (Ina)

Gaël Richard
Télécom ParisTech

Contents

9.1 Introduction

In the televisual domain, talk show programs are defined as broadcasts where one or several persons discuss various topics put forth by a host. Despite its history and popularity, this genre, originally invented in the 1950s, has been scarcely investigated.

This study proposes an analysis of this particular type of TV content with a view to suggest a *generic* talk show structuring scheme. If it seems that there is no consensual definition for *structuring*, which is a dedicated term for this type of process, one may however agree that its goal is the organization of content in sections conveying a proper type of information. In the field of audiovisual content analysis and indexing, several works were conducted on structuring. In [33] and [36], various approaches to extract the inner arrangement of TV streams were proposed. Also, in the domain of sports videos, [16] and [27] modeled structures for the automatic parsing of tennis broadcasts. Similar works may also be found for football [54], baseball [57], or basketball [55,58] match videos. However, to our knowledge, no analogous studies exist for talk show programs.

A number of semiotic works have studied the mechanisms of the talk shows, hence they offer significant prior knowledge on the structure of such programs. They stress out invariant aspects that appear to be characteristic of this genre of TV content. Since this type of insight is used, the approach followed here may be considered as semiotically motivated.

The outline of this chapter is then the following. After examining the talk show from a semiotic point of view, this task of talk show structuring is better specified by discussing specific use cases (e.g., the creation of a talk show table of contents for efficient browsing).

These considerations stress out the relevance of considering the speakers' interventions as elementary structural units for the extraction of generic talk show components. Thus, a panorama of various state-of-the-art segmentation and detection methods aiming at isolating the previously defined components is drawn, highlighting the importance of speaker-oriented detectors. However, the use of automatic speech-recognition approaches is discarded since it would lead to language-dependent and thus nongeneric systems. The accent is thus put on speaker diarization methods. Finally, a specific structuring scheme is proposed. This scheme is assessed in light of a specific use case through a user-based evaluation and conclusions are suggested.

9.2 Prior Knowledge on Talk Show Programs

Historically, after the Second World War, politicians and intellectuals defined the missions of television broadcasters as the trilogy: information, education, and entertainment [8]. At this time, radio and television were mostly produced by public national agencies, such as Office de Radiodiffusion Télévision Française (ORTF) in France. With the multiplication of TV sets in households and the advent of private networks, the television world underwent a slow but constant transformation. Due to the logic of profit peculiar to any industry, entertainment took an increasingly important place to respond to the need of gathering together a broader public and winning the audience ratings battles [7]. Thus, game shows, talk shows, variety shows, and reality TV went to occupy an always larger chunk of the program grid.

9.2.1 Semiotic Point of View

Talk shows appeared in the 1950s and became greatly popular. Over the years, scholars got more and more interested in studying this type of broadcast as it became clearer that it was returning an interesting image of the society.

In regard to the taxonomies proposed in semiotic works [8,14,52], talk show programs are positioned at the crossroads of informative, cultural, and entertaining TV programs. They generally feature celebrity guests talking about their professional and/or personal lives as well as their latest films, TV shows, music recordings, or other projects they wish to promote to the public.

However, defining the talk show as a genre has been an important issue due to the difficulty of developing a coherent picture of forms that vary so much from one another. The difficulty lies in identifying generic components from one show to another due to the heterogeneity of existing shapes [8,29]. Since its invention, the talk show format has been adopted in about every country. Thus, some cultural differences occur in the form of the show. For instance, studio sets may vary quite largely from one show to another. In French shows, the public generally surrounds the center of attraction that the couple host/guest forms [28], while in the USA a stage set is usually placed behind it. Besides, the host may seat behind a desk as it

Figure 9.1   Various talk show studio sets—Creative Commons license ⓒⓒ ⓑⓨ **(Flickr images—http://www.flickr.com/photos/65482984@N04/).**

usually happens with American talk shows or around a table, with the guests, for the French ones. Furthermore, the host may welcome these guests one at a time or all together. On American talk shows, the main presenter is often a humorist who opens the program with a monologue while in France he or she usually gives an introduction of the guest(s) and a brief outline of the show. Finally, in the USA, talk shows fall in two categories: daytime talk shows dealing more with public affairs and interviewing experts, and the more traditional late-night talk shows following the informal host/guest format and wrapped around with comedic or musical segments (Figure 9.1).

However, these differences tend to vanish nowadays since a general globalization process is observed, as it is in many other cultural fields. An important amount of semiotic studies, such as [28,29,31], tried to spell common features or components out of the disparity observed. The most striking of these generic components displayed by talk shows is the constant presence of host(s) and guest(s). The numbers may vary but the couple host/guest is always the center of attention in these programs. The polymorphic form of the show is another of the common features. Talk shows are usually built as a succession of interviews, musical passages, TV reports, film excerpts, jingles, etc. For each talk show, this succession reflects an inner organization of the content.

Talk show programs share the particularity of being structured around natural conversation. As shown in [7,20,22,46], no matter how spontaneous it seems to be, this talk is nevertheless highly planned and formatted. It is anchored around the host who is responsible for the tone, the direction, and for setting limits on the talk. In [13,34], it is shown that the language used during the talk show is very well defined. There are, for instance, very precise ways and codes to introduce a guest, launch a live performance, or change the subject of a conversation. The aim is to set for the viewer all the aspects of a daily conversation between the host and his or her guest while rigorously following a script written in advance all along the program.

Thus, while the course of the show may seem rather erratic, it is highly structured. Transitions are carried out by the host, but clear delimitations are also generally employed to switch from one part to the other. Jingles, cutaway shots, advertisements, or even applause are used as demarcation lines. The talk itself is precisely monitored, the host evoking in general only one discussion subject at a time with the guest in a speech section. Therefore, the comprehension of the internal organization of the speakers' interventions, and the talk in general, is the foundation for talk show automatic structuring.

9.2.2 Comparison between Two Talk Shows

Having identified common characteristics of the talk show from the semiotic point of view, it is of interest to evaluate their validity by comparing different programs. For this purpose we consider two collections of French programs: *Le Grand Échiquier* that was broadcasted monthly between 1972 and 1986 and presented by Jacques Chancel and *On n'a pas tout dit* that went on air each week from Monday to Friday between 2007 and 2008 and was presented by Laurent Ruquier. Both shows were designed to appeal to a wide audience. They were recorded 30 years apart, which has to be taken into account since the televisual production approach went through notable changes in the meantime. These two programs are thus supposed to be sufficiently representative of the talk show category presented in Section 9.2.1. The statistics given on audiovisual events (Table 9.1) were obtained on manual annotations of 22 shows for *Le Grand Échiquier* and 5 for *On n'a pas tout dit*. The corpus *Le Grand Échiquier* has been the object of previous works (see e.g. [2,10,24,49]) and is used again in this study while *On n'a pas tout dit* [6] is used to validate the genericity of the approach proposed and can thus be of smaller size. This explains the imbalance between the number of annotated shows. Speech statistics in Tables 9.2 and 9.3 were computed using six speaker-annotated shows of *Le Grand Échiquier*.

The study of the main constitutive parts of the two talk shows highlights some major differences. Table 9.1 shows the importance of several audiovisual events. *Musical performance* stands for parts where live music is played, *nonmusical*

Table 9.1 Audiovisual Events Statistics for 22 Shows of *Le Grand Échiquier* (GE) and 5 Shows of *On n'a pas tout dit* (OAPTD)

Event Corpus	Average Length		Standard Deviation		Average Number		Standard Deviation	
	GE	OAPTD	GE	OAPTD	GE	OAPTD	GE	OAPTD
Show	165'24" (100%)	50'41" (100%)	25'13" (15.2%)	4'03" (8.0%)	–	–	–	–
Participants	–	–	–	–	16.2	11.6	5.7	3.5
Music performance	85'43" (51.8%)	36" (1.2%)	25'07" (15.2%)	0 (0%)	26.4	1	8.5	0
Nonmusic performance	9'04" (5.5%)	–	16'17" (9.8%)	–	2.4	–	3.9	–
Inserts	16'55" (10.2%)	45" (1.5%)	10'47" (6.5%)	37" (1.2%)	7.8	1	5.8	0.7
Speech	40'31" (24.5%)	39'32" (78.0%)	23'31" (14.2%)	4'37" (9.1%)	–	–	–	–
Laughter	2'35" (1.6%)	3'59" (7.8%)	4'27" (2.7%)	2'35" (5.1%)	41.3	23.3	66.1	10.7
Applause	10'34" (6.4%)	5'26" (10.7%)	4'26" (2.7%)	41" (1.3%)	38.2	33.0	18.6	9.1
Jingles	–	24" (0.8%)	–	1" (0%)	–	1	–	0

Durations are given in minutes/seconds and percentages reflect the part of each event in the talk show.

Table 9.2   Speech Statistics for 6 Shows of *Le Grand Échiquier* (GE) and 5 Shows of *On n'a pas tout dit* (OAPTD)

Event	Average		Standard Deviation	
Corpus	GE	OAPTD	GE	OAPTD
Show	165'17" (100%)	50'41" (100%)	24'41" (14.9%)	4'03" (8.0%)
Speech	64'22" (38.9%)	39'32" (78.0%)	21'15" (12.9%)	4'37" (9.1%)
Speech overlap	5'10" (8.0%)	3'17" (8.3%)	2'31" (3.9%)	1'38" (4.1%)
Speech turns	1264	1348	432	237
First dominant speaker	26'08" (40.6%)	14'52" (37.6%)	4'03" (6.3%)	1'49" (4.6%)
Second dominant speaker	17'31" (27.2%)	6'15" (15.8%)	6'57" (10.8%)	1'02" (2.6%)
Average speaker	4'38" (7.2%)	3'43" (9.4%)	1'02" (1.6%)	1'11" (3.0%)
Average speech segment	3.1"	2.2"	0.6"	0.5"

Durations are given in minutes/seconds and percentages reflect the part of each event. Except for the first two lines percentages are computed over the total speech duration.

Table 9.3   Speech Statistics for the Host for 6 Shows of *Le Grand Échiquier* (GE) and 5 Shows of *On n'a pas tout dit* (OAPTD)

Event	Average		Standard Deviation	
Corpus	GE	OAPTD	GE	OAPTD
Speech	23'43" (36.8%)	12'38" (32.0%)	6'58" (10.8%)	1'08" (2.9%)
Speech turns	498 (39.4%)	398 (29.5%)	151 (12.0%)	118 (8.8%)
Average speech segment	2.9"	2.0"	0.5"	0.5"

Percentages are computed over the total speech duration.

performance for live performances where no music is produced (e.g., poetry reading and circus act) and *inserts* for any off-sequence shown on screen such as duplexes, TV reports, film excerpts, etc. Some of these events are unspecified, either because they do not exist or because they cannot be computed, as the number of speech sections, for instance. First, as expected, the formats of the programs are radically different. In the case of *Le Grand Échiquier*, the show lasts on average a bit less than 3 h but with great variations while for *On n'a pas tout dit* it is very precisely set around 50 min. *Applause* and *talk* components also contribute to characterize the reproducible pattern of *On n'a pas tout dit*, the standard deviations being very low compared to those obtained for *Le Grand Échiquier*. No *jingles* are used in *Le Grand Échiquier*, which could have been expected since it was not a common procedure in the TV world at that time.

Also, while a great diversity is observed in the form of the show itself for *Le Grand Échiquier* with numerous excerpts or musical passages and still a very important *talk* component, *On n'a pas tout dit* mostly features dialogues: 78% of the show duration against 25% or 39% (according to which of Table 9.1 or 9.2 is considered). This difference can be explained by the nature of the show, centered on the life and achievements of one or several guests in the first case and on humoristic chronicles in the second one as assessed by the large amounts of applause, laughter, and speech turns (see Table 9.2), where speech turns account for the number of changes from one active speaker to another. The great amount of speech turns indicates very short exchanges between participants. These are typically the differences between the late-night and daytime talk shows presented earlier. It explains the disparity observed in the treatment of the talk itself. In *Le Grand Échiquier*, two persons share about 70% of the speech load—namely, the host and the main guest—while in *On n'a pas tout dit*, the speech is more "democratically" distributed as can be seen in comparing the average speaker percentage (see Table 9.2). It is also notable that *Le Grand Échiquier* features on average four more participants than *On n'a pas tout dit* with 16 against 12.

However, while these two talk shows seem to display rather distinctive features, particularly in their inner construction, they still share a very similar distribution of the talk. In both programs, the spontaneity is put forward and the average speech intervention is about 2.5 s long. Besides, the importance of the overlap reinforces the feeling of natural conversation.

It has to be observed that the main host (Jacques Chancel or Laurent Ruquier) is always among the two most prominent speakers, which enables him to orchestrate the talk with savvy transitions as stated in the previous section. It is also interesting to study his speech activity. Table 9.3 highlights the fact that he is the conductor of the show since his speech load is characterized by a great number of turns. Thirty-nine percent of the *Le Grand Échiquier* speech turns are from Jacques Chancel while 29% of those of *On n'a pas tout dit* are from Laurent Ruquier. Besides, these speech turns are in general slightly shorter than the average over all the participants shown in Table 9.2 with 2.9 against 3.1 s for *Le Grand Échiquier* and 2.0 against 2.2 s for *On n'a pas tout dit*. This difference may look slim, it is however of importance since it accentuates the distinct roles of hosts and guests. The guest discusses his or her life and achievements while the host introduces and contextualizes it, as detailed in [13,34].

9.3 Specifying the Task of Talk Show Structuring

The previous section showed a number of features common to talk shows despite the great variability of this type of programs. These characteristics can be refined with a view of target applications. Therefore, it is crucial to assess specific examples of uses to circumscribe the properties of a good structuring process.

9.3.1 Use Cases

In a context of preservation, conservation, and dissemination of TV recordings, archiving industries have a strong need for indexing tools to be used in a variety of applications. The most prominent use cases include the following:

- The selection and retrieval of excerpts to be presented on a website (possibly for marketing or commercial purposes), which will be referred to as *UC1*: Use Case 1.
- The development of software to help archivists with the audiovisual indexing of programs (*UC2*: Use Case 2), which, to a large extent, is done manually.
- Complex cross-checking between various programs for intra-document or inter-document navigation (*UC3*: Use Case 3). This could, for instance, allow one to retrieve all the appearances of a given artist, the various versions of a particular song, etc.
- The timecoding of noticeable audiovisual events (*UC4*: Use Case 4).

The latter is quite popular. Many applications require the retrieval of audiovisual events given a corresponding description. Indeed, for archiving companies, most of the time a short outline or a selection of tags is the only available description of the programs stored. Thus, a very important chunk of the audiovisual archives lacks temporal information in the descriptions provided. A tool performing a temporal alignment of events of interest to video content is therefore one that would be very valuable.

In all the previous use cases, the problem of structuring actually boils down to the extraction of temporal indexes for structural elements defined beforehand. The definition of these various use cases reveals what invariant aspects of the talk show have to be emphasized in order to proceed to the automatic structuring of this kind of programs.

9.3.2 Generic Talk Show Components: The Importance of the Speakers

In light of the semiotic studies and the use cases mentioned earlier, we propose a set of *structural units* or *components* that characterize the vast majority of talk shows.

These units can be considered as general "talk show structural invariances" that stand as particularly relevant for the implementation of use cases of interest. They are specified hereafter and their relative importance is discussed.

Content elements alternate over the duration of a show (between the opening and the final credits). They are organized into three generic entities (as suggested by Section 9.2): talk, performance, and inserts:

- The *talk* component refers to every part where talk show participants (hosts and guests) are in an act of conversation. It is the skeleton of the talk show, linking together all constitutive elements.
- *Performance* refers to every live action that is not conversation, especially artistic actions. It includes musical performances, circus acts, but also comedy monologues or poetry recitation (that are not part of the talk component), etc.
- *Inserts* gather every sequence that is not shot inside the studio. They can be archives, reports, still images, etc.

It is worth noting that these three components can overlap or collide. Indeed, performances sometimes start before the host has finished announcing it; a guest may be asked to comment the insert being shown on the screen, etc.

Punctuation elements of diverse natures may also be defined. These markers are used to link together the various content units and make their succession smoother. They can take a wide number of forms. Events such as *applause* and *laughter* are natural delimiters. From the point of view of the production, *jingles* and *cutaway shots* play the same role as they indicate a shift from one content part of the show to another. *Commercials* are also a clear punctuation element as they can similarly be seen as a delimiter or separator. They are generally introduced by the host beforehand. The host himself being the conductor of the show sets numerous punctuation elements as asserted in the previous section by the semiotic studies [13,34] and the comparison of talk shows *Le Grand Échiquier* and *On n'a pas tout dit*; he announces performances or inserts, switches subjects in the conversation, introduces new guests, etc. The punctuation elements set by the host are the primary demarcation markers, since they delimit high-level "semantic" sections of the talk show. The rest of the structural elements belonging to the punctuation category generally only emphasize and put into perspective the information provided by the speakers and, most of the time, the host.

The last generic component of importance that can be defined here is the *location* of the action shown to the viewer, which may happen either *outside* or *inside* the studio. Outside refers to the broadcast elements shot at the exterior of the TV studio such as excerpts, duplexes, reports, etc., while inside can take several values such as *set* or *stage*. There is generally a strong overlap between the elements *content* → *insert* and *location* → *outside*.

It is important to note that while they explicitly appear only in the talk entity, speakers turn out to be crucial for the actual identification of most of the previous talk show components. This is particularly true for the host whose role as a conductor has, once more, to be emphasized. Practically, the speakers' interventions provide high-level indications on the occurrence of the various structural units. Performances, inserts, and commercials are, as a matter of fact, unavoidably introduced and identified by the host, as prescribed by the basic editing TV rules. Thus, the viewer is given information about the type of content (song, circus act, film excerpt, etc.) and, if relevant to the situation, the performer, title of the piece, composer, musicians, author, director, etc.

9.3.3 Link with Automatically Extracted Descriptors

Having defined a taxonomy for the generic structural units of the talk show programs, the focus is now put on how to retrieve them automatically. To this end, several detectors using audio and/or visual cues extracted from the video can be implemented. Table 9.4 gives a hierarchical classification of the various structural units previously specified as well as known technologies that can be used to detect them.

Some of the structural elements have been subdivided. For instance, performance leads to two categories: *musical*, where live music is produced, and *nonmusical* in the case of monologues, theater or circus acts, etc. This specific arrangement has been proposed to put in relation generic components and corresponding automatic descriptors. As a matter of fact, structural elements defined in this section often correspond directly to the decisions output by specific detectors that can be automatically run on the audio and/or the video signals. Dedicated classifiers can be exploited to detect events such as "applause," "laughter" [25,51], or "music" [38,40] using only the audio modality.

In other cases, such as "nonmusical performances" or "commercials," the structural units can be obtained using reasoning or inference techniques based on the outputs of the previously defined detectors. These outputs then serve as "mid-level descriptors," on the basis of which the occurrence of the higher-level structural elements is inferred. For instance, the work presented in [4] proposes a method for detecting the presence of commercials through dynamic Bayesian networks [32]. Similarly, generic inference methods are shown in [50] to detect "semantic" events in sport videos. A similar approach can be adopted for the detection of nonmusical performances such as theater acts, poetry reading, etc., where speech occurs. In a preliminary study, an inference system was built upon the combined outputs obtained from the applause and laughter detectors and speaker diarization and led to very convincing results for their detection. Thus, while there is only one talk-related structural element, one should keep in mind that the speakers' interventions convey a large proportion of the subjective information.

These descriptors turn out to be particularly efficient when dealing with talk show videos. For instance, in [40], an F-measure of 96.5% is obtained for speech/music

Table 9.4 Link between Generic Structural Elements and Their Automatic Detection

Structural Elements			Detection Method
Content	Talk	Speakers	Speaker diarization
	Performance	Musical	Music detector
		Nonmusical	Speaker diarization
			Laughter detector
			Applause detector
	Inserts	Photo	Still image detector
		Film-report	Environmental sound detector
			change in color distribution
			black stripes detection
Punctuation	Applause		Applause detector
	Laughter		Laughter detector
	Cutaway shot		High similarity shot detector
	Jingles		Music detector
			High similarity shot detector
	Commercials		Color coherency detector
			Monochrome frame detector
			Shot boundary detector
Location	Inside	Stage	Stage detector
		Set	Set detector
	Outside		Color coherency detector
			Environmental sound detector

discrimination on radiophonic streams. Obviously, while a radiophonic stream is not exactly the same content as a TV talk show, common characteristics are shared that ensure a pretty good reproducibility of the results. Commercials can also be extremely well detected, as shown in [4] with an F-measure of 91% for 10 h of video from French TV channels. In [25], the authors propose new features for the classification of impulse responses and obtain great results at detecting applause. In this case, sports videos are used; however, similar results would be expected with talk show videos. Finally, great performances can also be reached for speaker diarization methods on talk show content as detailed in Section 9.4.3.

9.4 Review of Key Relevant Technologies

Any effort in segmenting, indexing, or classifying an audiovisual document can be seen as a step in the process of automatic structuring as emphasized in state-of-the-art reviews [12,17]. Therefore, a huge variety of potentially useful technologies exist, with varying levels of "semantic" value. Some problems, such as shot boundary detection or music/speech segmentation, have become cornerstones of audiovisual analysis. Besides, methods can follow various learning schemes, ranging from supervised to unsupervised learning.

9.4.1 Use of Multimodal Approaches

In [45], the accent is put on the importance of the use of multimodal approaches. The joint exploitation of audio, video, or even text modalities has shown great results in the resolution of automatic structuring problems. Since a gap is observed between the low level of interpretation provided by basic detectors and the human level of interpretation of the content being analyzed (usually referred to as the "semantic" gap), a combination of different low-level detectors is expected to lead to the resolution of more complex problems.

The TRECVid* benchmarking activity has become, since 2001, a reference in the field of video information retrieval by providing large test collections and uniform scoring procedures for organizations interested in comparing their results. In this program, the detection of key audiovisual events is performed through the joint analysis of audio and video cues. At the same time, a lot of multimodal approaches for automatic structuring have been proposed, for instance, [16,27] for tennis broadcasts or [35] for Formula 1 races.

9.4.2 Segmentation Methods

The canonical segmentation problem in the field of audiovisual content analysis is the shot boundary detection problem [44]. Indeed, the shot is very often considered as the fundamental structural unit for audiovisual documents. In [23,56], the authors put forward the limitations of the use of the shot as a structuring element, owing to the lack of "semantic" value, and suggest to consider the "audiovisual scene" or "story unit" as an alternative. Story units are nevertheless gathered through the clustering of video shots, hence requiring a good shot boundary detection.

---

* TREC Video Retrieval Evaluation—http://trecvid.nist.gov/

In the audio community, *audio diarization* is a popular segmentation problem [39]. Different tasks are related to this general problem that are addressed either in a supervised or nonsupervised fashion. For instance, speech/nonspeech discrimination (where nonspeech generally refers to music and/or environmental sounds) is achieved using supervised approaches, often based on Gaussian mixture models (GMM) [41] or support vector machines (SVM) [40], while tasks such as speaker turn segmentation are tackled in a nonsupervised fashion (see, e.g., [15,21,24]). The previous are often used as preprocessing blocks for the task of speaker diarization that will be addressed specifically in the following section.

9.4.3 Speaker Diarization and Identification

Having highlighted the crucial role of the speakers for structuring talk show programs, a deeper look at the task of speaker information retrieval is proposed. Indeed, they are the fundamental description unit for building a coherent structure.

Speaker diarization is the process of partitioning an input audio stream into homogeneous segments according to the speaker identity. Speaker diarization systems are widely based on a GMM-hidden Markov model (GMM-HMM) architecture where two alternative approaches have been proposed: the bottom-up [53] and the top-down [9]. This task is usually exclusively audio oriented as stressed in [47]. The descriptors that are traditionally used in these systems are mel frequency cepstral coefficients (MFCC) [37] along with their first and second derivatives as they represent the short-term power spectrum of a sound in a homomorphic mapping. However, authors have recently proposed to include additional visual cues such as color histograms [10], gray-scale difference images [48], or visual activity features [19]. Indeed, the visual information is known to have a much steadier behavior than the audio and thus to allow better speaker model generation.

An alternative approach was proposed in [49], introducing a novel way of identifying speakers in a talk show program. For this task, the joint use of audiovisual features, namely, MFCC, dominant colors [30], and motion features [30], was investigated. A semiautomatic method was chosen in order to lead to the actual identification of the speakers. Indeed, while speaker diarization methods lead to good results, the problem of assigning a speaker to each cluster still needs to be addressed with the inconvenience that some speakers may not be found among the clusters due to the unsupervised nature of these approaches. Therefore, the scheme proposed is comparable to methods known as relevance feedback ones.

The originality lies in the use of a kernel-based method for a task generally assigned to generative ones. Once a segment of 5–15 s is given by the user (an archivist in the scenario proposed) for each speaker, an SVM classifier is run with several sets of audio and visual features. On top of classical MFCC features, visual speaker-oriented features were developed. Based on the assumption that most of the time the person shown on screen is the one speaking, several video features were

Figure 9.2 Face and costume bounding boxes—Creative Commons license ©
® **(Flickr images—http://www.flickr.com/photos/65482984@N04/).**

introduced, namely, the average dominant color of the clothing or motion features
for points of interest localized in the region below the face (see Figure 9.2).

Indeed, during a talk show program participants are not expected to change
outfit. Besides, some of them show a very distinctive body language while talking,
which is what the motion features are supposed to account for. The bounding boxes
are obtained using a face detection algorithm [11] and a set of heuristic rules for
the location of the costume [26]. The experiment was run on one talk show of the
corpus *Le Grand Échiquier* and a 100-fold cross-validation was performed on the
various candidate speech segments to assess the validity of the approach. Results
show that the use of multimodal features leads to an encouraging 8% increase of
the performance compared to an audio-only system using MFCC features. Indeed,
the error rate shifts from 35.4% with MFCC only to 27.4% for the combination of
MFCC, average dominant color, and motion features.

9.4.4 Concept Detection Systems

Audiovisual structuring can gain from using semantically richer descriptors. Some
automatic systems, either supervised or unsupervised, are built to detect audiovisual
concepts. For instance, a number of works prospected the field of key event recognition in sports videos. For instance, studies on football match videos addressed this
type of tasks using HMM structures, exploiting either the video only [3], the audio
only [5], or both modalities [54]. The audiovisual key events to be retrieved are here

typically the ones that would be included in a summary of the match: goals, penalties, faults, etc. In TRECVid, the task described as "high-level feature extraction" is also an instance of concept detection. In this case, participants are asked to automatically retrieve scenes such as *Sports, Desert, US flag, Car*, etc., from a database of videos. A key issue with this task is the variability in concept interpretation making the development of efficient detectors very challenging.

Another popular concept detection task is person detection. In [42], the authors retrieve the appearances of each person present in a TV sitcom using weak supervision from automatically aligned subtitles and script text with very encouraging results. Action recognition [18] is also a very active topic. It consists in temporally annotating a program with human actions in an automatic fashion. Action classes detected are in general of the following type: *opening door, drinking, sitting down*, etc.

Finally, audio concepts can also be detected in a similar manner. For instance, in [38], the authors propose discriminative methods based on SVM for the detection of vocal parts in music signals.

Thus, it is clear that there is substantial background that can be exploited for the implementation of the detectors to be used in extracting the talk show components described earlier.

9.5 Structuring Method Based on Speakers' Interventions

After defining generic structural elements and pointing to methods to retrieve them automatically, the focus is now put on their combination for the resolution of a specific use case.

9.5.1 Creation of the Structure

It has been shown that generic talk show components related to noticeable audio-visual events can be retrieved automatically using appropriate concept detectors. It is worth noting that these detectors become very reliable when their local outputs are integrated over longer temporal windows for decision making. The choice of the lengths of these temporal decision windows typically depends on the type of event to detect. For example, while 1–2 s length windows should be used for taking decision about the occurrence of "laughter," up to 1 min length windows could be used for musical or nonmusical performances.

The critical role of the speakers has also been largely commented since the structural units proposed are mostly based on speaker-related descriptors. It has been demonstrated that the talk component conveys the majority of the "semantic" knowledge. Though automatic speech recognition systems would deliver precious information on the structure, their use here was discarded. Indeed, these systems would lead to language-dependent and therefore nongeneric approaches. The focus is thus put on the study of the physical properties of the speech that may allow high-level reasoning such as the speech repartition between speakers and the prosody. The structure proposed here results from the combination of the various generic components defined in Table 9.4 (talk, musical performance, applause, etc.). This list can be refined if some structural units are obviously useless for specific talk show instances, as could have been jingles for a talk show like *Le Grand Échiquier* for which this procedure was not common at the time the program was released. The set of generic components defined here is thus expected to solve a wide variety of use cases on top of those presented earlier in Section 9.3.1.

To actually evaluate our structuring scheme to correctly capture the organization of a talk show document, we chose to apply it to the specific task of timecoding the noticeable audiovisual events selected by the archivists. This refers to the use case *UC4* presented in Section 9.3.1 where archivists' notes have to be temporally aligned with the corresponding video. The structural elements defined are expected to facilitate the navigation through the various events occurring during the course of the talk show and therefore simplify the task.

9.5.2 Evaluating the Structure

We propose an evaluation of our structuring scheme by applying it to the use case *UC4* (described in Section 9.3). To this end, we considered the corpus *Le Grand Échiquier* composed of talk show videos and corresponding audiovisual notes. Indeed, this corpus displays a great variety of audiovisual events of interest and has thus been the object of several studies (see, e.g., [2,10,24,49]). Sentences referring to audiovisual events were selected in the archivist's notes.

The task consisted in asking users to retrieve as fast as possible the audiovisual events corresponding to the chosen sentences. Each subject had to retrieve one half of these events using structural elements provided beforehand and the other half without. Reference sentences were manually selected to reflect a large range of aspects of the audiovisual programs. Some were, for instance, strongly linked to visual cues while some others were more complex in the sense of their high-level human interpretation. Such a choice was made to efficiently test the relevance of the approach proposed. A manual annotation locating the matching events was performed and is hereafter referred to as groundtruth.

9.5.2.1 Protocol

Users had to retrieve 16 audiovisual events from each of 4 shows (4 excerpts per show) within a time limit of 8 min for each event, thus, making it 2 shows with structural elements and 2 shows without. Twenty subjects took the test and the group was divided into two parts: A and B. Users belonging to group A had to retrieve events with the help of structural elements for shows 1 and 3 and without them for shows 2 and 4. It was the opposite for the subjects from group B.

In order to put the focus on the evaluation of the relevance of the chosen structure (rather than on the performance of low-level detectors), manually annotated structure components were actually used in this test. Indeed, using automatically obtained results could have caused interpretation issues since two major effects would then have been observed: the correctness of the detected elements and their actual usefulness for the retrieval task. Table 9.5 presents the sentences selected for the task.

Table 9.5 Excerpts to Retrieve in 4 Shows of *Le Grand Échiquier*

Show/Guest	Orchestra of the Opéra National de Paris (1982)	Jean-Pierre Rampal (1985)	Michel Sardou (1982)	Michel Berger (1985)
Length	2 h 58 min 37 s	2 h 40 min 3 s	2 h 51 min 0 s	2 h 17 min 10 s
Excerpt 1	Ella Fitzgerald sings "Smoke Gets in Your Eyes"	Jean-Pierre Rampal plays the flute solo in Gluck's "Orphee"	Seal taming act by Robby Gasser	Patrick Vigier presents a guitar with microprocessor
Excerpt 2	The orchestra directed by Alain Lombard plays "Alleluia"	Excerpts of an American program showing Rampal with the Muppets	Mireille Darc reads the poem "Colloque Sentimental" by Verlaine	Michel Berger sings "Y'a Pas De Honte"
Excerpt 3	Jacques Chancel talks with the union representative of the orchestra	The famous flute player presents his family: Françoise his wife, his daughter, and his son	Jean-Jacques Debout criticizes Jack Lang	24 h of violence: broadcast news from A2
Excerpt 4	Mechanic dismantling the piano in the studio	Alexandre Lagoya talks about Django Reinhardt	Michel Audiard post-syncing a scene of "Quest for Fire" by Jean-Jacques Annaud	Daniel Balavoine talks about his first album "Mur de Berlin"

Ideally, a dedicated navigation tool would have been designed for the task. However, since the evaluation was focused on measuring the contribution of various structural elements (regardless of presentation considerations), an existing software was chosen instead. Thus, the users were asked to retrieve the excerpts using the ELAN* program, a professional tool for the creation and visualization of audiovisual annotations (see [43]). This has actually raised ergonomic issues that were ignored since the default layout was considered as satisfactory.

Whether they were using the structural components or not, the subjects were always allowed to use the basic controls for video navigation (slider, play/pause, shift of 1 s, etc.). To get accustomed to the tool, the users were given a 15 min training with and without the structure elements on two other shows before proceeding to the actual test (Table 9.6).

Once the training phase had finished, the users were asked to proceed to the actual testing. They had to retrieve in a row all four excerpts of each program with pauses allowed only when switching shows. The objective was to limit the "learning" factor. Indeed, users would otherwise increase their score over time since they would jointly learn how to use the ELAN software and the organization of the show itself (Figure 9.3).

When an excerpt was identified, the users had to provide a timecode for its beginning and another for its end before being shown the next one. To be considered as correctly attributed, a video sequence had to overlap with at least 70% of the groundtruth. By this mean, we ensured the correct identification of the events without putting the focus on their slicing. In case of misdetection, the user was given by default the maximum retrieval time allowed for a single excerpt, i.e., 8 min.

9.5.2.2 Results and Discussion

The maximum time allowed for retrieving a given excerpt being 8 min, the time limit for the evaluation was theoretically of 2 h and 8 min (without counting the training phase and the pauses between the shows). However, the average time spent was slightly more than one hour (1 h 1 min 38 s with a standard deviation of 6 min 52 s). Group A performed on average in 1 h 4 min 7 s with a standard deviation of 6 min 4 s and group B in 59 min 9 s with a standard deviation of 7 min. The results in Table 9.7 highlight the fact that on average it takes less time to find a given excerpt with structuring elements than without: 3 min 31 s against 4 min 11 s.

Surprisingly, for several excerpts, such as 3, 4, 6, 9, and 14, it actually took more time in average to retrieve the excerpts with the structural elements than without. However, the presence of a generally large standard deviation has to be noted.

---

* EUDICO Linguistic Annotator—http://www.lat-mpi.eu/tools/elan/

Table 9.6   Structural Elements Available to the Users during the Test

Content			Punctuation				Location		
Performance	Insert	Talk	Applause	Laughter	Shot 1	Shot 2	Studio		Exterior
Musical / Nonmusical		Speakers					Stage	Set	

Figure 9.3 Illustrations of the ELAN software and of the interface collecting the timecodes—Creative Commons license ⓒ ⒝ (Flickr images—http://www.flickr.com/photos/65482984@No4/).

For some excerpts, such as 4 ("mechanic dismantling the piano in the studio"), structural elements did not really help users since it was not clearly linked to any of the proposed generic structural components. Subjects tended to spend some time to figure out which components could be useful (they wondered if it was an insert, a performance, if it happened on stage, etc.) instead of directly using the usual video navigation tools. Also, for excerpts easily identifiable visually, such as 6 ("the Muppets") or 9 ("seal taming act"), it actually took more time to think about what field the event actually belonged to than to just scroll along the show with the slider. This is another evidence that users had sometimes the tendency to forget to use basic navigation tools when provided with the structural components. This inclination seems, however, rectifiable.

For some other excerpts such as excerpt 3 for instance, many users relying on the structural elements tended to proceed hastily, got misled, and assigned the role of "union representative" to the wrong person. This is highlighted by the particularly high number of wrong detections for this excerpt. Thus, users with structural elements showed bad answers at a higher rate than users without. Since errors were penalized with the maximum allowed time of 8 min, greater average retrieval times were observed. It is a clear sign that users leaned toward trusting exceedingly the structural elements. They seemed to take a less active part in the search of the events. Feeling that they had the information at hand, they were indeed more eager to answer the question within the time limit.

The 16 excerpts can be classified in the four following categories that were defined as generic components earlier: talk, inserts, musical performance, and nonmusical performance. Due to their nature, some excerpts can belong to more than one single category. For instance, "Michel Audiard post-syncing a scene of 'Quest for Fire' by Jean-Jacques Annaud" belongs to nonmusical performance as much as insert (since

Table 9.7   Structural Elements Available to the Users during the Test

Excerpt	With Structuring Elements				Without Structuring Elements			
	Average Retrieval Time (s)	Standard Deviation (s)	% Wrong	% Overtime	Average Retrieval Time (s)	Standard Deviation (s)	% Wrong	% Over time
1	170.7	62.2	0	0	229.1	122.8	0	10
2	438.8	73.7	0	60	442.4	102.1	10	70
3	380.6	131.8	20	30	357.2	108.9	0	30
4	209.1	115.0	0	10	130.3	41.3	0	0
5	392.7	100.9	0	40	387.9	76.4	0	30
6	107.2	39.9	0	0	90.1	34.5	0	0
7	300.2	112.7	0	20	326.5	119.5	10	10
8	115.3	33.3	0	0	327.6	139.5	10	30
9	107.8	87.9	0	0	85.2	22.9	0	0
10	93.5	38.2	0	0	197.7	102.9	0	0
11	164.9	39.6	0	0	241.9	84.1	0	0
12	193.2	44.5	0	0	249.4	105.9	0	0
13	102.3	35.0	0	0	201.9	57.8	0	0
14	319.3	128.0	10	20	236.5	113.6	10	0
15	82.7	36.3	0	0	123.5	63.5	0	0
16	195.8	119.3	20	0	395.4	129.0	20	40
Average	210.9	118.4	2.5	11.3	251.4	112.3	3.8	14.8

% **Wrong** stands for the percentage of users who entered an incorrect audiovisual segment while % **overtime** indicates the percentage of users who did not locate the event within the allowed time.

the film is shown on screen). Thus, it is possible to compute the average retrieval time according to the type of the excerpts (Table 9.8).

Except for the musical performances where users without the structural elements at hand performed slightly better than the others, the results confirm the usefulness of the structuring for this application. Users with structure information clearly outperformed the others in the case of talk excerpts. This is furthermore asserted by the low percentages for answers exceeding the time limit, indicating that the information is, in this case, much easier to retrieve.

Following the experiment, users were asked to provide a feedback on the way they handled it. They were in particular asked what structural elements they used. The results of this questionnaire are summarized in Table 9.9.

As expected, content elements proved to be very useful to retrieve audiovisual events. This is due to the nature of these events. Indeed, since extracted from

Table 9.8   Retrieval Time With and Without Structuring Elements according to the Type of Excerpt

Excerpt	With Structuring Elements				Without Structuring Elements			
	Average Retrieval Time (s)	Standard Deviation (s)	% Wrong	% Overtime	Average Retrieval Time (s)	Standard Deviation (s)	% Wrong	% Overtime
Talk	193.2	101.2	3.8	6.3	287.2	74.2	5	13.8
Insert	152.6	55.0	0	2	164.5	70.3	0	2
Musical performance	285.7	142.4	2	24	277.2	140.1	4	22
Nonmusical performance	165.2	62.7	0	3.3	192.5	59.7	0	0

Table 9.9 Usefulness of the Various Structural Components according to the Users

Element	Musical perf.	Nonmusical perf.	Insert	Speakers	Applause	Laughter	Cutaway shot 1	Cutaway shot 2	Stage	Set	Exterior
Usefulness	3.9	2.9	3.6	3.9	1.5	1.4	1.4	1.4	1.9	1.9	1.8

4, Very useful; 3, Quite useful; 2, Not very useful; 1, Useless.

the archivists' notes, they pointed to an action of actual interest. There were, for instance, no events such as "*X* laughs at *Y*'s joke" or "*W* applauses *Z*'s performance," etc. The decrease in usefulness for nonmusical performance can be explained by the lack of nonmusical performances for users belonging to group B (since they did not have the structural elements for the show 3 where two nonmusical performances happened). It is interesting to observe that while it took slightly more time to find musical performances with the structural elements than without, it was still, on average, considered as very useful by the subjects.

It has to be noted also that the wide standard deviation on all results indicates that the ergonomics of the ELAN program plays a great role as well as the capacity of the users to browse at best the annotations available at hand. It is worth noting that it is difficult to single out the only merit of the structure proposed. Several aspects are evaluated at the same time: the ability of the subject to use the ELAN software efficiently, his or her retrieval strategy, as well as the "chance" factor. All the users were rather familiar with computers. However, large differences occurred in the way they retrieved excerpts. The fastest users tended to scroll through the whole show independently of whether they had the structure available or not to get a rough idea of the show. It turned out that the time spent in doing so allowed them to achieve a much faster retrieval since they had already figured out the form of the show. Indeed, the "learning" aspect is very important and hard to isolate. While looking for a given excerpt, users accumulate information that can allow them sometimes to retrieve future events (that are unknown to them at this point) much faster. This is clearly related to the user's capacity of memorizing and identifying what he or she sees on screen. It is also related to the "chance" factor that is as well impossible to eliminate. Besides, despite the training phase, users also learned how to handle the software as efficiently as possible along the experiment.

One has to keep in mind that this evaluation targeted specifically the use case *UC4*. The appeal of the generic structuring scheme proposed lies in the possibility to use it for other tasks, such as the retrieval of excerpts to be presented on a website (*UC1*) or the cross-checking of various shows, for instance, to retrieve the appearances of a given artist that is known to be present in the considered programs (*UC3*). In these circumstances as well, the structure proposed would be expected to simplify and speed up the execution of tasks that are usually fully manual. This evaluation is also a good starting point for the reflection on the construction of an efficient navigation tool as proposed in the use case *UC2*.

The results of this user-oriented experiment therefore prove the usefulness of the generic structural elements proposed in Section 9.3. Users retrieved audiovisual events more easily with the structural elements than without. It was particularly obvious for talk-oriented excerpts. The difference was not as marked for other types of events such as musical performances. However, the browsing through the video shows with the ELAN software seems to be improvable, indicating that ergonomics problems have to be carefully addressed.

9.6 Conclusion

In this chapter, a TV talk show structuring scheme has been proposed that does not depend on automatic speech recognition technologies. Inspired by semiotic works, a number of talk show common characteristics have been drawn that has led to the identification of key structural components. Use cases of interest have been proposed, on the basis of which the most relevant of those components have been cast out to form a generic structuring scheme. The link between the components defined and corresponding automatic detectors has been established that emphasized the importance of speakers' related processing modules (owing to the fact that the inference of most structural components depend on their outputs). Finally, a user evaluation has been proposed on a specific use case (of particular interest to archivits' activity) that confirmed the usefulness of the structuring scheme. This evaluation has pointed out the importance of presentation aspects for a proper exploitation of the structure. Efforts should be dedicated in this direction toward the design of efficient interfaces as part of the effort of implementation of particular use cases.

References

1. Flickr images (Owner Félicien Vallet TVCA)—http://www.flickr.com/photos/65482984@N04/
2. J. A. Arias, J. Pinquier, and R. André-Obrecht. Evaluation of classification techniques for audio indexing. In *European Signal Processing Conference*, Antalya, Turkey, 2005.
3. J. Assfalg, A. D. Bimbo, W. Nunziati, and P. Pala. Soccer highlights detection and recognition using HMMs. In *International Conference on Multimedia and Expo*, Lausanne, Switzerland, 2002.
4. S. Baghdadi, G. Gravier, C.-H. Demarty, and P. Gros. Structure learning in Bayesian network based video indexing. In *International Conference on Multimedia and Expo*, Hannover, Germany, 2008.
5. M. Baillie and J. M. Jose. An audio-based sports video segmentation and event detection algorithm. In *Conference on Computer Vision and Pattern Recognition Workshop*, Washington, DC, 2004.
6. M. Bendris, D. Charlet, and G. Chollet. Talking faces indexing in TV-content. In *Content-Based Multimedia Indexing*, Grenoble, France, 2010.
7. P. Bourdieu. *Sur la Télévision*. Raisons d'agir, Paris, France, 1996.
8. J. Bourdon. Propositions pour une semiologie des genres audiovisuels. *Quaderni*, 4:19–36, 1988.
9. S. Bozonnet, N. Evans, and C. Fredouille. The LIA-Eurecom RT'09 speaker diarization system: Enhancements in speaker modelling and cluster purification. In *International Conference on Acoustics, Speech, and Signal Processing*, Dallas, TX, 2010.
10. S. Bozonnet, F. Vallet, N. Evans, S. Essid, G. Richard, and J. Carrive. A multimodal approach to initialisation for top-down speaker diarization of television shows. In *European Signal Processing Conference*, Aalborg, Denmark, 2010.

11. G. Bradski and A. Kaehler. *Learning OpenCV: Computer Vision with the OpenCV Library*. O'Reilly Media, Sebastopol, CA, 2008.

12. R. Brunelli, O. Mich, and C.-M. Modena. A survey on the automatic indexing of video data. *Journal of Visual Communication and Image Representation*, 10:78–112, 1999.

13. S. Chalvon-Demersay and D. Pasquier. Le langage des variétés. *Terrain*, 15:29–40, 1990.

14. P. Charaudeau. Les conditions d'une typologie des genres télévisuels d'information. *Réseaux*, 15:79–101, 1997.

15. S. S. Chen and P. S. Gopalakrishnan. Speaker, environment and channel change detection and clustering via the Bayesian information criterion. In *DARPA Broadcast News Transcription and Understanding Workshop*, Lansdowne, VA, 1998.

16. M. Delakis, G. Gravier, and P. Gros. Audiovisual integration with segment models for tennis video parsing. *Computer Vision and Image Understanding*, 111:142–154, 2008.

17. N. Dimitrova, H.-J. Zhang, B. Shahraray, I. Sezan, T. Huang, and A. Zakhor. Applications of video-content analysis and retrieval. *Multi-Media, IEEE*, 9:42–55, 2002.

18. O. Duchenne, I. Laptev, J. Sivic, F. Bach, and J. Ponce. Automatic annotation of human actions in video. In *International Conference on Computer Vision*, Kyoto, Japan, 2010.

19. G. Friedland, H. Hung, and C. Yeo. Multi-modal speaker diarization of real-world meetings using compressed-domain video features. In *International Conference on Acoustics, Speech, and Signal Processing*, Taipei, Taiwan, 2009.

20. R. Ghiglione and P. Charaudeau. *La Parole Confisquée. Un Genre Télévisuel: Le Talk Show*. Dunod, Paris, France, 1997.

21. H. Gish, M.-H. Siu, and R. Rohlicek. Segregation of speakers for speech recognition and speaker identification. In *International Conference on Acoustics, Speech, and Signal Processing*, Toronto, Ontario, Canada, 1991.

22. E. Goffman. *Forms of Talk*. University of Pennsylvania Press, Philadelphia, PA, 1981.

23. A. Hanjalic, R. Lagendijk, and J. Biemond. Automated high-level movie segmentation for advanced video-retrieval systems. *IEEE Transactions on Circuits and Systems for Video Technology*, 9:580–588, 1999.

24. Z. Harchaoui, F. Vallet, A. Lung-Yut-Fong, and O. Cappé. A regularized kernel-based approach to unsupervised audio segmentation. In *International Conference on Acoustics, Speech, and Signal Processing*, Taipei, Taiwan, 2009.

25. C. Hory and W. J. Christmas. Cepstral features for classification of an impulse response with varying sample size dataset. In *European Signal Processing Conference*, Poznan, Poland, 2007.

26. G. Jaffré and P. Joly. Costume: A new feature for automatic video content indexing. In *International Conference on Adaptivity, Personalization, and Fusion of Heterogeneous Information*, Avignon, France, 2004.

27. E. Kijak, G. Gravier, L. Oisel, and P. Gros. Audiovisual integration for tennis broadcast structuring. *Multimedia Tools and Applications*, 30:289–311, 2006.

28. M. Lhérault and E. Neveu. Quelques dispositifs de talk-shows français (1998–2003). *Réseaux*, 118:201–207, 2003.

29. G. Lochard. Débats, talk shows: De la radio filmée? *Communication et Langages*, 86:92–100, 1990.

30. B. S. Manjunath, P. Salembier, and T. Sikora, eds. *Introduction to MPEG-7—Multimedia Content Description Interface*. Wiley, Chichester, U.K., 2002.

31. W. Munson. *All Talk: The Talk Show in Media Culture*. Temple University Press, Philadelphia, PA, 1993.

32. K. Murphy. *Dynamic Bayesian Networks: Representation, Inference and Learning*. PhD thesis, UC Berkeley, Computer Science Division, Berkeley, CA, 2002.

33. X. Naturel and P. Gros. Detecting repeats for video structuring. *Multimedia Tools and Applications*, 38:233–252, 2008.

34. H. Penz. *Language and Control in American TV Talk Shows: An Analysis of Linguistic Strategies*. Gunter Narr, Tübingen, Germany, 1996.

35. M. Petkovic, V. Mihajlovic, W. Jonker, and S. Djordjevic-Kajan. Multimodal extraction of highlights from TV formula 1 programs. In *International Conference on Multimedia and Expo*, Lausanne, Switzerland, 2002.

36. J.-P. Poli. An automatic television stream structuring system for television archives holder. *Multimedia Systems*, 14:255–275, 2008.

37. L. Rabiner and B.-H. Juang. *Fundamentals of Speech Recognition*. Prentice Hall PTR, Upper Saddle River, NJ, 1993.

38. M. Ramona, G. Richard, and B. David. Vocal detection in music with support vector machines. In *International Conference on Acoustics, Speech, and Signal Processing*, Las Vegas, NV, 2008.

39. D. A. Reynolds and P. A. Torres-Carrasquillo. Approaches and applications of audio diarization. In *International Conference on Acoustics, Speech, and Signal Processing*, Philadelphia, PA, 2005.

40. G. Richard, M. Ramona, and S. Essid. Combined supervised and unsupervised approaches for automatic segmentation of radiophonic audio streams. In *International Conference on Acoustics, Speech, and Signal Processing*, Honolulu, HI, 2007.

41. E. Scheirer and M. Slaney. Construction and evaluation of a robust multifeature speech/music discriminator. In *International Conference on Acoustics, Speech, and Signal Processing*, Munich, Germany, 1997.

42. J. Sivic, M. Everingham, and A. Zisserman. Who are you?: Learning person specific classifiers from video. In *International Conference on Computer Vision and Pattern Recognition*, Miami, FL, 2009.

43. H. Sloetjes and P. Wittenburg. Annotation by category—ELAN and ISO DCR. In *International Conference on Language Resources and Evaluation*, Marrakech, Morocco, 2008.

44. A. Smeaton, P. Over, and A. Doherty. Video shot boundary detection: Seven years of TRECVid activity. *Computer Vision and Image Understanding*, 114:411–418, 2009.

45. C. G. M. Snoek and M. Worring. Multimodal video indexing: A review of the state-of-the-art. *Multimedia Tools and Applications*, 25:5–35, 2005.

46. B. Timberg. *Television Talk: A History of TV Talk Show*. University of Texas Press, Austin, TX, 2002.

47. S. E. Tranter and D. A. Reynolds. An overview of automatic speaker diarization systems. *IEEE Transactions on Audio, Speech, and Language Processing*, 14 (5):1557–1565, 2006.

48. H. Vajaria, T. Islam, S. Sarkar, R. Sankar, and R. Kasturi. Audio segmentation and speaker localization in meeting videos. In *International Conference on Pattern Recognition*, Hong Kong, China, 2006.

49. F. Vallet, S. Essid, J. Carrive, and G. Richard. Robust visual features for the multimodal identification of unregistered speakers. In *International Conference on Image Processing*, Hong Kong, China, 2010.

50. F. Wang, Y.-F. Ma, H.-J. Zhang, and J.-T. Li. A generic framework for semantic sports video analysis using dynamic Bayesian networks. In *Multimedia Modelling Conference*, Melbourne, Australia, 2005.

51. P. Wilkins, T. Adamek, D. Byrne, G. J. F. Jones, H. Lee, G. Keenan, K. McGuiness, N. E. O'Connor, A. F. Smeaton, A. Amin, Z. Obrenovic, R. Benmokhtar, E. Galmar, B. Huet, S. Essid, R. Landais, F. Vallet, G. Th. Papadopoulos, S. Vrochidis, V. Mezaris, I. Kompatsiaris, E. Spyrou, Y. Avrithis, R. Morzinger, P. Schallauer, W. Bailer, T. Piatrik, K. Chandramouli, E. Izquierdo, M. Haller, L. Goldmann, A. Samour, A. Cobet, T. Sikora, and P. Praks. K-space at TRECVid 2007. In *TRECVid 2007—Text Retrieval Conference TRECVid Workshop*, Gaithersburg, MD, 2007.

52. R. Williams. *Television: Technology and Cultural form*. Fontana, London, U.K., 1974.

53. C. Wooters and M. Huijbregts. The ICSI RT07s speaker diarization system. *Multimodal Technologies for Perception of Humans*, 4625:509–519, 2008.

54. Z. Xiong, R. Radhakrishnan, and A. Divakaran. Generation of sports highlights using motion activities in combination with a common audio feature extraction framework. In *International Conference on Image Processing*, Barcelona, Spain, 2003.

55. M. Xu, L.-Y. Duan, C. Xu, M. Kankanhalli, and Q. Tian. Event detection in basketball video using multiple modalities. In *Pacific-Rim Conference on Multimedia*, Meritus Mandarin Hotel, Singapore, 2003.

56. M. Yeung and B.-L. Yeo. Time-constrained clustering for segmentation of video into story units. In *International Conference on Pattern Recognition*, Vienna, Austria, 1996.

57. D. Zhang and S.-F. Chang. Event detection in baseball video using superimposed caption recognition. In *ACM Conference on Multimedia*, Juan les Pins, France, 2002.

58. W. Zhou, A. Vellaikal, and C.-C. J. Kuo. Rule based video classification system for basketball video indexing. In *ACM Workshops on Multimedia*, Los Angeles, CA, 2000.

CONTENT
RECOMMENDATION

III

Chapter 10

Recommender Systems for Interactive TV

Riccardo Bambini
Fastweb

Paolo Cremonesi
Politecnico di Milano, DEI

Roberto Turrin
Moviri, R&D

Contents

10.1 Introduction

Interactive television (iTV), differently from conventional television, allows providers (a) to track user activity and (b) to personalize the content transmitted to the users. These tasks are accomplished by *recommender systems*, whose goal is to filter information from a large dataset—e.g., thousands of channels and movies offered by an iTV operator—and to recommend to the users only the content that is likely of interest and attraction to them. Recommender systems play an important role in iTV services because the presence of a large number of TV programs dramatically reduces the visibility of each one, potentially inhibiting users from finding interesting TV contents. From the provider's point of view, a large catalog is expensive to be maintained, due to the cost of the multimedia material itself, to the required storage space, and to the hardware infrastructure used to stream videos from the content provider to the users. Recently, many iTV recommender systems have been developed in academic as well as in corporate research labs, especially after the enormous resonance of the competition organized by the American movie rental provider Netflix. Differently from traditional e-commerce domains (e.g., iTunes, Last.fm, Amazon), recommender systems for iTV provide new challenges (e.g., real-time and scalability requirements, difficulties in collecting user ratings, difficulties in collecting TV content metadata).

The goal of this chapter is to give an overview of how to design and evaluate recommender systems for the iTV. The chapter is organized into three sections. In the first section, a comprehensive general background on recommender systems will be provided. The integration between iTV services and recommender systems will be explained. In the second section, a detailed overview of both statistical and user-based evaluation methodologies will be given, along with an explanation of how to use them to evaluate iTV recommender systems. Finally, in the third section, a case study on the development and deployment of a recommender system within Fastweb, one of the largest IPTV providers in Europe, will be presented.

10.2 Recommender Systems

In order to benefit from the rich set of channels and contents, iTV users need to be able to rapidly and easily find what they are actually interested in and do so effortlessly while relaxing on the couch in their living room, a location where they typically do not have easy access to keyboard, mouse, and close-up screen display typical of desktop web browsing. However, searching for a TV program or a video-on-demand (VoD) content is a challenging problem for iTV users [22]. When watching live television, users browse through a set of available channels until they find something interesting. Channel selection (zapping) involves two steps: (a) sampling the content to decide whether to continue or stop watching the channel and (b) switching across multiple channels for repeated sampling, until a desired channel is found. The problem of quickly finding the right channel becomes harder as the number of channel offerings grows in modern iTV services. Moreover, iTV channel switching time is not particularly responsive, compared to traditional TV, because of technological delays (e.g., buffering, coding/decoding, network) [21]. When searching for VoD content, iTV users generally have to either navigate a complex, predefined, and often deeply embedded menu structure or type in titles or other key phrases using on-screen keyboards or triple tap input on the remote control keypad. These interfaces are cumbersome and do not scale well as the range of content available increases. Moreover, the television screen usually is watched from a distance with respect to traditional personal computer screens, making traditional graphical user interfaces difficult to use.

Differently from conventional television, iTV allows an interactive navigation of the available content, and the system is able to acquire implicit usage data and explicit user preferences. Therefore, it is possible to integrate a recommender system into iTV services by providing a new and more effective way of browsing for interesting programs and movies. Recommender systems collect (either explicitly or implicitly) information about user preferences and provide user-oriented suggestions about items (e.g., movies and TV programs). However, iTV recommender systems need to satisfy particular requirements:

- The TV is used indistinctly by all the components of a family, and the iTV recommender system cannot identify who is actually watching a certain program.
- Differently from web-based domains, content-based iTV recommender algorithms make use of low-quality metadata; this aspect is particularly evident with linear channels, where new content is added every day at a very high rate, and the only available metadata can be found in the electronic program guide (EPG).
- The list of proposed items has to be small because of the limited screen definition and the reduced navigation capabilities.

- The generation of the recommended items must respect very strict time constraints (few milliseconds) because TV's customers are used to a very responsive system.
- The recommender system needs to scale up in a successful manner with both the number of users and the number of items.
- Part of the catalog is highly dynamic because of linear channels.

10.2.1 Input Data

The logical component in charge of preprocessing the data and generating the input of the recommender algorithm is referred to as *data collector*. The data collector gathers data from different sources, such as the EPG for information about the live programs, the content provider for information about the VoD catalog, and the service provider for information about the users. Formally, the available information is structured into two main matrices, practically stored into a relational database: the item-content matrix (ICM) and the user-rating matrix (URM).

The ICM, from here on denoted with $\mathbf{W}$, describes the characteristics (metadata) of each item. Columns and rows represent items and metadata, respectively, and the element w_{ci} represents the weight (relevance) of metadata c for item i. For example, the metadata can be the title of a movie, the actors, the director(s), the genre(s), or the plot. The ICM is generated from the analysis of the set of information given by the content provider (i.e., the EPG). The information stored into the ICM can be elaborated by means of techniques based on part-of-speech (PoS) tagging, stop words removal, and latent semantic analysis (LSA) [35]. Moreover, the ICM can be used to perform pre- or postprocessing on the items (e.g., parental control).

The URM, from here on denoted with $\mathbf{R}$, represents the ratings (i.e., preferences) of users about items. The element r_{pi} represents the rating of user p about item i. The user rating can be either explicit or implicit. Explicit ratings represent the true user opinion about TV programs and movies, even though they can be affected by biases due to (a) user subjectivity, (b) item popularity, and (c) global rating tendency [6]. The first bias depends on arbitrary interpretations of the rating scale. For instance, in a rating scale between 1 and 5, some user could use the value 3 to indicate an interesting item, someone else could use 3 for a not much interesting item. Similarly, popular items tend to be overrated, while unpopular items are usually underrated. Finally, explicit ratings can be affected by global attitudes (e.g., users are more willing to rate movies they like). On the other hand, implicit ratings are inferred by the system on the basis of the user-system interaction, which might not match the user opinion. For instance, the system is able to monitor whether a user has watched a TV program or whether the user has purchased a VoD movie.

Despite explicit ratings being more reliable than implicit ratings in representing the actual user interest toward an item, their collection can be annoying from the user's perspective.

10.2.2 Recommender Algorithms

In order to satisfy the strict real-time requirements of iTV services, recommender algorithms should be designed according to a *model-based* approach [15,36]. Recommendations in model-based algorithms are generated with a two-stage process. In the first stage, the algorithm processes the ICM and the URM in order to develop a "compact" model of the users' taste and/or item characteristics. Such computation is time-expensive and it is usually executed within a batch process during off-peak hours, with a frequency that depends on the rate new items/users are added into the system (e.g., once a day). In the second stage the model is matched with the user's profile in order to provide fast recommendations. This second stage is computationally light and can be performed online. The advantages of *model-based* algorithms are (a) the relatively low computational cost of the online stage, (b) the ability to provide recommendations for users new to the system without the need to update the model, and (c) the possibility to explain the recommendations in terms of items previously rated by the user.

Model-based recommender algorithms can be further classified into content, collaborative, and hybrid algorithms. The *content-based* approach to recommendation found its roots in information retrieval, which provides a set of tools for searching for textual information, e.g., in documents, websites, usenet news, and mail messages. Content-based systems [1,4,26] recommend items similar to those that a user liked in the past, by considering their features. For example, the features of a movie might be the actors, the producers, the genre, the directors, etc. Thus, if a user is used to watch many action movies, he will be recommended other action movies. In contrast to content-based, *collaborative systems* try to suggest items to a particular user on the basis of the other users' preferences [1,30]. In fact, in everyday life, we often rely on recommendations from other people such as by word of mouth or movie reviews. Such systems use the opinions of a community of users to help individuals more effectively identify content of interest. Collaborative systems assist and augment this process. Finally, *hybrid algorithms* make recommendations on the basis of multiple recommender algorithms. In the general case, whenever we merge two or more recommender algorithms we define a hybrid algorithm. However, the most interesting cases concern the union of collaborative and content-based algorithms.

10.2.3 Content-Based Filtering Algorithms

In content-based filtering (CBF) algorithms the model of an item is composed by a set of features (also referred to as metadata) representing its content, so that similar items contain similar features. In addition, features are assigned a weight indicating how representative they are of an item. Typically, the more items contain a feature, the less representative the feature is (i.e., it is less important in order to distinguish one item from another).

Feature extraction is probably the most critical phase of content-based algorithms and it can be particularly challenging with non-textual resources, such as audio/video streams. For instance, the textual features of a movie can be the genre (e.g., comedy), the list of actors, etc. While more interesting information could be obtained by analyzing the audio/video tracks, this technology [22] is fairly recent and it is necessary to examine whether it can really bring some improvement in this specific domain.

The classical way of representing items in content-based recommender is the *bag-of-words* (BOW) approach [10], where we consider textual features and we only retain frequencies of words, discarding any grammar/semantic connection. Usually the words are preprocessed by means of tokenization, stop-words removal, and stemming [35]. The former simply splits text into tokens (e.g., words). Tokens not useful for representing an item in a certain domain are discarded (stop-words). Finally, stemming is used to normalize some kind of grammar variability by converting tokens to their morphological root. For example, the words "play," "player," "playing," and "played" would all be converted to their root form, "play." After the preprocessing, each token has assigned a weight that is proportional to its frequency normalized using various schemes, the most known being the TF-IDF scheme [28,35]. The BOW representation can be summarized in the ICM, where columns and rows represent items and metadata, respectively, and the element w_{ci} represents the weight (relevance) of metadata c for item i.

In its simplest formulation, users can be represented as a set of weighted metadata. In fact, the profile of a user can be derived by means of a linear combination of the vectors corresponding to the items he has rated, weighted with the related user rating. Recommendations are then obtained by comparing the similarity between the vector representing the user profile and the vectors representing the items. The most similar items are then proposed to the user. Similarity between two vectors can be expressed by several metrics, such as the Euclidean distance and the cosine distance [28]. The fact that content-based systems recommend items with the same metadata as the items that a user liked in the past has two direct effects: it assures that the recommended items are coherent with the user's interests, but, at the same time, the set of recommended items could be obvious and too homogeneous. This issue is usually referred to as the *over-specialization* problem [4]. The main advantage of content-based techniques is that since they are based on evident features, they can provide an understandable and immediate explanation of the recommended items. Furthermore, CBF is based on a well-known and mature technology.

Once the ICM has been created, several algorithms can be used for generating recommendations, such as the Naïve Bayes approach and the LSA technique.

10.2.3.1 Naïve Bayes

The Naïve Bayesian Classifier is one of the most successful machine learning algorithms in many classification domains. Despite its simplicity, it is shown to be competitive with other complex approaches, especially in text categorization tasks [10]. Given a class Y and a set of characterizing features $f_1 \ldots f_n$, the *Naïve* Bayes, based on Bayes rule, assumes the attributes $f_1 \ldots f_n$ are all conditionally independent of one another, given Y; making the naïve assumption that features are independent given the class label, the probability of an item belonging to class Y given its n feature values, i.e., the *posterior probability* $p(Y|f_1, f_2, \ldots f_n)$, is proportional to

$$p(Y) \prod_{i=1}^{n} p(f_i|Y) \tag{10.1}$$

where

$p(Y)$ is called *prior probability*

$p(f_i|Y)$ is referred to as *likelihood*

Class Y can assume either binary values [24], e.g., "positive" and "negative" items, or non-binary values [23], e.g., items rated "1," rated "2," and so on.

10.2.3.2 Latent Semantic Analysis

LSA is a method well known in the settings of information retrieval for automatic indexing and searching of documents [14,17]. The approach takes advantage of the implicit structure (*latent semantic*) in the association of terms with documents. The technique consists in decomposing **W** into a set of orthogonal factors whose linear combination approximates the original matrix. The decomposition is performed by means of a trunked singular value decomposition (SVD).

W being a $c \times n$ matrix (c metadata and n items), it can be factorized into three matrices, **U** ($c \times l$), **S** ($l \times l$), and **V** ($n \times l$) so that

$$\mathbf{W} \approx \mathbf{USV}^{\mathsf{T}} \tag{10.2}$$

where l is the number of latent semantic characteristics of items. Generally l is unknown and it must be computed with cross-validation techniques. **S** contains the first l singular value of **W** that, roughly speaking, is related to the importance of each latent characteristic. The columns of **U** and **V** are orthonormal and represent, respectively, the left and right singular vectors. The product $\mathbf{USV}^{\mathsf{T}}$ is the best rank-l linear approximation of **W** in terms of the Frobenius norm [27]. Note that SVD is unique except for some linear combinations of rows and columns of the three resulting matrices and, conventionally, the diagonal elements of **S** are constructed so to be positive and sorted by decreasing magnitude.

The SVD defines a new low-rank vector space, whose dimensions are not the c metadata, but the $l \ll c$ latent semantic features. We can represent item i into the latent space by projecting (folding-in) the related column of $\mathbf{W}$; $\tilde{\mathbf{d}}_i$ being such a column vector, its projection $\tilde{\mathbf{d}}_i$ is given by:

$$\tilde{\mathbf{d}}_i = \mathbf{U}^{\mathrm{T}}\mathbf{d}_i \tag{10.3}$$

Similarly, metadata c can be represented into the latent space as the projection of the related row of $\mathbf{W}$, referred to as $\mathbf{w}_c$:

$$\tilde{\mathbf{w}} = \mathbf{w}_c \mathbf{V} \mathbf{S} \tag{10.4}$$

The advantages of LSA are in terms of memory and computation requirements and in terms of performance in analyzing textual features. In fact, once the SVD has been computed by the batch stage, the system works at real time on the low-dimensional space defined by the l latent semantic dimensions, much smaller than the BOW space. In addition, by keeping only the l most important characteristics, we filter out the data noise and we strengthen the relationships between items and metadata. For instance, if two metadata coappear in many items, this means they are somehow correlated (e.g., two synonyms) and they will be represented similarly in the latent space. The correlation might also be indirect, discovering hidden dependences [17,34].

As we represented items in the latent space, we represent users in the same space, expressing them as a linear combination—weighted by the user ratings—of the vectors $\tilde{\mathbf{d}}_i$ related to the items previously rated by the user. Let us denote the representation of user p in the latent space as $\tilde{\mathbf{r}}_p$. Once items and users have been represented in the same vector space, we can compute the estimated rating $\hat{r}_{pi}$ of user p about item i by means of any correlation metric among vectors. For instance, the cosine similarity is computed as

$$\hat{r}_{pi} = \frac{\sum_{e=1}^{l} \tilde{r}_{pe} \cdot \tilde{d}_{ie}}{\sqrt{\sum_{e=1}^{l} \tilde{r}_{pe}^2} \cdot \sqrt{\sum_{e=1}^{l} \tilde{d}_{ie}^2}} \tag{10.5}$$

where $\tilde{r}_{pe}$ and $\tilde{d}_{ie}$ indicate the eth element of vectors $\tilde{\mathbf{r}}_p$ and $\tilde{\mathbf{d}}_i$, respectively

Observe that this representation allows to integrate *explicit* user preferences, e.g., the actors a user has explicitly declared to like. In fact, a vector of explicit user preferences can be treated similarly to an item, i.e., a vector of metadata. Once the explicit preferences have been folded into the latent space, the projected user and the projected explicit preferences can be combined to form a new user profile biased toward the explicit preferences.

10.2.4 Collaborative Algorithms

Most recommender systems are based on collaborative filtering (CF), where recommendations rely only on past user behavior (to be referred to here as "ratings," though such behavior can include other user activities on items like purchases, rentals, and clicks), regardless of domain knowledge. There are two primary approaches to CF: the neighborhood approach and the latent factor approach. *Neighborhood* models represent the most common approach to CF. They are based on the similarity among either users or items. For instance, two users are similar because they have rated similarly the same set of items. A dual concept of similarity can be defined among items. *Latent factor* approaches model users and items as vectors in the same "latent factor" space by means of a reduced number of hidden factors. In such a space, users and items are directly comparable: the rating of user u on item i is predicted by the proximity (e.g., inner-product) between the related latent factor vectors.

Note that collaborative recommendation does not need to extract any feature from the items. Thus, such systems do not have the same shortcomings that content-based systems have. In particular, since collaborative systems use other users' preferences, they can deal with any kind of content. Furthermore, they can recommend any items, even the ones with a content that does not correspond to any item previously liked.

However, collaborative recommenders are affected by the *new item* (or first-rater) problem. In fact, since such systems recommend the items most correlated to those preferred by the current user, a new item cannot be recommended because nobody has rated it so far (the system cannot define a model for such item). Therefore, until the new item is rated by a substantial number of users, the recommender system will not be able to recommend it. For such reasons, collaborative algorithms are not practicable in live TV domains, where new programs enter the system at a very high rate and appear and receive ratings for a very limited time window (e.g., few hours). Note that content-based recommenders do not suffer for such a problem because when new items enter into the collection, their model is given by their own features (i.e., their metadata).

A second issue with collaborative algorithms is the *sparsity* problem. In fact, the effectiveness of collaborative systems depend on the availability of sets of users with similar preferences. Unfortunately, in any recommender system, the number of ratings already obtained is usually very small compared to the number of ratings to estimate. As a consequence, it might not be possible to recommend someone with unique tastes, because there will not be anyone enough similar to him.

As a consequence of these issues, at the beginning of its activity a brand new collaborative system will not be able to provide any accurate recommendation; it is called the *cold start* problem.

Finally, since popular items are the most rated, collaborative recommenders are likely to be biased toward the most popular items. For instance, if a movie has been rated by only few people, this movie would be recommended very rarely, because the predicted rating might not be reliable.

10.2.4.1 Nonpersonalized Models

Nonpersonalized recommenders present to any user a predefined, fixed list of items, regardless of his or her preferences [13]. Such algorithms serve as baselines for the more complex personalized algorithms.

A simple estimation rule, referred to as *movie average* (MovieAvg), recommends top-N items with the highest average rating. The rating of user u on item i is predicted as the mean rating expressed by the community on item i, regardless of the ratings given by u.

A similar prediction schema, denoted by *top popular* (TopPop), recommends top-N items with the highest popularity (largest number of ratings). Notice that in this case the rating of user u about item i cannot be inferred, but the output of this algorithm is only a ranked list of items. We will see in Section 10.3.3 how this prevents the use of error metrics—such as RMSE root mean square error (RMSE)—for evaluating the recommendation quality.

10.2.4.2 Neighborhood-Based Algorithm

The neighborhood approach is based on the assumptions that (a) groups of users with similar tastes rate the items similarly and (b) correlated items are rated by a group of users similarly.

Starting from the previous two assumptions, there exist two classes of collaborative recommenders, respectively, the user-based and the item-based [37]. Algorithms centered on user–user similarity predict the ratings of a user based on the ratings expressed by users similar to him about such item. On the other hand, algorithms centered on item–item similarity compute the user preference for an item based on his or her own ratings on similar items. In practice, user-based recommenders are seldom used because they are not model based and because of their poor quality [29]. For such reasons, we focus on item-based neighborhood algorithms.

In item-based algorithms, the similarity between item i and item j is measured as the tendency of users to rate items i and j similarly. It is typically based either on the cosine, the adjusted cosine, or (most commonly) the Pearson correlation coefficient [29]. Such similarity can be represented in a $m \times m$ matrix, referred to as $\mathbf{D}$, where the element d_{ij} expresses the similarity between item i and item j. Since each item receives ratings from a different set of users, item–item similarity is computed on the common raters. In the typical case of a very sparse dataset, it is likely that some pairs of items have a poor support, leading to a unreliable similarity measure. For such a reason, if n_{ij} denotes the number of common raters and s_{ij} the similarity between item i and item j, we can define the shrunk similarity d_{ij} as the coefficient $d_{ij} = \left(n_{ij}/(n_{ij} + \lambda_1) \right) s_{ij}$ where λ_1 is a shrinking factor. A typical value of λ_1 is 100 [18].

Neighborhood models are further enhanced by means of a kNN (k-nearest-neighborhood) approach. When predicting rating r_{ui}, we consider only the k items rated by u that are the most similar to i. We denote the set of most similar items by $D^k(u; i)$. The kNN approach discards the items poorly correlated to the target item, thus decreasing noise for improving the quality of recommendations.

Prior to comparing and summing different ratings, it is advised to remove different biases that mask the more fundamental relations between items, e.g., certain items tend to receive higher ratings than others and certain users tend to rate higher than others. A more delicate calculation of the biases would also estimate temporal effects [19]. We denote the bias associated with the rating of user u to item i by b_{ui}.

An item–item kNN method predicts the residual rating $r_{ui} - b_{ui}$ as the weighted average of the residual ratings of similar items:

$$\hat{r}_{ui} = b_{ui} + \frac{\sum_{j \in D^k(u;i)} d_{ij} \left(r_{uj} - b_{uj} \right)}{\sum_{j \in D^k(u;i)} d_{ij}} \tag{10.6}$$

We refer to this model as *correlation neighborhood* (CorNgbr), where d_{ij} is measured as the Pearson correlation coefficient. The denominator in (10.6) ensures that predicted ratings fall in the correct range, (e.g., $[1 \ldots 5]$). However, for a top-N recommendation task, exact rating values are not necessary. In such a case, we can simplify the formula by removing the denominator. A benefit of this would be higher ranking for items with many similar neighbors (that is high $\sum_{j \in D^k(u;i)} d_{ij}$), where we have a higher confidence in the recommendation. Therefore, Koren et al. propose in [13] to rank items according to the following coefficient $\hat{r}_{ui}$:

$$\hat{r}_{ui} = b_{ui} + \sum_{j \in D^k(u;i)} d_{ij} \left(r_{uj} - b_{uj} \right) \tag{10.7}$$

Here $\hat{r}_{ui}$ does not represent a proper rating, but is rather a metric for the association between user u and item i. The similarity d_{ij} is computed using the cosine similarity. Unlike the Pearson correlation that is computed only on ratings shared by common raters, the cosine coefficient between items i and j is computed over all ratings (taking missing values as zeroes), that is, $\cos(i, j) = \vec{i} \cdot \vec{j} / (||\vec{i}||_2 \cdot ||\vec{j}||_2)$. We denote such a model by *non-normalized cosine neighborhood* (NNCosNgbr).

10.2.4.3 Latent Factors Collaborative Algorithms

Recently, several recommender algorithms based on latent factor models have been proposed. Most of them are based on factoring the user–item ratings matrix [20], also informally known as SVD models after the related SVD.

The key idea of SVD models is to factorize the user–item rating matrix to a product of two lower-rank matrices, one containing the so-called user factors, and the other one containing the so-called item factors. Thus, each user u is represented with an f-dimensional user factors vector $\mathbf{p}_u \in \mathfrak{R}^f$. Similarly, each item i is represented with an item factors vector $\mathbf{q}_i \in \mathfrak{R}^f$. Prediction of a rating given by user u for item i is computed as the inner product between the related factor vectors (adjusted for biases), i.e.,

$$\hat{r}_{ui} = b_{ui} + \mathbf{p}_u \mathbf{q}_i^{\mathrm{T}} \tag{10.8}$$

Recent works learn factor vectors directly on known ratings through a suitable objective function that minimizes prediction error. The proposed objective functions are usually regularized in order to avoid overfitting (e.g., [25]). Typically, gradient descent is applied to minimize the objective function.

One of the most powerful factorization models that indeed represents users as a combination of item features is known as *asymmetric-SVD* (AsySVD) and is reported to reach an RMSE of 0.9000 on the Netflix dataset [18]. Let us denote by $R(u)$ the set of items rated by user u. AsySVD predicts r_{ui} according to the rule

$$\hat{r}_{ui} = b_{ui} + \mathbf{q}_i^{\mathrm{T}} |R(u)|^{-\frac{1}{2}} \sum_{j \in R(u)} \left(\left(r_{uj} - b_{uj} \right) \mathbf{x}_j + \mathbf{y}_j \right) \tag{10.9}$$

While pursuing a top-N recommendation task, we are interested only in a correct item ranking, not caring about exact rating prediction. Koren and coworkers [13] propose to consider all missing values in the user rating matrix as zeros, despite being out of the 1- to 5- rating range. Importantly, this allows to use highly optimized software packages for performing conventional SVD on sparse matrices, which becomes feasible since all matrix entries are now non-missing. Thus, the user rating matrix $\mathbf{R}$ is estimated by the factorization [5]

$$\hat{\mathbf{R}} = \mathbf{U} \cdot \mathbf{S} \cdot \mathbf{Q}^{\mathrm{T}} \tag{10.10}$$

where
  $\mathbf{U}$ is a $n \times f$ orthonormal matrix,
  $\mathbf{Q}$ is an $m \times f$ orthonormal matrix
  and $\mathbf{S}$ is an $f \times f$ diagonal matrix containing the first f singular values.

It can be proven (see [13]) that the prediction rule can be rewritten as

$$\hat{r}_{ui} = \mathbf{r}_u \cdot \mathbf{Q} \cdot \mathbf{q}_i^{\mathrm{T}} \tag{10.11}$$

where $\mathbf{r}_u$ denotes the uth row of the user rating matrix—i.e., the vector of ratings of user u.

In the following, we will refer to this model as *PureSVD*. As with item–item kNN and AsySVD, PureSVD offers all the benefits of representing users as a combination of item features (by (10.11)), without any user-specific parameterization. It also offers convenient optimization, which does not require tuning learning constants. Similarly to LSA, PureSVD has several interesting characteristics in terms of memory and computation requirements and in terms of capability of analyzing the available data. In fact, it represents items and users in a low-dimensional space and—by neglecting the singular values with low magnitude—reduces the noise in the data and strengthens the relationships among the data.

10.2.5 Hybrid Algorithms

Hybrid recommender systems combine two or more recommendation techniques to gain better performance with fewer of the drawbacks of any individual one. Most commonly, CF is combined with some other technique in an attempt to avoid the ramp-up problem. A taxonomy of existing and possible hybridization methods has been proposed by Burke [7], the most interesting being the following:

Weighted the ratings estimated by several recommendation techniques are combined (e.g., averaged) together to produce a single recommendation (e.g., [11]).

Switching the system chooses one among the available recommendation techniques depending on the situation (e.g., [33]).

Mixed recommendations from different recommenders are presented at the same time (e.g., [2]).

Feature combination features from different data sources are put together into a single recommendation algorithm. For instance, the hybrid system HYDRA [32] combines into the URM item features retrieved from IMDB (content-based) and user features (demographic data). The supplementary item features and user features are injected into the URM as additional users and additional items, respectively.

Feature augmentation the output from one recommender is used as an input feature of another. For example, Melville et al. [23] augment the ratings collected in the URM with ratings estimated by a Naïve Bayes content-based predictor; all the ratings are used as input to an item-based collaborative recommender.

10.3 Evaluation of iTV Recommender Systems

The effectiveness of a recommender system is related to the quality of its recommendations, which, in turn, is defined in terms of different attributes. The second section of this chapter will address the most important metrics and techniques that can be used to assess the quality of a recommender system.

10.3.1 Quality Attributes

As more and more recommendation techniques are proposed, researchers address the problem of estimating the value of recommendations. One particular problem is that the actors behind a recommender system (users and providers) have different perspectives. For instance, a good recommendation can be considered as one that makes the user happy as well as one that maximizes the sales margin at the same time. This section analyzes the evaluation of recommender systems from the user point of view, focusing on a number of quality attributes:

Relevance measures the ability of a recommender system to suggest TV contents that fit the user's preferences. Most evaluation techniques focus on the system's accuracy in supporting the "find good TV program" user's task. They measure
- How good the system is in predicting the exact rating value (value comparison)
- How well the system can predict whether the item is relevant or not (relevant vs. not relevant)
- How close the predicted ranking of items is to the user's true ranking (ordering comparison)

Coverage concerns the degree to which recommendations cover the set of available items and the degree to which recommendations can be generated to all potential users. The coverage is mainly associated with the percentage of the items for which the system is able to generate a recommendation. To give an example, CF systems are just able to make predictions for items that have been implicitly or explicitly rated. On the other hand, content-based systems are able to recommend only items that have been tagged with textual information (e.g., EPG).

Diversity is defined as the opposite of similarity, which means that the items in a recommendation list are similar to each other. For example, a recommendation list might be filled with episodes of the same TV serie. Similar recommendation achieves a high performance for accuracy and a low one for serendipity. Thus, a good quality system should be able to provide diverse recommendations.

Understandability measures the ability of a recommender systems to explains in natural language the reasons that led to a recommendation.

Novelty is the capability of a recommender system to help the user in finding surprisingly interesting TV contents that the user might have autonomously discovered but he was not aware of. If a system recommends items the user already has heard a lot about (TopPop, generally liked items), even a recommendation that matches the user's taste would not be too meaningful. This aspect is related to novelty.

Serendipity is the capability of a recommender system to surprise the user by suggesting fortuitous and unexpected TV content that the user might not have otherwise discovered. That means a highly serendipitous system would be capable of making nontrivial and surprising recommendations. Based on this definition we can see three important aspects related to serendipity: (a) a serendipitous item should be not yet discovered, i.e., it should be novel; (b) the item should also be relevant to the user; and (c) the item should not be expected by the user.

It is not hard to see that all these metrics are closely related and influence one another. For instance, in CF systems, coverage usually decreases as a function of accuracy. In fact, accurate recommendations are directly proportional to the amount of available ratings. As popular items receive much more ratings than others, an accurate system will tend to recommend items from this group.

10.3.2 Subjective Tests

User-centered approaches to quality evaluation have recently received some interest in the interactive TV arena of recommender systems. For instance, Celma and Herrera [9] report an experiment exploring the users' perceived quality of novel recommendations provided by a CF and a CBF algorithm in the music recommendation context. Shearer [31] describes an experiment with 29 subjects on a movie recommender systems to determine whether recommendations based on CF are perceived as superior to recommendations based on user population averages. The recommender systems suggested movies that subjects later viewed. Participants placed slightly more confidence in the recommendations with respect to the population averages algorithm, but the perceived quality of the two algorithms was almost the same. Ziegler et al. [39] and Zhang et al. [38] propose diversity as a quality attribute: recommender algorithms should seek to provide optimal coverage of the entire range of user's interests. This work is an example of the combined use of automatic and user-centered quality assessment techniques.

In this section, we describe the user-centric evaluation of different VoD recommender algorithms. The study involved approximately 200 participants, uniformly distributed between 20 and 50 years, about half male and half female. None of them had technical knowledge about recommender systems or had been previously exposed to the system used in our study. The evaluation took place in informal environments such as university (15%), interviewer's place (32%), and interviewee's place (31%). Each interview lasted 10–30 min.

The dataset used in our study is a subset of the movie dataset Netflix, integrated with data (e.g., movie plot, images, actors, director, and genre) collected from Internet sources. The dataset is formed by 2,137 movies and about 8 million ratings given by about 50,000 users. Our study considered several state-of-the-art recommender algorithms: four collaborative algorithms (CorNgbr, NNCosNgbr, AsySVD, PureSVD) and a content-based one (LSA). The algorithms have been described in Section 10.2.2. The experiment involved the commercial recommender framework ContentWise* [13]. The web-based interface supports functionalities such as browsing the movie catalog, retrieving movie details (e.g., director, actors, and summary), rating movies, and obtaining recommendations generated by a specified recommender algorithm.

Initially, each participant was asked to provide his/her personal information: age, gender, education, nationality, and number of movies watched per month. Afterward, any participant was allowed to browse the catalog and rate five movies (in a 1–5 rating scale). At this point, each subject was recommended five movies, according to a specific recommender algorithm. Thereafter, the participant was invited to reply to a set of questions related to the recommended movies. For each movie, we investigated how novel the item was for the user by asking the following questions: Have you ever watched this movie and Have you ever heard about this movie. In this case the subject neither had watched the movie nor had heard about it; he or she was shown the trailer of the movie. Finally, the participant was asked to give a rating about the movie in a 1–5 rating scale.

Figures 10.1 and 10.2 report the perceived relevance and novelty. Perceived quality values are calculated by considering, for each user, the values (in the 1–5 points scale) of each answer related to relevance on each recommended movie and by taking the average for all movies and for each set of users. Novelty values highlight the percentages of novel movies recommended by the algorithms. Box-and-whisker plots support the study of the variance in both the figures. Thick lines represent medians.

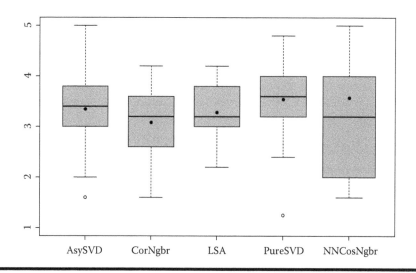

Figure 10.1 Perceived relevance of the recommended movies. Users can express the relevance in a 1-to-5 point scale.

---

* www.contentwise.tv

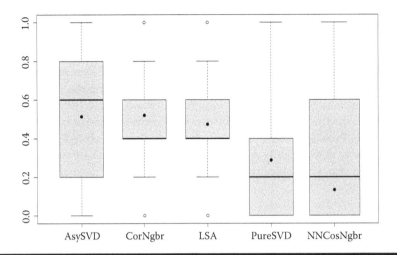

Figure 10.2   Perceived novelty of the recommended movies. Novelty can assume values in the interval [0, 1].

According to our study, all the algorithms have a comparable relevance, with PureSVD slightly outperforming all the other algorithms. As for novelty, AsySVD, CrnNgbr, and LSA are able to suggest 30% of novel movies, while PureSVD and NNCosNgbr are able to suggest 10% of novel movies. This is an important finding since it is believed that content-based methods (like LSA) are not able to recommend novel movies since they tend to suggest movies similar to those already watched by the user in the past. However our study does not confirm this belief. This happens mainly for two reasons. First of all, most collaborative algorithms are biased toward popular movies, thus reducing novelty. Moreover, if the size of the catalog is large, it is likely that it will contain movies novel to the user, even if such movies are similar to those already watched by the user in the past.

Novelty should not be limited to subjective evaluation, but it should also be taken into consideration when using automatic methods to evaluate relevance of recommendations, such as the off-line evaluation presented in Section 10.3.3. In fact, off-line methods compute accuracy or error of recommendations by exploiting previously rated movies, i.e., user's rankings of movies that they know about. Consequently, off-line techniques may underestimate the relevance of algorithms able to suggest novel movies and might penalize algorithms that, like LSA, have stronger novelty.

10.3.3 Off-Line Analysis

Most recommender algorithms are evaluated off-line using automatic approaches. Regardless of the quality of recommender algorithms depending on a number of attributes (see Section 10.3.1), off-line evaluation is typically focused on recommendation relevance, while neglecting other properties such as novelty and serendipity, more complex and articulated to operationalize. Two families of statistical metrics are usually adopted to automatically measure the relevance: *error metrics* and *accuracy metrics* [12,16]. Error metrics—such as RMSE—measure the capability of the system to accurately estimate the ratings real users would give to items. Accuracy metrics—such as precision and recall—measure the effectiveness of the recommender system in estimating whether an item is relevant or not. Both error and accuracy metrics can be automatically evaluated by means of well-known techniques developed in the field of machine learning, such as *k-fold cross validation, hold-out,* and *leave-one-out.*

Since the main goal of a recommender system in the settings of TV is to select a limited set of highly relevant items, in this chapter we focus on accuracy metrics—in particular on the recall—better suited for evaluating the so-called *top-N recommendation task* [13,15,18]. In information retrieval, recall specifies the percentage of relevant items that have been retrieved by, for instance, a search engine. In the recommendation domain, recall indicates how many movies watched by a user are recommended by the recommender system. To this purpose, recent evaluation methodologies (e.g., [13,18]) are based on a leave-one-out-like approach.

In the results presented in Section 10.4, the test set has been selected differently according to the kind of algorithm. In particular, for collaborative algorithms the URM has been split according to a 10-fold cross-validation approach, i.e., we have randomly split users into 10 folds and, in turn, one fold has been used as test set for computing the recall, while the remaining nine folds form the training set and have been used to generate the model. The reported results are the average recall among the 10 folds. On the other hand, content-based algorithms base their model only on the ICM, and so a cross-validation on the URM would be meaningless; thus all users form the test set.

Each test has been performed as follows. For each recommender algorithm being tested, the respective training data (which depends on the kind of algorithm) has been used to create a model. Then, for each user u to test, one of his ratings r_{ui}—in turn—has been removed from his profile. Therefore, all the ratings of user u but r_{ui} are used by the recommender algorithm for selecting the N items to recommend. Note that items already rated by the user are filtered out from the recommendation list. Whether item i falls into this list of N items we have a hit. The recall is defined as the percentage of hits with respect to the number of tests. In our results we will not show the precision because—as explained in [13]—in this family of tests precision is proportional to recall.

10.3.4 Online Analysis

Online evaluations of recommender systems are usually much more informative than off-line analysis because they provide a more accurate estimation of the actual quality of recommendations. However, online tests can only be performed on running recommender systems.

Similarly to off-line tests, also the online analysis usually focus on the relevance of recommendations. In order to empirically estimate the relevance, we assume that whether a user watches a movie after it has been recommended by the system, such movie is relevant for the user and this represents a *success* for the recommender system. Let us denote with $b(t)$ the *recommendation success*, i.e., the number of movies that have been watched within a time period t after being recommended. Similarly, let us denote with $w(t)$ the number of movies watched by the same set of users within time t. We can define an *empirical recall* as the percentage ratio between the recommendation success and the number of views:

$$\text{empirical recall}(t) = \frac{b(t)}{w(t)} \tag{10.12}$$

The empirical recall represents the percentage of views that have been triggered by the recommender algorithm. The specified indexes depend on the time period t that is taken into consideration after the recommendation has been provided to the user. Please note that a too long time period t could lose the dependency between the recommendation and the view. The results presented in Section 10.4.1 refer to the case t is 2 h, 24 h, or 7 days.

10.4 Case Study

This section of the chapter will describe, as a case study, the integration of a recommender system into the production environment of Fastweb,* one of the largest European IPTV providers.

Before deploying the recommender system in production, extensive performance analysis has been performed by means of k-fold cross-validation. The results suggests a 2.5% recall for the content-based algorithm, while the collaborative algorithms are able to reach a recall of more than 20%. The Fastweb recommender system has been released to production environment in October 2008 and implements both collaborative and content-based techniques. The system is actually providing, on average, 35,000 recommendations per day, with peaks of almost 130 recommendations per minute during peak hours (e.g., Saturday evening). The architecture of the recommender system will be described and the quality of its recommendations will be evaluated by means of off-line and online tests.

The recommender system implements one content-based algorithm, LSA, and two collaborative algorithms, NNCosNgbr and PureSVD. Despite the *model-based*

---

* Fastweb is the first company in the world to have launched fully IP-based broadband TV services, in 2001, and now serves hundreds of thousands of IPTV customers, with a catalog of thousands of multimedia contents. Since 2007, Fastweb has been part of the Swisscom group.

logical division of all the implemented algorithms, the model construction in real domains can still be challenging because of input data size and the related time and memory requirements. For this reason, the system implements high-performing, parallel versions of the most demanding matrix operations, optimized for sparse and big matrices, such as matrix–matrix and matrix–vector multiplication, matrix transposition, column/row normalization, and SVD.

The system is able to mix multiple recommendation lists (mixed hybridization) and to select the proper algorithm depending on the context (switching hybridization). For instance, if the user is reading a movie synopsis, looking for movies with his preferred actors, the system proposes similar items according to a content-based algorithm.

In the first stage of the integration, Fastweb exposed the full set of recommender services to a selected set of beta test users before the effective release. The services released to the full customer base concerned one of the catalogs of VoD domain and recommendations were based on LSA. The choice of focusing on content-based techniques is mainly motivated by the cold-start problem and by some legal issues. Recently, Fastweb is exposing also services based on collaborative algorithms (PureSVD and NNCosNgbr) to this set of VoD customers.

The recommender system does not rely on personal information from the users (e.g., gender, age, occupation). Recommendations are based on the past users' behavior (what they watched) and on any explicit preference they have expressed (e.g., preferred genres). The current deployment collects only implicit ratings, but the system is thought to work when implicit and explicit ratings coexist. The rating scale is between 1 and 5, where values less than 3 express negative ratings, values greater or equal to 3 express positive ratings. In the absence of explicit information, the rating implicitly inferred by monitoring the user behavior is assumed to be positive (i.e., greater than 3). In fact, whether a user starts watching a certain program, there must be some characteristic of this program appealing for the user (e.g., actors or genre). The fact that in well-known, explicit datasets, such as Netflix and Movielens, the average rating is higher than 3 motivates this assumption. The ratings stored in the URM, before being used by the recommender algorithms, are normalized by subtracting the constant value 2.5. This allows the algorithms to distinguish between positive and negative ratings, because values greater or equals to 2.5 (i.e., 3, 4, and 5) remain positive, while values less than 2.5 (i.e., 1 and 2) become negative. In the rest of the chapter we will assume that the recommender algorithms receive as input a normalized URM.

Finally, users can express *explicit preferences* about the content they would like to watch. For instance, by means of the graphical interface, a user can set his preferred actors. The content-based algorithm explained in Section 10.2.3 takes into consideration such information and biases the recommended movies toward the expressed preferences.

Users interact with the IPTV system by means of the set-top-box (STB), but typically we cannot identify who is actually in front of the TV. Consequently, the

STB collects the behavior and the preferences of a set of users (e.g., the component of a family). In order to simplify the notation, in the rest of the chapter we will refer to user and STB to identify the same entity. The user-disambiguation problem has been partially solved in Fastweb by separating the collected information according to the time slot they refer to. For instance, we can roughly assume the following pattern: housewives watch TV during the morning, children during the afternoon, the whole family in the evening, while only adults watch TV during the night. By means of time slots, the system can distinguish among different potential users of the same STB.

10.4.1 System Evaluation

In this section, we first discuss the quality of the recommender system—in terms of relevance—by means of accuracy metrics computed adopting an off-line testing. We later present some feedbacks from the online analysis of the recommender system.

10.4.1.1 Off-Line Analysis

The off-line tests are based on the views collected during 7 months of users' activity from one of the VoD catalogs. The average number of views per day is about 1600, with up to 3300 views during weeks.

Typical approaches for recommender system evaluation are based either on error metrics or classification accuracy metrics (see Section 10.3). Since Fastweb has collected so far only implicit, binary ratings, the quality evaluation is constrained to accuracy metrics. To this end, Table 10.1 presents the recall of the three algorithms implemented in Fastweb: LSA, NNCosNgbr, and PureSVD. Furthermore, the quality of recommendation of the three algorithms is compared with the trivial collaborative algorithm TopRated (see Section 10.2.4).

Let us first focus on the columns related to "Recall ALL" of the table, that show the recall of the recommender algorithms computed on all the items, both after 3 months of activity and after 6 months of activity, showing the time evolution of the system. The result is that during these 6 months of activity, the best algorithm is the collaborative algorithm NNCosNgbr, and the best configuration is with a neighborhood size k equal to 100.

Regardless we expect that as the system collects ratings, the quality of recommendations should improve, from Table 10.1 we can observe that in some cases the quality of recommendations after 6 months is lower than after 3 months. A similar behavior was highlighted, for instance, in [12]. Note that after 3 months of activity there are 510 active items, while after 6 months we have 621 active items. In terms of probability, after 3 months an algorithm has to pick up 1 item among 510 candidates, while after 6 months the number of candidates is 621. As a partial

Table 10.1 Recommendation Quality in One of the VoD Catalogs Computed on All the Items (Recall ALL) and Only on Long-Tail Items, i.e., Items Not in the Top-10 (Recall Non-Top-10) and Not in the Top-50% (Recall Non-Top-50%)

Algorithm	Parameter	Recall ALL		Recall Non-Top-10		Recall Non-Top-50%	
		3 months	6 months	3 months	6 months	3 months	6 months
NNCosNgbr	$k = 10$	16.8%	14.9%	14.0%	13.2%	7.7%	9.6%
	$k = 50$	18.7%	16.4%	**14.0%**	**13.8%**	6.8%	9.0%
	$k = 100$	**19.0%**	**16.6%**	13.8%	13.5%	6.2%	8.3%
	$k = 150$	18.8%	16.5%	13.5%	13.2%	6.1%	7.9%
PureSVD	$l = 5$	15.1%	12.7%	6.6%	6.8%	0.7%	1.4%
	$l = 15$	12.6%	13.3%	11.5%	10.2%	1.2%	3.5%
	$l = 25$	10.9%	11.5%	12.6%	12.0%	2.2%	4.9%
	$l = 50$	9.3%	9.9%	11.4%	11.2%	4.8%	7.8%
	$l = 100$	6.3%	8.0%	7.6%	9.3%	**9.8%**	**11.8%**
LSA	$l = 50$	1.9%	1.7%	2.1%	1.8%	1.8%	1.7%
	$l = 100$	2.3%	2.3%	2.3%	2.3%	2.0%	2.5%
	$l = 150$	2.4%	2.4%	2.5%	2.5%	2.1%	2.5%
	$l = 200$	2.5%	2.5%	2.6%	2.6%	2.2%	2.6%
TopRated		12.2%	7.7%	0.4%	1.0%	0%	0%

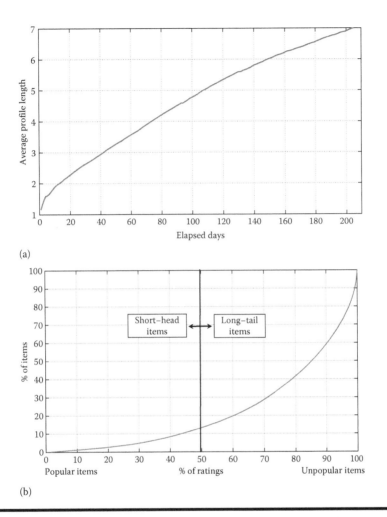

(a)

(b)

Figure 10.3 **(a) Time evolution of the average user profile length (computed on users active in one of the VoD catalogs). (b) Long-tail effect: 50% of ratings concerns 10%–12% of popular items (short head).**

counter-effect, while active items are increasing, users rate more items, and algorithms discard these items. Anyway, this minimally compensates the item-increase effect. In fact, while active items increase from 510 to 621, the average profile length increases from about 3 items per user to about 6 items per user, as shown in Figure 10.3a.

Furthermore, the quality of LSA is poor, even less than TopRated, that has a fairly good recall. The explanation is that the testing methodology based on the leave-one-out approach affects the estimated recall (e.g., [8,13]), which is biased toward the recall measured on popular items.* Thus, LSA quality is particularly low because it disregards item popularity, while TopRated results particularly advantaged.

For the aforementioned reasons, the columns "Recall non-top-10" and "Recall non-top-50%" of Table 10.1 present a further evaluation of the quality of the recommender algorithms, where the most popular items have been excluded from the tests and the recall is computed only on the unpopular items, addressing the well-known concept referred to as long-tail [3]. Figure 10.3b illustrates the distribution of ratings between popular and unpopular items. For instance, we can observe that about 50% of ratings is concentrated in the 10% of the most popular items (short-head), while the remaining 90% of items (long-tail) refers only to the 50% of ratings: one of the primary reasons for integrating a recommender system is to push up the sales of long-tail items, since they represent potential incoming for a service provider. However, recommending long-tail items is harder than recommending short-head items.

The two sets of reported metrics refer, respectively, to the recall computed when the 10 most popular items have been discarded (referred to as non-top-10) and when the short-head (most popular) items, representing the 50% of the total number of ratings, have been discarded from testing (referred to as non-top-50%).

We can note that the quality of the content-based algorithm is constant, not being affected by item popularity. On the other hand, collaborative algorithms decrease their quality when recommending unpopular items, and TopRated fails. Moreover, we can observe that for recommending non-top-10 items, the best algorithm is again the item-based collaborative algorithm. However, when we focus on the long-tail (non-top-50%), the dimensionality-reduction-based collaborative algorithm overtakes the item-based one. Finally, the results show that the latent-factors collaborative algorithm follows a positive trend as the system collects more ratings, increasing its capability in recommending unpopular items.

10.4.1.2 Online Analysis

In this section, we integrate the previous results obtained from off-line tests with an online analysis. The reported data refer to the content-based algorithm applied on one of the VoD catalogs.

According to the definition of *empirical recall* provided in Section 10.3.4, Table 10.2 shows the average quality of the system computed by monitoring the views within 2 h, within 24 h, and within 7 days from the recommendation. The reported results distinguish between popular and unpopular items. From the table we can observe that the empirical recall is larger for unpopular movies with respect to popular movies. In fact, popular movies are already known by users, even without

---

* The popularity of an item is measured as the number of users that have rated the item.

Table 10.2   Average Empirical Recall on the Considered VoD Catalog

	2 h	24 h	7 days
All	17.0%	19.8%	24.7%
Top 10	5.1%	7.0%	10.6%
Non-top 10	24.2%	27.6%	32.1%
Top 50%	9.4%	11.5%	16.2%
Non-top 50%	28.4%	32.2%	36.1%

Results refer to three time periods after the recommendation (2 h, 24 h, and 7 days) and are separated between popular and unpopular movies.

being suggested by the recommender system. For instance, either the user has already watched a popular movie (e.g., at cinema) or he is not interested in watching it.

As a further analysis, about 64% of the recommendation successes refers to unpopular movies (i.e., non-top 50%), while only 36% refers to popular movies (i.e., top 50%), i.e., the recommender system is stimulating users to watch unpopular movies, with a positive effect on the long-tail.

Moreover, we highlight the benefits of the recommender system by measuring the *lift factor* that it introduces in the number of views, i.e., the increase in views due to the recommender system. Generally speaking, the number of views in IPTV systems depends on the size of the customer base. Furthermore, we have to take into consideration that new users tend to view more movies than existing users. In addition to a constant incoming of new users, we have bursts of new users corresponding to marketing campaigns. For instance, Figure 10.4 shows the trend of the whole Fastweb customer base during a more than 2-year activity. The steep parts of new users are related to promotional campaigns. For privacy reasons, the real number of users is hidden and replaced with a proportional value.

In order to describe the correlation between users and views, we have defined an autoregressive moving average (ARMAX) model, whose inputs are the current size of the customer base and the number of new users. The parameters of the ARMAX model are estimated and validated by considering 50 weeks of users' activity before the integration of the recommender system. Figure 10.5a compares the actual number of views with the number of views estimated by the model. In order to smooth daily variability, views are aggregated by week. Splitting the data into training and validation sets, the RMSE on the validation set results below 2%.

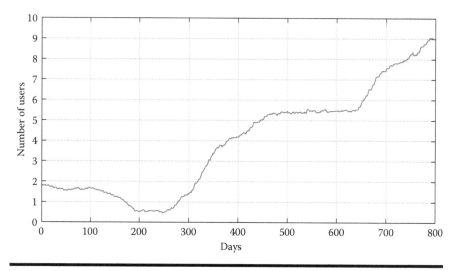

Figure 10.4 Number of Fastweb users. The real number of users is proportional to the reported value.

The model is then used to estimate the number of views in the first 20 weeks after the integration of the recommender system. As shown in Figure 10.5b, we have an increase of views with respect to the number of views estimated by the model, and this increase can be attributed to the impact of the recommender system, since the other potential factors (e.g., marketing campaigns) are included into the ARMAX model. On average, the lift factor within this period is equal to 15.5%.

Finally, Figure 10.6 shows the daily number of search requests by means of the recommender system, the keyword-based search engine, and the alphabetic browsing, respectively. The gap between the requests to the recommender system and the requests to the other searching tools indicates that users effectively utilize the recommender algorithm to search for movies.

10.5 Conclusions

The interactivity of TV is providing a set of new opportunities both to providers and to end users. In these settings, recommender systems can add interesting features to the actual TV that can positively impact both the customers and the service provider. In fact, three major considerations derive from the online analysis, confirming the positive effects of the recommender system: (a) users prefer to browse the VoD catalog by means of the recommender interface, (b) users tend to watch recommended movies within few hours, and (c) users increase the number of movies watched.

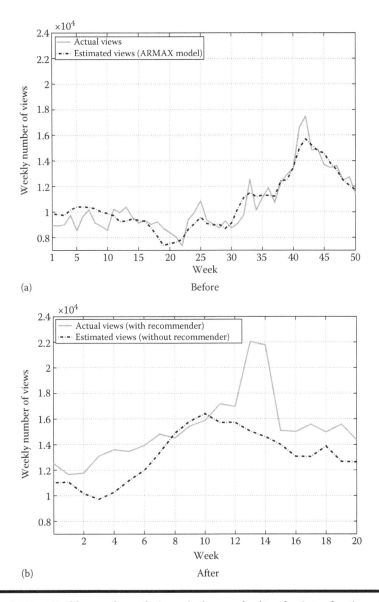

(a)   Before

(b)   After

Figure 10.5 **Weekly number of views *before* and *after* the introduction of the recommender system. Figure (a) shows the estimated views in order to validate the ARMAX model against the actual number of views. Figure (b) draws the estimated views that there would be without the recommender system, so to appreciate higher number of actual views (with the recommender system).**

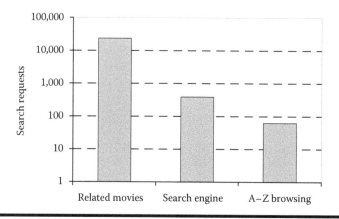

Figure 10.6 Comparison among different ways of searching for interesting content: the recommender system (related movies), the keyword-based search engine, and the alphabetic browsing. Values are reported in a logarithmic scale.

References

1. G. Adomavicius and A. Tuzhilin. Toward the next generation of recommender systems: A survey of the state-of-the-art and possible extensions. *IEEE Transactions on Knowledge and Data Engineering*, 17(6):734–749, 2005.
2. A.M. Ahmad Wasfi. Collecting user access patterns for building user profiles and collaborative filtering. In *Proceedings of the Fourth International Conference on Intelligent User Interfaces (IUI'99)*, Los Angeles, CA, pp. 57–64, 1999. ACM, New York.
3. C. Anderson. *The Long Tail: Why the Future of Business Is Selling Less of More.* Hyperion, New York, July 2006.
4. M. Balabanoviæ and Y. Shoham. Fab: Content-based, collaborative recommendation. *Communications of the ACM*, 40(3):66–72, 1997.
5. R. Bambini, P. Cremonesi, and R. Turrin. A recommender system for an IPTV service provider: A real large-scale production environment. In *Recommender Systems Handbook*, Springer, pp. 299–331, 2011.
6. R.M. Bell and Y. Koren. Scalable collaborative filtering with jointly derived neighborhood interpolation weights. In *Seventh IEEE International Conference on Data Mining*, Omaha, NB, pp. 43–52, 2007.
7. R. Burke. *Hybrid Recommender Systems: Survey and Experiments*, Vol. 12. Kluwer Academic Publishers, Hingham, MA, pp. 331–370, November 2002.
8. E. Campochiaro, R. Casatta, P. Cremonesi, and R. Turrin. Do metrics make recommender algorithms? In *IEEE 23rd International Conference on Advanced Information Networking and Applications (AINA-09)*, University of Bradford, Bradford, U.K., 2009.

9. Ò. Celma and P. Herrera. A new approach to evaluating novel recommendations. In *Proceedings of the 2008 ACM Conference on Recommender Systems (RecSys'08)*, Lausanne, Switzerland, pp. 179–186, 2008. ACM, New York.

10. K.M.A. Chai, H.L. Chieu, and H.T. Ng. Bayesian online classifiers for text classification and filtering. In *Proceedings of the 25th Annual International ACM SIGIR Conference on Research and Development in Information Retrieval*, Tampere, Finland, pp. 97–104, 2002.

11. M. Claypool, A. Gokhale, T. Miranda, P. Murnikov, D. Netes, and M. Sartin. Combining content-based and collaborative filters in an online newspaper. In *Proceedings of the ACM SIGIR Workshop on Recommender Systems*, Berkeley, CA, August 1999.

12. P. Cremonesi, E. Lentini, M. Matteucci, and R. Turrin. An evaluation methodology for recommender systems. In *Fourth International Conference on Automated Solutions for Cross Media Content and Multi-Channel Distribution*, Florence, Italy, pp. 224–231, November 2008.

13. P. Cremonesi, Y. Koren, and R. Turrin. Performance of recommender algorithms on top-n recommendation tasks. In *Proceedings of the 2010 ACM Conference on Recommender Systems (RecSys'10)*, Barcelona, Spain, pp. 39–46, 2010.

14. S.C. Deerwester, S.T. Dumais, T.K. Landauer, G.W. Furnas, and R.A. Harshman. Indexing by latent semantic analysis. *Journal of the American Society of Information Science*, 41(6):391–407, 1990.

15. M. Deshpande and G. Karypis. Item-based top-n recommendation algorithms. *ACM Transactions on Information Systems (TOIS)*, 22(1):143–177, 2004.

16. J.L. Herlocker, J.A. Konstan, L.G. Terveen, and J.T. Riedl. Evaluating collaborative filtering recommender systems. *ACM Transactions on Information Systems (TOIS)*, 22(1):5–53, 2004.

17. P. Husbands, H. Simon, and C. Ding. On the use of singular value decomposition for text retrieval. In *Proceedings of SIAM Computational Information Retrieval Workshop*, Raleigh, NC, October 2000.

18. Y. Koren. Factorization meets the neighborhood: A multifaceted collaborative filtering model. In *Proceedings of the 14th ACM SIGKDD International Conference on Knowledge Discovery and Data Mining (KDD'08)*, Las Vegas, NV, pp. 426–434, 2008. ACM, New York.

19. Y. Koren. Collaborative filtering with temporal dynamics. In *Proceedings of the 15th ACM SIGKDD International Conference on Knowledge Discovery and Data Mining (KDD'09)*, Paris, France, pp. 447–456, 2009. ACM, New York.

20. Y. Koren, R.M. Bell, and C. Volinsky. Matrix factorization techniques for recommender systems. *IEEE Computer*, 42(8):30–37, 2009.

21. Y. Lee, J. Lee, I. Kim, and H. Shin. Reducing IPTV channel switching time using h.264 scalable video coding. *IEEE Transactions on Consumer Electronics*, 54(2):912–919, May 2008.

22. S. Marchand-Maillet. Content-based video retrieval: An overview. Technical Report, Computer Vision Group, Computing Science Center, University of Geneva, Geneva, Switzerland, 2000.

23. P. Melville, R.J. Mooney, and R. Nagarajan. Content-boosted collaborative filtering for improved recommendations. In *Eighteenth National Conference on Artificial Intelligence*, Alberta, Canada, pp. 187–192, 2002. American Association for Artificial Intelligence, Menlo Park, CA.

24. R.J. Mooney and L. Roy. Content-based book recommending using learning for text categorization. In *Proceedings of the Fifth ACM Conference on Digital Libraries (DL-00)*, San Antonio, TX, pp. 195–204, 2000.

25. A. Paterek. Improving regularized singular value decomposition for collaborative filtering. In *Proceedings of the KDD Cup and Workshop*, San Jose, CA, 2007.

26. M.J. Pazzani and D. Billsus. Content-based recommendation systems. In *The Adaptive Web: Methods and Strategies of Web Personalization*, Springer-Verlag, Berlin, Germany, Volume 4321 of *Lecture Notes in Computer Science*, pp. 325–341, 2006.

27. Y. Saad. *Numerical Methods for Large Eigenvalue Problems*. Halsted Press, New York, 1992.

28. G. Salton (ed.). *Automatic Text Processing*. Addison-Wesley Longman Publishing Co., Inc., Boston, MA, 1988.

29. B. Sarwar, G. Karypis, J. Konstan, and J. Reidl. Item-based collaborative filtering recommendation algorithms. In *10th International Conference on World Wide Web (WWW'10)*, Hong Kong, pp. 285–295, 2001.

30. J. Schafer, D. Frankowski, J. Herlocker, and S. Sen. Collaborative filtering recommender systems. In *Adaptive Web-based Systems*, Springer, Heidelberg, Germany, pp. 291–324. 2007.

31. A.W. Shearer. User response to two algorithms as a test of collaborative filtering. In *CHI 2001 Extended Abstracts on Human Factors in Computing Systems (CHI'01)*, Seattle, WA, pp. 451–452, 2001. ACM, New York.

32. S. Spiegel, J. Kunegis, and F. Li. Hydra: A hybrid recommender system [cross-linked rating and content information]. In *Proceedings of the First ACM International Workshop on Complex Networks Meet Information & Knowledge Management (CNIKM'09)*, Hong Kong, pp. 75–80, 2009. ACM, New York.

33. T. Tran and R. Cohen. Hybrid recommender systems for electronic commerce. In *Proceedings of the 17th National Conference on Artificial Intelligence (AAAI'00)*, Austin, TX, 2000.

34. J.C. Valle-Lisboa and E. Mizraji. The uncovering of hidden structures by latent semantic analysis. *Information Sciences*, 177(19):4122–4147, 2007.

35. C.J. Van Rijsbergen. *Information Retrieval*, 2nd edn. Department of Computer Science, University of Glasgow, 1979.

36. E. Vozalis and K.G. Margaritis. Analysis of recommender systems algorithms. In *Proceedings of the Sixth Hellenic European Conference on Computer Mathematics and Its Applications*, Athens, Greece, 2003.

37. J. Wang, A.P. de Vries, and M.J.T. Reinders. Unifying user-based and item-based collaborative filtering approaches by similarity fusion. In *Proceedings of the 29th Annual ACM Conference on Research and Development in Information Retrieval (SIGIR'06)*, Seattle, WA, pp. 501–508, 2006. ACM Press, New York.

38. Y. Zhang, J. Callan, and T. Minka. Novelty and redundancy detection in adaptive filtering. In *Proceedings of the 25th Annual International ACM SIGIR Conference on Research and Development in Information Retrieval* (SIGIR'02), Tampere, Finland, pp. 81–88, 2002. ACM, New York.
39. C.-N. Ziegler, S.M. McNee, J.A. Konstan, and G. Lausen. Improving recommendation lists through topic diversification. In *Proceedings of the 14th International Conference on World Wide Web (WWW'05)*, Chiba, Japan, pp. 22–32, 2005. ACM, New York.

Chapter 11

Capturing Long-Term User Interests in Online Television News Programs

Frank Hopfgartner

University of California

Contents

11.1 Introduction

With the growing capabilities and the falling prices of current hardware systems, there are ever-increasing possibilities to store and manipulate videos in a digital format. Also with ever-increasing broadband capabilities it is now possible to view video online as easily as text-based pages were viewed when the web first appeared. People are now producing their own digital libraries from materials created through digital cameras and camcorders, and use a number of systems to place this material on the web, as well as store them in their own individual collections [9]. An interesting research problem is to assist users in dealing with such large and swiftly increasing volumes of video, i.e., in helping them to satisfy their information need by finding videos they are interested in. For example, a user who enjoys sitcoms might benefit from a personalized video retrieval system that automatically identifies this interest and, further, informs the user about other sitcoms he or she is not aware of. An important question that needs to be answered in this context is how users' personal information needs can be identified. A promising method is to employ relevance feedback (RF) techniques. RF can be split into two main paradigms: explicit and implicit RF. Employing explicit RF, users are asked to judge the relevance of videos. Unfortunately though, users tend not to provide constant feedback, which is rather problematic when feedback is required to identify users' interests over a longer period of time. Deviating from the method of explicitly asking the user to rate results, the use of implicit feedback techniques helps learning users' interest unobtrusively. The main advantage is that this approach relieves the user from providing explicit feedback. As a large quantity of implicit data can be gathered without disturbing the users' work flow, the implicit approach is an attractive alternative. In order to study these research challenges, we focus in this work on news videos. News broadcasts consist of many short independent news items that users can be interested in. Thus, news bulletins allow for the development of user profiling and recommendation techniques that rely on documents with similar features. In the context of this chapter, we hence assume that users' interests in certain news topics can be identified by identifying those news items that users' interacted most with. Further, we assume that users stay interested in certain news topics over a longer time period and thus might provide implicit RF over a longer time period, i.e., over multiple interaction sessions.

Within this chapter, we discuss how users' interactions such as viewing time or clicking behavior while consuming television news online can be exploited to identify their long-term interests in different aspects of news. We first introduce in Section 11.2 a fictitious application scenario in which a personalization system automatically provides multimedia content that matches a user's interest. The scenario provides a vivid introduction into challenges and research opportunities in the domain. In Section 11.3, we define the requirements that allow us to focus on studying the use of implicit RF for the generation of implicit user profiles. The main contribution is a proposal to analyze multimedia content that eases user profiling and corresponding recommendation of multimedia content. Section 11.4 introduces novel methodologies to tackle various research challenges toward the creation of implicit user profiles. We discuss the main challenges in exploiting implicit RF techniques to create efficient profiles and, further, how such profiles should be structured to separate different long-term interests.

11.2 Long-Term Personalization Scenario

In recent years, various application scenarios have been introduced to frame research activities in the field of personalized multimedia retrieval, e.g., within the European projects EU-MESH [32], PHAROS [33], and PetaMedia NoE [28]. It shows the increasing attention within the research community toward personalized multimedia retrieval. In this section, we discuss an exemplary multimedia personalization scenario, introduced by Sebe and Tian [36], that emphasizes arising challenges in the research field.

> John Citizen lives in Brussels, holds a degree in economics, and works for a multinational company dealing with oil imports. He enjoys travel with emphasis on warm Mediterranean sites with good swimming and fishing. When watching TV his primary interest is international politics, particularly European. During a recent armed conflict he wanted to understand different perspectives on the war, including both relevant historical material as well as future projections from commentators. When he returns home from work, a personalized interactive multimedia program is ready for him, created automatically from various multimedia segments taken from diverse sources including multimedia news feeds, digital libraries, and collected analyst commentaries. The program includes different perspectives on the events, discussions, and analysis appropriate for a university graduate. The video program is production quality, including segment transitions and music. Sections of the program allow him to interactively explore analyzes of particular relevance to him, namely the impact of war on oil prices in various countries (his business interest), and its potential effect on tourism and accommodation prices across the Mediterranean next summer. Some presentations may be synchronized with a map display which may be accessed interactively. John's behavior and dialog with the display are logged along with a record of the information presented to allow the

system to better accumulate his state of knowledge and discern his interests in order to better serve him in the future. When John is away from home for business or leisure, he may receive the same personalized information on his mobile device as well, emphasizing information reflecting the neighborhood of his current Mediterranean location.

In this scenario, a recommender system collates multimedia fragments from different sources to generate an interactive multimedia package that is tailored to a user's interests. By allowing the system to constantly keep track of his television viewing habits, John provides implicit RF on his personal interests over multiple sessions. For a more detailed discussion of the scenarios and on arising challenges in the field of multimedia personalization, the reader is referred to the survey paper Of Lu et al. [31].

In the remainder of this chapter, we discuss how this application scenario could be implemented, i.e., how users' implicit RF, given over a longer period of time, could be exploited to identify users' interests in multiple topics. In order to identify videos that match users' interests, a well-accepted statement (e.g., [5,39]) is that it is helpful to understand the content of the video. However, the difference between the low-level representation of videos and the higher-level concepts that users associate with video, commonly known as the Semantic Gap [38], provides difficulties. Bridging this gap is one of the most challenging research issues in multimedia information retrieval today. In Section 11.3, we discuss issues and problems arising when analyzing multimedia content.

According to Brusilovsky et al. [6], personalized retrieval systems exploit individual user profiles to adapt retrieval results or to recommend documents that match the user's information need. Having the users' interests captured in a profile, a challenge is how to identify *different* interest from their profile. One challenge is that users can show interest in multiple news topics. John Citizen, e.g., is interested in European politics and Mediterranean countries. He further could be interested in subcategories such as Greek islands, Spanish beaches, or Italian Dolce Vita. A specification for a user profile should therefore be able to automatically identify these multiple aspects. In Section 11.4, we introduce our methodology of multi-session user profiling and multimedia recommendation.

11.3 Requirements for a User Profile

John Citizen, the character in the application scenario introduced in the previous section, uses a news recommender system that automatically generates personalized multimedia packages that cover topics of his interest. In the scenario, these packages consist of many different multimedia segments such as news feeds or commentaries. When the packages are generated from up-to-date multimedia news broadcasts only, it becomes clear that they can either be collections of relevant *shots* from a given news story or collections of relevant news *stories*. Shots are often used to visually enrich the actual news story, e.g., by providing impressions of the location of the event. Sometimes, even archived video footage is used that is not in direct connection to the actual news. News stories consist of a series of shots. It is up to the editor of the television broadcast to decide which shots are used to report the news story. They should be seen as a means to assist the news consumer in understanding the news, rather than being the main unit conveying the news. We therefore define that the news video recommender system should focus on generating personalized multimedia packages consisting of news *stories*. We discuss in Section 11.3.1 challenges arising when focusing on news stories.

One challenge for recommending news stories is to analyze the content of these news stories. This is, due to the Semantic Gap, not trivial though. A promising approach to ease this problem is to set such multimedia documents into their semantic contexts (e.g., [3,14,42]). For instance, a video about David Cameron's visit to Italy can be put into different contexts. First of all, it shows an event that happened in a Mediterranean country, Italy. Moreover, it is a visit by a European politician, the prime minister of the United Kingdom. If the fictitious John Citizen follows news about Cameron's visit, it might indicate that he is interested in either politics, Italy, or both. Thus, the context expresses the "aboutness" of a document. Knowing the context of a video is useful for recommending other videos that match the users' information need. By exploiting these contexts, multimedia documents can also be linked to other, contextually related documents. Due to recent improvements in Semantic Web technologies, it is now feasible to automatically link concepts to the Linked Open Data Cloud,* where they are connected to other concepts. The Linked Open Data collection of ontologies unites information about many different freely available concepts. Section 11.3.2 discusses this technology further. Any news story's concepts can hence be set into its semantic context. Based on the state-of-the-art research, we hypothesize that exploiting this context can lead to appropriate news video recommendations. Thus, in this section, we introduce a methodology to set multimedia documents into their semantic context. We propose an approach of generating this semantic link in Section 11.3.2. In Section 11.3.3, we propose to categorize news stories based on their subject to ease access to the collection.

11.3.1 Capturing and Segmenting News Broadcasts

The most essential requirement for the previously presented multimedia recommendation scenario is to acquire up-to-date news broadcasts. In most countries, daily television news bulletins can be received by either aerial antenna, cable network, or satellite dish. Recently, some television stations started to offer their news bulletins as online download, e.g., the *BBC One O'clock News* on the BBC's iPlayer† portal or

---

* http://linkeddata.org/
† http://www.bbc.co.uk/iplayer/

the German *Tagesschau* as Podcast in the ARD Mediathek.* Consequently, a large amount of potential sources are available that could be used to create a personalized news broadcasting collection. Note that different copyright laws apply in each country. Cole [12] discusses issues related to copyright in a digital context from a UK perspective.

The next step after capturing the daily broadcast is to automatically segment it into semantically coherent sequences. A consumer-oriented segmentation approach is to identify story boundaries. News story segmentation is essentially finding the boundaries where one story ends and the other begins. Various text-based, audiovisual-based, and combinations of all features have been studied to segment news videos accordingly. Note that news story segmentation is not the main focus of this chapter and will therefore not be discussed further here. Detailed surveys on automatic news story segmentation are given by Arlandis et al. [1] and Chua et al. [11].

11.3.2 Exploiting External Knowledge

Multimedia documents are often enriched with additional metadata such as creation date, source, or descriptive tags [4]. The informative nature of news video broadcasts results in a large amount of potential textual tags, because news aim to provide a compressed overview of the latest events. Events are thus usually summarized by a background narrator, journalist or anchorperson, resulting in text-heavy transcripts. Indexing news videos based on such transcripts would enable textual retrieval and ease users' access to the corpus. Indeed, studies, e.g., within the evaluation workshop TRECVid, have shown that textual features are still the best source to perform multimedia retrieval [10].

A closer analysis of the state-of-the-art research within TRECVid, however, also indicates that the retrieval performance of news video is still far away from its textual counterparts. An interesting approach for narrowing this performance gap is to further enrich the textual transcripts using external data sources. Fernández et al. [16], for instance, have shown that ontology-based search models can outperform classical information retrieval models at a web scale. The advantage of these models is that external knowledge is used to place the content into its semantic context. Due to large community efforts such as the Linked Open Data project, broad collections of freely available concepts are available that are interlinked using different ontologies. The backbone of this cloud is DBpedia, an information extraction framework, which interlinks Wikipedia content with other databases on the web such as Geonames or WordNet. Figure 11.1 illustrates that the DBpedia Knowledge Base is a graph of linked concepts. As of April 2010, it contains more than 2.6 million graph elements that are interlinked. The nodes are concepts that are identified by unique identifiers, URIs. A semantic hierarchy between most neighbored nodes is defined

---

* http://www.ardmediathek.de/

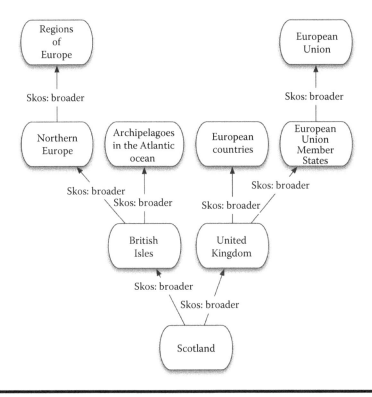

Figure 11.1   Hierarchy of the concept "Scotland" in DBpedia.

by the Simple Knowledge Organization system (SKOS) Reference data model. Figure 11.1 illustrates an example hierarchy, the hierarchy of the concept "Scotland" in DBpedia.

From a news personalization perspective, this semantic link provides the potential to improve interactive video retrieval and recommendation. For example, John Citizen could show interest in a story about the sunset at the Greek island Santorini. The story transcript might contain the following sentence:

> This is Peter Miller, reporting live from Santorini, Greece, where we are just about to witness one of the most magnificent sunsets of the decade. [...]

Since John enjoys travel with emphasis on warm Mediterranean sites, he might also be interested in a report about the Spanish island Majorca. For example, imagine the following story:

> Just as every year, thousands of tourists enjoy their annual sun bath here in Majorca. [...]

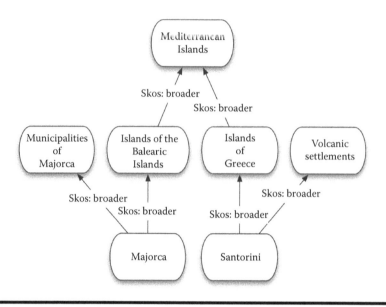

Figure 11.2   Linking "Santorini" and "Majorca" using DBpedia.

An interesting research question is how to identify whether this story matches John's interests. Lioma and Ounis [30] argue that the semantic meaning of a text is mostly expressed by nouns and foreign names, since they carry the highest content load. Indeed, most adaptation approaches rely on these terms to personalize retrieval results, e.g., by performing a simple query expansion. The two example stories, however, do not share similar terms. A personalization technique exploiting the terms only would hence not be able to recommend John the second story.

However, as Figure 11.2 illustrates, linking the concepts of the transcripts using DBpedia reveals the semantic context of both stories. It becomes evident that both stories are about two islands in the Mediterranean Sea. Exploiting this link could hence satisfy John's interest in warm Mediterranean sites. We therefore propose to set news broadcasts into their semantic context by exploiting the large pool of linked concepts provided by DBpedia.

11.3.3 Categorizing News Stories

Gans [17] argues that the modern time's news reports can be categorized into various categories such as Political news, Sports news or Entertainment news. For example, the following story transcript, taken from the BBC's news broadcast of March, 2010, could be categorized as belonging to the "Entertainment News" category.

Hollywood's biggest night of the year is almost upon it. The 82th Oscars Ceremony is taking place in Los Angeles on Sunday. Who is likely to walk away with the gongs? Will it be the box office hit Avatar or the gritty Iraqi hit The Hurt Locker. Rajesh Mirchandani is on the red carpet where preparations are under way. [...]

Various approaches have been studied to automatically determine a news story's subject and to categorize into such broad categories, e.g., [13,18,24]. The motivation for such a task is to ease access to the news corpus. Following this motivation, we suggest to categorize the news stories based on their subject since such categorization could help to separate users' interests.

In this section, we discussed requirements that should be fulfilled to ease the generation of user profiles. We first discussed the creation of a private news video corpus, which requires capture and segmentation of daily news broadcasts. Further, we suggest the enrichment of resulting news stories by identifying and linking concepts using a generic ontology. Various problems need to be handled when using such an ontology. The main problem is how to automatically identify the correct concept for a given term. Shadbolt et al. [37] argue in their survey on the development of Semantic Web technologies that this is the main problem within the domain and that in recent years, different techniques have been proposed. Another challenge is the quality of the existing ontology. Being a representation of Wikipedia, both quantity and quality of DBpedia links differ tremendously. While some nodes have many neighbors, others are linked to only a few related concepts. Further, the approach relies on the correctness of the information that is represented within DBpedia. Suchanek et al. [41] manually evaluate the quality of DBpedia as part of their Yago ontology, a semantic knowledge base that builds on DBpedia. They report a fact correctness of 95%, suggesting that DBpedia can be seen as a reliable source. Another problem is that DBpedia is created automatically every 6 months from the English language version of Wikipedia. Its content is hence out of date, which might be a problem when news contain concepts that have not yet been described on Wikipedia or that were recently created only. Examples are public figures such as new politicians, successful business tycoons, new inventions, and companies. Berners-Lee et al. [2] envisioned the Semantic Web as consisting of machine-readable information chunks that can be merged based on their semantic content. The current version of DBpedia can be seen as a milestone toward the development of such websites. With the increasing success of the Semantic Web, chances are that DBpedia (or similar approaches such as the Semantic MediaWiki project [27]) will become an essential part of the Wikipedia project. A desirable improvement would then be to update DBpedia concepts in real time whenever a Wikipedia page has been changed. Such a technical advance would bridge the problem of an outdated concept corpus. Nevertheless, major broadcasters such as the BBC [26] now already rely on DBpedia, indicating that even an outdated corpus can serve successfully to link documents. Finally, we suggest to categorize news stories into broader categories. These categories could ease the generation of user profiles.

11.4 Tackling User Profiling Problems

In the previous section, we suggested the creation of a private news video collection consisting of up-to-date news bulletins from different broadcasting stations. Further, we introduced our approach of exploiting the Linked Open Data Cloud to link concepts in the news broadcasts and suggested a categorization of stories into broad news categories. From a user profiling point of view, these links and categories can be of high value to recommend semantically related transcripts, hence creating a semantic-based user profile. In this section, we introduce our methodology of identifying user's long-term interests.

Providing feedback on a document is considered as evidence that this document is relevant for the user's current interest. Most personalization services rely on users explicitly specifying preferences. However, users tend not to provide constant explicit feedback on what they are interested in. In a long-term user profiling scenario, this lack of feedback is critical, since feedback is essential for the creation of such profiles. Hopfgartner and Jose [22] have shown that implicit RF can be used to balance this missing feedback. We therefore argue that user profiles should be automatically created by capturing users' implicit interactions with the retrieval interface (see [21–23]). Hence, our hypothesis is that implicit RF techniques can efficiently be employed to create implicit user profiles. The contribution of this section is thus a novel approach to generate such profiles. We discuss the generation process in Section 11.4.1.

Another challenge is to capture users' evolving interests in implicit user profiles. What a user finds interesting on 1 day might be completely irrelevant on the next day. In order to model this behavior, we therefore suggest in Section 11.4.2 to apply the Ostensive Model of Developing Information Needs. Further, we argue for the automatic identification of multiple aspects of users' interests.

In Section 11.4.3, we highlight and discuss the need to identify different aspects of interest and introduce our approach to solve this problem.

11.4.1 User Profile Model

Hopfgartner and Jose [20] analyzed representative video retrieval interfaces, revealing six user interactions that are commonly supported by most video retrieval interfaces. These include (1) hovering the mouse over a key frame; (2) clicking on a search result, e.g., to trigger; (3) playing back a video; (4) sliding through accompanying key frames; (5) looking at meta data; and (6) using the sliding bar to slide through the video being played. By treating these interactions as implicit indicators of relevance, they have shown that this implicit RF can be successfully employed to improve interactive video retrieval performed within single search sessions. The next challenge that needs to be addressed is how implicit RF techniques can be exploited to enable an application scenario as described in Section 11.2, i.e., the creation of efficient user profiles by implicitly capturing user interest. Unfortunately, even though the discussed scenario highlights various challenges in the field of multimedia content personalization, the scenario's setting makes it almost impossible to capture user interests. For example, the protagonist John might inform himself about the latest political developments by reading the newspaper, or by listening to the radio news. Consequently, he might not watch the news on television, since he is already aware of the current situation. Since we want to study whether implicit RF can be used to generate user profiles, we focus on the users' interactions with a news video recommender system, hence ignoring other sources.

By interacting with the graphical user interface of such system, users leave a "semantic fingerprint" indicating their interest in the content of the items they have interacted with. Hopfgartner and Jose [22] argue that the degree of their interest can be expressed by a weighting aligned with the different interface feature types. For example, the more interactions are performed on an item, the higher the weighting for this item, and the stronger the fingerprint that the user is interested in its content. The first challenge we then have to approach is how to capture this fingerprint.

A prominent way of capturing user interests is the weighted keyword vector approach. In this approach, the interests are represented as a vector of weighted terms where each dimension of the vector space represents a term aligned with a weighting. Considering the high semantics conveyed by each story users might interact with, generating user profiles on a term-based level only would ignore these semantics though. Defining a search session as a set of chronological user interactions that can be split into various iterations, we suggest a *weighted story vector approach* (*SW*) where each interaction I of a user i at iteration j of their search session is a vector of weights

$$\vec{I}_{ij} = \{SW_{ij1} \ldots SW_{ijs}\}$$

where s indexes the story in the whole collection. The weighting SW of each story expresses the evidence that the content of this story matches the user's interest. The higher the value of SW_{ijs}, the closer this match is. Thus, without further user input, the user interest is determined based on these implicit interactions alone, i.e., the previously mentioned semantic fingerprint.

Different from short-term adaptation services, a multi-session personalization system requires the storage of the user's semantic fingerprint. The next challenge is hence to store this vector of weights in a user profile. As explained in Section 11.3.3, we suggest classification of news stories into broad categories. This categorization can be exploited to model the user's multiple interests. For example, the character John from the previous scenario shows interest in both European Politics and Mediterranean countries, i.e., different aspects A. Having all interests in one profile is not effective. Since these are two different issues, it is reasonable to treat them separately. We therefore suggest to use this classification A as a splitting criterion. Thus, we represent user i's interest in an aspect A in a category profile vector $\vec{P}_i(A)$, containing the story weight $SW(A)$ of each story s of the collection:

$$\vec{P}_i(A) = \{SW(A)_{i1} \ldots SW(A)_{is}\}$$

Each $\vec{P}_i(A)$ hence contains a vector of stories that belong to the aspect in category A and in which the user showed interest at iteration j. This interest is expressed by the story weight SW, which is determined based on the implicit indicator of relevance that the user used to interact with the story.

Even though the user's interests can be split into different broad categories, two main problems remain. The first challenge is the capturing of user's evolving interest. Section 11.4.2 introduces our approach to handle this problem. The second challenge is the capturing of different sub-aspects of this interest. This problem is tackled in Section 11.4.3.

11.4.2 Capturing Evolving Interest

The simplest approach to create a weighting for each story in the profile is to combine the weighting of the stories over all iterations. This approach is based on the assumption that the user's information interest is static, which is, however, not appropriate in a retrieval context. The users' information need can change within different retrieval sessions [15,34,35]. Following the argumentation by Stvilia et al. [40] that information quality is sensitive to context changes such as time, an interesting research question is how this change of interest can be incorporated. Campbell and van Rijsbergen [8] state that the user's search direction is directly influenced by the documents retrieved. The following example illustrates this observation:

> Imagine a user who is interested in red cars and uses a video retrieval system to find videos depicting such cars. Their first search query returns several video clips, including videos of red Ferraris. Watching these videos, he or she wants to find more Ferraris and adapts the search query accordingly. The new result list now consists of video clips showing red and green Ferraris. Fascinated by the rare color for this type of car, he or she again reformulates the search query to find more green Ferraris. Within one session, the user's information need evolved from red cars to green Ferraris.

Based on this observation, Campbell and van Rijsbergen [8] introduce the Ostensive Model of Developing Information Need that incorporates this change of interest by considering *when* a user provided RF. In the Ostensive Model, providing feedback on a document is seen as ostensive evidence that this document is relevant for the user's current interest. The combination of this feedback over several search iterations provides ostensive evidence about the user's changing interest. The model considers the users changing focus of interest by granting the most recent feedback a higher impact over the combined evidence. Hence, they propose to consider a time factor when ranking documents, i.e., by modifying the weighting of terms based on the iteration in which user's interacted with the corresponding document. They distinguish between four different functions to calculate the weighting depending on the nature of aging:

- Constant weighting
- Exponential weighting
- Linear weighting
- Inverse exponential weighting

Considering the ostensive evidence as a method to model user interest in documents belonging to category A in a profile, we propose to manipulate the story weight in our category profile. Therefore, we define the story weight for each user i as the combination of the weighted stories s over different iterations j:

$$SW(A)_{is} = \sum_{j} a_j W_{ijs} \qquad (11.1)$$

We include the ostensive evidence, denoted a_j, to introduce different weighting schemes based on the ostensive model. Figure 11.3 plots this evidence a_j for up to 10 iterations. It can be seen that all functions, apart from the constant weighting, reduce the ostensive weighting of earlier iterations. The weighting depends on the constant $C > 1$.

In the remainder of this section, we discuss the functions in detail.

11.4.2.1 Constant Weighting

$$a_j = \frac{1}{j_{max}} \qquad (11.2)$$

The constant weighting function does not influence the ostensive weighting. As Equation 11.2 illustrates, all terms will be combined equally, ignoring the iteration when a term was added or updated. The constant weighting can be seen as a baseline methodology that does not include any ostensive factor.

11.4.2.2 Exponential Weighting

$$a_j = \frac{C^j}{\sum_{k=2}^{j_{max}} C^k} \qquad (11.3)$$

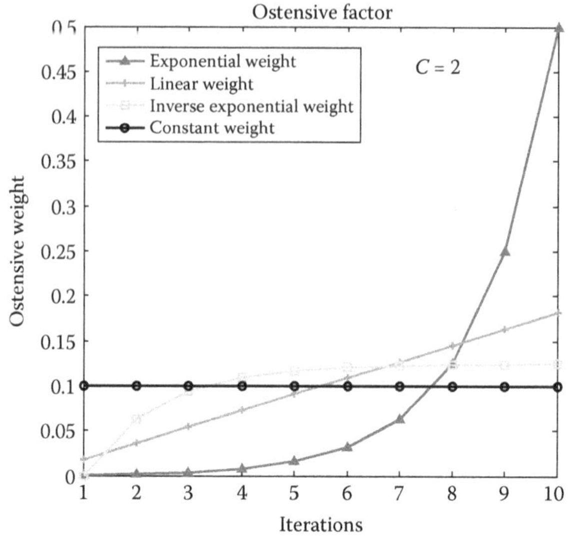

Figure 11.3   Effect of different ostensive weighting functions over 10 iterations.

The exponential weighting as defined in Equation 11.3 gives a higher ostensive weighting to terms that have been added or updated in older iterations. It is the most extreme function as the ostensive weighting of earlier iterations decreases steeply.

11.4.2.3 Linear Weighting

$$a_j = \frac{C^j}{\sum_{k=2}^{jmax} k} \tag{11.4}$$

Equation 11.4 defines the linear weighting function. The ostensive weighting of earlier iterations decreases linearly. This function linearly reduces the ostensive weighting of earlier iterations.

11.4.2.4 Inverse Exponential Weighting

$$a_j = \frac{1 - C^{-j+1}}{\sum_{k=2}^{jmax} (1 - C^{-k+1})} \tag{11.5}$$

The inverse exponential weighting defined by Equation 11.5 provides the "softest" decrease of the weighting for more recent iterations. Compared to the other introduced functions, the ostensive weighting of early iterations decreases more slowly.

This section has shown how the different weighting functions of the Ostensive Model of Evolving Information Need could be applied in our multi-session user profile. Each function supports different usage scenarios. In the context of modeling users' interests in news, we can, however, reduce the number of functions that fit into such scenario. We assume that a user's interest in certain news evolves over time. Consider, e.g., the following scenario. At the beginning of the credit crunch, John was following news about the financial troubles of big national banks. He showed some interest in it, but ignored the story after a while, since he was not directly affected. Day by day, however, more and more news appear, highlighting the complications of this bankruptcy case. At the same time, John's interest in the issue increases. Thus, his interest evolves from *low* interest to *high* interest.

A constant weighting does not provide any additional weighting to the user's profile. Exploiting corresponding profiles would hence not distinguish between recent and old feedback. The function thus cannot be used to model an evolving interest. Likewise, a profile created using an inverse exponential weighting does not support such a scenario. Both exponential weighting and linear weighting, however, consider more recent feedback as a stronger indicator of the user's interests than older feedback. While with the linear weight, this recent interest decays rather slowly over several iterations, the exponential weighting function decays very fast. Considering the nature of news, especially the sudden appearance of breaking news, the exponential weighting model seems to be the best function to model the user's evolving interest. Breaking news of rare events such as an earthquake will not have any similar stories in the profile; nevertheless, they might be of high importance for the user. Consequently, their weighting should be considerably higher than the weighting of other news. The linear weighting function gives a relative high weighting to stories of earlier iterations. Thus, the breaking news story might perish. The exponential weighting function gives a relatively high weighting to more recent iterations. Breaking news would hence be ranked higher in the user profile. The Ostensive Model has been applied in the image domain [7,29,43] and in web scenario [25]. In each case, the authors incorporate an exponential weighting as a decay function. Corollary: we propose to model this evolving interest in news by incorporating the exponential weighting as a decay function. An analysis of different approaches is given by Hopfgartner et al. [19].

11.4.3 Capturing Different Aspects of Interest

In Section 11.4.1, we suggest to split user profiles into broad news categories that can be derived from the classification procedure suggested in Section 11.3.3. Whenever a user interacts with a news document, the category vector $\vec{P}_i(A)$ of the corresponding category is updated with the new story weight. As some stories might belong to more than one broad category, we propose to add the corresponding story to every associated category profile. For example, a news story about the government's decision to bail out domestic banks might be categorized as belonging to both categories Politics and Business. The drawback of this approach is that during the early stages of the user profiling process, semantically related category profiles might contain exactly the same news documents. Thus, at later stages of the user's interactions, other documents might be added to either of the categories, resulting in different contents. These early duplicates are hence more a cold start problem that will decay in the process of user profiling.

The methodology introduced earlier results in a category-based representation of the user's interests. Each category profile consists of a list of weighted stories, with the most important stories having the highest weighting. Following this approach, the profile of the example user John would consist of two main category profiles: politics and tourism. Since these are very broad news categories, however, each category profile might still be very diverse. News reports about European Politics, for instance, might be about the internal politics of different European countries or about different aspects such as the negotiation of new trading agreements or the installment of new immigration regulations. Likewise, stories in the user's tourism profile might contain stories about Greece or Spain or different activities such as fishing and swimming.

Aiming to exploit the user profiles to recommend the user other stories that are related to each of these subcategories presents a challenge of identifying different contextual subaspects in their category profiles. This is an information filtering problem. Information filtering techniques exploit the fact that semantically related documents share certain textual features. A simple approach to address this problem is to cluster the documents based on these textual features, which should result in semantically related clusters where each cluster represents a subcategory of the user's interest. Note, however, that information filtering is a complex research challenge and thus, much more complex approaches exist that address the task of identifying subcategories in text documents.

In this section, we introduced the methodology for generating implicit user profiles. Our main research focus was on discussing how implicit RF can be exploited for the generation of such profiles. We proposed to store news stories that the user interacted with, aligned with an implicit feedback weighting, in structured user profiles. Each time a user provides new implicit RF, the corresponding user profile is updated. It is an iteration-based representation of the user's interests. We further argued that this interest is not static, since users will lose interest in old news. Aiming to smooth this decay, we proposed to apply the Ostensive Model of Evolving Information Need. We discussed different ostensive weighting functions and argued for the use of a decay function. Another problem we addressed is the user's interests in multiple topics. We first argued for the generation of category-based user profiles to separate these interests. Categories can be derived from the news stories the users interacted with. Whenever a user interacts with a news story, the corresponding category profile is updated automatically. Since these categories might be very broad, we further argued to identify subcategories by clustering the content of each category profile. Each cluster then represents the user's interest in a certain aspect of the broad news category.

11.5 Summary

In this chapter, we studied how multimedia could be analyzed to ease implicit user profiling. We, therefore, first discussed a visionary application scenario of a multimedia recommender system that generates personalized multimedia documents that satisfy a user's information need. We limited the conditions of the scenario, which allows us to focus on studying the use of implicit RF. Outlining the requirements for implicit user profiles, we proposed to generate personalized news video collections and argued to process this collection by segmenting each bulletin into semantically coherent news stories, categorizing them into broad news categories and, enriching these stories using a generic ontology. This data augmentation allows us to set news stories into their semantic context, which we then suggested to consider when creating the user profile. Thus, the first contribution of this chapter is a novel methodology to create such semantic link. We suggested to use implicit RF to store relevant news stories in a profile. Further, we suggested to apply the Ostensive Model of Evolving Information Need to compensate the user's losing interest in stories he or she showed interest in during earlier stages. Finally, we discussed that the user profiles should be split based on the user's different interests and suggested to perform clustering to identify the user's interests.

Hopfgartner and Jose [23] evaluate different recommendation approaches that are based on the introduced user profiling methodology. By employing the methodology that has been introduced in this chapter to categorize and enrich television broadcast data, they successfully capture user's interests in television programs. The results suggest the effectiveness of the introduced methodology.

Acknowledgment

This work was supported by a fellowship within the Postdoc-Program of the German Academic Exchange Service (DAAD).

References

1. J. Arlandis, P. Over, and W. Kraaij. Boundary error analysis and categorization in the TRECVID news story segmentation task. In W. K. Leow, M. S. Lew, T.-S. Chua, W.-Y. Ma, L. Chaisorn, and E. M. Bakker, eds., *CIVR'05: Proceedings of the Fourth International Conference on Image and Video Retrieval*, Singapore, July 20–22, 2005, Volume 3568 of *Lecture Notes in Computer Science*, pp. 103–112. Springer, 2005.

2. T. Berners-Lee, J. Hendler, and O. Lassila. The semantic web: A new form of web content that is meaningful to computers will unleash a revolution of new possibilities. *Scientific American*, 284(5):34–43, May 2001.

3. M. Bertini, A. D. Bimbo, and C. Torniai. Multimedia enriched ontologies for video digital libraries. *International Journal of Parallel, Emergent and Distributed Systems*, 22(6):407–416, 2007.

4. H. M. Blanken, A. P. de Vries, H. E. Bok, and L. Feng. *Multimedia Retrieval*, 1st edn., Springer Verlag, Heidelberg, Germany, 2007.

5. D. Brezeale and D. J. Cook. Automatic video classification: A survey of the literature. *IEEE Transactions on Systems, Man, and Cybernetics, Part C: Applications and Reviews*, 38(3):416–430, May 2008.

6. P. Brusilovsky, A. Kobsa, and W. Nejdl, eds. *The Adaptive Web*. Springer Verlag, Heidelberg, Germany, 2007.

7. I. Campbell. Interactive evaluation of the ostensive model using a new test collection of images with multiple relevance assessments. *Information Retrieval*, 2(1):85–112, 2000.

8. I. Campbell and C. J. van Rijsbergen. The ostensive model of developing information needs. In P. Ingwersen and N. O. Pors, eds., *CoLIS'06: Proceedings of the Sixth International Conference on Conceptions of Library and Information Sciences*, Borås, Sweden, pp. 251–268. The Royal School of Librarianship, October 1996.

9. M. Cha, H. Kwak, P. Rodriguez, Y.-Y. Ahn, and S. Moon. Analyzing the video popularity characteristics of large-scale user generated content systems. *IEEE/ACM Transactions on Networking*, 17:1357–1370, October 2009.

10. M. G. Christel. Establishing the utility of non-text search for news video retrieval with real world users. In R. Lienhart, A. R. Prasad, A. Hanjalic, S. Choi, B. P. Bailey, and N. Sebe, eds., *MM'07: Proceedings of the 15th International Conference on Multimedia*, Augsburg, Germany, pp. 707–716. ACM, 2007.

11. T.-S. Chua, S.-F. Chang, L. Chaisorn, and W. H. Hsu. Story boundary detection in large broadcast news video archives: Techniques, experience and trends. In H. Schulzrinne, N. Dimitrova, M. A. Sasse, S. B. Moon, and R. Lienhart, eds., *ACM MM'04: Proceedings of the 12th ACM International Conference on Multimedia*, New York, October 10–16, 2004, pp. 656–659. ACM, 2004.

12. L. Cole. Copyright in the digital age: A UK perspective. In *The E-Resources Management Handbook*, United Kingdom Serials Group, Newbury, U.K., February 2009.

13. A. Diriye, S. Zagorac, S. Little, and S. Rüger. NewsRoom: An information-seeking support system for news videos. In J. Wang, N. Boujemaa, N. O. Ramirez, and A. Natsev, eds., *MIR'10: Proceedings of the 11th ACM SIGMM International Conference on Multimedia Information Retrieval*, Philadelphia, PA, pp. 377–380. ACM, New York, 2010.

14. G. Durand, G. Kazai, M. Lalmas, U. Rauschenbach, and P. Wolf. A metadata model supporting scalable interactive TV services. In Y.-P. P. Chen, ed., *MMM'05: Proceedings of the 11th International Conference on Multi Media Modeling*, Melbourne, Australia, pp. 386–391. IEEE Computer Society, January 2005.

15. D. Elliott and J. M. Jose. A proactive personalised retrieval system. In D. W.-L. Cheung, I.-Y. Song, W. W. Chu, X. Hu, and J. J. Lin, eds., *CIKM'09: Proceedings of the 18th ACM Conference on Information and Knowledge Management*, Hong Kong, China, pp. 1935–1938. ACM, 2009.

16. M. Fernández, V. López, M. Sabou, V. Uren, D. Vallet, E. Motta, and P. Castells. Using TREC for cross-comparison between classic IR and ontology-based search models at a Web scale. In M. Grobelnik, P. Mika, T. T. Duc, and H. Wang, eds., *SemSearch'09: Workshop on Semantic Search at the 18th International World Wide Web Conference*, Madrid, Spain. April 2009.

17. H. J. Gans. *Deciding What's News: A Study of CBS Evening News, NBC Nightly News, Newsweek, and Time*. Northwestern University Press, Evanston, IL, 25th anniversary edn., February 2005.

18. P. J. Hayes, L. E. Knecht, and M. J. Cellio. A news story categorization system. In *Readings in Information Retrieval*, Morgan Kaufmann, San Francisco, CA, pp. 518–526, 1997.

19. F. Hopfgartner, D. Hannah, N. Gildea, and J. M. Jose. Capturing Multiple interests in news video retrieval by incorporating the ostensive model. In V. Christophides and G. Koutrika, eds., *PersDB'08: Proceedings of the Second International Workshop on Personalized Access, Profile Management, and Context Awareness: Databases*, Auckland, New Zealand, pp. 48–55. 2008.

20. F. Hopfgartner and J. M. Jose. Evaluating the implicit feedback models for adaptive video retrieval. In J. Z. Wang, N. Boujemaa, A. D. Bimbo, and J. Li, eds., *MIR'07: Proceedings of the Ninth ACM SIGMM International Workshop on Multimedia Information Retrieval*, Augsburg, Germany, pp. 323–331. ACM, 2007.

21. F. Hopfgartner and J. M. Jose. On user modelling for personalised news video recommendation. In G J. Houben, G. I. McCalla, F. Pianesi, and M. Zancanaro, eds., *UMAP'09: Proceedings of the 17th International Conference on User Modeling, Adaptation, and Personalization, formerly UM and AH*, Trento, Italy, Volume 5535 of *Lecture Notes in Computer Science*, pp. 403–408. Springer, 2009.

22. F. Hopfgartner and J. M. Jose. Semantic user modelling for personal news video retrieval. In S. Boll, Q. Tian, L. Zhang, Z. Zhang, and Y.-P. P. Chen, eds., *MMM'10: Proceedings of the 16th International Multimedia Modeling Conference*, Chongqing, China, Volume 5916 of *Lecture Notes in Computer Science*, pp. 336–346. Springer, 2010.

23. F. Hopfgartner and J. M. Jose. Semantic user profiling techniques for personalised multimedia recommendation. *Multimedia Systems*, 16:255–274, 2010.

24. T. Joachims. Text categorization with support vector machines: Learning with many relevant features. In C. Nedellec and C. Rouveirol, eds., *ECML'98: Proceedings of the Tenth European Conference on Machine Learning*, Chemnitz, Germany, Volume 1398 of *Lecture Notes in Computer Science*, pp. 137–142. Springer, 1998.

25. H. Joho, D. Birbeck, and J. M. Jose. An ostensive browsing and searching on the web. In B.-L. Doan, M. Melucci, and J. M. Jose, eds., *CIR'07: Proceedings of the Second International Workshop on Context-Based Information Retrieval*, Copenhagen, Denmark, pp. 81–92. 2007.

26. G, Kobilarov, T. Scott, Y. Raimond, S. Oliver, C. Sizemore, M. Smethurst, C. Bizer, and R. Lee. Media meets semantic web–How the BBC uses DBpedia and Linked data to make connections. In L. Aroyo, P. Traverso, F. Ciravegna, P. Cimiano, T. Heath, E. Hyvönen, R. Mizoguchi, E. Oren, M. Sabou, and E. P. B. Simperl, eds., *ESWC'09: Proceedings of the Sixth European Semantic Web Conference*, Heraklion, Greece, Volume 5554 of *Lecture Notes in Computer Science*, pp. 723–737. Springer, 2009.

27. M. Krötzsch, D. Vrandecic, and M. Völkel. Semantic MediaWiki. In I. F. Cruz, S. Decker, D. Allemang, C. Preist, D. Schwabe, P. Mika, M. Uschold, and L. Aroyo, eds., *ISWC'06: Proceedings of the Fifth International Semantic Web Conference, Athens, GA*, Volume 4273 of *Lecture Notes in Computer Science*, pp. 935–942. Springer, 2006.

28. I. Lagendijk, A. Hanjalic, N. Ramzan, and M. Larson. PetaMedia Deliverable D6.1—Integrative research plan, 2009 (last time accessed on February 4, 2010).

29. T. Leelanupab, F. Hopfgartner, and J. M. Jose. User centred evaluation of a recommendation based image browsing system. In B. Prasad, P. Lingras, and A. Ram, eds., *IICAI'09: Proceedings of the Fourth Indian International Conference on Artificial Intelligence*, Tumkur, India, pp. 558–573. IICAI, 2009.

30. C. Lioma and I. Ounis. Examining the content load of part of speech blocks for information retrieval. In *ACL'06: Proceedings of the 21st International Conference on Computational Linguistics and 44th Annual Meeting of the Association for Computational Linguistics*, Sydney, Australia. The Association for Computer Linguistics, 2006.

31. Y. Lu, N. Sebe, R. Hytnen, and Q. Tian. Personalization in multimedia retrieval: A survey. *Multimedia Tools and Applications*, 51:247–277, 2011.

32. MESH. Multimedia semantic syndication for enhanced news services—A view to the future of news, 2006 (last time accessed on February 25, 2010).

33. R. Paiu, L. Chen, C. S. Firan, and W. Nejdl. PHAROS–Personalizing users' experience in audio-visual online spaces. In V. Christophides and G. Koutrika, eds., *PersDB'08: Proceedings of the Second International Workshop on Personalized Access, Profile Management, and Context Awareness: Databases*, Auckland, New Zealand, pp. 40–47, 2008.

34. I. Psarras and J. M. Jose. A system for adaptive information retrieval. In V. P. Wade, H. Ashman, and B. Smyth, eds., *AH'06: Proceedings of the Fourth International Conference on Adaptive Hypermedia and Adaptive Web-Based Systems*, Dublin, Ireland, Volume 4018 of *Lecture Notes in Computer Science*, pp. 313–317. Springer, 2006.

35. I. Psarras and J. M. Jose. Evaluating a personal information assistant. In D. Evans, S. Furui, and C. Soulé-Dupuy, eds., In *RIAO'07: Proceedings of the Eighth International Conference on Computer-Assisted Information Retrieval (Recherche d'Information et ses Applications)*, Pittsburgh, PA. CID, 2007.

36. N. Sebe and Q. Tian. Personalized multimedia retrieval: The new trend? In J. Z. Wang, N. Boujemaa, A. D. Bimbo, and J. Li, eds., *MIR'07: Proceedings of the Ninth ACM SIGMM International Workshop on Multimedia Information Retrieval*, Augsburg, Germany, pp. 299–306. ACM, 2007.

37. N. Shadbolt, T. Berners-Lee, and W. Hall. The semantic web revisited. *IEEE Intelligent Systems*, 21(3):96–101, 2006.

38. A. W. M. Smeulders, M. Worring, S. Santini, A. Gupta, and R. Jain. Content-based image retrieval at the end of the early years. *IEEE Transactions on Pattern Analysis and Machine Intelligence*, 22:1349–1380, December 2000.

39. C. G. M. Snoek and M. Worring. Multimodal video indexing: A review of the state-of-the-art. *Multimedia Tools and Applications*, 25:5–35, 2005.

40. B. Stvilia, L. Gasser, M. B. Twidale, and L. C. Smith. A framework for information quality assessment. *Journal of the American Society for Information Science and Technology*, 58(12):1720–1733, 2007.

41. F. M. Suchanek, G. Kasneci, and G. Weikum. Yago: A core of semantic knowledge. In C. L. Williamson, M. E. Zurko, P. F. Patel-Schneider, and P. J. Shenoy, eds., *WWW'07: Proceedings of the 16th International Conference on World Wide Web*, Banff, Alberta, Canada, pp. 697–706. ACM, 2007.

42. C. Tsinaraki, P. Polydoros, F. G. Kazasis, and S. Christodoulakis. Ontology-based semantic indexing for MPEG-7 and TV-anytime audiovisual content. *Multimedia Tools and Applications*, 26(3):299–325, 2005.

43. J. Urban, J. M. Jose, and C. J. van Rijsbergen. An adaptive technique for content-based image retrieval. *Multimedia Tools and Applications*, 31(1):1–28, 2006.

Chapter 12

Personalized Content Access in Interactive TV-Based Cross Media Environments

Alcina Prata
University of Lisbon

Teresa Chambel
University of Lisbon

Nuno Guimarães
University of Lisbon

Contents

12.1 Introduction

This section explains the emergence of a cross media culture and addresses the motivations, benefits, and challenges of accessing additional and related interactive television (iTV) content in a cross media paradigm, supporting the viewers' cognitive modes and taking advantage of the strengths of each type of media and devices, in each situation and context of use. Then, it presents the main research questions underlying our research in this domain.

We are in a moment of transition, a moment when old media systems are dying and new media systems are born. The traditional "spectatorial" culture is giving way to a participatory culture [1]. Increasingly, interactive systems are becoming less restricted to a single media technology. In fact, the proliferation of new devices able to support human activities across a range of contextual settings [2], just like it happens in "real life," is one of the main motivations for media integration. Simultaneously, global access to information and technology is changing the relationship between people and knowledge, and the trends in convergence, integration, and coexistence of various media technologies are creating new opportunities for the globalization of learning and communication practices.

We are witnessing the growth of a new generation of systems, which are no longer limited to one single media technology, such as mobile devices, PC, or iTV, but, instead, include many of them. These systems are particularly interesting in what concerns the opportunities they create for communication, entertainment, learning, and others [3]. In terms of learning support, these systems are particularly promising due to the emerging era of lifelong learning, as learning will take place in a wide variety of contexts and locations and informal learning will tend to become as important as formal learning [3], calling for flexible environments.

These systems, often called cross media, are sometimes referred to in the literature as cross platform, cross device, and, more recently, transmedia by Jenkins [1]. Cross media and cross device are the most used concepts. The term cross media has emerged in the context of modern communications research, spanning the fields of computing and human–computer interaction (HCI) [4]. In this chapter, a cross media system is defined as a system that extends across a range of different devices, as part of a whole system with a structure of roles and functionalities, in order to achieve specific goals [2]. In our approach, we will refer to our system as cross media because it is the most spreading and well-known term, but it could also be considered, or referred to, as cross device or transmedia.

There are many advantages of cross media systems, especially the fact that they are already depicting the world, considering that reality is already cross media. In fact, reality is complex enough to allow us to have many different characters or many different stories on many different platforms. We are in the presence of different possible contexts that the viewer may experience. We can imagine the following scenario: a university student arrives from school and, after dinner, by chance, she/he comes across a documentary on TV that addresses some issues related to what she/he is studying in biology. She/he is very interested in knowing more about a certain number of those issues. However, since it is late, the intention is to watch the program through and just select some issues along the viewing, to be accessed as extra related selected content from the mobile phone, while in the train to the university next morning, or later on from the PC.

However, there are also aspects that affect the efficient use of cross media systems. Most users still feel more comfortable with the typical end-user computing environment and need to acquire practices in order to manage several devices [5]. This requires additional effort and there are often trade-offs between effort and benefit [2]. After a detailed literature review, it was possible to perceive that some of the proposed systems failed because too much effort was put into technical details, leaving behind cross media conceptual questions related to interaction design and underlying cognitive aspects, usability, affectivity, user experience, contextualization, continuity, media technology, or device characteristics. The handling of these dimensions was our starting point and main motivation. More than a high-tech solution or service, our main concern was to focus on these conceptual questions, to study and understand this emerging paradigm, the success of which requires not only technological solutions but also sustainable models and pedagogical solutions, where research has not been completed [2,6]. However, it was expected that the e-iTV system, designed to illustrate our research, would also technically allow us to propose a new and personalized type of service, which is, in the opinion of several researchers, the next direction to follow [7–9].

The designed e-iTV system that we will describe here generates personalized web content as additional information to the video being watched on iTV and in response to learning opportunities. The personalized web contents will be prepared to be viewed through iTV, PC, and mobile phones. Video was chosen as the departure media due to its richness, specific cognitive, affective, and entertainment features, and also for being a dominant media component in the cross media domain [10,11]. TV, and in particular iTV, was chosen since it is still the preferred device to deliver and access video. The history of iTV is full of pitfalls that have dictated a journey of advancements and recoils [12]. Nevertheless, iTV technology combines the appeal and mass audience of full-motion TV with the interactivity of the web and the Internet, providing new services, giving viewers more control over what they see, and creating a new and very rich environment. It is, in the opinion of many researchers and producers, a technology that is increasingly being used and that will conquer its market space [9,12]. This conviction is clearly supported by the number of research studies that were conducted on these last few years. Some studies have identified a potential for the use of iTV for increasing learning opportunities in the home, in particular through personalized options [3] and the need to find ways of utilizing the powerful combination of broadcast TV and interactive services to provide hooks to draw viewers into active learning environments [3].

The success of iTV requires technological solutions, sustainable models, and pedagogical solutions; and there is still limited research in this particular area, especially on cognitive and interaction aspects [3,13].

In spite of being a traditionally active or hot medium, inducing a passive or cold attitude in the viewers [14], TV may guide viewers into different cognitive states, more experiential or more reflective, in seconds. These cognitive states may appear inside or outside typical learning environments. For example, while watching a TV program, at some point in time, viewers may feel the need to know more about a specific issue that caught their attention. Viewers may prefer to remain in the dominant experiential mode of TV watching and follow a route to additional information at a later time and possibly through a different device, when they may engage in a more reflective cognitive mode, or explore it right away. As stated by [10,15], the medium is not neutral, influencing the message and its impact on us. Broadcast TV by itself does not provide the adequate support to reflection, especially important when learning is the goal. In spite of not augmenting human reflection in this sense, traditional TV may turn into a powerful tool for reflection when properly augmented [11,15,16]. Interactive TV has the potential to open doors to such a flexible environment in a cross media scenario, where media types are integrated and each device can contribute with its strengths to support learning.

The research questions concerned are therefore as follows: (a) Is there a real advantage in connecting these devices? (b) Are the iTV interfaces appropriate to provide an adequate support to create and follow extra web content, and are the iTV, PC, and mobile phone interfaces easy to use and understand? (c) What are the preferred interface designs for the relevant cognitive modes and needs in each scenario? (d) Are the personalized web contents appropriate to give sequence and continuity to the learning opportunities created by the visualization of the iTV video (are they able to contextualize viewers in relation to what they first saw and provide further content)? (e) What other functionalities would viewers like to have in this kind of environment? (f) Was the proposed framework adequate and efficient?

This chapter introduced the motivations, benefits, difficulties, and challenges of the cross media systems paradigm, with a particular focus on cross media systems that use iTV and video to access additional related content, and presented the main research questions. A review of related work and concepts is presented in Section 12.2. Section 12.3 describes the conceptual framework of the design of cross media personalized content access environments from iTV (as the e-iTV system) and addresses the most relevant cross media design challenges. Section 12.4 presents the e-iTV system, a specific case study designed in order to illustrate and evaluate the studied paradigm. Section 12.5 presents the user evaluation, followed by the conclusions and perspectives for future research and developments in Section 12.6.

12.2 State of the Art

This section presents the more relevant research studies, namely those systems where the additional related indexed information was based on a TV context and those where iTV has been used with other devices as part of cross media environments.

Due to the convergence between TV and the Internet, several research projects appeared in the last few years aimed at finding ways of combining TV and web content, with informational or communicational purposes, solely using iTV or being cross media. We refer to some of the more relevant to our work.

Dimitrova et al. [17] proposed two systems: MyInfo and InfoSip. MyInfo is a personal news application, which extracts specific web content listed in the user profile and displays personalized TV news programs—weather, traffic, sports, financial news, headlines, and local events—on the TV. To access the information, which is related to the program being watched, the viewer only needs to access one of the six mentioned "content zones." InfoSip is a movie information retrieval application, which analyzes the movie content and gives audiences information (overlaid onscreen) on such things as "who is the actor?" "what is the song?" "where are they?" In summary, the application answers most frequently asked questions. To access that information, the viewer only needs to press a specific button on the remote. Both systems were developed based on the belief that, while watching a program, the viewer may feel the need to know more about that story, so appropriate, personalized, summarized, and targeted information and references were provided. Both applications offered a new direction for personalization research "where the source of the content is less important than the actual delivered information to the viewer," but both were limited considering that the "extra information" available was previously categorized and limited to a small number of possibilities. As the e-iTV system, it also has an option with predefined categorized "extra information." However, viewers have the possibility to go much further considering that while watching the video, they may choose exactly in which topics they are interested in knowing more about, and almost everything that is said in the video is a possible choice.

Nadamoto and Tanaka [18] have developed a "TV-style presentation" system capable of searching the web, extracting related and relevant web pages, automatically transforming the text- and image-based web content found into audiovisual TV—program type content—through the use of character-animated agents and text readout, and fusing it with normal broadcasted TV program contents. In some aspects, the philosophy behind the work is similar to MyInfo. Miyamori and Tanaka [19] have developed the opposite idea, that is, a "web-browser-style presentation" system named Webified Video capable of automatically transforming traditional TV content into web content and integrating the result with related information such as complementary web content. Both systems addressed the need of extra and complementary content, however, that content was transformed in order to be integrated with the information source. In the Nadamoto and Tanaka [18] system, the final result may become too much intrusive of the TV viewing experience since TV is the only device being actually used by viewers. Contrary to our system, these two are not offering a personalized solution prepared to react to changes in viewers' cognitive modes.

Ma and Tanaka [20] have developed the Webtelop, a "parallel presentation" system to presenting the TV program and web content simultaneously on the TV, enabling viewers to browse the web content while watching the TV program. CoTV^{TM}[21] or coactive TV automatically presents, on a PC, web content related to the on-air program. It acts like a special web search engine that is continuously and automatically driven by the TV viewing context (not driven by the viewers' actions). CoTV^{TM} also includes a portal with traditional iTV services such as program guides, video on demand, DVR scheduling, and so on. As to the Webtelop, it is too much intrusive of the TV viewing experience and the CoTV^{TM} is distractive of the TV viewing experience. Due to their characteristics, and contrary to e-iTV, none of these two systems provided a personalized adequate answer to viewers needs while accommodating their changes in cognition modes. However, both addressed the need to provide viewers with extra content while watching a TV program and contributed with solutions to integrate web content with TV.

TV2Web developed by Sumiya et al. [22] is a cross media system, where a video and its closed captions were structured after being divided into units, such as segments, scenes, and shots. Units were then linked and displayed smoothly using zooming metaphors and providing a seamless user interface (UI) that could be moved between TV screens and web pages. This approach was interesting, since the final interface was developed with the smallest possible excerpts from the original video. In terms of contextualization, the use of small excerpts from the original video achieved good results. However, it was a limited cross media system due to the small number of devices involved and interaction possibilities. Our system also uses video excerpts from the original TV program in order to contextualize the web content. However, different approaches were tested (the video running, the video paused, etc.). As to the number of devices involved, we have spanned our system across three different environments (iTV, PC, and mobile phones).

A system proposed by Miyamori et al. [23] generates views of TV programs based on viewer's perspectives expressed in live web chats. They propose a new video indexing technique based on the view point of the users, collected from their participation in live web chats, where they express their emotions about the TV programs. This work was an attempt to integrate TV and the web in a personalized way and to take into account important dimensions such as the emotion and the sense of unity. In general terms, they defended the role of these two dimensions in the design process and the importance of personalizing the TV content, which are in accordance with our own belief and research.

The cross media TAMALLE project [24] developed a "dual device system" for informal language learning, based on iTV and mobile phones, supporting learners of English as a second language in their TV viewing, selecting what to access later on the mobile phone. This was an interesting cross media system capable to accommodate different cognitive modes since it was prepared to provide different types of information to be seen in two devices that typically require different cognitive modes. The system was flexible and able to accommodate different contexts of use due to the combination of two different devices. This work was important to our research due to the good results achieved by providing users with mobility in the use of the system. However, it is more limited in options and scope, considering that the only output device was the mobile phone and that no metadata was available.

Cronkite [25] provides extra information to viewers of broadcast news. While viewers are watching a news story, they feel the need to know more about it, they press the "interest" button on their remote control, and the system provides them with extra information on the computer display. The extra information, which also comprises pointers to other related stories, is about the story that they are watching rather than specific topics of interest inside the story, which is somehow limited. To have the system working, both TV and PC need to be simultaneously on. The system is limited considering that the extra information is not stored for later on view (which might be the viewers' preference: for example, to view the extra information next day). The work clearly addresses the need of further similar research in this area but with other program genres, namely, documentaries, which was exactly what we did but expanding the functionalities and without the limitations of the Cronkites' system. Our system stores the related information for later use, viewers may select very specific topics of interest inside a story instead of the whole story, and some specific functionalities, as asynchronous communication tools, were also contemplated.

Segerståhl [2] proposed a cross media fitness support system that includes a heart rate monitoring wrist unit, a web service, and data collection accessories such as the heart rate monitoring strap and a GPS sensor. The system provides information on factors such as heart rate, calories, time, and distance and tools for planning, monitoring, and following-up fitness activities. In order to access the complete information, users are supposed to consult the web service. In spite of the authors interesting contribution, this cross media system was not perceived by the users as cross media because the system was not presented as a whole unit. Since the wrist unit interface was not designed in a way that reminded the user that a web service was available, the contextualization failed. These typical cross media problems did not affect our system considering that it was presented to the viewers as a whole unit and designed to maintain viewers aware of all functionalities, and involved devices, while using the system.

Obrist et al. [26] developed a cross media "6 key navigation model" and its interface for an electronic program guide (EPG) running on the TV, PC, and mobile phone. The different devices were not used in a complementary way. In fact, the intention was basically to test a similar interface, on three different devices, which was based solely on six specific keys. They have reached important results since they have perceived what works best and what does not. In particular, viewers preferred a reduced number of navigation keys and a unified UI with the same functionalities across devices. This was an important contribution to our research since it supported our prototypes UI design decisions.

Newstream, developed by Martin and Holtzman [27], delivers a "cross medium (video, audio, text, etc.), socially aware news experience, focusing on relating virtually identical and similar content across varying media, community and personalized filtering, social dialogues, and multiple device delivery and interaction, delivering news stories through dynamically generated streams (sequence of news-related video clips, audio clips, text-based articles, or interactive experiences, aggregated according to specific themes, such as entertainment, politics, or technology)." The system provides extra information about what is being watched and related websites using TV, PC, and mobiles. Depending on the viewers' needs, that extra information may be viewed immediately, stored for later view, or pushed to another device. All devices maintain awareness of each other and are able to move interaction to the device that makes the most sense in a specific context, use several devices simultaneously, and use the mobile device as a TV remote.

What distinguishes their work from other experiences is the focus on cross media content. Limitations, in spite of the technically well-designed "ecosystem of devices," are the fact that the system relies almost exclusively on social networks to receive and share content, as well as for interaction and dialogues, and the limited viewer direct influence on the new contents presented as extra information. In fact, those contents are presented based on the whole story that the viewer is watching and not particular issues within that story. What distinguishes our work from Newstream is the viewers' possibility to choose exactly which issues they are interested in knowing more about, the ability to generate that extra information, which may be edited and complemented with the viewers' input (text, images, video, music), the fact that the system does not rely on social networks, in spite of having the possibility to share those extra contents with social networks contacts (if the viewer have them), and is not limited to a single genre, it was already implemented on two different genres: documentaries and film series. HyperSoap [28] explored interaction designs for the iTV paradigm, expecting a more passive audience, and allowing the indication of interest in topics to be later explored, in a more reflective mode at the end of the TV program. It was a soap opera where the user could inquire and get external information about purchasing clothes and furniture used in the show. This pioneer system, developed at MIT Media Lab, explored the need to access further information about a program that is being watched, taking into account users' attitudes while watching TV, just like our system does. However, contrary to our system, it was somehow limited considering that the only device used was iTV instead of a cross media environment, and that the additional information is accessed at the end of the program always in the same level of detail.

The 2BEON [12] is an iTV application, which supports the communication between viewers, allowing them to communicate textually, in real time, while watching a specific program. The system also allows viewers to see which of their contacts are online at a specific moment and which programs they are watching (due to privacy reasons, this functionality may be disconnected). This application allows instant messaging on the iTV, which, as demonstrated, is an important functionality to give viewers a sense of presence. This application, which started as a PhD project, has changed its name to WeOnTV and is now being implemented with smartphones as "secondary input devices," thus turning to a cross media application, which will be soon distributed by one of the most popular Portuguese TV cable companies. This work demonstrates the importance of the social presence by sharing information with viewer's contacts about what they are watching on the TV. This conclusion was important in the scope of our research since contributed to our decision of implementing a sharing functionality.

WebTV [29] appeared in the late 1990s and was a pioneer system, which enabled users to access the Internet via a TV set while watching it. This was not a cross media system but through the TV, users could send and receive e-mail, use live chats, shop online, and browse the Internet while also watching TV. Compared with 2BEON [12], this chat was limited since it was the traditional one directly implemented on a TV set and, thus, not integrated with the TV content. However, it offered other functionalities typical from the web environment. Both systems showed the importance of socializing while watching TV. This socialization feature was contemplated in our work considering that viewers may share extra contents, asynchronously, with their contacts.

Geerts et al. [30] built a system for sending and receiving enriched video fragments to and from a range of devices in order to understand which program genres were preferred for: talking while watching; talking about after watching (after the end of the program); and for sending to users with different devices. Their conclusions were important in the context of our research, since we needed to conceptualize and develop interfaces capable to accommodate the different characteristics of each program genre and devices as explained in Sections 12.3 and 12.4.

To illustrate emerging trends, we refer to two projects that aim to support and involve viewers with TV content in more active ways. Our new project ImTV [31] and the digital interactive television (iDTV)-HEALTH [32] are recent Portuguese projects in cooperation with the Austin University, Texas. ImTV addresses On-Demand Immersive-TV for Communities of Media Producers and Consumers, with the main goals of studying viewers' knowledge about key aspects of the new media workflow driving the entertainment industry; understanding and supporting the production side of the new media workflow, exploring the role of intelligent metadata and new digital formats in the production of video programs; developing richer immersive environments and novel feedback mechanisms inferred from richer interactions with media and among viewers; and improving viewers' experience by offering them a personalized combination of the mainstream TV content together with online user-generated content.

The iDTV-HEALTH is an inclusive service to promote health and wellness via iTV. The project main goal is to evaluate the potential of iDTV to promote original services, formats, and contents which can be relevant to support personal health care and wellness of individuals over 55 years of age. It is a cross media project since the intention is to develop an iDTV portal solution: a portal with video content, still images, and text, with associated navigation system both for IPTV and mobile.

Most of these related works present TV–web or web–TV approaches that allow access to versions of the same TV or web content (not additional and extra information) from different devices, in ways related to the TV content being watched but with limited or as only focused on the personalization. We believe that the challenge should be to go further and, as we have proposed in our system, to allow the access to related information that complements what is being watched and taking into account user preferences and the cognitive and affective aspects that influence user experiences in a variety of cross media scenarios. In our system, viewers may select general information and specific topics of interest in order to generate a personalized web content with extra related multimedia information. This web content is prepared to be viewed at any time, through TV, PC, or mobile phones, assuring the contextualization and continuity amongst these media and devices, and taking the best out of each medium, device, and context of use. Viewers may also share the generated web content with their social network contacts. More than a high-tech solution or service, the main concern was the focus on the identified conceptual questions that will be further detailed in the next section.

12.3 Conceptual Framework for the Design of iTV-Based Cross Media Environments

A successful application provides the best match between technology and the function it supports, along with flexibility in their combination. This raises a challenge when designing effective and consistent applications across media. An effective design takes cognitive and affective aspects into account in the use of, and interaction with, different media. We will explore the design of cross media environments taking into account design practices and guidelines in the integration of video in multimedia and hypermedia [10,11,16,33] and the challenges and approaches to the combination of different devices. This section describes the conceptual framework found relevant for the design of cross media personalized content access environments from iTV, as the e-iTV system, using an iTV design model [34] and addressing the cross media design challenges with a special focus on TV and PC/web.

12.3.1 Media and Cognition

Norman's [15] view defines two fundamental cognitive modes that are relevant to understand our relation with media: experiential and reflective. The *experiential mode* allows us to perceive and react to events efficiently and without effort. It is the mode of the expert behavior, the mode of perception, entertainment, motivation, and inspiration. In spite of being the key component of efficient performance, we need more if the goal is to create knowledge and human understanding. Reflection becomes fundamental in order to achieve and consolidate new ideas and concepts. The *reflective mode* of cognition is the one "of comparison and contrast, of thought, of decision making" of reasoning and contemplation.

One may alternate between these two modes, depending on several kinds of internal and external factors, and both are important in human cognition, but require different technological support.

Several communicational *media* may transmit the same information. However, the medium is not neutral. Due to its characteristics, the medium affects the way we interpret and use the message and its impact on us [10,14]. TV is usually watched in the experiential mode, commonly associated with entertainment, in a more relaxed and passive way, and it is easy to use since it does not require previous practice or much mental effort. However, as stated by [10–12,15] when properly constructed and augmented, TV may turn into a powerful tool for reflection, inducing and supporting a more active attitude. Study books induce a more active and reflective attitude, important in learning processes; while telephones were traditionally used for communication, greatly empowered by their current mobility and multimedia support.

Networked multimedia computers have somehow the ability to accommodate these properties, but in limited ways.

A successful integration should have each medium's support what it is most suited for, augmenting its capabilities. For example, an entertainment medium like TV can be extended with reflective content without forcing a change in its experiential nature, if the user is capable to easily select some program topics, without disturbing the TV viewing experience, for further reading through a PC. Thus, considering that there are several types of communication styles and tools, it is important to be able to identify which solution works best in a particular context based on the affordances of the different devices used in a cross media environment.

12.3.2 Cross Media Interaction

The challenges of cross media interaction design were grouped by Segerståhl [2] into three main areas: *Heterogeneity*: When several interaction devices and applications are part of a system, the user IT skills (also designated as technological literacy) need to be higher. Another challenge arises from the differences in terms of the devices and contexts of use, which are determinant in terms of adequacy between the system and its users. User expectations also vary in the presence of different devices; *Interoperability*: This concept, usually referred to as the system interconnectivity, is as relevant as the conceptual architecture—a fundamental tool since it shows how the system works, how each role is supported by each device, and how functionalities are distributed amongst them; *Consistency*: The system may vary in terms of goals, devices, and areas, increasing the risk of inconsistency in terms of semantics, interaction logic, industrial design, and technical standards.

The quality of a cross media system interaction cannot be measured only by the quality of its parts; it has to be measured as a whole. Following Segerståhl [2], there are three essential factors in order to determine the success of an information system: how easily it was adopted, how well it was implemented and to what level, and which characteristics and functionalities of the system are used. Thus, considering that a cross media system is a specific type of information system, these three factors will be applicable. However, it is our belief that, due to the complexity of a cross media system, measuring these factors will be a more complex task.

12.3.3 Cross Media User Experience and Conceptual Model

As stated by Segerståhl [2], user experience is a process that (1) is influenced by *different backgrounds*, such as previous experience, social and cultural factors, contexts of use, and so on; (2) is analyzed in *several dimensions*, such as emotional reactions and cognitive processes; and (3) contributes to *different cognitive effects*, such as emotion, learning, or acceptance.

Interaction is more manageable when a single device is being used. Different challenges arise if considering a cross media user experience. When multitask and multitechnology environments are being used, interaction must be designed in order to accommodate these different contexts [2]. Goodhue and Thompson [35] state that the "task-technology fit model" is based on the belief that information technologies are used only if their functions support (fit) users' activities. Thus, it is fundamental to correctly identify the contextual needs that justify and characterize the use of different media and how the different media support human activity. As in Segerståhl [2] "Task-technology fit can only be understood after analyzing the users' side of the story as well. That is, digging into the users' mental representations of the system at hand and understanding their experiential background."

12.3.3.1 Cross Media Conceptual Model

A conceptual model is a critical part of the design process. The *system image*, how the software will look like and act, influences how the system is constructed and should be used [36]. A mental image of a system is produced based on previous experiences and through concepts that come out when visualizing the system working [37]. When well designed, systems show people what functions they do and how they do it, being capable of participating in the human construction on how the system works [2]. This is a particularly important aspect in a cross media environment, since it involves several interaction scenarios and contexts.

12.3.3.2 Synergic Use and Coherent User Experience

Synergic use means using combinations of media in order to achieve a level of task support higher than it would be possible through the use of each one individually [38]. In a cross media environment, the user experience may be evaluated through how well it supports the synergic use of the devices and the different affordances provided. It is important to understand what makes the user pass the current device boundaries in order to use other devices as well. According to Segerståhl and Oinas-Kukkonen [38], in a cross media context, the user experience may be classified as distributed or coherent. *Distributed* user experience leads to the isolated perception of devices and thus is one of the biggest barriers to the efficient use and adoption of cross media systems, while *coherent* user experience leads to the perception of a cross media system as a whole unity. These perceptions, in terms of physical, semantic, and functional unity, "may help users to identify relevant functionality and intended use of the system components. They may also help narrowing down the conceptual gaps between media and encourage exploratory behaviors for discovering synergic use practices."

12.3.4 Supporting Cross Media Interaction

In a cross media system, the user activity may be supported by a variable number of different media that complement and enhance each other. In fact, the user may carry out a task through a sequence of devices. This migration of tasks is supported via cross media usability and *continuity*, influencing on how well and smoothly users' skills and experiences are transferred across the different media or devices. As stated by [39], users expect to reuse their interaction knowledge, and their user experience, when they switch device. Thus, in spite of the change of device, a *consistent* interaction (in terms of terminology, graphics, etc.) will obviously improve the usability of the system and help break barriers to the adoption of cross media systems. The consistent look and feel across media is an important requirement, keeping in mind the goal of having each device doing what it is the most suited for and extending its characteristics (synergic use) [40]. And for this, it is important to understand the devices and their affordability.

According to Robertson et al. [41], any attempt to create a taxonomy of devices, or media, is a complex problem since device usage patterns change over time and depend on their combination. The best approach is to study each particular situation, including device characteristics and cognitive and affective aspects associated to its use. Since TV is central in our approach, a more detailed explanation about the motivations and attitudes in watching TV and a review of other devices properties that influence cross media design options when TV is involved are presented.

12.3.4.1 Reasons and Ways of Watching TV

People have different reasons for watching TV and different ways of doing it. Goals when watching TV depend on the "time and context in which they are watching TV" [42]. Previous research has identified *three levels of TV viewing* [42]: *Level one* implies a low degree of viewer engagement and planning and usually happens when the viewer arrives from some sort of activity like work or school. His main goal is to relax and watch something interesting with the minimum effort. *Level two* implies a medium to high level of viewer engagement. It is normally associated with programs of general interest. The viewer's goal is to watch periodic programs of interest like news and soap operas. *Level three* implies a high level of viewer engagement and also some planning. This type of viewing is normally solitaire, since individual preferences are the motivation. This type of viewing is associated with programs of specific interest like documentaries, dramas, or current affairs.

While watching a certain program, the viewer's goals may change, as a result of internal or external factors, like a headache or a phone call. Several studies have identified four possible *levels of attention*, also dynamic, when watching TV, ranging from watching it as the only activity, and thus with a high level of attention, to using it only as a source of background noise and thus as a form of companionship [43].

The affective dimension of TV viewing may be supported by Uses and Gratifications theory. Previous research [44] states that traditional TV watching may be explained by this theory, which defends that consumers use media in order to satisfy four needs: *surveillance, personal identity, integration and social interaction,* and *diversion*. These needs may be categorized as ritualized (needs of entertainment, companionship, and escape) and instrumental or cognitive. *Ritualized use*, the predominant in current TV viewing, implies a viewer more passive mode and using a medium as diversion and to pass the time. *Instrumental or cognitive use* implies using a medium in order to seek information contents and cognitive involvement and requires a more active mode.

Thus, in *designing interactive applications*, we must consider that entertainment and communication applications (which cover ritualized needs) will be adopted easier by the mass audience; informational and transactional applications (which cover instrumental and cognitive needs) should be designed in order to offer entertainment or communication elements as well.

As to communication, a research study [30] has shown that news, soap, quiz, and sports are genres during which participants talk most while watching and are thus suitable for synchronous social iTV systems. As to film, news, documentaries, and music programs, they are potentially popular genres for asynchronous social iTV systems.

12.3.4.2 TV and Other Devices

Here, the focus will be on comparing TV with PC/web and mobile phones.

When compared with PC, the TV use implies a broadcast transmission; uniform speed in connection for all viewers; rare technical problems; a safer environment since hacking is not a risk on TV; expensive content production; limited interaction via a remote control; limited customization; limited vertical scrolling; only one window at a time; limited interface; more heterogeneous public, wide audience and group interaction, a relaxed and comfortable position, less attention, concentration, and instant interactivity, less specific goals, specific modes of interaction, and less interactivity; a compelling interface is fundamental, and ease of use is not enough, since entertainment or communication is also needed [3,8,17,45,46].

When compared with TV, the mobile phone use implies a simpler interaction (scrolling, navigation through touch, simple images resizing, etc.); smaller screen size; high mobility; functionalities not yet available through TV (GPS, MP3 player, games, Facebook, e-mail, etc.); a less safer environment since virus are a risk on mobile devices; more technical problems; different speed connections; more attention; more specific goals. In spite of maintaining some individual characteristics, as devices are converging, some of the mentioned distinguishing characteristics will become more blurred over time.

Concluding, in what concerns effective cross media design, it is important to understand the challenges and ways of supporting coherent and synergic use considering, amongst other factors, the user experience, the way people create mental images of a system, media and devices characteristics, considering the cognitive and effective aspects associated with their use.

12.4 e-iTV System Case Study Design

This section presents the e-iTV cross media system designed and developed to explore and illustrate the paradigm proposed in this chapter based on the framework described in Section 12.3. All options taken in terms of program genres, target population, and design are explained. The design options taken were explored to meet the most relevant challenges involved in the interaction with the different media and devices that are integrated. The more relevant research studies found in the iTV interface design area [8,46–52] show that no specific model can be found. Instead, some scattered UI principles, guidelines, heuristics, design patterns, processes, "steps," and "tips" are usually followed. For this reason, we proposed an iTV Design Model [34] for the planning, design, development, and evaluation of iTV applications, taking into account research in iTV interface design and HCI principles, integrating the aforementioned authors' UI principles, guidelines, and so on, and adopting a user-centered approach. This model was then used in the design of e-iTV.

12.4.1 TV Genres and Programs

For prototyping and evaluation purposes, there was a need to select and classify the television program considering that certain genres are more "compelling for inter-activity" [49] and some are more compelling for communication between viewers [12,30] than others. We adopted Livaditi et al. [44] classification: Documentaries belong to informational and transactional applications and thus cover instrumental and cognitive needs, and this type of program genre application interfaces design should contemplate entertainment and/or communication elements in order to be easily adopted by the mass audience. As to films, they belong to entertainment and communication applications and thus cover ritualized needs. According to Geerts et al. [30], both genres are more suitable for asynchronous social iTV, since people talk less while watching them. Since the intention was to develop an iTV system capable of responding to learning opportunities created by the program viewing, our choice was to use a film and a documentary. Both genres provide information and induce a state of attention adequate to this informal learning attitude.

In order to choose a documentary and a film that could be highly appreciated, a questionnaire was used with 243 persons (mainly students from the Superior School of Business Management: ESCE). The options available for the documentary category were animal life, natural phenomena, paranormal phenomena, space, physics, human body, or other. The preferred option (57%) was a documentary about space. The most common justifications were as follows: "it's different," "it's new," "it's something that everyone dreams to know more about," "it's something very far and thus mysterious," "it's thrilling because it's something that we cannot usually see."

The options available for the film category were specific series, action, police, horror, comedy, romance, science fiction, and drama. Within these options, the preferred one was specific series, namely, the popular CSI series (62%). The more common reasons were as follows: "it's very thrilling," "it's very cool," "it's the best series on TV at the moment."

12.4.2 Target Viewers

Another relevant dimension is to characterize the viewers in terms of demographic profile (e.g., age, sex, socioeconomic status), viewing patterns (e.g., social viewing, routines, preferences), and technological experience. The characterization of the potential users of a new type of application is a fundamental stage in a user-centered design process. However, and as stated by Eronen [53], the identification of the target population for an inexistent application is a complex task. A solution relies on observing and interpreting what happens in the use of other iTV applications. Lafrance [54], in a research study about the use of Internet, found out that the category of users more committed to the simultaneous use of TV and Internet services were the ones between 15 and 25 years old, since they already had that practice more deeply enrooted.

A more recent study [55] with people between 12 and 18 years old also demonstrated that in spite of preferring the use of Internet and mobile phones, watching TV is an important and significant activity for them (94.7%), which is done in a daily basis, and occupies a significant part of their free time (64.4% watch TV between 1 and 3 h/day). It was also possible to observe that the most traditional pattern in this group of young people is the realization of one or more activities at the same time while watching TV, which, in some points, reinforces the conclusion of Lafrance that the category of users more committed to the simultaneous use of TV and Internet services are young people.

The focus of the e-iTV system was on the population with more technological literacy or web access practice, which, as stated in [54,55], is typically found on younger populations. However, considering the importance of the lifelong learning trends, the system was also tested with other populations, namely, older people, and also those with lower technological literacy. According to the conceptual framework adopted (Section 12.3), it was important to test different levels of interactivity (more and less intrusive of the iTV experience, and more or less informational), and different ways of interacting, ways of integrating information and linking approaches in order to further contextualize the personalized web content viewers in relation to the original content (TV program).

A user-centered design approach for the e-iTV system design was followed [34, 45,56]. This process is divided into three main stages, namely, conceptual model, system architecture, design and prototyping as described next.

12.4.3 e-iTV Conceptual Model

The conceptual model defines the system image, how it will look like and act. According to Chorianopoulos and Spinellis [45], the quality of interactive products depends on three aspects: utility (usefulness), ease of use (usability), and enjoyment (affective quality) [45]. It will also have to avoid conflicting with, and instead augment and possibly improve, the TV viewer experience [49]. e-iTV works with the traditional iTV and aims at accommodating viewers' changes in cognition modes. The simplified scenario is the following: while watching a TV program, typically in an experiential cognitive mode, the viewer is able to select the specific topics of interest (related to the program content and meta-information, or metadata), for further access and learning in a more reflective cognitive mode. This selection is possible through interfaces, which differ in terms of level of detail, number, and type of available options, complexity, and more or less intrusion in the iTV experience. A personalized web content addressing all the selected topics and related web links is generated by the system, in a server (as described in Section 12.4.4), and made available to the viewer, via the Internet, in a format to be viewed on different media or devices: PC, iTV, and mobile phones. If the viewers' choice is to access the web content through a PC or mobile device, they receive an e-mail, an SMS, or both, with the web link address to the web content. If the viewers' choice is to access the web content through the iTV, the link is immediately available via the iTV application. These web contents are designed to satisfy the viewers' information needs, by containing more information in breadth, depth, and points of view than the original broadcast content, on the aspects directly related to the chosen content topics and program metadata. Thus, it provides an answer to the learning opportunities created by the entertainment environment of TV involving different media and, instead of being seen as the end product, the broadcast program can be the starting point to a cross media dynamically built learning space, a new cross media learning context to be further explored. It will also allow viewers to share their web content with their contacts, as a way to fulfill their communication needs while watching TV—a concept that was referred, by Geerts et al. [30], as "social TV" and that is growing due to the proliferation of different technological communication devices. In fact, since TV works as a promoter of interpersonal communication [12] and T-learning has social features [57], this communication functionality turns out to be important.

12.4.4 e-iTV System Architecture

A client-server architecture was adopted for the e-iTV system (see Figure 12.1). The server stores a database of the information modules delivered with the TV program (in order to serve as material to create the web contents); TV content meta-information; viewers' profiles; and specific templates to be used for each device. These templates are responsible for formatting the information to be presented to the viewer and the system selects them, essentially, based on the type of the access device and the viewer's profile, in order to personalize the system. The server also stores the web content generated by the system; the interactive applications in order to choose topics of interest, share contents, and so on.

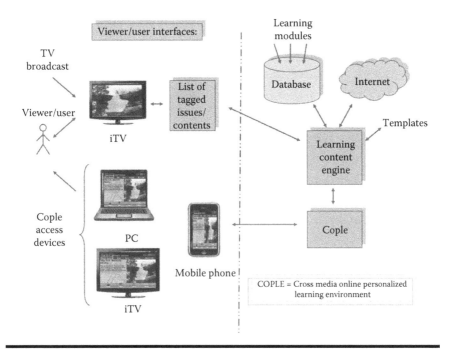

Figure 12.1   e-iTV system architecture.

The web contents are constructed dynamically, based on the viewers choices and profile, with information from two different sources: information modules and web links. The modules, developed under specific criteria and standards in order to be adequate to the server database, are supplied to the TV broadcaster in addition to the TV program. These modules provide a way of reusing resources. Producing TV programs is very expensive and, due to time constraints, usually, the amount of produced material is higher than the one that is actually used. Thus, we have proposed a system where that superfluous material may be used in learning modules. These modules will be complemented with information from reliable websites related with selected issues. The group of links will be made available in addition to the web content at the bottom.

Prototypes were developed using Action Script 3.0, PHP, MYSQL, HTML, and CSS Style sheets.

12.4.5 e-iTV Design Prototyping

In the study of the conceptual framework in Section 12.3, a considerable number of variables were identified in the cognitive, affective, communication and interaction, dimensions, informing the design of the e-iTV system. The e-iTV interactive features are described in the following categories: (1) personalization; (2) interacting with the

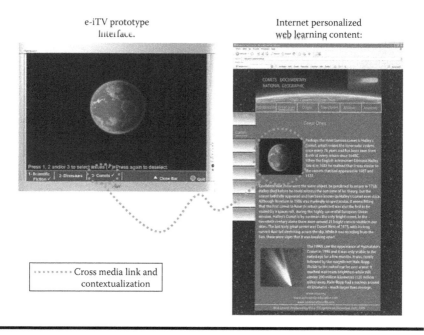

Figure 12.2   e-iTV system cross media links and contextualization.

TV program; (3) final choices and confirmation interface, including the possibility of sharing web content with friends; and (4) personalized web content interface generated in the cross media environment.

Most of the cross media design challenges are related to (2) and (4), the interaction with the program and the contextualization in the generated content (see Figure 12.2), so the design of these features received more attention, as described in Sections 12.4.5.2 and 12.4.5.4. All interfaces were designed based on the iTV design model proposed by the authors and latter adapted or improved according to evaluations feedback. Designed options accommodate different cognitive modes, levels of attention, goals, needs, interaction preferences, and affective dimension.

Prototypes were designed and implemented with the documentary about space and the CSI series as basic content. In general terms, both TV genres prototypes had the same features. The difference was that the first prototypes to be implemented were the ones on the documentary about space, which had a simplified interaction interface (see Figures 12.2 and 12.4). After their evaluation, the prototypes on the CSI series were then implemented with a considerable more elaborated interaction interface across devices and improved contextualization options. As to the interface, more navigation options were made available and the existing ones were refined. An option of having metadata available was included. As to the contextualization options, several possibilities were made available on the web content: to have the video playing, the video stopped, the list of topics presented by the chosen order but to be able to see them alphabetically ordered, and so on. These changes were made based on the previous prototypes feedback, and to test which option would be able to better accommodate people with different technological literacy, different cognition modes, levels of attention, goals, needs, and so on.

12.4.5.1 Personalization

This feature allows personalization of the service and adaptation of the web content to each user. After login, viewers may choose what to use, traditional iTV services, or the e-iTV system. When using the e-iTV system for the first time, viewers will be asked to register and define their profile (from iTV and via a wireless keyboard), which includes personal data and preferences like gender, age, e-mail, mobile phone, interests, the way in which viewers want to be informed about the web content location, which device(s) they want to use in order to view it, and so on. The viewer profile may be changed at any time.

12.4.5.2 Interacting with the TV Program

To interact with the TV program, the viewer needs to enter the interactive mode. During the first 3 min of the program, the interface presents, on the top right of the screen, the text "Press Enter to interact," which will be replaced by "Enter" after that period. The word "Enter" remains on screen for 1 min. Then, while not selected and until the end of the program, it appears for 10 s every 5 min. This solution will keep the viewer aware of the system presence, something fundamental for the success of a cross media system [2]. It was tested on previous prototypes in order to evaluate if it would be distracting but, as viewers referred, they are used to large amounts of dynamic text (e.g., the bottom bar of news programs) so this particular word was not considered intrusive on the iTV experience but helpful in order to remind them that the system was there.

To access additional information along the program, on the documentary prototypes, we have proposed simplified interaction interfaces (see Figures 12.3 and 12.4). In Figure 12.3, if interaction is selected, by pressing enter, we move to the interface presented in Figure 12.4, where viewers may choose their topics of interest for further information. On this interface, the selectable topics are presented to the viewer through numbers from 1 to 3 (Figure 12.4). As may be seen from Figure 12.4, the chosen topics were 1 and 3, the ones with the visual feedback ✓.

On the CSI prototypes, we have proposed more elaborated interaction interfaces where numbers were used to access different information levels instead of used to select topics (Figure 12.5). To accommodate viewers' changes in cognition modes and needs, we have proposed interfaces comprising two types of information and three information levels as described in the next subsection.

Figure 12.3   Interaction warning interface.

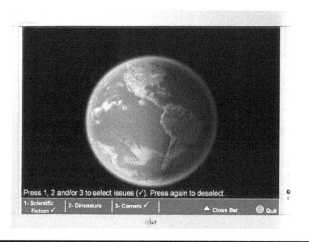

Figure 12.4   Content selection interface.

12.4.5.2.1 Information Types

Information made available about the TV program can differ in focus and scope:

- *TV content* refers to information on the TV program content, and what is being said, as presented in the subtitles, where some specific selectable topics are highlighted from time to time.
- *TV meta-information* refers to meta-information categorized as *specific*, the one that changes along the program and comprises information about the

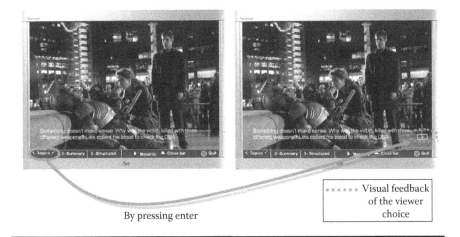

By pressing enter

Visual feedback
of the viewer
choice

Figure 12.5   Level 1: topics information.

on-screen scene, actors on the scene, props, shooting place, and so on; or
general, the one that relates to the whole program, as information about the
producer, director, actors, inspiration for that program, and so on.

Both types of information were made available on the three proposed interfaces
information levels as presented next.

12.4.5.2.2 Information Levels

This functionality accommodates viewers' changes in cognition mode, levels of
attention, goals, needs, and interaction preferences, since they will be able to choose
between three levels of interaction and detail, from less to high informative (see
Figure 12.5):

Level 1. Topics: Lower level of detail, requiring less viewer attention, probably
easier to follow and understand, where viewers are supposed to select their topics of
interest without having immediate extra information. The user maintains the typical
experiential cognitive mode, delaying the exploration of the selected additional
information in a more reflexive mode to a later time. This level only implies the use
of the *enter* button in order to select topics of interest. Each subtitle has, at most,
one selectable topic, which will appear underlined. The familiarity with previous
user experiences was considered, since underline is often associated with links. The
feedback on viewer choice is provided by a checked box that appears in front of
the subtitle. Note that there is at most one selectable topic in each subtitle (see
Figure 12.5).

Level 2. Summary: A higher level of detail, more informative and requiring more
viewer attention, where viewers are presented with immediate extra information

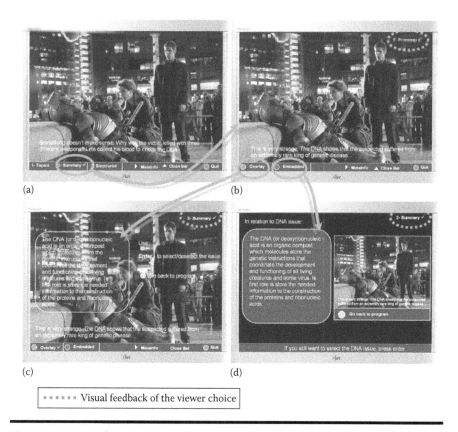

☐ ▪▪▪▪▪▪ Visual feedback of the viewer choice

Figure 12.6   Level 2: summary information. (a) Information level choice interface. (b) Interface when level 2 (summary) is chosen. (c) Summary information overlaid on-screen. (d) Summary information embedded on-screen.

as a brief summary about the topics *overlaid* or *embedded* on screen, depending on the viewers' preferences. In any case, the video automatically pauses, while the information is being shown. In addition, viewers still have the option to select that topic to generate a more detailed web content to be accessed at a later time (see Figure 12.6).

Level 3. Structured: The highest level of detail, very informative and requiring a high level of viewer's attention. Viewers are presented with immediate extra information, namely a structured list of that topic main aspects or options that the viewer may choose from, *overlaid* or *embedded* on screen. In any case, the video may pause, and the viewer may choose to get extra information about the different topics as generated web content (see Figure 12.7).

At any moment, the viewer is able to change between levels of information by pressing button 1, 2, or 3 on their remote (see Figure 12.5).

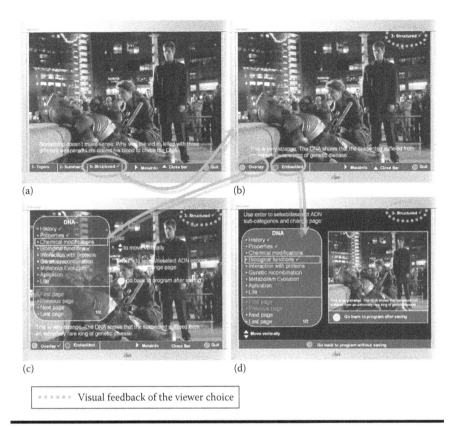

(a)

(b)

(c)

(d)

| ⠿⠿⠿⠿⠿ Visual feedback of the viewer choice |

Figure 12.7 Level 3: structured information. (a) Information level choice interface. (b) Interface when level 3 (summary) is chosen. (c) Summary information overlaid on-screen. (d) Summary information embedded on-screen.

12.4.5.3 Final Choices, Sharing, and Confirmation

At the end of the TV program, or when selected, the system presents the interfaces for the final choices.

12.4.5.3.1 Information and Device Confirmation

Presents the complete list of available TV content topics, highlighting those that were selected while watching the TV program, to be seen in more detail in the generated web content. Viewers may change their selected topics at this point, and may select additional meta-information to be included in the web content. They also have the possibility to change aspects obtained from their profile, like the device(s) they want to use in order to view the web content and the way to be warned about the web content location (SMS or e-mail), or cancel the web

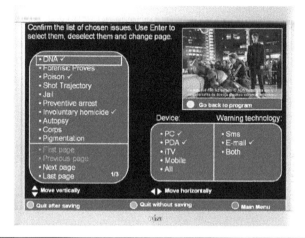

Figure 12.8 Information and device confirmation interface.

content production (see Figure 12.8). If the TV program ends, or if viewers decide to stop watching the program by pressing the quit button, they are automatically led to this interface. This interface accommodates changes in viewers' goals, needs, and attention levels.

12.4.5.3.2 Web Content Sharing

This feature allows viewers to share their web content. They are able to choose from a list of options including social platforms like hi5, Facebook, or LinkedIn (see Figure 12.9). They also have the possibility to add a text message to and about the web content (through a wireless keyboard). This functionality was developed in order to accommodate the viewers' affective dimension in TV viewing in terms of integration and social interaction.

12.4.5.3.3 Default Service Finalization

If the viewer turns off the TV or changes channel before the end of the TV program, and does not press the quit button, the system will prepare the corresponding web content with the selected issues and will use the warning device(s) defined in the viewer's profile. This feature was designed in order to accommodate changeable TV viewer's attention levels and focus.

12.4.5.4 Web Content Interface

An important part of our research goal is to explore effective ways of designing cross media dynamic informal learning contexts based on cognitive, affective, and

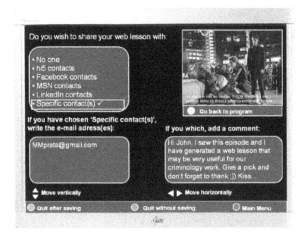

Figure 12.9   **Web content sharing interface.**

interaction aspects. Pointing the contents of the generated web, our main concern was to be able to efficiently contextualize the viewer in relation to the original TV program, providing for *coherence* and *unity*, through consistency and continuity, in the user experience. To achieve this goal, the choice of the look and feel matches the TV program aesthetics and the information included matches the users' choices and timings at the TV program. The smooth integration of different media was also taken into account [16,33].

Figure 12.2 shows an example of a generated web content for PC access, presenting more information and points of view than the original broadcast content, designed in the context of the documentary series. The left side menu contains all the topics selected by the viewer, presented by the *order* of selection in the TV program, to improve contextualization. On the CSI web contents, viewers may choose to see topics by alphabetical or logical (content-dependent) order. Subcategories of the topics are presented in the top menu.

Continuity and *contextualization* was further supported via the use of some excerpts from the original video, namely the excerpts that were being watched in the moment of the topic selection. By default, when reaching the web content, viewers are positioned in the first chosen topic and the first thing that they see is the excerpt of the video that was being watched when the topic was selected, which we believe might help creating a smooth and contextualized transition by reliving the moment of choice on TV. The viewer also has the option to stop the videos and just read the text and look at still images while navigating. As to the *video excerpt selection*, two options were made available: to have the videos beginning at the selection time (which sometimes cuts the sentences), or to begin in a previous position to include a consistent dialogue and context. Figure 12.10 illustrates the navigation in the iTV, and toward the contextualized and personalized web content.

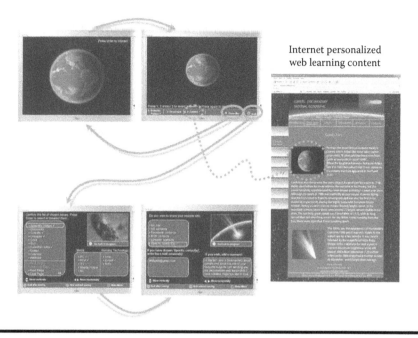

Internet personalized
web learning content

Figure 12.10 Overview and navigation in the iTV and contextualized web content using video.

12.4.5.5 Design Rationale Overview

In the conceptual framework in Section 12.3, a considerable number of variables was identified in the cognitive, affective, communication, and interaction. These variables were considered in the iTV interaction design model [34] and were used to plan, develop, design, and evaluate the e-iTV. To summarize our design rationale for e-iTV, some of the most relevant variables and design options are presented next:

1. In terms of *media and cognition*, the interfaces were designed to
   a. Support different levels of attention and cognitive modes, and changes among them, through the levels of information, layout styles, flexibility in the finalization, and the possibility to choose when and from which device to access the additional generated web content
   b. Accomodate viewers with different levels of technological literacy, levels of interest and current attention, namely through the use of different information levels (topics, summary, and structured) and through the use of shortcuts to the most technologically literate (access the options directly through the remote chromatic keys or through the directional keys plus enter)
2. In terms of *cross media design*, the interfaces were designed

a. In accordance with the devices characteristics. For example, on the iTV interface, due to the limited interaction possibilities associated to the use of a remote control, the number of navigation buttons was very small in order to assure an easy use of the functionalities that were identified as most important.

b. To be similar across the used devices. However, in spite of respecting that need of similarity to create a sense of continuity, the characteristics of each device were also considered. As a concrete example, the web content generated by the e-iTV system uses the same colors, buttons, and general look (when needed and where possible) but it also takes advantage of the scroll possibility offered through the access via PC. Figure 12.10 presents a documentary web content. When compared with the iTV interface presented, it is noticeable that in the web content shown on the PC, the navigation structure changed. However, some details were maintained in order to help creating a sense of coherence and continuity: a space theme template, the colors, the excerpt of the video in the moment of the topic choice, and the topics selected by viewers.

c. In a way that takes the best out of each device characteristics, considering what each one does best. The iTV is used in order to generate additional information to a certain program (since it tends to induce a lean-back attitude) while the PC or mobile devices were considered to present the generated additional web content (since they tend to induce a lean-forward attitude).

d. To support previous user experience. Thus, the guidelines already in use in this type of systems were followed. As an example, when a possible issue of interest comes up in the iTV, it appears underlined, the usual way to represent a text link in websites and most hypermedia systems. To provide feedback about the selection of an issue for further information, a checked box appears as a visual sign to signal that their action was accepted.

The e-iTV design options were implemented in the prototypes and evaluated. This evaluation is presented in the next section.

12.5 User Evaluation

Both genres prototypes, documentary and CSI series, were evaluated through a similar process: through low- and high-fidelity prototypes, with the same evaluation method, same number and category of evaluators, and so on. However, considering that the documentary was the first to be implemented, it was a simpler version. The results of this first prototype evaluation were used to improve the prototypes for the CSI series. Only the evaluation of these CSI prototypes is described. For details on the documentary evaluation results, the reader may refer to [6].

As to the CSI series, the first evaluation processes were carried out on low-fidelity prototypes. The collected feedback helped us to rethink the conceptualized models when evolving to high-fidelity prototypes. Both evaluation processes are described here.

The complete evaluation framework used, following a user-centered design perspective, is explained in detail in [34].

12.5.1 Evaluating the Low-Fidelity Prototypes

In an early phase, the CSI low-fidelity prototypes based on sketches were evaluated, more than once, in the following contexts:

■ An *expert usability evaluation* via heuristics and streamlined cognitive walk-throughs [49] was conducted. The group was composed of two HCI experts and one iTV expert.

■ A *viewer usability evaluation* using the "benchmarking lab studies" [56] was conducted via a group of 15 students from Higher School of Business Management: five from the human resources management degree (HRMD), five from the Marketing degree (MKD), and five from the information systems management degree (ISMD).

■ For both groups, an *affective evaluation* (details about this type of evaluation in [34]) was conducted.

Some usability problems were detected in this early evaluation phase, as for instance, the need of a more obvious back button, some confusion associated with the use of the chromatic buttons, small differences in terms of UIs were detected, and so on. The collected information and opinions helped us to rethink the conceptualized models when evolving to high-fidelity prototypes. The evaluation of the achieved high-fidelity prototypes is presented next.

12.5.2 Evaluating the High-Fidelity Prototypes

This evaluation was based on an empirical evaluation via experimentation, where viewers were asked to perform tasks that allowed using all the e-iTV system function-alities, under our observation followed by a questionnaire. This evaluation step was also repeated. The experimentation occurred in a specific room decorated to look like a typical domestic environment, a living room. It was preceded by an explanation of basic features of the system and was followed by a questionnaire to collect viewers' opinions. With the questionnaire, we intended to enrich the empirical evaluation and the direct observation. This gave us the possibility to check that the answers given to the questionnaire were in accordance with the reactions, denoting levels of difficulty or satisfaction that we observed in the viewers while using the system. Both tests and questionnaires had the participation of 33 persons divided into four groups: 3 experts (from HCI and iTV); 10 students, with ages between 19 and

53 years, with more technological literacy (ISMD); 10 students, between 18 and 45 years, with less technological literacy (MKD); and 10 persons from the general public with ages between 23 and 62 years and lower technological literacy. In order to classify and choose the evaluators among all the candidates, a questionnaire was used. The questions were, essentially, focused on their habits in terms of using PC, Internet, and new technologies (e.g., how many hours/day do you use the Internet? do you use Facebook, hi5, or equivalent? etc.).

As to the questionnaire, almost all of the questions were presented with a scale ranging from 1 to 5 meaning: 1 (strongly disagree), 2 (disagree), 3 (indifferent), 4 (agree), and 5 (strongly agree).

With this evaluation method and the participation of these groups, some of our main research questions were clarified:

(a) *Is there a real advantage in connecting these devices?* 21% of the tested population agreed and 64% strongly agreed meaning that a total of 85% agreed. As main advantages (they could indicate more than one from a predefined list): 91% indicated the possibility to have extra information about a program viewed on TV; 94% the flexibility (in terms of the possibility to see the web content through mobile phone anytime, anywhere); 82% the novelty of the system; and 76% the connection of the TV with other devices.

(b) *Are the iTV interfaces appropriate to provide an adequate support to create and follow extra web content, and are the iTV, PC, and mobile phones interfaces easy to use and understand?* At the moment of writing, mobile phone interfaces were being developed. From the questions used in order to validate this question, in what refers to iTV and PC, the most important were as follows:

(b1) Were the iTV interfaces adequate to create the web content? 10% agreed and 67% strongly agreed (a total of 77% agreed).

(b2) Were the iTV interfaces adequate to conduct you to the web content? 21% agreed and 48% strongly agreed (a total of 69% agreed).

(b3) Were the iTV interfaces easy to use? 39% agreed and 27% strongly agreed (a total of 66% agreed).

(b4) Were the iTV interfaces easy to understand? 42% agreed and 21% strongly agreed (a total of 63% agreed).

(b5) Were the PC interfaces easy to use? 18% agreed and 70% strongly agreed (a total of 88% agreed).

(b6) Were the PC interfaces easy to understand? 15% agreed and 79% strongly agreed (a total of 94% agreed).

The results obtained from (b3) and (b4) were good considering that viewers were not used to this level of TV interaction. However, it is our belief that we may achieve better results by the improvement of the interfaces navigational structure.

(b7) Were the iTV interfaces easy to read? In order to test all the details legibility, some changes on brightness and contrast were made (four levels above and below normal values were tested). In normal conditions: 21% agreed that all the interface elements were easy to perceive and 45% strongly agreed meaning that a total of 63% agreed; in lower and higher levels of brightness: 39% agreed that all the interface elements were easy to perceive and 21% strongly agreed (a total of 60% agreed); in lower and higher conditions of contrast: 39% agreed that all the interface elements were easy to perceive and 12% strongly agreed (a total of 51% agreed). In spite slightly different, these results may indicate that changes in contrast are more disturbing than changes in brightness. As a note, the time of response of the remote control was also tested in order to obtain a time of response similar to a real TV viewing experience.

(b8) All testers used the generated web content and were capable to evaluate if the interfaces were easy to use and easy to understand. The effective learning aspect of the system was not tested (if viewers are really capable to learn through the web contents). This type of evaluation requires different tests and, in our opinion, more important was to provide these extra contents with success considering that, when asked if they agreed with the level of development of the presented topics: 18% agreed and 70% strongly agreed meaning that a total of 88% agreed.

(c) *What are the preferred interface designs for the relevant cognitive modes and needs in each scenario?* 79% of the viewers preferred the *level 1* information interface in this evaluation context. However, this result should be analyzed more carefully because levels 2 and 3 paused the video, which was an option taken based on the first low-fidelity evaluation process. In fact, those evaluation groups' opinion was that the video should be paused or otherwise: "viewers' would not be able to follow the video," "might skip new link opportunities while reading the presented content," and "they would not have time to reflect about the presented content." Thus, the prototypes were not implemented with the possibility to use information levels 2 and 3 with the video playing. On the other hand, the high-fidelity prototypes evaluation groups stated that stopping the video is not a good option since they can be more interested in following the action while making the additional choices. Thus, and since we got different opinions in the two phases, we conclude that both options have perceived advantages and disadvantages, and that the low-fidelity prototypes do not provide a rich enough environment for a realistic evaluation of the interaction with dynamic media. In future prototypes and evaluations, viewers will be given the opportunity to change between video pausing or playing while on information levels 2 and 3, with the default being play, or the user preference if stated.

As to the *overlay* and *embedded* design options, in both information levels 2 and 3, 79% of the viewers preferred the embedded option, although not exactly the same viewers, two of them changed their preferences. Overlay is less intrusive for TV viewing, especially when there is not too much information, while embedded is less intrusive for information reading. Results align with this tendency to change the focus of interest from TV to additional information along information levels.

(d) *Are the web contents appropriate to give sequence and continuity to the learning opportunities created by the visualization of the iTV video (are they able to contextualize viewers in relation to what they first saw and provide further content)?* From the questions used to validate this research question the most important were (d1) and (d2):

(d1) Did the web content contextualization succeeded? 27% agreed and 52% strongly agreed (a total of 79% agreed).

(d2) Were the web contents capable to give continuity to the program? 21% agreed and 55% strongly agreed (a total of 76% agreed).

As to the *presentation of topics*, 73% preferred the selection order, 18% preferred the alphabetical order, and 9% preferred the logical order, indicating that a good choice would be to have the selection order as the default choice, and providing the possibility to change order.

As to the use of the *video excerpts to contextualize the content* in relation to the original TV program, 91% preferred the video playing and 9% preferred the video paused. Video playing will probably be the best default choice with the control to pause and play as the viewer wishes. This aligns with the continuity principle to provide more immersive and engaging user experiences, when coming from iTV, especially if users do not want to engage in more deep reflective cognitive modes.

As to the *video excerpts selection*, 9% preferred that the videos start at the time of selection, while 91% preferred the use of a previous video position in order to include a complete sentence in the video and improve the context.

(e) *What other functionalities would viewers like to have in this kind of environment?* Only three subjects provided feedback on this aspect, suggesting the provision of synchronous communication (chats). Being a new type of system, it is understandable that most viewers do not have clear ideas about future functionalities for now. Meanwhile, it is our job to devise some

It was possible to perceive a considerable higher enthusiasm from the group of experts and the groups of students. From the observed reactions, it was possible to foresee the success of this cross media application and to see how easy it was, for them, to use the three information level interfaces, in spite of preferring level 1. In fact, when not asked to use a specific information level, level 1 or 2 was always chosen, although it should be noted that this was not a completely realistic scenario in terms of viewers' intrinsic motivation to further navigate the information. As to the group of people with less technological literacy, the system was considered to be very easy to use. In spite of not having exactly the same expertise, they showed an "open mind" toward the use of this kind of new systems and technologies. In fact, and in spite of their initial difficulties, they used the prototype with higher facility than expected and, surprisingly, 70% of them said that they were interested in continuing to use this type of services (mainly in level 1) and recommend it to friends. As to the other groups, 90% of students, and 100% of experts, were interested in continuing to use this type of services and 100% (students and experts) would recommend it to friends.

(f) *Was the proposed framework efficient?* Considering that the design and use of the e-iTV system was conducted following the directions identified on the conceptual framework and that the achieved results were very promising, we have reasons to believe that we were capable to identify critical points and possible solutions to the design of iTV systems in this context.

12.6 Conclusions and Perspectives

In this chapter, the potential benefits and challenges that may affect the effective design of cross media systems were presented and discussed, along with the researchers' progresses in this area, to create cross media services in the context of an environment capable to generate extra related web content from iTV, accessible through iTV, PC, and mobile phones.

Following the directions identified in the conceptual framework, a study exploring the design and use of the proposed e-iTV system was conducted. The system is capable of creating, from iTV, cross media personalized web contents, as additional information, in order to give an answer to the learning opportunities created by the use of iTV, in informal learning contexts. Several low- and high-fidelity prototypes with interaction proposals were designed, developed, and evaluated. From those tests, it was possible to conclude that the system was considered: very appealing for the experts and students groups and very interesting to the group with poor technological literacy. In general, the majority of the evaluators considered that it is an advantage to connect these media, the interfaces are easy to understand, the web content is suitable to help contextualizing them in relation to the iTV program and providing continuity to it with smooth transitions between the different technologies tested. It is our belief that the presented study provided a contribute to addressing the identified research and design challenges identified in Sections 12.1 and 12.3, by providing new insights on how to design cross media systems in this context.

As to future work, the prototypes are already being redesigned, and will be re-evaluated, to accommodate the directions and suggestions raised in the previous evaluations and from our own insights. The redesigned prototypes will explore the video playing, as default and as an option, in the interface for information levels 2 and 3; a menu-based navigational structure common to all the devices, and making it possible to generate web contents (departure point) and to access the generated web contents (arrival point) from all the devices; an enhanced conceptual model, around the concept of a true "ecosystem of devices," that is to say, to make it possible that TV, PC, and mobile devices maintain awareness of each other and may work in a simultaneous or independent fashion. New functionalities will be researched in the direction of a more powerful and flexible cross media environment; for example, information cataloging and searching, and the possibility to edit and add user-generated content. The link to social networks and the use of chat tools will also be further explored, in order to evaluate if this type of cross media environment may provide a valuable support to collaborative learning and edutainment.

References

1. Jenkins, H. Transmedia. Video retrieved on December 10, 2010 from http://www.youtube.com/watch?v=bhGBfuyN5gg
2. Segerståhl, K. 2008. Utilization of pervasive IT compromised? Understanding the adoption and use of a cross media system. In *Proceedings of MUM'2008*, Umea, Sweden, December 3–5, pp. 168–175.
3. Bates, P. 2003. T-Learning—Final Report. Report prepared for the European Community IST Programme, pjb Associates. Retrieved on April 20, 2010 from http://www.pjb.co.uk/t-learning/contents.htm
4. Wiberg, C., Jegers, K., and Bodén, J. 2007. Cross media interaction design. Presented at the Workshop' HCI and New Media Arts: Methodology and Evaluation' at CHI.
5. Oulasvirta, A. 2008. When users "do" the ubicomp. *Interactions*, 15(2), March and April 2008. ACM, New York.
6. Prata, A., Chambel, T., and Guimarães, N. 2010. Generation of crossmedia dynamic learning contexts from iTV. In *Proceedings of ACM EuroiTV 2010*, Tampere, Finland, June 9–11, pp. 91–100.
7. Chorianopoulos, K. 2004. Virtual Television channels, conceptual model, user interface design and affective usability evaluation. Doctoral thesis, University of Economics and Business, Athens, Greece.
8. Eronen, L. 2004. User centered design of new and novel products: Case digital television. Doctoral thesis, Helsinki University of Technology, Helsinki, Finland.
9. Quico, C. 2004. Televisão Digital e Interactiva: o desafio de adequar a oferta às necessidades e preferências dos utilizadores. In *Proceedings of the Televisão Interactiva: Avanços e Impactos Conference*, Lisbon, Portugal, March 22.
10. Chambel, T. and Guimarães, N. 2000. Aprender com Vídeo em Hipermédia. *Sistemas de Informação*, 12, 85–98, ISSN: 0872-7031, July 2000. Special issue including best papers from CoopMedia 2000. Also as "Learning with video in hypermedia," Technical Report DI/FCUL TR-01-16, Department of Informatics, Faculty of Sciences, University of Lisbon, Portugal, December 2001.
11. Chambel, T. and Guimarães, N. 2002. Context perception in video-based hypermedia spaces. In *Proceedings of ACM Hypertext'02*, College Park, MD.

12. Abreu, J. 2007. Design de Serviços e Interfaces num Contexto de Televisão Interactiva. Doctoral thesis, Aveiro University, Aveiro, Portugal.
13. Lytras, M., Lougos, C., Chozos, P., and Pouloudi, A. 2002. iTV and e-learning convergence: Examining the potential of t-learning. In *Proceedings of European Conference on e-Learning*, Uxbridge, U.K., November 4–5, 2002, pp. 211–220.
14. McLuhan, M. 1964. *Understanding Media*. McGraw-Hill, New York.
15. Norman, D. 1993. *Things That Make Us Smart*. Addison Wesley Publishing Company, Reading, MA.
16. Chambel, T., Zahn, C., and Finke, M. 2006. Hypervideo and cognition: Designing video-based hypermedia for individual learning and collaborative knowledge building. In Alkalifa, E. (ed.), *Cognitively Informed Systems: Utilizing Practical Approaches to Enrich Information Presentation and Transfer*. Idea Group Publishing, Hershey, PA, pp. 26–49.
17. Dimitrova, N., Zimmerman, J., Janevski, A., Agnihotri, L., Haas, N., and Bolle, R. 2003. Content augmentation aspects of personalized entertainment experience. In *Proceedings of the UM 2003, Third Workshop on Personalization in Future TV*, Johnstown, PA, June 2, 2003, pp. 42–51.
18. Nadamoto, A. and Tanaka, K. 2005. Complementing your TV-viewing by web content automatically-transformed into TV-program-type content. In *Proceedings of the ACM Multimedia' 2005*, Singapore, November 6–11, 2005, pp. 41–50.
19. Miyamori, H. and Tanaka, K. 2005. Webified video: Media conversion from TV programs to web content for cross-media information integration. In *Lecture Notes in Computer Science*, Springer-Verlag, Berlin, Germany, pp. 176–185.
20. Ma, O. and Tanaka, K. 2003. Webtelop: Dynamic TV-content augmentation by using web pages. In *Proceedings of ICME' 2003, IEEE International Conference on Multimedia & Expo*, Baltimore, MD, Vol. 2, July 6–9, pp. 173–176.
21. CoTV site homepage http://www.teleshuttle.com/cotv/default.htm
22. Sumiya, K., Munisamy, M., and Tanaka, K. 2004. Tv2Web: Generating and browsing web with multiple LOD from video streams and their metadata. In *Proceedings of ICKS 2004*, Kyoto, Japan, pp. 158–167.
23. Miyamori, H., Nakamura, S., and Tanaka, K. 2005. Generation of views of TV content using TV viewers' perspectives expressed in live chats on the web. In *Proceedings of the ACM Multimedia' 2005*, Singapore, November 6–11, 2005, pp. 853–861.
24. Pemberton, L. and Fallahkhair, S. 2005. Design issues for dual device learning: Interactive television and mobile phone. In *Proceedings of mLearn'2005*, Cape Town, South Africa, October 25–28, 2005.
25. Livingston, K., Dredze, M., Hammond K., and Birnbaum, L. 2003. Beyond broadcast. In *Proceedings of ACM IUI'2003, The Seventh International Conference on Intelligent User Interfaces*, Miami, FL, January 12–15, 2003, pp. 260–262.
26. Obrist, M., Moser, C., Tscheligi, M., and Alliez, D. 2010. Field evaluation of a cross platform 6 key navigation model and a unified user interface design. In *Proceedings of the ACM EuroiTV 2010*, Tampere, Finland, June 9–11, 2010, pp. 141–144.
27. Martin, R. and Holtzman, H. 2010. Newstream. A multi-device, cross-medium, and socially aware approach to news content. In *Proceedings of the ACM EuroiTV 2010*, Tampere, Finland, June 9–11, 2010, pp. 83–90.

28. Dakss, S., Agamanolis, S., Bove, V., and Chalom, E. 1998. Hyperlinked video. In *Proceedings of SPIE Multimedia Systems and Applications*, Vol. 3528, Boston, MA, November 2–4, 1998.

29. WebTV. 2006. http://www.webTV.com/

30. Geerts, D., Cesar, P., and Bulterman, D. 2008. The implications of program genres for the design of social television systems. In *Proceedings of uxTV'08*, Silicon Valley, CA, October 22–24, 2008, pp. 71–80.

31. Magalhães, J. 2010. On-demand immersive-TV for communities of media producers and consumers, Project proposal, FCT UTAustin/Portugal Program on Future TV. Presented at National CoLab Event 2010, Lisbon, Portugal, September 21–22, 2010.

32. Damásio, M. 2010. iDTV-HEALTH: Inclusive services to promote health and wellness via digital interactive television. Presented at National CoLab Event, Lisbon, Portugal, September 21–22, 2010.

33. LiestØl, G. 1994. Aesthetic and rhetorical aspects of linking video in hypermedia. In *Proceedings of ACM HT'94*, Edinburgh, Scotland.

34. Prata, A., Guimarães, N., Kommers, P., and Chambel, T. 2006. iTV model—An HCI based model for the planning, development and evaluation of iTV applications. In *Proceedings of SIGMAP 2006*, Setúbal, Portugal, August 7–10, 2006, pp. 351–355.

35. Goodhue, D. and Thompson, R. 1995. Task-technology fit and individual performance. *MIS Quarterly*, 19(2), 213–236.

36. Norman, D. 2002. *The Design of Everyday Things*. Basic Books, New York.

37. Jonassen, D. and Henning, P. 1996. Knowledge in the head and knowledge in the world. In *Proceedings of the 1996 International Conference on Learning Sciences*, Evanston, IL, July 25–27, 1996, pp. 433–438.

38. Segerståhl, K. and Oinas-Kukkonen, H. 2007. Distributed user experience in persuasive technology environments. In de Kort, Y. et al. (eds.), *Lecture Notes in Computer Science 4744*, Persuasive 2007, Springer-Verlag, Berlin, Germany.

39. Florins, M. and Vanderdonckt, J. 2004. Graceful degradation of user interfaces as a design method for multiplatform systems. In *Proceedings of the IUI'04*, Madeira, Portugal, 2004.

40. Nielsen, J. 1989. *Coordinating User Interfaces for Consistency*. Neuauflage 2002 edn. The Morgan Kaufmann Series in Interactive Technologies, San Francisco, CA.

41. Robertson, S., Wharton, C., Ashworth, C., and Franzke, M. 1996. Dual device user interface design: PDAs and interactive television. In *Proceedings of ACM CHI 1996*, Vancouver, British Columbia, Canada, April 13–18, 1996, pp. 79–86.

42. Taylor, A. and Harper, R. 2002. Switching on to switch off: An analysis of routine TV watching habits and their implications for electronic programme design. Usable iTV, issue 3, pp. 7–13.

43. Ali, A. and Lamont, S. 2000. Interactive television programs: Current challenges and solutions. In *Proceedings of the Eight Annual Usability Professional's Association Conference*, North Carolina, 2000.

44. Livaditi, J., Vassilopoulou, K., Lougos, C., and Chorianopoulos, C. 2003. Needs and gratifications for interactive TV applications: Implications for designers. In *Proceedings of HICSS'03: The IEEE 36th Hawaii International Conference on System Sciences*, Honolulu, HI, January 6–9, 2003.

45. Chorianopoulos, K. and Spinellis, D. 2006. User interface evaluation of interactive TV: A media studies perspective. Universal Access in The Information Society. Retrieved on May 9, 2010 from http://itv.eltrun.aueb.gr/images/pdf

46. Prata, A. 2005. iTV Guidelines. In Margherita, P. (ed.), *Encyclopedia of Multimedia Technology and Networking*. Idea Group Inc., Hershey, PA. ISBN: 1-59140-561-0.

47. Ahonen, A., Turkki, L., Saarijarv, M., Lahti, M., and Virtanen, T. 2008. Chapter XII: Guidelines for designing easy-to-use interactive television services: Experiences from the ArviD programme. In *Interactive Digital Television: Technologies and Applications*, IGI Publishing, Hershey, PA, pp. 207–223.

48. Kunert, T., Kromker, H., and Kuhhirt, U. 2007. Navigation design guidelines for interactive television applications. In *Proceedings of EuroITV 2007*, Amsterdam, the Netherlands, May 24–25, 2007, pp. 17–23.

49. Lamont, S. 2003. An 8-step process for creating compelling enhanced television. In *Proceedings of the EuroiTV2003 the First European Conference on Interactive Television: From Viewers to Actors?* Brighton, U.K., April 2–4, 2003, pp. 133–136.

50. Lee, H., Ferguson, P., Gurrin, C., Smeaton, A., O'Connor, N., and Park, H. 2008. Balancing the power of multimedia information retrieval and usability in designing interactive TV. In *Proceedings of uxTV'08*, Silicon Valley, CA, October 22–24, 2008, pp. 105–114.

51. Lekakos, G., Chorianopoulos, K., and Spinellis, D. 2003. Intelligent user interfaces in the living room: Usability design for personalized television applications. In *Proceedings of the 2003 International Conference on Intelligent User Interfaces*, Miami, FL, January 12–15, 2003, pp. 230–232.

52. Matos, V. 2004. Design guidelines for iTV interface production. In Manuel José, D. (ed.), *Interactive Television: Contents, Applications and Challenges*. COFAC, Lisboa, p. 101.

53. Eronen, L. 2002. Early Stages of Digital Television: User Research and Application Innovation. In *Proceedings of the Fourth Nord Design Conference: Nord Design 2002, Visions and Values in Engineering Design*, Trondheim, Norway, August 14–16, 2002, pp. 65–72.

54. Lafrance, J. 2005. Le phénomène télénaute ou la convergence télévision/ordinateur chez les jeune, Réseaux, Paris, No. 129–130, Vol. 23, pp. 311–321.

55. Quico, C. 2008. Audiências dos 12 aos 18 anos no contexto da convergência dos *media* em Portugal: emergência de uma cultura participativa? Doctoral thesis, New University of Lisbon, Lisbon, Portugal.

56. Nielsen, J. 1994. *Usability Engineering*. Morgan Kaufmann, San Francisco, CA.

57. Aarreniemi-Jokipelto, P. 2007. T-learning and social interactive television. In *Proceedings of EuroITV 2007*, Amsterdam, the Netherlands, May 24–25, 2007, pp. 141–142.

CONTENT QUALITY

Chapter 13

Algorithmic Evaluation of Visual Appeal

The Effect of Content and Display Technologies on Perceptual Quality

Anush Krishna Moorthy
The University of Texas at Austin

Alan Conrad Bovik
The University of Texas at Austin

Contents

13.1 Introduction

According to a recent study, the amount of video traffic streamed over the Internet accounts for 51% of the total amount of data streamed over the Internet as against ~10% 5 years ago [5]. A large number of portable devices capable of streaming and playing videos over wireless/3G/4G networks are being produced and consumed at a rapidly increasing pace. It is obvious that in today's world, visual information, especially that transmitted over the Internet, is a major contributor to network traffic. As recent caps on bandwidth announced by AT&T demonstrate, current network capacities are not capable of managing the amount of traffic that such streaming generates. One possible solution to this problem of increasing bandwidth demand is to evaluate whether the current bandwidth allocated to a video stream is necessary for maintaining a certain level of perceptual video quality at the receiver. Specifically, the question that one seeks to answer is, if one reduces the bandwidth for a video stream by a factor of x, how does this affect perceptual video quality? Related to this is another relevant question—by what factor can one reduce the bandwidth of a video stream without any change in perceptual quality?

Since today's network devices treat video streams as simple bit-streams, these questions are almost impossible to answer. The reason for this is that unlike much of the information that is streamed over networks, the human visual system is the end receiver of visual stimuli such as videos. Since the ultimate goal is to display visual stimuli that are deemed palatable by the consumer, it is necessary to understand how human perception of video quality changes with a change in transmission parameters. One possible solution is to ask human observers to rate each and every video watched and relate these human ratings to transmission conditions. Obviously, such *subjective* assessment of quality is time-consuming, cumbersome, and impractical. Thus the need to develop algorithms that are capable of predicting the quality of visual stimuli, such that the algorithmic quality scores correlate well with human perception of quality. Such automatic assessment of visual quality is referred to as *objective* quality assessment (QA) and measures of objective quality may be used to gauge the perceptual quality of the visual stimulus at the receiver (human observer). Such measures can then be used to answer the questions that we posited earlier. QA and quality of experience (QoE) are becoming increasingly relevant in recent times. This is exemplified by the fact that the European Cooperation in Science and Technology (COST) has initiated a project titled "QUALINET"—European Network on Quality of Experience in Multimedia Systems and Services [17]. The goal of this project is to "develop and to promote methodologies to subjectively and objectively measure the impact in terms of quality of future multimedia products and services."

The way we have defined objective QA assumes that the information that the algorithm possesses is simply the (possibly) distorted stimulus that the human observes; such algorithms are referred to as no-reference (NR) or blind QA algorithms, since these algorithms are "blind" to the reference pristine stimulus being transmitted in that they do not have access to information on where the distortion (possibly) occurs. At the other extreme of such classification of QA algorithms are full-reference (FR) algorithms that have access to the original reference stimulus as well as the distorted stimulus whose quality needs to be assessed. The FR QA algorithm then produces a quality estimate for the distorted stimulus *relative* to the reference stimulus. Between these two extremes are reduced-reference (RR) QA algorithms that have access to additional information regarding the original reference stimulus, but not the actual reference. Obviously with reduced information, the complexity of the problem increases and NR QA algorithm development is possibly one of the most challenging problems to solve. In fact, although there exist a plethora of FR image and video QA algorithms (IQA/VQA) [75], algorithms for RR IQA/VQA are far fewer [46,89,95]. In the NR case, most algorithms for IQA/VQA are distortion-specific, that is, the algorithm assesses the quality of the stimulus under the assumption that the stimulus is corrupted with distortion x [12,19,49,52,62,83,88,94]. Such a relaxation of the NR problem simplifies the task at hand. Only recently have there been approaches to NR IQA that are distortion-agnostic [57,73]. Such distortion-agnostic NR VQA approaches are yet to make an appearance. In Figure 13.1, we illustrate these three different objective QA modalities.

Most present-day QA algorithms are general-purpose algorithms that are display and content-agnostic. These algorithms extract low-level features such as edges, correlations between windowed reference and distorted stimuli, and so on, and relate these measures to perceptual quality. Our focus in this chapter is not on these general-purpose algorithms. The interested reader is directed to [75,77] for a detailed analysis of these algorithms. Here, we focus on designing algorithms that take into account the display device under question as well as the content of the visual stimulus. With the wide-scale adoption of new display technologies such as HD TVs, 3D TVs, immersive environments, handheld devices, and so on, it is imperative that researchers design algorithms that take the display device into consideration. Further, the desirability of content and its relationship to quality should also be modeled for successful practical application of QA algorithms.

In this chapter, we summarize recent attempts at designing algorithms to evaluate the visual quality of a stimulus contingent upon the display device in question. We review approaches that have been proposed for handheld displays, HD displays, as well as 3D displays. We describe how generic objective QA algorithms may be extended to account for the display under consideration. Further, we review recent work in analyzing the relationship between content and perceptual quality. Recent findings indicate that content desirability masks the presence of distortions in many cases. We detail the relevance of these findings for algorithm design. Finally, we describe our own efforts in display-specific QA, and we detail databases that we have created/will create for this purpose.

This chapter is organized as follows. We explain the methods used to evaluate the performance of a QA algorithm. The field of QA for visual stimuli that are

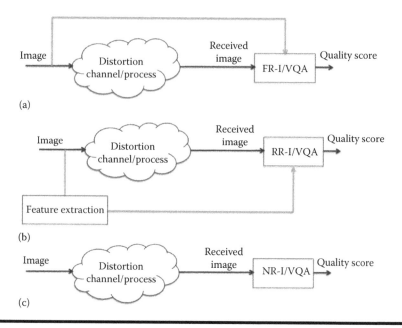

Figure 13.1 Illustration of the three objective quality assessment modalities. (a) Full-reference (FR) algorithms have access to the original stimulus, (b) reduced-reference (RR) algorithms have access to *some* information regarding the reference, and (c) no-reference (NR) algorithms have access only to the distorted stimulus whose quality is to be assessed.

displayed on large-screen devices is then introduced and algorithms for this purpose are detailed. This is followed by a discussion on handheld devices and 3D TVs. We then discuss the relationship between content and perceptual quality. A description of databases for the assessment of quality of 3D stimuli as well as one for HD QA follows. Finally, we describe future work that we think is relevant in this area of content-aware and display-aware QA.

13.2 Performance Evaluation of Quality Assessment Algorithms

Let us assume that we have an algorithm at our disposal that produces as output a perceptual quality score for a given input stimulus. As we have already discussed, the input could simply be the distorted video, or the reference and distorted video, or the distorted video coupled with some information regarding the reference stimulus. The question that we seek to answer now is: how well do the algorithmic quality scores correlate with human perception? The obvious answer to this question is to compare the scores produced by the algorithm for a set of stimuli with the ratings provided by human observers. In order to procure quality ratings from human observers, a large set of distorted stimuli spanning a variety of distortion categories and broad perceptual quality ranges that are bound to be encountered in the application phase of the algorithm under test are created. Then, a (large-enough) representative sample of the human populace is called in to rate each of these stimuli on a particular scale, for example, "bad," "poor," "fair," "good," and "excellent." These human opinion scores when averaged across human subjects produces what is known as the mean opinion score (MOS), which is representative of the perceived quality of the visual stimuli.

The reader will intuit that the subjective study described earlier could be conducted in various different ways. For example, one could display just a single stimulus (SS) at a time and ask the observers to rate the stimulus for its quality, or one could display the distorted stimulus along with the reference ("clean") stimulus and demand a comparative score for the distorted stimulus. The former is referred to as a SS study and the latter is a double stimulus (DS) study [9]. The SS/DS studies as well as various other study methodologies, along with recommendations on viewing distance, ambient lighting, number of subjects required, and subject rejection procedures before computing MOS are part of the standard recommendations from the International Telecommunications Union (ITU) [9]. All human studies for visual quality are expected to follow the ITU recommendations in order to produce the best estimate of subjective quality.

Once such human MOS are obtained for a large set of stimuli, the algorithmic scores produced for the same set of stimuli are compared with MOS. Such comparison is generally undertaken using the Spearman's rank ordered correlation coefficient (SROCC), the linear (Pearson's) correlation coefficient, and the root-mean-squared-error (RMSE). SROCC and LCC scores close to 1 indicate perfect correlation between algorithmic prediction and human opinion, while an RMSE score close to 0 indicates good algorithmic performance. One important note here is that the algorithmic scores need not correlate linearly with MOS, and since LCC and RMSE are *linear* correlation/error measures, the algorithmic scores are generally passed through a logistic nonlinearity to account for this nonlinear relationship. LCC and RMSE are generally computed after such nonlinear regression. Since SROCC is a rank-ordered measure, the SROCC value may be computed without any such regression.

Apart from measuring correlations between algorithmic scores and MOS, it is also prudent to measure the statistical significance of the produced correlations. Even if the correlation values between two algorithms are different, in a statistical sense, these algorithms may actually be indistinguishable in terms of their performance and the produced correlation numbers may simply be an artifact of the sampling distribution of the database in question. In order to measure the statistical significance of algorithms, researchers have used the F-statistic as well as ANOVA [82,90]. The interested reader is directed to [84] for a description of these techniques and to [82,90] for a demonstration of their application in algorithmic performance evaluation.

Currently, there exist many publicly available databases for such algorithmic performance evaluation of image quality assessment (IQA) algorithms [1,13,45,82] and video quality assessment algorithms [60,76,90]. For images, by far the most popular database is the LIVE IQA database [82]. The LIVE IQA database consists of 29 reference images and 779 distorted images spanning five different distortion categories—JPEG2000 compression, JPEG compression, additive white Gaussian noise, Gaussian blur, and a Rayleigh fading channel simulation. Each of the distorted images has associated with it a differential mean opinion score (DMOS),* which was computed from ratings provided by approximately 24 subjects/images. Figure 13.2 shows sample images from the LIVE IQA database and Figure 13.3 demonstrates sample distortions.

Apart from the LIVE database, there are some recently proposed databases, most of which are much smaller than the LIVE database [13,45]. The only other large-scale database is the TID2008 database [1] that consists of 25 reference images (24 natural images + 1 computer generated) and 1700 distorted images spanning 17

(a)   (b)

(c)   (d)

Figure 13.2 A sample of frames from the LIVE IQA database. (From Sheikh, H. R. et al., *IEEE Trans. Image Process.*, 15, 3440, 2006. Copyright 2006 IEEE. With Permission.)

---

* DMOS correlates inversely with increasing quality, while MOS correlates positively. Generally, DMOS is obtained from DS studies, or SS studies with a hidden reference [60].

Figure 13.3 Distortions from the LIVE IQA database: (a) JPEG2000 compression, (b) JPEG compression, (c) white noise, (d) Gaussian blur, and (e) Rayleigh fading channel simulation. (From Sheikh, H. R. et al., *IEEE Trans. Image Process.*, 15, 3440, 2006. copyright 2006 IEEE. With Permission.)

distortion categories, including compression, different varieties of noise, packet-loss, blur, luminance shifts, and contrast shifts.

For videos, the Video Quality Experts Group (VQEG) Phase-I database has generally been used to measure algorithmic performance [90]. However, the VQEG Phase-I dataset is a deeply flawed dataset in which humans and algorithms have difficulty making perceptual judgments [60]. The VQEG conducted many other studies [91,92]; however, none of the data was made publicly available to the research community. In order to overcome the flaws associated with the VQEG Phase-I dataset and to provide the research community with a publicly available, relevant database for algorithm evaluation, a VQA database as proposed by researchers at LIVE—the LIVE VQA database [76]. The LIVE VQA database consists of 10 raw YUV videos subjected to different distortions including compression and packet-loss over IP and wireless networks leading to 150 distorted videos along with the associated DMOS scores. Figure 13.4 shows sample frames from the LIVE VQA database, while Figure 13.5 shows the various distortions that the database incorporates. Other such subjective studies include those in [15,66].

As the reader would have noticed, all the databases mentioned earlier are general-purpose databases, that is, although these databases were created with a particular

(a)   (b)   (c)

(d)   (e)   (f)

Figure 13.4   A sample of frames from the LIVE VQA database: (a) pedestrian area, (b) river bed, (c) rush hour, (d) tractor, (e) station, and (f) sunflower. (From Seshadrinathan, K. and Borik, A. C., IEEE Trans. Image process., 19, 335, 2010. copyright 2010 IEEE. With Permission.)

(a)   (b)

(c)   (d)

Figure 13.5   Distortions from the LIVE VQA database: (a) MPEG-2 compression, (b) H.264 compression, (c) IP loss, and (d) wireless packet-loss. (From Seshadri-nathan, K. and Bovik, A.C., IEEE Trans. Image process., 19, 335, 2010. Copyright 2010 IEEE. With Permission.)

monitor resolution and viewing distance, the subjective scores have been used to evaluate algorithms without consideration of the display device resolution or the setting under which an observer views the content. Further, none of these databases account for interest in content and the effect that such an interest has in perceptual quality ratings. Indeed, most of these databases contain "boring" stimuli, that is, stimuli that are not attractive enough so that human attention is diverted by the content. This is ideal when one seeks to understand human perception of quality and to develop algorithms that seek to emulate such quality perception without heed for content. However, when one reaches a level of sophistication with these "general-purpose" algorithms, it is prudent to evaluate how practical stimuli (i.e., those that are interesting to the observer) and display resolutions affect viewing experience. In the following sections, we attempt to summarize this exciting, ill-explored area.

13.3 Display-Specific Quality Assessment

13.3.1 Large-Screen Displays

With large-format LCD and plasma devices becoming cheaper and cheaper everyday, large-screen displays are now pervasive in home entertainment. In this section, we chronicle research that aims at subjectively and objectively assessing the quality of visual stimuli on such displays.

Hoffmann and his colleagues performed a human study in order to gauge the bit-rates required for HD displays when critical content is coded using the H.264 standard [26]. The authors evaluated the performance of 1080p/50 versus 720p/50 and 1080i/25 in terms of perceived visual quality.* The authors utilized a 50″ plasma display panel (PDP) with a resolution of 1920 × 1080. The monitor was carefully calibrated and the study environment was set as per recommendations [9]. The lower resolution videos were upscaled to the native resolution of the monitor. Subjects were seated at a distance of three to four times the height of the picture from the screen. Twenty-one nonexpert subjects participated in the double stimulus impairment scale (DSIS) study, where subjects rated if the difference between the (uncompressed) reference and compressed/distorted video was observable on a scale of 1 (very annoying) to 5 (imperceptible).

Analog content captured on a 65 mm film at 50 Hz was digitized and down-converted to the appropriate resolutions. The distorted videos consisted of H.264 compressed versions of this uncompressed reference. Although an explicit training session was not part of the study, the first four scores from each subject were dropped before final opinion scores were conducted. Again, although the study design was not

---

* Video resolutions are generally written as *xx*F/*yy*, where *xx* indicates the number of horizontal lines (rows) of the video and *yy* indicates the frame-rate. "F" indicates the scanning type, "p" stands for progressive, that is, every row from each frame is transmitted, while "i" stands for interlaced, that is, only every alternate row from each frame is transmitted.

an explicit comparison between the three HD formats (since the DSIS was for each setting at a time), the authors draw some conclusions from the reported results. The authors state that the 1080i/25 format degrades more rapidly with decreasing bit-rate as against the 720p/50 and 1080p/50 formats. Although 720p/50 was presented on a large-screen display, the degradation curves for 720p/50 are very similar to those of the 1080p/50 videos. The authors also demonstrate that the coding efficiency of 1080p/50 is very similar to (and sometimes better than) the 1080i/25 format, thus concluding that the use of 1080p/50 for HD broadcasting is not only visually appealing, but also practical.

Péchard et al. studied the differences in the perceived quality of HD (1080i) and standard definition (SD) videos [65]. The authors used a subset of videos from that in [26] and compressed the HD videos using H.264 compression at seven different bit-rates chosen based on a small pilot study. SD videos were created by subsampling the HD content to approximate the 576i format (actual resolution = 960 × 540). Each SD sequence was compressed using 2 bit-rates. The procedure used for the human study was a derivative of the comparative method with adjectival categorical judgment described in [9]. A total of 21 subjects participated in the study and no restrictions on the viewing distance were placed. The average viewing distance chosen by the observer was measured to be 8H (H = height of picture), as against the recommended 3H. Results demonstrate that at low bit-rates (and hence low peak signal-to-noise-ratios, PSNRs), SD content is preferred to HD content. Further, the authors conclude that distortions in larger resolutions (display sizes) are more disturbing than in lower resolutions and, hence, the resolution plays an important factor in perceptual quality.

Wolf and Pinson applied the video quality metric (VQM) [67]—an FR VQA algorithm—to HD videos in [68], to evaluate its ability to assess the quality of large-resolution videos. The authors first conducted a human study using 12 30 s videos, compressed using five different software codecs and a wide range of bit-rates (2–19 Mbps). A total of 20 ratings per video were obtained using a single-stimulus continuous quality evaluation (SSCQE) with hidden reference methodology [60], where videos were displayed on a 50″ plasma HDTV with a native resolution of 1366 × 768 pixels. The viewing distance was set at 3H. The authors demonstrated that without any change in the VQM model (which was not designed with any particular display resolution in mind), correlations of 0.84 with subjective data could be obtained. Although the correlation is decent, the result implies that an addition to the VQM model accounting for the display device under consideration would provide better correlation with human perception.

Okamoto et al. developed an FR VQA algorithm based on fuzzy logic that was specifically geared toward assessment of visual quality of HD videos [61]. First, a database of human opinion scores was created using an absolute category rating (ACR) with hidden reference [70]. The study consisted of 24 human subjects who viewed videos at a resolution of 1920 × 1440 at 30 fps, distorted using H.264 compression at 6 different bit-rates (4–18 Mbps). The authors then applied an

ITU-recommended objective QA algorithm, J.247 [29] , and demonstrated that the algorithm was unable to correlate linearly with the data. The authors then proceeded to linearize the relationship using a fuzzy algorithm, and demonstrated that such enhancement produces better linear correlation. The use of the fuzzy logic is unclear, since nonlinear correlation with subjective opinion is acceptable as described earlier.

Keimel et al. described an NR HD VQA algorithm that extracts measures of blockiness, blur, activity, and predictability and relates them to perceptual quality [36]. Blocking and blur are computed using edge-strengths and edge-spreads, while activity is computed using the BTFR measure [36]. Predictability is gauged by a sum-of-absolute-differences (SAD) between each frame and its motion-compensated version from the previous frame. All features are extracted only from the center of the video for computational purposes. A variety of pooling strategies are then used to temporally collapse these measures, which are then combined using partial least squares regression (PLSR). The authors also use a series of correction mechanisms to account for content, including creating a low-quality version of the received distorted video in order to measure its resilience to coding distortions. The authors demonstrate good correlation with human perception. Since the algorithm was trained on an HD database, the NR algorithm is now capable of assessing HD video quality.

Pinson et al. evaluated the ability of the H.264 standard to achieve quality equivalent to that of the MPEG-2 standard at no more than half the bit-rate [68]. In order to evaluate this ability, the authors conducted a human study in which four different bit-rates were chosen for H.264 and MPEG-2 compression, respectively. The bit-rates chosen were such that they could fit within the allowed HDTV broadcast bandwidth of 19.4 Mbps. Twelve HD videos (available online [87]) shot using a commercial camera (i.e., not uncompressed, but high bit-rates for compression) were used along with one artificially generated sequence. Various combinations of the source videos and compression rates were used to simulate 132 distorted videos, which were viewed and rated by 24 naive observers in an ACR study. Their analysis indicated that the H.264 coded videos at 3.5 and 10 Mbps were statistically equivalent to the MPEG-2 videos at 8.5 and 18 Mbps, respectively. However, at lower bit-rates, H.264 videos at 2 and 6 Mbps were statistically worse than MPEG-2 videos at 6 and 12.5 Mbps. Thus, at least at higher bit-rates, H.264 achieves twice the compression efficiency as that of MPEG-2 for HD videos while maintaining the same perceptual quality. The authors also analyzed how increasing the bit-rate beyond a certain threshold (which is a function of the content) lead to diminishing returns in terms of increase in visual quality. Finally, the authors also analyzed the effect that packet-loss has on compressed HD videos, and concluded that even for low packet-loss rates, the drop in quality for H.264 compressed videos is much higher than that for MPEG-2 at higher compression rates (above 8–10 Mbps).

Barkowsky et al. detail a HD subjective database that is supposed to be publicly available and that has been developed by the video quality experts group (VQEG) [6]. The database consists of 9 reference videos (1080i/60) and 15 different distortion processes (referred to as hypothetical reference circuits [HRC] in VQEG literature), including compression using H.264, compression using MPEG-2, transmission losses, and transcoding losses. Not every reference video is distorted with every HRC however, and hence a total of 135 distorted videos were generated. A human study with 24 observers using an ACR with HR was conducted, and the ratings along with the videos will ostensibly be available for public use. We note that there seems to be some overlap between the dataset in [68] and that in [6].

Zlokolica et al. proposed an NR VQA algorithm to evaluate the quality of low bit-rate SD and HD videos [102]. The authors first compute a series of features including measures of blocking, ringing, global motion, local homegenity, contrast, color features, and so on. Then, using subjective opinion scores from a DSIS human study, a regression from feature space to DMOS is calibrated, where feature combination is performed using forward feature selection [23]. A neural network is trained to map the features to DMOS. The authors develop two different models for SD and HD videos and demonstrate that their approach works well in terms of correlation with human subjective judgments. The distortions that the algorithm is capable of assessing are those produced by MPEG-2 compression.

All of the databases described up to this point have generally been created following recommendations from the ITU [9]. However, some authors have argued for a different methodology to conduct subjective/human studies for HD videos. Keimel and Diepold [35] discuss the need to use reference monitors for subjective testing. They argue that reference monitors are expensive and their use in subjective QA may prove impractical for researchers in the field. Hence, they tested the difference in subjective perception of HD quality between reference monitors and high-quality calibrated monitors. They conclude that although the perceived quality ratings are generally lower on reference monitors, there is no statistically significant difference between human opinion scores on the reference monitor and the calibrated monitor.

Hoffmann et al. [27] evaluate the possibility of using a triple stimulus continuous evaluation scale (TSCES) to allow for direct comparison between various HD formats. The method consists of displaying three different HD formats sharing the same content on three separate displays, placed on a display rack one above the other. The top and the bottom display serve as anchors, with the top monitor displaying the uncompressed reference at 1080p/50 and the bottom one displaying videos at 576i/25 with either (1) a clear (undistorted) video or (2) video with impairments similar to that on the center screen. The authors then proceed to evaluate the quality of various HD formats and encoding settings using this setup and conclude that the results here mirror those in [26]. Further, the authors also demonstrate that the method is reliable and repeatable ratings for quality may be obtained by the use of the TSCES testing methodology.

An interesting study was undertaken by researchers at IRCCyN in Nantes, France, where they compared the effect of using a CRT versus an LCD for subjective QA [63]. Four 10 s long 1080i videos were used for the study, which were compressed using the H.264 encoder. SD sequences were computed from these HD videos by downsampling the HD streams to 540i. Again, the SD sequences were compressed using the H.264 encoder. For the actual study, two HD displays—a CRT and an LCD—were used, and at least 20 subjects viewed and rated these videos using the SAMVIQ protocol [42]. The authors observed that, in accordance with previous studies, LCD displays suffer from motion-blur and poor representation of darker areas in a frame. Further, with increase in resolution, these effects are more pronounced, that is, HD videos shown on LCD monitors received lower quality ratings than those shown on the CRT and the difference in rating was higher than that for the SD case.

It should be clear to the reader that although HD QA has seen some activity in the recent past, there is a lot more to be done. It is obvious that there exist many subjective databases (some of them public) for algorithmic performance evaluation. However, these databases utilize the same set of reference videos—evaluation of QA algorithms on a wide variety of content will ensure that the algorithm performance is truly robust across various contents. This implies that RAW HD video content sourced without any licensing issues is the need of the hour. Further, though there are many studies that compare different HD formats, there is room to develop databases that cater to a particular format, but allow for a variety of practical video distortions. On the algorithm development side, there does not seem to be any algorithm with parameters tailored for HD quality. In most cases, the approaches are simple extensions of general-purpose algorithms. Incorporation of viewing distance, lighting, and content acceptability are some issues that need to be modeled in order to develop a truly world-class HD VQA algorithm. Finally, researchers have generally focused on the display of HD content on large-screen displays; however, there remains tremendous room to evaluate the effect of perceived quality for HD content on handheld displays as well as to develop algorithms for this purpose.

13.3.2 Handheld Displays

Having journeyed through QA on large-screen displays, we move on to the other end of the spectrum—the increasingly important area of handheld devices. With the advent of the iphone and touch-screen devices, video on mobile handheld displays is becoming extremely relevant and researchers have aimed to study the perceptual quality of visual stimuli on such handheld displays.

Masry et al. conducted a human study to gauge the effect of extremely low bit-rates on perceptual quality [50]. Although the study was not conducted on a mobile device, the authors suggest that such a low-bit-rate scenario is common in wireless networks. Eight reference videos, each 30 s long, were selected from films and television and were re-sampled to 352 × 240 pixels. Three video encoders were utilized—a wavelet-based encoder [99], H.263+ [14], and the Sorenson Video® Coder. Each video was encoded using a combination of bit-rate and frame-rate, which ranged from 40 to 800 kbps and 10–30 fps, respectively. A controlled human study with 19 subjects was performed using the SSCQE methodology [9]. The authors then analyzed the results using objective measures of blocking and blur; they also evaluated the effect of frame-rate on perceived quality. Based on the analysis, the authors concluded that on an average, blocking and blurring were deemed to be equally annoying, in that, the subjects did not pick one as more annoying than the other. Further, the optimal frame-rate for a given bit-rate was a function of the motion in the sequence—videos with jerky motion benefited from increased quality (higher bit-rate) at lower frame-rates, while smooth motion sequences were not affected much by changes in frame-rate.

In [51], Masry and Hemami extend their work in [50] and develop an objective FR measure of perceived quality for low-bit-rate (i.e., severely distorted) videos. The reference and distorted videos are first temporally filtered using a low-pass and band-pass filter (they neglect the band-pass filter in the final implementation); the filtered videos are then subjected to a steerable pyramid decomposition [85] over multiple scales and multiple orientations. Each subband so formed is then normalized and weighted using a contrast sensitivity function (CSF). A Minkowski summation follows to produce a measure of error between the reference and distorted videos, which is then temporally pooled and transformed into a quality score. The "tuning" specific to the low-bit-rate case occurs in the CSF stage, where the parameters are chosen based on the results from [50], instead of the generally used ones drawn from psychovisual studies [64]. The argument here being that the psychovisual data is generally computed at threshold levels, while for extremely low quality videos, which are at suprathreshold levels, these psychovisual parameters may not hold.

Winkler and Dufax study the effect of transmitting MPEG-4 [2] and motion JPEG2000 [21] compressed videos over a WCDMA channel using a SSCQE study to collect subjective ratings from 21 subjects [96]. Eleven scenes from previous studies by the VQEG [90] and MPEG [2] were used in the study, including animations and scrolling texts. Videos compressed at 64, 128, and 384 kbps were then transmitted over a simulated WCDMA channel with two error patterns at a bit-error-rate of 10^{-4}. These distorted videos were viewed on an LCD monitor and rated by human subjects to produce MOS. The authors found that the MPEG-4 codec has a distinct advantage over the motion JPEG2000 codec, especially at lower bit-rates. The authors also analyze the effect that transmission losses have as a function of time on perceived quality. Finally, the authors demonstrate that PSNR is a poor measure of perceptual quality for these low-bit-rate settings.

Similar to the preceding work, Liu et al. conducted a study using clips from movies to assess the quality of low-resolution 320×240, low frame-rate 12/15 fps videos when encoded using the H.264 compression standard and transmitted over a simulated 3G channel [47]. The videos were displayed on an LCD monitor and at least 15 subjects rated each video. The quality scores were analyzed as a function of the error length, the loss severity (using PSNR as objective measure), error visibility, forgiveness effect, and so on. The authors also proposed a measure of visual quality based on objective measures of these quantities and demonstrated better correlation with human perception in comparison to other FR measures of quality such as PSNR , SSIM [93], and VQM [67].

Knoche et al. evaluate the effect that the resolution of the video displayed on handheld devices has on perceived quality [39]. The main goal of the study was to identify the minimum acceptable image resolution of mobile TV for a range of bit-rates and contents. The videos were displayed on an iPAQ 2210 with a native resolution of 240×320 pixels, by varying the resolution of the displayed video between 120×90 and 240×320 pixels. The viewing distance was not fixed, and each user was allowed to hold the device in a manner that they felt was most comfortable. Videos 140 s long were displayed on the mobile device, with the bit-rate for encoding being gradually varied from 224 to 32 kbps in 20 s intervals. Four reference videos from different content categories, such as news, sports, music, and animation, were used to produce a total of 16 such multi-bit-rate multi-resolution videos. Hundred and twenty-eight human subjects rated these videos on a binary-scale that assessed if the current quality is "acceptable" or "unacceptable." The authors concluded that across contents, there seems to be a saturating effect with increasing resolution; obviously, acceptability increases with increased bit-rate. Further, the authors also analyze the acceptability of the stimuli as a function of the content, and predictably, animation (which is the easiest to compress) has higher acceptability across resolutions as against other content categories, while sports has the lowest acceptability. In the news category, legibility of text is an important factor for acceptable presentation. Other reasons for unacceptability include object detail, facial detail, jerkiness, and so on. Approximately 10% of the subjects complained about visual fatigue with viewing videos on a small screen. Another finding from the study was that audio quality did not matter much in overall subjective video quality. Related work from the authors includes a study on the design requirements for mobile TV [38].

Jumisko-Pyykko and Hakkinen evaluated the effect of codecs and combinations of audio and video streams with low bit-rates and varied content on perceived quality [31]. Seventy-five subjects participated in the video study in which six different reference videos (from varied content categories) were compressed using H.263 [72], RealVideo 8, and H.264 [24] at a constant bit-rate and displayed on a Nokia 6600 mobile device at QCIF resolution. Subjects rated the perceived quality of these videos on a scale of 1–10. The authors concluded that the H.264-encoded videos possess higher visual quality than those encoded using other standards.

Ries et al. [71] studied various usage scenarios for mobile streaming content and defined various parameters that are algorithmically extracted from the video in order to characterize the perceived video quality at the receiver. The authors used six reference videos, including an animated clip, and distorted these videos using a combination of frame-rate and bit-rate to form two sets of videos. Using a total of 36 observers (26 for set I + 10 for set II), the ACR study methodology and a VPA IV UMTS/WLAN, MOS scores on a scale of 1–5 were computed. Viewing distance was not fixed during the study. Using motion estimates extracted from the video, the authors trained an ensemble of classifiers using set I and reported prediction results on set II. The authors demonstrate that their approach is better at mobile video QA than the ANSI standard for objective video QA [3].

Jumisko-Pyykko and Hannuksela evaluate an extremely interesting aspect of video quality ratings for mobile devices—context [32]. Context of use comprises of user characteristics, tasks, as well as technical, physical, and social environments. In their study, 30 subjects viewed 60 s videos and then rated the videos on (1) acceptability of quality, (2) overall quality, and (3) entertainment value and also participated in an information-recognition task. Such ratings were collected in various test environments, that is, contexts, including a train station, on the bus, and in a cafe. The videos themselves were compressed using H.264 at 128 kbps and a frame-rate of 12.5 fps. These compressed videos were then transmitted over a simulated DVB-H channel [18] with four different loss rates. Based on the results from the study, the authors conclude that there was no significant difference in the acceptability level or the overall quality with change in context; however, the entertainment value and the information-recognition tasks were context dependent. The authors found a saturating effect with reducing quality—error rates of 13.8% and 20.6% were statistically indistinguishable.

Eichhorn and Ni selected six reference 8 s videos at QVGA (320×240) and QQVGS (160×120) resolution and encoded these videos with the scalable video codec (SVC) [74] at various bit-rates and frame-rates [16]. A double stimulus continuous quality scale (DSCQS) study was conducted on an iPod classic with QVGA resolution in which 30 subjects rated the perceptual quality of the presentations. The authors then analyzed the ability of general purpose QA algorithms such as SSIM [93], PSNR, and the video quality metric (VQM) [67] in gauging perceptual quality on mobile devices. They also evaluated the performance of another algorithm—SVQM—that was designed specifically to assess the quality of SVC coded videos [37]. As expected, the SVQM measure did the best job in predicting perceptual quality, although, somewhat surprisingly, VQM and SSIM failed to correlate well—indeed, their performance was below that of the often-criticized PSNR.

13.3.3 3D Displays

In the recent past, 3D stimuli have found their way into the mainstream. With an increasing amount of industry attention being devoted to 3D content creation, compression, and transmission, QA of stereoscopic stimuli has become an extremely interesting area for study. Unfortunately though, much of the work in 3D QA has focused on simple extensions of already successful models for 2D QA without a deeper investigation into the problem at hand, as will be clear from the following discussion.

The 3D images/videos we consider here consist of a left and right stream, which are generally captured by calibrated cameras mounted on a stereo-rig, such that the cameras are laterally separated by ~65 mm—the adult inter-ocular distance. Disparity/depth information, when used, is computed by utilizing an algorithm that predicts disparity given the left and right image as input. Such disparity may be computed for the reference alone, or for both the reference and distorted image.

The field of algorithmically assessing the 3D QoE and/or 3D quality is an extremely challenging one, since, unlike the 2D realm, even in the FR case, we cannot have access to either the *perceived* original 3D stimulus or the *perceived* distorted 3D stimulus! While this might seem disconcerting at first, a little introspection will lead one to realize that this is true. This is due to the fact that the algorithm has access to the left and right views of the scene (and possibly associated a depth/disparity map that has been independently computed or measured), but does not have access to the 3D visuosensory experience—the *cyclopean image*—that the human re-creates. This is true for both "original" and impaired images and, hence, the problem is "double blind." The complexity of the problem, coupled with our yet nascent understanding of 3D perception and the increasing commercial shift toward 3D entertainment, makes the area of 3D QA interesting, formidable, and practically relevant.

Some researchers gauged the ability of 2D IQA algorithms (without any disparity/depth information) in predicting 3D quality [10,25,100]. Most of these studies concluded that 2D measures (such as those in [81,93]) alone fail to predict perceived 3D quality. The next step was to incorporate simple measures of differences in disparity between the reference and distorted stimuli. You et al. [100] demonstrated that the performance of 2D algorithms can be improved by incorporation of such disparity error. These results partially agree with those in [4], where the authors conclude that although the addition of disparity information (using differences in disparity maps) benefits a popular 2D IQA algorithm—the structural similarity index (SSIM) [93]—it does not help improve the performance of another such 2D IQA algorithm: C4 [11].

A variety of other measures have been proposed in the literature that revolve around a similar structure—2D QA algorithms for monoscopic QA and a measure of disparity difference for stereoscopic QA, including those that construct an "absolute disparity image" [98], those that use a multi-scale disparity difference-based approach [8], those that utilize SIFT [48] and RANSAC [20] and model contrast sensitivity [22], and those that evaluate the effect of color distortions on 3D quality [80].

Zhu and Wang developed a perceptually motivated measure for stereo video QA [101]. The authors decompose the videos using a 3D wavelet decomposition, the output of which is then subjected to a contrast masking function, followed by pooling and quality mapping. The authors demonstrate experimentally that their measure of quality is superior to that of PSNR.

There has been some interest in the development of stereo quality measures for handheld devices. Researchers conducted a survey indicating that prospective users are interested in the additional value generated by incorporation of 3D in handheld devices [34]. Human studies were also conducted for gauging visual quality of low-bit-rate videos used in mobile broadcasting [33]. The authors concluded that 2D stimuli have superior perceptual quality in comparison with 3D stimuli under these conditions. The authors also stated that face down viewing position, variable light, vibration circumstances, and diverted attention between the presentation and surrounding are challenges that need to be addressed before 3D on mobile devices attains commercial success. The European Mobile3DTV project [55] is currently in the process of developing technologies for streaming 3D content over DVB-H.

13.4 Content-Specific Quality Assessment

In this chapter, we have discussed various objective measures to predict the quality of visual stimuli—across resolutions and display devices. Most of these methods utilize a particular subjective database—either that created by the authors themselves, or one that is publicly available in order to test the performance of the proposed approach. What is missing in all of these databases is an account of how the content of the visual stimulus affects quality ratings. Some authors have hinted at the correlation between quality ratings and the desirability of content in the aforementioned studies [32]. It is obvious that "content" is extremely subjective and designing algorithms to account for the effect that content has is not as easy as one would hope. Although "content" by itself is defined in some sense by higher-level processing in the human visual system (HVS), as against the commonly used low-level features such as edges or corners, understanding how subjective ratings are influenced by content is an extremely interesting direction of research—one that has seen very little work in the image/video processing community.

A primary step in understanding "content" is possibly aiming to predict where humans look [28]. Such regions-of-interest can then be heavily weighted as compared to regions that the humans do not look at as much. Indeed, much work has gone into such gaze-based weighting of perceptual image and video quality scores [56], albeit to marginal success. The lack of success in such approaches may be attributed to the fact that algorithms that seek to predict gaze are themselves functions of low-level indicators of attention such as contrast or luminance or color [28]. In case the scene itself is "boring" (e.g., trees, forest scenes, etc.), these algorithms perform well in predicting human gaze [69]; however, in cases where the scene is interesting (e.g., fight sequence, fast action, etc.), the algorithms do not perform as well. Of course addition of higher-level features such as face detectors (which are great attractors of human attention) would help the prediction accuracy of these gaze-predictors, and ostensibly also help in better prediction of visual quality. Although this is another interesting area of research, our goal here is different. We wish to summarize efforts in gauging subjective reaction in terms of desirability of content. This implies that we do not seek to review algorithms that predict human attention using low (and possibly high) level features, but we seek to understand how the desirability of a stimulus on the whole affects perceptual ratings. Development of algorithms to predict this desirability may be of interest to certain researchers; however, our review here does not seek to describe approaches that may be capable of doing so. Instead, we take a more pragmatic approach.

Let us assume that for a user consuming visual stimuli, we have some sort of feedback mechanism that is able to capture the subjective desirability of content and the perceived quality from that user. We also assume that we have a general-purpose QA algorithm that has originally been developed using one of the above-mentioned techniques and tested on one of these databases to demonstrate its correlation with human perception, without regard for content (the algorithm assumed here is NR in nature). Given these content desirability ratings, one could then develop schemes to modify this algorithm in order to account for the individual tastes of that user. Thus, although the algorithm would not extract any high-level features to predict content desirability, it would "re-calibrate" itself in order to correlate better with the user; and such re-calibration would implicitly form a measure of content desirability.

The description in the preceding text is for one particular user; however, the description can be scaled based on the complexity of the problem—one could define desirability of a family or of a neighborhood. Further, one could define desirability as a function of time of the day or state of current affairs and so on (though in this case we are moving away from content desirability and into context and its influence on perceived quality). Of course all of this would only work in the case where content desirability has a definite impact on perceived quality, and there exist mechanisms to capture this effect. In the rest of this section, we review some studies that seek to understand the effect of content desirability on perceived quality.

Jumisko et al. conducted two studies, a video-only study and an audiovisual study [30]. Two hundred and seventy-four subjects participated in the video study, of which 20% were professionals in the field. The study was conducted in a laboratory, where a SS study with a quality rating scale of 1–10 was undertaken. A recognition task followed, and a rating for interest in content on a scale of 1–5 was obtained for each of the contents in the study. The study encompassed different genres, and videos were drawn from news, sports, television procedurals, animations, teletexts, and music videos. The selected videos spanned a wide range of spatial detail and motion. The videos were encoded using various codecs at 80 and 128 kbps, with a frame-rate of 12.5 fps and were displayed on multiple mobile devices.

The study consisted of a short interview following the ratings, where the participants were asked, "What were the factors you paid attention to while evaluating video quality?" Replies from these questions were analyzed as well. On average, content that the user was unfamiliar with elicited a higher quality score than content that the user had seen before. This result is not very surprising and is one the reasons researchers prefer to use obscure clips in human studies. This ensures that the human ratings are not biased due to previous viewing of the clip. The authors also observed a positive correlation between the level of interest and quality rating.

On average, across all videos, a higher level of interest implied a higher quality rating. Further, the correlation between interest and quality was higher when the subject was unfamiliar with the video being watched. Based on the verbal interviews conducted, the authors conclude that accuracy of reproduction, regions of interest, picture ratio, text, colors, and block distortion were some of the recurring themes that people spoke about.

Kortum and Sullivan greatly expand their earlier work [40] and study the effect that content has on perceptual quality ratings [41]. They argue that while the ITU recommendations and the studies that follow the recommendations are suited for a comparison of quality across various distortion severities, display resolutions, etc., these studies are not suited to answer the question, "Is this quality good-enough?" The authors realize that the definition of "good-enough" is subjective and is a function of time and experience in viewing and illustrate this with a couple of examples (black-and-white versus color TV). Further, the authors argue for using longer video clips than the generally used 8–10 s ones, pointing out that natural viewing consists of videos that are significantly longer than these short clips. Based on these observations, the authors design and conduct multiple experiments.

In the first experiment, 40 subjects who rented at least two movies a month were recruited and 20 movie clips, 2 min long, were used as stimuli. Each of these clips were compressed at 550, 770, and 1100 kbps and the participants viewed these clips on a CRT TV and rated the quality on a 9-point scale and the desirability on a 6-point scale. Additionally, 3.5, 4, and 5 Mbps clips were displayed as well. In the second experiment, 20 participants selected 10 movie titles from a list of 38 and these clips were used for the same study as before. Variations of these procedures were used for experiments 4 and 5.

As in [30], the results showed a strong correlation between desirability of content and quality, across the four experiments. As a function of the bit-rate used, the trend remained the same, showing strong positive correlation across bit-rates. In fact, the squared correlation coefficient was greater than 0.95 for 1.1, 3.5, and 5 Mbps videos! The results indicate that highly desirable low-quality content is rated equal to (if not higher than) undesirable high-quality content. However, surprisingly, when explicitly asked about why a particular quality score was provided, the participants failed to mention content as one of the driving factors, instead focusing on purely quality-driven aspects, such as pixelation, blur, etc. The results seem to indicate that immaterial of absence of cognition, content plays a critical role in subjective visual quality ratings.

13.5 Current and Future Work

By this juncture, we hope that we have conveyed to the reader that there is a wide spectrum of areas related to QA of visual stimuli that has been ill-explored, as compared to the work in FR visual QA. Further, there are some approaches to QA that cater to specific display devices in literature, and many of these approaches are tested on small-scale closed databases, thereby rendering any objective comparison among techniques impossible. There are a few databases that are supposed to be publicly available soon [6]; however, a set of large-scale databases that the research community at large can utilize to benchmark algorithms is missing.

Previously, we have addressed this need for general-purpose IQA with the LIVE IQA database, which is now the de facto standard for benchmarking IQA algorithms [82]. More recently, we also filled the void for video QA with the LIVE VQA [78] and LIVE wireless VQA [58] databases. In the future, we plan to provide such large-scale publicly available databases that have been viewed and rated by human subjects in the appropriate psychovisual setting.

We have already conducted a large-scale study for 3D images, and the LIVE 3D IQA database shall be made public soon (possibly by the time this chapter is printed). The LIVE 3D IQA database will be the only publicly available database that has not only stereoscopic pairs, but also "true" depth! It is unclear if this database will be public before this article goes to print, and the reader is referred to the LIVE website [43], which will be updated with the latest information on the LIVE 3D IQA database.

Other databases that we plan to release include one specifically geared toward mobile devices, where the videos and distortions will mirror real-world scenarios as closely as possible. With the spurt in "smart" mobile devices, we foresee a great demand for objective measures of quality catered toward small-screen devices, and we believe that this database will prove to be an invaluable asset to researchers in the field for such algorithm development and benchmarking. Further, we plan to release a database geared toward HD videos. Almost all HD video databases present today utilize digitized content from analog devices, owing to lack of digital RAW HD videos.* To this end, we have recently acquired an HD camera (the RED ONE) that is capable of capturing RAW digital HD videos. We are currently in the process of creating the content; the study is scheduled for Spring 2011. The database shall be made public soon after. Details regarding these upcoming databases will be posted on the LIVE website [43].

On the algorithm development front, we have already developed leading FR measures of quality such as SSIM [93] and the visual information fidelity (VIF) [81] for IQA, and the recently proposed motion-based video integrity evaluation (MOVIE) index [76] for VQA. Apart from our distortion-specific work on NR IQA, we have recently proposed measures that are distortion-agnostic (i.e., those that function across a range of distortion categories) [57,73]. Our future work in the area of such general-purpose algorithm development will include extensions of these distortion-agnostic NR IQA approaches to NR VQA, as well as

---

* We note that some RAW HD videos are available at The Open Video Project, as part of the LABRI-ANR ICOS-HD collection [44].

device- and application-dependent QA indices. We have already proposed preliminary approaches to 3D IQA [54] and our future work in the area of 3D QA will involve FR and NR measures of perceived 3D quality.

We believe that the area of content-aware QA has great potential, and we have explored this area in the past [56] and even recently [53,59]—as we seek to understand what draws human attention in distorted videos. Modeling such attention mechanisms, coupled with the "learning"-based approach that we described earlier, will lead to algorithms that are ostensibly content-aware.

Before concluding, we would like to reiterate that content and display-aware QA is closely related to the field of general-purpose QA. General-purpose QA encompasses many issues, such as multimedia streaming quality control at the end user [79,86,97]. Combining approaches for such quality monitoring with lessons learned from content and display-aware QA will allow for better estimation of end-user quality. Further, although we have not discussed audiovisual quality in this chapter, there has been interest in the field of audio QA and its relationship to video quality and overall QoE [7].

13.6 Conclusion

In this chapter, we summarized the field of QA of visual stimuli and described how algorithm performance is evaluated. We then went on to explore device-specific QA approaches for technologies that have great potential—HDTV, mobile TV, and 3D TV. We described general approaches, summarized strategies used, and hinted at possible ideas for better solutions to problems in the field. We then described the area of content-aware QA and detailed strategies that may be used in order to achieve an ostensibly content-aware quality assessment algorithm. Finally, we detailed directions that we seek to explore in our current and future work in this exciting area of QA.

Acknowledgments

This chapter was supported in part by the National Science Foundation under grant CCF-0728748 and by Intel Inc. and Cisco Corp. under the VAWN program.

References

1. Y. Horita. Toyama image database. http://mict.eng.u-toyama.ac.jp/mict/index2.html
2. ITU-T Recommendation H.262 and ISO/IEC 13818-2 (MPEG-2). Generic coding of moving pictures and associated audio information—Part 2: Video. ITU-T and ISO/IEC JTC 1, Geneva, Switzerland, 1994.

3. ANSI T1. 801.03-1996. Digital transport of one-way video signals. Parameters for objective performance assessment. American National Standard for Telecommunication. American National Standards Institute, New York, 1996.

4. B. Alexandre, L.C. Patrick, C. Patrizio, and C. Romain. Quality assessment of stereoscopic images. *EURASIP Journal on Image and Video Processing*, 2008, Article ID 659024, 2009.

5. C. Anderson and M. Wolff. The web is dead. Long live the internet. *Wired Magazine*, pp. 118–127, September 2010.

6. M. Barkowsky, M. Pinson, R. Pépion, and P. Le Callet. Analysis of freely available subjective dataset for HDTV including coding and transmission distortions. In *Proceedings of the Fourth International Workshop on Video Processing and Quality Metrics for Consumer Electronics (VPQM)*, Scottsdale, AZ, 2010.

7. J.G. Beerends and F.E. De Caluwe. The influence of video quality on perceived audio quality and vice versa. *Journal-Audio Engineering Society*, 47:355–362, 1999.

8. A. Boev, A. Gotchev, K. Egiazarian, A. Aksay, and G.B. Akar. Towards compound stereo-video quality metric: A specific encoder-based framework. In *IEEE Southwest Symposium on Image Analysis and Interpretation*, Denver, CO, pp. 218–222, 2006.

9. ITU-R BT.500-11. Methodology for the subjective assessment of the quality of television pictures. International Telecommunication Union, Geneva, Switzerland, 2002.

10. P. Campisi, P. Le Callet, and E. Marini. Stereoscopic images quality assessment. In *Proceedings of 15th European Signal Processing Conference (EUSIPCO07)*, Poznan, Poland, 2007.

11. M. Carnec, P. Le Callet, and D. Barba. An image quality assessment method based on perception of structural information. In *Proceedings of the International Conference on Image Processing, 2003 (ICIP 2003)*, Barcelona, Spain, Vol. 3. IEEE, Washington, DC, 2003.

12. J. Caviedes and S. Gurbuz. No-reference sharpness metric based on local edge kurtosis. In *Proceedings of IEEE International Conference on Image Processing*, Rochester, NY, Vol. 3, pp. 53–56, 2002.

13. D.M. Chandler and S.S. Hemami. A57 database, 2007. http://foulard.ece.cornell.edu/dmc27/vsnr/vsnr.html (accessed on November 2011).

14. G. Cote, B. Erol, M. Gallant, and F. Kossentini. H.263+: Video coding at low bit rates. *IEEE Transactions on Circuits and Systems for Video Technology*, 8(7):849–866, 2002.

15. D. Dalmi, T. Adam, and B. Formanek. Subjective video quality measurements of digital television streams with various bitrates. *Acta Universitatis Sapientiae, Electrical and Mechanical Engineering*, 4:133–142, 2009.

16. A. Eichhorn and P. Ni. Pick your layers wisely—A quality assessment of H.264 scalable video coding for mobile devices. In *Proceedings of the 2009 IEEE International Conference on Communications*, Dresden, Germany, pp. 5446–5451. IEEE Press, Washington, DC, 2009.

17. European Cooperation in Science and Technology. QUALINET European network on quality of experience in multimedia systems and services, 2010. http://www.cost.esf.org/domains actions/ict/Actions/qualinet (accessed on November 2011).

18. G. Faria, J.A. Henriksson, E. Stare, and P. Talmola. DVB-H: Digital broadcast services to handheld devices. *Proceedings of the IEEE*, 94(1):194–209, 2005.

19. R. Ferzli and L.J. Karam. A no-reference objective image sharpness metric based on the notion of just noticeable blur (JNB). *IEEE Transactions on Image Processing*, 18(4):717, 2009.

20. M.A. Fischler and R.C. Bolles. Random sample consensus: A paradigm for model fitting with applications to image analysis and automated cartography. *Communications of the ACM*, 24(6):381–395, 1981.

21. S. Fossel, G. Fottinger, and J. Mohr. Motion JPEG2000 for high quality video systems. *IEEE Transactions on Consumer Electronics*, 49(4):787–791, 2004.

22. P. Gorley and N. Holliman. Stereoscopic image quality metrics and compression. In *Proceedings of the SPIE Stereoscopic Displays and Applications XIX*, San Jose, CA, Vol. 6803, 2008.

23. I. Guyon and A. Elisseeff. An introduction to variable and feature selection. *The Journal of Machine Learning Research*, 3:1157–1182, 2003.

24. ITV/VCEG. H.264/AVC software coordination. http://iphome.hhi.de/suehring/tml/, 2007.

25. C. Hewage, S.T. Worrall, S. Dogan, and A.M. Kondoz. Prediction of stereoscopic video quality using objective quality models of 2-D video. *Electronics Letters*, 44(16):963–965, 2008.

26. H. Hoffmann, T. Itagaki, D. Wood, and A. Bock. Studies on the bit rate requirements for a HDTV format with 1920 × 1080 pixel resolution, progressive scanning at 50 Hz frame rate targeting large at panel displays. *IEEE Transactions on Broadcasting*, 52(4):420–434, 2006.

27. H. Hoffmann, T. Itagaki, D. Wood, T. Hinz, and T. Wiegand. A novel method for subjective picture quality assessment and further studies of HDTV formats. *IEEE Transactions on Broadcasting*, 54(1):1–13, 2008.

28. L. Itti, C. Koch, and E. Niebur. A model of saliency-based visual attention for rapid scene analysis. *IEEE Transactions on Pattern Analysis and Machine Intelligence*, 20(11):1254–1259, 2002.

29. ITU-T Recommendation J.247. Objective perceptual multimedia video quality measurement in the presence of a full reference. International Telecommunication Union, Geneva, Switzerland, 2008.

30. S.H. Jumisko, V.P. Ilvonen, and K.A. Vaananen-Vainio-Mattila. Effect of TV content in subjective assessment of video quality on mobile devices. In *Proceedings of SPIE-IS and T Electronic Imaging—Multimedia on Mobile Devices*, San Jose, CA, 2005.

31. S. Jumisko-Pyykko and J. Hakkinen. Evaluation of subjective video quality of mobile devices. In *Proceedings of the 13th Annual ACM International Conference on Multimedia*, Hilton, Singapore, pp. 535–538. ACM, New York, 2005.

32. S. Jumisko-Pyykko and M.M. Hannuksela. Does context matter in quality evaluation of mobile television? In *Proceedings of the 10th International Conference on Human Computer Interaction with Mobile Devices and Services*, Amsterdam, the Netherlands, pp. 63–72. ACM, New York, 2008.

33. S. Jumisko-Pyykko and T. Utriainen. User-centered quality of experience: Is mobile 3D video good enough in the actual context of use. In *Proceedings of VPQM*, Scottsdale, AZ, 2010.

34. S. Jumisko-Pyykko, M. Weitzel, and D. Strohmeier. Designing for user experience: What to expect from mobile 3D TV and video? In *Proceeding of the 1st International Conference on Designing Interactive User Experiences for TV and Video*, Silicon Valley, CA, pp. 183–192. ACM, New York, 2008.

35. C. Keimel and K. Diepold. On the use of reference monitors in subjective testing for HDTV. In *Second International Workshop on Quality of Multimedia Experience (QoMEX), 2010*, Trondheim, Norway, pp. 35–40. IEEE, Washington, DC, 2010.

36. C. Keimel, T. Oelbaum, and K. Diepold. No-reference video quality evaluation for high-definition video. In *IEEE International Conference on Acoustics, Speech and Signal Processing, 2009 (ICASSP 2009)*, Taipei, Taiwan, pp. 1145–1148. IEEE, Washington, DC, 2009.

37. C.S. Kim, S.H. Jin, D.J. Seo, and Y.M. Ro. Measuring video quality on full scalability of H.264/AVC scalable video coding. *IEICE Transactions on Communications*, 91(5):1269, 2008.

38. H. Knoche and J.D. McCarthy. Design requirements for mobile TV. In *Proceedings of the 7th International Conference on Human Computer Interaction with Mobile Devices and Services*, Salzburg, Austria, pp. 69–76. ACM, New York, 2005.

39. H. Knoche, J.D. McCarthy, and M.A. Sasse. Can small be beautiful?: Assessing image resolution requirements for mobile TV. In *Proceedings of the 13th Annual ACM International Conference on Multimedia*, Hilton, Singapore, pp. 829–838, 2005.

40. P. Kortum and M. Sullivan. Content is king: The effect of content on the perception of video quality. *Human Factors and Ergonomics Society Annual Meeting Proceedings*, 48(16):1910–1914, 2004.

41. P. Kortum and M. Sullivan. The effect of content desirability on subjective video quality ratings. *Human Factors: The Journal of the Human Factors and Ergonomics Society*, 52(1):105, 2010.

42. F. Kozamernik, V. Steinmann, P. Sunna, and E. Wyckens. SAMVIQ: A new EBU methodology for video quality evaluations in multimedia. *SMPTE Motion Imaging Journal*, 114(4):152–160, 2005.

43. Laboratory for Image and Video Engineering (LIVE). Live quality assessment research. The University of Texas, Austin, TX, 2010.

44. LaBRI. HD test database for the french national research project ICOS-HD, 2007. http://www.open-video.org/collection detail.php?cid=23 (accessed on November 2011).

45. P. Le Callet and F. Autrusseau. Subjective quality assessment IRCCyN/IVC database, 2005. http://www.irccyn.ec-nantes.fr/ivcdb/ (accessed on November 2011).

46. Q. Li and Z. Wang. Reduced-reference image quality assessment using divisive normalization-based image representation. *IEEE Journal of Selected Topics in Signal Processing, Issue on Visual Media Quality Assessment*, 3(2):202–211, April 2009.

47. T. Liu, Y. Wang, J.M. Boyce, H. Yang, and Z. Wu. A novel video quality metric for low bit-rate video considering both coding and packet-loss artifacts. *IEEE Journal of Selected Topics in Signal Processing*, 3(2):280–293, 2009.

48. D.G. Lowe. Distinctive image features from scale-invariant keypoints. *International Journal of Computer Vision*, 60(2):91–110, 2004.

49. P. Marziliano, F. Dufaux, S. Winkler, and T. Ebrahimi. Perceptual blur and ringing metrics: Application to JPEG2000. *Signal Processing: Image Communication*, 19(2):163–172, 2004.

50. M. Masry, S.S. Hemami, A.M. Rohaly, and W. Osberger. Subjective quality evaluation of low bit rate video. In *Proceedings of the SPIE Conference on Human Vision and Electronic Imaging*, San Jose, CA, pp. 195–195, 2001.

51. M.A. Masry and S.S. Hemami. A metric for continuous quality evaluation of compressed video with severe distortions. *Signal Processing: Image Communication*, 19(2):133–146, 2004.

52. L. Meesters and J.B. Martens. A single-ended blockiness measure for JPEG-coded images. *Signal Processing*, 82(3):369–387, 2002.

53. A. Mittal, A.K. Moorthy, W.S. Geisler, and A.C. Bovik. Task dependence of visual attention on compressed videos: Point of gaze statistics and analysis. In *SPIE Proceedings Human Vision and Electronic Imaging*, San Francisco, CA, 2011.

54. A. Mittal, A.K. Moorthy, J. Ghosh, and A.C. Bovik. Algorithmic assessment of 3D quality of experience for images and videos'. In *IEEE Digital Signal Processing Workshop*, Sedona, AZ, 2011.

55. Mobile 3DTV content delivery optimization over DVB-H system. www.mobile 3dtv.eu

56. A.K. Moorthy and A.C. Bovik. Visual importance pooling for image quality assessment. *IEEE Journal of Selected Topics in Signal Processing, Issue on Visual Media Quality Assessment*, 3(2):193–201, April 2009.

57. A.K. Moorthy and A.C. Bovik. A two-step framework for constructing blind image quality indices. *IEEE Signal Processing Letters*, 17(2):587–599, May 2010.

58. A.K. Moorthy and A.C. Bovik. LIVE wireless video quality assessment database. http:// live.ece.utexas.edu/research/quality/live wireless video.html (accessed on November 2011).

59. A.K. Moorthy, W.S. Geisler, and A.C. Bovik. Evaluating the task dependence on eye movements for compressed videos. In *Fifth International Workshop on Video Processing and Quality Metrics for Consumer Electronics (VPQM)*, Scottsdale, AZ, January 2010.

60. A.K. Moorthy, K. Seshadrinathan, R. Soundararajan, and A.C. Bovik. Wireless video quality assessment: A study of subjective scores and objective algorithms'. *IEEE Transactions on Circuits and Systems for Video Technology*, 20(4):513–516, April 2010.

61. J. Okamoto, K. Watanabe, A. Honda, M. Uchida, and S. Hangai. HDTV objective video quality assessment method applying fuzzy measure. In *International Workshop on Quality of Multimedia Experience, 2009 (QoMEX 2009)*, San Diego, CA, pp. 168–173. IEEE, Washington, DC, 2009.

62. E.P. Ong, W. Lin, Z. Lu, S. Yao, X. Yang, and L. Jiang. No-reference JPEG-2000 image quality metric. In *International Conference on Multimedia and Expo*, Baltimore, MD, Vol. 1, pp. 6–9, 2003.

63. P. Le Callet, S. Perchard, S. Tourancheau, A. Ninassi, and D. Barba. Towards the next generation of video and image quality metrics: Impact of display, resolution, content and visual attention in subjective assessment. In *Second International Workshop on Image Media Quality and Its Applications*, Chiba, Japan, Vol. 83, pp. 10–51, 2007.

64. S.E. Palmer. *Vision Science: Photons to Phenomenology*. MIT Press, Cambridge, MA, 1999.

65. S. Péchard, M. Carnec, and D. Barba. From SD to HD television: Effects of H.264 distortions versus display size on quality of experience. In *IEEE International Conference on Image Processing, 2006*, Atlanta, GA, pp. 409–412. IEEE, Washington, DC, 2007.

66. S. Pechard, R. Pepion, and P. Le Callet. Suitable methodology in subjective video quality assessment: A resolution dependent paradigm. In *International Workshop on Image Media Quality and Its Applications (IMQA 2008)*, Kyoto, Japan, 2008.

67. M.H. Pinson and S. Wolf. A new standardized method for objectively measuring video quality. *IEEE Transactions on Broadcasting*, 50(3):312–313, September 2004.

68. M.H. Pinson, S. Wolf, and G. Cermak. HDTV subjective quality of H.264 vs. MPEG-2, with and without packet loss. *IEEE Transactions on Broadcasting*, 56(1):86–91, 2010.

69. U. Rajashekar, I. van der Linde, A.C. Bovik, and L.K. Cormack. GAFFE: A gaze-attentive fixation finding engine. *IEEE Transactions on Image Processing*, 17(4):564–573, 2008.

70. Recommendation ITU-T P.910. Subjective video quality assessment methods for multimedia applications. ITU-T, Geneva, Switzerland, 1996.

71. M. Ries, O. Nemethova, and M. Rupp. Performance evaluation of mobile video quality estimators. In *Proceedings of the European Signal Processing Conference*, Poznan, Poland, 2007.

72. K. Rijkse. H.263: Video coding for low-bit-rate communication. *IEEE Communications Magazine*, 34(12):42–45, 1996.

73. M.A. Saad, A.C. Bovik, and C. Charrier. A perceptual DCT statistics based blind image quality metric. *IEEE Signal Processing Letters*, 17(6):583–586, 2010.

74. H. Schwarz, D. Marpe, and T. Wiegand. Overview of the scalable video coding extension of the H.264/AVC standard. *IEEE Transactions on Circuits and Systems for Video Technology*, 17(9):1103–1120, 2007.

75. K. Seshadrinathan and A.C. Bovik. Video quality assessment. In A.C. Bovik, ed., *The Essential Guide to Video Processing*. Academic Press, Burlington, MA, 2009.

76. K. Seshadrinathan and A.C. Bovik. Motion tuned spatio-temporal quality assessment of natural videos. *IEEE Transactions on Image Processing*, 19(2):335–350, 2010.

77. K. Seshadrinathan, R.J. Safranek, J. Chen, T.N. Pappas, H.R. Sheikh, E.P. Simoncelli, Z. Wang, and A.C. Bovik. Image quality assessment. In A.C. Bovik, ed., *The Essential Guide to Image Processing*. Academic Press, Burlington, MA, 2009.

78. K. Seshadrinathan, R. Soundararajan, A.C. Bovik, and L.K. Cormack. LIVE video quality assessment database. http://live.ece.utexas.edu/research/quality/live video.html (accessed on November 2011).

79. D. Shabtay, N. Raviv, and Y. Moshe. Video packet loss concealment detection based on image content. In *16th European Signal Processing Conference*, Lausanne, Switzerland, August 25–29, 2008.

80. H. Shao, X. Cao, and G. Er. Objective quality assessment of depth image based rendering in 3DTV system. In *Proceedings of the IEEE 3DTV Conference*, Potsdam, Germany, 2009.

81. H.R. Sheikh and A.C. Bovik. Image information and visual quality. *IEEE Transactions on Image Processing*, 15(2):430–444, 2006.

82. H.R. Sheikh, M.F. Sabir, and A.C. Bovik. A statistical evaluation of recent full reference image quality assessment algorithms. *IEEE Transactions on Image Processing*, 15(11):3440–3451, November 2006.

83. H.R. Sheikh, A.C. Bovik, and L. Cormack. No-reference quality assessment using natural scene statistics: JPEG 2000. *IEEE Transactions on Image Processing*, 14(11):1918–1927, 2005.

84. D. Sheskin. *Handbook of Parametric and Nonparametric Statistical Procedures*. CRC Press, Boca Raton, FL, 2004.

85. E.P. Simoncelli, W.T. Freeman, E.H. Adelson, and D.J. Heeger. Shiftable multiscale transforms. *IEEE Transactions on Information Theory*, 38(2):587–607, 1992.

86. N. Teslic, D.V. Zlokolica, V. Pekovic, T. Tekcan, and M. Temerinac. Packet-loss error detection system for DTV and set-top box functional testing. *IEEE Transactions on Consumer Electronics*, 56(3):1311–1319, August 2010.

87. The Consumer Digital Video Library. http://www.cdvl.org, 2010.

88. H. Tong, M. Li, H.J. Zhang, and C. Zhang. No-reference quality assessment for JPEG2000 compressed images. In *IEEE ICIP*, Singapore, pp. 24–27, 2004.

89. G. Valenzise, M. Naccari, M. Tagliasacchi, and S. Tubaro. Reduced-reference estimation of channel-induced video distortion using distributed source coding. In *Proceeding of the 16th ACM International Conference on Multimedia*, Vancouver, British Columbia, Canada, 2008.

90. Video Quality Experts Group (VQEG). Final report from the video quality experts group on the validation of objective quality metrics for video quality assessment phase I, 2000. http://www.its.bldrdoc.gov/vqeg/projects/frtv phaseI (accessed on November 2011).

91. Video Quality Experts Group (VQEG). Final report of video quality experts group multimedia phase I validation test, TD 923, ITU Study Group 9. International Telecommunication Union, Atlanta, GA, 2008.

92. Video Quality Experts Group (VQEG). Final report from the video quality experts group on the validation of objective quality metrics for video quality assessment phase II, 2003. http://www.its.bldrdoc.gov/vqeg/projects/frtv phaseII (accessed on November 2011).

93. Z. Wang, A.C. Bovik, H.R. Sheikh, and E.P. Simoncelli. Image quality assessment: From error measurement to structural similarity. *IEEE Signal Processing Letters*, 13(4):600–612, April 2004.

94. Z. Wang, H.R. Sheikh, and A.C. Bovik. No-reference perceptual quality assessment of JPEG compressed images. In *Proceedings of IEEE International Conference on Image Processing*, Rochester, NY, Vol. 1, pp. 477–480, 2002.

95. Z. Wang, G. Wu, H.R. Sheikh, E.P. Simoncelli, E.H. Yang, and A.C. Bovik. Quality-aware images. *IEEE Transactions on Image Processing*, 15(6):1680–1689, 2006.

96. S. Winkler and R. Campos. Video quality evaluation for Internet streaming applications. In *Proceedings of SPIE Human Vision and Electronic Imaging*, Santa Clara, CA, 5007:21–24, 2003.

97. T. Yamada, Y. Miyamoto, and M. Serizawa. No reference video quality estimation based on error concealment effectiveness. In *16th International Packet Video Workshop*, Lausanne, Switzerland, 2007.

98. J. Yang, C. Hou, Y. Zhou, Z. Zhang, and J. Guo. Objective quality assessment method of stereo images. In *3DTV Conference: The True Vision-Capture, Transmission and Display of 3D Video, 2009*, Potsdam, Germany, pp. 1–4, 2009.

99. Y. Yang and S.S. Hemami. Generalized rate-distortion optimization for motion-compensated video coders. *IEEE Transactions on Circuits and Systems for Video Technology*, 10(6):942–955, 2002.

100. J. You, L. Xing, A. Perkis, and X. Wang. Perceptual quality assessment for stereoscopic images based on 2D image quality metrics and disparity analysis. In *Proceedings of the International Workshop Video Processing and Quality Metrics*, Scottsdale, AZ, 2010.

101. Z. Zhu and Y. Wang. Perceptual distortion metric for stereo video quality evaluation. *WSEAS Transactions on Signal Processing*, 5(7):241–250, 2009.

102. V. Zlokolica, D. Kukolj, N. Lukic, and M. Temerinac. Evaluation on the selection of video quality metrics for overall visual perception. In *Second International Workshop on Quality of Multimedia Experience (QoMEX), 2010*, Trondheim, Norway, pp. 23–28. IEEE, Washington, DC, 2010.

Chapter 14

Mobile TV Content Design Rules

Shelley Buchinger
University of Vienna

Julia Wippersberg
University of Vienna

Klaus Lojka
University of Vienna

Karin Macher
Film Academy Vienna

Werner Robitza
University of Vienna

Matej Nezveda
University of Vienna

Patrik Hummelbrunner
University of Vienna

Helmut Hlavacs
University of Vienna

Contents

14.1 Introduction

Mobile TV on mobile phones is an important example for convergence of telecommunications and broadcasting services and of telephones and television devices; the mobile phone is becoming a multimedia mobile integration medium. Television on the mobile phone is also referred to as television on the "third screen" [13].

The fact that it is possible to watch television on mobile phones brings about certain characteristics typical of Mobile TV content. If television is indeed consumed site-independently, its use will rarely be free from disturbances, owing to background noise, exposure to light, and increased distractions. Mobile TV is, thus, television under less favorable conditions [7,26]:

- The screens are small, even if their quality is excellent (4.3" TFT display, qHD 540 × 960 pixels resolution).
- Mobile TV is frequently used in situations featuring severe background noise and/or other people, hence, rarely undisturbed, for example, during waiting times on the go [3,20,23].
- Television usage on mobile phones is usually (and unsurprisingly) limited to rather short viewing periods [17,25].

The question arises of how to design clips for Mobile TV in order to be viewable for end users. This question concerns two components: content-related (selecting appropriate presentation formats, dramatic structure) and creation (types of shots, editing, sound). Additionally, technical aspects of encoding and compression have to be taken into account.

Design rules for made-for-mobile content are set out in Section 14.3. This manual comprises guidelines for content and practical implementation, advising on the production and technical execution of made-for-mobile material. The aim is to make the material as easy to assimilate as possible, and to ensure that viewers' quality of experience as defined in [31] is maximized.

A fundamental premise is that viewing must not be too taxing for the human visual and auditory systems, and the cognitive process [2,11], and additionally meet time constraints [17]. Initially, at least until the audience has become accustomed to new guidelines, presentation should with familiar viewing experiences. This facilitates decoding and visuals.

14.2 Investigation Procedure

Professional production of TV content is very expensive. Unfortunately, this fact is also valid for Mobile TV. Therefore, the investigation procedure to be adopted for setting out Mobile TV production guidelines had to be made with care. Iterative methods where results are repeatedly refined and corrected during the entire process had to be excluded. Similar to most movie productions, financial means only allowed to create the clips once. Therefore, the rules had to be defined in their last and definite version before the content production was started.

First, we decided to rely on available information: Literature on users' and also experts' opinions, experiences, and visions concerning Mobile TV content were found. Fortunately, a certain amount of made-for-mobile content is already available on the web. However, the quality of this content and the suitability of adopted production techniques have not been investigated yet. Since normal users are not able to relate their viewing experience to single production techniques, it seemed to be most convenient to involve experts in our investigation.

A comprehensive theoretical background on mobile multimedia was acquired based on the available literature. Eight experts from several disciplines were asked to analyze the collected, existing made-for-mobile clips to discuss and merge their findings and finally to define guidelines for the production of Mobile TV content. Related work and details on the adopted procedure are provided in this section, whereas the results of the so-called expert viewing study, that is, the guidelines for Mobile TV content creation, are described in Section 14.3.

14.2.1 Available Literature

The first step of our research activities consisted in an extensive literature survey performed by all involved partners. Several types of documents such as scientific papers, conference contributions, or magazine articles from academia as well as from industry have been taken into consideration. For the most part, the usage of Mobile TV, economical aspects, the content, technical aspects, and results of empirical studies were described in the collected literature. Furthermore, future trends, the arrangement, legal aspects, commercials, and the general usefulness have been addressed. Less than 15% of the considered previous work has focused on the challenge of producing made-for-mobile content. In the frame of this work, the previously published survey on QoE for Mobile TV [4] has been extended by several aspects, putting a stronger focus on the issue of creating Mobile TV content.

Independent of adopted business models in different countries [19], the success of Mobile TV is still below expectations all over the world. In [33], the situation is presented, possible reasons for existing problems are discussed, and some possibilities on how to improve the situation are presented. One issue represents the lack of interesting services or content.

In [4], results of user studies carried out in different countries were analyzed. It was concluded that news, sports, and soaps are the content types that users would mainly like to watch on their mobile phones. However, it has been understood that younger consumers are more attracted by music clips than by news content. This result is confirmed by the study of Lee et al. [16], where college students in South Korea have stated to use their mobile phones for entertainment purposes rather than for information retrieval. Interactivity seems to be a very attractive aspect—in particular for entertaining content. The TV comedy *Accidental Lovers** represents a typical example for interactive content creation. The unfolding of the drama is developed according to SMS messages that users have sent to the broadcaster.

In previous studies, two major physical contexts for Mobile TV consumption have been found: on the way or during short waiting times. Those studies were conducted in Japan [21], in Austria [23], and in Germany [3]. Hence, in the mobile context, the total duration of an episode in a series, a short film, or other program for Mobile TV is also of importance. Nonetheless, there is some contention about what exactly constitutes the ideal length. On the whole, the most agreeable duration for episodes in series is perceived to be 1–3 min (and no more than 5 min), as this is long enough to create and sustain interest, but not so long that the viewer gets overburdened or bored [12,17].

The importance of other technical parameters such as the shot type [15] and the text size [14] have already been taken into consideration. Sound, that is, speech, music, and noise, poses a fundamental, so far unanswered question: Is Mobile TV mainly consumed with or without sound? Learned viewing habits, based on

---

* http://crucible.mlog.taik.fi/productions/accidental-lovers/

television being transmitted and watched with sound, point in the direction of consumption with sound. Assuming solitary use, for example, at home, the question of sound does not pose a problem even if no head phones are used: Nobody else is being disturbed when a mobile phone's speakers are used. However, if Mobile TV is used outside the home, for example, during waiting periods or on public transport, it is assumed that viewers exclusively use headphones in order not to disturb others. Interestingly, available test data is contradicting these statements [4]; therefore, the question of viewing Mobile TV with or without sound is still open. Assuming that the sound is generally turned off, Mobile TV actors would need to change their style of playing and provide a similar performance as former silent movie actors. This has been realized in [5]. Furthermore, classical sets such as the talking head of news content would become completely obsolete [34].

The question of usage with or without sound presents two new format options. It is striking that both original formats (silent film and audio drama) are forms of representation from the early days of audiovisual media [35]. If Mobile TV is watched with sound, illustrated audio dramas might be an option, that is, formats whose predominant feature is sound and whose images only serve to complement the sound. Simple images, used sparingly, would accompany those features. Audio versions of diaries, consisting of images with voice-over narration, are conceivable. Clear and distinct language is especially important here, and the images have to be designed in enthralling ways.

The second option is based on silent films: The action shown must be intelligible without sound. One possible term for this would be "Silent TV." Clips whose design is based on "silent films" can be consumed without sound, because viewers have to concentrate on images and, if present, subtitles only. No voice is necessary for understanding, and it is solely the pictures that matter. In this scenario, it is crucial that images are easily recognizable in any environment. However, it is likely that Mobile TV is more often consumed with sound since mobile users are already used to wearing headphones when listening to music.

14.2.2 Collecting and Analyzing Made-for-Mobile Content

In general, transcoded standard TV content is currently used for Mobile TV [1,14]. However, some efforts on creating made-for-mobile content have already been performed and results have been broadcast or offered over video on demand platforms. Typical examples of such kind of content are *Anna und Du/Anna and You** or *When Evil Calls.*[†]

Anna und Du is the first interactive daily comedy in Austria. After each episode, two possibilities on how to continue the story were offered to the spectators. They

---

* http://www.myvideo.at/channel/anna_und_du

[†] http://www.pocketpicks.co.uk/index.php/2006/10/27/when-evil-calls-mobile-tv-horror-videos/

Table 14.1   Overview of Collected Clips and Their Length

Genre	Number	Min Length (s)	Max Length (s)	Mean Length (s)	Std Dev
Adventure	5	68	81	74.2	5.2
Animation	24	26	318	82.2	76.6
Comedy	68	27	316	129.1	73.7
Drama	40	58	664	140	111
Information	19	61	285	170.4	73
Music	4	37	336	180	137.3
Reality show	14	50	449	162.1	124.2
Soap	49	16	265	111.2	80.2
All clips	251	16	664	127	86.7

had the opportunity to send an SMS indicating their preference. The comedy is still available today at Lala TV. *When Evil Calls* has been the first made-for-mobile horror show that started with 20 episodes of 2 min length. In 2006, a DVD has been produced.

Altogether, 251 videos of eight genre types (soaps, adventure, comedy, animation, music show, drama, reality-show, and information) could be found on the web. They served as reference for our expert test viewing experiment. Detailed information on the number of clip types, their minimum, maximum, mean length, and the standard deviation of clip lengths of each type is provided in Table 14.1.

Content analysis: After studying available literature, eight experts from different disciplines started to watch and analyze the collected content. In order to be able to verify and shape their thoughts through discussions, the experts were split in three different teams. Since one major goal of this evaluation is to collect the opinions from different points of view, the teams were not equally formed.

In detail, team 1 comprised one screen-play writer, one camera expert, and one director. Team 2 was composed of one director, one cutting expert, and one publication and mass media scientist. One screenplay writer and one mass media and communication scientist formed team 3. A senior scientist from the Film Academy Vienna, the expert viewing experiment leader, was responsible for the team building procedure and the member selection.

Each group was asked (1) to watch the same selection of 51 clips on a Nokia N96 mobile phone in the order of their choice under different viewing conditions, and (2) to identify the cases in which the observed dramaturgical, camera guidance, and cutting techniques yield in especially attractive or repellent viewing experiences.

In particular, the experts were instructed to watch the clips inside (also in a dark room) as well as outside a building, with natural (particularly in bright sunlight) as well as artificial environmental lighting for both cases, alone and together with the team members, in silent and in noisy areas, in a stationary (e.g., while sitting) and in a mobile (e.g., while walking) consumption mode.

During and after the viewing task, each group of experts had designed their own preliminary design rules for Mobile TV content production—with the assistance of the experiment leader if necessary. The result needed to be shaped as a list organized into different thematic areas. Two columns, one for positive and one for negative properties and examples, were associated to each area. Hence, the evaluators could use the assessment approach, vocabulary, or scales of their choice since they were considered to be the experts in their field.

Finally, the experiment leader merged the three lists together by defining general concepts to which the single list elements have been associated. Repetitions were eliminated at this stage. The summarized version contained some contradictions, which had been emphasized. This summarized version was then reviewed by all experts. The contradicting elements were discussed: Different authors explained their motivation and meaning to find a common and consistent view on the topic. Finally, the design rules have been reduced to an acceptable and readable size.

14.3 Guidelines for Mobile TV Content Creation

The production guidelines presented in the following text represent the discussed, merged, and condensed result of the expert viewing test described in Section 14.2.2 supplemented by their knowledge acquired during the literature analysis described in Section 14.2.1. In order to provide practical examples that might help the reader to visualize the mentioned positive or negative effects of the experts' suggestions, the title of clips available on the web are mentioned in the text within quotes.

Single expert statements are not included in this document because it would exceed the available space for this chapter. All the collected statements have been assigned to four major categories that seem to be most important for Mobile TV content production: (1) image and camera, (2) editing, (3) sound, and (4) dramatization and genres. We would like to additionally mention that these guidelines cannot guarantee the attractiveness of a clip for the users. The idea behind each script and setting will still play the essential role. These rules should help the producer to avoid unnecessary errors that might be responsible for the rejection of certain attractive contents, for example, because they are tiring to watch.

14.3.1 Image: Camera

When creating design rules, it is crucial to take into account the reduced size of the display the videos will be watched on. Today, several phones with larger display size than the one of the Nokia N96 are already available on the market. But still, with respect to watching standard television, their sizes remain small. Hence, our guidelines are likely to remain equally valid for 3.5 in. screens. However, the consumption of Mobile TV content on tablets might represent a different case. Unfortunately, at the time the expert viewing test had been performed, no such devices had been available on the market. This aspect represents an open issue to be addressed within future work.

In the following, not all possible parameters related to image and camera are taken into account. Only a selection of aspects that have to be estimated by the experts to be most relevant for the creation of Mobile TV content have been extracted. They formulated suggestions related to (1) contrast and light, (2) text on the screen, (3) screen layout, (4) shots, and (5) movements within the image.

Contrast / light: Clear color contrasts and black-and-white footage are easy to be seen on a small screen, whereas night shots are generally difficult to comprehend. Viewers are prevented from recognizing images that are too dark or too light if there is much light reflection, or if the environment is too dark. It is, therefore, crucial to pay heed to contrasts and corresponding lighting. High color saturation is more agreeable to the eye, and black-and-white materials that are rich in contrast also result in a pleasant viewing experience, although shades of gray should be used with caution (positive example *Little Devil*).

In terms of light and sound, interior shots (in rooms or in a studio) are probably easiest to create, and hence to consume (positive examples *Clean Slate*,* *Forget the Rules*[†]). Careful lighting is always highly important, but particularly for Mobile TV content the central object always has to be illuminated well because of the small screen and possible environmental disturbances. In a mobile consumption scenario, it is usually not possible to make out persons standing against the light or whose faces are supposed to be perceived dimly. Effects such as strobe lighting or flashlights are perceived as extremely intrusive, as they obscure the characters and create an atmosphere of disquiet (negative example *Forget the Rules*).

Light conditions cause particular problems when viewers attempt to assimilate videos in bright environments (in the sunshine). One option for improvement would be to use corresponding lighting during filming, or another solution could be found in the mobile devices, so that the screen contrast automatically adapts to the environment in order to achieve an optimal image.

The backdrop should not form a distraction, and be kept as simple as possible and not contain too much color. Protagonists should be clearly delineated against the background (positive example *Stephen King's N*[‡]): The heads are drawn slightly lighter compared to the rest of the body. This results in a higher contrast and makes the depiction easily distinguishable—even when watched in sunlight).

---

* http://www.youtube.com/user/owwzone
[†] http://www.forgettherules.com/
[‡] http://www.youtube.com/watch?v=OCEkgM3Kp_4

A white or light-colored background with boldly colored figures is always beneficial, whereas a busy colorful background and busy costumes are perceived as being disruptive. When choosing costumes, one must opt for garments that form a visual contrast to the environment and the background. This can support quick recognizability of the figures. In principle, it is recommended to use dark backgrounds and light persons or faces. Things such as very dark backgrounds or shadows on faces are awkward to see. Recognizability represents an important issue for any content production. However, in Mobile TV it is of even higher importance because of the short clip duration. More precisely, if the entire clip duration is, for example, 1 min the available time for user's orientation is reduced to a few seconds only. Hence, it seems convenient to use clearly recognizable locations. A similar set during each episode of a series ensures easier orientation (positive example *Forget the Rules*: the series always starts on the same premises, which creates a familiar environment; this prevents location changes from distracting viewers from the central characters and the plot sequence).

Text on the screen: Material is often supported and complemented by superimposed writing. Text may be used for titles, as a comprehension tool or for subtitles. It can also form the missing link if, despite all efforts, information gets lost on the image or sound level.

Short sentences and a distinctive sans serif font are best; playful or fragile fonts are difficult to read (negative example *Sofia's Diary**: the writing is far too playful and curly). The font size should be between 1/5 and 1/4 of the size of the screen, and the height of the letters should be between 40 and 80 pixels in digital video (DV) and between 70 and 150 pixels in high definition (HD; positive examples *Girl Friday,*[†] *Stephen King's N, Anna und Du*). The font size for titles should measure approximately 2/5 of the screen's diagonal.

Good contrast also has to be maintained for inserted writing: black script is hard to perceive or even illegible except against a pure white background, even when the letters are fairly large (negative example *When Evil Calls, The GYM*[‡]). On the other hand, light colored writing against a dark background is much more legible. The black bar below the 16:9 image can be used for this purpose. When text is being shown on paper, this absolutely has to be enlarged to fit the screen in order to be properly legible (positive example *Stephen King's N*: anything written on sheets of paper is also shown in close-up. Shadows, movement within text, or animated scripts are generally undesirable. If animated text is to be used, it has to appear gradually or one has to zoom in on it slowly. It is preferable to leave the writing up on the screen for longer instead. Maps are a special case for script and graphics. Maps are particularly difficult to see on displays. If a map is required, for example, on a

---

* http://vimeo.com/3062813
† http://vimeo.com/16190895
‡ http://vimeo.com/8243302

news program, one should definitely enlarge and show the relevant details (negative example *Highly Dubious News**).

Shots: Due to the display restrictions, extremely long shots cannot be used. Detailed long shots are also problematic because small, distant objects blur together. Medium close-ups and close-ups work better (e.g., *Clean Slate*). The recommended shots are thus close-ups, medium close-ups, and medium shots. The aim should be to produce clearly visible situations; important characters and scenes should be shown in close-up or medium close-up, as otherwise there is a risk of details being lost. The maximum shot size that still allows the viewer to follow the action is the medium shot. We observed that a typical duration for a medium shot presentation is about 5–15 s long. Generally, it is best to work mainly with medium close-ups [15,32].

Stationary television clips transformed for Mobile TV without a change of concept attract negative attention. What looks majestic on big-screen television or on a cinema screen can easily look puny on a mobile phone display and is hard to identify. The recognition of elements might be improved by using high resolutions but the sensation caused by the small size of the content can only be avoided by using larger screens. Situations that are easy to grasp, that is, the presented content format is familiar to the viewer, constitute an exception to this rule, for example, an establishing shot: a band at a performance (e.g., *Anna und Du/Anna and You*) or a tram journey (e.g., *Girl Friday*). Close-up shots of heads open up the material and relax the eyes of the viewer because there is no struggle to make out all the details. Furthermore, this does not distract from the essence but directs the recipient's focus toward a single aspect: the central figure (positive example: *THMBNLS*[†]).

Over-the-shoulder shots look rather good on a large television screen, but those types of shots are disruptive on a small display. Persons with their backs turned to the camera are unnecessary, as they merely obscure the more important elements (negative example *When Evil Calls*).

Movement within the image: A video contains several types of motion: (1) moving content elements, for example, running persons or a car race, (2) camera work, depending on the velocity of the camera movement, for example, during a pan or tilt, and (3) scene changes. Recognition is difficult when the image shows too much or rapid movement. The image quality deteriorates with rapid movement and soon becomes unacceptable for the user. Images are pixelated and blurred, and viewers are unable to discern much of what is shown on the screen. This is due to the fact that high-motion clips, for example, sports or action movies, require more encoding bit rate to obtain the same video quality than low motion clips, for example, a news speaker. Since available transmission bandwidth for Mobile TV is generally limited, high-motion videos may contain more compression artifacts.

---

* http://vimeo.com/8566932
† http://vimeo.com/20057670

To keep the amount of motion within certain bounds, camera work should be slow and steadier than average, for example, for standard TV. Panning, tilting, and zooming should also be simple, that is, only one type of movement using only a small angle, and complicated shots with excessive movement in the picture ought to be avoided.

Slow motion is an appropriate style in this context. It is particularly useful for action sequences and leads to better spatial orientation and comprehension. Moderate track-in and track-out movements promise to make shots recognizable, whereas handheld camera shots are less beneficial. Thus, a tripod should be used at all times. Since the mobile phone already wobbles in the viewer's hand, "wobbly" shots would lead to "double wobbling," seriously impairing intelligibility. It is, therefore, problematic to depict unavoidable movements such as flashing emergency lights, falling snow, and flowing water.

The low resolution of mobile phone displays waives any need to use sophisticated recording equipment. However, it makes sense to use high-quality lenses, which allow to vary the definition of the image. In general, the definition of the image should be rather low.

14.3.2 Editing

Classic, that is, invisible, editing is usually best. For stories, soaps, and news, a cut every 2 s (on average) is easy on the eye. For music videos, dance scenes, short action/fight scenes can certainly contain faster cuts (several per second). In contrast to standard TV production, such sequences should never last too long (20–30 s maximum), and longer close-ups, etc., should resume immediately afterward.

A change of camera axis is generally not advantageous. It should always remain on the right optical axis to guarantee effortless orientation. Compared to a large screen, the small display is already significantly more prone to causing disorientation. On the other hand, this technique can be used to support the action to signal disorientation and to build up the pace. The classic left-right rules of cinema and TV do not have to be adhered to the same degree when it comes to spatial orientation. The language of film is evolving toward more associative editing, abbreviated plot depiction (especially with Mobile TV), and emancipation from causally constrained storytelling that is tied to physical space. More and more frequently only "highlights" are being picked out without regard to causal sequences.

This generates an increased scope for parallel plots, as viewers can jump between different locations and characters. The locations and characters just have to be clearly distinguishable from one another, for example, by using expressive symbols. A difference in light ambience can also be helpful (positive example *Traffic*,* where each plot thread/location has its own color code).

---

* http://vimeo.com/5362466

14.3.3 Sound

Sound should be used sparingly and pointedly: few dialogues, no parallel stream, little noise or music. To create a harmonic and realistic atmosphere, noise related to background content elements, for example, the blowing of wind or rumors of leaves, is usually added to Standard TV clips. In the case of Mobile TV, important information carried by one sound-emitting source must not be obscured by others. This can be achieved, for example, by using only marginal or no background noise whenever an actor is talking.

Good sound quality is crucial in Mobile TV, as much is already lost through low-quality headphones or interference through noisy surroundings. Furthermore, the dynamic volume has to be adapted to the mobile phone, that is, the volume range between loud and soft sounds should not be too wide, to avoid having to continually adjust the phone volume. An alternative strategy to the use of noise-blocking earphones that fully isolate the users from their surroundings could consist in adopting an automatic sound setting adjustment in respect to the experienced environmental conditions [26]. Every environment has its own optimal dynamical profile considering to environmental noise (loud street, living room, quiet cinema) and content source (TV, cinema audio installation, headphones). First, the nomadic behavior of mobile content consumers causes that these consumers are confronted with noisy and not so noisy environments. The environmental noise must be masked by a signal on the headphones with a larger energy density then this noise. Increasing this energy density can be done by decreasing (compressing) the dynamic range of the content, single or multiband. Multiband compression can be used when environmental noise properties must be adapted. Second, too big a fluctuation in the energy density is not only annoying when noise is interfering during quiet scenes, but is also highly uncomfortable. The goal is that each content item (clip, program, file) must have an average loudness to get rid of sudden loudness changes while zapping or program changes (e.g., scene changes). Therefore, the European Broadcast Union (EBU) describes an LRA (loudness range) and a loudness anchor at -23 LUFS (loudness unit full scale) in dB in the EBU R128 recommendation (or loudness normalization). In the past, LUFS was called LKFS by ITU-R, described in ITU-R BS.1770-1 recommendation. Not only broadcasters can implement this, but also mobile phones should be able to auto-level the content they have (e.g., mp3 files).

Sound often skips and exhibits static, so it is important to ensure loud and clear sound mixing on the video, so that it is not necessary to maximize the sound volume just to achieve intelligible sound. In Standard TV content, sound plays an essential role in semantics. However, its effect for Mobile TV is limited due to a frequent use of low-quality headphones or due to environmental disturbances. Hence, a loud and clear sound mixing represents the most essential condition.

Sounds supporting the action have to be definite and significant. Pointless background noises often hinder comprehension, especially during dialogue. Background noises should, therefore, be avoided as a matter of principle. They merely interfere with the spoken text and make it unintelligible. Additional noises such as from a television do not create a richer atmosphere but act as annoying background noises that make it impossible to hear central characters' voices, etc. Water is a particularly detrimental background noise. Faint, quiet sounds, designed to enhance the atmosphere, are not appropriate for Mobile TV because they quickly get drowned out by ambient noise. A selective use of music might constitute an alternative. The selection of the type of music strongly depends on the genre and the story. Music should be used less frequently than in Standard TV movies, or only when no other sound-emitting source is active and its duration shorter.

The sound arrangement has to be distinct: different sound levels are to be separated and treated independently (dialogue, music, noises, voice-over). Whether modern sound systems such as Dolby Surround will be used much in Mobile TV is an open question.

Until now, sound properties addressing speech, music, and noise all together has been discussed. However, during the expert viewing study described in Section 14.2.2 statements on specific areas, that is, language, music, and old formats, have been collected and the result is presented in the following text.

Language: Spoken language should favor recognizable voices with clear, distinctive, and loud enough diction. They should be easy to tell apart by their timbre and, therefore, be highly identifiable. Parallel conversations and deep voices are difficult to understand (negative examples *Dubplate Drama**). Artistic gimmicks like whispering are counterproductive (negative example *Shame*†) because they might not be intelligible and, therefore, be perceived as annoying by the users.

In case of Mobile TV, sound perception is likely to be subject to several disturbances. Experts have noticed that it is nearly impossible to follow quick dialogue spoken by characters facing away from the camera. Since lip reading in general (also in case of Standard TV clips) significantly contributes to comprehension, it is of even higher importance that the characters' face is clearly visible when the screen is small.

It may be best to steer clear of original sound material as the low sound quality makes it laborious to distinguish between competing noises. For several content types, a narrator in the background (voice-over) presents an excellent alternative to actors who speak. For Mobile TV content production, this narrative option should be considered also in cases where it is usually considered to be less appealing (e.g., Standard TV). Viewers pay more attention to the plot and to what the narrator is saying (positive example *Foreplay*‡). Inner monologue works equally well as a voice-over, because it makes it easier for viewers to identify with the characters.

Music: Deep voices (and the bass register in general) are lost due to the low volume capacity of mobile phone speakers, or they sound indistinct, diluted, or distorted,

---

* http://vimeo.com/8076017
† http://www.chickenfactory.co.uk/shortspage.html
‡ http://www.youtube.com/watch? v=UkIE5Uu0Jkw

especially in combination with music with low frequencies. High notes and voices are not necessarily more agreeable, but are, on the whole, easier to understand.

Background music is subject to the same limitations as background noise: it is distracting and interferes with the essence of the action. Music should not be employed in lieu of atmosphere; a selective use of it, however, can be a relaxing break from spoken word or information.

14.3.4 Dramatization and Genres

Buildup of suspense: The short duration and assorted technical limitations make it especially challenging to develop tension. While a loss of suspense has to be avoided, the dramatic buildup must not be too complex either.

Naturally, an episode of a series has to build suspense; otherwise nobody wants to watch the next episode. To maximize the viewers' curiosity, each episode should, therefore, end with a cliff-hanger. Suspense should, however, contain an element of relaxation. Too much character development or plot advancement in a single episode may overstrain the viewer. This entails a rush from one suspenseful moment to the next without any opportunity to digest the material. The episodes must, therefore, not be overloaded with too much material.

Opening credits, commonly used in normal TV, should be avoided in Mobile TV. Opening credits that last more than 5 s are basically a waste of time (negative example *Crime Scene*). This time would be better spent on a recap, so one should simply employ a logo at the beginning of the episode to identify the series. The recap should be brief and succinct and last 15 s at the most.

The dramatization of content that is produced especially for Mobile TV (e.g., mobisoaps, mobile news) should focus on essential content. One would assume that there will be fewer story threads than in conventional television. Stereotypes and clichés as well as simplification support the decoding of highly abbreviated narratives. Characters are pared down to their basic significant traits [35]. There is no reason to expect any major comprehension problems on the viewers' part, as they are already familiar with highly abbreviated narratives through advertising and jingles, making this format a cultural standard. One may expect further developments here, as it takes a while for media to infiltrate people's viewing habits. When considering the fact that existing Mobile TV spin-offs such as *24*,* *Stephen King's N*, or *Diário de Sofia* experience a certain success, it seems to be likely that compressed versions of familiar formats will become established first. Furthermore, by building on those, several specific parameters of Mobile TV will probably emerge.

Screen layout: If the display additionally shows another smaller screen (e.g., a TV or computer screen), this should be enlarged to fit the display. Otherwise, space is wasted "unnecessarily": If what is on the screen is relevant, it might as well be shown in close-up. If a clip is shown on a TV screen, several objects can be shown to enrich

---

* http://www.24.tvheaven.com/conspiracy.htm

the atmosphere of the scene, but in the case of Mobile TV it is always a disadvantage to not use the entire display for the most important element. The screen is small already, so it is important to fully use the available space for the most significant part of the picture to facilitate the users' comprehension. Split screens do not make sense due to the reduced screen size, although some series do use them. Dividing the screen merely makes it more challenging to decipher what is shown.

Genres: There is the basic question about which genres are suited to Mobile TV. In our opinion, all short dramatized materials are suitable. This is particularly true for materials that are suited for Mobile TV based on their nature, especially their inherent length, and that can be interrupted and resumed any time without affecting comprehension (e.g., music videos, comedy clips, funny home videos of mishaps, and pornography). News of all types are equally suited, as viewers are already familiar with short news segments. These formats can be transmitted as stand-alone content. Stationary television content can be condensed or edited for Mobile TV, and may function as a teaser, preview, or summary. Summaries of films and series raise questions of copyright that have to be resolved on an individual basis.

News: News programs work rather well on Mobile TV because they deliver all relevant daily news to the viewer in a limited amount of time, for example, *TV 100*,* the news in 100 s. It has the advantage that, if necessary, the viewer can merely listen and still absorb the important information. Clarity of expression and good sound quality are, therefore, paramount. The presenter is often of marginal importance and does not have to be shown in close-up, as it is only his narration that counts (similar to voice-over); in fact, they need not be shown at all. The news images should at any rate be much larger than the presenter (positive and negative example *Highly Dubious News*).

Sports: Sports broadcasts will rarely show entire matches due to the short attention span inherent to Mobile TV usage, and will tend to show highlights only (goals, victories, etc.). Since "normal speed" may be too fast for the small display, slow motion shots are often advisable. It is, however, conceivable that special or exceptionally exciting competitions might be viewed in full length. A challenge is posed by sports that are dominated by a single color due to the venue (green for ball games, white for skiing), or where a small ball moves around an extended area (e.g., football, tennis, hockey).

Series, adaptations, and spin-offs: Series work well if they do not require too much (prior) knowledge to follow the plot; also, it is difficult to convey complex plots. Humorous formats appear to be better suited to Mobile TV because of their routine exaggeration of characters and manipulation of clichés. There is no lengthy explanation of the circumstances or characters, which facilitates immersion for the viewer.

Realistic psychological drama series are, therefore, not suited for Mobile TV, simply because its limitations make it difficult to be turned to a profound story and to develop empathy for complex characters.

---

* http://fm100.gr/portal/index.php/webtv

In principle, it seems a good idea to adapt existing programs from Standard TV or to create spin-offs (there is an existing fan base, viewers are familiar with the setting and characters, and, unlike programs produced specifically for Mobile TV, they do not require a serious readjustment from the viewer). The short duration, however, neither allows for any complex psychology of characters, nor for elaborate plot development, and consequently the result may be perceived as shallow and unsatisfactory. Additionally, familiarity with the plot and the central protagonist is usually presupposed [30].

In line with "customary" dramatizations of short films, it is best to do without too many location changes and temporal leaps. The small display prevents their "usual" impact, and the viewer is supposed to be drawn into a dense and enthralling situation that is created in only a few minutes.

Animated films, cartoons, and comics: Cartoons and animated films in children's television are appropriate not only due to their short duration but also due to their visual storytelling style that is supported by judicious sound design. Many short animated films are rather action-oriented and use easily distinguishable characters, making this genre highly suitable for Mobile TV.

An interesting new hybrid in the Mobile TV sector is the series *Stephen King's N*, which has arisen from collaboration between Stephen King and Marvel Comics. Stephen King's story is told through fixed comic images (limiting movement to mimic camera motion, e.g., track-in, zoom, panning). The comic style perfectly fits to the requirements of Mobile TV, bestowing novel and exciting aesthetics. It furthermore permits light and color contrasts to be adapted so that perception does not suffer from dark environments, etc. Strong outlines help to make characters clearly visible. Also, the fixed images reduce the viewers' risk of missing something important if they briefly glance away.

Characters: One or two central characters and two to four minor characters are recommended, using more might turn out to be problematic. In Section 14.3.1, it is mentioned that shots from close-up to medium should be generally used. On small screens, at most two persons can be presented within such a shot type. Consequently, the number of characters needs to be limited.

Ideally, all central characters should be present from the very first episode and be given an introduction. In Mobile TV, time constraints preclude the usual exposition of full-length films, that is, spending time to introduce the characters and the circumstances, before a conflict might be developed. It is necessary to get straight to the point in order to grab the viewer and kindle their desire to watch to the end of the episode, as well as the next one. Most series, therefore, opt to delve into the action directly with a conflict, and to gradually incorporate information normally provided through exposition (positive example: the Mobile TV spin-off of *24*). However, it is important to do without heavy-handed explanations that function as a mere time-saving device for character development. It is generally dangerous to compensate for missing exposition by letting characters account for themselves.

Again, due to Mobile TV time constraints it is challenging to establish multi-faceted characters who reveal their dimensions slowly. A Mobile TV character should be concise and clear-cut. Exaggeration seems a useful tool as it makes characters more memorable and recognizable than if they were described as average people. Clichés are a great help when launching or introducing characters. The short program length precludes any in-depth introductions, so clichéd and exaggerated characters fit perfectly to Mobile TV. Additionally, they improve and accelerate the viewer's orientation within the plot.

Extroverted characters work best because they reveal their character traits more rapidly. Introverted characters can disclose their motivation quite efficiently through inner monologue. Explicit differences in characters' appearance or hyperbolic and unique body language facilitate the characters' positioning and recognition. Much can be conveyed in a minimum of time (positive example *Girl Friday*: the protagonist is scatterbrained, imaginative, slightly eccentric, and tends to make blunders; her friend, on the other hand, is loyal, respectable, and sensible).

Interactivity: Because of mobile phones' many applications (including television, telephone, camera, video camera, Internet portal, game boy), it makes sense to build an increased interactive element into clips or programs. The viewer can intervene in programs through the active back channel inherent to the mobile phone. The prospect of influencing or contributing to the course of programs, or even creating a platform for one's own videos (open channel) makes this medium particularly attractive.

If a series works exceptionally well, and many viewers develop an emotional attachment to it, an actual "coauthoring" of the plot through viewers' votes is certainly conceivable, especially among the younger user group that has grown up with multimediality.

This might lead to a disappearance of the boundaries between consumption and production in Mobile TV: Consumers could (and should) produce their own television content that will be broadcast in designated programs.

Production is low-threshold and simple for participants, and user-generated content is already being disseminated via appropriate platforms and open channels. This special brand of interactivity will probably be used quite rarely, whereas other kinds of interactivity will occur rather more frequently in Mobile TV due to the existing integrated back channel of mobile phones. What comes to mind are polls, commentary [29] and betting functions [22], and similar applications [10,18].

14.4 Mobile TV Guideline–Based Example Clips

In the scope of this work, several video clips have been professionally produced. Following the guidelines described in Section 14.3, these clips seek to provide highly usable examples of contents that were specifically made for mobile viewing scenarios. However, to evaluate the differences between made-for-mobile video sequences and standard-television sequences, certain clips have been edited in different versions. The set of content will be available for testing purposes in order to simplify research on mobile-television video and audio quality.

In this chapter, the production stages and the content of the videos are described. Section 14.4.1 provides a general overview of the material and outlines the production circumstances. In the subsections following, for each class of content, all different versions will be outlined and described by their differences from each other.

14.4.1 Summary of All Available Clips

Content classification: There are a total of 20 different clips that can be classified according to their content, their language (German and English), and editing type (i.e., made-for-mobile or standard television). Made-for-mobile as well as standard television clips have been produced in order to be able to compare both editing types in future user studies, where positive and negative examples will be needed.

- News Show (also dubbed "Handy TV"): A news show that focuses on three main topics and a weather forecast. It is available in made-for-mobile and standard television versions.
- Mobisode (also dubbed "Loved Shelter"): A fictitious story involving an animal shelter that consists of three episodes. Each episode is available in two edits.
- Sports Clips: One clip shows a match of handball, the second clip is a report on an outdoor running event. They are only available in one edit and thus follow the made-for-mobile guidelines.

The total amount of different versions can be seen in Table 14.2.

Production: All clips have been professionally recorded and processed on HD equipment—for more technical information, see Section 14.5. The editing process took place in dedicated studios, and the companies involved provide footage for

Table 14.2   Overview of Different Versions of the Produced Content

Clip	Episodes	Versions per Episode	Languages
News show	1	2 (made-for-mobile, standard TV)	2 (German, English)
Mobisode	3	2 (different edits)	2 (German, English)
Ice hockey	1	1	2 (German, English)
Outdoor running	1	1	2 (German, English)

major television networks in Austria on a regular basis. This footage is, therefore, expected to consist of highly professional-level material.

The news and sports clips mostly depict real-life content and do not include actors or actresses. Only the news anchorwomen are actresses. All the other clips mostly show interviews with real persons or footage of real television scenes that may have been used for broadcasting.

The content has been chosen to serve for as many purposes as possible. The news show is a mixture of cultural, informational, and sports-related reports and, therefore, appeals to a wide variety of users. Each news clip can also be used separately as they are not coherent with regard to content. The whole news show is of a length of approximately 7 min. The mobisodes instead feature a memorable storyline and are condensed to approximately 3 min. Each episode can be viewed individually as the story will be self-explanatory. The sports clips cover a range of team sports and provide for short entertainment and information.

14.4.2 News Show

The news show is a series of reports, each announced by an anchorwoman. With a duration of approximately 7 min, it is typical for a short news broadcast, and can be shown during the day or between two movies to give a short update.

In the beginning, the anchorwoman welcomes the viewers and announces the first topic. She stands in front of a neutral gray background. The mobile version fills the frame with the person, whereas in the standard television version a large LCD monitor is also showing a picture related to the following topic. Subtitles also give the headline of the following report, but they differ in letter size in the two versions.

Report 1: The first report gives an overview of the opening of an arts exhibition in Vienna, Austria. It is mainly composed of interior scenes from the exhibition site. Several interviews are shown—subtitles inform about the interviewed persons' names. Again, the subtitle size is adjusted. Most of the interviewees are of public interest (including the federal president of Austria who is shown on Figure 14.1)— this ensures that when subjectively testing the content, test persons are more likely to feel immersion into "real" television content. In between the interviews, details of the architecture or overviews of the audience are presented.

Color and contrast: Due to the event filmed taking place in an art gallery, mostly interior shots are shown. Also, the opening ceremony is at night, which means that exterior shots will be very dark and only lit by street lamps. Interviews are lit by dedicated camera light making the background appear darker. The colors range from dark brown to red tones due to the decoration of the exhibition site.

Report 2: The second report is a short documentation about Vienna's main sewage treating plant. Again, a spokesman is interviewed and gives a brief explanation of the plant's different facilities. While the sound of the interview plays, detailed shots of the architecture and water are included. The mobile and standard version differ in the shot types (see Section 14.3).

Figure 14.1   Report 1—Federal President of Austria.

Color and contrast: Contrary to the first report, the second is filmed mostly outside of buildings in bright overcast daylight. Due to the sewage plant being a concrete building and the overcast weather conditions resulting in a diffuse light, there is little contrast in the shots. The water color ranges from dark subtle greens to gray, therefore, blending with the facility. Sometimes in the background green scenery can be seen, but still the amount of different colors is rather small.

Report 3: The third report is a sports report of an ice hockey match. As it can be viewed separately, it will be described in Section 14.4.4 together with the other sports clips.

Weather forecast: After the reports, a weather forecast is shown. The presentation depends on the version—the mobile version only shows a map of Austria, colored in blue, with large gray patches as indicators for the temperature and cloudiness. In the standard television version, however, the anchorwoman points out the different regions on the LCD display. The temperature indicators are considerably smaller and feature no background patch.

Shot types: In the made-for-mobile version, counting the different types reveals that the majority of shots are taken from a medium range (about 50%). Around 20% and 15% are full and medium close-up shots, respectively. Another 15% are close-ups.

In the standard television version, full and medium shots are equally distributed (about 40% each), with almost no medium close-ups or close-ups (around 5%). The amount of long shots is also increased (10% in contrast to only 5% in the made-for-mobile cut).

As mentioned before, there is a relatively large amount of interviews in the news show. This is the main reason for the predominance of medium shots. In total, there are six different interviews, one of them filmed at various locations.

Shot length: When analyzing the average length of shots for the news show, we can identify the difference between the made-for-mobile and Standard TV version. For example, in the made-for-mobile version, the first report is composed of "normal" scenes and interviews. On average, those normal shots are 3.4 s long (with a standard error of 1.67). The interviews are 11.6 s long (standard error 3.5). The standard TV version, however, has much longer shots. Normal scenes average on 6.4 s with a standard error of 1.62. The duration of interviews is roughly the same. It has to be noted, however, that this version includes seven camera pans with an average of 5.8 s (standard error 1.29).

Sound: As the news show compromises several different types of footage, the sound differs in each clip. The first report shows interviews and contains many spoken words and voice-overs from the narrator. Noise in the background is due to other visitors talking. With this clip, the perceivability of speech can be measured. The second report also features a narrator and an interviewed person. Noise can be heard from the machines in the treatment plant.

14.4.3 Mobisodes

The Mobile TV episodes created are an important part of the work, as they convey a whole story over three episodes and are available in different versions. There is a good chance that the attitude toward a certain topic might influence the test person's ratings; therefore, the content was chosen in order to be adequate for a large group of possible users (e.g., from children to elderly people).

The three episodes of *Loved Shelter* tell the story of a dog trying to stay at a rescue shelter. Every episode starts with a 1 min long introduction, including title screens and small computer animations. The introduction is the same for all episodes, making them viewable in any order. Every episode first shows the future owners choosing the dog while seated on a table, looking through the catalog. In the first episode, a woman chooses the dog as a companion for running. While jogging in the park, she gets mocked by her friends and the dog leaves the scene, returning to its shelter. The second episode tells the story of a child receiving the dog as a birthday present—the animal destroys part of the interior during the celebration. In the third episode, a pair of elderly people takes the dog to an outdoor restaurant, where it runs away over the tables, smashing plates and glasses. Every episode concludes with a scene at the shelter and then rolling credits or a simple title screen.

Shot types: The mobile episodes try to cover a broad range of possible shot types. Typical close-up and medium shots are very dominant, but also full shots are used. Many shots show dialogs between actors. Others depict details of the locations used. Especially, the second episode features scenes with fast cuts, therefore, including more close-ups.

Some differences can be spotted within the different episodes when counting the different shots. The first one has a higher emphasis on medium close-ups (about 40% of all) and medium shots (also about 40%). Close-ups make up 15%, while full shots are only used twice. The second episode features more close-ups than before. Medium shots, medium close-ups, and close-ups are equally distributed (around 30%). The third episode again focuses on medium shots (50%).

Color and contrast: In the first episode, the location used is a park in bright daylight. Saturated greens make up most of the visible area, while the main actress wears a bright pink. This was introduced to test contrast handling and the visibility of color. On the contrary, the second episode plays in an apartment. The actors wear clothes of the same light brown color as the rest of the apartment and the props on the set. The contrast is drastically reduced. The last episode is balanced in terms of color.

Sound: The mobisodes cover a wide range of audio content. As each episode begins with an introduction, a signation soundtrack is heard. In most shots, people can be heard talking to each other or to the dog. The first episode features ambient noise from a park, whereas in the second episode, no background noise can be heard. The third episode again plays outside, therefore, natural ambient noise is audible.

14.4.4 Sports Clips

Sports coverage comprises a major part of today's television content and is also very popular on mobile devices. Because of this, different sports scenes have been included into the content.

Hockey match: Taken from the news show, this report focuses on an ice hockey match, recapitulating the events and showing the most important scenes and replays. All goals are shown, including subtitles that show the current score and the player who achieved the goal, as can be observed in Figure 14.2. In between, parts of the audience are filmed. Some scenes also show the players greeting each other. One interview is conducted.

Shot types: The main difference between the mobile and standard version lies in the different shot types. Whereas the standard version mostly shows long shots (overviews of the hockey field), the mobile version provides more full shots that help to identify the puck.

Figure 14.2　Hockey match—goal scene.

Color and contrast: Strong contrasts make up the hockey scenes, since the players (with yellow and dark blue dresses) stand out against the bright white ice. The audience shots, however, show less contrast since they are filmed from a farther away camera position. The color palette is reduced.

Handball match: Being a separate report, the handball match features not only scenes from the game field, but also a few shots of the audience and the coach. There are no subtitles included and no different versions for mobile and standard television.

Shot types: The match is filmed from the side of the game field and, therefore, features some wide angle (full) shots as well as some medium shots of players. Full shots make up for almost 60% of all shot types. The whole game field is never shown.

Color and contrast: Being an interior match, the colors are dominated by browns from the floor. The player's dresses are yellow/black and white/black. While the audience is kept in a darker background, there are some differently colored advertisement banners and blue parts of the hall floor.

Outdoor running: This is a report on an outdoor running game taking place in a rural environment in Austria. Contestants are equipped with sensors and have to run along a specific route. There are three interviews, mixed with shots from the contest.

Shot types: In this report, there is a fair amount of different shot types. Medium shots are used in interviews (about 40% of all shots). Scene details and long-distance shots are also included (35% and 10%, respectively).

Color and contrast: As the contest takes place outside, there are many scenes dominated by green and brown colors. The overcast weather, however, lowers the contrast a bit, so do the long-distance shots.

Sound: Both, the hockey and the handball match, have a very distinct sound scape, composed of a commentator and the loud background noise from cheering fans. Here, artificial background noise could be inserted to test the audibility of a commentator over the loud audience.

14.5 Subjective Analysis

To perform some first investigations of the impact of made-for-mobile content production according to the expressed design rules, a subjective user study has been performed.

14.5.1 Technical Clip Description

Fifty-two test sequences, that is, clips, with a duration of around 10 s were extracted from the available material to avoid an additional bias caused by the recency effect. This has been shown to occur for test sequences of a longer duration than 10 s. For longer sequences, observers will emphasize the parts at the end of the clip when rating its quality [9]. The average video length was 8.4 s, with a standard deviation of 2.3. The shortest sequence was 2.8 s long, whereas the longest had a duration of 15.5 s. The lengths were almost evenly distributed, 24 videos being shorter than the average, 28 longer. Each clip showed only one shot type. Due to the high number of sports-related videos, 23 long shots can be observed (e.g., in the ice hockey match, where no other camera position is available). For the other clips, there are 6 close-up shots, 12 medium close-ups, and 11 medium shots.

When technically classifying video material, two common characteristics are used: the spatial detail and the temporal activity. Spatial detail, also referred to as spatial information (SI), is a measure for the amount of detail visible in video. It is calculated by applying a filter over each frame. Temporal activity (or temporal information, TI) is a similar measure that calculates the difference between two subsequent frames on a pixel-by-pixel basis.

Both measures have been computed according to [9] and results are depicted in Figure 14.3. The clips that have been produced according to the formulated guidelines are marked with dots—the others with a square symbol. Over all sequences, SI ranges between 5 and 13 and TI between 3 and 67.

Assessment of those numbers is important for several reasons [24]:

■ Both are related to difficulties in encoding the scene, so that when compressed with the same bitrate, a video with high spatial detail and high temporal motion will exhibit poor quality in comparison to a video with low spatial detail and little temporal motion.
■ In a subjective test, the viewers will become less bored if the videos span a wide range of possible combinations.
■ Viewers will not become trained to certain types of material when they have to see it over and over again.

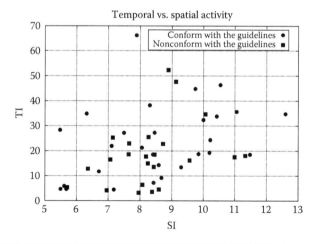

Figure 14.3   Temporal and spatial activity of all presented clips.

It can be observed in Figure 14.3 that most guideline conform clips have lower temporal activity than the others. This result is in accordance with the recommendations made by the experts, where frequent and fast camera movements should be avoided and where it is stated that the content should not contain too much motion.

14.5.2 Test Setting

All sequences have been shown in random order to 26 test persons on an HTC Hero mobile phone in horizontal holding position. To match a realistic consumption scenario where environmental differences might occur, we decided to perform a mobile test that would—at least in some aspects—differ from the ITU recommendations described in [8,9]. Hence, the test was not carried out under fully controlled conditions. On the other hand, we wanted to limit possible environmental influences to a certain point. Therefore, the tests were performed indoor, at two places. In each place, a different user group was engaged:

- Researchers at work, on their own working place, sitting in their chair. The group was composed of scientific staff of the university.
- Students at home, sitting in their room like in their spare time. The group had some minor experience with Mobile TV.

In the future, the entire set of clips as they are described in Section 14.4 will be evaluated in outdoor as well as indoor scenarios.

In the beginning, the test persons were introduced to the aims of our research that consists of understanding which content production schemes seem to be most attractive for consumption on mobile phones.

We handed the device to the user and left the decision on where and when the different sequences were presented up to the evaluator. While presentation, the observers remained in the same room as the evaluator. The evaluator was neither watching the clip nor observing the rating procedure. The clips were presented without sound. We used two similar phones (the HTC Desire and the HTC Hero) in parallel in different places equipped with our own mobile subjective player depicted in Figure 14.4. It can be used on most Android* phones and, thus, allows for quick and easy testing.

After each sequence, the test person was asked to rate the perceived quality in terms of adequateness for the use on a mobile phone by positioning a slider on the desired value of a continuous 11-grade scale (from 0 to 10). The recorded score was then transformed to a value between 0 and 100.

The clips were presented in a resolution of 480 × 320 with a frame rate of 25 Hz. MPEG-4/AVC h.264 with a baseline profile was used for encoding. The presented content comprised six different talking head clips, where three of them

---

* http://www.android.com/

Figure 14.4   Using the SubjectivePlayer on a mobile device.

followed the guidelines expressed in Section 14.3 and the remaining three did not. Similarly, 9 videos showing interviews and 11 hockey match clips were shown. Four interview and four hockey clips were produced in compliance to the guidelines and the remaining five and seven clips were not. Six handball and seven outdoor running scenes as described in Section 14.4.1 showing running athletes and interviews were added. Two water scenes (one of which has been made according to the guidelines) as well as five pans (pans in general have been estimated not to be convenient for mobile content) were used. Furthermore, a clip presenting the federal president talking on a podium was selected. Its purpose is to attract the evaluators' attention. Finally, a weather forecast—often contained in news clips—and a queue of waiting people in front of a building with high spatial activity were selected.

14.5.3 Results

Test persons are likely to use the available scale in different ways. Some persons are more confident than others and use the entire range to perform their rating, while others—more cautious characters—might express their opinion by choosing the values from a small interval only. Furthermore, some people are more optimistic than others and are likely to assign higher mean opinion scores to the same clip than others. To avoid inconsistencies in the data analysis, we decided to preprocess the collected data according to the procedure defined in [8]. It mainly consists in centralizing and normalizing the single user ratings.

In Table 14.3, it can be observed that clips created following our guidelines in average reached a higher MOS than the others. Hence, it can be stated that users preferred the clips produced according to our guidelines in general. To demonstrate the validity of each single rule separately, a more comprehensive user study needs to be performed. It might not even be possible to consider each single aspect because the amount of clips that could be produced within this investigation was limited.

Table 14.3 Test Results

Clip Type	Avg. MOS	Std Dev(s)
Conform	63.65	13.25
Nonconform	61.3	11.13
All	61.95	11.05

However, this fact might not be sufficient to prove the significance of the result because the values of the standard deviations presented in Table 14.3 seem to be too high. Therefore, we decided to perform an analysis of variance (ANOVA) [6] with the statistical tool R.* The null-hypothesis H_0 was that "producing mobile TV content according to the expressed guidelines has no impact on the perceived quality (collected MOS values)." Unfortunately, the obtained p-value was not small enough to reject the hypothesis from this general point of view. This result can generally be explained when we take into consideration that clips of only 10 s length might not give enough hints for the viewer to perceive the implications of made-for-mobile content.

However, when having a closer look at the data it can be observed that the insignificant results are due to the fact that ratings assigned to different content types are not homogeneous. Therefore, the data has been divided by clip types: (1) videos showing a talking head, (2) interviews, and (3) hockey match scenes. These are the genres for which both guideline conform and nonconform clips have been produced.

Now the ANOVA test was repeated for the single categories: The p-values for the first two categories are 0.01993 and 0.002889, respectively. Hence, in both cases the null hypothesis H_0 can be rejected—the guidelines that were formulated and taken into account when producing the videos have a significant impact on the user experience. In the third case, the p-value is 0.3569. This means that no indication could be found that the guidelines have an impact on the perceived quality for hockey matches. One reason might be that the sports scenes contain significantly more temporal activity than the others. Hence, the impact of changing the image's setup is more difficult to assess than for other content types. However, a larger user test in the future might probably prove more insights on this research question.

14.6 Conclusion and Future Work

In this chapter, the important issue on how content for Mobile TV needs to be created to attract the consumers is addressed. An interdisciplinary team comprising experts from mass media and communication science, from the Film Academy

---

* http://www.r-project.org/

in Vienna, and researchers from computer science has collaborated to extract the critical elements for creating a guideline on the production of mobile TV content. In a second step, videos have been professionally produced according to these guidelines. To verify the validity of the formulated guidelines, sequences showing similar content that do not conform to the proposed concept have been additionally produced.

With the means of a subjective test, it could be shown that users do prefer the clips produced according to our rules and that in most cases this result is also significant. In the future, it seems to be promising to continue investigations on single rules defined by the experts to obtain more detailed results on certain aspects. The relation between the movement velocity of content elements, for example, sports, and their recognition will be studied in future work.

However, the major goal that we had in mind during our investigation was the creation of a Mobile TV content database that can be used in the future by the research community for quality assessment purposes of different types. The quality evaluation described in this chapter represents only a starting point for our future research. To reach this main goal, we need to perform a deeper analysis of the obtained clips and we have to carry out at least two large-scale user tests (lab based and outdoor) comprising all clips and not only some short sequences of 10 s length. The collected results will be used to finalize the database. Additionally, the data will be used to find some answers to several open questions: We would like to understand if the currently adopted quality assessment procedure, for example, where the clips of the LIVE database [27,28] are frequently used, can be improved by using our Mobile TV clips instead. We would like to know if we succeeded in improving the users' feeling of being more involved when a realistic content is presented. Furthermore, it is interesting to know whether the subjective perception of quality is the same for any presented content containing a similar error pattern or not.

References

1. *Mobile TV Guide in Austria*, http://www.androidlounge.at/lounge/?p=2400 [Referred to March 24, 2011].
2. L.V. Berens and N. Dario. *Understanding Yourself and Others: An Introduction to the Personality Type Code*. Telos Publications, Huntington Beach, CA, 2004.
3. C. Breunig. Mobile television in Germany. *Media Perspektiven*, 11(4):220–234, 2006.
4. S. Buchinger, S. Kriglstein, S. Brandt, and H. Hlavacs. A survey on user studies and technical aspects of mobile multimedia applications. *Entertainment Computing*, 2(3):175–190, 2011.
5. Guardian. Mini-series for upwardly mobile Chinese. *Guardian News & Media*, 2008, http://www.buzzle.com/editorials/6-28-2005-72274.asp, June 2005.
6. J. Hartung, B. Elpelt, and K.-H. Klösener. *Lehr-und Handbuch der angewandten Statistik*. Oldenbourg, München, Wien, 2002.

7. K. Hummel, A. Hess, and T. Grill. Environmental context sensing for usability evaluation in mobile HCI by means of small wireless sensor networks. In *Proceedings of MoMM'08*, New York, 2008.

8. ITU-R BT.500-11. Methodology for the subjective assessment of the quality of television pictures. ITU-R BT.500–11, 2002.

9. ITU-T P.910. Subjective video quality assessment methods for multimedia applications. ITU-T P.910, ITU, 1999.

10. S. Jumisko-Pyykkö, M. Weitzel, and D. Strohmeier. Designing for user experience: What to expect from mobile 3d tv and video? In *Proceedings of UXTV'08*, New York, 2008.

11. C.G. Jung. *Psychological Types, Collected Works*. Princeton University Press, Princeton, NJ, p. 6, 1921.

12. E. Kaasinen, M. Kulju, T. Kivinen, and V. Oksman. User acceptance of mobile TV services. In *Proceedings of MobileHCI'09*. ACM, New York, 2009.

13. D. Kleine. Content für Mobile TV-Erfahrungen und zukünftige Entwicklungen aus Sicht der ProSiebenSat1 Media AG, October 2006.

14. H. Knoche, J. McCarthy, and M.A. Sasse. Reading the fine print: The effect of text legibility on perceived video quality in mobile TV. In *Proceedings of ACM Multimedia*, Santa Barbara, CA, October 2006.

15. H. Knoche, J. McCarthy, and M.A. Sasse. How low can you go? The effect of low resolutions on shot types in mobile TV. In *Personalized and Mobile Digital TV Applications in Springer Multimedia Tools and Applications Series*, 36(1–2):145–166, 2008.

16. H. Lee, D. Kim, J. Ryu, and S. Lee. Acceptance and rejection of mobile TV among young adults: A case of college students in South Korea. *Telematics and Informatics*, 28(4):239–250, 2011.

17. B. Lievens, E. Vanhengel, J. Pierson, and A. Jacobs. Does mobile television enhance a new television experience? In A. Marcus, A. Cereijo Roibás, and R. Sala, eds., *Mobile TV: Customizing Content and Experience, Human-Computer Interaction Series Part 1*. Springer-Verlag, London, U.K., pp. 81–96, 2010.

18. M. Maguire and N. Bevan. User requirements analysis: A review of supporting methods. In *Proceedings of the IFIP'02*, Deventer, the Netherlands, 2002.

19. H. Mittermayr, S. Schneiders, and B. Canstein. Mobile broadcast business models, Generic Business Models and Country-specific Implementations, bmcoforum, 2010.

20. K. Miyauchi, T. Sugahara, and H. Oda. Relax or study?: A qualitative user study on the usage of mobile tv and video. In *Proceedings of EuroITV'08*, Vol. 5066/2008, Salzburg, July 2008.

21. K. Miyauchi, T. Sugahara, and H. Oda. Different attitudes concerning the usage of live mobile tv and mobile video. In A. Marcus, A. Cereijo Roibas, and R. Sala, eds., *Mobile TV: Customizing Content and Experience, Human-Computer Interaction Series*. Springer, London, U.K., pp. 165–193, 2010.

22. S. Orgad. This box was made for walking. Nokia Mobile TV Report, 2006.

23. O. Petrovic. Mobile TV in Austria. *Schriftenreihe der Rundfunk und Telekom Regulierungs-GmbH*, Vol. 2, Wien, Austria, 2006.

24. M. Pinson. Considerations for video scene selection. Presentation, VQEG Meeting, Berlin, Germany, 2009.

25. Projektgruppe Mobiles Fernsehen. Mobiles Fernsehen: Interessen, potentielle Nutzungskontexte und Einstellungen der Bevölkerung. *Media Perspektiven*, 2007.

26. M. Sack, S. Buchinger, and H. Hlavacs. Loudness and auditory masking compensation for Mobile TV. In *Proceedings of BMSB'10*, Shanghai, China, 2010.

27. K. Seshadrinathan, R. Soundararajan, A.C. Bovik, and L.K. Cormack. Study of subjective and objective quality assessment of video. *IEEE Transactions on Image Processing*, 19(6):1427–1441, 2010.

28. K. Seshadrinathan, R. Soundararajan, A.C. Bovik, and L.K. Cormack. A subjective study to evaluate video quality assessment algorithms. *SPIE Proceedings Human Vision and Electronic Imaging*, San Jose, CA, Proc. 7527, 75270H, January 2010.

29. P. Alexandra Silva and A. Dix. Usability—Not as we know it! [Referred December 10, 2010]. Lancaster: British Computer Society. http://www.bcs.org/upload/pdf/ewic hc07 sppaper26.pdf, 2007.

30. L. Stockbridge and A. Mughal. Usability guidelines for developing mobile TV services. [Referred December 10, 2010]. http://www.serco.com/experiencelab/blog/articles/guidelines.asp, 2006.

31. Study Group 12. Quality of experience requirements for IPTV services. ITU-T Recommendations G.1080, ITU, 2008.

32. O. Svec. Handys zeigen großes Kino im Kleinformat [Referred December 10, 2010]. http://www.welt.de/wams print/article799297/Handys zeigen grosses Kino im Kleinformat. html, 2007.

33. K. Taga, C. Niegel, and L. Riegel. Mobile TV, turning in or switching off, 2009.

34. M. Vangenck, A. Jacobs, B. Lievens, E. Vanhengel, and J. Pierson. Does mobile television challenge the dimension of viewing television? An explorative research on time, place and social context of the use of mobile television content. In *Proceedings of Eur oITV'08*, Vol. 5066/2008, Salzburg, July 2008.

35. J. Wippersberg. Die Forderung nach "sehbarem Fernsehen". In *TV 3.0 Journalistische und politische Herausforderungen des Fernsehens im Digitalen Zeitalter*, Berlin, Germany, March 2008.

WEB AND SOCIAL TV

Chapter 15

Hierarchical Semantic Content Analysis and Its Applications in Multimedia Summarization and Browsing

Junyong You
Norwegian University of Science and Technology

Andrew Perkis
Norwegian University of Science and Technology

Moncef Gabbouj
Tampere University of Technology

Touradj Ebrahimi
Norwegian University of Science and Technology
Ecole Polytechnique Fédérale de Lausanne

Contents

15.1 Introduction

With the rapid growth of television (TV) content in digital libraries, information redundancy of the content is increasing at an even higher pace. A large portion of the TV material is, however, redundant even after editing and postprocessing. Consequently, efficient content management, for example, content classification, representation, retrieval, summarization, is becoming a kernel task for TV content providers as well as end users. Traditional management of TV content is usually conducted manually, which is quite expensive in terms of time and labor, especially with the dazzling increase of TV content. Therefore, it is critical to develop automatic content management solutions. On the other hand, in order to enable the end users of TV services to deal with large amounts of content, it has to be presented in a form that facilitates the comprehension of the content and allows judging the relevance of segments of the content quickly. However, a practical difficulty in automatic content management is how to bridge the gap between low-level content characteristics that can be processed and recognized by machines and high-level semantics as requested by users, which usually cannot be easily processed by machines, because they lack cognitive processing abilities similarly to human beings. Therefore, semantic content analysis methods are required in order to connect low-level characteristics to semantic meanings of TV content [1–3].

Semantic multimedia content analysis refers to the computerized understanding of the semantic meanings of a multimedia signal, which is an important step bridging the gap between the syntax of the multimedia stream and some high-level applications, such as browsing, retrieval, summarization. In this chapter, we will mainly focus on rapid multimedia content browsing using the format of content summarization based on semantic analysis. Content browsing deals with how to help viewers browse the multimedia content rapidly. This is because a lot of original TV material usually contains a lot of content redundancy, even after editing and postproduction by content providers. In order for viewers to rapidly browse the multimedia content and understand the main meanings of a TV program, the original multimedia content should be represented in a convenient structure that can describe the most important information for the viewers. Content summarization is an enabling technology that facilitates easy and quick access to multimedia sequences from digital archives. Generally, multimedia summarization technologies can be classified into two categories: static key frames and dynamic skimming. The former is a small collection of frame images that have been extracted or generated from the underlying multimedia sources, and can express the main or the most important meanings of the original sequences. Static key frames can be presented based on different visualization techniques, such as storyboard [4], mosaic [5], and tree-map, which provide intuitive ways to show the main content and internal structure of the original video. The dynamic skimming refers to a collection that consists of some continuous frames extracted from the original sequences. As the summarized results in a multimedia content summarization method are usually much shorter than the original version, it is naturally convenient to use the summary in rapid multimedia browsing. However, multimedia summarization is a highly subjective task, and different viewers might have different requests on the summary. On the other hand, the semantic meaning of a given content is not unique, as the content can be perceived and explained in many different ways by different viewers. Therefore, each way of perceiving the content requires a particular type of information in order to index, classify, summarize, or organize the multimedia collection correspondingly. In this chapter, we will present a semantic importance analysis framework to parse the content based on a general structure of an audiovisual sequence, that is, from sequence to scene, shot, and finally frame, based on low-level or middle-level audiovisual features. Accordingly, state-of-the-art algorithms for audiovisual feature extraction and modeling, multimedia content analysis, summarization, and rapid browsing will be reviewed and discussed.

The reminder of this chapter is organized as follows. Section 15.2 reviews related work on audiovisual feature modeling, semantic content analysis, and their applications. Section 15.3 presents the semantic importance analysis model for the hierarchical structure (scene → shot → frame) of a TV program based on audiovisual cues. The multimedia summarization method and its application in rapid content browsing are presented in Section 15.4. Experimental results on evaluating the proposed summarization method and some discussions are reported in Section 15.5, and finally, concluding remarks are given in Section 15.6.

15.2 Review of Multimedia Content Analysis and Applications

Generally speaking, a TV program usually consists of two main modalities, namely, audio track and video sequence. Accordingly, semantic TV content analysis usually relies on the analysis of audio and video signals, respectively [1,6,7]. The first step in any content analysis task is the parsing or segmentation of its presentation. This is motivated by the fact that human understanding of a TV program is usually based on the combination and interaction between different segments (from here onward, we use the word "multimedia" to refer to TV programs containing both video frames and their associated audio track). A multimedia presentation is combined with different scene segments, each of which represents a single story unit. Furthermore, each scene might include many different shots. According to movie production terminology, a shot is "one uninterrupted image with a single static or mobile framing" [8], and it usually contains many frames whose auditory and/or visual characteristics are coherent within a shot. Based on the definition of shot, it is natural to employ the coherence between consecutive temporal clips for shot segmentation. Most existing work on shot segmentation is primarily focused on using visual information, for example, comparing intensity, color, motion, histogram, and so on, between two video frames [9,10]. The resulting segments usually correspond to individual camera shots that have been captured with single cameras. However, the situation becomes more complicated in scene segmentation, because there is no a clear boundary between two scenes. Different viewers might have different judgments on scene changes. Audio characteristics are often employed in scene segmentation, in addition to visual features, as a scene change is usually associated with simultaneous changes of auditory attributes [11,12]. For example, a TV commercial usually consists of many shots, but the audio in a same commercial follows the same tone and rhythm. Temporal segmentation of multimedia content can be broadly classified as operating on uncompressed sequences, or working directly with the compressed information, using the data that can be extracted from the compressed streams, such as macroblock types, motion vectors, or DC-coefficient images [13,14].

Both the scene segmentation and the shot segmentation are performed by comparing audio or visual features, such as tone, motion, and color. An important step for multimedia content analysis is to model audiovisual features in a way that it can be implemented by machines. Such audiovisual features are usually classified as low-level semantics, which means that they are not connected to the high-level semantics directly. Many audiovisual features have been employed in the literature [1,12,15–17]. For example, volume (loudness), zero crossing rate (ZCR), pitch, frequency, and their derived features are often used in audio characterization while color, motion, texture, and so on are useful for image/video analysis. In practice, an audio waveform is artificially divided into different frames with or without overlap, as there are no borders within the audio waveform like in the video sequence. An audio frame is defined as a group of neighboring samples lasting a short period, within which it can be assumed that the audio signal is stationary. Audio features can be computed from each frame or a set of frames. Volume is a widely used feature, which can normally be approximated by the root mean square of the magnitude of the audio signal in a frame. ZCR is defined as the number of times that the audio waveform crosses the zero axis. Pitch is the fundamental frequency of an audio waveform and is an important parameter in analyzing speech and music signals

[18]. For example, the typical pitch frequency of a voice is between 50 and 450 Hz, while its range for music is much broader. In addition, many features based on the audio spectrum (the Fourier transform of the samples in a frame) have also been widely used in audio signal processing, for example, frequency centroid (FC) and band width (BW). Mel-frequency cepstral coefficient (MFCC) is another important audio feature widely used in speech and music modeling [19], as it takes into account the nonlinear property of the human auditory system (HAS) with respect to different frequencies.

Visual features of multimedia presentations can be in principle categorized into two domains: spatial and temporal. An important attribute for image presentation is color, including luminance and chrominance components. For example, color histogram representing color distribution in an image is usually used to compare whether or not two images have similar characteristics [17] and to identify the dominant colors, which are widely used in image retrieval [20]. However, color histogram ignores the spatial structure of pixels, such as the location information, which potentially influences the performance of a video segmentation algorithm. For example, two images that have similar histograms might be drastically different in appearance. Hence, some improved methods have been proposed to include other information to complement color histogram. In [21], not only the distribution of a color component, but also mean, variance, and entropy of pair-wise distances among pixels with the color are used in an augmented image histogram for image similarity analysis. Texture and shape are two other important spatial features that can be modeled, for example, using Gabor and Fourier descriptors, respectively. Motion is the most important attribute in the temporal domain, which depicts the inter-frame activities and behavior of a video sequence. Usually, motion information is expressed by motion vectors extracted from block-matching motion estimation, or optical flow techniques. Global motion caused by a moving camera and local motion of moving objects are two main components of motion information in video sequences. Many camera motion models have been proposed to extract global motion parameters, for example, affine or bilinear, which can further be used in estimating the ego-motion in a camera, such as tilting, zooming, and panning [22]. Motion of a moving object, obtained from the motion vector compensated by global motion, is widely used in moving object extraction and tracking systems [23].

In addition to be used in audio and video segmentation, extracting appropriate audiovisual features plays an important role in multimedia content analysis. Actually, the semantic meaning of an audiovisual clip is usually not unique as it can be perceived in many different ways by viewers. Thus, audiovisual features can be extracted and modeled in different manners for respective purposes of multimedia content analysis systems. In a previous work, we have proposed to use some semantic features such as the state of global motion, dominant colors, the magnitude of motion vectors, and behavior of moving objects, as inputs for probabilistic models in order to classify and recognize video genres and the contained events [24]. In [25], a motion representation scheme is developed using an energy distribution function and three motion filters, and then fed into a multilevel hidden Markov model (HMM) framework to detect and recognize video shots and events. Currently, most multimedia content analysis algorithms are constructed at a cognitive level extracting information that describes the "fact" of the content, for example, the structure of the story, the composition of a scene, and the objects captured by the camera. Moreover, multimedia content can further be analyzed or represented at a higher level, such as at affective level [26,27]. The affective multimedia content is defined as the amount and type of human feelings or emotions which are related to high-level perception mechanisms. In [26], auditory and visual features, for example, motion, rhythm, and sound energy, have been employed to model three affective dimensions: valence, arousal, and control.

Semantic content analysis provides an efficient approach to model the syntax of multimedia presentations. However, as explained earlier, a lot of redundancy might exist in original TV materials, and the TV content should be presented to users in an efficient way, that is, allowing them to rapidly browse the content. Within a large amount of multimedia content, viewers might be only interested in the most representative excerpts while the redundant or less interesting parts may not attract viewers' attention, especially when they are searching for specific content collections. Multimedia summarization techniques provide an efficient approach for rapid content browsing, in which users can skin through the summaries and retrieve the most attractive content [28]. Typical video summarization methods aim at finding and extracting the most important frames, also known as key frames, or video clips. For example, the first or the last frame in a shot can be treated as a key frame, after shot segmentation [29]. Most existing work on multimedia browsing and summarization has concentrated on content representation by using low-level features rather than from a viewpoint of high-level semantic understanding. However, since multimedia summarization is a subjective task, it is important to generate the summary based on the general understanding of viewers. As an important attribute of the human perception system, the psychological attention mechanism has been adopted in multimedia content representation and summarization [30,31]. Ma et al. [30] have proposed a user attention model based on some low-level audiovisual features, such as motion, image contrast, camera motion, audio energy, and speech features, and a feasible solution for generating video summary is also proposed to extract those frames or clips that can attract viewers' attention more than other video segments. Similarly, we have proposed a multiple visual models–based perceptive analysis framework by using visual features, including motion, contrast, special scenes, and statistical rhythm. A multilevel video summarization can be generated based on a constructed perception curve corresponding to human perception changes when watching a video sequence [31]. Each of the existing techniques in multimedia content analysis and summarization can in principle be categorized into domain-specific and nondomain-specific methods. The former refers to techniques that deal specifically with a domain to which multimedia content belongs. Commonly used content domains include sports (e.g., basketball, soccer), news, ordinary movie, home video,

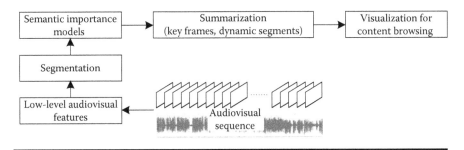

Figure 15.1   Flowchart of semantic importance–based multimedia summarization and browsing.

and so on [32]. Domain-specific analysis techniques can usually reduce the level of ambiguity because prior knowledge about the domain can be applied in analyzing the multimedia content. A large part of existing content analysis and summarization algorithms follows the domain-specific technique, especially for sports content [25,33]. On the other hand, nondomain-specific techniques usually propose generic solutions to multimedia content analysis and summarization in any content domain, rather than a specific one [24,30,31,34].

However, existing multimedia analysis and summarization methods usually take into account local audiovisual features only, that is, the features are computed based on only the current frame and a couple of the closest frames while the relationship between the frame/segment and the whole content is neglected. Thus, the computed peak points on either the attention curve [30] or the perception curve [31] are usually the local maxima such that the corresponding frames/segments might not be the most important or representative collections for understanding the whole content. Another disadvantage of existing summarization algorithms [28,30–34] is that many duplicate frames even in a same scene or shot are extracted because the content is modeled in a local manner rather than a global fashion. In this chapter, we will propose a multimedia summarization method for rapid TV content browsing that selects key frames and clips in a holistic structure based on analyzing the semantic importance of scenes, shots, and frames, which can avoid these disadvantages of the traditional methods. Figure 15.1 illustrates the flowchart of the proposed semantic importance analysis framework for multimedia summarization and rapid content browsing.

15.3 Audiovisual Cues–Based Semantic Importance Analysis

15.3.1 Audio Scene Segmentation and Classification

As explained in Section 15.2, the first step for multimedia content analysis is usually to divide an audiovisual sequence into different segments or clips, as different clips might have drastically different characteristics. Therefore, we first segment a sequence into different scenes, and further, shots. Past experiments have demonstrated that audio track within a scene is often consistent in terms of the signal characteristics; hence, scene segmentation can be performed based on comparing audio features between two consequent scenes.

The audio waveform is divided into different frames, which is defined as 2048 continuous samples with 50% overlap between two consecutive frames. As an important index in psychoacoustics, loudness can express the ability to catch human attention. In our work, we have adopted a method to measure the loudness of audio frames based on a psychoacoustic model [35]. This model can accurately model the physical strength of sound. For example, if the loudness of an audio clip is lower than 3 dB, we can reasonably assume that such clip cannot attract viewers' attention. The loudness is calculated as follows in Equation 15.1:

$$L = \frac{24}{Z} \cdot \sum_{k=0}^{Z} \max(N(k), 0) \tag{15.1}$$

in which

$$N(k) = 1.07664 \cdot \left(\frac{1}{s(k)} \cdot \frac{ET(k)}{10,000} \right)^{0.23} \cdot \left[\left(1 - s(k) + \frac{s(k) \cdot E(k)}{ET(k)} \right)^{0.23} - 1 \right]$$

where

$$ET(k) = 10^{0.364 \cdot f^{-0.8}}$$

$$s(k) = 10^{\frac{1}{10} \cdot \left\{ -2 - 2.05 \cdot \mathrm{atan}\left(\frac{f}{4} \right) - 0.75 \cdot \mathrm{atan}\left[\left(\frac{f}{1600} \right)^2 \right] \right\}} \tag{15.2}$$

where
  f denotes the frequency representation of the transformed result of an audio frame, which is grouped into critical bands
  Z is the number of the critical bands in a peripheral ear model
  k is the centroid frequency of each band
  E denotes the energy of each frequency representation

This model can accurately estimate the physical strength of sound forms, and thus, it provides a psychoacoustic measure to model the semantic audio importance (SAI). In our experiments, the loudness computed in Equation 15.1 usually ranges from 1 to 80 dB, for example, the typical loudness level of normal speech is around 45 dB.

Audio features can be modeled in different units, such as a frame or a clip that might contain several frames. Some experiments in audio analysis have demonstrated that using clip as a processing unit is usually better than using frame, in recognizing and analyzing audio signals. We will report some experimental results on audio classification using different processing units later. However, even an audio signal is processed at the unit of clips, some basic features, for example, volume, ZCR, are first computed within an audio frame, and then short-term temporal features within a clip can be derived from the basic features. In our experiments, an audio track was divided into different nonoverlap clips with a constant duration of, for example, typically 1 s.

Some commonly used features in audio signal analysis can be summarized into the following categories:

Volume based: The most widely used frame feature is volume, which is closely related to loudness. Normally, volume is approximated by the root mean square within each frame. Subsequently, some other features based on volume, such as short-time energy (STE), volume standard deviation (VSTD), and volume dynamic range (VDR), can be calculated.

ZCR based: ZCR is another widely used temporal feature, which is one of the most indicative and robust measures to discern unvoiced speech. To compute the ZCR of a frame, the number of times that the audio waveform crosses the zero axes can be counted. In addition, ZCR standard deviation (ZSTD) can also be used in audio content classification [12].

Pitch based: Pitch is the fundamental frequency of an audio waveform and is an important parameter in the analysis of speech and music signals. Normally, only voiced speech and harmonic music have well-defined pitch. It is not easy to reliably and robustly estimate the pitch value for an audio signal. The average magnitude different function (AMDF) is often used to estimate the pitch value. On the AMDF curve of voiced speech and harmonic music signals, there are periodic valleys, which are defined as local extremes that satisfy additional constraints in terms of their values relative to the global minimum and their curvatures. The pitch frequency can be estimated by the reciprocal of the time period between the original and the first valley on the AMDF curve [18]. After estimating the pitch frequency for an audio track, pitch contour (PC), pitch standard deviation (PSTD), smooth pitch ratio (SPR), and non-pitch ratio (NPR) are some effective features for classifying audio signals into different categories, such as speech and music.

Frequency based: Frequency-based features are usually based on the spectrum of an audio frame using the Fourier transform. BW and FC are two widely used spectral features.

MFCC based: MFCC is another important feature in the frequency domain, which is widely used in speech recognition and speaker identification. MFCC can provide a smoothed representation of the original spectrum of an audio waveform, and further considers the nonlinear attributes of the human hearing system with respect to different frequencies. Its extended features, such as delta MFCC and autocorrelation MFCC, are often used in speech and speaker recognition [1,36,37].

Scene changes can be detected based on the comparison of the audio features between two consecutive clips. Actually, it is unnecessary to employ all the features mentioned earlier to detect the scene change, and some of them are enough to express the coherent characteristics within an individual scene. According to our experiments, we suggest using the volume-, ZCR-, and pitch-based features in order to detect the change between two scenes, based on a scene change index (SCI) defined as follows [12]:

$$
\text{SCI} = \frac{\left\| \left(\sum_{i=-N}^{-1} f(i) - \sum_{i=0}^{N-1} f(i) \right) \big/ N \right\|^2}{\sqrt{(c + \text{avg}(f(-N), \ldots, f(-1)) \cdot (c + \text{avg}(f(0), \ldots, f(N-1)))}}
\tag{15.3}
$$

where $f(i)$ denotes the feature vector of the ith clip, while $i = 0$ represents the current clip, $\| \cdot \|$ is the $L2$ norm, avg denotes the average of the squared Euclidean distances between each vector and the mean feature vector of the i clips considered, and c is a small constant to prevent division by zero. In our experiments, we have found that $N = 6$ provides a robust and promising result for scene change detection.

Audio classification is important for analyzing the semantics of an audio track. There are many different kinds of audio signals, for example, speech, pure music, speech + music, applauses, background sound, and even music content contains many different genres [38]. To keep the computational cost reasonably low, we have predefined five genres in audio classification, including speech, music, noise, silence, and others. The silent clips can be first detected based on the loudness ($< 3\,\text{dB}$), as humans cannot hear sounds lower than 3 dB measured by the psychoa-coustic model in Equation 15.1. The classification of each audio clip into the other four genres is achieved based on the aforementioned features by using a Gaussian mixture model (GMM). GMM is an extension of the single Gaussian probabilis-tic function, and it can simulate most probabilistic distributions with arbitrary shapes [39]. The GMM has one state containing multiple Gaussian distributions, that is, $P(X|\lambda) = \sum_{i=1}^{M} w_i b_i(X)$ where X denotes a D-dimension random vector, $\{w_i, i = 1, 2, \ldots, M\}$ denote the fusion weights, and $\{b_i(X), i = 1, 2, \ldots, M\}$ are subdistributions of D-dimension-combined Gaussian distributions. Then, a GMM is composed of a mean vector, a covariance matrix, and fusion weights, namely, $\lambda = \{w_i, \mu_i, \Sigma_i\}$, $i = 1, 2, \ldots, M$, where $\sum w_i = 1$. In our experi-ments, we have used STE-, ZCR-, PC-, and MFCC-based features to estimate the GMM parameters using the EM algorithm based on a large number of training audio signals lasting about 4.6 h in total, in which the average duration of audio clips is 12.3 s, and the training audio signals have already been categorized into dif-ferent classes. In our experiments, the following audio classes were included: speech (sole speech of one person), music, speech + speech (combined speeches of two or more people), speech + music (music usually as background), speech + noise (noise as background), and noise (pure noise). The classification was performed on other audio clips that have not been employed in the training. In total, about 3.5 h audio clips with the average duration being 12 s were included in the classification. Table 15.1 gives the classification results using different sets of audio features and different processing units (frame vs. clip with different duration). According to the

Table 15.1 Experimental Results of Audio Classification in Different Configurations

Audio Features	Classification Accuracy with respect to Different Feature Sets (Clip Based) (%)					
	Speech	*Music*	*Speech + Speech*	*Speech + Music*	*Speech + Noise*	*Noise*
Volume-, ZCR-based features	74.7	68.2	72.1	70.6	57.3	79.0
MFCC	91.4	94.2	95.5	93.7	70.2	82.1
STE, ZCR, PC, and MFCC	93.0	94.9	96.2	93.9	73.2	89.4
Frame/clip	Classification Accuracy with respect to Different Units (Frame vs. Clip) Using Same Features: STE, ZCR, PC, MFCC (%)					
Frame based	82.9	87.7	80.4	76.4	71.2	74.3
Clip based (0.5 s)	90.4	94.5	94.9	95.1	80.2	88.5
Clip based (1 s)	93.0	94.9	96.2	93.9	83.2	90.4
Clip based (2 s)	93.7	92.4	96.8	95.6	85.7	86.1
Clip based (5 s)	95.7	96.2	97.0	94.9	90.2	88.3
Frame/clip	Classification Accuracy for Speech, Music and Noise Only (%)					
Frame based	84.2	86.5	—	—	—	77.5
Clip based (1 s)	91.3	93.7	—	—	—	86.4

experimental results, the GMM classifier achieves a promising performance in classifying different audio genres based on the efficient features. This provides a solid base for semantic audio content analysis. Furthermore, audio classification can also be performed using other classifiers, for example, HMM [40].

15.3.2 Shot Clustering and Semantic Scene Importance

According to the SCI computed in Equation 15.3, an audiovisual sequence can be divided into different scenes, each of which describes an individual story unit. Every scene contains a few shots, each of which is usually taken with a single camera. Shot segmentation can be performed by comparing the similarity between two adjacent frames. In principle, there are two main change types between shots, namely, cut and transition. Many advanced shot change detection methods have been proposed in the literature [13]. In our experiments, we have employed the luminance histogram of image frames to detect the cut change. If the correlation coefficient of the histograms of two adjacent frames is below an empirical threshold (0.9 in our experiments), we assume that a cut is detected. Shot transition detection is a little complicated, since there is no clear boundary during the transition change between two different shots. We have adopted a detection method using the dynamic partial function, which can dynamically selects a partial feature subset to measure the inter-frame distance, in order to detect the transition shot changes [41]. Subsequently, the middle frame during the transition is selected as the boundary between two shots.

However, some shots within a scene may be originated from the same camera and their contents might be similar to each other. We assume that such duplicated or similar shots cannot represent more semantic meanings than a single shot. The goal of multimedia summarization is to find the most representative segments or frames, and hence, only one among all the similar or duplicated shots will be extracted for the summary. We use a representative histogram of a shot, which is defined as the average of all frame histograms in this shot, to determine if two shots have similar contents. All the representative histograms within a scene are compared using the correlation coefficient to classify shots that are close to each other into the same cluster. Another empirical threshold 0.8 is used to compare two representative histograms. Finally, all the shots in a scene can be classified into different clusters through the K-means algorithm, from each of which a shot is extracted for deriving a scene representative index (SRI). We assume that a scene can present more abundant contents if it contains more unrelated shot clusters. On the other hand, a shorter scene with more unrelated contents is more important for content browsing and summarization than a longer scene with less different contents. Hence, the SRI is defined as the ratio of the number of the classified shot clusters against the length of the scene.

Audio characteristics are quite important for helping understand the content of a scene. Especially, viewers usually pay more attention to those clips containing speech and music tracks, and louder sound is able to attract more attention than other audio clips. Thus, the semantic importance index (SII) of an audio clip is defined as follows:

$$SII = AW \cdot \bar{L} \qquad (15.4)$$

where

$\bar{L}$ denotes the average loudness over all the audio frames in the clip

AW is a weight corresponding to different audio genres

In our experiments, three weights have been set: 1 for speech and music, 0 for silence and noise, and 0.5 for others. Finally, the average of the SIIs over all the audio clips in a scene is taken as the SAI of the scene.

In general, viewers are usually interested in video frames containing dominant faces, while texts can also provide more useful information for understanding the semantics of a scene. Many face and text detection methods have been proposed [42,43]. We have employed a Bayesian classifier to detect face and text regions in a frame. The human skin-tone characteristics of two chrominance components (Cb and Cr) are used to generate statistics of skin-tone color distribution directly on the Cb–Cr plane in the classification process. Based on the Bayesian decision rules, the color of each image block (8×8 pixels) can be classified into face or non-face regions. Text regions in a video frame can also be detected using the Bayesian classifier based on the energy of each image block. In this chapter, we take into account the size and location of face and text regions in deriving a face and text importance (FTI) index of a frame, which is calculated as follows:

$$\text{FTI} = \sum S \cdot W \qquad (15.5)$$

where

W denotes a weight determined by the region location, as shown in Figure 15.2
S is the size of the face and text regions in number of pixels
$\sum$ denotes the sum operation over all the face and text regions in the image

Furthermore, the ratio of the detected frames containing faces and texts weighted by FTI compared with the scene length is defined as the FTI index for that scene.

Moreover, affective cues are important for content analysis at a high level. A TV program, especially movie, can usually be classified into a special affective genre, for example, comedy, thriller, tragedy, and so on. However, the difficulty of bridging the semantic gap between low-level features and affection remains very hard, as human perception on the affection is strongly individual. In the proposed semantic importance analysis framework, we have adopted some general conclusions on the

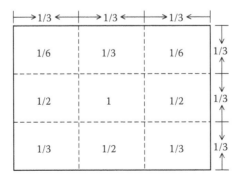

Figure 15.2 Weights {*W*} of different locations in a frame image. The rectangle denotes a frame image, values inside the rectangle are the weights, and the number 1/3 outside the rectangle denotes the current location in the frame image.

relations between the low-level audiovisual features and the affection, and attempted to derive a comparative relationship index between the emotion of a scene and the global emotion of the whole sequence. Based on the results obtained by Murray and Arnott [44], as well as those reported by Picard [27], vocal effects present in the sound track of an audiovisual sequence may bear broad relations to the affective content. For example, the loudness and speech rate are often faster for fear or joy and slower for disgust or romance, while the inflection, rhythm, voice quality (breathy, resonant), and especially the pitch- and motion-related features (pitch average, pitch range and pitch changes, motion magnitude) are commonly related to affective valence. Although it is a challenging issue to discriminate different emotions from audiovisual content, we can use the distance between the affective features in one scene and the whole sequence to express the affective relationship of this scene to the entire sequence. If the emotion of one scene is closer to the global emotion, we assume that this scene can represent the sequence better than those scenes that are not related to the whole sequence, affectively speaking. The distance between the emotion of a scene and the global emotion of the sequence is computed as follows. First, the pitch and loudness of every audio frame, as well as the luminance and representative motion vector of every video frame, are computed as affective features. Next, the averages of the affective features without the maximal and minimal 1% feature values are calculated and taken as the global affective features of the whole sequence. Furthermore, the averages of the affective features in each scene are defined as the affective scene features. Finally, the reciprocal of the Euclidean distance between the scene affective features and the global affective features is taken as the relationship index between the scene emotion and the global emotion.

After deriving the four semantic feature importance indices, including the SAI, the SRI, the FTI in a scene, and the emotional relationship index (ERI), a critical issue is to appropriately combine them into an overall semantic index representing the comparative importance indices of the divided scenes. Generally, the formation of visual perception can be considered as a combination of different factors. There are two representative mechanisms, namely, addition theory and average theory [45]. However, fusing different feature importance indices is difficult, because they were modeled in different ways and they might represent modalities that are not easy to compare. We have performed a statistical analysis (ANOVA) on the feature indices over all the video sequences employed in our experiments. The ANOVA results demonstrated that these feature importance indices are in principle independent from each other, while the dependency between different features within the same modality, for example, features related to both visual stimuli, is stronger than that across different modalities, for example, auditory features against visual features. Therefore, we can basically adopt the addition theory to combine different feature indices. Additionally, the studies of audiovisual multisensory integration have confirmed that the overall perception can be measured by an additive term and a multiplication of auditory and visual perception [46].

Consequently, in our experiments, we first normalize each of the feature indices into the range [0, 1] over all the segmented scenes in order to eliminate the modality-dependent amplitude differences. As SRI and FTS are related to visual information and independent from each other, they are summed into a semantic scene visual importance (SSVI) index as in Equation 15.6:

$$SSVI = SRI + FTI \tag{15.6}$$

Furthermore, ERI is modeled at an affective level, which is not only related to the audiovisual stimuli, but also correlative with some other perception mechanisms in the human brain. The SAI index is derived from the auditory stimuli. Thus, we employ the following fusion method, as explained in Equation 15.7, combining the different indices related to different perception modalities to compute a semantic scene importance (SScI):

$$SScI = SAI + SSVI + ERI + SAI \times SSVI \times ERI \tag{15.7}$$

We have also tested different fusion methods, such as averaging fusion, using different weights for each term, and found out that Equation 15.7 usually provides an accurate and robust result.

15.3.3 Semantic Shot Importance

The construction of semantic shot importance (SShI) model is similar but not identical to the scene importance model. Here the SAI and FTI of frames are still taken into account, while the processing unit is changed from a scene to a shot. Additionally, we believe that motion information, including camera motion and local motion, and shot length are two other factors in modeling SShI.

Different types of camera motion are used to represent the objective reality for catching the attention of viewers. Hence, camera motion is a useful clue for semantic importance analysis. A shot usually contains a certain types of camera motion, such as panning, tilting, rolling, tracking, booming, dollying, zooming, and still. Each camera motion has its own expressive ability. For example, zooming/dollying is always employed to emphasize the details or an overview scene, and the importance emphasis is proportional to the motion speed. On the other hand, panning or tilting usually reveals the surroundings horizontally or vertically while they cannot catch viewers' attention in fast motion [47]. Although other camera motion types have the respective expressive effect, it is difficult to map them to a single semantic purpose because of the scene complexity and directors' subjective intention. In our experiments, only zooming/dollying and panning/tilting are taken into account. We use a four-parameter affine model as in Equation 15.8 to detect zooming/dollying and panning/tilting motion types using a recursive outlier-rejecting least square algorithm based on the motion vectors, and the camera motion speed is approximated by the corresponding motion parameters [48]:

$$MV_{camera} = \begin{pmatrix} zoom & rotate \\ -rotate & zoom \end{pmatrix} \cdot \begin{pmatrix} x \\ y \end{pmatrix} + \begin{pmatrix} pan \\ tilt \end{pmatrix} \quad (15.8)$$

A shot usually contains one camera motion type, but sometimes zooming/dollying and panning/tilting exist simultaneously in some special scenes. Therefore, the camera motion importance (CMI) is defined as follows:

$$CMI = \begin{cases} 0, & \text{no zooming/dollying or panning/tilting} \\ \log(\max\{zoom, 1\}), & \text{only zooming/dollying} \\ \log\left(1 + \frac{1}{\max\{pan, tilt\}}\right), & \text{only panning/tilting} \\ \log\left(\max\left\{\frac{zoom}{\max\{pan, tilt\}}, 1\right\}\right), & \text{simultaneously} \end{cases} \quad (15.9)$$

Object motion, defined as the motion of the foreground object, is an important clue for video analysis, which can be obtained by the global motion compensation to motion vectors. Viewers generally pay more attention to those objects with fast moving speed. In addition, the temporal motion coherence is another useful clue for shot motion importance. The sensory data is processed in a continuous fashion, creating a continuous internal representation of the outside world. Comparatively speaking, a continuous and homogeneous motion with fast speed can attract more attention than slow and incoherent motion. Thus, we define the entropy of motion vectors of the macroblocks lying at the same location to express the temporal motion coherence of this location, as described in Equation 15.10:

$$E_{TM} = -\sum_{n=1}^{N} h_k(n) \cdot \log(h_k(n)) \quad (15.10)$$

where
   h_k denotes the probability density function of the phase histogram of motion vectors within the shot
   N is the number of the histogram bins

Then, we compute the average of all the entropies avg(E_{TM}) as the temporal motion coherence of this shot, and the importance index of the object motion is defined as follows:

$$OMI = \frac{avg(MA)}{avg(E_{TM})} \quad (15.11)$$

where avg(MA) denotes the averaged motion activity over all video frames in a shot, which is computed by the magnitude of motion vectors.

Additionally, as for the SShI in a scene, we assume that a longer shot is more important than a shorter one, because it can describe more story contents. Hence, the ratio (SLI) of the shot length compared with the scene length is considered as another index for SShI. Similar to the SScI model, all the SIIs are normalized into the interval [0, 1] over all the shots in a scene. Since these features are both related to the visual stimuli, the following additive fusion method is used to model semantic visual importance of a shot first:

$$ SVI = FTI + CMI + OMI + SLI \qquad (15.12) $$

where SLI denotes the shot length importance index.

Finally, following the similar fusion method between the semantic visual and auditory importance, the SShI is defined as

$$ SShI = SAI + SVI + SAI \times SVI \qquad (15.13) $$

15.3.4 Semantic Frame Importance

Since an isolated audio frame is semantically negligible for human perception, we only take visual information into account when computing semantic frame importance (SFrI). The FTI as well as the motion information are utilized. However, human faces and texts might not be present in all types of video content and all frames in a sequence. If face or text regions are not detected in a frame, we employ an image saliency model proposed by Itti and Koch [49] to extract salient regions for those videos or frames without human activity. The image saliency model is inspired by the behavior and neuronal architecture of the early primate visual system, and then multiscale image features, such as color, intensity, orientations, are combined into a single topographical saliency map. Salient regions that might attract more visual attention can be detected based on the saliency map. Figure 15.3 illustrates an example with an original frame image and the detected face, text, and salient regions. Subsequently, based on the detected face/text/salient regions, the size of these regions weighted by the location weight in Figure 15.2 is used as a region importance index (RI).

Furthermore, motion activity (MA) in terms of the magnitude of motion vectors of a frame is used while the spatial motion coherence is taken into account when constructing the SFrI model. Similarly, we define the entropy of all the motion vectors in a frame to express the spatial motion coherence:

$$ E_{SM} = - \sum_{n=1}^{N} h_k(n) \cdot \log(h_k(n)) \qquad (15.14) $$

(a)   (b)

Figure 15.3 An example of (a) original image and (b) upper rectangle: detected face, lower rectangles: text, and irregular shapes: salient regions. (From You, J. et al., Perceptual quality assessment based on visual attention analysis, in *ACM International Conference on Multimedia (MM)*, Beijing, China, October. 2009, pp. 561–564.)

where h_k denotes the probability density function of the phase histogram of motion vectors in a same frame. Finally, the SFrI is modeled as follows:

$$\text{SFrI} = \text{RI} + \frac{\text{MA}}{E_{\text{SM}}} \tag{15.15}$$

Figure 15.4 summarizes the proposed semantic importance analysis model for TV program structures: scene, shot, and frame. In addition, as many audiovisual features or terms have been derived in analyzing the semantic importance of different units, Table 15.2 lists all the abbreviations that we have defined in this chapter.

15.4 Hierarchical Multimedia Content Summarization for Rapid Browsing

Rapid content browsing from a large number of TV volumes requires an efficient representation of multimedia content, which allows viewers to quickly localize the most attractive segments. Content summarization that extracts the most representative excerpts from a long audiovisual sequence with many redundant contents is a useful tool for rapid browsing, as it can provide a much shorter collection of the original sequence for viewers to understand the main stories. Viewers usually have their preferred duration of a video summary for rapid browsing. On the other hand, we assume that a scene is usually more important than a shot in helping viewers understand the whole content, which in turn is more important than a

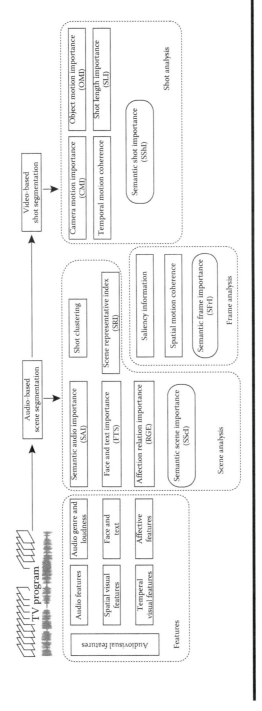

Figure 15.4   Semantic importance analysis for scene, shot, and frame.

Table 15.2   List of Abbreviations

Abbreviation	Full Term
STE	Short-time energy
VSTD	Volume standard deviation
VDR	Volume dynamic range
ZCR	Zero crossing rate
ZSTD	ZCR standard deviation
AMDF	Average magnitude different function
PC	Pitch contour
PSTD	Pitch standard deviation
SPR	Smooth pitch ratio
NPR	Non-pitch ratio
BW	Band width
FC	Frequency centroid
MFCC	Mel-frequency cepstral coefficient
SCI	Scene change index
GMM	Gaussian mixture model
HMM	Hidden Markov model
SAI	Semantic audio importance
FTI	Face and text importance
SRI	Scene representative index
ERI	Emotional relationship index
SSVI	Semantic scene visual importance
SScI	Semantic scene importance
CMI	Camera motion importance
OMI	Object motion importance
SLI	Shot length importance
SVI	Semantic visual importance in a shot
SShI	Semantic shot importance

Table 15.2   (*continued*)   List of Abbreviations

Abbreviation	Full Term
RI	Region importance
MA	Motion activity
SFrI	Semantic frame importance

frame, because continuous frames can represent the continuous behavior of objects while a single frame cannot express enough information for content understanding. Thus, we propose the following summarization approach based on the semantic content importance models in order to extract the most important or representative audiovisual clips for rapidly browsing the content of a TV program.

Step 1: For rapid content browsing, we empirically assume that half of all the scenes with lower semantic importance in a TV program can be dropped, as another half scenes should be able to represent the main contents of this program. It is worth noting that the duration of dropped scenes is dependent on the content genre. In this case, a genre classification algorithm might be required first to choose appropriate target duration of the scenes to be dropped.

Step 2: For the remaining scenes, viewers can browse them following the order of the SScI, from high to low. In addition, viewers might attempt to browse and understand the content as much as possible within a limited duration. For example, if a user prefers to view a summary of a given duration, which can be translated into frame numbers by the frame rate, for example, LF frames, we will compute the proportion ($p1$) of the semantic importance of a scene against the sum of the importance of all the remaining scenes, and then, the number of key frames of this scene is set as $ScL = [p1 \cdot LF]$, where $[\cdot]$ denotes the rounding operation. Then, we will go to *Step 3* to choose which shots being presented to the user in individual scenes.

Step 3: For a set of shots containing similar visual contents within each selected scene, only the shots having the highest SShI (in this case, the highest SShI usually corresponds to the highest SAI) are selected for the extraction of a representative excerpt. Therefore, a few representative shots with different visual contents can be obtained. For each selected shot, the proportion ($p2$) of its semantic importance against the sum of the importance indices of all the selected shots is computed, and the number of key frames in this shot is set to $SpL = [p1 \cdot ScL]$.

Step 4: In a selected shot, the key frames are determined according to the order of the SFrI, till the number of key frames of this shot achieves SpL.

Previously, we have presented a key frame extraction scheme for rapid content browsing. However, key frames can only provide a static representation of the multimedia contents, while they are not able to show continuous changes in the contents. We also propose the use of another dynamic summarization made up of a

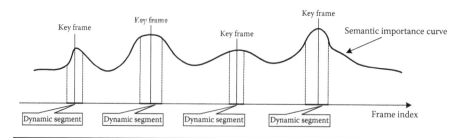

Figure 15.5 **Extraction of key frames and dynamic segments according to the semantic importance.**

group of segments from one sequence. Similar to the extraction of key frames, we assume that the predefined duration of the dynamic summarization of an audiovisual sequence is LD in terms of the number of all frames included in the dynamic summarization. LD is usually much longer than LF. We can also determine the number of frames that will be extracted in individual scenes and shots, as in the extraction of key frames. However, in generating the dynamic summarization, we extract those frames around a key frame and compose them as the dynamic summary. Figure 15.5 illustrates the extraction of key frames and dynamic segments.

Rapid multimedia content browsing can be performed by allowing the users to select the most important or representative frames/segments that can express the main story of the original program. According to the construction methodology of the proposed semantic analysis model, we believe that the portions (scenes, shots, or frames) extracted from the original sequence based on their semantic importance can describe the main content. Hence, viewers can recognize the main content of a TV program by watching the extracted portions. Though this chapter is mainly focused on extracting visual frames from the multimedia sequence, audio information is also important to convey the main content of a TV program. Therefore, audio content summarization can be generated by analyzing the interaction between auditory and visual stimuli based on the proposed visual summarization scheme. Additionally, another important issue in rapid content browsing is the way to present the generated content summary. As introduced in Section 15.1, either image set, mosaic, or tree-map can be used in the presentation of content summary. An important clue of video sequences is the temporal relations between different scenes. Therefore, it is critical to develop appropriate browsing presentation methods that can map the temporal dimension into a fast easy-to-grasp view. Subsequently, based on the generated multimedia content summary, an audiovisual sequence can be browsed rapidly without viewing the original sequence containing a lot of unimportant, redundant contents. On the other hand, as another important application of the semantic importance analysis, multimedia content retrieval can also be easily performed based on the extracted small portions with the help of audiovisual features.

15.5 Experiments and Discussions

The performance of either a multimedia content browsing method or a summarization system can be evaluated by the representative ability of the extracted collections. If a collection of key frames or clips with a small storage requirement can tell the main stories of a TV program to viewers, such collection can be used for rapidly browsing the original program or taken as a summary of the original version. However, accurately evaluating the performance of a content browsing/summarization system is a difficult task, as different viewers might have their individual preference or requirements for the representative frames or clips. Basically, two methods can be used to evaluate the performance of a multimedia content browsing system or a summarization scheme. One method is to evaluate the generated content summary itself in terms of its capability to describe the content of original sequences by subjective judgment. The other method is to ask viewers to generate their own preferred summary first, and then compare it with the summarized result generated by the summarization scheme using some evaluation criteria, such as correlation. However, such an evaluation method is usually difficult to perform in practical applications. The reasons are twofold. First, different viewers might extract significantly different summaries on a same original sequence, because they have different understandings on what clips are more important for themselves. Second, it is quite expensive for individual viewers to generate their own summary for each TV program. Hence, in our experiments, we employed the first evaluation method. Key excerpts are first extracted from an original audiovisual sequence, and viewers are asked to judge to what extent the extracted excerpts can express the original content in a subjective evaluation experiment by watching the original sequence and the extractions, respectively. The extracted image sets were presented to the viewers in their original temporal order in order to maintain the temporal relations of the extracted summaries in the original sequences. Another important issue in designing the evaluation experiment is the presentation order of the original content and the generated summary. Since a normal multimedia sequence usually lasts tens of minutes, a subject might lose his/her memory on the content summary if it was presented before the original content. Therefore, we first presented the original multimedia sequence such that a subject can understand the main content of the sequence. Subsequently, extracted key frames or dynamic segments were shown, and the subject can compare the content summary with the main content stored in his/her memory. Whereas, this presentation methodology might produce a hindsight bias because a subject might have prior expectation on the content summary since he/she has understood the original content. Therefore, designing appropriate test methodologies plays an important role in evaluating multimedia content summarization algorithm, which has not drawn enough interests from the research community so far.

In order to compare the performance of the proposed summarization algorithm, two other human-attention- and perception-based video summarization methods have been included in our experiments. Ma et al. [30] proposed an attention-based video analysis and used it to detect and extract key frames and important clips. The analysis model is constructed based on some low-level audiovisual features, such as object motion, static scenes, face, camera motion, and audio energy. An attention curve over all the frames in a sequence is then generated based on the combination of different attentive cues. Finally, static key frames can be taken as those frames corresponding to the local maximum points on the attention curve, and the frames around the local maximum points are extracted for generating the dynamic summary. In previous work, we have also proposed a human perception–based video analysis framework and applied it in video summarization [31]. Different visual perception models have been developed based on four salient factors that can influence viewers' perception when watching a video sequence, including local motion, contrast, special scene, and statistical rhythm. A perception curve of a video sequence can be generated by fusing four individual curves that correspond to the changes of the four perceptive cues. Key frames or clips are then extracted from the original sequence by searching for the local maxima on the perception curve. As explained in Section 15.2, these two analysis and summarization systems are both attempting to localize the local maxima on the attention or perception curve, and then the corresponding frames or clips are extracted as a video summary. In this manner, the extracted frames or clips might contain many unimportant or redundant contents because the analysis models do not take into account the relationship between a local part of the sequence and the whole content. However, the proposed analysis model in this chapter analyzes the content of an audiovisual sequence in a holistic structure, and the relationship between scene/shot/frame content and the whole sequence content has further been taken into account. Thus, in principle, the extracted key frames and dynamic segments using the proposed algorithm can accurately describe the most important content of the original sequence.

We have employed six typical TV program genres to evaluate and compare the performance of the proposed content summarization method and the two algorithms in [30,31]. These TV programs include sports program, news interview, nature documentary, ordinary movie, comedy, and tragedy. The comedy and tragedy programs were extracted from their original sequences by randomly selecting the excerpts, for example, the first, the middle, and the last half, as well as the entire sequences. These contents cover a range of different genres and are of different durations, therefore, providing a good test of the robustness and generality of the proposed method. Table 15.3 summarizes these TV programs, and Figure 15.6 illustrates an example of the proposed semantic content analysis model and the extracted key frames in two adjacent shots from a comedy program.

Before the actual subjective evaluation, we have conducted a trial test to determine appropriate length of key frames and dynamic summarization. In the trial test, five naive viewers were presented the extracted key frames and dynamic summaries with different durations, including 1%, 3%, 5%, 10%, and 20% for the key frames in respect to the original length, and 5%, 10%, 20%, 30%, and 50% for the dynamic

Table 15.3 Summary of the Employed TV Program Genres

Program Genre	Descriptions	Duration (min)
Sports	Football match containing abundant motion information	45
News	A news interview with different story units containing human faces, captions, and close-up	30
Documentary	A documentary describing the behavior of animals	50
Movie	A general movie with multicues, e.g., multiple actors, different scenes	90
Comedy	*Bruce Almighty* starring Jim Carrey; containing a lot of funny scenes	40
Tragedy	A disaster film containing a lot of depressive and horrific scenes	50

summaries. According to the trial test, 5% and 20% regarding the original length were chosen by the naive viewers for the duration of the key frames and dynamic summaries, respectively, which achieved the best trade-off between the capability of describing the original content and the time cost for content browsing. In the actual evaluation experiments, we have used different multimedia contents from those in the trial test. In generating static key frames, we extracted those frames having the highest values on the attention or perception curve as the key frames in the algorithms proposed in [30,31], till the total duration of these frames achieved the predefined length. For generating the dynamic summarization, a segment around the peak points on the attention or perception curve have been extracted, and the duration of each segment can be accordingly determined by the attention curve value and the perception curve value in [30,31], respectively.

In the subjective evaluation, we invited 20 nonexpert volunteers to evaluate the key frames or dynamic segments extracted by the three summarization methods in term of representative ability of the excerpts. The volunteers were asked to watch the original TV programs first, and then the key frames or dynamic segments, which were shown as an image set or a group of continuous video clips in their original temporal order, as long as the volunteers thought they have understood the meaning of these images or segments. Subsequently, the volunteers were asked to judge whether the key frames or the dynamic segments can accurately express the original content. The judgments were classified into five score levels of 100%, 75%, 50%, 25%, and 0%, in which 100% indicates that a volunteer can totally understand the main content by watching the extracted excerpts based on his/her own judgment, and

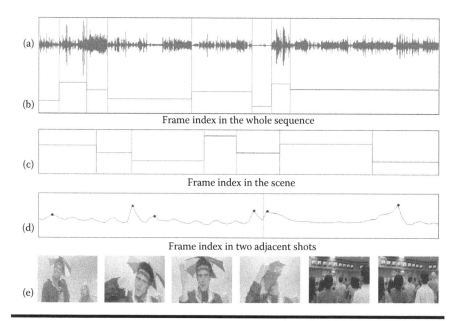

Figure 15.6   Semantic analysis results for a comedy program and the extracted key frames. (a) Audio samples; (b) semantic scene importance (gray vertical lines denote the scene boundaries); (c) semantic shot importance in the last scene in (b) (gray vertical lines denote the shot boundaries); (d) semantic frame importance in the fourth and fifth shots in (c) (gray vertical lines denote the shot boundary, and the dots denote the positions of the extracted key frames); and (e) extracted key frames in two adjacent shots. (From You, J. et al., Semantic audiovisual analysis for video summarization, in *IEEE Region 8 EUROCON2009*, St. Petersburg, Russia, May 2009, pp. 1358–1363.)

0% means that the extracted excerpts cannot express any meaning of the original sequence. The number of the volunteers corresponding to each score level was marked as vn_1, vn_2, vn_3, vn_4, and vn_5. Subsequently, the representative capability of a summarization method is calculated as follows:

$$E = \sum_{i=1}^{5} s_i \cdot \frac{vn_i}{20} \qquad (15.16)$$

where s_i denotes the score level. As a benchmark, if the volunteer numbers corresponding to each score level are equal to each other, the representative ability is 0.5.

Tables 15.4 and 15.5 report the evaluation results of the three summarization methods for extracting key frames and dynamic segments, and Figure 15.7 shows the overall scores as well as the 95% confidence interval of these methods with respect to different program genres, respectively. In order to eliminate the memory effect

Table 15.4 Evaluation Results of Representative Capability of Different Key Frame Extraction Methods

Program Genre	Proposed Method	Key Frame Extraction Method in [30]	Key Frame Extraction Method in [31]
Sports	0.83	0.81	0.72
News	0.75	0.79	0.78
Documentary	0.73	0.66	0.64
Movie	0.80	0.68	0.39
Comedy	0.75	0.63	0.44
Tragedy	0.79	0.71	0.74

Table 15.5 Evaluation Results of Representative Capability of Different Dynamic Segment Extraction Methods

Program Genre	Proposed Method	Dynamic Segment Extraction Method in [30]	Dynamic Segment Extraction Method in [31]
Sports	0.88	0.75	0.77
News	0.79	0.71	0.79
Documentary	0.74	0.59	0.68
Movie	0.78	0.64	0.57
Comedy	0.82	0.69	0.53
Tragedy	0.84	0.76	0.81

on evaluating the representative capability, different sequences have been used in generating key frames and dynamic segments in each program genre. According to the evaluation results, the proposed semantic analysis model is in principle more efficient for extracting key frames and dynamic segments in terms of both the representative capability and the confidence interval, compared with other two methods. The only exception exists in the news program. In our opinion, the possible reason is that the news programs contain a lot of different irrelevant news stories, and, thus, there is no a coherent narrative spanning the whole length, but a collection of independent stories. Consequently, even in the proposed summarization method, the key frames and dynamic segments were extracted according to the local maxima on the semantic importance curve, because the relationship between scene/shot contents and the global content is not significant. For other program genres, especially

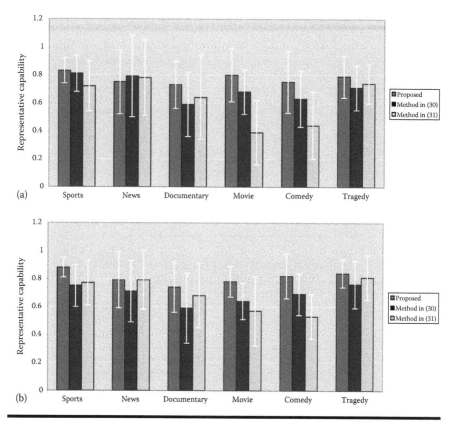

Figure 15.7 Overall representative capability and 95% confidence interval of content summarization methods: (a) Key frames; (b) dynamic summarization.

the movie, comedy, and tragedy, which have a master clue in an individual genre, the proposed summarization algorithm significantly outperforms other methods. This is because the semantic importance of different units in a TV program has been analyzed by taking into account the relationship between local units, such as scene and shot, and the entire sequence. Additionally, Figure 15.7 shows that the proposed summarization method provides a consistent result for the sports, comedy, and tragedy genres across different viewers, in comparison with other content genres. This is because these three content genres usually have coherent characteristics that can be captured by the proposed semantic content analysis algorithm, while the rest genres might contain various narratives.

According to the evaluation results across the static key frame and dynamic segment, we can find that the latter has only a little stronger capability to describe the main content of the original sequence, even though it usually has much longer duration than static key frames. The reason is that a dynamic segment usually contains a lot of redundant or duplicated frames which cannot provide more information for understanding the whole content. However, the use of dynamic summarization can bring more enjoyable experience for viewers compared with the static key frames. Furthermore, the evaluation results on the dynamic summarization are often more consistent than those with the key frames, which indicates that dynamic summarization can reduce the misunderstanding in conveying the original content as it usually maintains more temporal relationship of the original scenes than static frames.

15.6 Conclusions

In this chapter, we have reviewed state-of-the-art multimedia content analysis methods for structure and representation of the semantic meanings of audiovisual sequences. Two important applications of semantic content analysis, video summarization methods for rapid browsing, have also been investigated. Based on some carefully designed audiovisual features, we have proposed a hierarchical model for analyzing semantic content importance of different units: sequence → scene → shot → frame, in an audiovisual sequence in a holistic structure. Traditional multimedia content analysis methods usually attempt to extract important frames or clips corresponding to the local maxima from a generated curve that can describe the semantic importance in the temporal domain. However, such a methodology has some intrinsic disadvantages. In the proposed analysis model, we consider not only the local importance of frames and clips, but also the relationship between the local clips and the whole sequence. Therefore, the semantic importance analysis of the proposed model can always find and localize the most important parts globally from the original sequence for viewers to understand the entire content.

We have applied the proposed semantic content analysis model in extracting key frames and dynamic segments for rapid content browsing. With respect to different types of TV programs, we have extracted short excerpts of key frames and dynamic segments from the original sequences. A subjective evaluation experiment has been conducted to evaluate the performance of the proposed summarization algorithm as well as the comparison with two other video summarization methods. The evaluation results have demonstrated a promising performance of the proposed semantic analysis model and its applications in multimedia content summarization and browsing.

References

1. Y. Wang, Z. Liu, and J.-C. Huang, Multimedia content analysis using both audio and video clues, *IEEE Signal Processing Magazine*, 17(6), 12–36, 2000.
2. A. Cavallaro, O. Steiger, and T. Ebrahimi, Semantic video analysis for adaptive content delivery and automatic description, *IEEE Transactions on Circuits and Systems for Video Technology*, 15(10), 1200–1209, 2005.

3. J. You, G. Liu, and H. Li, A novel attention model and its application in video analysis, *Applied Mathematics and Computation*, 185(2), 963–975, 2007.

4. G. Ciocca and R. Schettini, Dynamic storyboards for video content summarization, in *Proceedings of 8th ACM SIGMM International Workshop on Multimedia Information Retrieval*, Santa Barbara, CA, October 2006.

5. A. Aner-Wolf and J. R. Kender, Video summaries and cross-referencing through mosaic-based representation, *Computer Vision and Image Understanding*, 95(2), 201–237, 2004.

6. M. R. Naphade and T. S. Huang, Extracting semantics from audio-visual content: The final frontier in multimedia retrieval, *IEEE Transactions on Neural Networks*, 13(4), 793–810, 2002.

7. W. H. Adams, G. Iyengar, C.-Y. Lin et al., Semantic indexing of multimedia content using visual, audio, and text cues, *EURASIP Journal of Applied Signal Processing*, 2, 170–185, 2003.

8. D. Bordwell and K. Thompson, *Film Art: An Introduction*, 4th edn., McGraw-Hill, New York, 1993.

9. C. Cotsaces, N. Nikolaidis, and I. Pitas, Video shot detection and condensed representation: A review, *IEEE Signal Processing Magazine*, 23(2), 28–37, 2006.

10. H. Zhang and S. S. A. Kankanhalli, Automatic partitioning of full-motion video, *ACM Multimedia Systems*, 1(1), 10–28, 1993.

11. J. Huang, Z. Liu, and Y. Wang, Integration of audio and visual information for content-based video segmentation, in *Proceedings of IEEE International Conference on Image Processing*, Vol. 3, Chicago, IL, October 1998, pp. 526–530.

12. Z. Liu, Y. Wang, and T. Chen, Audio feature extraction and analysis for scene segmentation and classification, *Journal of VLSI Signal Processing*, 20, 61–79, 1998.

13. I. Koprinska and S. Carrato, Temporal video segmentation: A survey, *Signal Processing: Image Communication*, 16(5), 477–500, 2001.

14. D. Lelescu and D. Schonfeld, Statistical sequential analysis for real-time video scene change detection on compressed multimedia bitstream, *IEEE Transactions on Multimedia*, 5(1), 106–117, 2003.

15. E. Wold, T. Blum, D. Keislar, and J. Wheaton, Content-based classification, search, and retrieval of audio, *IEEE Multimedia Magazine*, 3, 27–36, 1996.

16. T. Zhang and C.-C. J. Kuo, Video content parsing based on combined audio and visual information, in *Proceedings of SPIE's Conference on Multimedia Storage and Archiving Systems IV*, Boston, MA, September 1999, pp. 78–89.

17. X. Wan and C.-C. J. Kuo, A new approach to image retrieval with hierarchical color clustering, *IEEE Transactions on Circuits and Systems for Video Technology*, Vol. 8, September 1998, pp. 628–643.

18. W. Hess, *Pitch Determination of Speech Signals*, New York: Springer-Verlag, 1983.

19. B. Logan, Mel frequency cepstral coefficients for music modeling, in *Proceedings of International Symposium Music Information Retrieval*, Plymouth, MA, 2000.

20. Y. Deng, B. S. Manjunath, C. Kenney et al., An efficient color representation for image retrieval, *IEEE Transactions on Image Processing*, 10(1), 14–147, 2001.

21. Y. Chen and E. K. Wong, Augmented image histogram for image and video similarity search, in *Proceedings of SPIE Conference on Storage and Retrieval for Image and Video Database VII*, San Jose, CA, January 26–29. 1999, pp. 523–532.

22. Y.-P. Tan, D. D. Saur, S. R. Kulkarni et al., Rapid estimation of camera motion from compressed video with application to video annotation, *IEEE Transactions on Circuits and Systems for Video Technology*, 10(1), 133–146, 2000.

23. A. Ylimaz, O. Javed, and M. Shah, Object tracking: A survey, *ACM Computing Surveys*, 38(4), 1–45, 2006.

24. J. You, G. Liu, and A. Perkis, A generic framework for video event and content analysis, *Signal Processing: Image Communication*, 25(4), 287–302, 2010.

25. G. Xu, Y.-F. Ma, H.-J. Zhang et al., An HMM-based framework for video semantic analysis, *IEEE Transactions on Circuits and Systems for Video Technology*, 15(11), 1422–1433, 2005.

26. A. Hanjalic and L.-Q. Xu, Affective video content representation and modeling, *IEEE Transactions on Multimedia*, 7(1), 143–154, 2005.

27. R. Picard, *Affective Computing*, Cambridge, MA: MIT Press, 1997.

28. S. Pfeiffer, R. Lienhart, S. Fischer, and W. Effelsberg, Abstracting digital movies automatically, *Journal of Visual Communication Image Representation*, 7(4), 345–353, 1996.

29. S. W. Smoliar and H. J. Zhang, Content based video indexing and retrieval, *IEEE Multimedia*, 1(2), 62–72, 1994.

30. Y. F. Ma, X. S. Hua, L. Lu et al., A generic framework of user attention model and its application in video summarization, *IEEE Transactions on Multimedia*, 7(5), 907–919, 2005.

31. J. You, G. Liu, L. Sun, and H. Li, A multiple visual models based perceptive analysis framework for multilevel video summarization, *IEEE Transactions on Circuits and Systems for Video Technology*, 17(3), 273–285, 2007.

32. A. G. Money and H. Agius, Video summarisation: A conceptual framework and survey of the state of the art, *Journal of Visual Communication and Image Representation*, 19(2), 121–143, 2008.

33. D. Tjondronegoro, Y. Chen, and B. Pham, Highlights for more complete sports video summarization, *IEEE Transactions on Multimedia*, 11(4), 22–37, 2004.

34. A. M. Ferman and A. M. Tekalp, Two-stage hierarchical video summary extraction to match low-level user browsing preferences, *IEEE Transactions on Multimedia*, 5(2), 244–256, 2003.

35. ITU-R Recommendation 1387-1, Method for objective measurement of perceived audio quality, ITU Telecommunication Standardization Sector, 1998–2001.

36. G. Peeters, A large set of audio features for sound description (similarity and classification) in the Cuidado Project, Cuidado Project Report, Ircam, 2004.

37. J. A. Morales, A. M. Pernado, V. Sanchez, and J. A. Gonzalez, Feature extraction based on pitch-synchronous averaging for robust speech recognition, *IEEE Transactions on Audio, Speech, and Language Processing*, 19(3), 640–651, 2011.

38. N. Scaringella, G. Zoia, and D. Mlynek, Automatic genre classification of music content: A survey, *IEEE Signal Processing Magazine*, 23(2), 133–141, 2006.

39. J. F. Brendan, *Graphical Models for Machine Learning and Digital Communication*, MIT Press, Cambridge, MA, 1998.

40. L. R. Rabiner, A tutorial on hidden Markov Models and selected applications in speech recognition, *Proceedings of the IEEE*, 77(2), 257–286, 1989.

41. Y. Wu, E. Chang, and B. Li, Shot transition detection using a perceptual distance function, in *Proceedings of IEEE International Conference on Multimedia and Expo*, Lausanne, Switzerland, 2002, pp. 293–296.

42. E. Heelmås and B. K. Low, Face detection: A survey, *Computer Vision and Image Understanding*, 83(3), 236–274, 2001.

43. D. Chen, J.-M. Odobez, and H. Bourlard, Text detection and recognition in images and video frames, *Pattern Recognition*, 37, 595–608, 2004.

44. I. R. Murray and J. L. Arnott, Toward the simulation of emotion in synthetic speech: A review of the literature on human vocal emotion, *Journal of the Acoustic Society of America*, 93(2), 1097–1108, 1993.

45. J. Norman, Two visual systems and two theories of perception: An attempt to reconcile the constructivist and ecological approaches, *Behavioral Brain Science*, 25(1), 73–144, 2002.

46. C. Spence, Audiovisual multisensory integration, *Journal of Acoustical Science and Technology*, 28, 61–70, 2007.

47. Y.-F. Ma, L. Lu, H.-J. Zhang, and M. Li, A user attention model for video summarization, in *Proceedings of 10th ACM International Conference on Multimedia*, Juan-les-Pins, France, December 1–6, 2002, pp. 533–542.

48. R. Wang and T. Huang, Fast camera motion analysis in MPEG domain, in *Proceedings of IEEE International Conference on Image Processing*, Kobe, Japan, October 24–28, 1999, pp. 691–694.

49. L. Itti and C. Koch, Computational modeling of visual attention, *Nature Reviews Neuroscience*, 2(3), 194–203, 2001.

50. J. You, A. Perkis, M. Gabbouj, and M. Hannuksela, Perceptual quality assessment based on visual attention analysis, in *ACM International Conference on Multimedia (MM)*, Beijing, China, October. 2009, pp. 561–564.

51. J. You, M. M. Hannuksela, and M. Gabbouj, Semantic audiovisual analysis for video summarization, in *IEEE Region 8 EUROCON2009*, St. Petersburg, Russia, May 2009, pp. 1358–1363.

Chapter 16

Elaborating the Convergence of TV and Web (2.0) Content

Austrian and Finnish Field Study with Special Respect to Program Formats

Sabine Bachmayer
Johannes Kepler University Linz

Pauliina Tuomi
Tampere University of Technology

Contents

16.1 Introduction

The digitalization, internationalization, and marketing of the media have created new competitive online and mobile communication forms that have changed both television (TV) and radio. This development manifests in the increased competition and cooperation with online media (Ala-Fossi et al., 2008). It is very common for TV channels to offer additional information, content, and interaction between broadcasts and the web. "TV meets the Internet" is a global expression that characterizes digital and interactive TV (e.g., Jensen and Toscan, 1999). TV has become a part of the bigger puzzle of interconnected devices that operate on several platforms instead of just one.

Therefore, the main objective of this study is to elaborate on the current ways to link web and television since TV can no longer be seen as a separated platform. It is rather part of a bigger picture and getting connected to several platforms (such as web and telephone) not only by offering additional services and information on these platforms but also by TV program formats, inviting the viewer to interact and participate on these platforms. The questions are how is this connection done and at which level and characteristics? and is there potential for more, for example, by taking TV content analysis into account? With this focus, we addressed the following problem classes:

1. Survey of existing linkage mechanisms
2. Applicability of TV content for getting linked with web content
3. Describing the nature of the linkage mechanism
4. Identifying the potential of TV content analysis to bridge the gap for converging TV and web

The focus is not on reopening the field of interactive television like adding interactive elements to the TV content or similar. Also, we do not actualize a technical analysis of TV and web platform. In brief, our study gives the basic knowledge to develop the current situation, which was not found in literature at the moment of writing this chapter. To cover these questions, an analysis is performed on a sample set of TV program formats that feature convergence to the web. To narrow the sample set down, the focus is set on mainstream Austrian and Finnish TV channels and program formats. Details on the sample selection (including the Austrian and Finnish TV channels) are mentioned in Section 16.2. The description of the sample set (selected Austrian and Finnish TV program formats) is listed in Appendix 16.A.

The analysis of the selected program formats is in a first step accomplished by exploring how both platforms are connected. This is done by multiplatform analysis based on a developed catalog of criteria. Section 16.2 gives background information to the used methodology. Section 16.3 describes the developed catalog in detail. In a second step, we summarized the outcome of the analysis by defining classes from the most frequently observed combinations of criteria, which are mentioned in Section 16.4. The outcome of this classification serves as a basis for the concluding discussion in Section 16.5. Finally, in Section 16.6, this chapter is finalized by adducing ideas and assumptions how TV content analysis methods could impact the linkage of TV and web contents. The conclusion closes the chapter.

Please take into account that the used terminology is listed and described in alphabetical order in the Glossary at the end of this book.

16.2 Theory and Background

The meeting between mass and digital media opens a number of suggestive avenues for research (Deuze, 2006). In general, it is clear that research both on the production and reception side needs to draw on and combine existing traditions of research on broadcasting, web-based and mobile media (Ytreberg, 2009). New methods emerge for getting TV content via the web and interacting with TV content on set-top boxes (Borgotallo et al., 2010).

This study first analyzed the currently existing linking mechanisms between the TV and the web based on analyzing case studies in both Austria and Finland. Second, it investigated the potential of TV content analysis and a possible idea how TV content analysis could bridge the gap for the convergence of TV and web contents.

Our research view has not been addressed in any state-of-the-art work. The previous research concentrates on studying different technical solutions in order to combine TV and web contents. For example, Ma and Tanaka (2005) and Tanaka (2007) have concentrated on the fusion of the web and TV broadcasting. In their research, several ways to acquire information from diverse information sources of different media types, especially from web and TV broadcasting, are proposed. For these studies, three different prototype systems (e.g., TV2Web), for enabling users to watch web content in the same way as they watch TV, have been developed.

Bellekens et al. (2008) present their tool "iFanzy," which is a personalized TV guide application aiming at offering users' television content in a personalized and context-sensitive way. TV content and background data from various heterogeneous sources (set-top box, mobile phone, web) are integrated. Also, Ma and Tanaka (2003) have studied a method for dynamic integration of TV program content and related web content but eventually mainly demonstrated their prototype system called *WebTelop*. The European NoTube project has focused on the scenario of personalized semantic news. With the advancement of web technologies and with the convergence of various platforms for the access of multimedia content, new added value services were explored (Borgotallo et al., 2010). One more accurate study on TV formats is done by Bachmayer et al. (2009). In their work, they provided a simple categorization according to narration character, content types, and interactivity types of program formats. There is also some research on today's participatory and multiplatform TV formats already done (Tuomi, 2010; Ytreberg, 2009).

As research questions in the context of interactive digital television differ from those in traditional "lean-back" TV, an amalgamation of methodologies and methods is often necessary to fully comprehend the character and impact of the interactivity (Scannell, 1996). Therefore, our method of investigation is due to Espen Ytreberg's (2009) idea of a multidisciplinary platform analysis. In this chapter, based on his idea, the term *multiplatform* is used to include formats that feature a *central cluster* of television and web platforms, as well as various *peripheral* platforms from very different angles. "Multiplatform" itself as a term, in the computer industries and occasionally in media research, tends to focus on digital technology as providing a technological and design framework for incorporating existing media (e.g., text-based or audiovisual), platforms (e.g., chats, blogs, discussion groups), and/or software systems (e.g., Linux or Windows, gif or jpeg) (Jeffery-Poulter, 2003).

Besides this, our methodology is in turn based on a catalog of criteria that relies on preview literary research work followed by an analysis of existing work. Our goal was to define a complete scheme of criteria to provide an overview and multiplatform analysis of the state of the art. This is followed by researching and identifying gaps in this field with special focus on applied linking mechanisms. The research was executed by observing the current state of the linkage of (non)linear TV and web contents. The research material consists of observations from the web and TV formats broadcast by the most popular Austrian and Finnish TV channels. The overall research process is the following:

1. Selected the most popular Austrian (23 channels) and Finnish (13 channels) channels concerning their market share.
2. Analyzed current (in the scope of 2 years) TV formats on the selected channels to build the sample set. Every format that had a connection point to the web was taken into the sample set for the next step of the study.
3. Categorized selected formats and their connections to the web and summarized them in Table 16.1.
4. Identified the most frequent co-occurrences of criteria and combined them into six classes to exemplify the current situation on TV/web formats and the linkage between them.

16.2.1 Sample Selection

In both countries, Austria and Finland, there are few different ways how TV content is linked to the web. The sample set consists of 10 Austrian and 10 Finnish TV program formats (listed in Tables 16.1 and 16.2), which possess connection to the web. We have chosen representatives by analyzing the most present Austrian and Finnish TV channels. They were selected concerning their market share in 2010. In the following, we present a list of the analyzed TV channels as well as a list of the chosen TV program formats and web references for our sample set.

The research was executed by observing the current state of the linkage of (non)linear TV and web contents. The research material consists of observations from the websites and TV formats broadcast by the most popular Austrian and

Table 16.1 Summary of the Application of the Presented Methodology to Selected TV Program Formats

Example	TV Content		Web Content	Linkage		Purpose
	Structure	Genre		Technically	Thematically	
ZIB	Linear	News	Web page with video on demand and live streams, appearance in social network	Coexistence, linkage to media (live stream)	Content	Transmission
Helden von Morgen	Participatory	Casting show	Web platform including video on demand and social features, appearance in social network	Coexistence, linkage to media (live stream)	Story line	Additional information, transmission, influence
Bauer sucht Frau	Linear	Reality show	Web platform including video on demand and social features, appearance in social network	Coexistence	Content	Additional information, transmission
Willkommen Österreich	Linear	Comedy show	Web platform including video on demand and social features, appearance in social network	Coexistence	Content	Additional information, transmission
Am Punkt	Participatory	Talk and discussion show	Web platform including video on demand and social features, appearance in social network	Coexistence, linkage to content	Story line	Influence, additional information, transmission

Vote	Participatory	Music	Web page with voting gadget	Linkage to content	Story line	Influence
Alpenpanorama	Linear	Weather	Web page including live stream	Linkage to media	Content	Transmission, additional information
RTL Exclusiv	Linear	News	Web platform including video on demand, appearance in social network	Coexistence	Content	Additional information, transmission
Open Space	Interactive		Web page	Linkage to content	Story line	Influence
Battlestar Galactica	Linear	Drama series	Web page, video on demand, appearance in social network	Coexistence	Content	Shift
Aamu-TV	Linear	News	Web platform, appearance in social network	Coexistence, linkage to media	Content	Transmission
Summeri	Participatory	Youth program	Web platform, additional videos and social features, appearance in social network	Coexistence, linkage to content	Story line, content	Additional information, transmission, influence, participation

(continued)

Table 16.1 (continued) Summary of the Application of the Presented Methodology to Selected TV Program Formats

Example	TV Content		Web Content	Linkage		Purpose
	Structure	Genre		Technically	Thematically	
Maajussille morsian	Linear	Reality show	Web platform, additional videos and social features, appearance in social network	Coexistence	Content	Additional information, shift
Glee	Linear	Musical comedy drama	Web platform, additional videos and social features, appearance in social network	Coexistence	Content	Additional information, extra material
Kuorcsota	Participatory	Casting show	Web platform, additional videos and social features, appearance in social network	Coexistence, linkage to content	Story line, content	Participate, additional information, transmission
Heräämö	Interactive	Music	Web platform, additional videos and social features, appearance in social network	Coexistence, linkage to content	Story line, content	Influence, transmission

Linnan Juhlat	Linear	Media spectacle: independence day celebrations	Web platform, additional videos and social features, appearance in social network	Coexistence, linkage to content, linkage to media	Content	Additional information, participate, shift
Salatut Elämät	Linear	Soap opera	Web platform, additional videos and social features, appearance in social network	Coexistence	Content	Additional information, shift, transmission, extra material
Mitä tänään syötäisiin	Linear	Cook show	Web platform, additional videos	Coexistence	Content	Additional information
Ajankohtainen Kakkonen	Linear	Talk and discussion show	Web platform, additional videos and social features, appearance in social network	Coexistence, linkage to content, linkage to media	Story line, content	Shift, influence, participation, transmission

Table 16.2 Classifications of Selected TV Program Formats

Class #	Example Formats
I	Reality: *Bauer sucht Frau*, comedy: *Willkommen Österreich*, news: *RTL Exclusiv*, music: *Vote* and *Heräämö*, casting: *Helden von Morgen*, talk and discussion: *Ajankohtainen Kakkonen*
II	News: *ZIB* and *RTL Exclusiv*, reality: *Bauer sucht Frau*, casting: *Helden von Morgen*, misc: *Summeri*, music: *Heräämö*
III	Drama: *Battlestar Galactica* and *Salatut Elämät*
IV	Talk and discussion: *Am Punkt*, misc: *Summeri*
V	Music: *Vote* and *Heräämö*, casting: *Helden von Morgen*, misc: *Open Space*, talk and discussion: *Ajankohtainen Kakkonen*
VI	Weather: *Alpenpanorama*, news: *ZIB* and *Aamu-TV*

Finnish TV channels. In the following, we give a brief overview of the channels that broadcast program formats relevant to this study. The detailed description of the selected TV program formats can be found in Appendix 16.A.1.

16.2.1.1 Relevant Austrian TV Channel

16.2.1.1.1 Channel Description

Austria's national public service broadcast company is the ORF (37.8%*). Its main channel, ORF1 (14.6%), presents content in all genres ranging from children's programs in the morning and early afternoon to sitcoms and soap operas at noon and in the afternoon, and movies, shows, and TV series in the evening and at night. ORF2 (23.2%) focuses on national issues, arts, culture, and educational programs. Both channels broadcast news and sports reports between programs. ATV (3.5%) is a commercial free-to-air channel that targets youth and adults aged fewer than 50. It offers diverse entertainment 24 h/day ranging from foreign TV series and movies to its own productions of news reports and various shows. The free-to-air music channel GoTV (1.1%) also focuses on youth and young adults and broadcasts news, reports, and clips about national and foreign music scenes, recommendations, commercials, and sales for tickets to upcoming events. The noncommercial channel DORF TV is located and broadcasts in Upper Austria. "Der offene Rundfunk" (DORF) is a German acronym for "The Open Broadcaster," and the channel offers Upper Austrian viewers, organizations, and artists in movie/cultural/media production the

---

* Market shares (%) source: AGTT/GfK Austria/Teletest 2010. http://www.agtt.at/show_content.php?sid=23

ability to broadcast their own videos and contributions. The market share for DORF is unknown. It was chosen because of the user-centered focus. RTL Austria (6.3%), RTL2 Austria (2.4%), and 3Sat Austria (1.9%) are Austrian versions of German TV content. RTL and RTL2 are each specialized on an age-defined target group and broadcast mainly applied productions from children's programs to TV series and movies in all genres. 3Sat is a cooperation between German, Austrian, and Swiss public TV channels. The focus is on culture, arts, literature, and knowledge.

These eight channels represent a good overview about Austria's TV channel landscape since they are market leaders in Austria (covering a total share of 53%) and free to receive for all Austrians. Therefore, results are thus valid for most of the Austrian population.

16.2.1.2 Relevant Finnish TV Channel

16.2.1.2.1 Channel Description

Yle is Finland's national public service broadcasting company. Yle's channels 1 (22.2%*) and 2 (18.9%) produce and present programs dealing with national arts, educational programs, and children's programs. Yle's operations are financed mainly by television fee (€231.05 per year), and programming carries no advertising. The company is 99.9% state owned and supervised by the Administrative Council appointed by Parliament. MTV3 (21.6%) is a commercial free-to-air provider of entertainment and information, with its programming founded on news and current affairs, top sports, Finnish entertainment and drama, and international series and movies. SubTV (6.5%) is MTV3's daughter channel and it is clearly targeted to youth and young adults. It is a free-to-air channel, offering diverse entertainment 24 h/day. Sub is a mix of foreign series, Finnish productions, reality TV, and movies and classic series from the past. Nelonen (9.3%) is a commercial channel as well. It focuses on major Finnish entertainment, international series, and movies. TV Viisi (2.0%) is a free TV channel that airs feature films, documents, and series. These six channels were chosen for this study because of their popularity and market share and since every Finn is able to watch them. Results are then valid for most of the Finnish population.

16.2.2 Establishing a Catalog of Criteria for Multidisciplinary Content Analysis

16.2.2.1 Inclusion of Uncataloged Criteria

In this chapter, we propose a catalog of criteria for a structured classification and evaluation of existing mechanisms for linking TV and Web (2.0) contents. Our

---

* Market shares (%) source: Finnpanel 2010. http://www.finnpanel.fi/tulokset/tv/vuosi/share/
viimeisin/

rationale was to provide a fine-grained catalog as a prerequisite for an in-depth classification of existing approaches which allows evaluating the applied linking mechanisms.

The criteria for the classification were, in the first step, derived in a bottom-up manner from the TV content structure to the linkage mechanism itself. In the second step, each criterion was again split into subcriteria, derived partly in a top-down manner, leading in turn to other subcriteria. Criteria and subcriteria definitions found in other surveys were partly adopted and, if necessary, refined. In the course of the criteria description in the following, we indicate whether and how a criterion from related work was adopted or refined.

16.2.2.2 Excluding Nonrelevant Criteria

Some criteria that may be obvious for specific approaches or were proposed in related surveys had to be excluded from our catalog. Approaches can be classified in many different ways, for instance, with regard to their performance, implementation, platforms, usability and user acceptance, or provided functionality. Hence, different criteria may apply to different approaches. Obviously, some criteria had to be excluded because they would have increased complexity and cannot be measured without user studies and/or extensive case studies, for which resources were not available.

16.2.2.3 Establishing a Schema for Criteria Definition

A further goal was to provide unambiguous definitions of and values for the criteria. Therefore, each criterion is described by a set of properties:

- A *name* and *reference* to the source(s) when a criterion was adopted or refined from another source and a description of how the refinement was justified.
- A *case* or *example* to illustrate the description of the criterion. The cases and examples mentioned are not a complete list of all the cases and examples identified so far.
- When a criterion was redefined, a *line of argument* emphasizes its necessity in this approach.
- A *definition* specifying the criterion as clearly as possible with an optional discussion in case of difficulties or ambiguity.

16.2.2.4 Expanding the Selected Criteria

As previously mentioned, three main criteria (see Figure 16.1) were identified and expanded into several subcriteria. "TV Content" classifies TV content according to structure and therefore also according to its ability to immerse the viewer in

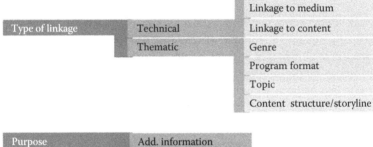

Figure 16.1   Catalog of criteria.

the story. "Web Content" addresses the technical formatting of the web content. "Type of Linkage" describes the level of connectivity between TV content and web content, according to technical and thematic linkage. "Purpose" addresses the purpose of the established linkage.

The following sections provide a detailed description of each criterion and its correlations.

16.3 Criteria in Detail

The following four main criteria (see Figure 16.1) help to elaborate the nature of the linkage between TV and web contents. In general, the linkage (or linkage mechanism) defines the level and characteristics of connectivity of at least two elements on involved platforms. As already mentioned, we focus on the element "program format" on the television's side. Since the focus is on television, the focus on web is kept more general as "Web Content." The connectivity in turn is realized by the usage of hooks that are given on both sides (TV and web) and defined and connected on different levels, namely, on technical and thematic level.

16.3.1 TV Content

This criterion classifies the selected TV program formats according to structure and genre. Additionally, we get the following information:

- Those kinds of program formats that are conveyed with the web
- The role of the TV content structure in the conveyance of TV and web contents (e.g., whether linear program structures are conveyed similarly via the web as nonlinear program structures)
- If existing, patterns within the genre (e.g., genre to web application, which genres have the strongest web presences)

16.3.1.1 Content Structure

To define the term "content," it is necessary to define its constituent parts essence and metadata first.

Essence: "Raw program material is referred as essence. Essence is the data that represents pictures, sound and text. Types of essence include video, audio and data of various kinds, including captions, graphics, still images, text enhancements and other data as needed by each application" (EBU, 1998).

Metadata: "Metadata is a generic term for all sorts of captured data that relates in one way or another to program material. It ranges from time code and details of technical conditions when material was created to the scripts used, the publicity materials created and descriptions of the shooting locations" (EBU, 1998).

According to the SMPTE taskforce, "Content equals metadata plus essence" (EBU, 1998).

Note: Please consider that we did not take into account any technical details concerning TV and web contents (e.g., MPEG coding or general standards as presented in (Morris et al., 2005)) since no technical connection between the encoding of the broadcast TV content and the web standards exists.

The content structure describes the geometric design or the media narrative space of a story. A narrative is defined as a series of events that are linked in various ways, including by cause and effect, time, and place. Something that happens in the first event causes an action in the second event, and so on (usually moving forward in time) (Garrand, 2006; Lugmayr et al., 2004; Samsel and Wimberley, 1998).

The media narrative space (or media/content structure) is defined as a place for immersing the viewer in the story flow not only explicitly as a kind of codirector, but also by building virtual communities, by communication with other viewers, and by obtaining natural or narrated multimedia assets. The literature distinguishes four narrative spaces: linear, branched, nondeterministic, and evolutionary. In TV, only the linear and branched narrative spaces have been applied. Therefore, this criterion does not provide any further distinction between the geometric structures mentioned and fuses nonlinear program formats into participatory formats.

Linear: Sequential structure is the basic building block of linear and interactive media projects. Linear (or sequential) structure, the most common type found in broadcasting media, has no links or interactivity. User navigation follows a strictly defined procedural path, as Figure 16.2a shows, without the possibility to jump or skip one node. In interactive media projects, the linear structure is not primary course, but a recurrent theme that keeps the story moving along. Its beginning and ending are known in advance.

Interactive: The main feature of interactive program formats is instant feedback (e.g., by sending an SMS* to a chat or a game on TV with the outcome immediately visible). We can further differentiate interactive content according to structure. To make a linear content structure, interactive means adding elements that are embedded within, and broadcast as part of, the TV content. A variant of the linear structure is adding cul-de-sacs (dead ends with only one entry/exit application) to individual nodes (see Figure 16.2b). This offers the user the possibility to step off

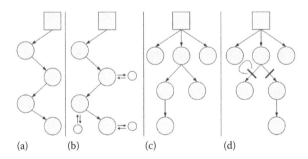

(a) (b) (c) (d)

Figure 16.2   Geometric design structures of content. (a) Linear, (b) cul-de-sac, (c) branches, and (d) conditional branches. (Adapted from Lugmayr, A., et al., *Digital Interactive TV and Metadata—Future Broadcast Multimedia. Signals and Communication Technology*, Springer New York, 2004.)

---

* Short message service used on mobile phones.

the procedural path into areas that are unrelated to the critical objective of the piece. For instance, they provide additional information about an athlete linked to TV content.

Participatory: This content format invites the viewer to become an active participant. It allows the user to explore several variants of a story (see Figure 16.2c and d). The participating viewer unfolds the points of variants collaboratively, but due to the broadcasting character of TV, there is usually a delay before the result becomes visible. In addition, individual participants cannot be sure whether their participation (e.g., voting for/against a person or an item) made a difference.

16.3.1.1.1 Genre

The Merriam Webster online dictionary defines genre as "a category of artistic, musical, or literary composition characterized by a particular style, form, or content" (cited from http://www.merriamwebster.com/dictionary/genre). However, in the context of video content, defining the term *genre* is difficult because of the myriad of already established categories. For instance, there are groupings by period or country ("American films of the 1930s"), by director/star/producer/writer/studio, by technical process ("CinemaScope films"), by cycle ("the 'fallen women' films"), by series ("the James Bond movies"), by style ("German expressionism"), by subject or theme ("thriller") just to name some (Bordwell, 1991).

We used the following categories:

Casting show: This type of show features the casting of, for instance, potential singers, models, or dancers. The main element is a group of candidates trying to prove their talent to a jury and the audience. Over several rounds, both jury and audience judge and vote for or against candidates until the winner is determined.

Comedy show: Comedy shows are usually fictive and serial type. The story line is mainly humorous and it is intended to spark the audiences' laughter.

Cooking show: It is a TV program that is hosted by famous chefs who teach people how to cook.

Drama series: It is a fictional and dramatically TV story featuring serious actors.

Music: A TV show where the majority of content clearly consists of music and musical elements.

News, sports, and weather: In general, they report world events as they unfold. Television news programs report current national and international events a day. News broadcasts often have sports sections that feature the latest events and results in sports. Weather provides daily forecasts.

Reality show: A reality show purports to be unscripted, although evidence points to scripting. Nonactors are filmed while interacting with each other or dealing with invented or contrived challenges. Reality shows are filmed in a fashion similar to that of documentaries, but with greater emphasis on interpersonal conflict, emotional reactions, or unusual events.

Sitcom: An amusing TV series about fictional characters, which is also known as a situation comedy.

Talk and discussion show: This type of TV show usually features a celebrity host who interviews, ordinary and/or celebrity, people. In talk shows there are generally several guests interviewed separately, when in discussion shows it is common that the group of people are discussing over a certain theme simultaneously.

16.3.2 Web Content

The second criterion "Web Content" addresses the technical formatting of the web content, whether it is realized as Web 1.0 or 2.0 but not on the technical standards used for implementation (e.g., service oriented architecture, Ajax).

Web page: A web page is an information resource that is suitable for the World Wide Web and can be accessed through a web browser. The web page contains additional information, gadgets (e.g., the possibility to vote for something), or videos related to the TV content in Web 1.0 phase.

Web platform: As Tim O'Reilly mentioned in his article (O'Reilly, 2005), Web 2.0 treats the web as a platform where users control their own data. Core features of a web platform are services, participative architecture (e.g., uploading videos, comment functionality, votes), availability of social features (e.g., blogs, discussion forums, like/dislike functionality, polls), and may also include video clips.

Social networking: The term "social networking" currently describes how people socialize or interact with each other throughout the web. It mostly refers to social networks (such as Facebook, MySpace, and Twitter). In our context, social networking refers to the presence of a TV program format in social networks as a special interest group, game, user, or similar.

16.3.3 Type of Linkage

The third criterion "Type of Linkage" describes the level of connectivity between TV and web contents. To link both sides, the so-called hooks are necessary (whether they were defined consciously or unwittingly) which can be defined on a thematic or technical level.

16.3.3.1 Technical

This subcriterion describes if TV and web contents are just coexistent or if technical linkage is realized in the form of defining hooks in the delivery medium or content.

Delivery medium (hence termed as medium) denotes the technical realization and representation of the content. Well-known standards are, for example, MPEG-2 and MPEG-4 as employed in the digital video-broadcasting (DVB) standard in Europe. Characteristics of the medium are metadata, frames, time stamps, and other features that are defined by the used standard. Content defines the substance that is transmitted via the medium as abstract model (e.g., a movie or radio show) and consumed by the audience. Characteristics of the content are, for instance, start and end point(s), scenes, and characters in scenes. Its course is defined by the narrative structure, timing, and pace. Access to the content is provided via the medium by a mapping mechanism (mapping characteristics of the medium to those of the content).

Coexistence: The web provides information and gadgets in addition to the TV content, in this case TV and web contents coexist. For instance, the web platform http://www.thesimpsons.com/, officially affiliated with the TV series *The Simpsons*, includes several services for fans (e.g., newsletter, shop, media library). However, series and platform features no technical linkage.

Linkage to medium: This category addresses the technical dependency on the broadcast medium (e.g., simultaneous TV and web transmission of content)—not only to a channel, player, or set-top box. Linkage to the medium can have influence or no influence to the medium.

Noninfluencing linkage: Does not affect the characteristics of the linked medium. For example, to define a certain scene or frame in the medium as hook previously. After the player detects this scene or frame for the first time, a noninfluencing web service is provided.

Influencing linkage: Affects the characteristics of the linked medium. One example would be to provide a 60-s chat as a joker in *Who Wants to Be a Millionaire*. This service is linked to the medium, as it is provided for a specified time interval. Influencing the medium means, for example, adapting the duration of the interval depending on the intensity of the collaborative activity.

Linkage to content: Web services relate to characteristics of the TV content and in turn affect its course and characteristics. For example, the story line or topic of a live discussion show is changed by the activity in the corresponding chat. Viewers can vote on a web page of a music channel for the music clips to be aired in the next show.

Noninfluencing linkage: Does not affect the characteristics of the linked content (e.g., course and/or characteristics). For example, to provide a chat on a web platform that is automatically enabled and disabled with the beginning and ending of the content.

Influencing linkage: Affects the course and the characteristics of the content. Taking the example of a 60-s chat as a joker in *Who Wants to Be a Millionaire*, this chat is linked to the content and influences its course.

16.3.3.2 Thematic

The thematic linkage is given purely by the topic, and there is no technical linkage. The following thematic linking types were observed:

Genre: Web content for specific genres (e.g., the web page http://www.aliena.de/
buntes/tv/tvkult.html about cult children series or a Facebook group about soap
operas).

Program format: Web content for a certain program format (e.g., prototypic
web platform for the program format *Who Wants to Be a Millionaire*). In this case,
a program format is a license to produce and broadcast a national version of a
copyrighted foreign television program and to use its name. Formats are a major
part of the international television market.

Topic: Web content that refers to the topic of certain TV content (e.g., web page
of *The Simpsons*).

Content structure/story line: Web content that refers to the TV content structure
and/or is (de)/activated at a certain stage, or time stamp of the story line. Therefore,
this kind of web content allows influencing the story line (e.g., by a voting functionality or by uploading video content to be broadcast). The linkage to the content
structure/story line also implies a linkage to the topic.

16.3.4 Purpose

This criterion addresses the purpose of the link between web and TV content. In
the following, we present a list of possible purposes:

Additional information: Providing web information in addition to the TV content
or its elements/objects.

Advertisement: Advertising the TV content or its elements/objects.

Interact with/participate in content: The viewer has the possibility to interact
with/participate in the TV content. Interaction is characterized by giving immediate
feedback to the viewer. For example, chatting in a TV chat. The viewers can see
their chat messages immediately on TV and they might get immediate response to
it. The viewer can also participate on different discussions, for example, on the chats
and discussions on the web platform.

Influence the content: To give the viewers, the possibility to influence the course
and/or characteristics of the TV content (e.g., by a voting mechanism) and to
offer viewers the possibility to participate in the show (e.g., by concurrent forum
and live TV discussion; the outcome of the forum discussion is introduced to the
discussion on TV). Influence can happen active or passive. Passive influence was,
for example, realized by the IST-LIVE project (Grünvogel et al., 2007). The LIVE
system observes the behavior of the viewers and adapts the TV content concerning
this observation. For instance, if many viewers were switching the channel during a
sports report, they changed reporting from soccer to skiing. Influencing the television
content actively comes along with interaction or participation. For example, voting
for a candidate influences the broadcast content by participation. However, contrary
to interaction, a participating viewer might not get an immediate feedback about

his/her participation. It even might not be clear whether the participation had any effect or not.

Transmission: Web transmission of content that is broadcast on TV. For instance, a newscast is offered as a video-on-demand stream after the (live) broadcast on TV.

Shift: The content is broadcast alternate on different platforms (it is shifted from TV to web and back again). For example, the main episodes of a drama series are broadcast on TV. To shorten the waiting time between seasons, mini episodes are made available on the web.

In both countries, there are few different ways how TV content is actually linked to the web which are described in the next sections. More precisely, the next section represents a summary of the analysis of the presented TV program formats in Table 16.1.

16.4 Classification

Table 16.1 is a compact representation of our analysis. It shows the evaluation of the earlier listed TV program formats concerning the proposed criteria.

To summarize the results in Table 16.1, the most frequent co-occurrences of the linkage criteria were combined into the following six classes:

16.4.1 Class I: Advertising Additional Web Content and/or Social Network Presence on TV

This class is characterized by coexisting TV and web contents that may be linked to the topic, depending on the purpose. In case only additional information is provided, the linkage is realized by advertising the additional web content or social network presence on TV. This is a dead end: there is no channel back to TV.

When participation or influence on the TV content is provided, linkage to the content exists. In all approaches analyzed, the linkage is realized by advertising the web content or social network presence on TV. Although there is no technical linkage, this is not a dead end. The link back to TV is realized by analyzing web activity manually or by using simple automated mechanisms (e.g., counting votes) and including the results in the content, for instance, by excluding a candidate in a live show. Representatives of Class I:

- *Additional information*: *Bauer sucht Frau*, *Willkommen Österreich*; *Maajussille morsian*, *Glee*
- *Presence in social network*: *RTL Exclusiv*; *Kuorosota*
- *To influence or participate via web*: *Vote*, *Helden von Morgen*; *Heräämö*, *Ajankohtainen Kakkonen*

16.4.2 Class II: Transmission of TV Content on the Web or Vice Versa

The transmission is characterized by coexisting TV and web contents linked thematically with the purpose of sharing between TV and web. The linkage is again realized by advertising web content on TV and vice versa. Representatives of Class II:

- *Media library* (TV content to web): for example, *ZIB*, *RTL Exclusiv*
- *Simultaneous TV and web broadcast*: for example, *Summeri* (TV and web), *Heräämö* (TV, web, and radio)
- *Internet-connected TV sets*: Web content to TV set (e.g., Google TV), YouTube content broadcast on TV

16.4.3 Class III: Shifting of Content from TV to Web and Back

This class is also characterized by coexisting TV and web contents linked thematically with the purpose of shifting the content from TV to web and back again. The linkage is implemented by advertising the shift of video content on TV or in the web. Representatives of Class III:

- *Battlestar Galactica*: TV series with mini episodes on the web between second and third season.
- *Salatut Elämät*: A few subplots are broadcast only online (e.g., during the breaks of the actual show).

16.4.4 Class IV: Linkage between Social Activity and TV Content

Although no technical linkage is given in this class, linkage to the TV content and thematic linkage to the story line exist. The purpose of this class is to influence or participate by activity in social applications or networks. Linkage is realized by the design of the TV content structure. Activity (e.g., answering questions in a forum) of the influencing and participating viewer is analyzed and integrated manually by the production team. Representatives of Class IV:

- *Am Punkt*: It invites the viewer to participate in the web discussion. The director integrates the outcome of the discussion and arising questions into the live discussion.
- *Summeri*: It offers possibilities to influence the TV discussions, for instance, via polls and interviewee suggestions.

16.4.5 Class V: Linkage between Web Activity and TV Content

This class is similar to the previous one. Although no technical linkage is given in this class, linkage to the TV content and thematic linkage to the story line exist. The purpose is to influence or participate by activity on a web page. Linkage is realized by the design of the content structure of the TV content. The story line invites the viewer to influence or participate, and the web activity (e.g., vote on a web page for a music track) of the influencing and participating viewer is analyzed and integrated/incorporated manually by the director or the team. Representatives of Class V:

- *Helden von Morgen*: It invites the viewers to vote for their favorite candidate via telephone or on the web page.
- *Vote*: It invites the viewer to vote for music tracks they want to be played in the show.
- *Open Space*: It invites the viewers to design content by uploading their own videos.
- *Heräämö*: It lets the audience suggest music and music videos they would want to see on the web platform.
- *Ajankohtainen Kakkonen*: It enables people to take part through different themed questions and so on.

16.4.6 Class VI: Linkage between Broadcast and Web Medium

Technical linkage between the TV medium and the web medium is hardly realized in practice. The only case we could observe is realized by synchronous transmission of the content on TV and web (e.g., live stream of news) as mentioned in Class II. Representatives of Class VI:

- *Alpenpanorama*: It broadcasts live views simultaneously on TV and web. The live stream is permanently available on the web and at specific times also on TV. The *ZIB* live stream is broadcast simultaneously on TV and web.
- *Aamu-TV* and Yle's *News*: Its live stream is broadcast simultaneously on TV and on the web.

As the summary in Table 16.2 shows, the main linkage between TV and web in Austria and Finland is the use of a web platform as a place for additional information and social consumer participation. The linkage is mainly at the levels of coexistent TV and web contents. As previously mentioned, both Austrian and Finnish TV make extensive use of the web to provide additional information, but notably the majority of the TV formats offer web platforms rather than just websites.

To conclude the discussion of the situation in Finland, it can be said that much could be achieved in the field of TV and web broadcasts. There is great potential in the participatory features of web platforms and social media in general that are not exploited at the moment. For example, Finnish TV history has gone through numerous trials that explored the interactive potential of TV formats. In some ways, Finland can be seen as one of the pioneers in the field of interactive TV entertainment (TV chats, TV mobile games, and interactive call quizzes) (Tuomi, 2008). Finnish iTV had its golden era around the year 2005 and, when nearly 50% of the TV formats were to some extent interactive (Aslama and Wallenius, 2005). Many of these interactive features that are and have been used in SMS-based TV interaction (symbiosis between the TV screen and the mobile phone) could also be used in web/TV participation. There are some more innovating ways TV content and watching experience can be supported also with the assistance of the web platform, for example, *Linnan Juhlat*, which is a yearly event that is held to celebrate and honor the independence of Finland. The president of Finland invites Finnish people that have been noteworthy and have forwarded equality and good values during the present year. This event is one of the most followed TV broadcasts in Finland. In 2010, YLE enabled people to watch the event and at the same time follow the Twitter conversation on the Text TV in real time. There were tweets coming from inside the Finnish Castle as well, which really widened the whole TV experience.

Yet another example of convergence and divergence between TV and other media technologies is the try out concerning the *Big Brother* "online real TV" spin-off from 2009 called *Nipsu-TV* (based on one of the contestants in season 2009). It was supported by SMS messages and one could buy viewing time via SMS (€1.50/h) and then insert the received SMS code to the website. The show was then broadcast on the website and it had lots of similarities to the *Big Brother* format itself. This is one of the ways that could be utilized when building the same kind of symbiosis of TV and mobile phone mentioned before, since the producers and TV channels are looking for ways that are also profitable. These financial considerations are probably one of the reasons why the web's potential has not been exploited accordingly. Like Syvertsen states, the competition and the loss of audiences to digital media threaten broadcasters' profit margins, leading them to explore the digital realm in search of new audiences and new sources of revenue (Syvertsen, 2006).

To conclude the situation in Austria, linkage between TV and web contents is practically not given and not well-established on the open market outside of the academic research area (at the moment of writing this chapter). The main reasons are the majority of TV sets on the market which are not connected to the Internet, as well as missing suitable interfaces and input devices. But we have to mention that the technical improvement of our TV sets goes well into the direction of converging TV and web contents. If we think of the situation a few years ago, one crux was the low resolution of TV sets. Today full HD Plasma, LCD, or LED TV devices with a mean resolution of 1440 × 1080 pixels are common. In addition, the trend is going to connect TV sets with the Internet as AppleTV and Google TV demonstrate. These trends open up the gates to scenarios as we mention in the following section. However, similar to the situation in Finland, no "real" technical linkage exists.

In both cases (Austria and Finland), the main realization of converging TV and web contents is limited to coexistent web content to TV content (for instance, web pages including specialized, additional information to the TV content) or transmitting TV content into the web. The social activity that is often initiated by offering social features on the coexisting web pages or by presence in social networks is barely integrated into the TV content—only two Austrian approaches were found when writing this chapter (one is listed in Table 16.1 which is *Am Punkt*). One reason may be the time-consuming, manual analysis of this social activity. Adaptations of web content to a changing story line in the TV content must be done by hand as well which are permanent time, effort, and money. For example, the casting show *Helden von Morgen* allows additional content and voting on the web. Since web lives on up-to-datedness, web content must be changed by hand (deleting web content and deactivating the voting for this candidate) if a candidate leaves the show. TV content analysis could find a remedy for automating those responsibilities. Additionally, most of the Austrian TV content is made for watching it passively. It does not invite the viewer to explore additional content or services on the web. Exceptional cases are TV shows offering some voting on the web.

16.5 Discussion

Currently, audience involvement and/or interaction with TV content via the web are almost nonexistent. There are a few examples of viewer involvement, for instance, by voting or commenting online. There are even fewer possibilities to influence TV content, as, for example, it is done via SMS (e.g., in reality TV spectacles such as *Big Brother*). This is undoubtedly due to financial considerations. Voting via chargeable SMS is much more profitable than free online voting. Next, we will thematically cover the topics that rose during our study and discuss the current situations in both countries.

Viewer participation: As mentioned earlier, there really is not that much concrete audience interaction via web to the TV content in the year 2010. There are few examples where people are allowed to take part in the actual broadcast via web, for example, by voting or giving a comment to the show online, via web platform.

Participatory program formats: This kind of program format is rare, although the few existing examples are quite popular (e.g., casting shows). Linkage to TV content exists, but it is paired with coexisting web mechanisms, and implemented manually.

Technical linkage: In general, we can say that aside from the simultaneous transmission of content on TV and web, there is no "real" technical linkage to influence course and characteristics of content via the web. This may be due to a lack of analysis functionality of social and web activity. Except in voting, the presented approaches of activity are analyzed and incorporated manually.

Patterns in content characteristics: When linkage exists, linear and nonlinear program formats are represented similarly, even though in the case of linear TV content the linkage is limited to coexisting web pages. In general, the genre does not play an important role. However, we were able to identify correlations between genre and linkage mechanisms. For example, voting mechanisms are suitable for casting shows and blogs suitable for talk shows.

What about association: It is noticeable that associations (e.g., providing web activity at certain time and state in the course of the TV content) between TV and web contents hardly exist. Also in the social TV area, social applications are mostly offered on a certain channel, but completely independent from the broadcast content. However, it is indicated that reference to the broadcast content is quite important for the success of such applications.

What about collaboration: The web remains highly collaborative and social used in combination with TV. One of the most frequently used collaborative mechanisms in this context is voting. However, various social applications, for example, likes/dislikes, discussions, small-scale voting, and polls on social networks such as Facebook, are changing the TV experience. Collaborative content creation takes place on the same platform, mainly at the content level.

Net–TV service is common: Almost every channel mentioned in this study has some kind of net–TV service. This enables the audience to watch episodes on demand. However, not all of the formats are available and some of them are also chargeable. Shorter video clips are often free of charge. In fact, just one of the TV show examples (*Salatut elämät*) offers the possibility to watch the next episode online before it is actually broadcast. This costs €2.95 per pre-webisode. It is obvious that TV broadcasters and channels struggle with the competition from online viewing, which is why they are eager to strike a balance between TV shows, online episodes, and other extra material.

Use of social media: Social media are definitely one of the easiest ways of linking TV and web. For example, Facebook is used for many of the purposes listed in our criteria. It can be used for voting, for polls, and obviously also for social purposes. It can also offer additional information and content transmitted from TV, for instance, in the form of video clips. Furthermore, it is a place for audiences to influence and to create content for the actual TV broadcasts. Since it is free, it is also a very cost-effective place for advertisements. It can be argued that the potential of the nonchargeable ways of linkage between TV and web rely heavily on the features and possibilities of social media. It may not bring any revenue to the broadcasters, but it bridges the gap between TV and online watching, engages the audience, and enables the incorporation of self-created content on TV for free. As mentioned in Chapter 15, social networks are also places to participate in polls and tests and to advertise online shops affiliated with TV programs and their contents.

Summing up, to make convergence of TV and web contents entirely successful in both countries, the following are necessary:

- Connect TV sets to the web by default.
- Connect TV content to web content by defining hook points on both parts.
- Provide adequate interfaces and input devices.
- Provide automatism (analyzing TV content, analyzing web activity, updating information, connecting to TV content).
- Provide nonlinear television content to invite the viewer to web activity.

Identifying criteria that cover all aspects of linking TV and web contents is at the same time necessary and challenging. In our study, we struggled to find common terms and to handle the differences between Austria and Finland. However, as a result, our criteria can now be applied worldwide, since we studied a wide range of areas and themes. By means of these criteria it is possible to enumerate the various and most common linkages between TV and web. There are also lots of difficult decisions to be made when analyzing the linkage itself. One of the inevitable problem areas is the overlapping categorization on the use of videos on the web platform to give one example. There are differences in whether the web platform actually offers whole episodes or just video clips as extra material and additional information. This gets even trickier when one tries to study the phenomena on the international level since there are certain phases every nation is at the moment of the study, for example, on IPTV and mobile TV usage.

However, our criteria can be used worldwide since the areas and themes are on a very broad level. With this criterion, it is possible to define the different and most common linkages between TV and web. Naturally, wider research (geographically and channel-based) is in order in the future. However, this research can be seen as a first step, and in whole the position of the paper is important for the research about TV and web since there is hardly any organized research on the matter. Earlier research concentrates mainly on different solutions more than coherent studies on that matter (Bellekens et al., 2008; Ma and Tanaka, 2003; Tanaka, 2007).

16.6 Future Scenario

In literature, different approaches concerning TV and web contents exist, as, for example, converting web content into TV content in (Nadamoto and Tanaka, 2005). In this section, we present some reference examples, which should demonstrate how TV content analysis could be used as a method for automating the linkage of TV and web contents in theory—more precisely, how the outcome of TV content analysis could be used for the linkage. The initial point builds TV content analysis methods presented in this book. With these examples, we try to provide a basis for future research, for instance, the elaboration of feasibility and factors, which could break and promote such scenarios. We do not provide a cost-benefit analysis or an analysis concerning their marketability (like pros and cons for broadcaster). In the following we present six scenarios, all using different TV content analysis techniques for linking TV and web contents. Due to the lack of space, the first scenario is described in detail; the remaining five scenarios are kept short.

16.6.1 Scenario #1: Using TV-Structuring Techniques

TV-structuring techniques are needed to precisely extract full programs in broadcasts and one step further to extract fragments or chapters out of a TV program (Manson and Berrani, 2010). Identifying the extracted components can help enable or disable web content and services automatically for the whole or in several fragments or chapters of the TV program as Figure 16.3 illustrates.

16.6.1.1 Example Scenario

A casting show for finding the world's greatest singer is given. In the current episode, eight candidates are fighting to pass this round and reach the next episode. Each candidate has to perform one solo song and one song in a group of two to four. Therefore, the show can logically be divided into several blocks, concerning the

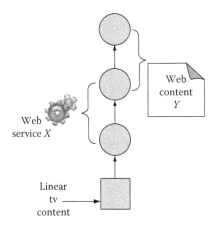

Figure 16.3   Linking fragments or chapters of a program with web content.

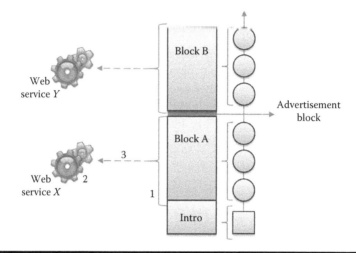

Figure 16.4   Illustration of the application flow of Scenario #1.

candidates, performances (see Figure 16.4). Those blocks can in turn be linked to several web services (e.g., voting service) as shown in Figure 16.4, which illustrates the application flow:

1. Recognizing and distinguishing the blocks: Identification of blocks (beginning, ending, id, content) can be done by using mechanisms provided by the medium, like metadata or scenes as defined in MPEG-4. In case of live TV shows, the critical issue is to add metadata to the medium in real time—in live TV shows.

2. Providing and identifying corresponding web services: Predefined and preselected web services are provided, for example, in a pool of services (on client or server side) or already running on a server and waiting for input from the medium. The web service is enabled and disabled concerning the progress of the medium.

3. Linking both parts: Points 1 and 2 define hooks that can be connected among others with a simple communication protocol between the player (in case of client-side web services) or the point of time when the certain frame of the block is broadcast and the server-side web service. For instance, the player recognizes metadata that identify the ending of block A. Therefore, it enables the web service X and disables it after the advertisement block that follows block A.

To realize the given steps, no special technology is necessary, just the implementation of a player and a communication mechanism between the player and web service(s). Barriers could be the real-time demands.

16.6.2 Scenario #2: Using Automatic Cast Detection

As the title of this paragraph assumes, TV cast detection is a technique to detect and recognize the cast of certain TV content. The outcome of this analysis can be used to load additional information, for instance, from the movie database http://www.imdb.com. This additional information can be provided on TV during the broadcast of this TV content in several designs and formats like in the form of an overlay, or just providing an icon in the right upper corner of the TV which can be activated by the viewer. Taking object detection into account, as presented in Takahashi et al. (2010), it is also possible to link web content directly to the character in the movie.

16.6.2.1 Example Scenario

Recognize Johnny Depp in the movie *Alice in Wonderland* and link his character in the video automatically to his personal web page on http://www.imdb.com. Or the other way around, delete web content automatically if a candidate leaves a casting show.

16.6.3 Scenario #3: Using Advertisement Detection, Commercial and Trademark Recognition

Advertisement and commercial detection attend to estimate the beginning and the end of an advertisement block and commercials (Naturel and Berrani, 2009; Schoeffmann et al., 2009). Trademark recognition is about recognizing trademarks in the broadcast TV content (Ballan et al., 2008). Detecting an advertising block in a first instance and recognizing trademark in the commercial in a second step may be a powerful tool to provide web content and services related to the actual commercial.

16.6.3.1 Example Scenario

An advertisement for delivering food is actually broadcast. Additionally to the phone number of this delivery service, a web service is provided to order pizza immediately during the broadcast of this advertisement. Or more easy, a link is provided to the web page of the delivery service including order mechanisms.

16.6.4 Scenario #4: Using Overlay Detection

In today's television, the viewer is confronted with overlays in the broadcast content permanently, as Figure 16.5* demonstrates. At the same time, the scientific

---

* Figure 16.5 shows a screenshot taken from the TV format *RTL-Shop* broadcasted on Channel 21.

Figure 16.5   Overlay on a home shopping format.

community is confronted with the challenge of designing applicable interfaces and input devices for TV. Automatic overlay detection, which is about the recognition and feature extraction of currently visible overlays, may be an easy mechanism to provide areas and objects for linking and including web content to the TV content. The prototypical platform "Overlay TV" http://www.overlay.tv demonstrates how to make noninteractive video content interactive and clickable. The platform allows creating overlays to current visible objects in a scene. The created overlay is linked to additional content concerning the underlying object (see Figure 16.6*) and may also be suitable as web links.

16.6.5 Scenario #5: Using Metadata

One mighty but maybe underestimated mechanism for convergence is the usage of metadata. Metadata allows embedding additional information into the TV broadcasting delivery medium, which is mainly MPEG-2 in Austria and Finland. Embedding metadata combined with a video player that is able to analyze the received video content concerning existing metadata, extracting and interpreting them. Metadata opens up a bunch of possible applications (see Figure 16.7), ranging from embedded links that are in turn addressed to overlays, to calling web services hosted on servers (as described in Scenario #1) or on their own computers up to services that in turn connect viewers, watching the same TV content, to allow collaborative participation.

---

* Overlay TV Inc.

Figure 16.6 **Screenshot of the platform "Overlay TV." (Taken from http://www. overlay.tv)**

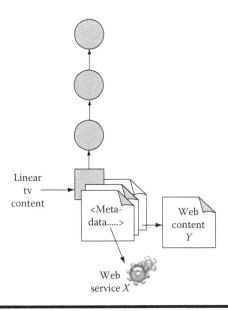

Figure 16.7 **The usage of metadata for linking TV and web contents.**

16.6.6 Scenario #6: Using Nonlinear TV Content

The trend is still going into the direction of adding web content or services to linear TV content which by force ends in coexisting TV and web contents. Linear TV content is constructed for watching it passively not for providing any additional activity. Although several trials of nonlinear television content have shown their popularity by the viewers, only casting shows could really establish. This may be caused by the higher production costs and the lack of deployed standards.

However, the convergence of TV and web contents, besides coexisting information, may need a rethinking of TV content design from linear to influencing/participatory/interactive, by planning a consideration of the web from the beginning (by the director in scripting phase): for instance, the levels of the broadcast content and its story line at which the web is applied (e.g., fractional or during the whole content); the design of the points of contact; should web activity have influence to the story line and if so, the analysis of the web activity; the integration of the web into the story line (e.g., inviting the viewers to be active on the web and indicating the additional web content), just to mention some. The contents from the web are also exploited directly in TV broadcasts. The user-generated content has been used in TV broadcasts. For example, the material uploaded to YouTube is used in different home video–based comedy shows. There is also an official TV show that reviews and shows only video clips from YouTube (http://www.rudetube.tv/). This is naturally very profitable for the TV producers since the content of the program is totally free and quite easily accessible. The owners of the videos usually do not get any reward other than becoming famous both in the web and TV. This also emphasizes the current trend. It is said that people want content and communication in short snack-size bites (Guber, 2007). This new trend toward brevity has implications for the next round of popular social media tools (Postman, 2009). The web material is perfect for this and it also suits the TV formats when gathered together as one show, for example, the funniest/most shocking/most popular YouTube videos.

16.7 Conclusion

Although TV and the Internet are the most popular entertainment media people use in their every day lives, the linkage between these two major platforms has so far been the focus of just a small number of scientific studies. More detailed research on the linkage and its potential is necessary, as both industry and academia have become interested in the topic. Our study can be seen as one of the first steps in this direction. Within our study, we analyzed the level of converging TV and web contents in Austria and Finland. Our sample set consisted of 10 Austrian and 10 Finnish TV program formats which feature linkage to the web. To analyze the sample set, we developed a scheme consisting of the categories "TV Content," "web Content," "Linkage," and "Purpose." This allows first a multiplatform analysis of each element in our sample set and second shaping the provided linkage mechanism.

Our hypothesis, of the television's current role with the web in TV spectacles and as additional source of information to the TV content, was confirmed. In addition, the prevailing application of coexisting TV and web contents, limited to thematic linkage, was noticeable.

Overall, TV is in major transition where it is evolving from just scheduled broadcast to being always-on, participatory, and social. The web remains highly collaborative and social used in combination with TV. Various social applications, for example, likes/dislikes, discussions, small-scale voting, and polls on social networks such as Facebook, are changing the TV experience. Collaborative content creation takes place on the same platform, mainly at the content level. Almost every channel mentioned in this study has some kind of net–TV service. This enables the audience to watch episodes on demand. However, not all of the formats are available and some of them are also chargeable. It is obvious that TV broadcasters and channels struggle with the competition from online viewing, which is why they are eager to find a balance between TV shows, with the help of online episodes and other extra material. Social media are definitely one of the easiest ways of linking TV and web. For example, Facebook is used for many of the purposes listed in our criteria. It can be used obviously for social purposes and to advertise online shops affiliated with TV programs and their contents. It can also offer additional information and content transmitted from TV, for instance, in the form of video clips. Furthermore, it is a place for audiences to influence and to create content for the actual TV broadcasts. Since it is free, it is also a very cost-effective place for advertisements.

It can be argued that the potential of the nonchargeable ways of linkage between TV and web rely heavily on the features and possibilities of social media. It may not bring any revenue to the broadcasters, but it bridges the gap between TV and online watching, engages the audience, and enables the incorporation of self-created content on TV for free. These nonchargeable ways to take part in TV broadcasts via web platforms will become more common in the future when engaging people with the happenings on TV (Tuomi, 2010). Also new, more innovative ways will be invented; for example, the Finnish (YLE's) tryout of using Twitter tweets on Text TV application in real time during the TV show is experimental. This broadens the TV experience and at the same time brings the web and social media closer to the TV content. It is noticeable that it is actually done through quite an old service, Text TV, which emphasizes the fact that new connections can also be made with the help of the older devices.

To conclude, the broadcasters alone do not make things happen. Some of the best innovations often come from the audiences and their practices. Technology can be used and combined in more ways than producers may imagine. For example, in Finland there are a few innovative ways the audience has created to establish linkage between the web and TV, for example, watching football on TV while chatting on the PC using a webcam, thus shaping today's TV watching experience with people at various locations. Also, the use of social media is reshaping the linkage between TV and web. Social aspects that it brings are affecting the collective TV experiences as well. The social side, all the talks concerning certain formats and shows, of TV cannot be forgotten since it is one of the pleasures TV offers—whether it occurs in coffee tables or in social networks. When it comes to TV shows and actors/actresses, the watching experience does not end in front of the TV. Often it emerges in discussions and in different social actions concerning the TV shows itself (Nikunen, 2005).

Like Gary Hayes has stated (Hayes, 2009), the conventional TV is going to keep its ground despite the fact that social mobile media and the Internet with the help of different mobile devices have gained more and more ground in TV production. TV is, however, still holding the center position among the other platforms. There are lots of activities in other platforms, for example, web and telephony, but still the fuel for this comes from TV content and broadcast. There have been speculations concerning the death of television, at least in its traditional sense. TV is reshaping itself in this struggle of other media by converging itself to others. On the contrary, TV is not dead, it is just transforming (Tuomi, 2010).

Appendix 16.A

16.A.1 Selected Austrian TV Program Formats

Alpenpanorama: *Alpenpanorama* on 3Sat Austria presents live panoramic views of the Austrian Alps with background. The corresponding web page http://www.3sat.de/alpenpanorama_index.html provides locations and live streams of the cameras also on the web, plus information and search functions for the background music that is played on TV. The show is produced and broadcast in Austria.

Am Punkt: *Am Punkt* is a live and participatory discussion show on ATV. Live guests participate in a moderated discussion about current topics (about politics or other events). Viewers have the possibility to influence the TV content and course of the discussion by using social media provided on the web platform http://atv.at/contentset/410627-am-punkt. During the live broadcast, the web platform provides a blog and a forum, which are observed and analyzed by the producer. The outcome of this analysis is integrated in the live discussion. The show is produced and broadcast in Austria. The show is available on Twitter.

Battlestar Galactica: *Battlestar Galactica* is a remake of the 1980 science fiction classic *Galactica*. The story line is about the human race searching for a new home called "Earth" after its 12 colonies were destroyed by the Cylons (artificial intelligent creatures created by the human race). The series was produced in the United States/Canada and broadcast all over the world (in Austria on RTL 2 Austria). The period between the second and third seasons was bridged by webisodes with the title *Battlestar Galactica: The Resistance*. The webisodes were provided on the web page http://video.syfy.com/shows/battlestar/the_resistance as streams, which represent a shift of the story line from the TV to the web and back again.

Farmer Wants a Wife (original title: *Bauer sucht Frau*): This is a casting show for single farmers looking for a wife (or the other way around). After an interview with a lonely farmer is broadcast, interested women can apply. The farmer chooses three candidates, who are invited to compete. The show is produced and broadcast in Austria, via ATV. A web platform http://atv.at/contentset/855462-Bauer%20sucht%20Frau offers additional information about the single farmers and their amour, and an RSS-Feed. Furthermore, additional video material on episodes, farmers, and candidates and Google maps to the location of the production plus comment functions are provided. The show is available on Facebook.

Helden von Morgen: *Helden von Morgen* is a casting show to find Austria's best singer. Fourteen candidates are selected from casting events in each federal state and then compete in a reality show. In Austria, the program format has been produced and broadcast since 2009. A web page http://heldenvonmorgen.orf.at/ provides additional information about the progress of the show and its candidates, additional video material, a blog, a forum, and web applications to comment and vote for/against a certain candidate. The show is represented on Facebook (21,323 fans).

Open Space: The channel "Dorf TV," which broadcasts the format *Open Space*, is a nonprofit open TV channel that gives everyone the possibility to publish and broadcast TV content. The format *Open Space* airs video content that is submitted by people to the web platform http://www.dorftv.at/pages/174. After the director has examined the submitted content, it is placed in the next broadcasting loop. The sender of the video is then notified by e-mail about the broadcasting time. "Dorf TV" is a local channel in Linz.

RTL Exclusiv: *RTL Exclusiv* is a gossip magazine about celebrities, produced in Germany and broadcast also in Austria (on RTL Austria). Its content is transmitted to the web and available as podcast, breaking news, e-mail, and compact video news on their web page http://www.rtl.de/cms/information/rtl-exclusiv.html. In addition, the show is represented on Facebook (4743 fans) and Twitter.

Vote: GoTV's *Vote* is a music clip show that allows the viewer to vote for music clips they want to be played in the show. The voting happens via the web page http://www.gotv.at/vote.php, based on a given list of clips. The list can be extended by one's own suggestions. The show is produced and broadcast in Austria.

Willkommen Österreich: This is a weekly Austrian late-night comedy show presented by the comedians Dirk Steermann and Christoph Grissemann (http://www.willkommen-tv.at/). The show is produced and broadcast in Austria on ORF1. It provides an additional web platform including social media, such as a forum, mailing list, and newsletter, and a calendar function, additional videos, and information. The show is available on Facebook.

ZIB (Original title: *Zeit im Bild*): *ZIB* is a newscast broadcast several times a day. It provides news at different levels of detail, depending on the time of the broadcast (e.g., *ZIB* at 7:30 PM gives a detailed overview of current events whereas *ZIB* Flash at 4:15 PM provides just a quick overview). The TV format has been produced and broadcast in Austria, via the channels ORF1 and ORF2. In November 2009, an online video-on-demand http://tvthek.orf.at/ and live stream http://tvthek.orf.at/live platform, called "ORF TVThek," to which content is transmitted, were launched. *ZIB* is available on Facebook.

16.A.2 Selected Finnish TV Program Formats

Aamu-TV: It is a Finnish news-based magazine program that airs every morning. It processes all the major national and international news topics. *Aamu-TV* is a conventional TV format with live stream. On the web platform http://yle.fi/uutiset/ohjelmat/aamu-tv/, *Aamu-TV* offers video clips, which means that morning highlights (interviews, news stories) are available on demand. *Aamu-TV* also has a traditional website mainly for additional information.

Ajankohtainen Kakkonen (A-Tuubi): It is a magazine show addressing important Finnish issues. The web platform http://atuubi.yle.fi/ohjelmat/ajankohtainen_kakkonen provides numerous social applications and polls. The audience can use the platform to vote and/or express their feelings by sending comments to the show and submit their video/photo content. After reviewing the video, the director and editors edit it.

Glee: It is a typical example of a foreign TV show in Finland. It is based on conventional broadcasting. The web platform http://www.sub.fi/glee/ offers additional information around the show (extra material, trivia on characters, etc.), tests, polls, background, pictures, blogs, discussions, episode summaries, and spoilers. *Glee* is on Facebook (9,992,259 fans). *Glee* is produced by Fox in the United States and broadcast in Finland.

Heräämö: It is a Finnish youth morning show that combines TV, web, and radio platforms. The audience is invited to take part by watching the live stream on TV. The live stream is also available online together with on-demand videos. It also provides the possibility to interact with the content during live broadcasts by asking questions and discussing topics in the blog and forum. Furthermore, viewers can use the website http://www.voice.fi/heraamo to vote for music clips they want to be played in the show. The show is also on Facebook (940 members).

Kuorosota: It is a talent/casting show for Finnish choirs. It features ordinary people who are directed and tutored by famous Finnish singers. People are able to vote for the best choirs, and every Sunday the choir with the fewest votes is eliminated from the competition. The web platform provides tests, contests, videos, discussion forums, video commenting, and additional information. The show is also represented on Facebook (1348 fans).

Linnan Juhlat: It is a yearly event that is held to celebrate and honor the independence of Finland. The president of Finland invites Finnish people who have been noteworthy and have forwarded equality and good values during the present year. This event is one of the most followed TV broadcast in Finland and, for example, the invitees' dresses and appearance are discussed weeks after in discussions and in press. Year 2010 YLE enabled people to watch the event and at the same time follow the Twitter conversation on the Text TV in real time. *Linnan Juhlat* is available on Facebook (487 fans) (http://yle.fi/linnanjuhlat/2010/).

Maajussille morsian: It is based on the international reality format *Farmer Wants a Wife*. It is a conventional reality TV format that follows Finnish farmers seeking the love of their lives via TV. The web platform offers additional information. For example, one can learn more about the farmers and their backgrounds and watch related video clips. There are also social applications available—discussion forums and a blog. The web platform http://www.mtv3.fi/maajussillemorsian/ is also used for advertising the format. The show is on Facebook (2833 fans).

Mitä tänään syötäisiin: It is a cooking show and is broadcast as a conventional stream. However, the website http://www.mtv3.fi/mitatanaansyotaisiin/ also provides video clips of each show (available for a certain amount of time) and all the recipes used and other additional information and material. Recipes are published on the web platform that also offers contests and cooking tips.

Salatut Elämät: It is a Finnish soap opera about common people and their everyday lives in Helsinki. Web platform http://www.mtv3.fi/salatutelamat/ offers video clips, social applications, webisodes, and extra material about the plot and the characters. The episodes can be watched in advance on a pay-per-view principle. The web platform provides tests, contests, videos, discussion forums, video commenting, additional information, and fictional blog texts by one of the characters as add-ons to the story line. The soap opera is on Facebook (107,504 fans).

Summeri: It is a popular Finnish format that handles youth themes and diverse content. It is a conventional TV format with occasional live streams. The web platform provides extensive additional information and participatory effects, for example, polls and extra material. The web platform also offers social applications such as a discussion forum and a blog. The audience can vote, for example, what themes and/or interviewees *Summeri* should present in future shows. Moreover, viewers can create their own video content and submit it to the TV show via the web platform http://summeri.squarespace.com/. Especially through the connection with Facebook (29,979 fans), viewer questions are transferred from the web to live shows.

Uutiset: The major national and international news are broadcast several times daily on TV. The Finnish Broadcasting Company's news appear on the website (all broadcasts are available online) http://yle.fi/uutiset/. The website lists the most significant news topics and offers additional information and video clips. The audience is able to participate in various discussions.

References

Ala-Fossi, M., Herkman, J., and Keinonen, H. (2008) *The Methodology of Radio- and Television Research*. University Press, Juvenes Print, Tampere, Finland.

Aslama, M. and Wallenius, J. (2005) *Suomalainen televisiotarjonta 2004.* Liikenne-ja viestintäministeriön julkaisuja 47/2005. Edita, Helsinki.

Bachmayer, S., Lugmayr, A., and Kotsis, G. (2009) New social and collaborative interactive TV program formats. In *Proceedings of the 7th International Conference on Advances in Mobile Computing and Multimedia (MoMM2009)*, Kuala Lumpur, Malaysia, pp. 121–128, ACM ISBN: 978-1-60558-659-5.

Ballan, L., Bertini, M., and Arjun, J. (2008) A system for automatic detection and recognition of advertising trademarks in sports videos. In *Proceeding of the 16th ACM International Conference on Multimedia (MM '08)*. ACM, New York, pp. 991–992. DOI=10.1145/1459359.1459544. http://doi.acm.org/10.1145/1459359.1459544 (accessed on October 25, 2011).

Bellekens, P., Sluijs, K., Aroyo, L., and Houben, G. (2008) Convergence of Web and TV broadcast data for adaptive content access and navigation. In *Proceedings of the 5th International Conference on Adaptive Hypermedia and Adaptive Web-Based Systems (AH '08)*, Nejdl, W., Kay, J., Pu, P., and Herder, E. (Eds.). Springer-Verlag, Berlin, Heidelberg, Germany, pp. 361–365. DOI=10.1007/978-3-540-70987-9_54. http://dx.doi.org/10.1007/978-3-540-70987-9_54 (accessed on October 25, 2011).

Bordwell, D. (1991) *Making Meaning: Inference and Rhetoric in the Interpretation of Cinema.* Harvard University Press, Cambridge, U.K.

Borgotallo, R. et al. (2010) Personalized semantic news: Combining semantics and television. User centric media: Lecture notes of the Institute for Computer Sciences, Social Informatics and Telecommunications Engineering, Vol. 40, Part 6, pp. 137–140. DOI: 10.1007/978-3-642-12630-7_16.

Deuze, M. (2006) Collaboration, participation and the media. *New Media & Society*, 8(4): 691–698.

EBU, S. (1998) Task force for harmonized standards for the exchange of program material as bit-stream—Final report: Analyses and results. Technical report, SMPTE/EBU.

Garrand, T. (2006) *Writing for Multimedia and the Web, Third Edition: A Practical Guide to Content Development for Interactive Media.* Focal Press, Oxford, U.K.

Guber, P. (2007) Let's do snacks. http://www.wired.com/wired/archive/15.03/snack filmtv.html (accessed on October 25, 2011).

Grünvogel, S., Wages, R., Bürger, T., and Zaletelj, J. (2007) A novel system for interactive live TV. In *ICEC'07: Entertainment Computing*, Springer, Berlin, Heidelberg, Germany, pp. 193–204.

Hayes, G. (2009) Social IPTV: Interactive and personal. In *Proceedings of the 24th conference of Screen Producers Association of Australia (SPAA 2009)*, Sydney, Australia.

Jeffery-Poulter, S. (2003) Creating and producing digital content across multiple platforms. *Journal of Media Practice*, 3(3), 155–165.

Jensen, J. and Toscan, C. (1999) *Interactive Television: TV of the Future or the Future of TV? Media & Cultural Studies 1.* Aalborg University Press, Aalborg, Denmark.

Lugmayr, A., Niiranen, S., and Kalli, S. (2004) *Digital Interactive TV and Metadata— Future Broadcast Multimedia. Signals and Communication Technology.* Springer, New York.

Ma, Q. and Tanaka, K. (2003) WebTelop: Dynamic TV-content augmentation by using Web pages. In *Proceedings of IEEE International Conference on Multimedia and Expo (ICME2003)*, Baltimore, MD, Vol. 2, pp. 173–176.

Ma, Q. and Tanaka, K. (2005) Topic-structure-based complementary information retrieval and its application. *ACM Transactions on Asia Language Information Processing*, 4(4): 475–503.

Manson, G. and Berrani, S.-A. (2010) Automatic TV broadcast structuring. *International Journal of Digital Multimedia Broadcasting*, 2010, Article ID 153160.

Morris, S. and Smith-Chaigneau, A. (2005) *Interactive TV Standards—A Guide to MHP, OCAP and JavaTV*. Elsevier, Focal Press, Oxford, U.K.

Nadamoto, A. and Tanaka, K. (2005) Complementing your TV-viewing by Web content automatically-transformed into TV-program-type content. In *Proceedings of the 13th Annual ACM International Conference on Multimedia (MULTIMEDIA '05)*. New York, pp. 41–50. DOI=10.1145/1101149.1101157. http://doi.acm.org/10.1145/1101149.1101157 (accessed on October 25, 2011).

Naturel, X. and Berrani, S.-A. (2009) Content-based TV stream analysis techniques toward building a catch-up TV service. In *Proceedings of the 2009 11th IEEE International Symposium on Multimedia (ISM '09)*. IEEE Computer Society, Washington, DC, pp. 412–417. DOI=10.1109/ISM.2009.99. http://dx.doi.org/10.1109/ISM.2009.99 (accessed on October 25, 2011).

Nikunen, K. (2005) Time for Fandom—Three Cases of TV-Show Fandom in Finland. Doctoral Dissertation, University of Tampere, University press, Tampere, Finland.

O'Reilly, T. (2005) What is Web 2.0?—Design patterns and business models for the next generation software. http://oreilly.com/Web2/archive/what-is-Web-20.html (accessed on October 25, 2011).

Postman, J. (2009) *Social Corp: Social Media Goes Corporate*. New Riders, Berkeley, CA.

Samsel, J. and Wimberley, D. (1998) *Writing for Interactive Media: The Complete Guide*. Allworth Press, New York.

Scannell, P. (1996) *Radio, Television and Modern Life*. Blackwell, Oxford, U.K.

Schoeffmann, K., Lux, M., and Boeszoermenyi, L. (2009) A novel approach for fast and accurate commercial detection in H.264/AVC bit streams based on logo identification. In *Proceedings of the 15th International Multimedia Modelling Conference*. Sophia-Antipolis, France.

Syvertsen, T. (2006) *Medien und Demokratie/Media and Democracy. Europäische Erfahrungen/Experiences from Europe*, chapter TV and Multi-Platform Media Hybrids. Corporate Strategies and Regulatory Dilemmas. Haupt, 1st edn., pp. 253–273.

Takahashi, T., Sugano, M., and Sakazawa, S. (2010) Important object detection from TV programs based on production technique estimation. In *Consumer Electronics (ICCE), 2010 Digest of Technical Papers International Conference*, Las Vegas, NV, January 9–13, pp. 251–252. Doi: 10.1109/ICCE.2010.5418807. http://ieeexplore.ieee.org/stamp/stamp.jsp?tp=&arnumber=5418807&isnumber=5418683 (accessed on October 25, 2011).

Tanaka, K. (2007) Research on fusion of the web and TV broadcasting. In *Second International Conference on Informatics Research for Development of Knowledge Society Infrastructure-Cover*, Kyoto, Japan, pp. 129–136. 10.1109/ICKS.2007.24.

Tuomi, P. (2008) SMS-based human-hosted interactive TV in Finland. In *ACM International Conference Proceeding Series*, Vol. 291 archive, UxTV, Silicon Valley, CA, pp. 67–70.

Tuomi, P. (2010) The role of the traditional TV in the age of intermedial media spectacles. In *Proceedings of the 8th International Interactive Conference on Interactive TV & Video 2010*, Tampere, Finland, June 09–11, 2010, pp. 5–14.

Ytreberg, E. (2009) Extended liveness and eventfulness in multiplatform reality formats. *New Media & Society*, 11(4): 467–485.

Chapter 17

Enhancing Social TV through Social Media Mining

Ovidiu Dan
Lehigh University

Junlan Feng
AT&T Labs Research

Bernard Renger
AT&T Labs Research

Contents

Social TV was named one of the 10 most important emerging technologies in 2010 by the *MIT Technology Review*. This general term covers many areas, including the integration of voice and chat capabilities into television sets, TV recommendations, video conferencing, etc. From a social network perspective, Social TV is concerned with mining information related to TV programs from social media and integrating the results into TV services.

This chapter will give an overview of recent social media mining technologies and their applications to TV-related services. In particular, we will cover three main themes related to Social TV. First, we will discuss retrieving social media content related to a TV program. Some TV shows such as *Lost* and *Heroes* have titles that are also common terms. Using these titles as keywords to search for relevant messages will lead to low precision. Conversely, many shows have long titles, which result in low recall as users do not use the full name of the shows. Appropriately retrieved social media content can be used to display social discussions on certain TV shows. Furthermore, retrieving such data with high precision and recall is crucial for a wide spectrum of applications and data-mining algorithms.

The second theme is social media mining for TV services. We will focus on sentiment analysis and detection of influential users in social networks. Analyzing messages for sentiments can help uncover the aggregate opinion of a large number of users with respect to certain TV shows or episodes. It can also be useful in presenting opposing views on the same subject. Graph analysis can be used to determine the most influential users that discuss certain TV programs.

The third theme is integrating the information mined from social media into a Social TV interface. This section describes the technologies that enable a user to interact with social media through television sets. We will present VoiSTV, a voice-enabled Social TV prototype system created at AT&T Labs Research.

In this chapter, we review the related work of Social TV as well as the recent technologies that have been developed to address the three themes we discussed earlier. Though we concentrate on TV programs and shows in this chapter, the underlying technologies can be ported to online media resources such as YouTube videos.

17.1 Related Work

Prior research in Social TV includes CollaboraTV [1], a PC-based system that allows avatars to share TV content synchronously and asynchronously using annotations and a closed social network (buddy system). Buddies can watch shows simultaneously, create text comments or share emotions (happy, sad, angry, etc.), which effectively provide recommendations or highlight interest points for those watching the show in real time or for those who watch the TV show asynchronously at another time. The Lancaster University ResNet.TV IPTV system [2] is a web-based system with a navigation interface that combines access to live TV/video on demand and web content, such as YouTube, with social media awareness. The PC interface allows the user to view the content in a picture-in-picture (PIP) window and see messages from social media sites such as Facebook and Twitter. In particular, tweets are pulled in from Twitter by searching for the program title using the Twitter search API. The system also has hooks in place for recommending content based on direct feedback and channel usage but this seems mostly geared toward recommending channels rather than specific shows. The queveo.tv is a Web 2.0 TV program recommendation system [3,4]. It combined both content-based filtering and collaborative filtering approaches to recommend programs for TV viewers. Collaborative filtering approaches rely on the availability of user ratings information and make suggestions to a target user base on the items that similar users have liked in the past. Content-based filtering relies on item descriptions and generates recommendations from items that are similar to those the target user has liked in the past.

Today, cable providers, software companies, and hardware manufacturers are launching products with Social TV functionalities. Boxee [5] provides software and also manufacturers a hardware device that allows viewing of photos and playing of music, movies, and TV shows. Twitter, Facebook, and Google Buzz integration are included so that any content that is shared will show up as a status update on these social media sites as well as on the Boxee website. Moreover, content that is posted on these other social media sites will also show up on the Boxee website (e.g., Twitter updates). But there is no notion of crowd sharing a live entertainment viewing experience since the content is not live. Various mobile device applications such as yap.TV [6] and Miso [7] let users follow what their friends are watching live or shortly after the live broadcast. These are used in conjunction with the TV set that the viewer uses to consume the video content. yap.TV integrates the actual TV guide grid and a list of trending shows, whereas Miso only has a list of trending shows or requires the user to search for the program name and "check in" (sort of like joining a chat room about that TV show). Either way, users of both can share the experience by messaging about the selected TV show. yap.TV has recently integrated Twitter feeds about the shows you are watching or following so users can follow yap.TV messages as well as Twitter messages. yap.TV does not appear to be doing any data mining as the Twitter messages all appear to have hashtags for particular shows.

Some cable and IPTV providers are integrating the social media experience so that a separate laptop or mobile device is not needed for reading or posting social media messages. Verizon FiOS [8], Yahoo! Connected TV [9], Google TV [10], and our VoiSTV system all have the advantage that allows users to access the full Twitter experience on the TV in a PIP window, so that the user can watch TV in one window or PIP and experience the Twitter experience in another portion of the TV screen. The Yahoo! Connected TV and Google TV products use either Internet ready TVs or a separate set top box (STB) to enable the marriage of TV and Internet with access to online or TV content. Verizon FiOS and VoiSTV only use a separate STB and much of the content is delivered over the IPTV-based format.

Verizon FiOS provides Twitter and Facebook widgets [8] that enable live Social TV such that the viewer can read social media messages about the program currently being watched. The Twitter widget uses the title of the current program as a search term to the Twitter API in order to retrieve tweets. Our VoiSTV system goes beyond issuing simple title search queries and uses data mining to find higher quality tweets. The Verizon widget does support most of the basic Twitter functions (search, view and post updates, follow trending topics, reply to tweets). However, users must type updates or select them from a list of canned entries using the remote control, whereas the VoiSTV system uses speech to speak the status update (or reply).

Yahoo! Connected TV [9] also provides a social media widget that supports traditional Twitter features. Viewers can watch TV in a PIP window while reading personal tweets. However, the widget does not display tweets relevant to the show being watched.

Similarly, Google TV [10] includes Twitter integration but does not show tweets related to what the user is watching. Otherwise, Google TV provides the expected Twitter functions (via an Android application) including viewing and posting status updates and interacting with tweets (reply, retweet, view URLs, and search Twitter functions using typed text or hashtags). Like in the case of the Verizon FIOS widget, users need to use the remote control or a keyboard to enter text.

Although Facebook is not a content provider, it is possible that they will be a big player in Social TV in the near future [11] by combining large amounts of video content and a very large social network. The Facebook Connect API already makes it easy for any website to integrate Facebook's social media capabilities. Furthermore, Facebook's "live stream" widget has been used by websites such as CNN to combine live streaming of video content with Facebook updates from others watching the live content (or from only your friends). Facebook has also unveiled a live video streaming channel, Facebook Live, which allows comments from users.

17.2 Social Media Content Filtering

This section studies the problem of filtering social media messages for use in Social TV applications. A common functionality among available Social TV applications is displaying social media posts relevant to the TV program the user is currently watching. The messages are displayed either alongside the video or on a companion device such as a mobile phone or tablet. The messages can be displayed individually or in some cases as aggregate statistics. Current Social TV applications search for these messages by issuing queries to social networks with the full title of the television program. This naive approach can lead to low precision and recall. As an example of a query that results in low precision, consider the popular television show *House*. Searching for the title of the show often yields results unrelated to the show. The word "house" could have several meanings, including "White House," "House of Representatives," building, home, etc.

Our main task is developing a method for determining which television show (if any) is referenced by a microblogging message. Filtering messages from microblogging websites poses several challenges. First, in the last decade alone television networks have aired more than a thousand new television shows. New shows are aired every 6 months. Obtaining training data for every show would be prohibitively expensive. Consequently, we need to make use of bootstrapping techniques to derive a classifier. Second, social media posts tend to be sparse. For instance, posts to the microblogging website Twitter are limited to 140 characters. Determining the context of such messages is challenging. Third, many messages lack proper grammatical structure, capitalization, or punctuation. This makes traditional natural language processing algorithms less effective. Fourth, most social media websites offer access to their posts through search APIs that have rate limits.

In order to filter messages, we first need to collect them by issuing queries to these services. For each show, we require a set of keywords that offers the best possible coverage while respecting the rate limits. Such queries could include the title of the show as well as other related strings such as hashtags and usernames related to the show. Determining which keywords best describe a TV show can be a challenge.

Assuming we can devise a robust filtering method with high precision, it could be used as a basis for several applications, including displaying messages related to particular television shows, measuring the popularity of television programs, displaying accounts and hashtags related to a show, TV program recommendation, and generating training data for speech recognition grammars for each television program (see Section 17.4). Properly filtering messages would also enable sentiment analysis and other aggregate statistics for each show. Last but not least, such an algorithm could give us insights in filtering other types of messages, such as messages related to organizations, products, important individuals, etc.

17.2.1 Overview of Bootstrapping Approach

Before any classification step can take place, we first retrieve candidate messages from the social media website. This retrieval step is needed because most social media websites offer search APIs that require keywords. Let $S = \{s_1, s_2, \ldots, s_n\}$ be a set of n television shows and let k_i be the set of keywords we use to search for candidate messages that might be relevant to show s_i, $\forall i = 1 \ldots n$. For now, we define k_i to only contain variants of the title of the show s_i. Let m be a message retrieved by searching for keywords in k_i. Then, we would like to train classifier $f(i, m)$, which outputs 1 if the message makes a reference to show s_i, and 0 otherwise. Note that i is an input of f, along with the message m. Since we know m was retrieved by searching for k_i, we can use this context when we compute the values of the features. This is a key aspect of our approach. Labeling training data for hundreds or thousands of television shows is a costly and time-consuming process. Instead, we will propose a method of training a classifier that generalizes to hundreds of television programs, but it only requires a small amount of training data and some domain knowledge. The features are designed to capture the general characteristics of messages that discuss TV programs instead of training to classify a specific show. For instance, the classifier could "learn" that messages that mention the names of some actors that play in the current show s_i are likely relevant to that show. The actors in the example would change depending on the context i.

We will next turn to another aspect of our bootstrapping approach. Figure 17.1 presents the process by which we use training data, domain knowledge, and a small training dataset to iteratively train the classifier. We start by training an initial classifier on the training data. As we will see, some of the classifier's features use domain knowledge on television shows. Next, the initial classifier is used to assign labels to a large corpus of unlabeled messages. From this corpus of messages, we derive more features that are combined with the ones from the initial classifier to form an improved classifier. Optionally, we can iterate this step using the improved classifier to improve the quality of the extra features.

17.2.2 Datasets

For training and evaluation, we use three datasets: $D1$, $D2$, and DU. We used Amazon Turk (AMT), an online labor market [12], to generate dataset $D1$. The labelers were asked if the message references the show. The possible answers were:

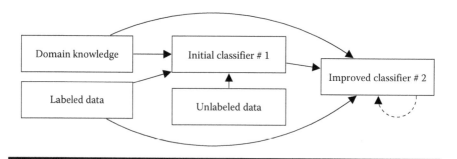

Figure 17.1   Overview of bootstrapping method.

"*Yes,*" "*No,*" and "*Not sure / Foreign language.*" Labelers were asked to successfully complete a test before being allowed to label data. We also requested that they have at least a 95% historical approval rating and that they have a mailing address in the United States. To generate the list of unlabeled messages for the AMT task, we picked three television shows with ambiguous names: *Fringe, Heroes,* and *Monk.* For each of these shows, we randomly sampled 1000 messages from our dataset *DU* described in the following text. In total, for *D*1 we have 2629 labeled messages. We conducted the labeling task in October 2010.

Dataset *D*2 contains 1082 messages labeled by our team. It is smaller in size but covers more shows than *D*1. The messages were sampled randomly through the Twitter Search API between May and September 2010. It does not contain messages where we were unsure of the label as we just skipped them while labeling. For most of the evaluation experiments, we will combine datasets *D*1 and *D*2.

The bootstrapping method described in Figure 17.1 makes use of a large amount of unlabeled data to improve features used by Classifier 2. We will call this corpus of data *DU*. The dataset consists of 10 million messages collected in October 2009 using the Streaming API provided by Twitter.

17.2.3 Initial Classifier

Before constructing the features for the first classifier, we need to determine the set *S* of television programs. For the purpose of this chapter, we will focus on popular television programs broadcasted primarily in the United States and United Kingdom. We collected lists of popular shows for each genre by crawling TV.com, a well-known website that offers information on television programs. Next, we developed features that capture the general characteristics of messages that discuss television shows.

While studying TV-related microblogging messages, we noticed that some of them contain general terms commonly associated with watching TV. Starting from this observation, we have developed three features: *tv_terms, network_terms,* and *season_episode. tv_terms* and *network_terms* are short manually compiled lists of keywords. *tv_terms* are general terms such as *watching, finale, episode, netflix,* etc. The *network_terms* list contains names of television networks such as CNN, BBC, PBS, Fox News, etc. Some users post messages that contain the season and episode numbers of the television show they are currently watching. Since Twitter messages are limited in length, this is often written in shorthand. For instance, "S06E07," "06x07," and even "6.7" are common ways of referring to season six, episode seven of a particular television show. The feature *season_episode* is computed with the help of a limited set of regular expressions that can match these types of patterns. All three features described earlier are in the range from 0 to 1. For example, if a message matches one of the patterns in *season_episode*, this feature will have the value 1. Otherwise, it will have the value 0. Also, throughout this chapter, we will assume that all features are normalized when needed.

Table 17.1   Examples of General Positive Rules

\<start> watching \<show_name>
episode of \<show_name>
\<show_name> was awesome

Next, we describe the process of deriving the feature *rules_score*. The motivation behind this feature is the fact that many messages that discuss TV shows follow certain patterns. Table 17.1 shows such patterns. *\<start>* means the start of the message and *\<show_name>* is a placeholder for the real name of the show in the current context s_i. When a message contains such a rule, it is more likely to be related to television shows.

We developed an automated way of determining such general rules and their probability of occurrence. We start from a list of 10 unambiguous television show titles. The list was compiled manually by our team in a few minutes. It contains titles such as *MythBusters, The Simpsons, Grey's Anatomy,* etc. We searched for these titles in all 10 million messages from *DU*. Each message was processed to extract the rules. The system replaced the title of the unambiguous show found in the message with the term *\<show_name>*, mentions of patterns recognized by feature *season_episode* with the term *\<episode>*, and it also replaced quotes with *\<quote>*. Mentions to other Twitter users ("*@user*") were replaced with *\<user>*, URLs with *\<url>*, and mentions of time such as "*9 AM EST*" or "*10:20*" with *\<time>*. After splitting the messages into a vector of words, and adding the elements "*\<start>*" and "*\<end>*" at the beginning and end of the vector, respectively, it used a sliding window of three word trigrams to extract rules around the title *\<show_name>*. The result is general rules such as the ones we have seen in Table 17.1. Furthermore, we also compute the occurrences of these rules in dataset *DU* to determine which ones have a higher chance of occurring. Using these rules, we can then give a value between 0 and 1 for the feature *rules_score* to each new message.

Although many social media messages lack proper capitalization, when users do capitalize the titles of the shows, this can be used as a feature. Consequently, our classifier has a feature called *title_case*, which has the value 1 if the title of the show is capitalized, otherwise it has the value 0. Another feature that makes use of our list of titles is *titles_match*. Some messages contain more than one reference to titles of TV shows. Some examples are listed in Table 17.2. If any of the titles mentioned in the message (apart from the title of the current context s_i) are unambiguous, we can set the value of this feature to 1. For the purpose of this feature, we define *unambiguous title* to be a title that has zero or one hit when searching for it in WordNET [13].

One of our assumptions is that if a message contains names of actors, characters, or other keywords strongly related to the show s_i, the probability of $f(i, m)$ being 1

Table 17.2 Examples of Messages That Mention the Titles of Several Shows

If I'm sick call **HOUSE**, if I'm dead call **CSI**
grey's anatomy & **supernatural**
Lets see - **Jericho**, **Heroes**, and now **Caprica**.
Don't tell me to watch a series you like.
If I like it, it'll get the axe for sure :-/ #fb

increases. To capture this intuition, we developed three features: *cosine_characters*, *cosine_actors*, and *cosine_wiki*, which are based on data crawled from TV.com and Wikipedia. This feature captures the cosine similarity between a message and the list of characters, actors, and the Wikipedia article of the assumed show s_i, respectively.

17.2.4 Improved Classifier

Once we have an initial classifier, we can label the messages in DU and derive new features. Two such features, *pos_rules_score*, and *neg_rules_score*, are natural extensions of the feature *rules_score*. Whereas *rules_score* determined general positive rules, now that we have an initial classifier, we can determine positive and negative rules for each show in S separately. For instance, for the show "*House*" we can now learn positive rules such as *episode of house*, as well as negative rules such as *in the house* or *the white house*.

Using messages labeled by Classifier #1, we can determine commonly occurring hashtags and users that often talk about a particular show. These features are *users_score*, and *hashtags_score*, respectively. Furthermore, these features can also help us expand the set k_i for each show, thus improving the recall by searching for hashtags and users related to the show, in addition to the title.

Lastly, having a large number of messages allows us to create one more feature, *rush_period*. This feature is based on the observation that users of social media websites often discuss about a show during the time it airs. Knowing this, we keep a running count of the number of times each show was mentioned in every 10 min interval. When a new message needs to be classified in the context s_i, we check how many mentions of show s_i there were in the previous window of 10 min. If the number of mentions is higher than a threshold equal to twice the mean of the mentions of all previous 10 min windows, we set the feature to 1. Otherwise, we set it to 0.

17.2.5 Evaluation of Classifiers

We begin our evaluation by running a 10-fold cross-validation of the initial classifier on the $D1 + D2$ dataset. By $D1 + D2$, we mean the dataset composed of messages

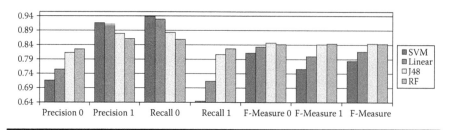

Figure 17.2   Classifier 1–10-fold cross-validation on *D1* + *D2*.

in $D1 \cup D2$. The results are shown in Figure 17.2. To save space, we will refer to labels "*Yes*" and "*No*" as 1 and 0, respectively. Along the X-axis, we displayed the precision, recall, and F-Measure of the two labels. Precision is the fraction of classified tweets as Label *Y* that are correct. In our case, *Y* is either 0 or 1. Recall is the fraction of tweets that should be classified as label *Y* and are correctly classified. F-Measure combines precision and recall to give a single performance measurement. We use the harmonic mean of precision and recall as the F-Measure. We also plotted the combined F-Measure of the two labels. We ran the experiment on four classifiers: *SVM* [14], *Linear* [15], *J48* [16], and *Rotation Forest (RF)* [17], which also uses [16].

We ran all classifiers with their default settings. Although we report results for both labels, we are mainly interested in the performance of the *Yes* label. Figure 17.2 shows that we can achieve a precision of over 90% with both the *SVM* and *Linear*. In fact, all four classifiers achieve a precision over 85% for the label. Unfortunately, the results suffer from poor and inconsistent recall. *SVM* and *Linear*, which had the best precision, have especially bad results. Overall, the best classifier for this experiment is RF, which achieves an F-Measure of 83.9%.

Next, we turn our attention to the improved classifier. We first run the same evaluation as for the initial classifier. Figure 17.3 shows the results of the 10-fold cross-validation on the *D1* + *D2* dataset. We can easily see that the recall has improved significantly for label *Yes* for all four classifiers. Again, the best-performing classifier is RF, with an F-Measure of 87.8%. Also, the Linear classifier

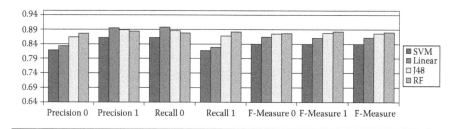

Figure 17.3   Classifier 2–10-fold cross-validation on *D1* + *D2*.

yields the best precision of 89% while still maintaining a respectable F-Measure of 85.6%.

17.3 Social Media Data Mining for Social TV

17.3.1 Sentiment Analysis

Sentiment analysis is an area of research at the intersection of natural language processing, computational linguistics, and text mining. Generally speaking, sentiment analysis aims to determine the opinion or attitude of the writer. There is a large body of work in this field, especially on news and product review datasets [18]. Sentiment analysis can be attempted at several granularities, such as at the document, sentence, or word level. There are several subtasks of sentiment analysis: polarity (negative, positive, or neutral), subjectivity (subjective and objective), and aspect-based (sentiments toward certain aspects of a topic). There have been attempts at testing [19] and recently adapting [20] sentiment analysis algorithms to microblogging messages.

Sentiment analysis is a valuable tool in Social TV as messages that discuss TV shows can be analyzed for polarity to determine the aggregate sentiment of viewers. This information can then be used to recommend content and to present opposing views about TV shows. With the increasing popularity of online social media, TV viewers tend to share more of their TV watching experience on social network sites in the form of short posts, blogs, and videos. Sentiment analysis of TV-related social media content is complimentary to information provided by traditional TV program rating organizations such as Nielsen, which focus on reporting audience size. Aggregated sentiment for TV programs can be valuable for TV content providers, TV network operators, or TV viewers.

In many previous studies, research on sentiment classification is conducted on review-type data, such as movie or restaurant reviews [21], blogs [22], and news [18,23]. Most of these systems were built based on machine-learning models such as support vector machines (SVMs) for sentiment detection. Features used are word-based (n-grams), lexicon-based, or based on the output of natural language parsers. The involved datasets often consist of relatively well-formed, coherent, and at least paragraph-length pieces of text. Furthermore, resources such as polarity lexicons and parsers are usually available for these domains. Sentiment analysis of social media posts, however, faces different challenges, where most posts or comments are short (one or two sentences) and informal, with abbreviations, typos, or ungrammatical language usage.

Sentiment analysis of Twitter messages has recently received great attention from both research and industry. Barbosa and Feng [20] reported a two-step sentiment analysis method for Twitter using noisy training data. It first classified tweets as subjective (polar) and objective (nonpolar), and further distinguished polar tweets as positive and negative. The classification model is based on SVMs. The training data were collected from three popular real-time tweet sentiment detection websites.

It emphasized using more abstract features beyond simple n-grams such as meta-features and tweet syntactic features. Meta-features include part-of-speech tags, dictionary-based word prior subjectivity and polarity, and negative expressions. Tweet syntax features include retweet, hashtag, reply, hyperlinks, punctuations, emotion expression symbols, as well as upper cases. These features have proved to be more robust than n-grams.

Celikyilmaz et al. [24] proposed to use latent Dirichlet allocation (LDA) to build polarity lexicon from a given subset of tweets and extract features based on this obtained lexicon. The argument is that in cases with noisy text, such as with tweets, the use of off-the-shelf polarity lexicons may not be as useful as using lexicons extracted from the given dataset. Davidov et al. [25] presented an approach for using hashtags and smileys in tweets to improve sentiment detection.

Social media posts concerning TV programs are a special subset, where TV program-related entities such as program titles, specific episodes, and character names are referred to in a variety of ways. Correctly detecting these entities is important for improving the performance of sentiment detection, since instantiations of these entities often contain emotional words such as the word "love" in the TV show *I Love Lucy*. These words without preprocessing will be extracted as word-level features and confuse the sentiment classifier. Another observation is that many TV-related posts are sarcastic or ironic such as a comment "a great show, wonder who wastes time on it," which makes sentiment analysis more challenging.

Technologies underlying sentiment analysis will continue to improve. Sentiment analysis will play an important role in the evolution of Social TV.

17.3.2 Social Network Influencers

Social influence can be described as power—the ability of a person to influence other persons' thoughts or initiate other persons' actions. Information and influence propagation in social networks have been actively studied for decades in the fields of psychology, sociology, communications, marketing, and political science. In 1955, psychologists Morton Deusch and Harold Gerard described two psychological needs that lead humans to compete for the attention of others [26]. One is informational social influence (our need to be right) and the other is normative social influence (our need to be liked). For Social TV applications, knowing influencers for a given TV program is useful for tracking how viewers exchange their thoughts.

For online social networks, [27] has summarized the social structures into three categories: pyramid, circular, and hybrid. An example of the pyramid structure is Twitter. Influencers such as CNN have millions of followers, while the influencer does not follow back. Facebook is an example of a circular social structure, where Facebook users befriend only a select number of people or brands. The hybrid social structure combines the circular and pyramid-shaped community frameworks. Automatically detecting influencers on online social networks has recently received a great amount of attention from both research and industry.

In industry, Klout [28] tracks influence of users on online social networks including Twitter and Facebook. It measures users' influence using the Klout score, which is calculated based on 35 variables such as follower/follow ratio, unique retweeters, unique messages retweeted, and username mention count. The scores range from 1 to 100 with higher scores representing a wider and stronger sphere of influence. The size of this sphere is calculated by measuring true reach (engaged followers and friends vs. spam bots, dead accounts, etc.). The strength of influence is calculated by tracking interactions across your social graph to determine the likelihood of someone listening to or acting upon any specific message. TunkRank [29] is another tool to measure user influence on Twitter. The TunkRank score is a reflection of both how much attention your followers can directly give you and how much attention they bring you from their network followers.

In research, there has been a broad spectrum of algorithms proposed to measure influence on online social networks such as the number of retweets and the number of followers, PageRank, H-index, Passive-Influence algorithm, and k-shell decomposition. Measuring influence based on the number of retweets and followers has been widely used as a baseline. More advanced metrics are based on models such as the k-shell model.

PageRank is a link analysis algorithm that assigns a numerical weight (PageRank value) to all elements of a linked graph [30]. The PageRank value is calculated recursively depending on the number and PageRank metric of all pages that link to it. Weng et al. [31] extended the original PageRank algorithm to measure the influence of Twitter users. The proposed algorithm, TwitterRank, considers both the topical similarity between users and the link structure between the user accounts.

The Hirsch index (or H-index) [32] is used in the scientific community in order to measure the productivity and impact of a scientist. A scientist gets index i if he has i articles published that have been cited at least i times each. In a social network, a user has index i if i of his messages have been retweeted or mentioned at least i times each. The higher the H-index, the more influential the user is expected to be.

The IP algorithm was recently proposed in [33] to address the observation that the majority of users on Twitter act as passive information consumers and do not forward the content to the network. The IP algorithm interactively estimates the influence and passivity of users based on their information-forwarding activity.

Kitsak et al. [34] proposed to apply k-shell decomposition to identify influential spreaders in complex networks. The basic method behind k-shell decomposition is to group all nodes in the network that have k (or less) connections or that are only connected to nodes with k (or less) connections. Nodes in the higher groups are more influential. The motivation behind the k-shell decomposition algorithm is to find the core of a given social network, which can spread information more efficiently.

These previously applied algorithms and frameworks can also be used in detecting influencers for TV-related social media content. The main difference is the focus on a narrower domain.

17.4 Integrating Mined Data into Social TV Interfaces

In this section, we will present VoiSTV, which allows users to interact, follow, and monitor the main social media messages (tweets) on Twitter related to a TV show being watched. More specifically, VoiSTV first collects relevant tweets for each show, by employing a novel bootstrapping algorithm based on machine learning to suggest query expansions and determine if a candidate tweet is truly relevant to a given TV show (see Section 17.2). VoiSTV archives and mines the collected tweets in order to capture trending topics, detect sentiments on the tweets, as well as estimate the popularity of shows. The collected corpus along with the mined metadata is valuable for a number of TV applications such as TV program navigation, search, and recommendation. VoiSTV presents its results in a graphical interface on the TV STB to enable Twitter access capabilities through the TV as well as to provide access to the archived corpus and metadata. From this interface, users can also compose tweets using speech and post the recognized speech as a status update.

17.4.1 VoiSTV Architecture

The VoiSTV architecture, as shown in Figure 17.4, has three major function blocks: Data Manager, Data Mining Module, and Application Manager. The Data Manager retrieves tweets relevant to TV shows and archives them. The crawler takes the TV

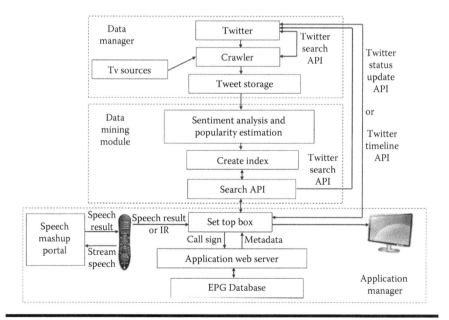

Figure 17.4 VoiSTV architecture.

program sources as input and retrieves relevant tweets for each TV show through Twitter search APIs and archives them in the Tweet Storage for later analysis and indexing.

The Data Mining Module focuses on mining the archived data and creating the search index that is used by the Application Manager through search APIs. It returns relevant tweets for a given TV show, ranks the messages based on recency, returns tweets with positive and negative sentiment, returns the most popular messages for each show (most retweeted), provides aggregated statistics such as sentiment analysis (percentage of positive, neutral, negative), provides a popularity chart showing the number of messages about a particular show in the last week, and provides a word cloud of trending topics.

The Application Manager integrates the archived Twitter data, Twitter stream data, and the generated data from the Data Mining Module into an interactive interface on the TV. Speech input from the voice-enabled remote control is streamed to the Speech Mashup Portal [35], which provides the speech recognition result. The underlying speech recognition engine is AT&T Watson [36]. The STB displays the recognition result and allows the user to confirm it before sending the tweet using the Twitter status update API. The role of the Application Web Server is to host the application web page that runs on the STB. Essentially all the capabilities described earlier about the STB are possible because of the Application Web Server. The Application Web Server also runs a web service to handle database requests to the EPG database for metadata for a given channel. This is needed in order to determine the show title currently playing on that channel.

The Data Manager and the Data Mining Module run in the backend independent of any user action on the STB, whereas the Application Manager handles the real-time interaction of the user with the STB.

In terms of hardware and operating systems, the Data Manager and Data Mining Modules each use Dell M605 Blades with two Quad-Core AMD Opteron(tm) Processor 2350 (2.00 GHz and 16 GB memory) running CentOS release 5.6. The Application Manager uses the Dell PowerEdge 610 with X5680 Processor (3.324 GHz with 16 GB memory) running CentOS release 5.6. The Speech Mashup Portal as described in [35] is a dedicated cloud solution for supporting various AT&T speech services but could, for example, be implemented on the Amazon Elastic Compute Cloud (Amazon EC2) [37]. The STB hardware is a Motorola VIP1216 and the Motorola KreaTV SDK [38] was used to support the portal application environment that enabled us to use HTML/JavaScript to develop the application web page running on the STB.

17.4.2 VoiSTV User Interface Capabilities

The STB is the center point of the system from the userŠs point of view. Traditionally, the remote control is used for changing channels and navigating TV menus. In our system, user's can navigate the TV menus, read tweets (personal or about the current TV program), speak tweets by pressing a TALK button on the voice-enabled remote, see the speech recognition output on the STB/TV, send tweets (status update), reply to tweets, and retweet tweets. Every time the user switches channels, the STB fetches the TV show information from the electronic program guide (EPG) database, which contains schedule and show information for the upcoming 14 days, and uses the program name to retrieve tweets relevant to the current show through the Search APIs in the Data Mining Module. The STB displays the TV content (high definition video) and the relevant tweets on the same screen. Instead of tweets relevant to the current program, it can also show the user's personal tweets on the same screen as the TV show. Other data that can be displayed on the TV include top tweets (most retweeted) for the current program, positive/negative tweets, various charts (aggregate positive/neutral/negative sentiment percentages, word cloud of hot topics about the program, and popularity), and Twitter trend data using Twitter APIs (top trends overall, in last day, in last week).

17.4.3 VoiSTV User Interface

This section will focus on what the user sees on the TV screen and how the user interacts with the TV and Twitter. The main menu options are *Program Tweets*, *My Tweets*, *Program Trends*, *General Trends*, and *Send Tweets*. The menu options are shown on the left and navigated by using the up and down arrows. Each menu option except the *Send Tweets* option has more options that can be reached by hitting the OK button. This reveals another level of menus with more options. The context window is to the right of the menu options. At the top level, the context window is the TV program being watched. As the user uses the arrow keys to move up or down, the bottom bar updates with relevant information.

Most of the discussion will focus on the *Program Tweets*, *Send Tweets*, and *Program Trends* options. The *My Tweets* option shows personal tweets that are posted by the user and those that the user follows using the timeline Twitter API. The *General Trends* option shows various Twitter trends (top trends overall, in last day, in last week) that are retrieved using the appropriate general trend Twitter API.

These capabilities allow the user to have access to general trends, personal updates, and crowd intelligence about the program being watched and be able to interact with the social media crowd in the expected manner (by posting updates, reading tweets, retweeting, and replying to tweets).

17.4.3.1 Option One: Program Tweets

For the *Program Tweets* option, the tweets for the current program are shown in the bottom bar as shown in Figure 17.5. Only one tweet is shown at a time. The user can see more tweets by using the right and left arrows. The left most tweet is the most

Figure 17.5 Program tweets option.

recent tweet and the tweets are numbered so the user can keep track of which tweet is being displayed. As new tweets arrive for the current program being watched, the numbering will be updated appropriately while keeping the currently viewed tweet in the bottom bar. If the user changes the channel, the video will change to the current program on the selected channel and the tweets in the bottom bar will be replaced with tweets relevant to the new program. If the user presses the OK button, more options will be shown for the *Program Tweets* selection. This includes the *Program Tweets* browsing screen, where the user can see and interact with a list of four tweets per screen. In this case, the user can retweet or reply to any highlighted tweet. The reply would be created using speech. In either case, instructions would appear in the bottom bar to help the user along.

17.4.3.2 Option Two: Send Tweets

For the *Send Tweets* options, the bottom bar shows instructions on how to create a tweet using speech as shown in Figure 17.6. The instructions indicate that the user

Figure 17.6 Send tweets option.

should press the TALK button on the remote, speak the message, and then press the OK button to send the tweet. The speech result will appear in the bottom bar moments after speaking into the remote so the user has the option of confirming the speech result and can press the OK button to send the tweet if it is acceptable. Otherwise, the user can speak into the remote again to overwrite the last result.

17.4.3.3 Option Three: Program Trends

As described earlier, the data mining backend is used to retrieve the most relevant program tweets. The *Program Trends* option gives the user access to much more information that is generated by the data mining component of our system. For example, the Summary option for *Program Trends* as shown in Figure 17.7 provides a chart showing the results of sentiment analysis (negative, neutral, and positive), a word cloud containing words (hot topics) that occur most frequently in tweets about the current program, and a popularity chart that shows the number of tweets in the last week about the current program. The *Top Tweets* option shows the tweets about the current program that are retweeted the most. *Recent Tweets* are the same tweets as those that were shown in the top-level *Program Tweets* option. Finally, the *Most Positive* and *Most Negative* are the most positive and negative tweets about the show from the sentiment analysis.

17.4.4 Evaluation of the VoiSTV Interface

Evaluating the effectiveness of this interface design and the usefulness of each capability is a challenging task. We have not yet conducted a full usability study of the VoiSTV system. Among the users whom we talked to, the feature of being able to view relevant tweets while watching a TV show is broadly welcome. Viewers in general are curious about the opinions of the crowd about a show, especially the

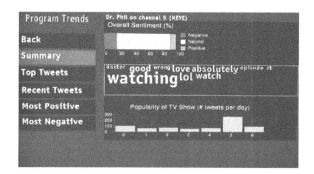

Figure 17.7 Summary option in program trends.

opinions of their friends. The aggregate sentiment received many viewers' attention because it helps the viewer decide what to watch. More specifically, reviewing positive and negative tweets allows the user to see exactly why others have favorable or unfavorable impressions about a show. Users prefer to speak tweets rather than type out tweets because it is faster and text input can be cumbersome on a remote control or on a mobile phone. However, users' satisfaction of this feature will be heavily dependent on the speech recognition word accuracy.

Designing a complete study to evaluate the overall performance of VoiSTV is a challenging task and will be part of our future work. It is still not clear if users will prefer an integrated one-screen experience (where the TV screen is used for displaying both the TV program and social media content as in the VoiSTV interface) or a two-screen experience (where a companion device such as a smartphone or tablet is used to consume the social media content and the big screen TV is used to watch the TV program). This is one of the key questions that needs to be addressed in our future work.

17.5 Conclusion

This chapter presented an overview of the recent social media mining technologies and their applications to TV-related services. This field is still in its infancy. Most available Social TV applications in the market just display raw data gathered from online social networks without much mining or aggregation. The VoiSTV system filters and mines the retrieved social media posts before presenting them to the user.

After describing previous work on mining social media for Social TV and presenting some of the current commercial products that are evolving in this direction, we focused on three main themes.

First, we presented our work on filtering social media messages for TV shows, with an emphasis on content from Twitter. Retrieving messages relevant to the show currently being aired with high precision and recall is a challenging task due to the inherent ambiguity of some TV show titles such as "Lost" and "House." We described a bootstrapping method that requires a small labeled dataset, some domain knowledge collected automatically, and a large unlabeled dataset to derive a classifier that can generalize to television shows it was not trained on. Our evaluation shows that our classifier achieved an F-Measure of 87.8%.

Second, we summarized previous work on two important social media mining tasks: sentiment analysis and social network influencer detection. The output of these technologies can benefit a broad range of Social TV applications. Sentiment analysis can be used to determine the aggregate sentiment of viewers for a TV show. Influencer detection determines which users are more influential in spreading opinions about a given show.

Third, we presented VoiSTV, a state-of-the-art system for integrating online social media and TV. The system allows users to view TV content and the associated social media content on the same screen. While watching a TV program, users can opt to view Twitter messages relevant to that program. The interface also presents several aggregate statistics on the shows, such as overall sentiment and popularity. VoiSTV uses speech recognition technologies to enable users to reply to messages or post new messages by speaking to the remote. We included evaluation results of several key components of VoiSTV. However, evaluating the overall user satisfaction of VoiSTV is still ongoing work.

References

1. M. Nathan, C. Harrison, S. Yarosh, L. Terveen, L. Stead, and B. Amento. CollaboraTV: Making television viewing social again. In *Proceedings of the First International Conference on Designing Interactive User Experiences for TV and Video (UXTV'08)*, Silicon Valley, CA, pp. 85–94, 2008. ACM, New York.
2. K. Mitchell, A. Jones, J. Ishmael, and N.J.P. Race. Social TV: Toward content navigation using social awareness. In *Proceedings of the Eighth International Interactive Conference on Interactive TV & Video (EuroITV'10)*, Tampere, Finland, pp. 283–292, 2010. ACM, New York.
3. A.B. Barragáns-Martínez, E. Costa-Montenegro, J.C. Burguillo, M. Rey-López, F.A. Mikic-Fonte, and A. Peleteiro. A hybrid content-based and item-based collaborative filtering approach to recommend TV programs enhanced with singular value decomposition. *Information Sciences*, 180:4290–4311, 2010.
4. A.B. Barragáns-Martínez, E. Costa-Montenegro, J.C. Burguillo, M. Rey-López, F.A. Mikic-Fonte, and A. Peleteiro. Exploiting social tagging in a Web 2.0 recommender system. *IEEE Internet Computing*, 14:23–30, 2010.
5. Boxee—Watch movies, TV shows and clips from the Internet on your TV. http://www.boxee.tv/ (accessed April 12, 2011).
6. yap.TV. http://yap.tv/ (accessed April 12, 2011).
7. Home|Miso. http://gomiso.com/ (accessed April 12, 2011).
8. Verizon|FiOS TV Central Widgets|Cool Widgets|Interactive Television|Free TV Widget. https://www22.version.com/fiostv/web/unprotected/Widgets.aspx (accessed April 12, 2011).
9. Yahoo! connected TV: Movies, TV shows, Internet on demand. http://connectedtv.yahoo.com/ (accessed April 12, 2011).
10. Features—Google TV. http://www.google.com/tv/features.html (accessed April 12, 2011).
11. N. Evans. Why Facebook TV would beat Google TV & Apple TV platforms. http://www.reelseo.com/facebook-tv, November 2010 (accessed April 12, 2011).
12. B. O'Connor, R. Snow, D. Jurafsky, and A.Y. Ng. Cheap and fast—But is it good?: Evaluating non-expert annotations for natural language tasks. In *Proceedings of the Conference on Empirical Methods in Natural Language Processing*, Honolulu, HI, pp. 254–263, 2008. Association for Computational Linguistics.

13. C. Fellbaum. *WordNet: An Electronic Lexical Database*. The MIT Press, Cambridge, MA, 1998.
14. C.-C. Chang and C.-J. Lin. LIBSVM: A library for support vector machines, 2001. Software available at http://www.csie.ntu.edu.tw/cjlin/libsvm
15. R.-E. Fan, K.-W. Chang, C.-J. Hsieh, X.-R. Wang, and C.-J. Lin. LIBLINEAR: A library for large linear classification. *Journal of Machine Learning Research*, 9:1871–1874, 2008.
16. J.R. Quinlan. *C4.5: Programs for Machine Learning*. Morgan Kaufmann, San Mateo, CA, 1993.
17. J.J. Rodrguez, L.I. Kuncheva, and C.J. Alonso. Rotation forest: A new classifier ensemble method. *IEEE Transactions on Pattern Analysis and Machine Intelligence*, 28(10):1619–1630, 2006.
18. B. Pang and L. Lee. Opinion mining and sentiment analysis. *Foundations and Trends in Information Retrieval*, 2(1–2):1–135, 2008.
19. B.J. Jansen, M. Zhang, K. Sobel, and A. Chowdury. Twitter power: Tweets as electronic word of mouth. *Journal of the American Society for Information Science and Technology*, 60(11):2169–2188, 2009.
20. L. Barbosa and J. Feng. Robust sentiment detection on Twitter from biased and noisy data. In *Proceedings of the 23rd International Conference on Computational Linguistics: Posters*, Beijing, China, pp. 36–44, 2010. Association for Computational Linguistics.
21. A. Kennedy and D. Inkpen. Sentiment classification of movie reviews using contextual valence shifters. *Computational Intelligence*, 22:2006, 2006.
22. P. Melville, W. Gryc, and R.D. Lawrence. Sentiment analysis of blogs by combining lexical knowledge with text classification. In *Proceedings of the 15th ACM SIGKDD International Conference on Knowledge Discovery and Data Mining (KDD'09)*, Paris, France, pp. 1275–1284, 2009. ACM, New York.
23. N. Godbole, M. Srinivasaiah, and S. Skiena. Large-scale sentiment analysis for news and blogs. In *Proceedings of the International Conference on Weblogs and Social Media (ICWSM'07)*, Boulder, CO, 2007.
24. A. Celikyilmaz, D. Hakkani-Tur, and J. Feng. Probabilistic model-based sentiment analysis of Twitter messages. In *Workshop on Spoken Language Technology*, Berkeley, CA, pp. 79–84, December 2010. IEEE.
25. D. Davidov, O. Tsur, and A. Rappoport. Enhanced sentiment learning using twitter hashtags and smileys. In *Proceedings of the 23rd International Conference on Computational Linguistics: Posters*, Beijing, China, pp. 241–249, August 2010. Association for Computational Linguistics, COLING 2010 Organizing Committee.
26. M. Deutsch and H.B. Gerard. A study of normative and informational social influences upon individual judgment. *Journal of Abnormal and Social Psychology*, 51(3): 629–636, 1955.
27. Digital influence in news and politics. http://sparxoo.com/wp-content/sparxoo_digital_influence_news_politics.pdf, September 2009 (accessed April 12, 2011).
28. Klout|The standard for influence. http://klout.com/ (accessed April 12, 2011).
29. TunkRank::Measuring influence by how much attention your followers can give you. http://tunkrank.com/ (accessed April 12, 2011).

30. L. Page, S. Brin, R. Motwani, and T. Winograd. The pagerank citation ranking: Bringing order to the web. Technical Report 1999-66, Stanford InfoLab, November 1999. Previous number = SIDL-WP-1999-0120.

31. J. Weng, E.P. Lim, J. Jiang, and Q. He. TwitterRank: Finding topic-sensitive influential twitterers. In *Proceedings of the Third ACM International Conference on Web Search and Data Mining (WSDM'10)*, New York, pp. 261–270, 2010. ACM, New York.

32. J.E. Hirsch. An index to quantify an individual's scientific research output. *Proceedings of the National Academy of Sciences of the United States of America*, 102(46):16569, 2005.

33. D.M. Romero, W. Galuba, S. Asur, and B.A. Huberman. Influence and passivity in social media. In *Proceedings of the 20th International World Wide Web Conference (WWW'11)*, Hyderabad, India, 2011.

34. M. Kitsak, L.K. Gallos, S. Havlin, F. Liljeros, L. Muchnik, H. Eugene Stanley, and H.A. Makse. Identifying influential spreaders in complex networks. *Arxiv Preprint arXiv:1001.5285*, 2010.

35. G. Di Fabbrizio, T. Okken, and J.G. Wilpon. A speech mashup framework for multimodal mobile services. In *Proceedings of the 2009 International Conference on Multimodal Interfaces*, Cambridge, MA, pp. 71–78, 2009. ACM.

36. V. Goffin, C. Allauzen, E. Bocchieri, D. Hakkani-Tur, A. Ljolje, S. Parthasarathy, M. Rahim, G. Riccardi, and M. Saraclar. The AT&T Watson speech recognizer. In *Proceedings of the IEEE International Conference on Acoustics, Speech, and Signal Processing (ICASSP'05)*, Philadelphia, PA, pp. 1033–1036, March 2005. CiteSeer.

37. Amazon Elastic Compute Cloud (Amazon EC2). http://aws.amazon.com/ec2/ (accessed April 12, 2011).

38. KreaTV Software Development Kits Specification Sheet. http://broadband.motorola.com/downloads/kreatv sdk.pdf, July 2006 (accessed April 12, 2011).

CONTENT PRODUCTION

Chapter 18

A Survey of Advanced Content Management Tools for TV Postproduction

Werner Bailer
JOANNEUM RESEARCH

Klaus Schoeffmann
Klagenfurt University

Frank Hopfgartner
University of California

Contents

18.1 Introduction

Users in TV postproduction need to deal with large amounts of audiovisual content that is often sparsely annotated and contains a high degree of redundancy. Their task is to efficiently organize content and select the most appropriate segments for the productions they are working on, often under time pressure. Traditionally, these processes rely crucially on the knowledge and memory of people who were involved in preproduction and content capture. This is not only an issue of production costs but it also hinders the transformation of production processes toward more flexible and distributed workflows.

Digital media asset management systems (DMAMS) provide storage, search, and retrieval functionality for audiovisual content items, supporting users in navigating, viewing, and finding relevant content items. Today, these systems still rely mostly on textual metadata. Content-based tools can efficiently support specific tasks in the entire process of content management (e.g., content navigation, content selection and filtering, content annotation) and can play an important role in facilitating TV postproduction. Most commercial systems rely on key frames displayed in result lists, as well as low-resolution proxies for preview. Browsing is mostly restricted to using directory structures or links to different versions of content. Only few systems provide storyboard or light table views in their user interfaces. Autonomy Virage [106] is one of the few commercial systems integrating a range of automatic content analysis tools.

The focus of the chapter is on tools targeting professional users in a production context and excludes tools for end users. We describe tools and algorithms for *abstracting* multimedia content in order to allow for efficient presentations of large content sets, such as interactive video browsing, navigation, and content filtering. The term *video abstract* is defined in [82] as "a sequence of still or moving images presenting the content of a video in such a way that the respective target group is rapidly provided with concise information about the content while the essential message of the original is preserved." The authors of [102] use the term *video abstraction* to denote all approaches for the extraction and presentation of representative frames and for the generation of video skims. We use the term *content abstraction* to include all approaches that aim at providing condensed representations of segments of a relevant or salient single media item or a collection of such items, independent of the purpose, context, form, creation method, and presentation style of the abstract.

The existing approaches differ in many aspects, including user interfaces and usage paradigms, requirements in terms of available metadata, and the type of content for which they are designed. In the following, we discuss some of these aspects that are relevant in the context of multimedia abstraction for TV postproduction. For a comprehensive overview and comparison of video abstraction methods, see, for example, [102].

Content abstraction can be done manually, automatically, or semiautomatically (e.g., using user input to define examples of relevant content segments [79]). A basic aspect when creating the abstract is its **purpose**, which can be to objectively summarize the content conveying all of the original message or to deliberately bias the viewer (e.g., when creating a movie trailer or a teaser for a program, cf. [64]). In the postproduction use case, the purpose is to maximize the amount of information in the abstract that is needed to judge the relevance of a content item for the current task.

Somewhat related to the purpose is the **context** of the abstract, which may be undefined and independent of the initial input of the user (e.g., when a user starts browsing), it can be defined by user input, or it can be predefined, for example, when abstracts are used for representing search results and the user's query is known [21]. Domain knowledge also contributes to the definition of the context, as it helps defining the relevance of content segments. Most video abstraction approaches for sports content exploit this knowledge (e.g., goal scenes in soccer games are relevant). The context in TV postproduction is given by the current production a user is working on. However, while this context is possibly defined in scripts and storyboards, it is usually not formalized in a way that is directly usable by content management tools.

A number of aspects are related to the media type of the content to be extracted. The **dimension** of the content may be a single media item (e.g., one video) or a collection of items (an example for the visualization of a content set is presented in [84]). In the latter case, all items may be of the same or of different types (e.g., a mixed collection of videos, still images, and audio clips). The media type also determines whether the content set has a defined **order**. For example, a video or audio stream has an intrinsic temporal order, and it is in many cases desired to keep it in the abstract. In TV postproduction, the dimension is given by the set of content related to a certain production. For fictional content such as movies or series, this is often 30 times or more of the duration of the final content, and the ratio can be potentially much higher, if a production (e.g., a documentary) makes extensive use of archive content.

One of the most important aspects is the **content structure**. In [112], the authors discriminate *scripted* (e.g., movies) from *unscripted* content (e.g., sports or news). Of course, the boundaries between the two are very fuzzy. Another dimension of structure is *edited* versus *unedited* ("rushes," "raw video") content, and there exist rushes for both scripted and unscripted content. For edited scripted content, the abstraction algorithm can attempt to detect and use the structure of the content (such as dialogs, e.g., in [64]), while for unscripted (and especially also unedited) content other approaches are required (e.g., [19]). Content structure exists not only on the level of the single media item, but also on the level of the collection in the case of multi-item abstracts. In some cases, the collection has a "macrostructure," such as a set of rushes produced according to a script. The content encountered in production is mostly unedited (except for existing programs, from which extracts might be needed), but depending on the type of content it can be both scripted and unscripted.

There is a large variety of approaches for the **presentation** of abstracts. It can be interactive or non-interactive, sequential or hierarchical, and different media types and visualizations can be used.

This chapter discusses tools based on different ways of usage paradigms and presentation methods. Section 18.2 starts with an overview of domain-independent tools for browsing and navigating content collections in postproduction. The section then focuses on tools for two important content domains in TV production: news and fictional entertainment content. Section 18.3 discusses the different usage patterns and the considerations on user interfaces that are derived from them. In Section 18.4, we provide an overview of methods and initiatives for evaluating content abstraction tools and provide information on the level of maturity. Section 18.5 concludes the chapter and outlines future research topics.

18.2 Tools for Video Browsing and Navigation

The main goals of a video browsing tool are to enable interacting users to (a) quickly get an overview of the content of a video and to (b) quickly find specific-video segments in it. The first goal is important in cases where users are not yet familiar with the content, for example, an editor starting with a new project and trying to get an overview of the raw material. The second goal is important for nearly all use cases in TV postproduction. Users need efficient ways to quickly locate specific scenes, shots, or single frames in the video through appropriate interaction means and advanced visualizations of video content.

In the audiovisual media production process, different classes of content need to be treated differently. The reasons are the different amount of metadata that are available (or that one can afford to annotate), the different temporal granularity of productions (i.e., the lengths of clips being used), the level of reuse of content, and the production schedules. Two important classes of audiovisual content, also commercially, are news and fictional entertainment content, such as TV movies or series. The first consists of rather short segments that are heavily reused (especially when they are new, but sometimes also over longer periods), well annotated, and typically need to be brought into productions in a hurry. The second consists of rather longer segments, specifically produced for a production according to a script, but otherwise typically not well annotated. This section first discusses approaches that are not targeting a specific content domain, and then discusses tools focusing on news and fictional entertainment content, respectively. Sports is the third important content domain in TV production, but due to the large amount of quite specific approaches for different types of sports, there is not enough room to include the topic in this chapter.

A remarkable amount of work can be found in the literature that focuses on automatic detection of content classes (e.g., sports, news, and fictional entertainment). These *multimedia genre classification* methods usually employ machine-learning algorithms (such as SVM [39]) on content descriptors (e.g., bag-of-visual-words [113]) in order to train classifiers that are able to automatically detect different genres, often also with fine granularity (e.g., different kinds of sports content). However, multimedia genre classification is a large field of research; a complete survey on that topic is out of the scope of this chapter. The interested reader is referred to recent literature, such as [57,71,108].

18.2.1 Domain-Independent Approaches

18.2.1.1 Simple Video Players

An example of a simple but commonly used video browsing tool is a video player providing a time-slider, often also a fast-forward feature, in addition to the playback feature. Such a video player is a very convenient tool for video browsing as it uses simple and well-known interaction means. Maybe more important, it is immediately usable for any video file without any preprocessing delay, which an advanced video retrieval tool would require for content analysis. On the other hand, however, a common video player is very poorly suited for the task of quickly locating specific parts in a long video, because the resolution of the time-slider is way too coarse in order to be efficiently used for frame-based search. Moving the time-slider by just one pixel may result in a jump of several seconds or minutes instead of only one frame.

This type of video player with a time line is commonly used in content management tools, and is also included in all 28 commercial media asset management systems we surveyed.

18.2.1.2 Enhanced Video Players

In order to overcome the limitations of a common time-slider (also known as *seeker-bar*), several improvements of the interaction model have been proposed [30,50,51,85]. Hürst et al. [49–51] propose the *zoom slider* (see Figure 18.1), which is a virtual hidden time-slider available on the entire player window. When the user clicks on any position in the player window, a time-slider for moving backward or forward appears. The granularity of that time-slider is dependent on the vertical position of the mouse in relation to the entire height of the player window. When the mouse is moved in a vertical direction, the scaling of the time-slider changes in a linear way. The finest granularity is used at the top and the coarsest granularity is used at the bottom of the window. Therefore, a user can zoom in or zoom out the scaling of the time-slider by selecting different vertical mouse positions.

Traditional video tape recorders also allow improved navigation in video by *shuttle* and *jog* controls. A shuttle control enables to easily change playback speed through wheel-rotation. Complementary, a jog control enables to quickly change the direction of play (forward, backward) through an additional wheel. The combined usage of shuttle/jog controls allows for a convenient navigation through a video. This interaction model has been adopted by video players and video editing products (e.g., Apple's Final Cut [53], Avid's DS System [54], or MAGIX's Movie Edit Pro [3]) that

Figure 18.1   Video navigation with the *zoom slider*. (From Hürst, W. and Jarvers, P., Interactive, dynamic video browsing with the zoomslider interface, in: *International Conference on Multimedia and Expo (ICME 2005)*, Amsterdam, the Netherlands, p. 4, 2005. © 2005 IEEE. With permission.)

provide a virtual wheel for improved navigation. It allows a user to more accurately locate specific positions/frames in video.

Dragicevic et al. [30] propose *relative flow dragging* as an alternative to improved time-sliders and shuttle/jog controls for frame-accurate positioning. Relative flow dragging is a technique to move forward and backward in a video by direct mouse manipulation of content objects. They use an optical flow estimation algorithm based on SIFT [66] salient feature points of two consecutive frames, which is very computationally intensive and, thus, time-consuming. A user study was conducted, where specific events in videos had to be found (e.g., *Where does the car start to move?* or *Where does the ladybug pass over a specific point?*). In a *2 technique* × *2 task* within-participant design, subjects were asked to solve tasks either with relative flow dragging or with a traditional seeker-bar. The results of their study show that participants were at least 2.5 times faster with relative flow dragging than with the traditional seeker-bar.

Pongnumkul et al. [85] propose an interaction model for a time-slider that integrates both *low-speed* navigation and *high-speed* navigation into one single control element. Their *elastic time line* dynamically switches navigation granularity based on the horizontal and vertical distance of the mouse pointer to the handle (thumb) of the time-slider. If the user keeps the mouse pointer close to the handle, the time-slider works in low-speed browsing mode. When the user pulls the mouse pointer far away from the handle, the time-slider enters high-speed browsing mode.

Such improved interaction models allow a more flexible navigation in the video and/or more accurate locating of specific content units (scenes, shots, frames). However, they do not give any additional visual information about the content structure. Therefore, several visual enhancements of the common time-slider have been proposed in the literature. For instance, Barbieri et al. [11] propose to enhance the background of the time-slider with vertical color lines (see Figure 18.2), representing information about the content (e.g., the *dominant color* of every frame, or the *volume level* of the corresponding audio channel). This idea helps to reduce the number of interactions with the time-slider as it can directly show where shots start or stop and where segments of a specific dominant color of audio volume are located. In order to be appropriate for both short and long videos, they propose to use two time-sliders of different sensibility, for example, the first one for fast navigation and the second one for slow navigation in a particular segment. A similar idea has been presented by Moraveji [74], who proposed to display distinctive colors in the background of the time-slider as abstraction for different semantic concepts (e.g., cars, persons, and faces). Chen et al. [17] use the same idea to visualize emotions of a specific actor/actress in sitcoms with the *EmoPlayer*. Rehatschek et al. [89] use *frame stripes* as time-slider to improve navigation in a video. Frame stripes are images constructed by adjacent visualizations of the center columns of frames. This kind of content abstraction implicitly conveys information about content structure and the motion of a scene (in addition to the general color tone of a scene).

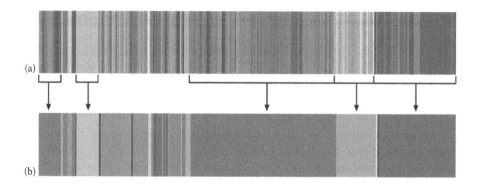

Figure 18.2 Visualization of the *ColorBrowser* without (a) and with (b) a smoothing filter. (From Barbieri, M. et al., The color browser: A content driven linear video browsing tool, in: *IEEE International Conference on Multimedia and Expo* (ICME 2001), Tokyo, Japan, pp. 627–630, 2001. © 2005 IEEE. With permission.)

A more general concept of *interactive navigation summaries* (INS) is proposed by Schoeffmann and Boeszoermenyi [94]. An INS consists of an *overview* component that contains a zoom-window for a specific time segment of a video, which can be moved and resized by the user. The zoom-window defines the time segment of the video shown in the *detailed* component. Both components act as time-sliders but visualize abstract information about the content in the background. Several examples of content abstractions (see Figure 18.3) for INS have been presented (e.g., *color flow* [95] and *motion flow* [97]).

The fast-forward mode (e.g., 2×, 4×, 8× playback speeds) provides not only a simple way of getting a quick overview about the content of a video, but also a convenient way to jump to the next segment of interest. In a large user test with 200 users, Crockford and Agius [24] found out that when searching for specific content in a video with a VCR-like control set (play, pause, fast-forward, fast-reverse, stop) *speed-switching* is the predominant search technique (most-used and fastest). Speed-switching is defined as a combination of play and fast-forward, where the user switches the playback speed according to the experienced level of interest (e.g., play, 2×, 4×, 2×, play). So when users believe the searched content is hardly to appear in the current segment, they switch to fast-forward and switch back to play when they think the searched scene is just to appear. Therefore, improving fast-forward may have a high significance for the performance of search tasks in videos.

Peker and Divakaran [81] propose to use an *adaptive fast playback* feature (see Figure 18.4) that is based on the complexity of scenes in the video. The main idea is to enable quick skimming through a video by an adaptive playback function that automatically plays complex scenes at lower (or normal) speed and less complex

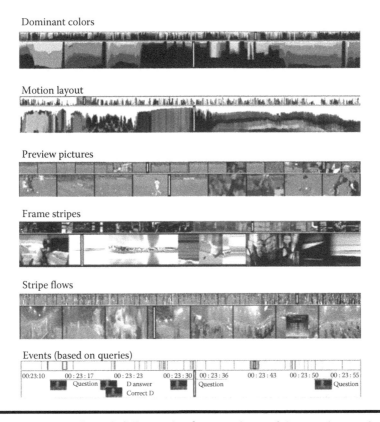

Dominant colors

Motion layout

Preview pictures

Frame stripes

Stripe flows

Events (based on queries)

Figure 18.3 **Examples of different implementations of** *interactive navigation summaries* **(for details see [93]).**

scenes at higher speed. In order to determine the complexity of scenes, content analysis is used. The same idea was used by Cheng et al. [18] for the *SmartPlayer*. It uses an automatic *playback speed adaptation* function that is based on scene complexity, which is learned through motion analysis. Their player has been designed in accordance with the "scenic car driving" metaphor, where a driver slows down at interesting areas and speeds up through unexciting areas.

Pongnumkul et al. [85] also propose a similar feature for dynamic video skimming, which is, however, more sophisticated. They argue that fast-forwarding at very high speed is very hard to perceive by a human because only unrelated frames are shown to the user. So instead of simply speeding up the whole content, they play short clips (1 s) at a playback speed of 2× and perform a discrete jump forward to maintain the desired average video speed. In order to perform "good jumps," they use a shot-boundary detection method to find out all key frames and generate *key-clips* that are located 1 s around the key frame. The jump is always performed

Figure 18.4 Video browsing enhanced personal video recorder. (From Divakaran, A. and Otsuka, I., A video-browsing-enhanced personal video recorder, in: *14th International Conference on Image Analysis and Processing Workshops (ICIAPW 2007)*, Modena, Italy, pp. 137–142, 2007. © 2007 IEEE. With permission.)

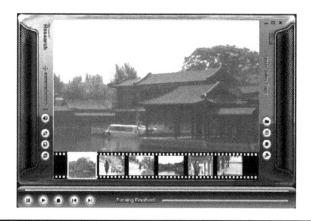

Figure 18.5 Smart Video Player. (From Chang, L. et al., Smart video player, in: *2008 IEEE International Conference on Multimedia and Expo (ICME'08)*, Hannover, Germany, June 23–April 26, 2008, pp. 1605–1606, 2008. © 2008 IEEE. With permission.)

to the nearest key-clip. (Chang et al. [16] propose the *Smart Video Player* (see Figure 18.5) to facilitate browsing and seeking in videos. It provides a filmstrip view in the bottom part of the screen, which shows key frames of the shots of the video. The user can set the level of detail for that view and, thus, extend or reduce the number of shots/key frames displayed within the filmstrip.

18.2.1.3 Approaches Based on Key Frames

18.2.1.3.1 Storyboards

A *storyboard* is a grid-like alignment of key frames of shots that is used to browse through the content of a video or through the results of a query in a video retrieval application. As one of the first, Arman et al. [5] proposed to use the concept of *key frames*, which are representative frames of shots, for chronologically browsing the content of a video sequence. For every shot, a key frame is selected and the storyboard as a chronological list of key frames is used to browse through the content of a video. For visualization of the results, they propose to display good results in original size (e.g., 100%), somewhat similar results in smaller size (e.g., 33%), and bad results in an even smaller size (e.g., 5%). A user study of Komlodi and Marchionini [61] in 1998 revealed that simple storyboards are preferred by users over dynamic approaches, even if additional time is required to interact with the user interface (scroll bars) and for eye movements. Dynamic approaches such as slide shows often display the content with a fixed frame rate and do not allow the user to adjust it. Storyboards have been used as basis for many tools, especially in the field of video retrieval. A comprehensive study is out of the scope of this chapter but can be found in [96]. More recent approaches, such as the *VisionGo* system [76], use keyboard shortcuts to quickly scroll through the list of key frames and/or to provide relevance feedback. Practically all commercial media asset management systems extract key frames for representing media items (many shot-based or at fixed intervals) and use them in storyboards or content time lines. In the latter case, either time line or light table visualizations are used.

18.2.1.3.2 Content Hierarchies

Jansen et al. [56] propose to use *VideoTrees* for navigation through a video (see Figure 18.6). A VideoTree is a hierarchical tree-like temporal presentation of a video through key frames. The key frames are placed adjacently to their parents and siblings such that no edge lines are required to show the affiliation of a node. With each depth level, the *level-of-detail* increases as well until shot-level granularity. For example, a user may navigate from a semantic root segment to one of the subjacent scenes, then to one of the subjacent shot groups, and finally to one of the subjacent shots. The current selected node in the tree is always centered, showing the context (i.e., a few of the adjacent nodes) in the surrounding area. In a user study with 15 participants, they show that the VideoTrees can outperform storyboards (a matrix-like alignment of key frames) regarding the search time (1.14 times faster). However, the study also reveals that users find the classical storyboard much easier and clearer.

Eidenberger [34] proposes a video browsing approach that uses similarity-based clustering. More precisely, a *self-organizing map* (SOM), which is a neural network

Figure 18.6   Video browsing with the *VideoTree*. (From Jansen, M. et al., Videotrees: Improving video surrogate presentation using hierarchy, in: *IEEE International Workshop on Content-Based Multimedia Indexing (CBMI 2008)*, London, U.K., pp. 560–567, 2008. © 2008 IEEE. With permission.)

that uses feed-forward learning, is employed as a similarity-based clustering method. Visually similar segments of a video are grouped together and visualized in hierarchically organized index trees. The clusters are visualized as hexagonally shaped cells showing key frames of shots. The user can interactively select a certain cell and step one layer deeper in the hierarchical tree structure to see more details of the selected shot. del Fabro et al. [26] propose a hierarchical video browser that enables uniform temporal decomposition of a video by interaction. The browser uses an $m \times n$ storyboard that contains key frames uniformly sampled from the video content. The user is able to specify the size of the storyboard (e.g., select m and n) and go into details of a selected segment by a left-mouse click. For instance, if $m = 2, n = 2$ the four key frames at the top level are uniformly selected from the whole video (one key frame per quarter) and when the user clicks on the second key frame, for instance, the storyboard is reloaded with new key frames from the second quarter segment of the video. In that way, a user can delve into details of a specific segment until frame-level granularity and go back the hierarchy by a right-mouse click. Each segment can be further inspected by an own time-slider and a double click will start playback for the corresponding segment. The browser is called the *Instant Video Browser* as it requires no content analysis and is immediately usable for a newly recorded video.

Bailer et al. [10] argue for an automatic generation of condensed abstracts that shall ease access to videos. Therefore, they introduce a multimedia content abstraction process that aims at providing a condensed representation of segments of video

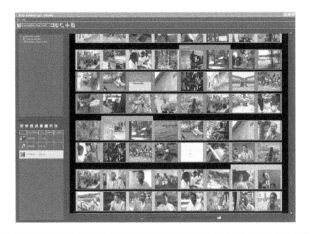

Figure 18.7   Video browsing tool as proposed by Bailer et al. [10].

documents. The process can be divided into five generic steps, the most important ones being clustering of video content in order to identify similarities, selection of representative clusters, and the presentation of these clusters in a graphical user interface (see Figure 18.7). In their paper, they introduce a video browsing tool for content management, which is designed based on these steps. The central component of their graphical user interface is a light table where video segment clusters are displayed by representative key frames. The user can manipulate this representation by selecting different features used for clustering (e.g., camera motion, visual activity, and faces). The user can further decide to select a subset of clusters that seem to be relevant and discard the others. This way, the system supports the user in exploring the video content step by step.

18.2.1.3.3 3D(-Like) Visualizations

In the last decade, most computer systems became equipped with hardware to support 3D graphics. Therefore, video search and navigation tools could also take advantage of 3D graphics: (a) use 3D transformations (e.g., rotation) in order to display more key frames on a 2D screen at a glance instead of planar arrangements, (b) allow users to interactively navigate through a 3D space of content representation and focus on content of interest only. Instead of making all key frames equally visible, 3D graphics would also inherently allow to display more important key frames at larger size and less important key frames in smaller size. With interactive navigation, users would be able to change the perspective to their current needs, so that key frames considered as less important by the system will be larger in size. However, it is not clear yet whether such a 3D representation is beneficial for interactive search tasks. In the literature, only a few approaches for video search and navigation can be found that take advantage of real 3D graphics.

In an early work, Manske [68] proposes to use a *cone-tree*-like representation of key frame hierarchies. A "side view" has been chosen as perspective enabling to see many transformed key frames at a glance. A user is able to open and close sub-trees in order to inspect specific segments in more detail and to switch to a front-view perspective based on a selected key frame. Moreover, a feature for an automatic *walk through* the whole video-tree in its temporal sequence is supported. Unfortunately no evaluation has been done, which would assess the performance of such a content representation. The Mitsubishi Electric Research Laboratories (MERL) propose several techniques for improved navigation within a video through content presentation with rather simple 3D transformations. For example, the *Squeeze* layout and the *Fisheye* layout [27] (see Figure 18.8) are proposed for improved fast-forward and rewind with personal digital video recorders. With a user study, they show that their approach can significantly outperform the VCR-like navigation set in accuracy. However, no significant difference was found in the task completion time.

de Rooij et al. [25] propose the *CrossBrowser* that uses a 3D-like visualization of key frames. The interface consists of two key frames/shot paths, called *video threads*. The *horizontal* video thread adheres to the temporal sequence of shots in the video, while the *vertical* video thread displays visually (or semantically) similar shots according to the user-selected center-shot of the horizontal thread.

18.2.2 News Content

An important characteristic of news content is the fact that clips are entirely or partially reused in many broadcasts not only within one organization, but also across organizations, using, for example, content from distribution networks such as Eurovision. When analyzing complete news broadcasts, the segmentation into the individual news stories is also a relevant topic. In addition, near duplicates exist, as at many events the cameras of different broadcasters record the same scene from different but nearby positions. Finally, news stories develop over time; thus, there is content often showing the same scene at different times, and in some cases the content differs only marginally. Grouping related clips of news content is thus an important tool to organize news content, known as news topic threading.

18.2.2.1 Browsing

For browsing story-based video content like news, interviews, or sports summaries, Goeau et al. [35] propose the *table of video contents* (TOC). Several types of content features are used to decompose the content into semantic units, which are the basis for an improved visualization that facilitates browsing and navigation. Their visualization uses a *video backbone* that can effectively show the content structure.

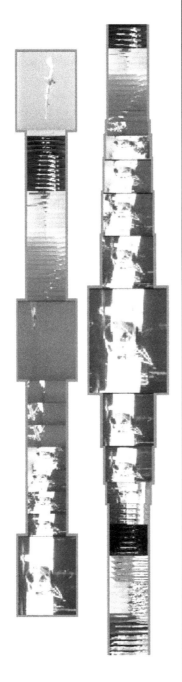

Figure 18.8 *Squeeze and Fisheye* layout for improved fast-forward and rewind. (From Divakaran, A. et al., Augmenting fast-forward and rewind for personal digital video recorders, in: *IEEE International Conference on Consumer Electronics (ICCE), Digest of Technical Papers*, pp. 43–44, 2005. Copyright 2005 IEEE. With permission.)

For a news video, every news story is shown as a loop of key frames originating from that backbone, while the rather short moderation scenes appear directly along the backbone. Tang et al. [101] propose the *NewsEye*, an application for improved news story browsing. With unsupervised fuzzy k-means clustering, the content is first segmented into shots. Then, the shots are grouped together in order to form several different news stories. Their VideoPlayer-like interface contains an own panel showing key frames of all the shots in the current news story as well as the detected caption text based on OCR, which can also be used with a text-based search. Liu et al. [65] propose a news video browsing system called *NewsBR*, which is very similar to the aforementioned NewsEye. The news story segmentation uses a shot detection method, silence clip detection, and OCR to detect text of a news topic. Their interface shows a TOC (in combination with a key frame preview) according to the story segmentation that can be used as navigation means. It also provides a keyword-based search on the extracted caption text. Vakkalanka et al. [104] describe a news video indexing, browsing, and retrieval system called *NVIBRS*. Their system performs shot detection and news story segmentation based on localization of anchor person frames. The interface of their application provides a tree view of all detected news story units in a video and shows key frames of the currently selected story as a navigation means. It also allows a user to perform a textual query by specifying the desired video category as the news content is categorized into a few categories.

18.2.2.2 News Story Segmentation

In the news video domain, the coherent segments of a broadcast are news stories, commonly defined as segments with a coherent news focus that contain at least two independent declarative clauses. Chaisorn and Chua [15] argue that the internal structure of news stories depends on the broadcast station's style. While some stories consist of anchor person shots only, often with a changing background image, other stories can consist of multiple different shots, for example, other anchor persons, graphics or animations, interview scenes, or shots of meetings. News story segmentation is essentially finding the boundaries where one story ends and the other begins.

Various text-based, audiovisual-based, and combinations of all features have been studied to segment news videos accordingly. Based on the observation that the structure depends on the broadcast station, some methods use prior knowledge for the segmentation. The detection of the repeated appearance of anchor person shots is exploited by several methods, either by using classifiers for anchor person shots [47,83] or similarity search [107,115].

The basic features employed in many of the approaches are visual similarity between shots within a time window and the temporal distance between shots, for example, [33,38,78,99]. Some approaches use additionally the similarity of faces appearing in the shots [38]. The audio signal is used in many approaches to detect pauses, speaker changes, or changes between music and speech. Other audio-based methods are the detection of jingles [88] and the detection of changes in the acoustic environment, such as changes of the signal-to-noise ratio (to discriminate studio from outside shots) [38]. A number of approaches also use text from transcripts or automated speech recognition. Some use the text to find similar word appearances in different shots [38,47] or watch for trigger phrases that indicate certain types of shots [33].

Some of the reported approaches are based on supervised learning approaches. The approaches discussed in [47,99] are based on classifying boundary candidates into story boundaries and nonstory boundaries using the expectation-maximization (EM) algorithm and support vector machines (SVMs), respectively. The approach in [15] is based on shot classification using a hidden Markov model (HMM). The approach reported in [115] uses a model called shot connectivity graph (SCG). Shots are classified and each node in the graph represents a shot; the edges are transitions from one shot to another. As it is expected that anchor person shots reappear, the task is to search for cycles in the graph. Special types of shots are detected using other features, such as word spotting for detecting sports shots and greenish/bluish color impression to detect weather shots. Detailed surveys of the earlier research on news story segmentation are given by Arlandis et al. [4] and Chua et al. [22].

Recently, research has moved to combining more modalities, applying more powerful language processing, including multilingual approaches (e.g., [90]), and using contextual knowledge. In [70], anchor shots are detected based on both visual and speaker features. In addition, the fact that most story changes are related to a change of the type of camera shot is exploited. Misra et al. [73] use latent Dirichlet allocation (LDA) on the text transcript in addition to the detection of anchor person shots. Also the approach presented in [67] uses latent semantic indexing (LSI) in addition to cue word spotting, anchor shot detection, and audio-type detection. The authors of [105] model the social network between the persons appearing in the news, and create a segmentation based on the assumption that persons appearing in the same news story are stronger than those appearing in different stories. The authors of [86] have conducted a thorough survey of the performance of different types of features for news story segmentation.

18.2.2.3 News Story Threading

Near-duplicate detection is used for topic tracking of news stories as they develop over time. Some approaches work on a story level and use features such as speech transcripts [48] that are often not available in other content such as rushes. The approach proposed in [52] uses a transcript (obtained, e.g., from ASR) to perform news story segmentation and topic threading.

The approach proposed in [32] works on matching sequences of key frames, tolerating gaps and insertions. Starting from single matching key frames, the search for matching sequences is performed temporally around these key frames. The authors of [111] propose a co-clustering approach for near-duplicate key frames based on a bipartite graph model including both visual and textual information. In [116], an approach combining textual matching of ASR transcripts, matching of extended face regions for key frames showing faces and affine matching of non-face key frames is proposed. An approach using visual concept detection together with time constraints is proposed in [59]. An important result of this paper is that the most useful concepts for story tracking are settings, followed by named persons.

In [92], a near-duplicate video detection approach based on feature point trajectories is proposed. An inconsistency descriptor is extracted from a spatiotemporal patch around the feature points and a binary discontinuity sequence is determined by detecting local maxima after Gaussian smoothing of the inconsistency sequence. Efficient matching is performed using the discontinuity sequence representation and histograms representing temporal offsets.

18.2.3 Fictional Content

In film and video production large amounts of raw material ("rushes") are shot and only a small fraction of this material is used in the final edited content. The reason for shooting that amount of material is that the same scene is often taken from different camera positions and several alternative takes for each of them are recorded, partly because of mistakes of the actors or technical failures, partly to experiment with different artistic options. The action performed in each of these takes is similar, but not identical, for example, it has omissions and insertions, or object and actor positions and trajectories are slightly different. In addition, there are takes that stop earlier (mostly due to mistakes) or start in the middle of the scene ("pickups"). The result of this practice in production is that users dealing with rushes have to handle large amounts of audiovisual material that makes viewing and navigation difficult. In postproduction, editors need to view and organize the material in order to select the best takes to be used. The ratio between the playtime of the rushes and that of the edited content is often 30:1 or more.

The task of the editor can be facilitated by identifying near-duplicate video segments in order to group them. One of the most prominent applications for near-duplicate detection is finding illegal copies of video content (cf. [36,37]). A related problem is the identification of known unwanted content in public access video databases [23]. These applications are based on the following assumptions: (a) the actual content of the videos to be matched is identical, (b) partial matches need to be identified, and (c) the algorithm needs to be robust against a number of distortions, such as changes of sampling parameters, noise, encoding artifacts, cropping, change of aspect ratio, etc. The first assumption is not valid for clustering takes of fictional content, while robustness to distortions is only necessary to a limited degree in this application, as the content to be matched is captured and processed under similar conditions.

The authors of [91] propose an approach for clustering repeated takes into scenes using agglomerative hierarchical clustering of feature vectors. In [77], a near-duplicate key frame detection approach based on PCA-SIFT matching between feature points extracted using the Hessian-affine detector is proposed. Using an efficient indexing structure, approximate k-NN matching between PCA-SIFT descriptors is performed, looking for parallel or zoom-like patterns of matching between key frames. The matching sequences are found using transitivity of matches and temporal proximity constraints.

The problem of matching video segments can also be transformed into a problem of matching sequences of feature vectors extracted from the video segments. The feature vectors can contain arbitrary features and can be sampled with different rates from the videos. The task is then to find suitable distance measures between sequences of these feature vectors. Two classes of approaches have been proposed for this problem. One is based on the dynamic time warping (DTW) paradigm [75], which tries to align the samples of the sequences so that the temporal order is kept but the distance is globally minimized. The approach has been applied to detecting repeated takes in rushes video [60]. The authors of [100] propose a method that is conceptually very similar to DTW but includes further strict constraints; for example, it is assumed that the start and end of the two video segments are temporally aligned and only the content in between may vary in timing. The distance measure nearest feature line (NFL) [117] is also conceptually related. It does not align samples of the two sequences but calculates the nearest point as the intersection of a line that is orthogonal to the line between two samples in feature space and passes through a sample of the other sequence. The distances in feature space between the intersection points and the corresponding points in the other feature sequence are summed to yield the total distance of the sequences.

The other class of distance measures is based on the idea of the edit distance between strings, that is, the cost of inserting, deleting, or replacing samples in the sequence. The authors of [2] propose such a measure called vString edit distance. The values of vectors in the feature sequence are mapped to a set of discrete symbols and three new edit operations are introduced: fusion/fission of symbols (in order to deal with speed changes), swapping of symbols or blocks of symbols, and insertion/deletion of shot boundaries. The distance is defined as a weighted linear combination of the traditional edit distance (using only equality or inequality of the symbols) and a modified one taking also the difference between the symbol values into account. The drawbacks are that the sequence of feature vectors needs to be mapped to a discrete set of symbols and that operations such as fission/fusion and handling of shot boundaries need to be modeled separately. In [7], a method based on the longest common subsequence (LCSS) model, a variant of the edit distance supporting gaps in the match, has been proposed. The method addresses the problem of clustering repeated takes of a scene, which might have insertions, omissions, or different timings. The authors of [12] also propose a method for matching clips in video databases using color similarity and edit distance, avoiding discretization of the feature vectors. A similar approach using the edit distance and different costs for substitution, deletion, and insertion is proposed in [114]. The method for clustering takes into scenes that is proposed in [31] also uses a variant of the edit distance. Hierarchical clustering of segments with a duration of one second is performed and yields the cost for matching two segments, which together with a cost for gaps is used to determine the optimal alignment.

18.3 Paradigms for Interactive Search, Browsing, and Content Navigation

An important concept in interactive video search is the design of graphical user interfaces that allow the users to both express their information need and to interact with the retrieval results. As we have shown in the previous section, the specific nature of video data requires rather complex graphical user interfaces. In this section, we introduce different interaction patterns that can be observed when interacting with such systems. Understanding usage interactions is of particular interest in the field of adaptive retrieval since users' implicit interactions can be interpreted in order to identify users' interests and to adapt retrieval results accordingly (e.g., [43,46]). These usage patterns have the potential to significantly improve the performance of content management tools. A large variety of different interface designs exist and, thus, the way users interact with these interfaces differs significantly from their textual counterparts. Graphical user interfaces of both textual and multimedia domains are designed to assist users in their information seeking task. Dix et al. [29] argue that user interactions in interactive systems can be represented as a series of low-level events, for example, key presses or mouse clicks. These events are the most basic interactions that users can perform during their interaction. The interfaces that have been surveyed in [96] provide various low-level events that users can trigger while interacting with given documents. Any action that users perform during their information seeking activity, further referred to as their search session, consists of a series of these events. A further analysis reveals the following six events:

- *Previewing:* Hovering the mouse over a key frame. This can result in a tool tip showing neighbored key frames and additional text or in highlighting the query terms in the text associated with the key frame. This low-level event indicates further interest in a key frame as the user receives additional information about the result.
- *Clicking result:* Click, for example, on a key frame, to trigger playback of a video shot or to perform further actions. This event indicates the users' interest in the video shot that is represented by the key frame.
- *Sliding:* Using the sliding bar to navigate through a video. This event indicates further interest in the video. Users appear to slide through a video when the initial shot is not exactly what they were searching for but when they believe

that the rest of the video might contain other relevant shots. Hence, the initial shot might not be an exact match of the users' need but raises hope to find something of relevance in the same video.

■ *Exploring:* Looking at metadata (date of event, capture location, production notes, etc.). By performing this event, users show a higher interest in the current shot, as they want to get additional information. This information can help them judge the relevance of the shot. A user, for example, might search for a specific news event such as a certain speech of the president of the United States. In such cases, the direct correlation between capture date and event date can help to identify relevant shots of the speech itself, comments on expectations from just before, and reactions of politicians and commentators shortly afterward.

■ *Browsing:* Browsing through a video by clicking on its neighbored key frames. Similar to using the sliding bar to navigate through a video, this feedback indicates users' interest in this shot. Unlike using the sliding bar, browsing indicates that users suspect a relevant shot in the neighborhood of the current shot.

■ *Viewing:* Viewing a video. The playing duration of a video might indicate users' interest in the content of the video.

Bezold [13] describes such event series as probabilistic finite-state automata. Considering that each low-level event combination within a user's interaction sequence depends on the preceding event, we argue that user interactions can be simplified in a Markov chain [72]. Markov chains consist of states and transitions between these states. A state change is triggered by a certain event with a certain probability. In the remainder of this section, we introduce the example of Markov chains that represent possible user action sequences consisting of low-level events when users interact with a given document using an interactive video retrieval system. Note that due to simplicity reasons, the scenarios cover some possible user interaction, not necessarily a user interaction including all features an interface can provide.

18.3.1 User Action Sequence S_1 (Preview-Click'n'View)

Sequence S_1 combines three different low-level events, encompassing all interfaces that provide the minimal functionalities of previewing, clicking on a key frame in the result set, and viewing the video shot. Due to these functionalities, we refer to this sequence as "Preview-Click'n'View." Example interfaces that allow this event combination have been presented in [20,44]. Possible low-level event combinations are visualized in Figure 18.9.

Given a displayed document, denoted "retrieval result presentation" in Figure 18.9, this sequence models users (a) hovering the mouse over listed key frames to get some additional information of the shot, for example, in a tool tip (previewing). Further,

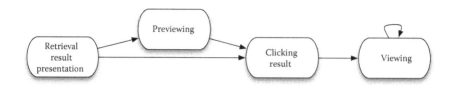

Figure 18.9 Possible event combinations on a given document in sequence S_1.

the users may (b) click on the key frame (clicking result) to (c) start playing a video (viewing).

18.3.2 User Action Sequence S_2 (Click'n'Browse)

Sequence S_2, referred to as "Click'n'Browse," combines two low-level events that can be given when interacting with a document: clicking a result on a result list to display the video and its key frames, followed by browsing these key frames. An example interface supporting this sequence is introduced by Heesch et al. [40]. In this interface, information is presented on different panels. Retrieval results are represented by key frames. Clicking on one key frame in a result panel will set focus on that key frame and update all other panels. One panel contains the neighbored key frames in a fish-eye presentation. In this panel, a user can browse through the results. Possible low-level event combinations are visualized in Figure 18.10.

In this sequence, users can (a) click on a key frame in the result list (clicking result) and (b) browse through its presented neighbored frames (browsing).

18.3.3 User Action Sequence S_3 (Click-View-Explore'n'Slide)

The third sequence S_3 covers an event combination that can be achieved when interacting with a document using the text-only video retrieval system provided by Browne et al. [14]. Their web interface ranks retrieved results in a list of relevant video programs. Each row displays the most relevant key frame, surrounded by its two neighbored key frames. Below the shots, the text associated with the result is presented. The query terms that are associated with the key frame are highlighted when

Figure 18.10 Possible event combinations on a given document in sequence S_2.

Figure 18.11   Possible event combinations on a given document in sequence S_3.

the user moves the mouse over the key frame. When clicking on a key frame, the represented video shot can be played. Different from S_1 and S_2, this sequence considers two additional low-level events: highlighting metadata (exploring) and using a sliding bar (sliding). We refer to this scenario as "Click-View-Explore'n'Slide." Possible low-level event combinations are visualized in Figure 18.11.

In this sequence, users can (a) click on a key frame (clicking result) to (b) trigger video playback (viewing). They can (c) highlight associated query terms (exploring) and (d) navigate through the video using a sliding bar (sliding).

18.3.4 User Action Sequence S_4 (Preview-Click-View'n'Browse)

This sequence models the users' interaction on a given document using the system provided by Hopfgartner et al. [44]. In their interface, retrieved video shots, represented by a key frame, are listed in a result panel. Hovering the mouse over a key frame will highlight a tool tip showing its neighbored key frames and the associated text (previewing). When clicking on a key frame, the corresponding video is played (viewing). The video that is currently played is surrounded by its neighbored key frames. Users can click on them and browse through the current video (browsing). We refer to this sequence as "Preview-Click-View'n'Browse." Possible low-level event combinations are visualized in Figure 18.12.

In this sequence, users can (a) highlight additional information by moving the mouse over a retrieved key frame to get some additional information of the shot (neighbored key frames and text from the speech recognition software) (previewing), (b) click on a key frame of a result list (clicking result), and (c) play a video (viewing). Also, they can (d) browse through the video to find new results in the same video (browsing).

Figure 18.12   Possible event combinations on a given document in sequence S_4.

18.3.5 User Action Sequence S_5 (Click'n'More)

Sequence S_5 is the most complex of all introduced sequences. It is based on the retrieval interface by Christel and Conescu [20]. In this interface, retrieved results are represented by key frames and presented in a list. Clicking on one key frame, the user can choose to explicitly mark a shot as relevant (providing explicit relevance feedback) to play the video (viewing) or to display additional information (exploring). Further, it allows to browse displayed key frames (browsing) and slide through the video (sliding). We refer to this sequence as "Click'n'More." Possible low-level event combinations are visualized in Figure 18.13.

In this sequence, users can (a) click on a key frame in the result list (clicking result) and (b) play a video (viewing). They can also (c) use the sliding bar (sliding). Users may (d) browse through the video to find new results in the same video (browsing). Moreover, they can (e) show additional video information and sort results by date and broadcasting station (exploring). Besides, they can explicitly judge the relevance of a video shot (providing explicit relevance feedback).

The introduced user interaction scenarios illustrate that the design of graphical video retrieval interfaces directly influence user behavior patterns. Even though users might follow the same aim, that is, finding documents of interest, the interface design forces them to interact differently. Sequence S_2, for example, shows that users can interact with video results without viewing the actual video. In sequence S_3, however, viewing a video is essential while interacting with the results. Consequently, Hopfgartner and Jose [41] argue that the interpretation and importance of the implicit indicators of relevance depend on the interface context. By applying the scenarios introduced earlier, they simulate users providing implicit relevance feedback while performing a retrieval task over multiple iterations. They conclude that these features can be seen as implicit indicators of relevance and, thus, retrieval

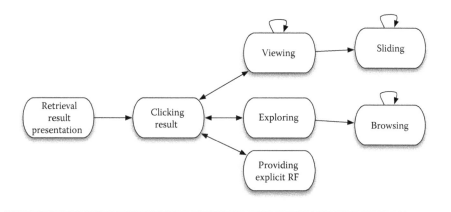

Figure 18.13 Possible event combinations on a given document in sequence S_5.

results can be adapted to the user's current interest. Further applications of this implicit relevance feedback in the video domain have been presented in [42,45].

18.4 Evaluation and Benchmarking

This section reviews the evaluation methods for browsing and interactive search, near-duplicate detection, as well as for event detection and linking video content by occurrence of objects, persons, and places.

18.4.1 Browsing and Interactive Search

As pointed out in [109], the evaluation of browsing and exploratory search tools is still an open issue. In the information retrieval and multimedia information retrieval community, evaluations following the Cranfield paradigm, which is also used by the TREC (text) and TRECVID (video) [98] retrieval benchmarks, have been widely adopted. This type of evaluation is system or component centric and answers a well-defined information need, that is, question answering or fact finding. In browsing or exploratory search, the user's information need may not be well defined [110]. User-centric evaluation methods such as surveys take the context of the user's task when using a system into account. The issue of limited correspondence between these evaluation methods has been discussed for information retrieval systems [103].

Most of the literature on evaluation of exploratory search deals with text documents. In the multimedia domain, evaluation approaches for summarization and skimming systems often deal only with single multimedia documents, rather than with collections. The following classes of evaluation approaches have been proposed (of course combinations of the methods from different classes are sometimes used).

Survey The users are asked about their experience with the tool, their satisfaction with the results, and the relevance of certain features of the tool (e.g., [87]). This type of evaluation does not require any ground truth or specific preparation of a data set.

Analysis of system logs This approach uses either server-side logs [1] or specific client applications that log user actions [55]. The main advantage is that evaluation does not interfere with the user's work with the system and that the approach can be used for long-term studies. However, comparison across different types of tasks and systems might be difficult.

Question answering Users are asked fact-finding questions about the content in order to evaluate whether they have found the correct segment of content or were able to extract information from the collection of multimedia documents (e.g., [58]). The questions can be open or in the form of a multiple choice test (quiz). The correctness of answers to open questions needs to be checked by a human, while multiple choice tests can be very efficiently evaluated once the ground truth for a specific data set has been created.

Indirect evaluation The user performs a task using the tool or system. Based on the success of this task, the effectiveness of the tool can be measured. The task can, for example, be a content-retrieval task [9] or gathering information from a meeting archive browser [62]. Once the ground truth for theses tasks has been created, the answers can be checked automatically.

In [8], two TRECVID style fact-finding approaches, a retrieval and a question answering task, and a user survey were applied to the evaluation of a video-browsing tool for use in movie and TV postproduction. The retrieval task correlates better with the user experience according to the survey than the question answering tasks. As retrieving relevant content is also closer to the real-world application of the tool than finding facts about the content, it seems to be the more appropriate evaluation method in this case, although it is a costly method due to the efforts for data set and ground truth preparation. The authors conclude that surveys are rather suitable for comparing the general usability of tools for certain applications than for getting information about strengths and weaknesses of specific functionalities of a tool.

In 2005 and 2006, the TRECVID video retrieval benchmarking initiative [98] organized a pilot task for exploring rushes material. Some participants used interactive search and browsing approaches. For the pilot task, no specific evaluation scheme was defined, and most participants evaluated specific feature detectors rather than the overall systems. In general, the results show that the recall scores are lower than precision in such an application. The difficulty in evaluating such a task led TRECVID to move to video skimming of rushes video from 2007 onward.

18.4.2 Near-Duplicate Detection

Different measures for evaluating near-duplicate video detection are found in literature. A recent study [6] found the following measures are applied for evaluating near-duplicate video detection: three variants of precision/recall-based measures, a measure based on normalized mutual information, and three measures coming from classic copy detection, that is, two measures used in the MUSCLE VCD benchmark [63] and the one used in the TRECVID benchmark [98] content-based copy detection task. The measure differs in several dimensions, such as providing frame or segment precision, requiring the same segmentation for ground truth and results and support for evaluation of clustering per scene/topic. There are further methods used for evaluating near-duplicate detection that require additional metadata (e.g., topic labels), such as the measure for evaluating news story threading in [32]. However, as they are not generally applicable this additional metadata are not available in all tasks that are relevant for near-duplicate detection.

In the TRECVID 2007 and 2008 rushes summarization experiments, the redundancy of the summaries was judged by the evaluators, which is an indirect measure of how well removal of near duplicates works in the summary generation process. The evaluators used a five-point scale. The results are in the range from 2 to 4, with both mean and median 3.33 [80]. Other results for near-duplicate detection are difficult to compare due to different task context, data sets, and measures. On the TRECVID data set, equal precision/recall of around 0.7 [7] or precision of up to 0.85 at recall of 0.3 [31] are reported.

In [6], the correlations of the different measures on real algorithm results as well as on simulated results have been analyzed, as well as their correlation with human judgment of redundancy from the TRECVID rushes experiments. The results show that depending on the type of differences (segments added, dropped, shifted) between ground truth and results, the correlation between the measures can in some cases be quite low, so that results obtained from different measures cannot be compared as it is sometimes found in literature. Shifting segment boundaries has the strongest impact on the correlation of the measures, and does not only affect frame-based measures, but also shot-based ones that assume alignment between result and truth segments. In general, there is no grouping into frame- and segment-based measures. However, the different variants of precision/recall-type measures have higher correlations among them than others. For obtaining comparable evaluation results, choosing one of the measures from the well-correlated group seems to be advantageous. The aligned cluster and frame-based precision/recall measures both do not require the same segmentation on ground truth and result set and support clustering. These are useful properties for many practical problems. The correlation of the measures with human perception is generally weak, but rank correlation is slightly higher. The frame-based precision/recall measure performs best with a correlation coefficient of 0.37. Human perception seems to take a broader range of factors into account than covered by near-duplicate detection methods.

18.4.3 Event Detection and Instance Linking

Related emerging topics are event detection in video and linking of video segments based on recurring objects, persons, or places. In 2010, TRECVID included new tasks to address these emerging research topics. The multimedia event detection task aims at finding complex events in video. A normalized detection cost measure has been used, and the results were quite good, that is, most runs were clearly below the baseline cost of reporting no events (and thus no false positives). However, some groups tried dynamic features for representing the events that did not outperform static features. The other new task targets detecting the occurrence of the same object instance, person, or location in a moderately large database. The instances differ strongly in terms of size, pose, lighting, etc. The results show that automatic systems perform very poorly, with top mean average precision around 0.030, and top median average precision around 0.005. However, the experiment also shows that interactive systems can reach a mean average precision of around 0.5 on the same data. This clearly underlines the potential of interactive search and browsing approaches.

A somewhat related task, that is, determining the location of images, was part of the MediaEval 2010 [69] benchmark. In the top runs, nearly half of the images were placed in a 1 km radius of the target; however, most approaches relied only or mainly on tags provided with the images.

18.5 Conclusion and Outlook

In this chapter, we have reviewed tools for browsing, navigating, and organizing audiovisual content in TV postproduction. We find a broad range of tools for this purpose, ranging from simple or extended video players, which are already widely used today, to much more advanced approaches, which are based on various automatic analysis methods and provide sophisticated user interfaces. Such tools are currently still research prototypes, partly because of the fact that the underlying content analysis methods are not robust enough for production use. However, such tools have the potential to change workflows and enhance productivity in TV postproduction.

The graphical user interfaces of the tools directly influence user behavior patterns, as is illustrated by the user action sequences we have modeled based on representative video retrieval interfaces that have been surveyed in [96]. Each sequence models different user interaction scenarios, where users trigger different events while interacting with a given document. Even though users might follow the same aim, that is, finding documents of interests, the interface design forces them to interact differently. Sequence S_2 (Click'n'Browse), for example, shows that users can interact with video results *without* viewing the actual video. In sequence S_3 (Click-View-Explore'n'Slide), however, viewing a video is essential while interacting with the results.

The review of benchmarking methods and results highlights two important facts. First, fully automatic content-based methods for organizing and cross-linking are limited in terms of their performance, and providing additional metadata to support the process is too costly. Benchmarking results show that finding reoccurring objects, persons, and locations under general conditions, as well as identifying complex dynamic events in video, are hard problems. Both are emerging research topics, and while we can expect significant progress in coming years, the results are still not sufficient to be directly used in production. However, benchmarking results also show that having the "human in the loop" can boost the results of such tasks. This means that interactive browsing and navigation tools, combining content-based methods with intelligent user interfaces, can already provide solutions to practical problems in TV postproduction workflows.

The second conclusion from the state of the art in benchmarking is that evaluating interactive search and browsing tools still poses open research questions. The focus of evaluation is on automatic tasks, which is clearly a simpler problem, and tries to transfer these methods also to interactive tools. However, this neglects many important aspects of browsing and navigation tools.

Finally, there are new trends in TV production that also need to be reflected by future content management tools. One is 3D TV, which at present means stereoscopic, but that might change to a larger number of views or actual 3D information with future display technologies. The consequence for postproduction is that even more content has to be handled, and that further properties of the content (e.g., the depth of objects) are relevant for selection, and also need to be visualized appropriately. Another trend is the integration of broadcast content with web and social media content, for example, in Hybrid TV, that is, delivering Internet content together with the main audiovisual stream, or "Second Screen" approaches, that is, delivering personalized content related to the broadcast to devices such as smart phones or tablets. While production tools for interactive TV, which have been thoroughly studied in the recent years, provide some relevant solutions, there are new challenges in terms of content management. For example, not all information is local at the production site, but might be accessed from anywhere on the Internet, and the content to be delivered is potentially dynamically changing over time.

Acknowledgments

The first author's work has received funding from the European Union's Seventh Framework Programme (FP7/2007-2013) under grant agreement no. 215475, "2020 3D Media—Spatial Sound and Vision" (http://www.20203dmedia.eu/). The third author was supported by a fellowship within the Postdoc-Program of the German Academic Exchange Service (DAAD).

References

1. S.F. Adafre and M. de Rijke. Exploratory search in Wikipedia. In *SIGIR Workshop on Evaluating Exploratory Search Systems*, Seattle, WA, 2006.
2. D.A. Adjeroh, M.C. Lee, and I. King. A distance measure for video sequences. *Computer Vision and Image Understanding*, 75(1–2):25–45, 1999.
3. MAGIX AG. Movie Edit Pro. http://www.magix.com/us/movie-edit-pro/, 2011. [Online; accessed March 24, 2011.]
4. J. Arlandis, P. Over, and W. Kraaij. Boundary error analysis and categorization in the TRECVID news story segmentation task. In *CIVR'05: Proceedings of the Fourth International Conference on Image and Video Retrieval*, Singapore, July 20–22, 2005, pp. 103–112.
5. F. Arman, R. Depommier, A. Hsu, and M.Y. Chiu. Content-based browsing of video sequences. In *Proceedings of the Second ACM International Conference on Multimedia*, San Francisco, CA, pp. 97–103, 1994.
6. W. Bailer. Evaluating detection of near duplicate video segments. In *ACM International Conference on Image and Video Retrieval*, Xian, China, pp. 197–204, July 2010.

7. W. Bailer, F. Lee, and G. Thallinger. Detecting and clustering multiple takes of one scene. In *Proceedings of the 14th Multimedia Modeling Conference*, Kyoto, Japan, pp. 80–89, 2008.

8. W. Bailer and H. Rehatschek. Comparing fact finding tasks and user survey for evaluating a video browsing tool. In *Proceedings of ACM Multimedia*, Beijing, China, October 2009.

9. W. Bailer, C. Schober, and G. Thallinger. Video content browsing based on iterative feature clustering for rushes exploitation. In *Proceedings of the TRECVID Workshop*, Gaithersburg, MD, pp. 230–239, November 2006.

10. W. Bailer, W. Weiss, G. Kienast, G. Thallinger, and W. Haas. A video browsing tool for content management in post-production. *International Journal of Digital Multimedia Broadcasting*, 2010:1–17, March 2010, Article ID 856761.

11. M. Barbieri, G. Mekenkamp, M. Ceccarelli, and J. Nesvadba. The color browser: A content driven linear video browsing tool. In *IEEE International Conference on Multimedia and Expo* (ICME 2001), Tokyo, Japan, pp. 627–630, 2001.

12. M. Bertini, A.D. Bimbo, and W. Nunziati. Video clip matching using MPEG-7 descriptors and edit distance. In *Proceedings of the ACM International Conference on Image and Video Retrieval (CIVR'06)*, Amsterdam, the Netherlands, pp. 133–142, 2006.

13. M. Bezold. Describing user interactions in adaptive interactive systems. In *UMAP'09: Proceedings of the 17th International Conference on User Modeling, Adaptation, and Personalization, formerly UM and AH*, Trento, Italy, pp. 150–161, 2009.

14. P. Browne, C. Czirjek, G. Gaughan, C. Gurrin, G. Jones, H.L.S. Marlow, K. McDonald, N. Murphy, N. O'Connor, N. O'Hare, A.F. Smeaton, and J. Ye. Dublin City University video track experiments for TREC 2003. In *Proceedings of TRECVID Workshop*, Gaithersburg, MD, 2003.

15. L. Chaisorn and T.-S. Chua. The segmentation and classification of story boundaries in news video. In *(VDB'02): Proceedings of the IFIP TC2/WG2.6 Sixth Working Conference on Visual Database Systems*, Brisbane, Australia, pp. 95–109, 2002.

16. L. Chang, Y. Yang, and X.-S. Hua. Smart video player. In *2008 IEEE International Conference on Multimedia and Expo (ICME'08)*, Hannover, Germany, June 23–April 26, 2008, pp. 1605–1606.

17. L. Chen, G.C. Chen, C.Z. Xu, J. March, and S. Benford. EmoPlayer: A media player for video clips with affective annotations. *Interacting with Computers*, 20(1):17–28, 2008.

18. K.-Y. Cheng, S.-J. Luo, B.-Y. Chen, and H.-H. Chu. Smartplayer: User-centric video fast-forwarding. In *CHI'09: Proceedings of the 27th International Conference on Human Factors in Computing Systems*, Boston, MA, pp. 789–798, 2009. ACM, New York.

19. P. Chiu, A. Girgensohn, W. Polak, E. Rieffel, and L. Wilcox. A genetic algorithm for video segmentation and summarization. In *Proceedings of the IEEE International Conference on Multimedia and Expo*, Vol. III, Salt Lake City, UT, pp. 1329–1332, 2000. ACM, New York.

20. M.G. Christel and R.M. Conescu. Addressing the challenge of visual information access from digital image and video libraries. In *JCDL'05: Proceedings of the ACM/IEEE Joint Conference on Digital Libraries*, Denver, CA, June 7–11, 2005, pp. 69–78.

21. M.G. Christel, A.G. Hauptmann, A.S. Warmack, and S.A. Crosby. Adjustable film-strips and skims as abstractions for a digital video library. In *Proceedings of the IEEE Forum on Research and Technology Advances in Digital Libraries*, Baltimore, MD, pp. 98–104, 1999.
22. T.-S. Chua, S.-F. Chang, L. Chaisorn, and W.H. Hsu. Story boundary detection in large broadcast news video archives: Techniques, experience and trends. In *ACM MM'04: Proceedings of the 12th ACM International Conference on Multimedia*, New York, October 10–16, 2004, pp. 656–659.
23. M. Covell, S. Baluja, and M. Fink. Advertisement detection and replacement using acoustic and visual repetition. In *IEEE Workshop on Multimedia Signal Processing*, Victoria, British Columbia, Canada, pp. 461–466, October 2006.
24. C. Crockford and H. Agius. An empirical investigation into user navigation of digital video using the VCR-like control set. *International Journal of Human-Computer Studies*, 64(4):340–355, 2006.
25. O. de Rooij, C.G.M. Snoek, and M. Worring. Query on demand video browsing. In *Proceedings of the 15th International Conference on Multimedia*, Augsburg, Germany, pp. 811–814, 2007. ACM Press, New York.
26. M. del Fabro, K. Schoeffmann, and L. Boeszoermenyi. Instant video browsing: A tool for fast non-sequential hierarchical video browsing. *HCI in Work and Learning, Life and Leisure*, Klagenfurt, Austria, pp. 443–446, 2010.
27. A. Divakaran, C. Forlines, T. Lanning, S. Shipman, and K. Wittenburg. Augmenting fast-forward and rewind for personal digital video recorders. In *IEEE International Conference on Consumer Electronics (ICCE), Digest of Technical Papers*, Las Vegas, NV, pp. 43–44, 2005.
28. A. Divakaran and I. Otsuka. A video-browsing-enhanced personal video recorder. In *14th International Conference on Image Analysis and Processing Workshops (ICIAPW 2007)*, Modena, Italy, pp. 137–142, 2007.
29. A. Dix, J. Finlay, and R. Beale. Analysis of user behaviour as time series. In *HCI'92: Proceedings of the Conference on People and Computers VII*, pp. 429–444, 1993. Cambridge University Press, New York.
30. P. Dragicevic, G. Ramos, J. Bibliowitcz, D. Nowrouzezahrai, R. Balakrishnan, and K. Singh. Video browsing by direct manipulation. In *Proceeding of the 26th Annual SIGCHI Conference on Human Factors in Computing Systems (CHI'08)*, Florence, Italy, pp. 237–246, 2008. ACM, New York.
31. E. Dumont and B. Mérialdo. Rushes video parsing using video sequence alignment. In *CBMI 2009, Seventh International Workshop on Content-Based Multimedia Indexing*, Crete Island, Greece, June 3–5, 2009.
32. P. Duygulu, J.-Y. Pan, and D.A. Forsyth. Towards auto-documentary: Tracking the evolution of news stories. In *MULTIMEDIA'04: Proceedings of the 12th Annual ACM International Conference on Multimedia*, New York, pp. 820–827, 2004. ACM Press, New York.
33. D. Eichmann and D.-J. Park. Boundary and feature extraction at the University of Iowa. In *Proceedings of TRECVID Workshop*, Gaithersburg, MD, 2004.
34. H. Eidenberger. A video browsing application based on visual MPEG-7 descriptors and self-organising maps. *International Journal of Fuzzy Systems*, 6(3):125–138, 2004.

35. H. Goeau, J. Thievre, M.L. Viaud, and D. Pellerin. Interactive visualization tool with graphic table of video contents. In *IEEE International Conference on Multimedia and Expo*, Beijing, China, pp. 807–810, 2007.

36. A. Hampapur and R.M. Bolle. Comparison of distance measures for video copy detection. In *IEEE International Conference on Multimedia and Expo*, Tokyo, Japan, pp. 737–740, August 2001.

37. A. Hampapur, K. Hyun, and R.M. Bolle. Comparison of sequence matching techniques for video copy detection. In M.M. Yeung, C.-S. Li, and R.W. Lienhart (eds.), *Storage and Retrieval for Media Databases 2002*, volume 4676 of Society of Photo-Optical Instrumentation Engineers (SPIE) Conference, pp. 194–201, December 2001.

38. A.G. Hauptmann and M.J. Witbrock. Story segmentation and detection of commercials in broadcast news video. In *Proceedings of the Advances in Digital Libraries Conference*, Santa Barbara, CA, 1998.

39. M.A. Hearst, S.T. Dumais, E. Osman, J. Platt, and B. Scholkopf. Support vector machines. *IEEE Intelligent Systems and Their Applications*, 13(4):18–28, 1998.

40. D. Heesch, P. Howarth, J. Magalhães, A. May, M. Pickering, A. Yavlinski, and S. Rüger. Video retrieval using search and browsing. In *Proceedings of TRECVID Workshop*, Gaithersburg, MD, 2004.

41. F. Hopfgartner and J.M. Jose. Evaluating the implicit feedback models for adaptive video retrieval. In *ACM MIR'07: Proceedings of the Ninth ACM SIGMM International Workshop on Multimedia Information Retrieval*, Augsburg, Germany, pp. 323–331, 2007. ACM Press.

42. F. Hopfgartner and J.M. Jose. Semantic user modelling for personal news video retrieval. In *Proceedings of Multimedia Modeling Conference*, Chongging, China, pp. 336–346, 2010.

43. F. Hopfgartner and J.M. Jose. Semantic user profiling techniques for personalized multimedia recommendation. *Multimedia Systems*, 16(4–5):255–274, 2010.

44. F. Hopfgartner, J. Urban, R. Villa, and J.M. Jose. Simulated testing of an adaptive multimedia information retrieval system. In *CBMI'07: Proceedings of the Fifth International Workshop on Content-Based Multimedia Indexing*, Bordeaux, France, pp. 328–335, 2007. IEEE.

45. F. Hopfgartner, T. Urruty, P.B. Lopez, R. Villa, and J.M. Jose. Simulated evaluation of faceted browsing based on feature selection. *Multimedia Tools and Applications*, 47(3):631–662, 2010.

46. F. Hopfgartner, D. Vallet, M. Halvey, and J.M. Jose. Search trails using user feedback to improve video search. In *ACM Multimedia*, Vancouver, Canada, pp. 339–348, 2008.

47. W. Hsu, S.-F. Chang, C.-W. Huang, L. Kennedy, C.-Y. Lin, and G. Iyengar. Discovery and fusion of salient multimodal features toward news story segmentation. In *Proceedings of the Storage and Retrieval Methods and Applications for Multimedia*, San Jose, CA, pp. 244–258, 2004.

48. W. Hsu and S.-F. Chang. Topic tracking across broadcast news videos with visual duplicates and semantic concepts. In *International Conference on Image Processing (ICIP)*, Atlanta, GA, October 2006.

49. W. Hürst, G. Goetz, and M. Welte. Interactive video browsing on mobile devices. In *Proceedings of the 15th International Conference on Multimedia*, pp. 247–256, Augsburg, Germany, 2007. ACM.

50. W. Hürst and P. Jarvers. Interactive, dynamic video browsing with the zoom-slider interface. In *International Conference on Multimedia and Expo (ICME 2005)*, Amsterdam, the Netherlands, p. 4, 2005. IEEE.

51. W. Hürst, G. Götz, and P. Jarvers. Advanced user interfaces for dynamic video browsing. In *Proceedings of the 12th Annual ACM International Conference on Multimedia (MULTIMEDIA'04)*, New York, pp. 742–743, 2004. ACM.

52. I. Ide, H. Mo, N. Katayama, and S. Satoh. Topic threading for structuring a large-scale news video archive. In *International Conference on Image and Video Retrieval*, Dublin, Ireland, pp. 123–131, July 2004.

53. Apple Inc. Final cut studio. http://www.apple.com/at/finalcutstudio/, 2011. [Online; accessed March 24, 2011.]

54. Avid Technology Inc. Avid DS system. http://www.avid.com/US/products/dssystem, 2011. [Online; accessed March 24, 2011.]

55. B.J. Jansen, R. Ramadoss, M. Zhang, and N. Zang. Wrapper: An application for evaluating exploratory searching outside of the lab. In *SIGIR Workshop on Evaluating Exploratory Search Systems*, Seattle, WA, 2006.

56. M. Jansen, W. Heeren, and B. van Dijk. Videotrees: Improving video surrogate presentation using hierarchy. In *IEEE International Workshop on Content-Based Multimedia Indexing (CBMI 2008)*, London, U.K., pp. 560–567, 2008.

57. Y.G. Jiang, J. Yang, C.W. Ngo, and A.G. Hauptmann. Representations of keypoint-based semantic concept detection: A comprehensive study. *IEEE Transactions on Multimedia*, 12(1):42–53, 2010.

58. V.B. Jijkoun and M. de Rijke. A pilot for evaluating exploratory question answering. In *SIGIR Workshop on Evaluating Exploratory Search Systems*, Seattle, WA, 2006.

59. J.R. Kender and M.R. Naphade. Visual concepts for news story tracking: Analyzing and exploiting the NIST TRECVID video annotation experiment. In *2005 IEEE Computer Society Conference on Computer Vision and Pattern Recognition (CVPR)*, San Diego, CA, Vol. 1, pp. 1174–1181, 2005.

60. J. Kleban, A. Sarkar, E. Moxley, S. Mangiat, S. Joshi, T. Kuo, and B.S. Manjunath. Feature fusion and redundancy pruning for rush video summarization. In *TVS'07: Proceedings of the International Workshop on TRECVID Video Summarization*, Augsburg, Germany, pp. 84–88, 2007. ACM, New York.

61. A. Komlodi and G. Marchionini. Key frame preview techniques for video browsing. In *Proceedings of the Third ACM Conference on Digital Libraries*, Pittsburgh, PA, pp. 118–125, 1998.

62. W. Kraaij and W. Post. Task based evaluation of exploratory search systems. In *SIGIR Workshop on Evaluating Exploratory Search Systems*, Seattle, WA, 2006.

63. J. Law-To, A. Joly, and N. Boujemaa. Muscle-VCD-2007: A live benchmark for video copy detection, 2007. http://www-rocq.inria.fr/imedia/civr-bench/

64. R. Lienhart, S. Pfeiffer, and W. Effelsberg. Video Abstracting. *Communications of the ACM*, 40(12):54–63, December 1997.

65. J. Liu, Y. He, and M. Peng. NewsBR: A content-based news video browsing and retrieval system. In *The Fourth International Conference on Computer and Information Technology (CIT'04)*, Wuhan, China, pp. 857–862, 2004.

66. D.G. Lowe. Distinctive image features from scale-invariant keypoints. *International Journal of Computer Vision*, 60(2):91–110, 2004.

67. C. Ma, B. Byun, I. Kim, and C.-H. Lee. A detection-based approach to broadcast news video story segmentation. In *International Conference on Acoustics, Speech and Signal Processing*, Taipei, Taiwan, pp. 1957–1960, 2009.

68. K. Manske. Video browsing using 3D video content trees. In *Proceedings of the 1998 Workshop on New Paradigms in Information Visualization and Manipulation*, Bethesda, MD, pp. 20–24, 1998. ACM.

69. Mediaeval benchmarking initiative. http://www.multimediaeval.org. [Online; accessed December 15, 2010.]

70. A. Messina, R. Borgotallo, G. Dimino, D. Airola Gnota, and L. Boch. Ants: A complete system for automatic news programme annotation based on multimodal analysis. In *Workshop on Image Analysis for Multimedia Interactive Services*, Lausanne, Switzerland, pp. 219–222, 2008.

71. A. Messina and M. Montagnuolo. Fuzzy mining of multimedia genre applied to television archives. In *IEEE International Conference on Multimedia and Expo*, Hannover, Germany, pp. 117–120, 2008. IEEE.

72. S.P. Meyn and R.L. Tweedie. *Markov Chains and Stochastic Stability (Communications and Control Engineering)*. Springer Verlag, London, U.K., 1996.

73. H. Misra, F. Hopfgartner, A. Goyal, P. Punitha, and J. Jose. TV news story segmentation based on semantic coherence and content similarity. In *Advances in Multimedia Modeling*, Springer, Berlin/Heidelberg, Germany, pp. 347–357, 2010.

74. N. Moraveji. Improving video browsing with an eye-tracking evaluation of feature-based color bars. In *Proceedings of the 2004 Joint ACM/IEEE Conference on Digital Libraries*, Tucson, AZ, pp. 49–50, 2004.

75. C.S. Myers and L.R. Rabiner. A comparative study of several dynamic time-warping algorithms for connected word recognition. *The Bell System Technical Journal*, 60(7):1389–1409, September 1981.

76. S.-Y. Neo, H. Luan, Y. Zheng, H.-K. Goh, and T.-S. Chua. VisionGo: Bridging users and multimedia video retrieval. In *CIVR'08: Proceedings of the 2008 International Conference on Content-based Image and Video Retrieval*, Niagara Falls, Canada, pp. 559–560, 2008. ACM, New York.

77. C.-W. Ngo, W.-L. Zhao, and Y.-G. Jiang. Fast tracking of near-duplicate keyframes in broadcast domain with transitivity propagation. In *MULTIMEDIA'06: Proceedings of the 14th Annual ACM International Conference on Multimedia*, Santa Barbara, CA, pp. 845–854, 2006. ACM, New York.

78. N.E. O'Connor, C. Czirjek, S. Deasy, N. Murphy, S. Marlow, and A.F. Smeaton. News story segmentation in the Fischlar video indexing system. In *Proceedings of the International Conference on Image Processing*, Thessaloniki, Greece, pp. 418–421, 2001.

79. J.H. Oh and K.A. Hua. An efficient technique for summarizing videos using visual contents. In *IEEE International Conference on Multimedia and Expo (ICME)*, New York, pp. 1167–1170, 2000.

80. P. Over, A.F. Smeaton, and G. Awad. The TRECVID 2008 BBC rushes summarization evaluation. In *Proceedings of the Second ACM TRECVid Video Summarization Workshop (TVS'08)*, Vancouver, British Columbia, Canada, pp. 1–20, 2008.

81. K.A. Peker and A. Divakaran. Adaptive fast playback-based video skimming using a compressed-domain visual complexity measure. In *IEEE International Conference on Multimedia and Expo (ICME'04)*, Taipei, Taiwan, Vol. 3, 2004.

82. S. Pfeiffer, R. Lienhart, S. Fischer, and W. Effelsberg. Abstracting digital movies automatically. *Journal of Visual Communication and Image Representation*, 7(4):345–353, December 1996.

83. M.J. Pickering, L.W.C. Wong, and S.M. Rüger. ANSES: Summarisation of news video. In *Proceedings of the International Conference on Image and Video Retrieval*, Urbana-Champaign, IL, pp. 425–434, 2003.

84. D. Ponceleon. Hierachical brushing in a collection of video data. In *HICSS'01: Proceedings of the 34th Annual Hawaii International Conference on System Sciences (HICSS-34)*, Maui, HI, Vol. 4, p. 4045, 2001. IEEE Computer Society, Washington, DC.

85. S. Pongnumkul, J. Wang, G. Ramos, and M. Cohen. Content-aware dynamic timeline for video browsing. In *Proceedings of the 23rd Annual ACM Symposium on User Interface Software and Technology*, New York, pp. 139–142, 2010. ACM.

86. G.-J. Poulisse and M.-F. Moens. Multimodal news story segmentation. In *Proceedings of the First International Conference on Intelligent Human Computer Interaction*, Allahabad, India, pp. 95–101. 2009.

87. Y. Qu and G.W. Furnas. Model-driven formative evaluation of exploratory search: A study under a sensemaking framework. *Information Processing and Management*, 44(2):534–555, 2008.

88. G.M. Quénot, D. Mararu, S. Ayache, M. Charhad, and L. Besacier. Clips-lis-lsr-labri experiments at TRECVID 2004. In *Proceedings of TRECVID Workshop*, Gaithersburg, MD, 2004.

89. H. Rehatschek, W. Bailer, H. Neuschmied, S. Ober, and H. Bischof. A tool supporting annotation and analysis of videos. In S. Knauss and A.D. Ornella (eds.), *Reconfigurations. Interdisciplinary Perspectives on Religion in a Post-Secular Society*, Vienna, Austria, pp. 253–268, 2007.

90. A. Rosenberg and J. Hirschberg. Story segmentation of broadcast news in English, Mandarin and Arabic. In *Proceedings of the Human Language Technology Conference of the NAACL*, Companion Volume: Short Papers, New York, pp. 125–128, 2006.

91. E. Rossi, S. Benini, R. Leonardi, B. Mansencal, and J. Benois-Pineau. Clustering of scene repeats for essential rushes preview. In *International Workshop on Image Analysis for Multimedia Interactive Services*, London, U.K., pp. 234–237, 2009.

92. S. Satoh, M. Takimoto, and J. Adachi. Scene duplicate detection from videos based on trajectories of feature points. In *MIR'07: Proceedings of the International Workshop on Multimedia Information Retrieval*, Augsburg, Germany, pp. 237–244, 2007. ACM, New York.

93. K. Schoeffmann. Facilitating interactive search and navigation in videos. In *Proceedings of the ACM International Conference on Multimedia*, Firenze, Italy, October 2010.

94. K. Schoeffmann and L. Boeszoermenyi. Video browsing using interactive navigation summaries. In *Proceedings of the Seventh International Workshop on Content-Based Multimedia Indexing*, Chania, Crete, June 2009. IEEE.

95. K. Schoeffmann and L. Boeszoermenyi. Enhancing seeker-bars of video players with dominant color rivers. In Y.-P.P. Chen, Z. Zhang, S. Boll, Q. Tian, and L. Zhang (eds.), *Advances in Multimedia Modeling*, Chongqing, China, January 2010. Springer.

96. K. Schoeffmann, F. Hopfgartner, O. Marques, L. Boeszoermenyi, and J.M. Jose. Video browsing interfaces and applications: A review. *SPIE Reviews*, 1(1):018004-1–018004-35, 2010.

97. K. Schoeffmann, M. Taschwer, and L. Boeszoermenyi. Video browsing using motion visualization. In *Proceedings of the IEEE International Conference on Multimedia and Expo*, New York, July 2009. IEEE, New York.

98. A.F. Smeaton, P. Over, and W. Kraaij. Evaluation campaigns and TRECVid. In *MIR'06: Proceedings of the Eighth ACM International Workshop on Multimedia Information Retrieval*, Santa Barbara, CA, pp. 321–330, 2006. ACM Press, New York.

99. M. Sugano, K. Hoashi, K. Matsumoto, and Y. Nakajima. Shot boundary determination on MPEG compressed domain and story segmentation experiments for Trecvid 2004. In *Proceedings of TRECVID Workshop*, Gaithersburg, MD, 2004.

100. Y.-P. Tan, S.R. Kulkarni, and P.J. Ramadge. A framework for measuring video similarity and its application to video query by example. In *Proceedings of International Conference on Image Processing*, Kobe, Japan, Vol. 2, pp. 106–110, October 1999.

101. X. Tang, X. Gao, and C.Y. Wong. NewsEye: A news video browsing and retrieval system. In *Proceedings of 2001 International Symposium on Intelligent Multimedia, Video and Speech Processing*, Hong Kong, pp. 150–153, 2001.

102. B.T. Truong and S. Venkatesh. Video abstraction: A systematic review and classification. *ACM Transactions on Multimedia Computing Communications and Applications*, 3(1):3, 2007.

103. A.H. Turpin and W. Hersh. Why batch and user evaluations do not give the same results. In *Proceedings of the 24th Annual International ACM SIGIR Conference on Research and Development in Information Retrieval (SIGIR'01)*, New Orleans, LA, 2001.

104. S. Vakkalanka, S. Palanivel, and B. Yegnanarayana. NVIBRS-news video indexing, browsing and retrieval system. In *IEEE International Conference on Intelligent Sensing and Information Processing (ICISIP-05)*, Chennai, India, pp. 181–186, 2005.

105. A. Vinciarelli and S. Favre. Broadcast news story segmentation using social network analysis and hidden Markov models. In *Proceedings of the 15th International Conference on Multimedia*, Augsburg, Germany, pp. 261–264, 2007.

106. Autonomy virage. http://www.virage.com/. [Online; accessed March 21, 2011.]

107. T. Volkmer, S.M.M. Tahahoghi, and H.E. Williams. RMIT University at TRECVID 2004. In *Proceedings of TRECVID Workshop*, Gaithersburg, MD, 2004.

108. J. Wang, C. Xu, and E. Chng. Automatic sports video genre classification using pseudo-2D-HMM. *Pattern Recognition*, 4:778–781, 2006.

109. R.W. White, B. Kules, S.M. Drucker, and M.C. Schraefel. Supporting exploratory search. *Communications of the ACM*, 49(4):36–39, 2006.

110. R.W. White, G. Marchionini, and G. Muresan. Editorial: Evaluating exploratory search systems. *Information Processing and Management*, 44(2):433–436, 2008.

111. X. Wu, C.-W. Ngo, and Q. Li. Threading and autodocumenting news videos: A promising solution to rapidly browse news topics. *IEEE Signal Processing Magazine*, 23(2):59–68, March 2006.

112. Z. Xiong, R. Radhakrishnan, A. Divakaran, Y. Rui, and T.S. Huang. *A Unified Framework for Video Summarization, Browsing and Retrieval: With Applications to Consumer and Surveillance Video*, Academic Press, Burlington, MA, 2005.

113. J. Yang, Y.G. Jiang, A.G. Hauptmann, and C.W. Ngo. Evaluating bag-of-visual-words representations in scene classification. In *Proceedings of the International Workshop on Multimedia Information Retrieval*, Augsburg, Germany, pp. 197–206, 2007. ACM.

114. M.-C. Yeh and K.-T. Cheng. Video copy detection by fast sequence matching. In *ACM International Conference on Image and Video Retrieval*, Island of Santorini, Greece, July 2009.

115. Y. Zhai, X. Cao, Y. Zhang, O. Javed, A. Yilmaz, F. Rafi, S. Ali, O. Alatas, S.M. Khan, and M. Shah. University of Central Florida at TRECVID 2004. In *Proceedings of TRECVID Workshop*, Gaithersburg, MD, 2004.

116. Y. Zhai and M. Shah. Tracking news stories across different sources. In *ACM Multimedia*, Singapore, pp. 2–10, 2005.

117. L. Zhao, W. Qi, S.Z. Li, S.-Q. Yang, and H.J. Zhang. Key-frame extraction and shot retrieval using nearest feature line (NFL). In *MULTIMEDIA'00: Proceedings of the 2000 ACM workshops on Multimedia*, Los Angeles, CA, pp. 217–220, 2000. ACM, New York.

Chapter 19

Enriching the Viewing Experience of TV Programs Using Virtual Content Insertion

Yu-Tzu Lin
National Taiwan Normal University

Chia-Hu Chang
National Taiwan University

Ja-Ling Wu
National Taiwan University

Contents

19.1 Introduction

Over the years, the rapid technical advances in multimedia compression and broadband network delivery have led to a huge amount of multimedia content created and distributed. With the advanced digital TV technologies and easy-to-use electrical devices, for example, digital cameras, digital camcorders, and smart phones, creating multimedia contents will no longer be peculiar to the professionals and power users. In addition, with dramatically boosted social media services, such as YouTube, AudioBoo, Flickr, Facebook, Plurk, and so on, people can easily create, share, and watch tremendous amounts of multimedia contents in their daily lives. Therefore, people can access rich multimedia content through various media easily. In order to attract more viewers, the TV programs should be refined to be more interesting and useful according to different requirements of various types of TV services (e.g., advertising, education, or entertainment, etc.). Nowadays, users can shape their vivid personal lives via the uniqueness, creativity, and interest of their own multimedia contents and thereby share experiences and knowledge with each other. This phenomenon of personal branding has become a popular culture trend and the market now pays high attention to the latent yet amazing economic benefits of advertising that accompanied with the trend. Besides advertising, digital TV service is also opening up opportunities for interactive learning services to reach mass audiences. It is popular to record the lecture as a digital video for efficient distribution through the Internet. However, general lectures take at least 1 h and will produce a large video file. Consequently, it becomes difficult for learners to browse the lecture content efficiently. In addition, while watching the traditional lecture video, students usually feel bored because it lacks interaction with the teacher or classmates. Therefore, additional interactive content should be incorporated in the self-paced learning environment to help students learn efficiently.

According to different purposes, such as advertising, education, entertainment, or information enhancement, TV programs usually are overlaid by the brand, commercial logos, interesting images, informative windows, or whatever message where deemed to be needed during production or annotate. Since the additional contents, which are virtually inserted into TV programs, can be considered as the virtual content compared with the original content, such insertion techniques are also called *virtual content insertion* [Li07,Li08,Liu08]. By using the techniques for virtual content insertion, specific objects or regions in TV programs can be virtually replaced with the additional content as seamlessly as possible after the program is complete. We define such TV program, which is postproduced to augment its information by using virtual content insertion, as the augmented TV program. The augmented information with well-designed representations or animations can turn TV programs into visually appealing ones. Audiences can watch the original TV programs or the augmented TV programs according to their needs. As a result, the viewing experience of TV programs can be enriched, and a new opportunity to increase audience ratings and advertising revenue will be brought. The previously mentioned concept is illustrated in Figure 19.1.

Although augmented TV programs are popular, there are many crucial issues that need to be addressed in designing strategies and developing systematic techniques for

Figure 19.1 The augmented TV programs can be served by using techniques of virtual content insertion to enrich the original TV programs and thereby increase broadcast content attractivity. For example, the automatically inserted virtual content can assist in indicating the important lecture content (i.e., the monkey approaches the teacher's fingers in the lecture video) or provide an attractive presentation for advertising (i.e., the Nike logo which is transforming in the sports video).

virtual content insertion to be effective and efficient, specifically, how to efficiently insert the semantically relevant virtual contents at the appropriate place and time with the impressive yet less-intrusive representation in the TV programs, so as to maximize the effectiveness of visual communication. The posed problems, which are relating to "what," "where," "when," and "how" are significant and challenging. Most existing related works have proposed various solutions to handle the problems about what, where, and when, but how to elaborately represent the virtual content is rarely touched. Specifically, they focus on the source-oriented content analysis (e.g., camera calibration [Yu08]), detections of insertion points [Mei08,Mei09a,Mei10b], and selections of relevant virtual contents [Hua08,Mei10a,Wang08a], rather than the representation of virtual contents.

Motivated by the previously mentioned observations, there is a need to investigate how to develop systematic techniques for virtual content insertion to efficiently and effectively integrate additional information into the TV programs in a well-orchestrated way. Various media types can be used for conveying additional messages to consumers, for example, texts, still images, audios, videos, and animations. Understanding the characteristics of the TV program productions (e.g., applied media aesthetics [Zett99]) and the psychological responses of audiences supports the effective and efficient visual communication and thus reaches the goal of enriching the viewing experiences. Therefore, different applications need different theoretical bases. For example, in the field of advertising and marketing, lots of advertising strategies [Mori91] were developed and widely adopted in practice based on the advertising theory and psychology. In addition, the design principles for virtual product placement was posed and discussed in our previous study [Chan10c]. On the other hand, in order to grab and keep audiences' attention in a pleasing manner, teachers can bring creativity into lectures according to the principles and theories of education. By integrating the related techniques and the design guidelines, the comprehensive framework for virtual content insertion is shown in Figure 19.2.

In the following sections, we will describe the related theories and practice of virtual content insertion: the techniques of content analysis and media representation are detailed in Sections 19.2 and 19.3, respectively. Section 19.4 describes the prototypes and gives some examples of possible applications in which techniques of virtual content insertion are utilized. The summary is contained in Section 19.5.

19.2 Multimedia Content Analysis for TV programs

In order to automatically insert virtual content into TV programs and provide virtual interactions, audiovisual features should be extracted by analyzing the content of TV programs. Since the focus of attention is usually driven by semantic features or neurological stimulus, the features for constructing the attention model range from low level to high level and even the fusion of them. The extracted low-level features are usually derived from rigid experiments on human perception processes. On the

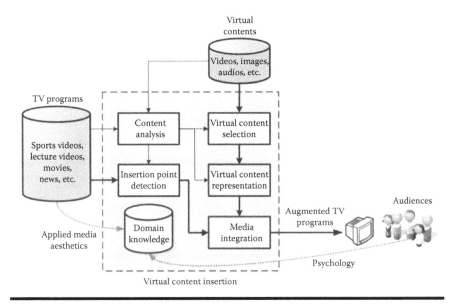

Figure 19.2   The comprehensive framework for virtual content insertion.

other hand, the utilized high-level concepts are based on the implicit prior knowledge or semantic understanding of visual contents. In the following paragraphs, we introduce the essential analysis methods that can be utilized to extract features from low to high semantic level.

19.2.1 Visual Analysis

Visual analysis can be used to understand the video semantically by merely finding low-level features (color, texture, pixel histogram, etc.) or further extracting semantic-level features (gesture, expression, action, etc.) from low-level visual features, which will be detailed by examples in the following.

19.2.1.1 Low-Level Feature Analysis

Low-level features can be extracted by directly analyzing the visual characteristics in the spatial or frequency domain, which contains no semantic meaning for humans at first glance. In lecture content, color features are used to counting the chalk pixels. At first, the lecture content should be extracted by finding the blackboard area in the video frame. System parameters can be tuned according to different blackboard/chalk colors. Since the color of the blackboard and handwriting are influenced by the light, the frame image is converted to the $L^*a^*b^*$ color space, which can be resilient to the light influence. Then, the frame pixels are segmented

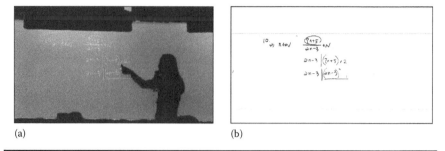

(a)   (b)

Figure 19.3   Lecture content extraction: (a) the blackboard region and (b) the extracted lecture content.

into several regions by clustering pixels with similar colors based on the k-means algorithm [Chen07]. The blackboard region is then obtained by extracting the regions of the blackboard color and merging them (Figure 19.3a). After deciding the blackboard region, the set of chalk pixels P_{chalk} can be computed as

$$P_{chalk} = \cup \left\{ x | I(x) > I_{cp} \right\}, \qquad (19.1)$$

where
   $I(x)$ is the luminance of pixel x
   I_{cp} is the luminance threshold

Figure 19.3 shows one example of lecture content extraction.

   The chalk text or figures written on the blackboard by the lecturer are undoubtedly the most important information for students. It is obvious that the more there is lecture content (chalk handwriting or figures), the more semantics are contained in the lecture video. Therefore, the attention values are evaluated by extracting the lecture content on the blackboard and analyzing the content fluctuation in lecture videos. As a result, the students can easily review and learn the lecture content through the well-structured lecture video according to the estimated lecture content attention curve. Lecture content analysis includes blackboard extraction, content extraction, and content-based attention model construction, which are described in the following paragraphs (see Figure 19.4).

   Another important low-level feature for videos is motion extracted in the pixel or compression domain. Many sophisticated motion estimation algorithms have been developed in the literature, for example, the optical flow in [Beau95] and the feature tracking in [Shi94]. However, they often have high computational complexity because the operations are executed in the pixel domain and the estimated motions are accurate. In the work of [Chan10a], accurate motion estimation is not needed, so the motion information can be directly extracted from the motion vectors of a compressed video. Since the process is done directly in the compression domain, the

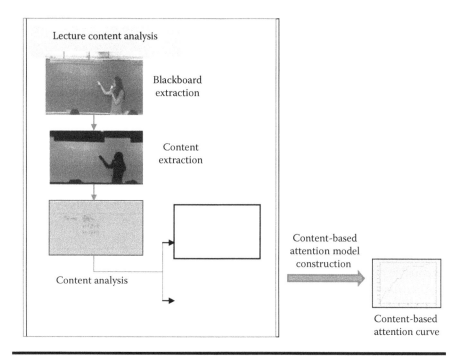

Figure 19.4 **The framework of lecture content analysis for the construction of lecture content attention curve.**

induced complexity is very low. Therefore, the motion information in each video frame can be efficiently obtained.

19.2.1.2 Semantic-Level Feature Analysis

Low-level feature provides only limited information for human perception, for example, the DCT coefficients could not be understood well by humans, even though these features play an important role in pattern recognition. Therefore, semantic understanding for videos can be improved by extracting semantic-level features like gestures, expression, actions, and so on. For instance, the posture of the lecturer will generally change with the delivered lecture content or the situation in lecture presentation. For example, when teaching the math problems, the lecturer may first write the lecture content on the blackboard and shows their back to the students. Next, he starts to narrate the written equations and moves sideways to avoid occluding the content which students should focus their gazes on. After writing the complete lecture content, the lecturer will face the students to further explain the details. All of the lecturing states and postures mentioned earlier will repeatedly occur with alternative random order in a course presentation. Different

Figure 19.5 Teacher skeleton extraction.

states represent different presentation states and also different semantics. Therefore, the lecturing states can be decided according to the changes of the lecturer's posture. In [Lin10a], the skeleton of the lecturer is extracted to represent the posture and then the lecturing states are identified by using the SVM approach. The regions of the head and hands are detected by using the skin-color features [Garc99]. The lecturer's skeleton is then constructed by considering the relations between the positions of head and hands.

After constructing skeletons, several features derived from the skeleton are used for posture discrimination to estimate the lecturing state, including the distance between end points of the skeleton, the joint angle of the skeleton, and the orientation of the joint angle. Besides, some features of skin-color region are also selected for discrimination, including the number of detected skin-color regions, the aspect ratio of the bounding box for the detected skin-color regions, and the distances between detected skin-color regions. Figure 19.5 shows the three types of skeleton, which represent the teaching states in the class: the writing state, the narration state, and the speaking state. Then a binary decision tree is utilized to classify the lecturing state of the lecturer, as shown in Figure 19.6. At first the writing state is discriminated from other states based on a heuristic criterion:

The shortest distance between two arms is approximately the width of a human body and, at the same time, the face region is not detected.

Then features mentioned earlier are used to train a SVM classifier, so that the other defined lecturing states can be identified. Note that SVM is not applied in the first step. Since the writing state has very different characteristics than other two states, it can be differentiated from other states using the simplified heuristic criterion to decrease the computational complexity.

19.2.2 Aural Analysis

Aural information in multimedia contents is also an important stimulus to attract viewers and should be utilized to affect the inserted virtual content. Compared with visual saliency analysis, researches on aural saliency analysis are rare. In [Ma05], an aural attention modeling method, taking aural signal, as well as speech and music into account, was proposed to incorporate with the visual attention models for benefiting video summarization. Intuitively, a sound with loud volume or sudden

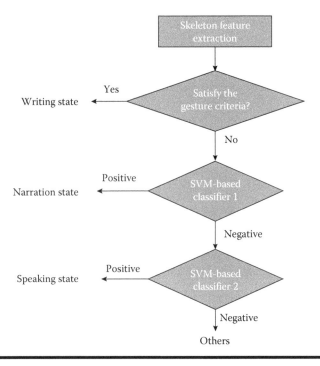

Figure 19.6 **The decision tree for discriminating the lecturer's posture.**

change usually grabs human's attention no matter what they are looking at. If the volume of sound keeps low, even if a special sound effect or music is played, the aural stimulus will easily be ignored or be treated as the environmental noise. In other words, loudness of aural information is a primary and critical factor to influence human perception and can be used to model aural saliency. Similar to the ideas stated in [Ma05], the sound is considered as a salient stimulus in terms of aural signal if the following situation occurs: loudness of sound at a specific time unit averages higher than the ones within a historical period which human continued listening so far, especially with peaks.

Based on the observations and assumptions, the aural saliency response, $AR(T_h, T)$, is defined at a time unit T and within a duration T_h, to quantify the salient strength of the sound. That is,

$$AR(T_h, T) = \frac{E_{\mathrm{avr}}(T)}{\hat{E}_{\mathrm{avr}}(T_h)} \cdot \frac{E_{\mathrm{peak}}(T)}{\hat{E}_{\mathrm{peak}}(T_h)}, \qquad (19.2)$$

where $E_{\mathrm{avr}}(T)$ and $E_{\mathrm{peak}}(T)$ are the *average sound energy* and the *sound energy peak* in the period T, respectively. In addition, $\hat{E}_{\mathrm{avr}}(T_h)$ and $\hat{E}_{\mathrm{peak}}(T_h)$ are the *maximum average sound energy* and the *maximum sound energy peak* within duration T_h, respectively.

In order to suppress the noises from low frequencies, the sound energy is defined as the weighted sum over the power spectrum of an audio signal at a given time as follows:

$$E \triangleq \int_{0}^{f_s} W(f) \times 10 \log(|\mathrm{SF}(f)|^2 + \varsigma) df, \qquad (19.3)$$

where

$\mathrm{SF}(f)$ is the *short-time Fourier transform* of the frequency component f and f_s denote the sampling frequency

Figure 19.7 shows the weighted sound energy for an input audio. In addition, $W(f)$ is the corresponding weighting function defined as follows:

$$W(f) = \frac{1}{1 + e^{-f_1(f - f_2)}}, \qquad (19.4)$$

where f_1 and f_2 are parameters for adjusting inflection points. Generally, $f_1 = 3.2$ (kHz) and $f_2 = 6.4$ (kHz).

After analyzing the aural saliency of the video, an *AS feature sequence* (see Figure 19.8) is generated which describes the aural saliency response with the range [0, 1] at each time unit T.

In [Lin10a], besides gesture and posture, making sounds or changing tones is another way that lecturers usually use to grab students' attentions while narrating the lecture content. Therefore, aural information of lecturers is an important cue to estimate the saliency for lecture videos. Since more words are spoken by lecturers within a period may imply more semantics are conveyed or delivered in such duration, the aural attention can be modeled based on the lecturer's speech speed. Generally, each Chinese character corresponds to at least one syllable, so we can analyze the syllables by extracting the envelope [Iked05] of audio samples to estimate the lecturer's speech speed (see Figure 19.9) as 19.5:

$$W_{\mathrm{syllable}}(t) = \begin{cases} 1, & \text{if } e(t) > C_w \mathrm{Max}\{e(T)\} \\ 0, & \text{otherwise} \end{cases}, \qquad (19.5)$$

where

$W_{\mathrm{syllable}}(t)$ represents whether it is a syllable ending at time t
$e(t)$ is the envelope size at time t
T is a time period
C_w is a threshold

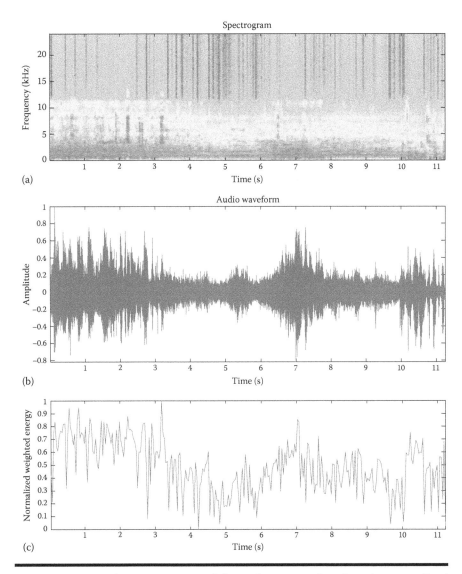

Figure 19.7 (a) **The spectrogram of (b) an input sound and (c) its normalized weighted energy.**

19.2.3 ROI Estimation

The virtual content should be inserted at suitable spatial and temporal location, which is often an area attractive to humans, that is, the ROI region. While considering the human perception and viewing experience, a compelling multimedia content is usually created by artfully manipulating the salience of visual and aural stimulus.

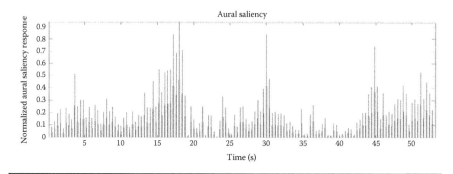

Figure 19.8   The normalized aural saliency response of the audio segment given in Figure 19.7.

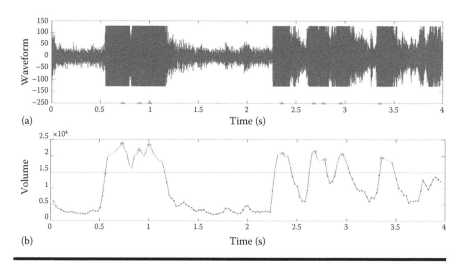

Figure 19.9   Sample results that show (a) the waveform of input audio samples and (b) the waveform smoothed by moving averaging.

Therefore, attractive regions or objects are usually utilized to direct and grab viewers' attention and play an important role in multimedia contents. Algorithms of both spatial and temporal ROI estimation will be discussed in this section.

19.2.3.1 Region Segmentation

In order to discriminate the regions in the video frame, segmentation techniques are applied to segment the video frames into partitions. There have been several segmentation algorithms and schemes proposed in the literature [Chen05,Meza04,Bore08,Kokk09,Wang08b]. In the implementation, an unsupervised image segmentation algorithm was adopted, which is called JSEG [Deng01], to segment each motion-vector-embedded video frame into several disjoint color-texture regions. Note that the motion vectors that are illustrated on the video frame can be considered as some kind of texture information for image segmentation. Therefore, in addition to color and texture, the motion vectors are also cleverly used to segment a video frame into disjoint regions. In this way, the segmentation map for each video frame can be constructed. The segmentation map of the nth frame is denoted by S^n and is defined as

$$S^n = \bigcup_j s_j^n, \quad \text{where } s_j^n \cap s_{j'}^n = \phi \text{ if } j \neq j' \tag{19.6}$$

where s_j^n represents the jth disjoint color-texture region in the nth frame. Each segmentation region is considered as an independent background with different influence to the virtual content and the region boundary would restrict or affect the movement of virtual contents according to the user-defined behavior modeling.

19.2.3.2 Spatial ROI Estimation

In order to automatically identify the attractive information in visual contents, a great deal of research efforts on estimating and modeling the visual attention in human perception have proliferated for years. The systematic investigations about the relationships between the vision perceived by humans and attentions are provided in many existing researches [Chun01,Itti01,Chen03,Ma05,Liu07,Zhan09]. Instead of directly computing a bounding contour for attractive regions or objects, most existing approaches construct a saliency map to represent the attention strength or attractiveness of each pixel or image block in visual contents. The value of a saliency map is normalized to [0, 255] and the brighter pixel means higher salience. Several fusion methods for integrating each of the developed visual feature models have been developed and discussed in [Dymi00]. Different fusion methods are designed for different visual attention models and applications. The goal of this module is to be able to provide a flexible mechanism to detect various ROIs as the targets, which the inserted virtual content can interact with, according to the users' requirements. For this purpose, we utilize linear combinations for fusion, so that users can flexibly set each weight of corresponding feature salience maps.

The ROI saliency map, which is denoted as S_{ROI}, is computed as

$$S_{\text{ROI}} = \sum_{i=1}^{n} w_i \times F_i, \tag{19.7}$$

where

F_i is the ith feature map of that frame

w_i is the ith weight of the corresponding ith feature map F_i with the constraints of $w_i \geq 0$, and $\sum_{i=1}^{n} w_i = 1$

The ROI can be easily derived by evaluating the center of gravity and the ranging variance [Bow02] on the basis of the saliency map.

In our implementation, four types of video-oriented visual features, selected from low level to high level, including contrast-based intensity, contrast-based color [Itti98], motion [Ho03], and human skin color [Garc99] are adopted to construct corresponding feature maps independently. Therefore, using different weights to linearly combine the constructed feature maps can produce various saliency maps with different meanings. We construct two types of ROI saliency maps, that is, HROI and LROI, which are defined by emphasizing the human skin color and the contrast-based color, respectively, to distinguish the attractive salient regions perceived by the virtual content in different phases.

A human visual system has been introduced for finding ROIs in many researches. In [Lee06] and [Kank98], an HVS was used to improve the quality of a watermarked image. In [Geis98], an HVS was used to skip bits without influencing the visual perceptibility of video encoding applications. It can also be applied to build the user-attentive model proposed in [Cox97] for selecting the ROI. In [Lin10b], the user-attentive model is constructed based on the gray level and texture features of the image. Regions with mid-gray levels will have a high score for selection because regions with very high or low gray levels are less noticeable to human beings. In addition, the strongly textured segments will have low scores. The distances to the image center are also considered because human beings often focus on the area near the center of an image. Therefore, the user-attentive levels of areas can be evaluated using the values of C_R, L_R, and T_R, which estimate the closeness to the center points, the moderate of gray levels, and the roughness of region R, respectively. The following steps are followed when selecting the embedding region:

1. Define the region size ε and the checking interval s.
2. For each checking area R with ε and s, compute

$$E = \alpha C_R + \beta L_R + \gamma T_R \tag{19.8}$$

where

$$C_R = 1 - \frac{\sum_{(x,y) \in R} \sqrt{((x-x_c)/w)^2 + ((y-y_c)/h)^2}}{|R|}$$

$$L_R = 1 - \frac{\sum\limits_{(i,j)\in R}\left[\left(128 - I_{i,j}/128\right)^2\right]^m}{|R|}$$

$$T_R = \sum\limits_{(k,l)\in R}\left(\frac{(C_{k,l})^2 - (C_{0,0})^2}{(C_{0,0})^2}\right)$$

in which $I_{i,j}$ is the gray level of the pixel (i,j), $C_{k,l}$ is the DCT coefficient of the positions (k, l) after applying the DCT to the region block R, m is an empirically determined constant that adjusts the degree of the gray level's influence (a large m increases the distance among values of the base number), and $|R|$ denotes the number of pixels in the region R. α, β, and γ are also empirically decided constants and result in different weights for C_R, L_R, and T_R.

3. Select the area R_a with the largest value E as the embedding region; this region is the most attractive area (the ROI).

19.2.3.3 Temporal ROI Estimation

The temporal ROI is the video clip that is attractive to humans. As mentioned in Section 19.2.1.1, the curve derived from extracting the chalk text and figures captures the variance of importance of the lecture content. From this curve, the temporal ROI can be estimated based on the obtained attention value. In fact, besides lecture-content-based attention curve, [Lin10a] constructs the learner attention model by integrating the attention model derived from lecture content, lecturer's posture, and speech speed.

As shown in Figure 19.10, the final attention curve is obtained by fusing three types of attention curves (the posture-based attention curve, the voice-based attention curve, and the content-based attention curve). The video frames corresponding to the peeks of the curve then represent the temporal ROIs for this application, in which the virtual content is then embedded. Figure 19.11 shows the produced attention curve of the proposed system, compared with the curves drawn by the teacher and students.

19.3 Virtual Content Analysis and Media Representation

Based on the results of the multimedia content analysis, the virtual content can be created and then inserted into TV programs properly for different applications. In this section, we will address two important issues of virtual content insertion: how the virtual content is characterized by analyzing visual features, and how to decide the insertion policy.

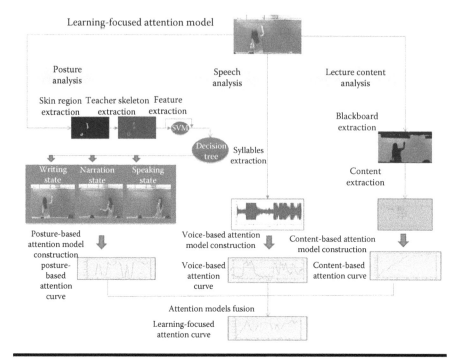

Figure 19.10 The system framework of learner-focused attention model construction. (From Lin, Y.-T. et al., Learning-focused structuring for blackboard lecture videos, in *Proceedings of the Fourth IEEE International Conference on Semantic Computing (ICSC'10)*, Carnegie Mellon University, Pittsburgh, PA, September 22–24, 2010.)

19.3.1 Virtual Content Analysis

The virtual content should be analyzed to extract its visual (e.g., color, shape) feature at first, and then the suitable behavior will be shaped up for being embedded into the TV program.

19.3.1.1 Characterization

Characterization aims at understanding the features of the virtual content. The visual features are analyzed to decompose the virtual content into a number of visual patterns, and generate descriptors for creating an informative or attractive representation for animated virtual content in terms of appearance. Although some existing researches have been involved in the seeking of characteristic representations for images [Han09] and videos [Dore09,Lia09] by using hierarchical approaches on

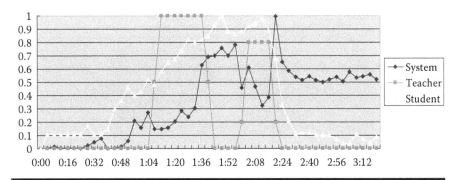

Figure 19.11 **The learner attention curves produced by the proposed system of [20] and the curves drawn by the teacher and students. These three curves have the same trend approximately, which implies that the proposed system can catch the major variation of the teaching focus in accordance with teacher's and students' opinions. However, the system can detect more detailed visual or aural events and reflect that on the curve.**

the basis of segmentation techniques, it is still an open issue and an application-dependent problem. For example, for advertising application, more controversial issues should be considered by advertisers and companies. In addition, advertisement providers may try to design their own representations for their advertisements with uniqueness and attractiveness. The color-texture segmentation algorithm JSEG [Deng01], which is mentioned in Section 19.2.3, can segment the virtual content image into several disjoint color-texture regions. From the perspective of biology, each region can be thought of as a *cell* of the virtual content. The segmentation map H for the virtual content is defined as

$$H = \bigcup_{i=1}^{N} h_i, \quad \text{where } h_i \cap h_{i'} = \phi \text{ if } i \neq i' \tag{19.9}$$

where
   h_i is the ith disjoint region in the segmentation map
   N is the total number of regions

Figure 19.12 shows an example of the virtual content segmentation and the associated segmentation map.

After segmenting the virtual content into several regions, a suitable order is computed for each region in the obtained segmentation map. The order is used to present the cells of the virtual content in sequence to simulate the cell proliferation process and provide less-intrusive insertions at the same time. The scheme proposed to determine the presentation order of cells is summarized in Algorithm 19.3.1.1 [Chan09].

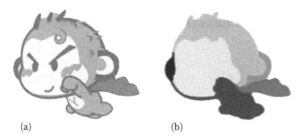

(a)   (b)

Figure 19.12   Sample results of the segmentations. (a) Virtual content (VC) and (b) VC segmentation map.

Algorithm 19.1 $(\tilde{H}) = \text{ReOrder}(H)$
Given the set of segmentations $H = \{h_1,\ h_2,\ \ldots,\ h_N\}$, construct the ordered set of segmentations $\tilde{H}$

1. Calculate the area of each element in H
2. Sort all elements in H from small area to large area
3. Construct the ordered set $A = \{A_1, A_2,\ \ldots,\ A_N\}$, where $A_1 \le A_2 \le \ldots \le A_N$
4. Construct the adjacent matrix of A
5. Initially, take out the segmented region with the smallest area A_1 as the first element of $\tilde{H}$. That is, $\tilde{H}(1) = A_1$
6. Repeat
7. Select the element with the smallest area from the neighborhood of $\tilde{H}(i-1)$
8. Add the selected element to $\tilde{H}$
9. Until all elements in A are added to $\tilde{H}$
10. Return $\tilde{H}$

With the determined order, the shape of the virtual content can be evolved by controlling the opacity of each region to simulate an effect of growing up, as shown in Figure 19.13.

Figure 19.13   An example for showing the effect of growing up.

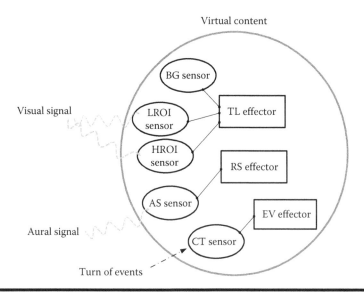

Figure 19.14 The architecture of behavior modeling.

19.3.1.2 Behavior Modeling

Based on the obtained characteristics, the virtual content is then assigned behavior interactively to the TV program content in the behavior modeling module. In [Chan09], various *sensors* and *effectors* are constructed and can be assigned to virtual contents for simulating a living thing, as shown in Figure 19.14. An effector is designed to generate a series of actions to react to the signals or data that are received or accessed by a sensor. By gradually establishing links between sensors and effectors, virtual contents will be able to trigger the visual evolving process and artificial phase evolutions, and then interact with contents in TV programs. To separately capture the data belonging to different feature maps that are mentioned in Section 19.2.3, four types of sensors are constructed, that is, *BG sensor*, *LROI sensor*, *HROI sensor*, and *AS sensor*. Specifically, BG sensor can access the extracted motion data and discriminated regions of each video frame from the BG feature map. LROI and HROI sensors can, respectively, detect the positions of low-level ROI and high-level ROI in the video and obtain the values in the ROI saliency map. AS sensor can get the aural saliency response at each time unit in the AS feature sequence. On the other hand, there are two effectors constructed to react to the sensor data and synthesize rich behaviors, that is, *TL effector* that generates movements by using translation operation and *RS effector* that generates motions by using rotation or scaling operations. Furthermore, *CT sensor* is constructed to detect the predefined turn of events for triggering evolutions and *EV effector* to control the colors and opacities of cells to animate virtual advertisements in terms of shape, color, and texture.

Laws in physics and mechanism are also considered to make synthesized behaviors physically plausible. For instance, the generated movements of virtual content should obey *Newton's law*. There are three types of forces defined in the behavior modeling system:

1. *The external force* of the region R, where the virtual content is emplaced, is defined as the resultant force exerted on the region R by the surrounding regions B, and denoted by $\mathbf{F_e}(B, R)$. The surrounding regions is given by $B = \{s_j \in S | s_j \cup R\}$.
2. *The internal force* of the region Q is defined as the resultant force contributed in the region Q, and denoted by $\mathbf{F_o}(Q)$.
3. *The spontaneous force* is defined as the inherent force of the virtual content for moving actively, and denoted by $\mathbf{F_s}$. Note that the direction of the spontaneous force is determined by the position of ROI which the virtual content intends to touch.

Accordingly, *TL effector* is in charge of estimating the resultant force of the virtual content $\mathbf{F_{va}}$ and calculates the displacement for translation in a range of activity based on *Newton's second law* and the *law of reflection* while colliding with boundaries. [Chan09] proposed a three-phase construction methodology for virtual content evolution, which will be described as the following.

19.3.1.2.1 Cell Phase

Initially, only BG sensor is activated to simulate the sense of touch and thereby the received surrounding force is the only factor that affects movements of the virtual content. With the sensor data, TL effector continues updating the resultant force of the virtual content $\mathbf{F_{va}}$ to $\mathbf{F_e}$ in each video frame. The scopes, which the virtual content can freely move around, are restricted to its initial insertion regions. Therefore, the virtual content will be inserted and restricted in a specific region, which can be determined by insertion point detection techniques or user intervention, regardless of how the virtual content moves.

The event for triggering the shape-evolving process of the virtual content is denoted as ToE_{v1} and defined as that the change of direction of $\mathbf{F_{va}}$ is larger than a threshold $\mathrm{TH}_\theta^{\mathrm{BG}}$ (in degrees). Once the event is detected by CT sensor, EV effector will immediately control the opacity of cells to present one of them according to the ordered advertisement segmentation map; otherwise, all cells will be presented piece by piece within a user-defined duration D_{shape} (in seconds). By setting the parameters $\mathrm{TH}_\theta^{\mathrm{BG}}$ and D_{shape}, users can create their own shape-evolving tempos for inserting the virtual content.

In order to reduce the visual intrusiveness in terms of colors, EV effector will manipulate color of cells before presenting them. First, the virtual content is

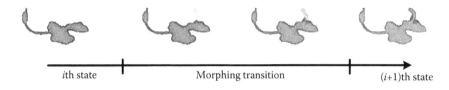

ith state | Morphing transition | $(i+1)$th state

Figure 19.15 **An example for showing the morphing transition between two consecutive states. The source (i.e., the leftmost one) and the destination (i.e., the rightmost one) are warped and cross-dissolved throughout the metamorphosis. Note that the contour of the objects is darkened.**

harmonized with its background, that is, the target video frame for insertion, by using the color harmonization method [Chan08]. Then, the harmonized color of each presented cell is simplified to a single color by averaging. Finally, the contour of each presented cell is darkened to enhance the shape information of the virtual content. Moreover, the technique of morphing [Wolb98,Beie92,Rupr95] is utilized to generate realistic transitions between two consecutive states in presenting cells, to further improve the viewing experience of shape evolving, as illustrated in Figure 19.15.

To trigger the phase evolution for the virtual content to leave the cell phase, the event is denoted as ToE_{p1} and is configured as that all the cells are presented.

19.3.1.2.2 Microbe Phase

In the microbe phase, LROI sensor is activated to simulate the preliminary sense of sight and a low-level ROI can be detected. TL effector will update the resultant force of the virtual content as follows to let the virtual content be attracted by the low-level ROI and move toward it:

$$\begin{cases} \mathbf{F_{va}} = \mathbf{F_e}(\overline{Q_L}, R) + \mathbf{F_s} \\ \angle(\mathbf{F_s}) = \tan^{-1} \dfrac{\|y_{Q_L} - y_R\|}{\|x_{Q_L} - x_R\|} \end{cases} \qquad (19.10)$$

where

(x_R, y_R) and (x_{Q_L}, y_{Q_L}), respectively, denote the centers of R

Q_L and $\overline{Q_L}$ represents the non-LROI region

Note that the resultant force of the virtual content $\mathbf{F_{va}}$ will not be updated until a low-level ROI is detected by the LROI sensor. The virtual content is restricted to move in the $\overline{Q_L}$ region to avoid occluding the low-level ROI, which may include salient visual information.

The visual evolving of the virtual content in this phase is designed based on color-texture features, which gradually replaces the simplified appearance of cells by

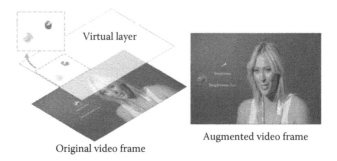

Original video frame

Augmented video frame

Figure 19.16 An example for showing the way to produce the effect of absorbability.

their original color-texture information. The event for triggering the color-texture-evolving process is denoted as ToE_{v2} and is defined as that a collision between the virtual content and the low-level ROI occurs. Each time the virtual content touches the boundary of the low-level ROI, one of cells will be replaced by its original color-texture features with a fading-in effect and its opacity will be modulated by a Gaussian function.

Besides considering the visual and aural signals of the TV programs, an additional functionality for the EV effector is developed to provide dramatic and impressive interactions between the virtual content and salient contents in TV programs. Specifically, EV effector can be configured to produce textures for the low-level ROI except the virtual content. As a result, the low-level ROI will look like being removed in the scene if we overlays such produced textures on it. We also applied inpainting techniques [Crim03,Patw07] to fill holes while removing target regions so that the EV effector can synthesize textures used for covering the low-level ROI. The sample result is illustrated in Figure 19.16.

19.3.1.2.3 Creature Phase

In the creature phase, the virtual content will be more like a creature, which has the ability to act with the perceived aural stimuli and interacts with the high-level ROI of the TV program. Both AS and HROI sensors are activated to simulate the sense of hearing and develop a more penetrative sight. For AS sensor data, two thresholds (TH_L^{AS} and TH_H^{AS}) were defined for RS effector to trigger the rotation or the scaling animation for the virtual content. If AS sensor value is larger than TH_L^{AS} but smaller than TH_H^{AS}, RS effector will rotate the virtual content with the parameter ϖ_r (in degrees) to generate the jiggling effect. On the other hand, if AS sensor data is larger than TH_H^{AS}, RS effector will resize the virtual content by a user-defined scaling factor ϖ_s to simulate the effect of astonished expression. Note that RS effector can replace the automatically generated rotation and scaling animations by the user-provided animations for the virtual contents.

For HROI sensor data, the virtual content is simulated to begin to interact with high-level ROI and TL effector updates the resultant force of the virtual content as follows:

$$
\begin{cases}
\mathbf{F_{va}} = \mathbf{F_e}(\overline{Q_H}, R) + \mathbf{F_s} \\
\angle(\mathbf{F_s}) = \tan^{-1} \dfrac{\|y_{Q_H} - y_R\|}{\|x_{Q_H} - x_R\|}, & \text{if } \mathbf{F_o}(Q_H) > \text{TH}^{\text{HROI}} \\
\mathbf{F_{va}} = \mathbf{F_e}(\overline{Q_H}, R) + \mathbf{F_o}(Q_H), & \text{otherwise}
\end{cases}
\tag{19.11}
$$

where
$\overline{Q_H}$ is the non-HROI region
TH^{HROI} is a threshold
(x_{Q_H}, y_{Q_H}) is the center of HROI region Q_H

The virtual content is restricted to movie within the $\overline{Q_H}$ region to avoid occluding the high-level ROI. Note that the threshold TH^{HROI} is used for TL effector to produce different reactions. Specifically, if the internal force of HROI region is smaller than the threshold TH^{HROI}, the virtual content tends to imitate the behavior of the high-level ROI. On the other hand, if the high-level ROI has larger internal force, the virtual content will move to touch it.

19.3.2 Media Representation

After creating the virtual content, the system automatically generates impressive animations with evolutions on the *virtual layer* according to the aural and visual features extracted from videos and the configured behaviors for the virtual contents. Then, the virtual layer and the input video are integrated to produce the augmented video.

19.3.2.1 Animation Generation

After determining the insertion position of the virtual content for a TV program, the animation generation module acts on the effectors and sensors of the inserted virtual content. The effectors begin to react to the features perceived by the sensors and automatically animate the inserted virtual content for each video frame, according to the configured behavior modeling. The received motion vectors are mapped to the forces, as described in Section 19.3.1, to quantify the influence induced from the videos. Specifically, the external force is computed as the weighted vector sum of motion vectors in the surrounding region of the nth video frame, that is,

$$\mathbf{F}(R^n, R^n) = \sum_{(x,y) \in B^n} G(x, y, x_{R^n}, y_{R^n}) \cdot \widehat{\mathbf{MV}}^n(x, y) \cdot I_{R^n}(x, y)$$

where

$$G(x, y, x_{R^n}, y_{R^n}) = e^{\left(-\dfrac{(x - x_{R^n})^2 + (y - y_{R^n})^2}{2\sigma^2} \right)} \tag{19.12}$$

$$I_{R^n}(x, y) = \begin{cases} 0, & (x, y) \in R^n \\ 1, & \text{otherwise} \end{cases}$$

Note that (x_{R^n}, y_{R^n}) in Equation 19.12 is the central macroblock in the region R of the nth video frame, and I_{R^n} is used to indicate whether the macroblock is in the region R of the nth video frame. In addition, $\widehat{\mathbf{MV}}^n(x, y)$ denotes that its direction is opposite to $\mathbf{MV}^n(x, y)$. Similarly, the internal force is computed as

$$\mathbf{F_o}(Q^n) = \sum_{(x,y) \in Q^n} G(x, y, x_{Q^n}, y_{Q^n}) \cdot \widehat{\mathbf{MV}}^n(x, y) \tag{19.13}$$

Accordingly, the displacement of the virtual content in the $(n + d)$th frame $\mathbf{P}^n(d)$ can be calculated by

$$\mathbf{V}^n(d) = \mathbf{V}^n + \frac{\mathbf{F}^n_{\mathbf{va}}}{M^n_{\mathbf{va}}} \cdot d \tag{19.14}$$

$$\mathbf{P}^n(d) = \mathbf{V}^n(d) + \frac{\mathbf{F}^n_{\mathbf{va}}}{2 \cdot M^n_{\mathbf{va}}} \cdot d^2 \tag{19.15}$$

where
   $\mathbf{V}^n(d)$ is the simulated velocity of the virtual content in the $(n + d)$th frame
   $\mathbf{F}^n_{\mathbf{va}}$ and $M^n_{\mathbf{va}}$ represent the resultant force and the mass of virtual content in the nth frame, respectively
   d is the duration of the nth frame

Note that all the animations of virtual content are constructed on the virtual layer and are associated with corresponding video frames by the animation generation module. Thus, the original video can be protected from modifications to avoid annoying the users and provide possibilities to increase commercial value of TV programs by enriching the viewing experience.

19.3.2.2 Layer Composition

The final task of the media representation stage is to produce the augmented video by integrating the virtual layers with the input video. To provide flexible usages of the augmented video in satisfying different scenario demands, we can overlay the virtual layers onto corresponding video frames to produce the output video with overlays or a single augmented video. The augmented videos with overlaid virtual layers can be implemented by using the techniques of Flash; as a result, the inserted virtual contents can be hidden if viewers want to see the original video. Furthermore, users can easily choose different virtual contents with different behaviors to overlay on the same source video for targeting the online audiences based on their demographic information [Hu07] or cultures.

19.4 Prototype of Interactive Virtual Content Insertion and Its Possible Applications

We propose a prototype of interactive virtual content insertion for developing the appearance evolving mechanism of the virtual content. As shown in Figure 19.17, the TV program is at first processed by visual and aural analysis. On the other hand, the virtual content is characterized and assigned with suitable behavior. Finally, the system automatically generates impressive animations with evolutions on a virtual layer according to the video features and the virtual content behaviors, and the virtual layer is overlaid onto the TV program to produce an augmented TV program with separated layers.

In this section, two example applications are then provided to illustrate the design flow and show the feasibility of the proposed prototype. The first example is virtual interactive advertising [Chan09] for commercial applications, and another is the virtual learning e-partner for education [Chan10b].

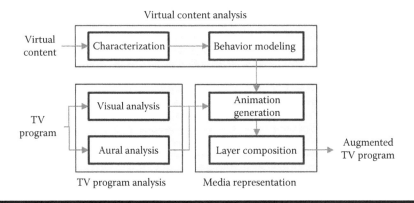

Figure 19.17 The prototype of interactive virtual content insertion. (From Chang, C.-H. et al., Evolving virtual contents with interactions in videos, in *Proceedings of the ACM International Workshop on Interactive Multimedia for Consumer Electronics (IMCE)*, Beijing, China, pp. 97–104, 2009.)

19.4.1 Virtual Interactive Advertising

In the TV program analysis stage, both the visual and aural analyses are applied to the input TV program. As for the visual analysis, to each frame of the input TV program the frame profiling is applied to estimate the motion information and discriminate the regions according to visual features. On the other hand, the ROI estimation module localizes the region-of-interest in each video frame as described earlier. In addition to the visual analysis, aural saliency analysis is performed to characterize the sound that accompanies the TV program. Finally, by combining the result of each module in the TV program analysis stage, a multimodal feature space for each frame of the input TV program is automatically constructed.

In the virtual content analysis stage, the characterization module is used to analyze the appearance of the virtual content for visually evolving in terms of shapes, colors, and textures. With the information of characterization, various sensors and effectors are assigned to the virtual content for generating progressive behaviors with evolutions in the behavior modeling module.

Then, in the virtual content insertion stage, the animation generation module acts on the effectors and sensors of the inserted virtual content. Therefore, according to the features perceived by the sensors of the virtual content, the effectors automatically generate the corresponding reactions. In the layer composition module, the virtual layer, in which the virtual content is animated on, is integrated with the video layer. Eventually, the augmented TV program with virtual content overlay is produced. Figure 19.18 shows the additionally inserted image (i.e., Nike logo) animates to virtually interact with the contents in the broadcast tennis program.

19.4.2 Virtual Learning e-Partner

The framework of virtual learning e-partner scheme is shown in Figure 19.19. In the e-partner behavior modeling module, any given image can be selected as the e-partner and be assigned life-like behaviors through the evolution process. In the cell phase, the e-partner is made like a single-celled organism. The e-partner would perceive the force from the environment (the lecture content, the lecturer's posture, and the lecturer's speech speed) and evolve. The technique of morphing is used to generate realistic transitions during the evolution. In the microbe phase, the e-partner is assigned the ability to seek for the salient objects, which is detected by finding the ROIs based on the algorithms described in Section 19.2. The original colors of cell would be presented with the fading-in effect and the opacity would be modulated by a Gaussian function. At the same time, the e-partner is simulated to obtain the color and texture by absorbing the energy of the salient object, just like the microbe organism. In the creature phase, the e-partner is simulated to own the ability to dance with the music or show the astonished expression while perceiving loud sound. Besides, the e-partner would interact with the moving salient object in an intelligent manner. The e-partner would either tend to imitate the behavior

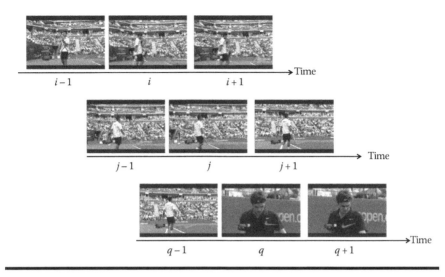

Figure 19.18   Snapshots of sample results showing the additionally inserted image (i.e., Nike logo) animates to virtually interact with the contents in the broadcast tennis program.

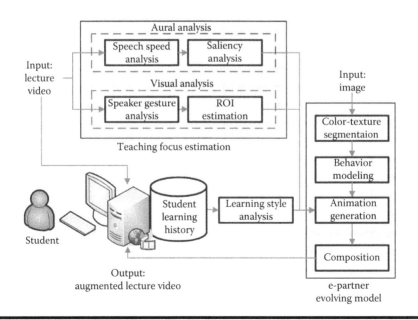

Figure 19.19   The framework for virtual learning e-partner.

Evolving process

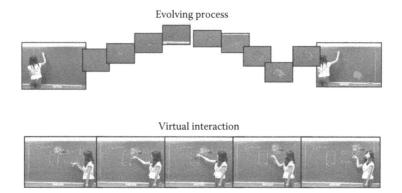

Virtual interaction

Figure 19.20 Snapshots of sample results of the virtual learning e-partner. In the beginning, the e-partner will evolve its appearance according to some predefined events. For example, the e-partner gradually changes its shape to simulate the growing effect. If the student's feedback is positive, the e-partner will reveal more colors and textures. Finally, the e-partner will interact with the teacher in an intelligent manner. For example, the e-partner moves to the teacher and the pointed lecture content and produces special behavior according to the sound of the teacher.

of the moving salient object or move to the salient object for further interactions. With the extracted feature space of the lecture videos and the behavior modeling of the e-partner, the proposed system automatically generates impressive animations on a virtual layer. Finally, the virtual layer, in which the e-partner is animated on, is integrated with the video layer. Figure 19.20 shows sample results of the virtual learning e-partner, in which the e-partner can evolve according to the lecturer's teaching behavior in the lecture video and assist in pointing out or enhancing the important lecture content. It is apparent that watching the produced lecture video may be more attractive than seeing the lecture content in class.

19.5 Summary

In this chapter, we have stated the new possibilities that virtual content insertion can bring to digital TV services. With the developed virtual content insertion techniques, more interesting and useful TV services can be provided, and a win–win relationship can be built for the TV ecosystem that includes, but is not limited to, content producers, advertisers, publishers, and audiences. The viewing experiences can be enriched by carefully designing the appearance and behavior of the virtual content and inserting the virtual contents into the TV programs appropriately to add interaction, interest, and helpfulness of the programs, so that audiences can be attracted and the business opportunities increase accordingly. Note that, since objective evaluation of the viewing experience is very difficult, subjective experiments are generally taken to investigate the generic performance of virtual content insertion. However, the selection of data sets and performance metrics depends on the application scenarios and there are no standard methods to make a fair comparison currently. In [Mei10a], such issues were explicitly discussed.

We have also presented the technologies of virtual content insertion from the multimedia content analysis techniques, which are the basis of virtual content insertion. The multimedia content can be analyzed from the low-level visual/aural features at first and then be further understood by interpreting the low-level features semantically. After deriving the features of the program content, the virtual content should be characterized and assigned with applicable behaviors. The virtual content is then embedded into the TV programs as seamlessly as possible to interact with contents of videos according to different requirements of various applications, and it often acts as one of the objects/actors in the program, so that the audiences would notice the existence of the virtual content without feeling uncomfortable. Algorithms and feasible prototypes were also discussed to illustrate the design strategies. We then gave possible applications, including advertising and learning, to provide suggestions of implementation of virtual content insertion for TV programs. The concept of virtual content insertion will be more and more important for digital TV services to create high-quality programs for customers, so that they can not only enjoy the viewing experience, but also benefit a lot from the programs.

References

[Bow02]   S. T. Bow, *Pattern Recognition and Image Preprocessing*, Marcel Dekker, New York, 2002.

[Beau95] S. S. Beauchemin and J. L. Barron, The computation of optical flow, *ACM Computing Surveys*, 27, 433–467, 1995.

[Beie92] T. Beier and S. Neely, Feature-based image metamorphosis, *ACM SIGGRAPH Computer Graphics*, 26(2), 35–42, 1992.

[Bore08] E. Borenstein and S. Ullman, Combined top-down/bottom-up segmentation, *IEEE Transactions on Pattern Analysis and Machine Intelligence*, 30(12), 2109–2125, 2008.

[Chan08] C.-H. Chang, K.-Y. Hsieh, M.-C. Chung, and J.-L. Wu, ViSA: Virtual spotlighted advertising, in *Proceedings of the 16th ACM International Conference on Multimedia (MM)*, Vancouver, Canada, pp. 837–840, 2008.

[Chan09] C.-H. Chang, M.-C. Chiang, and J.-L. Wu, Evolving virtual contents with interactions in videos, in *Proceedings of the ACM International Workshop on Interactive Multimedia for Consumer Electronics (IMCE)*, Beijing, China, pp. 97–104, 2009.

[Chan10a] C.-H. Chang, K.-Y. Hsieh, M.-C. Chiang, and J.-L. Wu, Virtual spotlighted advertising for tennis videos, *Journal of Visual Communication and Image Representation (JVCIR)*, 21(7), 595–612, 2010.

[Chan10b] C. H. Chang, Y. T. Lin, and J.-L. Wu, Adaptive video learning by the inter-active e-partner, in *Proceedings of the Third IEEE International Conference on Digital Game and Intelligent Toy Enhanced Learning (DIGITEL'10)*, Kaohsiung, Taiwan, pp. 207–209, 2010.

[Chan10c] C.-H. Chang, A study of content analysis based virtual product placement, PhD dissertation, Department of Computer Science and Information Engineering, National Taiwan University, Taiwan, 2010.

[Chen03] L. Chen, X. Xie, X. Fan, W. Ma, H. Zhang, and H. Zhou, A visual attention model for adapting images on small displays, *Multimedia Systems*, 9(4), 353–364, 2003.

[Chen05] J. Chen, T. N. Pappas, A. Mojsilović, and B. E. Rogowitz, Adaptive perceptual color-texture image segmentation, *IEEE Transactions on Image Process*, 14(10), 1524–1536, 2005.

[Chen07] W.-H. Cheng, C.-W. Wang, and J.-L. Wu, Video adaptation for small display based on content recomposition, *IEEE Transactions on Circuits and Systems for Video Technology*, 17(1), 43–58, 2007.

[Chun01] M. M. Chun and J. M. Wolfe, Visual attention, in B. Goldstein (ed.) *Blackwell Handbook of Perception*, Wiley-Blackwell, Oxford, U.K., Chapter 9, pp. 272–310, 2001.

[Cox97] I. Cox, J. Kilian, F. Leighton, and T. Shamoon, Secure spectrum water-marking for multimedia, *IEEE Transactions on Image Processing*, 6(12), 1673–1687, 1997.

[Crim03] A. Criminisi, P. Perez, and K. Toyama, Object removal by exemplar-based inpainting, in *Proceedings of the IEEE Computer Society Conference on Computer Vision and Pattern Recognition*, Madison, WI, Vol. 2, pp. 721–728, 2003.

[Deng01] Y. Deng and B. S. Manjunath, Unsupervised segmentation of color-texture regions in images and video, *IEEE Transactions on Pattern Analysis and Machine Intelligence (T-PAMI)*, 23(8), 800–810, 2001.

[Dore09] C. C. Dorea, M. Pardas, and F. Marques, Trajectory tree as an object-oriented hierarchical representation for video, *IEEE Transactions on Circuits and Systems for Video Technology (T-CSVT)*, 19(4), 547–560, 2009.

[Dymi00] R. Dymitr and G. Bogdan, An overview of classifier fusion methods, *Computing and Information Systems*, 7(1), 1–10, 2000.

[Garc99] C. Garcia and G. Tziritas, Face detection using quantized skin color regions merging and wavelet packet analysis, *IEEE Transactions on Multimedia (T-MM)*, 1(3), 264–277, 1999.

[Geis98] W. S. Geisler and J. S. Perry, A real-time foveated multiresolution system for low-bandwidth video communication, *SPIE Proceedings: Human Vision and Electronic Imaging (VCIP'98)*, Vol. 3299, pp. 294–305, 1998.

[Han09] F. Han and S. Zhu, Bottom-up/top-down image parsing with attribute gram-mar, *IEEE Transactions on Pattern Analysis and Machine Intelligence (T-PAMI)*, 31(1), 59–73, 2009.

[Ho03] C.-C. Ho, W.-H. Cheng, T.-J. Pan, and J.-L. Wu, A user-attention based focus detection framework and its applications, in *Proceedings of the Fourth*

	IEEE Pacific-Rim Conference on Multimedia (PCM), Singapore, pp. 1341–1345, 2003.
[Hu07]	J. Hu, H. Zeng, H. Li, C. Niu, and Z. Chen, Demographic prediction based on user's browsing behavior, in *Proceedings of the 16th International Conference on World Wide Web (WWW)*, Banff, Alberta, Canada, pp. 151–160, 2007.
[Hua08]	X. Hua, T. Mei, and S. Li, When multimedia advertising meets the new Internet era, in *Proceedings of the 10th IEEE Workshop on Multimedia Signal Processing (MMSP)*, Cairns, Queensland, Australia, pp. 1–5, 2008.
[Iked05]	O. Ikeda, Estimation of speaking speed for faster face detection in video-footage, in *Proceedings of the IEEE International Conference on Multimedia and Expo (ICME)*, Amsterdam, the Netherlands, pp. 442–445, 2005.
[Itti01]	L. Itti and C. Koch, Computational modelling of visual attention, *Nature Reviews. Neuroscience*, 2(3), 194–203, 2001.
[Itti98]	L. Itti, C. Koch, and E. Niebur, A model of saliency-based visual attention for rapid scene analysis, *IEEE Transactions on Pattern Analysis and Machine Intelligence (T-PAMI)*, 20(11), 1254–1259, 1998.
[Kank98]	M. S. Kankanhalli and K. R. Ramakrishnan, Content based watermarking of images, *ACM Multimedia'98*, Bristol, U.K., pp. 61–70, 1998.
[Kokk09]	I. Kokkinos, G. Evangelopoulos, and P. Maragos, Texture analysis and segmentation using modulation features, generative models, and weighted curve evolution, *IEEE Transactions on Pattern Analysis and Machine Intelligence (T-PAMI)*, 31(1), 142–157, 2009.
[Lee06]	H. Y. Lee, H. Kim, and H.-K. Lee, Robust image watermarking using local invariant features, *Optical Engineering, SPIE 2006*, 45(3), 2006.
[Li07]	S. Li and B. Lu, Automatic camera calibration technique and its application in virtual advertisement insertion system, in *Proceedings of the Second IEEE Conference on Industrial Electronics and Applications (ICIEA)*, Harbin, China, pp. 288–292, 2007.
[Li08]	L. Li, T. Mei, X. Hua, and S. Li, ImageSense, in *Proceedings of the ACM International Conference on Multimedia (MM)*, Vancouver, British Columbia, Canada, pp. 1027–1028, 2008.
[Lia09]	T. Lia, T. Mei, S. Kweona, and X.-S. Hua, Multi-video synopsis for video representation, *Signal Processing*, 89(12), 2354–2366, 2009.
[Lin10a]	Y.-T. Lin, H.-Y. Tsai, C.-H. Chang, and G. C. Lee, Learning-focused structuring for blackboard lecture videos, in *Proceedings of the Fourth IEEE International Conference on Semantic Computing (ICSC'10)*, Carnegie Mellon University, Pittsburgh, PA, September 22–24, 2010.
[Lin10b]	Y.-T. Lin, C.-Y. Huang, and G. Lee, Rotation, scaling, and translation resilient watermarking for images, *IET Image Processing*, 5(4), 328–340, 2011.
[Liu07]	H. Liu, S. Jiang, Q. Huang, C. Xu, and W. Gao, Region-based visual attention analysis with its application in image browsing on small displays, in *Proceedings of the 15th International Conference on Multimedia (MULTIMEDIA)*, Augsburg, Germany, pp. 305–308, 2007.

[Liu08]   H. Liu, S. Jiang, Q. Huang, and C. Xu, Lower attentive region detection for virtual advertisement insertion, in *Proceedings of the IEEE International Conference on Multimedia and Expo (ICME)*, Hannover, Germany, pp. 1529–1532, 2008.

[Ma05]   Y. Ma, X. Hua, L. Lu, and H. Zhang, A generic framework of user attention model and its application in video summarization, *IEEE Transactions on Multimedia (T-MM)*, 7(5), 907–919, 2005.

[Mei08]   T. Mei, X. Hua, and S. Li, Contextual in-image advertising, in *Proceedings of the 16th ACM International Conference on Multimedia (MM)*, Vancouver, British Columbia, Canada, pp. 439–448, 2008.

[Mei09a]   T. Mei, X. Hua, and S. Li, VideoSense: A contextual in-video advertising system, *IEEE Transactions on Circuits and Systems for Video Technology (T-CSVT)*, 19(12), 1866–1879, 2009.

[Mei10a]   T. Mei and X. Hua, Contextual Internet multimedia advertising, in *Proceedings of the IEEE, Special Issue on Internet Vision (PIEEE)*, issue 99, pp. 1–18, 2010.

[Mei10b]   T. Mei, J. Guo, X. Hua, and F. Liu, AdOn: Toward contextual overlay in-video advertising, *ACM/Springer Multimedia Systems (MMSJ)*, 16(4–5), 335–344, 2010.

[Meza04]   V. Mezaris, I. Kompatsiaris, and M. G. Strintzis, Video object segmentation using Bayes-based temporal tracking and trajectory-based region merging, *IEEE Transactions on Circuits and Systems for Video Technology (T-CSVT)*, 14(6), 782–795, 2004.

[Mori91]   S. E. Moriarty, *Creative Advertising: Theory and Practice*, Prentice-Hall, Englewood Cliffs, NJ, 1991.

[Patw07]   K. A. Patwardhan, G. Sapiro, and M. Bertalmio, Video inpainting under constrained camera motion, *IEEE Transactions on Image Processing (T-IP)*, 16(2), 545–553, 2007.

[Rupr95]   D. Ruprecht and H. Muller, Image warping with scattered data interpolation, *IEEE Computer Graphics and Applications*, 15(2), 37–43, 1995.

[Shi94]   J. Shi and C. Tomasi, Good features to track, in *Proceedings of the IEEE Conference on Computer Vision and Pattern Recognition (CVPR)*, Seattle, WA, pp. 539–600, 1994.

[Wang08a]   J. Wang, Y. Fang, and H. Lu, Online video advertising based on user's attention relavancy computing, in *Proceedings of the IEEE International Conference on Multimedia and Expo (ICME)*, Hannover, Germany, pp. 1161–1164, 2008.

[Wang08b]   W. Wang, J. Yang, and W. Gao, Modeling background and segmenting moving objects from compressed video, *IEEE Transactions on Circuits and Systems for Video Technology*, 18(5), 670–681, 2008.

[Wolb98]   G. Wolberg, Image morphing: A survey, *The Visual Computer*, Vol. 14, pp. 360–372, 1998.

[Yu08]   X. Yu, N. Jiang, L. Cheong, H. Leong, and X. Yan, Automatic camera calibration of broadcast tennis video with applications to 3D virtual advertisement insertion and ball detection and tracking, in *Computer Vision and Image Understanding (CVIU)*, 113, 837–840, 2009.

[Zett99]   H. Zettl, *Sight, Sound, Motion: Applied Media Aesthetics*, Wadsworth, Belmont, CA, 1999.

[Zhan09]   H. Zhang, X. Tian, and Y. Chen, A distortion-weighing spatiotemporal visual attention model for video analysis, in *Proceedings of the International Congress on Image and Signal Processing*, Tianjin, China, pp. 1–4, 2009.

.

Chapter 20

Analysis of the TV Interactive Content Convergence and Cross-Platform Adaptation

Aitor Rodriguez-Alsina
Universitat Autònoma de Barcelona

Jordi Carrabina
Universitat Autònoma de Barcelona

Contents

20.1 Introduction

Interactive television represents the adaptation of this communication media to an environment in which viewers demand greater significance and new services that suit their preferences. These interactive services are implemented by means of interactive applications, which can be defined as those additional programs related to television content which are accessible and can run in an interactive TV decoder. The user decides whether or not to view the interactive applications through a simple action with the remote control device. In order to inform the user concerning how to access interactive applications, operators and television channels must provide a small menu that tells the user that they can see an application or a group of interactive applications. The number of different devices that can access TV services and the interactive content is growing rapidly due to the technological advances in consumer devices and communication networks. A clear example of this are smartphones, which can be considered as handheld computers with powerful processors, abundant memory, and larger screens than contemporary feature phones, that is, low-end mobile phones that have less computing ability than a smartphone, but more capability than the largely obsolete portable cellular telephones made from 1983 to 1999, known as "dumb phones." The new wave of devices also rely on and take advantage of the mobile broadband networks (i.e., third-generation mobile networks) that provide the required speed and support for Internet browsing, enabling a new generation of interactive services for mobile devices. Smartphones, however, are not the only newly available consumer devices capable of accessing iTV services. Based largely on the success of Apple's iPad, the market seems to be in a race to introduce new tablet personal computers (tablet PCs) equipped with a touch screen as a primary input device, wireless adapters for Internet browsing, and screens that are larger than that of smartphones. That said, the traditional home environment for watching TV is also evolving to meet the needs of the modern consumer with Internet access, the production of user-generated content, the participation in social networks, and the provision of on-demand content. The implementation of these features over the broadcast channels and their efficient combination with IP services is an ongoing challenge that is faced in the interactivity provided by the TV consumer platform, which is based on interactive applications. These new devices that integrate Internet into the traditional TV sets and set-top boxes (STBs), also known as connected TVs (e.g., Google TV), most often have a much higher focus on online interactive media, over-the-top content, and on-demand streaming media that in previous generations of TV sets and STBs were simply not available. This scenario of new platforms and converged networks suggests that interactive contents are becoming more and more important in the leisure activity that is watching TV and suggests the need for an analysis of interactive content as well as of its production in a platform-independent way.

Nowadays, the design of user interfaces for interactive TV is recognized as the main problem in terms of the design convergence for any device that can present TV contents [9]. In other words, it is not unusual for an interactive application provider to establish different development lines to provide the same interactive application for different devices and distribution networks. This represents an extra development effort that needs to be addressed by the industry in the form of standard formats for creating, transmitting, and presenting platform-independent interactive applications for TV. Typically, these application formats can be classified depending on the runtime environment into declarative or procedural application formats. Declarative application environments (DAEs) are based on a browser for the presentation of user interfaces written in a declarative language, which is typically based on XML and includes scripting support for interaction with network server-side applications and access to the APIs of the target client middleware. DAE applications are associated with a collection of documents written commonly in HTML, JavaScript, CSS, XHTML, and SVG. This is the most widespread solution for deploying interactive applications on IP-based networks like Internet and proprietary IPTV networks. On the other hand, procedural application environments (PAEs) are those that are able to locally execute an application written in a procedural programming language, which is any programming language in which the programmer specifies an explicit sequence of steps to follow in order to produce a result (i.e., an algorithm). Examples of procedural programming languages are C/C++, Java, Perl, and Python; however, Java is the core of the most widely used middleware programs that are key to the presentation of interactive applications on broadcast TV environments. These environments are typically PAE based, especially if the client platform does not have access to a two-way communication channel such as an IP network. The adoption of different standards and the deployment of middleware frameworks for iTV [6–8] depend to a large degree on geographical location; for example, the Multimedia Home Platform (MHP) [1] is an open middleware system used in some European countries as well as in Korea, Colombia, Uruguay, and Australia; MHEG-5 [2] is used in the UK, New Zealand, Hong Kong, and South Africa; the Open-Cable Application Platform (OCAP) [3] and the Advanced Common Application

Platform (ACAP) [4] are used in North America; and the Integrated Services Digital Broadcasting (ISDB-T) [5] are used in Japan and South America. This diversity implies not only a change in the instruction sets, but also different application environments based on declarative and procedural programming languages [10,11]. The translation from one specific iTV application format to another could be considered as a form of short-term solution; however, this approach is usually avoided due to the underlying data and programmatic model differences between the target formats [12]. This kind of direct mapping solution between interactive application formats can provide an explicit mapping from one format to another but reduces the flexibility of the system by having to implement a cloud of mapping functions to perform the translation from one format to another. In this case, the number of mapping functions increases exponentially with the number of formats. A different approach is to integrate all interactive application formats for TV into a new single format, which satisfies the requirements of all of the relevant platforms. This is an independent way to minimize the total number of mapping functions (particularly, in the case of three or more interactive content formats), which increases linearly with the number of formats. Figure 20.1 depicts the basic schemas for both mapping models.

Based on the integration model solution for a unified design of interactive applications for TV environments, the DVB consortium published the PCF content format [13] in 2006. It can be easily translated into any other interactive application format in a platform-specific conversion step that is also called "transcoding." PCF facilitates that conversion avoiding the implementation complexities of each separate platform and tries to represent the desired user experience of the interactive application. In other words, this content format tends to focus on defining user perception and responses that result from the use of an interactive application rather than defining the implementation issues in detail. This enables the production of platform-independent iTV applications that can be provided to any TV service provider in a standard way, facilitating the business-to-business (B2B) interchange by providing a common application format that can be easily adapted to any iTV

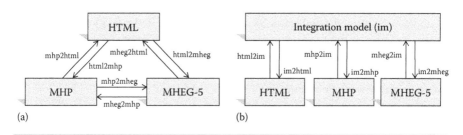

(a)

(b)

Figure 20.1 Mapping models for the format conversion. In (a), formats are directly translated across formats and, in (b), outlines of a single higher-level format that provides for better scalability and flexibility.

platform. The translation into the platform-specific format is generally done by the service provider, who knows the required configuration for the deployment; however, the PCF description of an iTV service can also be pre-translated by the application provider if the parameters required for the application deployment can be configured subsequently by the service provider. In the case of the conversion into a web-based format, which is addressed in this chapter, this can be achieved through the generation of Rich Internet Applications (RIA) [14] and a simple XML configuration file. On the other hand, the PCF standard recommends that the suitable scaling algorithms for each specific target platform must be implemented in the transcoding step. However, it does not define the mapping rules for the scenario where the resolution of the display differs from the reference screen or indeed when the interactivity model changes because of the different usability requirements for a specific device (e.g., the use of the remote control for a TV set, a mouse for a computer, and a touch screen for a mobile). These adaptations must also be taken into account in the transcoding step to be able to generate applications for any target device without modifying (or at least keeping modifications to a minimum) the usability and functionality of the designed interactive application.

In a related field of work, many innovative research studies have explored PCF as an option for the production of iTV services [15,16] but the lack of tools to visualize, edit, and translate PCF descriptions has been the main handicap until now for this format. Although the standard was published in January 2006 and the BBC research and development group successfully implemented a translation from PCF to MHEG-5 [12], the technical details of their implementation have not as yet been revealed. In order to facilitate research and development concerning this format and based on our previous work, some tools have been published and made freely available as an open source project [17]. Other works have addressed the translation between XML presentation formats as presented in [18], which proposes the generation of iTV user interfaces for mobile devices through a customized XML schema. Moreover, the interoperability problem between Digital Terrestrial Television (DTT) broadcasting systems has been explored in [19], which proposes a solution based on the Globally Executable MHP (GEM) [20] to support application interoperability across different frameworks.

The content analysis presented in the rest of this chapter is related to the production and management of platform-independent TV interactive services by the use of an integration model that is based on the DVB's PCF. The reader will learn the mechanisms that make this approach an effective way for interactive content providers to build and maintain iTV services for its deployment across different networks, devices, and geographical areas. In that regard, Section 20.2 presents the common scenario for designing and providing interactive services for TV and its involved actors, which are basically the audiovisual content provider, the interactive application provider, and the actor who offers the service to users, that is, the service provider. Section 20.3 introduces PCF as a high-level format that can describe an interactive service in a platform-independent way and an integration model. In this section, the reader will find an overview of this XML-based format and a comparison with other format candidates which could be applied to provide a similar solution. Section 20.4 summarizes the adaptation mechanisms for translating a PCF service into a web-based application for its deployment on an IPTV or WebTV platform and Section 20.5 presents the architecture that enables service providers to efficiently manage interactive content using the PCF standard. Section 20.6 presents an example of this methodology applied on two different iTV services for learning environments: a content management application for a university and a distance learning seminar. Finally, the reader will find in Section 20.7 the conclusions about the concepts provided in this chapter and the experimental work conducted by its authors.

20.2 Interactive Service Design Scenario

As discussed earlier, the environment for the production and deployment of iTV services is changing rapidly due to the increased supply of new platforms that can access this kind of content as well as the user demand for converged services that can be accessed anytime, anywhere. Typically, the main actors involved in the production of iTV services can be classified into three categories: (1) audiovisual content providers, (2) interactive application providers, and (3) the service provider. Audiovisual content providers are those that generate and provide the audiovisual material that is supposed to be the main thread of a TV program. This is, for instance, the role of a news service that provides different recorded content to many TV channels. The second category actors are the interactive application providers who design and develop interactive applications for deployment along with the related audiovisual content. The implementation of these interactive applications has traditionally been carried out by third-party development companies at the request of the TV service providers. Currently, with the rise of Internet-connected platforms and the emergence of online application stores as Google Android Market and Apple App Store, the production and deployment of this interactive content is being democratized by allowing independent developers and even the users themselves an easy deployment of their content into the distribution network underpinned by a clear business model. Finally, the service provider is the actor who takes all the content related to a TV program (i.e., the audiovisual content plus the related interactive applications), deploys it on a particular distribution network (i.e., terrestrial, satellite, Internet, etc.), and makes it accessible to the users. This category includes the TV operators for terrestrial, cable, and satellite as well as the IPTV providers and the website that provide webTV contents via the Internet. Sometimes, the three roles involved in the production and deployment of iTV services are centralized in one company that controls the whole process, but usually there are different entities involved that must cooperate in order to effectively deploy an interactive service.

Although most of the iTV services are based on standardized middleware platforms, the content producer and the application provider usually need some knowledge of the platform to apply their contents properly. Producing iTV services in a platform-independent way through an integration model for the description of the interactive applications also implies high levels of cooperation between the parties involved in the deployment of the service to the end user. The adaptation of an interactive application written in a unified application format as an integration model into the runtime environment of the access platform requires a platform-dependent step in the iTV service production chain that can be assumed by the service provider as well as the interactive application provider. The service provider usually has enough information about the target platform and as such one of the key objectives is to design, build, and deploy an interactive application that is not subject to rework for different platforms. In addition, the service provider generally wants to maintain control of the viewer experience in the deployed application post-translation, so it can verify the requirements of their own customers. For example, the exact position on the screen of an advertisement can be a key consideration for an advertiser based on their own market studies and it must not be modified. Figure 20.2 shows a basic scheme of the adaptation options for an interactive application which are defined by the means of an integration model with two possible scenarios: (1) the application provider gives the integration model of the interactive application to the service provider, who adapts this application code to the specific format required by the access platform to present the interactive content, that is, the

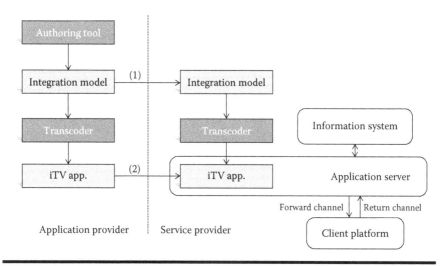

Figure 20.2 Two possible scenarios for the production and deployment of platform-independent iTV services that are based on the integration model for describing interactive applications.

target application format and (2) the application provider implements the adaptation from the integrated model and supplies it to the service provider as deployable iTV application.

The first scenario would be the desired one. It assumes that the integration model behaves like a real B2B interchange format and the service provider has the required tools to adapt the service to its runtime application environment. However, this requires an industry agreement that has not been achieved to date which will benefit the proprietary solutions and walled gardens that enable the service providers to maintain control over applications, content and media on distribution, and access platforms such as some IPTV platforms as well as the highly successful application markets for mobile phones. The great success of some of these proprietary solutions makes the adoption of open and shared standards for the production of iTV services difficult to achieve. In contrast, an application provider can benefit from the second scenario described earlier, that is, the adaptation of the integration model of an interactive application by implementing or deploying the required translation modules to transform the integration model of the interactive application into the target application format. This transformation step, also known as "transcoding," represents the direct digital-to-digital conversion of one code to another; and the module that is responsible for this is the "transcoder." The configuration parameters necessary to deploy the interactive service must be sufficiently configurable to facilitate the application interchange and the adaptation to the target iTV platform.

20.3 DVB Portable Content Format Overview

In order to unify the design and production of iTV services, the DVB consortium explored the viability of defining a new content format as an integration model for representing interactive TV applications that abstract the implementation issues and programming interfaces for each target platform. The result was published in 2006 under the name Portable Content Format (PCF).

This section covers the basic aspects of the DVB's PCF, its scope, how it works, an example of its use, how to manage the differences between platforms, a comparison with other languages and other important features such as the media synchronization and the return channel.

20.3.1 Introduction to Content Format

PCF is a high-level and platform-independent declarative description of an iTV service that defines its basic aspects as they relate to the user experience, that is, the content, presentation, and behavior and leaves to one side the implementation details for each TV platform that will access it. This content format follows an integration model approach to address the portability problem of interactive applications for TV. It defines a common interface that enables the adaptation to other application formats through a transcoding step, which is platform-dependent by nature. This conversion generates the code of the iTV application that can be then deployed in the target application format (e.g., MHEG-5) and executed in the access platform (e.g., STB) using its programming interface. To enable a service to be described efficiently, and in a way that best conveys the author's intent, the format uses a referencing mechanism. This allows the service description to be flexibly partitioned and gives the transcoder considerable freedom to decide how to package the service optimally to suit the target platform. PCF is based on existing industry standard formats such as Extensible Markup Language (XML), Multipurpose Internet Mail Extensions (MIME), Unified Modeling Language (UML), and Uniform Resource Identifiers (URI) [21]. PCF can describe in a declarative way the main features of the existing iTV services, especially those related specifically to TV environments such as the audiovisual consumption, information-driven services, games without many reactive requirements, and video synchronized applications. Moreover, PCF also tries to unify the production of iTV services by defining a standard format that could be generated from any existing authoring tool. Therefore, as shown in Figure 20.2, PCF can be seen as a meeting point between the authoring tools of iTV services and the target platforms that will access to the generated service.

The core aspects of the PCF description of an iTV service can be summarized in the following list:

1. *Scenes*—The PCF service item is subdivided into scenes that represent the different destinations that can be accessed within the service.
2. *Components*—The building blocks of a PCF service description. They can be included directly in the service level to define shared objects in all the scenes or in a specific scene of the service.
   a. *Visual components*—Visual "widgets" used to describe the visual appearance of the service at a particular point, for example, TextBox, Video, Menu, and geometric shapes like pixel, line, ellipse, and rectangle.
   b. *Nonvisual components*—These are used for the presentation of nonvisual content or providing other aspects of service functionality, for example, audio and stream.
3. *Layout*—In order to place the visual components on the screen, the layout of each scene can be explicit and the exact positions of the components can be defined. It can also define a flow layout with specific flow rules to position the components according to the other component positions in the scene.
4. *Content*—It is managed and presented using PCF components.
5. *Behavior*—It is the response to events generated at runtime.

Figure 20.3 shows a basic example of a PCF service description. In the example, the core aspects of the format are shown, that is, content, components, and behavior (user interaction and navigation between the scenes). Moreover, it contains a stream component, which includes a video component, shared by all the scenes

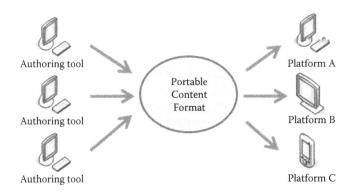

Figure 20.3 PCF scope.

in the service. This service contains two scenes named *scene_1*, where some PCF components are defined, and *scene_2*, respectively. This first scene only contains a text component named *str_press_red* and its behavior, which defines the trigger (a key event) and the "to do" action (switch to the second scene). The item named *firstScene* is used to declare the scene that will be displayed when the service loads.

20.3.2 Behavior

In PCF, the behavior of the service and its components is event-driven and it is defined through XML event items and the PCF action language, which allows the specification of the actions to be executed in an event firing response. There are four types of events:

- *System events*: Events independent of the user's interaction and include file/object updates in the transmission stream, media synchronization, and in-band triggers.
- *User events*: Events generated by the user interaction with the remote control keys.
- *Component events*: A component provides information about a change in its internal state through this type of events. This mechanism allows notifications about the state of the event (e.g., selection and focus) and the event propagation.
- *Error events*: Specialization of component events that define the rules for propagating the component error conditions within a service.

20.3.3 Structuring a Service Description

The PCF provides a referencing mechanism that allows the distribution of the service description in different local or remote files to accommodate the modularity required for an efficient authoring and for B2B interchanges. This is possible due to the "href" property present in all PCF components, which allows any PCF item to be specified by reference rather than by its stated value. It also enables a clear separation of the service layout from its data to facilitate the work of each role involved in the service production and the B2B interchange. The file structure of a PCF service can take advantage of the PCF referencing model. Although for small services the PCF document structure could be simpler, even in a unique file, a smart PCF document structure enables the distinction between layout documents, which can be updated by an authoring tool, and the data files, which can be generated automatically from the information in a database. Figure 20.4 shows a proposal for this PCF file distribution.

The service scene catalog is defined in the *service.xml* file and it contains references to the corresponding data and layouts for each scene and shared components. Each data file is related to a particular scene, that is, those that are in the folder *data* are referenced from their corresponding layout file in order

```
<PCF xmlns="http://www.dvb.org/pcf/pcf">
 <Service name="hello_pcf">
  <String name="pcfSpecVersion"value="1.0"/>
  <URI name="firstScene"value="#scene_1"/>
  <Background name="bg"fillcolor="EAF1DD00"/>
  <Stream name="tv">
   <StreamData name="content">
    <ExternalBodycontent-type="video/x-MP2T-P"
    uri="dvb://<sample_address>"/>
   </StreamData>
   <Video name="film">
    <Position name="origin"value="46020"/>
    <Size name="size"value="960540"/>
   </Video>
  </Stream>
  <Scene name="scene_1">
   <TextBox name="str_press_red">
    <Position name="origin"value="600650"/>
    <Size name="size"value="200 30"/>
    <String name="content"
     value="Press Red"/>
   </TextBox>
   <OnEvent name="press_red">
    <Trigger eventtype="KeyEvent">
     <UserKey name="k"
     value="VK_COLORED_KEY_0"/>
    </Trigger>
    <SceneNavigate>
     <URI name="target"value="#../../scene_2"/>
    </SceneNavigate>
   </OnEvent>
  </Scene>
  <Scene name="scene_2"> … </Scene>
 </Service>
(a)
```

Press red

(b)

Figure 20.4 (a) Basic PCF service description example: code and presentation. (b) Document structure of PCF services.

to display this information in the desired component for a specified scene. This information can be generated dynamically by content producers and published as PCF files.

20.3.4 Managing Differences between Platforms

PCF also provides a profile mechanism to describe the minimum features of a platform necessary to achieve the requirements of an interactive service. The profiles define pragmatic subsets of PCF functions based on the ability of the platforms to support specific features and the ease of implementing a supporting PCF transcoder. A PCF profile shall be defined by reference to one or more profile packages, which contain sets of PCF features (e.g., return channel). These features shall be grouped into one or more levels that embody the boundaries in platform capabilities (e.g., the presence of a specific feature) and the significant steps in the complexity of PCF transcoder implementation. Although custom profiles can be defined, PCF defines three main profiles:

- *Basic*: It encapsulates the minimum useful subset of PCF features for providing a high degree of portability with the minimum requirements for the target platform.
- *Core*: It includes what is believed to be the maximum subset of PCF features that can be expected to offer a high degree of portability.
- *Full*: It encapsulates all the PCF features.

Once the PCF profile is defined, it is associated with a service description in the *Service* element of the service description itself.

20.3.5 Media Synchronization

The media temporal synchronization mechanism provides the mechanism to coordinate the audiovisual stream contents and the interactive ones. It is defined in PCF through StreamEvents, which control the generation of stream events from a specified elementary stream within the stream component. These events have attributes to represent the event group, the time code for firing, and an optional String payload field to define the parameters of the event. This feature is particularly interesting for iTV environments because of the high load of multimedia contents, which are sometimes related to each other. For example, an interactive application can show real-time additional information concerning a live event (e.g., sports) or acquire and display subtitles synchronously in a language not supported by the provider. A further example of the presented technology shown in this chapter is based on a use case for learning environments.

20.3.6 Return Channel

The PCF standard provides three main items that enable the return channel definition: (1) the *ReturnPath* component, (2) the *Transaction* component, and (3) a *TransferCollection* component.

The *ReturnPath* component defines the properties of the return path itself and manages the data transaction process between the iTV service and the application server. It includes the connection address of the target server via a URI and the start-up behavior of the return path, which can be opened or closed depending on the channel connection status. The connection target value is an abstract URI to be resolved by the later transcoding step. It is defined as a URN, which identifies a resource without taking into account its specific location. The portability achieved with URN must be resolved in the transcoding process in order to get a unique name of the actual resource depending on the target platform (e.g., a URI for a broadband platform and a telephone number for a dial-up capable platform). The *Transaction* component manages the status of the data transfer processes and generates events regarding the success or failure of the transaction. It embodies a pair of *TransferCollection* components, for the request and the response, that define the sequence of serialized data to be transferred over the return path. This mechanism enables the straightforward generation of an RIA from a PCF description. Two more PCF components complete the list of the return channel definition items: (1) the *Indicate* component, a cut-down version of the *ReturnPath* component (without transaction process) that only establishes a connection with the server for very simple applications (e.g., voting, counter, etc.) and (2) the *SecureReturnPath* component, for secured data transactions.

20.3.7 Comparison with Other Languages

Other declarative application formats based on XML as the HyperText Markup Language (HTML), the eXtensible Hypertext Markup Language (XHMTL) [22], the Scalable Vector Graphics (SVG) [23], and the Worldwide TV Markup Language (WTVML) [24] are platform-specific presentation formats that are interpreted by the browser engine. Their description of the user interface must detail all the implementation issues to ensure an accurate visualization; this increases the complexity of the transformations between different application formats, especially for the translation to procedural application formats like MHP and MHEG-5. The PCF describes how the components of an iTV service must be presented, that is, layout and behavior, without taking into account the implementation details of a given browser engine. The User Interface Markup Language (UIML) [25], similar to PCF, provides a platform-independent solution for the presentation of multimedia content and, although more tools are available for this format, the accurate management of the time-related issues (e.g., the synchronism) of PCF, despite its specialization in regards to iTV services, make it a good candidate as a platform with independent presentation format. The major technological problem of the aforementioned formats is that they are text-centric solutions that require the use of scripting in order to synchronize XML-based applications with the audiovisual content and to produce playlists. This is because those formats do not include time-related considerations. Other declarative languages like the Synchronized Multimedia Integration Language (SMIL) [26] and the Nested Context Language (NCL) [27] also include time information and thus provide a more media-centric solution. However, PCF has been developed to facilitate the automatic translation into platform-specific formats, leading to a significant reduction in cross-platform costs.

In contrast, the controlled delivery of multimedia content to a user's personal device (e.g., Personal Video Recorder [PVR]) has been addressed by the set of specifications covered by TV-Anytime. It seeks to exploit the evolution in convenient, high capacity storage of digital information to provide consumers with a highly personalized TV experience. TV-Anytime manages the metadata related to the description of the TV content, such as program title and synopsis. In TV-Anytime program, metadata describe the audiovisual content in a formal way and allows the consumer to find, navigate, and manage content from a variety of internal and external sources including enhanced broadcast, interactive TV, Internet, and local storage. The management and personalization of TV contents from a user's personal device is out of the scope of PCF, which is focused on defining and producing the interactive contents that are available to users rather than the management of their preferences in the local platform. In other words, PCF enables the generation of interactive content that can be searched and selected from a user platform with TV-Anytime.

20.4 PCF Transcoding Use Case: Generating Web-Based Contents

Once a PCF description is created or acquired, it must be translated into the format supported by the target platform. This transformation is slightly different for declarative and procedural application formats due to their programmatic models, but the required steps to implement a transcoder are basically the same. This chapter shows the main features of a PCF translation to a declarative application format, which is based on web technologies. The test, deployment, and visualization of web-based applications are simpler than the broadcast ones and there are many more tools available for web-based environments than for other presentation formats, so it is easier to test the resulting applications on different platforms. In the following section, this chapter summarizes the steps involved in the implementation of a PCF transcoder and, in particular, for transcoding from PCF to HTML, CSS, and JavaScript.

20.4.1 PCF Validation and Parser

For a PCF transcoder that is not integrated in an authoring framework (as such its validation may not be ensured), the first step is to validate the correctness of the documents against the PCF Schema and parse them to have a memory object structure, which allows the management of the PCF data. A DOMParser has been chosen for this step as validation is required just prior to generating the object model and a back-and-forth fast is needed in order to read the PCF components across its multiple possible documents and its references [28].

20.4.2 Translating the Layout and Its Components

Although PCF supports pixel-accurate positioning of the visible components as well as flowed layout according to an automated layout algorithm, our work has been centered on the pixel-accurate positioning and assumes that the service author knows the screen resolution of the target platform renderer. In this case, any visible PCF component can be translated to a HTML container, for example, a DIV container, and put on the reference screen through absolute positioning.

In order to translate the PCF components, a component analysis is needed to identify the components that can be directly adapted to the platform-dependent middleware language. Those components that cannot be directly adapted will form complex objects, that is, widgets, in the final application. Figure 20.5 summarizes

PCF Components to HTML			
Visual Components		Nonvisual Components	
Simple (Direct Translation)	Complex (Widget Generation)	Simple (Direct Translation)	Complex (Widget Generation)
Background	Basic shapes (rectangle, ellipse, etc.)	Audio	Return path
Hint text box	Clock	Cookie	Stream
Image	Connect status image	Current time	Stream event
Text box	Image animated	Random	
Input components	Image scalable	Timer	
Video	Menu		
	Numeric navigator		
	Spin control		
	Subtitles		
	Ticker		

Figure 20.5 PCF component clustering based on its adaptation complexity to a web-based platform.

the cluster of the main PCF components depending on the translation complexity in the conversion from PCF to HTML, CSS, and JavaScript.

The components of a simple adaptation are transformed into an HTML tag and its CSS data for styling. As its definition and transformation is quite simple, it is highly likely that the implementation of this transformation will be regular. This is not the same for the components with a complex adaptation, which can be interpreted differently depending on the transcoder implementation. For example, a SpinControl component can be written and rendered in several ways for a web-based environment. In the following lines are described the PCF components that form complex widgets in a translation into HTML. The basic shapes components such as rectangle, line, and pixel can be translated within a Canvas element, which is part of HTML5 and is supported by the main web browsers. The Clock, Connect-StatusImage, SpinControl, and Ticker components are visual widgets implemented in HTML layers and managed by JS functions. Fortunately, the HTML5 *video* tag allows the overlay of other HTML objects in a relatively straight forward way, so components such as Clock, Ticker, Subtitles, and any other widget can be presented on the video without any plug-in or additional code. The ImageAnimated is a component used to display a simple sequence of images and ImageScalable displays a still image with control over its scaling and presentation. Both of them can be easily implemented with JS functions to form a widget. The Menu and NumericNavigation are navigation components explained in the following with the user interaction and navigation issues. The ReturnPath set of components provides control over the return path and its status when this communication path is not always available, as is the case with dial-up or some satellite connections. Finally, a stream component controls the connection to a set of one or more elementary media streams, such as video, audio, and subtitles. Depending on its defined complexity, it can be translated directly into a *video* tag component or, if advanced functions are required (e.g., subtitles), into a more complex widget. The stream component also may contain StreamEvent components to provide media synchronization.

20.4.3 User Interaction and Navigation

The user interaction is mainly defined through custom key events that fire a specific behavior or by a component class default behavior. For example, the PCF Menu component reacts to the UP/DOWN user keys by moving its highlights over its menu items without the explicit service author description of this behavior. The custom events are divided in two parts: the trigger and the "to do" action. For user events, the trigger is a key-stroke event activated by the remote control that fires the behavior specified in the event node. This mechanism is implemented by defining the JavaScript onkeydown event and the key code matching between the defined PCF virtual keys (e.g., the VK_COLORED_KEY_0 key code) and the specific platform key codes from the remote control. This matching is defined in a key matching configuration table within the platform profile provided to the PCF transcoder. In platforms where users interact through a mouse or a touch panel, that is, where the user events are fired through pointing on the screen instead of pressing keys, the input mode must be adapted according to this interaction mode.

HTML does not define complex widgets such as the PCF Menu component, so a direct translation is not possible. The PCF Menu component allows the navigation and selection of one of a set of options presented in a visually coherent ordered list. The PCF NumericNavigator component provides the navigate capability through the service using the numeric keys. In both cases, the component contains a label array to specify the item order and, in the Menu component, it is also possible to define the looping behavior of the menu items through the menuLoop property. The translation of these components can be implemented in a similar way as the custom user key events by adding a JavaScript object to manage an identifier array of HTML nodes and by controlling its behavior through the specified component properties.

Finally, the scene navigation within the scene is mainly done by the translation of the HistoryNavigate PCF component to the JavaScript History object and the SceneNavigate translation to the JavaScript Location object. While the former allows navigation through the document history stack, the latter enables the transitions to any specified URL.

20.4.4 Media Synchronization

The PCF does not define how the target platform ensures that events take place at the right moment. For the web-based PCF transcoder presented in this work, the implementation of this mechanism is based on the creation of a time table within a JavaScript Timer that fires the corresponding functions to meet the event required actions. The timetable is initialized at the moment that the stream composition component is loaded and by reference to the time specified in the counterPosition property of the target stream, the position in the composition that the stream starts playing is defined. A simpler solution, but perhaps less portable, is the implementation of the synchronism through SMIL. It allows an accurate definition of the time and includes easy mechanisms to ensure that different service contents are presented synchronously. This solution is nowadays less portable due to the lack of support in most of the exiting platforms; however, the increasing level of support for SVG (closely related to SMIL) in all of the more widely used web browsers and its recommendation by the Open IPTV Forum (OIPF) [29] as an advanced graphic format means that one should not forget this technology in relation to time-related behaviors in multimedia presentations.

20.4.5 Client-Server Communication: AJAX

The Asynchronous JavaScript and XML (AJAX), as defined in [30], is a set of technologies used to build rich web applications usually with improved performance, interactivity, and user experience. It is based on HTML/XHTML and CSS for the presentation; the Document Object Model (DOM) updating is based on the dynamic behavior; XML and XSLT are used for the interchange and manipulation of data between the server and client platform; an *XMLHttpRequest* object or an equivalent ActiveX is used for the asynchronous communications; and JavaScript binds everything together [31]. AJAX enables the request and the display of specific contents without reloading the entire current page. It reduces the amount of required data for each transaction and enhances the user experience. Moreover, the reduction in bytes of HTTP responses is significant, over 56% average according to [32]. This saves transmission time between server and client, reduces the required bandwidth, and improves the response time of the application. That said, these techniques are necessary for iTV applications based on web environments to enable, for example, the interactive content browsing while a live stream video is consumed.

For a translation from PCF into an RIA, making an intensive use of AJAX, the PCF transcoder can generate a unique HTML page that is the application root and may contain the appropriate AJAX requests to apply the scene changes and manage dynamic data transfers with the server, the first scene of the service and the components shared by all the scenes (e.g., header logo). When a dynamic data transfer is needed, the PCF description includes a transaction component and its behavior. Application developers are free to specify the return path–related items as shared components as well as scene-specific components. The rest of the scenes are translated to the necessary JavaScript code that embodies the scene items in HTML and the functions to update the specific DOM elements. When a scene change is requested, the components of the previous scene are replaced with the new ones in order to avoid increasing unpredictably the DOM memory size in the client platform. To complete the deployment of the generated service, the application server must include the suitable request attention module to process the dynamic data request, access the system information (if needed), and return information related to the client STB. This last part of the service implementation is strongly dependent on the application server technology, but by applying AJAX techniques, it can be fully independent from the application layout, where the specification of the user experience of the iTV service resides.

20.5 Production Architecture

A PCF transcoder is the required tool to overcome the portability problem between formats and generate a platform-specific iTV application based on a platform-independent description. But what is the relationship between the transcoder and the other key modules of an iTV production chain such as the authoring tool, the information system, and the application repository? How can an application provider manage different PCF layouts and apply it correctly according to the target platform? This section presents a complete architecture for generating and maintaining platform-independent iTV services using the PCF. This architecture can be implemented entirely by a single company or organization (e.g., an application provider) but it can be also distributed between the actors involved in the iTV production chain, as it fits within the two possible PCF scenarios described earlier. This architecture spans the process lifecycle starting at the custom service authoring and the B2B interchange all the way to the service provided in a platform-specific format. Figure 20.6 outlines this architecture at system and subsystem

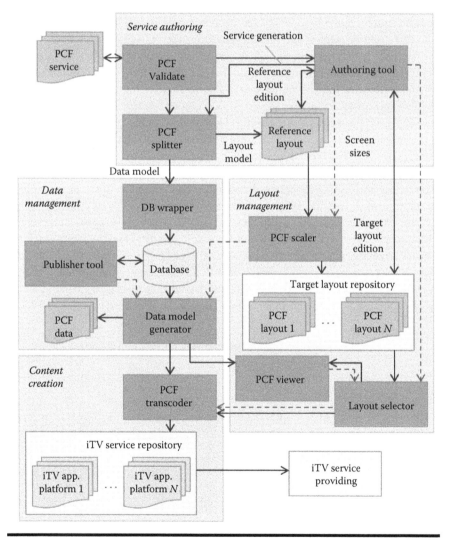

Figure 20.6 **Overall system and subsystem architecture for platform-independent iTV production.**

level, which consists of (1) the Service Authoring, (2) the Data Management, (3) the Layout Management, and (4) the Content creation

The Service Authoring subsystem is responsible for generating new services, acquiring external applications from the B2B interchange and controlling the design and adaptation processes. It consists of the PCF Validator, the Authoring Tool, and the PCF Splitter. The PCF Validator component verifies the document schema and generates the object model structure. The Authoring Tool component is one of the key components because besides generating new service descriptions and modifying the current ones, it manages the scaling process allowing a redesign when necessary in order to achieve the best possible user experience in the target application format. The PCF Splitter extracts the editable data from the PCF description and provides the reference layout description, which can be updated by the Authoring Tool. The implementation of a basic authoring tool for building PCF-based interactive services which is published in [17] can be seen in Figure 20.7.

This authoring tool allows the graphical design of simple iTV services with the typical presentation components for this kind of multimedia environment. This tool is not intended to be a commercial tool nor a complete solution for the designing of PCF layouts. However, it enables PCF descriptions of an entire iTV service for testing and research to be easily created as well as the management of the PCF transcoding and scaling processes, the source code verification of the designed PCF description, and its visualization at different scale levels.

The Data Management subsystem consists of the DB Wrapper component, which receives a service data model and stores it in the database; the Publisher Tool, which allows the maintenance of the service data by content publishers; and the Data Model Generator, which generates a PCF service description when a change in the service data is executed. The data and layout models can be managed across the architecture both in the PCF format (better for B2B interchange) and in its

Figure 20.7 **The developed authoring tool for the design and generation of PCF services.**

programmatic object representation if the interchange between modules is done in the same runtime system (which is more performant).

In the Layout Management subsystem, the PCF Scaler, automatically adapts the reference layout to the different screen resolutions of the target layouts. This preliminary transformation is a suggested scaled version of the reference layout that must be verified by the Authoring Tool. This step can imply relevant changes in the application design in order to take the maximum advantage of a specific screen resolution, taking into account the recommendations for a specific target platform, such as the bandwidth optimization for mobile devices. The combination of the automatic scaling and the design control through the Authoring Tool with data independency gives full control over the application scaling reducing the time associated with design. The generated target layouts are stored in a Layout Repository and acquired by the Layout Selector component, which provides the requested PCF layout documents to be translated. The PCF Viewer displays in real time the PCF service descriptions before providing it to the Content Creation subsystem.

The Content Creation subsystem transforms a PCF description into a specific iTV content language for a concrete iTV platform. This subsystem includes the PCF Transcoder, which is the second key component of the proposed architecture, and the repository of generated services. The PCF Transcoder component uses a PCF data document and the root file of a PCF layout description to generate the code of the service for the desired iTV language and platform. This implies that the transcoder must implement a different set of transformations for each target content language but the service parsing and signaling can be shared by all the platforms. Moreover, several target platforms can support the same content language with little changes in implementation or instruction set (e.g., generic HTML-based services for different platforms). Finally, the repository of generated services stores the platform-dependent application set. Each one can be supplied independently to a different service provider system.

20.6 Use Case for Interactive Services: Learning Environments

The architecture presented earlier has been applied in the generation of interactive applications for learning environments where students can access multimedia contents from a TV set with a STB for IPTV, a personal computer for WebTV, and a mobile phone for mobile TV. Two specific interactive applications have been built: (1) a content management system and (2) a distance seminar. The first application could be for a university TV channel and it is a site that allows students the management of their subjects and personal information, shares video contents generated by themselves, and defines text notifications for reminders that are shown as a note on the screen. This application consists of some browsable scenes with the live TV channel on continuous play while the event management is demonstrated through the creation and display of the reminders. A student can, for example, create a reminder from his mobile phone when he Is In the university and in the evening, when he is watching the TV at home, the notification is shown on the screen at the selected time. The second application is a distance seminar about the soldering process of complex chips with Ball Grid Array (BGA) packages to electronic printed circuits boards for the Technology of Digital Systems course of the Autonomous University of Barcelona. This seminar is described in depth in [33]. The complexity involved in showing the real soldering process in a live environment was the motivation behind creating the seminar, which includes three synchronized video streams in a unique scene: (1) the teacher's speech, which helps the students to understand the process; (2) the real-time soldering machine camera signal, which consists of two cameras (the reflow process camera and the placement camera) that are manually switched depending on the step of the process; and (3) the screen capture of the PC that controls the soldering machine, which shows useful process information such as the current temperature, the reflow profile parameters, and the actual temperature/time curve. In addition to the video streams, the seminar application provides access to a question form to allow students to write their questions while the seminar is running.

These two applications have been initially build as PCF descriptions with the help of the authoring tool outlined earlier. Each application includes various common features from iTV services such as the video management (live and on-demand), content synchronization, navigation, and event handling. The application layouts for each platform have been created in the authoring tool adapting the interfaces for the different user input modes (i.e., pointer or keys) and screen sizes. After that, the PCF transcoder generates the web-based applications for the three platforms; that is, TV, PC, and mobile. Although most of the transformations have been done automatically by the Java application, some issues required more detailed management, particularly, those related with the video (and audio) components. Video components are displayed in PC environments through common video players embedded in HTML code. However, in TV environments, the STB is responsible for decoding the contents and managing the video issues. Due to the fact that there is not yet a standardized common management interface for STB, the generated code must be completed with the specific management instructions of the target STB. Finally, although nowadays most of the mobile devices play video contents, designers should keep in mind the fact that mobile computational constraints limit them to playing one video at a time and sometimes the video playback is not embedded with the rest of the application.

Figure 20.8 shows the two interactive applications displayed in three selected platforms: (1) a Full HD Philips TV and decoded with a Neuros Link v1.1 Media Center corresponding to (a) and (b), (2) a Google Chrome browser on a Ubuntu desktop distribution corresponding to (b) and (c), and (3) an Android 2.1-update1 running on the Android Emulator provided by Google and corresponding to (e) and (f). While the differences between the TV and PC versions are mainly the user

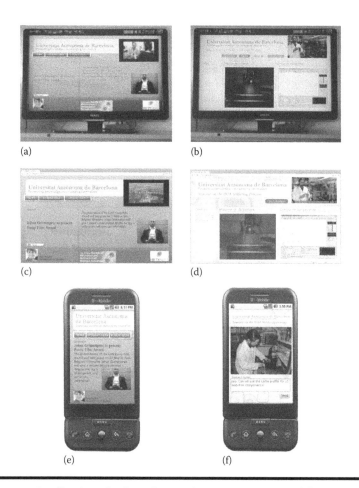

Figure 20.8 Applications for learning environments generated from PCF for TV (a,b), PC (c,d), and mobile (e,f).

input mode, the mobile version requires further changes on the layout model to ensure that contents fit on the screen and are readable and usable by the users.

20.7 Conclusion

This chapter has introduced a platform-independent design of iTV services through a higher-level declarative format and its translation into the format supported by the target application. It has presented an overview of the PCF as the presentation metadata, the core aspects of its translation into a web-based format, and a proposed architecture to generate and maintain this kind of service. Finally and as part of our use cases for the presented methodology, two interactive applications for learning environments have been shown.

While real interoperability between iTV content formats is by no means assured, this can be achieved through high levels of cooperation in the industry, the usage of a common standards, and the use of effective tools by application and service providers to generate content in a platform-independent way that can be used on any iTV device. The extra effort currently undertaken by application providers in the repeated rework and development of user interfaces for different platforms can be reduced dramatically through the use of platform-independent design techniques such as that presented in this chapter. However, the lack of professional tools can still be a handicap for a rapid deployment of this methodology in a real scenario as currently most of the development work has to be done from the scratch. Meanwhile, application providers can evaluate the benefit and effort involved in implementing these design techniques in terms of offering their interactive content to any iTV platform. Moreover, the platform-independent user interface design enables applications to be prepared in such a way that they support future formats (e.g., HTML5), thereby allowing easier entry to new markets where different standard formats (e.g., MHEG-5 for the British market) are in place.

20.8 Acknowledgment

This chapter is supported by the Catalan Government Grant Agency Ref. 2009SGR700.

References

1. European Telecommunications Standards Institute (ETSI). Digital Video Broadcasting (DVB); Multimedia Home Platform (MHP) Specification 1.1.1. ETSI TS 102 812 V1.2.2, August 2006.
2. Digital Television Group Digital Television MHEG-5 Specification, 2010, http://www.dtg.org.uk/publications/books_mheg.html (accessed on December 10, 2010).
3. CableLabs, OpenCable application platform specification, OCAP 1.0 profile OC-SP-OCAP1.0-I07-030522, 2004.
4. ATSC, ATSC Candidate Standard 101A, Advanced common application platform (ACAP), August 2005.
5. M. Takada, M. Saito, Transmission system for ISDB-T, *Proceedings of the IEEE*, 94(1), 251–256, 2006.
6. OpenTV, OpenTV middleware, 2010, http://www.opentv.com (accessed on December 10, 2010).
7. MediaHighway middleware, 2010, http://www.nds.com/solutions/mediahighway.php (accessed on December 10, 2010).
8. Microsoft TV, The Microsoft TV Platform, 2010, http://www.microsoft.com/mediaroom/ (accessed on December 10, 2010).
9. G. Hölbling, T. Rabl, H. Kosch, Overview of open standards for interactive TV (iTV). *Multimedia Semantics—The Role of Metadata*, 2008, pp. 45–64.

10. Open IPTV Forum (OIPF). Release 2 specification. Volume 6—Declarative Application v2.0, September 2010.

11. Open IPTV Forum (OIPF). Release 2 specification. Volume 6—Procedural Application v2.0, September 2010.

12. BBC R&D White Paper #134. Portable Content Format: A Standard for Describing an Interactive Digital Television Service, 2010, http://www.bbc.co.uk/rd/pubs/whp (accessed on December 10, 2010).

13. Digital Video Broadcasting; Portable Content Format Specification 1.0, ETSI TS 102 523.

14. M. Driver, R. Valdes, G. Phifer. Rich internet applications are the next evolution of the web. Technical report, Gartner, May 2005.

15. D. Van Deursen, F. De Keukelaere, L. Nachtegaele, J. Feyaerts, R. Van deWalle, a scalable presentation format for multichannel publishing based on MPEG-21 digital items. In *Lecture Notes in Computer Science*, vol. 4105, pp. 650–657. Springer, Heidelberg, Germany, September 2006.

16. H.-T. Chiao, F.-C. Chen, K.-S. Hsu, S.-M. Yuan, Video everywhere through a scalable IP-streaming service framework. In *Proceedings of the 3rd International Symposium on Wireless Communication Systems (ISWCS '06)*, Valencia, Spain, pp. 190–194, September 2006. ISBN: 978-1-4244-0398-1.

17. Portable Content Format Java Tools (PCF-JTools), 2010, http://code.google.com/p/pcf-jtools/ (accessed on December 10, 2010).

18. E. Tsekleves, J. Cosmas, Semi-automated creation of converged iTV services: From macromedia director simulations to services ready for broadcast. In *Proceedings of the 4th European Interactive TV Conference (EuroITV'06)*, Athens, Greece, 2006.

19. J. Amatller Clarasó, D. Baldo, G. Benelli, G. Luca Daino, R. Zambon, Interactive digital terrestrial television: The interoperability challenge in Brazil. *International Journal of Digital Multimedia Broadcasting*, Article ID 579569, 17pp, Hindawi Publishing Corporation, June 2009.

20. Digital video broadcasting (DVB) globally executable MHP (GEM) specification 1.0.0. ETSI TS 102 819 v1.1.1.

21. IETF RFC 2141: URN Syntax.

22. W3C, *The Extensible HyperText Markup Language*, 2nd edition, 2010, www.w3c.org (accessed on December 10, 2010).

23. W3C, *Scalable Vector Graphics*, 2010, www.w3c.org (accessed on December 10, 2010).

24. Specification for a lightweight microbrowser for interactive TV applications, based on and compatible with WML, ETSI TS 102 322.

25. M. Abrams, C. Phanouriou, A. Batongbacal, S. Williams, J. Shuster, UIML: An appliance-independent XML user interface language, *Computer Networks*, 1999, 1695–1708.

26. W3C, *Synchronized Multimedia Integration Language*, 2010, www.w3c.org (accessed on December 10, 2010).

27. *Nested Content Language 3.0 Part 8—NCL Digital TV Profiles*, 2010, http://www.ncl.org.br (accessed on December 10, 2010).

28. T.C. Lam, J.J. Ding, J.C. Liu, XML Document parsing: Operational and performance characteristics, *Computer* 41, 30–37, 2008.

29. Open IPTV Forum (OIPF), 2010, http://www.openiptvforum.org (accessed on December 10, 2010).
30. L. Paulson, Building rich web applications with AJAX, *IEEE Computer*, 38(10), 14–17, 2005.
31. J. Garrett, AJAX: A new approach to web applications, *Adaptive Path*, 2005.
32. C.W. Smullen, S.A. Smullen, An experimental study of AJAX application performance, *Journal of Software*, 3, 30, 2008.
33. A. Rodriguez-Alsina, E. Cespedes-Borras, R. Puig-Fargas, M. Moreno-Berengue, J. Carrabina, Unified content design for ubiquitous learning: The soldering seminar use case, in *Proceedings of the 4th EEE International Conference on E-Learning in Industrial Electronics (ICELIE '10)*, Phoenix, AZ, November 2010.

Glossary

ABox (assertional box): It contains axioms and definitions describing a specific instance of the domain under investigation. Namely, ABox is the data of the knowledge base.

Adaboost (adaptive boost): General method for generating a strong classifier out of a set of weak classifiers.

AMDF (average magnitude different function): Measurement used in audio processing.

ANOVA (analysis of variance): A set of statistical procedures to test whether the means of several groups are equal or not.

ASR (automatic speech recognition).

BW (bandwidth): Measurement used in audio processing.

CBCD (content-based copy detection).

CBF (content-based filtering): The process of filtering for items whose content (e.g., item descriptions) is of particular interest to the user.

CF (collaborative filtering): The process of filtering for relevant items using techniques involving collaboration among multiple users.

CFG (context-free grammars): Formal grammars providing simple and mathematically precise mechanisms for describing the methods by which constructs (i.e., scenes, phrases) are built from smaller blocks (i.e., shots, words), capturing the "block structure" of constructs in a natural way.

Closed caption: Text displayed on the TV screen during the broadcast of different TV programs.

Consistency checking: Ontology consistency checking evaluates whether the devised model contains any implicit contradictions.

Content: It defines the substance that is transmitted via the medium as abstract model (e.g., a TV or radio show) and consumed by the audience. Characteristics of the content are, for instance, start and end point(s), scenes, and characters in scenes. Its course is defined by the narrative structure, timing, and pace. Access to the content is provided via the medium by a mapping mechanism (mapping characteristics of the medium to those of the content).

Co-training: A meta-learning algorithm that exploits unlabeled in addition with labeled training data for classifier learning.

Data features: The measurements/numerical values/statistics extracted from physical properties of the data under investigation (e.g., mean of pitch, color histogram).

Delivery medium: Delivery medium (also termed as "medium") denotes the technical realization and representation of the content. Well-known media standards are, for example, MPEG-2 and MPEG-4 as employed in the digital video broadcasting (DVB) standard in Europe. Characteristics of the medium are metadata, frames, time stamps, and other features that are defined by the used standard.

DL (description logics): A family of object oriented Knowledge Representation formalisms extensively studied in artificial intelligence.

DMAMS (digital media asset management system): Software and system to manage and distribute digital media.

DTW (dynamic time warping): A sequence alignment method.

DV (digital video).

Early fusion: Multimodal fusion approaches that integrate single modality feature vectors in a unique feature representation before further processing.

EBU (European Broadcasting Union): Standardization organization.

Editing effects: Special effects used in video editing with the goal to create more complex transitions between scenes and to capture viewers' attention and amplify their feelings. Examples of editing effects are dissolve, wipe, fade, replay, and so on.

EIT (event information table): It provides scheduling data about broadcasted programs and also information about the program being broadcasted (i.e., the title, the start time, the duration, etc.) and about the next one. The EIT is broadcasted along with the audiovisual stream.

EM (expectation–maximization algorithm): Algorithm to estimate model probabilities.

EPG (electronic program guide): It provides applications with continuously updated menus displaying scheduling information for current and upcoming TV programming of several TV channels over several days.

FC (frequency centroid): Measurement used in audio processing.

FPS (frames per second): The amount of still frames shown per second in a video clip.

Gamelog: A file that can be found on the Internet and that describes the activity over an entire broadcasted sports video. It is used for ranking players but also to help viewers to follow the game.

GMM (Gaussian mixture model): It is a parametric probability density function represented as a weighted sum of Gaussian component densities. GMMs are commonly used as a parametric model of the probability distribution of continuous measurements or features. GMM parameters are usually estimated from training data using the iterative expectation–maximization (EM).

HCO (harmful content ontology): Harmful content ontology is the formal representation of violence and pornography domain knowledge in movies/TV content, defined to drive corresponding events/acts detection.

HD (high definition): Mostly related to video, meaning a higher spatial and/or temporal resolution than standard video. For example, HD video is typically broadcast at a resolution of 1920 × 1080 or 1280 × 720 pixels, whereas typical standard definition (PAL) is transmitted at 720 × 576.

HMM (hidden Markov model): It is a joint statistical model for an ordered sequence of variables. It is the result of stochastically perturbing the variables in a Markov chain (the original variables are thus "hidden"). HMM assign patterns to a class based on a sequential model of state and transition probabilities.

Image segmentation: The process of automatically partitioning an image/frame into smaller connected areas with common attributes (same color, shape, texture, motion, etc.) to simplify image representation, extract meaning, and ease analysis.

Inference: The process of deriving logical conclusion from premises known or assumed to be true.

ISO (International Standardization Organization): Standardization organization.

ITU (International Telecommunication Union): Standardization organization.

kNN (k-nearest neighbor): k nearest neighbor is a classification approach applied to predict the category of an object. To classify feature vector x, take the k nearest training feature vectors and choose the most popular class among them.

Knowledge base: It represents knowledge of a specific domain in a formal machine readable way. A knowledge base is usually composed of an ABox (i.e., data) and a TBox (i.e., schema).

Late fusion: Multimodal fusion approaches first reduce single modality features to separately learned concept scores and then these scores are integrated to learn concepts.

LCSS (longest common subsequence): A sequence alignment method.

LDA (latent Dirichlet allocation): Generative model using latent variables.

LRA (loudness range): It measures the variation of loudness on a macroscopic time scale. A short but very loud event would not affect the loudness range of a longer segment. Loudness range is measured in loudness units (LU), as described in EBU recommendation R 128.

LSH (locality-sensitive hashing): Algorithm for fast approximate search.

LSI (latent semantic indexing): Indexing technique that identifies the most important latent variables to describe the set of data points.

LUFS (loudness unit full scale): A standard on measuring audio program loudness, as defined in ITU recommendation BS.177.

MediaEval: A benchmarking initiative dedicated to evaluating new algorithms for multimedia access and retrieval.

MFCC (mel-frequency cepstral coefficient): Mel-frequency cepstral coefficients are commonly used audio features in speech recognition, music information retrieval, and audio analysis in general. MFCC are coefficients collectively representing the short-term power spectrum of a sound, based on a linear cosine transform of a log power spectrum on a nonlinear mel-scale of frequency. Mel-scale approximates more accurately the human auditory response system than linear-spaced frequency bands.

MOS (mean opinion score): A numerical measure of perceived quality in transmission, as defined in ITU-T recommendation P.800.

MPEG (Moving Picture Experts Group): A family of standards used for coding audiovisual information (e.g., movies, video, music) in a digital compressed format.

MPEG-1: ISO/IEC standard developed by the Moving Picture Experts Group (MPEG) defining coding of moving pictures and associated audio for digital storage media at up to about 1.5 Mbit/s. MPEG-1 is composed from several frame/picture types that serve different purposes.

MPEG-7: Multimedia Content Description Interface. MPEG-7 is an ISO/IEC standard developed by the Moving Picture Experts Group (MPEG) that provides structural and semantic interfaces for multimedia content description.

MPEG-21: ISO/IEC standard developed by the Moving Picture Experts Group (MPEG) that defines an open framework supporting the creation, management, manipulation, transport, distribution, and consumption of content.

MSO (movie sound ontology): It is the ontological definition of the structure, properties, and logical correlations of events extracted from the audio modality of movies/TV content.

MVisO (movie visual ontology): It is the ontological definition of the structure, properties, and logical correlations of objects and events extracted from the visual modality of movies/TV content.

NN (neural networks): These are networks of interconnected artificial neurons aiming toward simulating the real human biological nervous system usually used for artificial intelligence and pattern recognition.

NPR (non-pitch ratio): Measurement used in audio processing.

OCR (optical character recognition).

Ontological/knowledge engineering: Refers to the set of activities concerning the ontology/knowledge development process, the ontology/knowledge life cycle, the methodologies, tools and applications for building ontology/knowledge bases, and the reasoning on top of ontology approaches.

Ontology: Formal explicit specification of a shared conceptualization.

Ontology classification: The computation of all subsumption relationships between named classes.

Open world assumption: Every logical statement is true unless there is a formal definition that proves it is false.

OWL (web ontology language): A description logic-based formalism/language designed for knowledge representation and reasoning on the web.

PASCAL VOC: A challenge evaluating performance on object class recognition organized by the PASCAL network of excellence.

PC (pitch contour): Measurement used in audio processing.

Postproduction: Stage of the media production process after recording of the content, including, for example, editing, adding special effects, and color grading.

POWDER (protocol for web description resources): It provides mechanisms for individuals or organizations to describe web resources through the publication of machine-readable metadata.

PSTD (pitch standard deviation): Measurement used in audio processing.

PVR personal video recorder, also called digital video recorder.

QoE (quality of experience): The subjective quality a user experiences from a service, often used in transmission and multimedia systems.

QoS (quality of service): All quality indicators that can be measured objectively.

RANSAC (random sample consensus): Algorithm for visual point matching.

RS (recommender system): Information-filtering technique that attempts to recommend personalized items (movies, TV program, video on demand, music, books, etc.) that are likely to be of interest to the user.

RuleML (rule markup language): A markup language defined by the Rule Markup Initiative to express rules in XML format.

Rushes: raw, unedited video material.

Scene: Set of consecutive shots displaying either the same event or interchanging actions that compose a higher level event (i.e., a series of consecutive shots of alternating people speaking conveys a dialogue scene).

Scene detection: The process of automatically detecting the meaningful temporal boundaries between scenes in video.

Shot: A sequence of consecutive frames taken with a single camera movement/recording.

Shot boundary detection: The process of automatically detecting the temporal boundaries between shots in video. The detection of temporal boundaries is fundamental to video analysis and video application since it enables temporal segmentation of video data into their basic temporal components.

SI (spatial information): A measure to indicate the amount of spatial detail in an image or video, as defined in ITU-T recommendation P.910.

SIFT (scale-invariant feature transform): Algorithm for extracting and describing salient image features.

SOM (self-organizing maps): Invented by Teuvo Kohonen, SOM is a vector quantization technique aiming to represent multidimensional vectors in spaces of lower dimensions (i.e., one or two) further preserving topological relationships within the training set.

Speaker diarization: Process of partitioning an input audio stream into homogeneous segments according to the speaker identity. Speaker diarization is a combination of speaker segmentation and speaker clustering. The first aims at finding speaker change points in an audio stream. The second aims at grouping together speech segments on the basis of speaker characteristics.

SPR (smooth pitch ratio): Measurement used in audio processing.

STE (short-time energy): Measurement used in audio processing.

SURF (speeded-up robust features): Image descriptor partly inspired by the SIFT descriptor. The standard version of SURF is several times faster than SIFT.

SVM (support vector machines): Linear classifiers with a maximum-margin fitting criterion.

SWRL (semantic web rule language): It is a horn-like rule language combining OWL with RuleML.

Talk show: A television program where one person (or group of people) discuss various topics put forth by a talk show host.

TBox (terminological box): It contains axioms and definitions about the general structure of the conceptual domain under investigation. In other words, TBox is the schema of the knowledge base.

TI (temporal information): A measure to indicate the amount of temporal complexity (i.e., motion) in a video sequence, as defined in ITU-T recommendation P.910.

TREC (Text REtrieval Conference): A benchmarking initiative for text retrieval.

TRECVid (TREC video retrieval evaluation): The video "track" of TREC conference series devoted to research in automatic segmentation, indexing, and content-based retrieval of digital video.

TV-anytime: It is a TV program-oriented metadata specification allowing for detailed content classification and description.

TV program format/TV program/TV format: It defines the content (see glossary entry "content") that is broadcast by television, for example, a certain TV show or a movie. The format specifies the type (layout, course, etc.) of the program.

VCD (video copy detection).

VCR (video cassette recorder).

VDR (volume dynamic range): Measurement used in audio processing.

VSO (video structure ontology): It is the ontological definition/description of the broad class of multimodal documents (composed of audio, visual and textual information), their structure, and the corresponding authoring information.

VSTD (volume standard deviation): Measurement used in audio processing.

VTR (video tape recorder).

ZCR (zero crossing rate): Measurement used in audio processing.

ZSTD (zero crossing rate standard deviation): Measurement used in audio processing.

Index